...is a marvellous achievement' John

...rapher is to establish a living sense of
...other is to trace the development of
...athan Bate's biography, the first full-
...ceeds splendidly on both counts . . . It is time
...from the stereotypes of "peasant poet" and "mad
...unquestionably major author he is' *TLS*

...e enables us to see for the first time the complex development of
...'s relationships . . . This biography will be central to our appreciation
...e poet for many years to come' *Independent*

...athan Bate, as surefooted a biographer as he is sympathetic, rejects the
...n of Clare as victim of poverty-grinding land-enclosers, interfering edi-
...s and ignorant doctors . . . [this biography] makes the reader wish to have
...t Clare and to read his poetry' *Tablet*

...d with detailed biographical finding, splendidly lively and readable'
...*ly Telegraph*

...Clare's biography by Jonathan Bate is glorious' Andrew Marr, *Sunday*
...*d* 'Books of the Year'

...inating . . . I could hardly put it down' Trevor McDonald, *The Times*
...*ks* of the Year'

'A heart-breaking account of the life of the great English poet whose place has
been almost as hard to locate as that of the corncrake' Paul Muldoon, *Times
Literary Supplement* 'Books of the Year'

'Bate brings a vary rare mixture of tenderness and scholarship to a subtle,
thought-provoking reconstruction of lost landscapes, lost childhood, lost love
and finally lost identity' Richard Holmes, *Guardian* 'Books of the Year'

'An impressive tribute to a neglected poet' Tom Paulin, *Guardian* 'Books of
the Year'

Jonathan Bate is a well-known biographer, critic, writer and broadcaster, Provost of Worcester College, and Professor of English Literature in the University of Oxford. He is also the editor of John Clare's *Selected Poems*. *John Clare* won the Hawthornden Prize and the James Tait Black Memorial Prize, and the NAMI (New York) Book Award.

JOHN CLARE

JONATHAN BATE

John Clare

A BIOGRAPHY

PICADOR

First published 2003 by Farrar, Straus and Giroux, New York

First published in Great Britain 2003 by Picador

First published in paperback 2004 by Picador
an imprint of Pan Macmillan, a division of Macmillan Publishers Limited
Pan Macmillan, 20 New Wharf Road, London N1 9RR
Basingstoke and Oxford
Associated companies throughout the world
www.panmacmillan.com

ISBN 978-0-330-37112-4

5 7 9 8 6 4

A CIP catalogue record for this book is available from
the British Library.

Printed and bound in Great Britain by
CPI Group (UK) Ltd, Croydon, CR0 4YY

Visit **www.picador.com** to read more about all our books and to buy
them. You will also find features, author interviews and news of any author
events, and you can sign up for e-newsletters so that you're always first to hear
about our new releases.

As new things meet thy childish eyes …

CONTENTS

ILLUSTRATIONS

PLATES

(following pages 170 and 458)

TEXT ILLUSTRATIONS

This book was written out of the conviction that John Clare is the one major English poet never to have received a biography that is worthy of his memory. It is based on a thorough examination of all the available sources, both published and unpublished.

Our knowledge of Clare's early years, from his birth in 1793 to the beginning of his literary career in 1819, is dependent on his own autobiographical prose. His memory cannot, however, be trusted in every particular: it is impossible to piece together a precise chronology of his passage from schoolboy to casual labourer to soldiering and back to work in the fields. In 1821 he wrote a brief autobiography for his publisher, 'Sketches in the Life of John Clare'. Three years later he drafted a more complete (untitled) autobiography, but he never published it. The two documents are not always consistent with each other or with external evidence such as parish records.

Because of the gaps and uncertainties in the record of Clare's first twenty-five years, Part One of this biography is structured as much thematically as chronologically: chapters on heredity and childhood are followed by a general account of Clare's geographical and social environment, then a chapter on his life as a labourer and then one on the friendships, erotic entanglements and writing activities of his leisure hours. Only with the final chapter of Part One, when Clare is 'discovered' as a poet in the autumn of 1818, do we have firm facts of the kind that are provided by dated correspondence.

The most fully documented period of his life spans his debut as a writer and his move, a dozen years later, from his home village of Helpston to nearby Northborough. These were the years when celebrity came suddenly and departed as swiftly. His journal and the great majority of his poetic manuscripts belong to this period, as does the bulk of his surviving correspondence. Here, in contrast to the earlier and later years, there is an embarrassment of biographical riches.

Clare kept the letters he received and stitched them together into hand-made books, an exceptionally valuable source: it is an unusual privilege for a biographer to see his subject through the eyes of so many friends and acquaintances. The most intimate and revealing letters, written throughout the 1820s and 1830s, are from a London admirer called Eliza Emmerson. She intended to publish both sides of the correspondence, but Clare's letters to her seem to have been destroyed. Tantalising fragments of them are glimpsed when Mrs Emmerson refers to and quotes from them in her replies.

After his move to Northborough, Clare's mental health became increasingly unstable and his writing grew more spasmodic and fragmentary. He went on composing poetry after he was confined to lunatic asylums (in Essex from 1837 to 1841 and in Northampton until his death), but we have no journal and only a few letters from these years. For a picture of his life in the two madhouses, we are mostly reliant on the correspondence and (sometimes unreliable) reminiscences of staff, family, fellow-inmates and visitors—though his own account of his walk home from the Essex asylum to Northborough survives as one of the most remarkable autobiographical fragments in the English language.

In 1865, a year after Clare's death, a biography of him was written by Frederick Martin, a German-Jewish émigré. It is a lively read and a significant resource—Martin almost certainly had access to a now-lost fair copy of Clare's autobiography—but its colourful detail must be taken with a very large grain of salt. Separating truth from invention in this first *Life of John Clare* is an intricate task: many errors of fact and misrepresentations of image have passed from Martin's text to subsequent biographies and critical studies.

But the greatest difficulties arise when we examine Clare's own manuscripts. He was among the most prolific of all English poets, survived by nearly ten thousand pages of manuscript writings—poems, autobiography, journal, letters, essays, natural history writings and more. Much of this work remained unpublished until the late twentieth century; some of it has never appeared in print. Partly because of Clare's 'peasant' origin and partly due to the sheer speed of his writing, the manuscripts are fragile, fragmentary, confusing and often barely legible. They have very little punctuation and are highly irregular in grammar, spelling and capitalization.

Four collections of Clare's poems, representing less than a quarter of his overall output, appeared in print in his lifetime: *Poems, Descriptive of Rural Life and Scenery* (published in 1820, when he was twenty-six years old), *The Village Minstrel, and Other Poems* (published a year later), *The Shepherd's Calendar; with Village Stories, and Other Poems* (1827) and *The Rural Muse* (1835). These volumes were 'regularised' for the press by his editors and publishers. The effect of the procedure was a matter of concern to Clare; it has also become the single point of greatest controversy among modern scholars of his work. Is justice done to Clare by the presentation of his manuscripts in the raw, free from the shackles of prescriptive grammar? Or does the reproduction of their idiosyncrasies unintentionally perpetuate the image of him as a semi-illiterate primitive, an eternal child?

In view of the intractability of this debate, I have been eclectic in my habits of quotation. When I have quoted with the specific purpose of evoking Clare in the very moment of writing, I have reproduced the manuscripts as exactly as possible, though with the introduction of light punctuation—the occasional dash, comma and apostrophe—where the sense requires some form of pointing. This seemed the most appropriate way to reproduce some of the extracts from his letters and journal. When I have sought to show how his works were presented to his original public, I have reproduced the texts printed in his lifetime. For the most part, though, I have quoted his writings as manifestations of his vision of himself and his world; in the majority of my quotations I have therefore edited his manuscripts with a light touch. I believe that this is how he wanted them to be handled. That is to say, I have done what he expected his editors to do: normalised his spelling (*I'm* for *Im*, *used* for *usd*, *and* for *&*, *than* in place of the old spelling *then*, etc.) and introduced a degree of punctuation for the sake of clarity, but not over-regularised his grammar or diluted the regional dialect that is so essential to his voice. So, for instance, his use of a singular verb with a plural noun, as in 'my parents was illiterate', is retained—the usage remains common to this day in the spoken language of the fens of eastern England. Some distinctive spellings, such as *childern* for *children*, are also retained to give the feel of Clare's own rural accent. A certain purposeful inconsistency in the presentation of quotations has seemed the best way of giving the flavour of Clare's erratic orthography whilst avoiding such an excess of irregularities that his 'peasant' origin would outweigh all other impressions of his writing.*

An equally difficult question is the extent to which the poems should be regarded as autobiographical. In particular, there is a strong temptation to read Clare's relationship with his childhood sweetheart Mary Joyce through his many 'Mary' poems and to wonder about the many other women's names that occur in his work. Throughout this biography, I have sought to show how the life illuminates the poems and vice-versa, whilst also recognising that— even in the case of a poet who drew as extensively on his own experience and environment as Clare did—a body of poetry offers an imaginative reshaping of a life, not a direct report on it.

'In writing such Biographs', remarked Clare in an unpublished fragment, 'one can only repeat what has been written—for it cannot be expected that new discoverys can be made . . . so long after the lives of those whom the writers celebrate.' Matters of fact, he continued, thus become 'little better than guesses at truth—from hearsay acquaintance—therefore doubts exist not as tenants at will but on leases that cannot be broken—and the doing away with an old doubt to find a new one in its place has been so long the usage of commentators that it ought to be out of fashion.' Though I have been able to correct scores of local errors and larger misconceptions in the re-

---

*The question of the presentation of Clare's texts is discussed at greater length in the Appendix.

ceived biographical record, I have inevitably made many 'guesses at truth' and will have introduced new doubts in place of the old ones that I have resolved. I have relied above all on my 'hearsay acquaintance' with John Clare via his papers and correspondence: to have spent five years in the company of his remarkable written voice has been the most exciting and humbling adventure of my own writing life.

JOHN CLARE

PROLOGUE

BESIDE THE ROAD TO THE NORTH

Thursday 22 July 1841. Morning. A countryman sits by the Great York Road, the main coaching route that joins London to the north of England. He is just over five feet tall, his hair receding and his girth increasing with middle age. A week ago he passed his forty-eighth birthday far away from his family. He is probably smoking a pipe. He has walked over fifty miles from the Epping Forest and is now just south of Buckden in Huntingdonshire.

In the following century the road will be paved and widened and named with a number instead of a destination: the A1. Driving its dual carriageway today, one covers those fifty miles in less than an hour, bypassing villages like Buckden in a flash. It is impossible to imagine a man walking this route, tired, confused, cold at night and hungry by day. He will soon resort to eating the grass by the roadside, cheering himself with the observation that its taste is a little like that of bread.

As he sits resting, he takes out his six-by-four-inch pocket memorandum book. In a scratchy, barely legible hand, he writes:

> The man whose daughter is the queen of England is now sitting
> on a stone heap on the high way to bugden without a farthing in
> his pocket and without tasting a bit of food ever since yesterday
> morning—when he was offered a bit of Bread and cheese at

Enfield—he has not had any since but If I put a little fresh speed on hope too may speed to morrow—O Mary mary If you knew how anxious I am to see you and dear Patty with the childern I think you would come and meet me.

He is walking home from Dr Allen's private lunatic asylum, in which he has been confined for four years. Some gypsies had offered to help him escape by hiding him in their camp, but he has chosen to go it alone. He is walking home to his wife, Patty, and his seven children. He thinks that he is also walking home to Mary Joyce, the sweetheart of his youth and the obsession of his later years. He does not know that a year after he entered the asylum Mary, unmarried and childless, died of burns sustained in a freak accident.

He still has over thirty miles to go. The next day, he arrives at his cottage in the windswept fenland village of Northborough. Though 'compleatly foot foundered and broken down', he starts work on an account of his journey. 'Returned home out of Essex,' he begins, 'and found no Mary—her and her family are as nothing to me now though she herself was once the dearest of all—and how can I forget.' In his pocket he finds some notes he has scribbled along the way, written in pencil on scraps of old newspaper: '1st Day—Tuesday—Started from Enfield and slept at Stevenage on some clover trusses—cold lodging.'

The day after his homecoming, he writes up a fair copy of his 'Reccolections etc. of journey from Essex' in a foolscap manuscript book of brown half-suede with marbled boards. But he is not at peace. 'So here I am homeless at home', he concludes, 'and half gratified to feel that I can be happy any where'.

In the early 1820s John Clare achieved short-lived metropolitan fame under the soubriquet 'the Northamptonshire Peasant Poet'. He was the son of an agricultural labourer who never found regular employment. As a boy he worked as a thresher, a bird-scarer, a ploughboy and a pot-scourer in a pub. As a young man he was variously a gardener in the grounds of a stately home, a militiaman, a casual field-worker like his father, and a lime-burner. He was born and raised—and remained to raise his own children—in a cottage with no running water. His family had to share a single outdoor privy with the neighbours in their row of tenements. When a man from such a background writes in his notebook that he is the father of Queen Victoria, one may assume that he is not in his perfect mind. But when he recollects his journey in minute detail, and when he says 'and how can I forget', one may only feel that he is all too fully in possession of himself.

There were times when Clare believed that Dr Allen's lunatic asylum was a prison in which he had been incarcerated for bigamy—for marrying and having children with his youthful flame Mary as well as his real wife Patty. There were times when he said he was Lord Byron, the greatest poet and most notorious lover of the age. The notebook that he took from his pocket beside the Great North Road included a poem he had just written, full of sexual disgust, called 'Don Juan'. 'The lunatic, the lover, and the poet,' wrote Shakespeare in *A Midsummer Night's Dream*, 'Are of imagination all compact.'

Five months later John Clare was committed again, this time to a public rather than a private institution: the Northampton General Lunatic Asylum. Among the questions asked on his admission papers was whether insanity had been 'preceded by any severe or long continued mental emotion or exertion'. Dr Fenwick Skrimshire—who also inserted and underlined the information that Clare had 'escaped' from the asylum at High Beech, Epping—answered: 'after years addicted to Poetical prosing'.

PART ONE

Early Years

1793–1819

I was a lover very early in life…

■■■

CHAPTER ONE

'HEREDITARY'

D r Skrimshire also had an answer to the question 'What are
the supposed causes of Insanity?' He noted that they were
'hereditary'. There is no sure ground for this claim, but there is no
doubt that the public image of Clare as 'the Northamptonshire Peasant Poet' was heavily dependent on his humble heredity.

Here is how the story begins in the first biography of him:

> Some thirty years previous to the birth of John, there came into
> Helpston* a big, swaggering fellow of no particular home, and,
> as far as could be ascertained, of no particular name: a wanderer
> over the earth, passing himself off, now for an Irishman, and
> now for a Scotchman. He had tramped over the greater part of
> Europe, alternately fighting and playing the fiddle; and being
> tired awhile of tramping, and footsore and thirsty withal, he re-
> solved to settle for a few weeks, or months, at the quiet little vil-
> lage. The place of schoolmaster happened to be vacant, perhaps
> had been vacant for years; and the villagers were overjoyed
> when they heard that this noble stranger, able to play the fiddle,
> and to drink a gallon of beer at a sitting, would condescend to

---

*In Clare's own time, the name of his native village in Northamptonshire was
spelt *Helpstone*.

9

teach the A B C to their children. So 'Master Parker,' as the great unknown called himself for the nonce, was duly installed schoolmaster of Helpston. The event, taking place sometime about the commencement of the reign of King George the Third, marks the first dawn of the family history of John Clare.

According to biographer Frederick Martin, 'the tramping schoolmaster' soon made the acquaintance of the pretty daughter of the parish clerk. Her name was Alice Clare. She had to walk through the schoolroom each day on her way to wind the church clock. As skilled with words as with his fiddlestick, Master Parker seduced her, and on discovering that the girl was pregnant, he quit the village. The parish clerk's daughter gave birth to a boy, who was given his mother's surname but christened for the absent father. Such, says Martin, was the origin of Parker Clare, father of John Clare.

The original source for this story—minus the colourful narrative embroidery that Martin always added—was the autobiographical 'Sketches in the Life of John Clare':

> My father was one of fate's chancelings who drop into the world without the honour of matrimony—he took the surname of his mother, who to commemorate the memory of a worthless father with more tenderness of lovelorn feeling than he doubtless deserved, gave him his surname at his christening, who was a Scotchman by birth and a schoolmaster by profession and in his stay at this and the neighboring villages went by the name of John Donald Parker—this I had from John Cue of Ufford, an old man who in his young days was a companion and confidential to my run-a-gate of a grandfather, for he left the village and my grandmother soon after the deplorable accident of misplaced love was revealed to him, but her love was not that frenzy which shortens the days of the victim of seduction, for she lived to the age of 86.

Old John Cue had once been head-gardener to Lord Manners of nearby Ufford Hall. He remembered Clare's renegade grandfather as a man of somewhat mysterious identity, an outsider and a wanderer, a rogue and a lady's man, but also a teacher of letters.

It does not matter whether the transmission of these attributes to John Clare was genetic or part of the family folklore. Either way, we will see the shade of old John Donald Parker in Clare's own life—the unstable identity and the sense of exile, but also the sexual activity and the commitment to reading and writing. Genetically speaking, three-quarters of Clare belonged to Helpston and the immediate neighbourhood, while the other quarter was Scots. He felt an affinity with Robert Burns. In the asylum years, he wrote in many different voices, one of which was the Scottish vernacular.

Clare, who was usually wry and uncensorious when writing of sexual matters, calls the seduction nothing more than a 'deplorable accident of misplaced love'. He clearly admired the robust common sense of his grandmother, who got on with her (long) life and did not pine for what was lost. He himself lacked the gift of putting the past readily behind him.

Hard labour on the land was written into the very name of the family: *Clare* derives from *clayer*, one who manures or marls agricultural land. The soil in the fields of some of the parishes around Helpston is heavy, clayey, difficult to work. 'I cannot trace my name to any remote period,' wrote Clare, 'a century and a half is the utmost and in this I have found no great ancestors to boast in the breed—all I can make out is that they were Gardeners, Parish Clerks and fiddlers'. His own talents were not so very different from those of his ancestors. He was trained as a gardener and became a fine fiddler. And parish clerks would, by definition, have been able to use a pen.

There seem to have been at least two Clare families in the village of Helpston in the early eighteenth century. A John Clare became senior parish clerk. For this reason, his name often appears in the parish register as a witness at weddings. He had a careful writing hand. He was buried in June 1781, aged about eighty. He and his wife Alice (née Gorge) had eleven children, at least four of whom died in infancy or early childhood. Their daughter Alice, who succumbed to the charms of John Donald Parker, was born in 1737 and died on 1 January 1820, the very day on which a London literary magazine published a profile of her grandson and the news that his first book would soon be published. Longevity was in the Clare genes.

The birth in 1765 of Parker Clare was not recorded in the Helpston register. Perhaps the parish clerk was ashamed of the illegitimacy. But Parker was brought up in his grandparents' home in the village. In adult life he was employed on a day-to-day basis as a farm labourer, and was especially known as a thresher. Considerable physical strength was required to wield the flail that separated grain from husk and straw, so when Parker developed rheumatism in his later years, he found it increasingly hard to earn a living. He did not take well to immobility. As a young man he had been a noted wrestler in the village sports. He would come to share with his son an obsession with professional prize-fighting, a world known as the Fancy. A glimpse of their conversations on the subject may be caught from one of Clare's letters to a London friend: 'as soon as he knew I was writing to you [he] reminedded me to be sure and ask you to tell us who wins in Curtis's and Jones's Battles to day and if you take in any of the daily papers which contains the fights we should be very much obliged to you for the loan of one'.

In October 1792, Parker Clare married Ann Stimson, fourth of the six children of John and Elizabeth Stimson of Castor, a village beyond the open land of Emmonsales Heath, some five miles to the south. John Stimson was a 'town shepherd', responsible for the local landowners' livestock, which grazed on the common fields and wastelands. His stewardship seems to have extended to Marholm, closer to Helpston, for it was in that parish's church that his daughter's wedding took place. At thirty-five, Ann Stimson was eight years her husband's senior and swarthy in appearance. She was sometimes ill-tempered. Her parents were probably relieved to see her leave home, even though a casual labourer such as Parker Clare was not an especially attractive match. Given her age, Ann could not have hoped to have a large family. She conceived twins immediately.

'Both my parents was illiterate to the last degree,' Clare would remark. The statement's bluntness and grammatical roughness have served the myth of Clare as child of nature, a pure untutored genius.

However, in the eighteenth century *illiterate* meant not 'unable to read' but 'ignorant of polite letters'. The Clares who formed a line of parish clerks would have been among the more literate of the Helpston villagers. Parker could certainly read. He owned a Bible, but preferred 'the superstitious tales that are hawked about a sheet for a penny, such as old Nixon's Prophesies, Mother Bunch's Fairy Tales, and Mother Shipton's Legacy'. A poor man does not spend his hard-earned pennies on broadsheets if he is incapable of reading them. Ann Stimson, by contrast, did not know a single letter of the alphabet and, like many country people, regarded book-learning as a kind of witchcraft.

It was through his father that Clare first encountered storytelling and folk songs. Best of all, Parker Clare liked ballads. Over a horn of ale at the Blue Bell public house—conveniently situated next door to his cottage—he would boast to his friends that he could sing or recite over a hundred of them. Clare could recollect his father's 'tolerable good voice' and how he would be called upon to entertain the company during many a convivial evening. Parker's son grew up to become not only a teller of tales in verse, but also a highly accomplished musician and collector of songs and tunes. In all probability he was the earliest folk-song collector in southern England. His poetry grew out of an oral tradition that was fully alive in his village and his childhood home.

In the autumn of 1792 Parker and his bride moved into a steep-roofed thatched tenement on Helpston High Street. It was there that Ann gave birth to the twins in the heat of the following July. They had four rooms at their disposal, two up and two down, for which they paid a rent of thirty shillings a year. One bedroom would have been occupied by old Alice Clare, Parker's mother, and the other by Parker, Ann and the children. The bedrooms were reached by a ladder leading up to a trap-door.

Though there was no proper stairway, to have two rooms downstairs was a comparative luxury. Clare said that his childhood home was 'as roomy and comfortable as any of our neighbours'. He 'never felt a desire to have a better'. Often he drew comfort from the thought of home: in an early sonnet he remembered how he would stand watching the light-blue smoke pour from the chimney and think of his family gathered round the fire within. His eye would be drawn to the yellow flowers of the leeks grown in the thatch as a charm against lightning. In a letter he wrote fondly of his snug 'hut': it was so low that if you stood outside and held a walking stick in the air you could reach the upstairs window; you had to stoop to enter the front door, the chimney corner was open to the sky and the hearth always full of soot; but all in all it felt solid and homely with its thick walls and absorbent thatch. His favourite place was a 'corner chair' by the fire— though 'when the rain comes down the chimney it often falls plump on the book I am reading and I am forced to put away the book till the rain is gone'.

There was a large garden. Parker Clare dug vegetables before and after work each day. The family owed much to a Golden Russet apple tree, as Clare explained years later: 'the tree is an old favourite with my father and stood his friend many a year in the days of adversity by producing an abundance of fruit which always met with ready sale and paid his rent.' In better times, Clare sent some of the apples down to his publisher in London: 'their peculiar flavour makes them esteemed here but how your cockney pallets are I know not yet'.

John Clare and his twin sister were born on 13 July 1793. Into what sort of a world did they arrive?

The year had begun with the people of France putting their king on trial for treason. Louis XVI was executed on 21 January. Within three weeks the French republic had declared war on Britain. By summer, the navy was busy in action. On 9 July, William Waldegrave —who later became the first Baron Radstock—celebrated his fortieth birthday aboard a man-of-war he was captaining in the Mediterranean. On the day of Clare's birth, a little-known young poet of radical sympathies and high ideals watched from the Isle of Wight with sorrow in his heart as the British fleet gathered in the Solent. His name was William Wordsworth. That evening in Paris one of the leaders of the revolutionary Jacobins, Jean Paul Marat, was stabbed to death in his bath by Charlotte Corday.

In July 1793 London saw a spate of arson attacks and countless Jacobinical handbills circulated in the streets. In Oxford it was business as usual—the Earls Fitzwilliam and Spencer attended a grand ceremony for the installation of a new University chancellor—but in Cambridge a Mr John Cook was tried and imprisoned for uttering seditious words against king and government.

Some forty miles north of Cambridge stands the mellow-stoned market town of Stamford, where in mediaeval times there had been a short-lived attempt to establish a third English university. This was a region of great houses and estates, owned by the British counterparts of those French aristocrats who were daily being dispatched to the guillotine by Marat's compatriots: the Spencer seat at Althorp; Milton Park, the principal southern residence of the Fitzwilliams; and, most imposing of all, Burghley House, built for Queen Elizabeth's chief minister and now the home of his descendant, the tenth Earl of Exeter. Burghley is on the southern outskirts of Stamford, Helpston four and a half miles further along the same road.

In the week of Clare's birth, the *Stamford Mercury* reported (over-optimistically) that 'the unfortunate delusion that had overspread France is fast dissipating'. But for the people of the village, war and revolution were far away. There was trouble closer to home: a depressed rural economy. Northamptonshire wheat was fetching a price well below the national average. The *Mercury* listed a higher-than-usual number of bankruptcies, auctions of bankrupts' possessions, and creditors' meetings.

Everywhere people were saying that something had to be done about the state of British agriculture. A correspondent in the July *Gentleman's Magazine* proposed a design for a new drill-plough which would reduce the necessity for superfluous men and horses. He informed readers of other devices he had in hand—a machine for dibbling corn, a pedometer for measuring land.

The government was also seeking to measure and to improve.

Prime Minister William Pitt the Younger was working towards the institution of a national Board of Agriculture. Its remit was announced the following month: to inquire into the ownership of land, the state of the soil, livestock, crops and their rotation, the use of ploughs and other machines. To ask 'What advantages have been found to result from inclosing land, in regard to the increase of rent,— quantity or quality of produce,—improvement of stock, etc.' To gather information regarding the size and nature of enclosures, their effect on population and on common lands. The rate of agricultural labour. The extent of wastelands and the upkeep of woodlands. The condition of roads and farmhouses.

The effects of enclosure had not yet been felt in Helpston. The parliamentary act that initiated the change in its landscape would come sixteen years later.

Year in, year out, before and after enclosure, July was a month of back-breaking labour in the fields. In 1793 it would have been particularly arduous because of the weather: Clare was born in the middle of a heat wave. The temperature rose into the eighties on ten out of eleven days around Saturday the thirteenth. It reached ninety degrees as Ann went into labour with the twins. The *Mercury* noted that it was the hottest spell for years. In Stamford the paper's proprietor, Richard Newcomb, announced that he had received a special consignment of Mr Cox's Nitre Tablets, Calcined Magnelia and Pearl Seeds, 'peculiarly serviceable to *every* constitution during the extreme hot weather in particular'.

In Clare's poetry July is a month of 'sultry days and dewy nights'. The time for making hay. Flies everywhere, boys beating them off with boughs while shepherds eat their noontide dinner. Teams of horses wait to cart away the hay, swishing their tails and turning their heads in order to nip—though Clare's word is *knap*—'the gadfly's teazing wound'. There are turnip seeds to be planted, ploughshares to be 'laid' (re-edged) by the blacksmith. And on the margin of the scene, a gypsy with a reaping hook tied to the end of a long pole cuts down bulrushes to hawk around the neighbouring towns.

Since Clare was the son of a day labourer, the expectation would have been that by the age of ten he would follow his father into the fields. No one in the village could have imagined that one day he would be not just experiencing rural labour but also writing about it, as in these vignettes from the 'July' he intended for his *Shepherd's Calendar*.

The initial fear was that he would be lucky to survive at all. Though born first, the boy twin was weakly. His mother joked that she could fit him into a pint pot—a suitable receptacle for the son of a drinker, who became a drinker himself. The girl was 'as much to the contrary a fine lively bonny wench'. But, as Clare said in his autobiographical 'Sketches', the weakest does not always go to the wall: it was the girl who died after a few weeks. The search for something lost— something innocent, female, and associated with childhood—was bound into Clare's mental state and at the heart of his poetry. For the first few weeks of his life, but never again, he lay with his closest kin.

John was baptised on 11 August 1793. His sister was dead by then. No grave is marked. She was to have been christened Elizabeth, after her maternal grandmother. The family remembered her as Bessy. They talked about her enough to ingrain her in John's memory. Years later, shortly before the birth of his own second child, fearful for its prospects after his wife's difficult pregnancy, he wrote a poem for his lost twin:

> Bessey—I call thee by that earthly name
> That but a little while belonged to thee—
> Thou left me growing up to sin and shame
> And kept thy innocence untained and free
> To meet the refuge of a heaven above
> Where life's bud opens in eternity . . .

The sonnet goes on to imagine what it would have been like if the twins had 'gone together' into an early death, if John had been a stranger to the world as Bessy all too soon became a stranger to her mother's love. 'What years of sorrow I had never seen', writes Clare. Growing up meant departing from unblemished innocence and untamed freedom, growing into shame and sorrow.

This movement of thought recurs throughout his poetry. Prospects are closed down with the passing of earthly time; childhood is represented as a lost paradise that can be regained only in eternity. Clare longs for the day when he will at last once again lie at peace beneath the vault of heaven, as a child lies upon the grass, free from care, looking up in wonder at the vastness of the sky.

CHAPTER TWO

CHILDHOOD

John Clare is England's greatest poet of childhood. That he wrote so much and so well on the subject perhaps conspired to give the impression that there was always something childlike about him. But to suppose that Clare was always a child within is to mishear him. He remembered the joy of childhood because he was acutely conscious of the pain and complexity—in his own plain phrase, the 'ups and downs'—of adulthood.

In his poetry he frequently imagined childhood as a kind of Eden, but the point about Eden is that those who write about it have been expelled from it. He interpreted Adam and Eve's expulsion from paradise as an allegory for growing up: 'surely the garden of Eden was nothing more than our first parents' entrance upon life and the loss of it their knowledge of the world.' He considered childhood existence to be synonymous with 'real simple soul-moving poetry'—'the laughter and joy of poetry', though 'not its philosophy'. By the same account, the only poetry available to the adult is 'the reflection and the remembrance of what has been—nothing more'.

Clare is at his freshest as a poet when remembering the simple pleasures of boyhood. He knows the power of a child's imagination:

SCHOOL EXERCISE BOOK, WITH CLARE'S
SIGNATURE AT AGES TEN AND THIRTEEN

Our fancies made us great and rich,
No bounds our wealth could fix,
A stool drawn round the room was soon
A splendid coach and six;
The magic of our minds was great
And even pebbles they
Soon as we chose to call them gold
Grew guineas in our play.

And he remembers how every child rejoices in the freedom of the open air. School is out for the day and it's a race into the fields:

Harken that happy shout—the schoolhouse door
Is open thrown and out the younkers teem.
Some run to leapfrog on the rushy moor
And others dabble in the shallow stream,
Catching young fish and turning pebbles o'er
For mussel-clams—Look in that mellow gleam
Where the retiring sun that rests the while
Streams through the broken hedge—How happy seem
Those schoolboy friendships leaning o'er the stile,
Both reading in one book—anon a dream
Rich with new joys doth their young hearts beguile
And the book's pocketed most hastily.
Ah happy boys, well may ye turn and smile
When joys are yours that never cost a sigh.

The boys play and dream and share companionship without a worry in the world, whereas for the man every joy will be paid for with sighs. But this is a retrospective idealisation: Clare's childhood was not without its share of pain and toil.

Ann Clare bore two further daughters. A few days before John's third birthday, a baby sister was baptised, but she died before the year was out. Fortune changed in the spring of 1798 with the birth of a healthy girl, Sophy.

In most of Clare's vividest childhood recollections, he is either alone or with his schoolmates. He does not often write of Sophy. But the shadow of a younger sister may be glimpsed via the pronoun *we* in an evening memory such as this:

> and round the fire
> We sat—what joy was there:
> The kitten dancing round the cork
> That dangled from a chair
> While we our scraps of paper burnt
> To watch the flitting sparks.

Sophy learnt to read and write, but it is not known for how long she attended school. Ann Clare favoured her son's education, convinced that she had suffered from her own ignorance and hoping that—given she had relatively few mouths to feed—at least her boy could be made 'a good scholar'. So it was that at the age of five young John began attending Mrs Bullimore's dame school in the village. Two years later, he moved on to Mr Seaton's makeshift schoolroom in the vestry of the parish church at Glinton, a two-mile walk away. The image of a boy walking across the fields to school, drinking in his environment, is a recurring memory in his mature poetry:

> The youth, who leaves his corner stool
> Betimes for neighbouring village-school,
> Where, as a mark to guide him right,
> The church spire's all the way in sight,
> With cheerings from his parents given,
> Beneath the joyous smiles of Heaven
> Saunters, with many an idle stand,
> With satchel swinging in his hand,
> And gazes, as he passes by,
> On every thing that meets his eye.

His attendance at school was patchy. When times were hard, his father withdrew him in order to save on the fees. When they were very hard, he took his son to work with him in the fields and barns. He made a light flail so that the boy could assist in the threshing. 'Though one of the weakest', writes Clare, '[I] was stubborn and stomachful and never flinched from the roughest labour—by that means I always secured the favour of my masters and escaped the ignominy that brands the name of idleness'. His employers characterised him as 'weak but willing'. In all his labours, poetic as well as physical, he pushed himself harder than his body could endure.

Threshing in the dusty barn was mainly a winter task, which Clare regarded as 'imprisonment'. He much preferred his spring and summer jobs: tending sheep or horses in the fields, scaring birds from the grain, weeding. The old women of the village assisted with the weeding and helped the time pass with their tales of 'Giants, Hobgobblins, and fairies'. An ancient cowherd known as Granny Bains taught him village lore, weather signs and old songs.

Until he was eleven or twelve, his family managed to keep him in the classroom for three months or more per year, mainly through the worst of the winter when farmwork was limited. He began his ABC at Mrs Bullimore's and was a quick learner. His mother proudly claimed that he could read a chapter of the Bible before he was six. Mrs Bullimore inspired affectionate memories in her pupil. She was not an over-severe disciplinarian and she varied the curriculum. The Bible held a pre-eminent, but not an exclusive place. She would recite old tales to the children—'how Johnny Armstrong fought and how he fell', the poisoning of 'fair Rosamond' by Queen Eleanor, the sufferings of King Edward IV's mistress Jane Shore—and every day they would ask to hear them again. Clare paid a simple but heart-felt tribute to her in one of his earliest poems: 'And by imbibing what she simply taught / My taste for reading there was surely caught.'

Home also provided material for reading practice. He began with the family Bible and prayer book. He started to learn the Psalms by heart, nurturing his instinct for poetry. Then a neighbour lent him an old volume of essays that had lost its title-page, together with a large farming manual. Clare used them to try spelling out words and guessing at the meaning of ones he did not understand. Among his father's penny chapbooks were 'Robin Hood's Garland and the Scotch Rogue'. He also got hold of a pile of sixpenny romances and fairy tales, including 'Cinderella', 'Little Red Riding Hood', 'Jack and the Beanstalk', 'Zig Zag' and 'Prince Cherry'. He loved the stories and took them for fact.

His first introduction to the higher sort of poetry was a book that his uncle, a drover, brought from London. It was a volume by the Reverend John Pomfret, which included a poem called 'Love triumphant over Reason. A Vision'. According to Clare, this was 'more known among the lower orders than any thing else of poetry—at least with us'. Falteringly, his father would recite the poem, a didactic work intended to teach the reader to quell sexual desire, to avoid the physical charms of woman. In the poet's vision, the lovely 'Delia' is transformed from woman to goddess, so that 'Love' triumphs in the form of divine *caritas* as opposed to earthly lust. Clare was not old enough to understand the moral lesson, but looking back on the poem he remarked that 'the relating any thing under the character of a dream is a captivating way of drawing the attention of the vulgar'. The dream or vision became one of his own favoured poetic forms.

What he did remember about the old book of Pomfret's 'was that it was full of wooden cuts and one at the beginning of every poem, the first of which was two childern holding up a great Letter'. It had been the woodcuts that had persuaded his Stimson uncle to pay a shilling for the book. The boy so liked the pictures that he cut them out and burnt the rest of the book to avoid detection. The vividness of his memory of the image of the two children supporting the giant letter suggests that he saw himself and his sister in it: perhaps it served him as an icon of the power of literacy.

He learnt to write at the school in Glinton, where he swiftly proved himself as enthusiastic a pupil as he had been for Mrs Bullimore. Ambitious to do well, he practised his penmanship even when his parents could not afford to send him to school. Mr Seaton 'was always surprised to find me improved every fresh visit, instead of having lost what I had learned before'. Seaton liked to reward his best pupils with 'premiums' and took special delight in questioning and rewarding Clare, even though the boy was an outsider from another village. He saw John's commitment and sought to nurture him. Throughout his writing life, Clare responded positively to encouragement and praise, whilst being all too easily hurt by criticism. When he rose to the challenge of learning an entire chapter of the Book of Job by heart (in the week's holiday over Christmas), Seaton gave him six-pence and warm congratulations. After that, the other boys became reluctant to compete with Clare: 'I got the prizes without trouble and have come in for some time as much as threepence a Week—this I saved unknown to my parents to buy books etc'.

John Seaton was succeeded by a Mr James Merrishaw. In a poem 'To the Memory of James Merrishaw A Village Schoolmaster', Clare offered similar gratitude to that expressed in the poem to Mrs Bullimore:

> For thou it was, dear injur'd man, that gave
> This little learning which I now enjoy,
> A Gift so dear that nothing can destroy.

He also praised Merrishaw for his versatility. The schoolmaster was gifted in music as well as reading and writing, while

> Through Mathematics' hidden depths he'd pry,
> Trace all her windings with a skilful eye.
> And in Geometry his searching view
> Could draw a figure admirably true.

When Clare was sixteen and long out of school, Merrishaw died 'friendless' and in poverty. He was buried in an unmarked grave. Clare wrote two indignant poems about the absence of a headstone to mark the resting-place of this worthy man. His own verse-tributes would have to stand in for the missing memorial inscription. Some years later a correspondent located the grave on Clare's behalf, and made some amends: 'His place of rest is a quiet and retire[d] corner of the church-yard, at the greatest possible distance from the school room. I have directed his grave to be covered with verdant turf.'

One of Clare's school exercise books survives. On the inside front cover he has written in a flowing hand 'John Clare His Book Helpston Northamptonshire 1803'. Three years later, he added an old schoolboy rhyme: 'Steal not this book for fear of Shame / For here doth Stand the owners Name. / John Clare'. Most of the pages are filled with mathematical rules and calculations. To begin with, there is simple addition, calculation of pounds, shillings and pence, and enumeration of weights and measures ('ale or beer measure—4 Quarts make 1 Gallon / 54 Gallons make 1 Hogshead'). Then Clare advanced to subtraction, multiplication, division, compound multiplication and division, square measure and rule of three. On later pages there are practical applications: rule of barter, loss and gain, building measures for carpenter's work ('Of Roofing, Of Walling, Of Chimnees'), rules of thumb for joiners and painters, measurements of timber. Decimals, square roots and geometric figures appear in Clare's most careful hand, and the last thirty pages or so are covered with complex algebraic equations.

It is not clear how far Merrishaw took Clare in his maths. The schoolmaster's name, with the date 1803, appears beneath the twelve-times-table early in the exercise book, but on a later page Clare has written 'J C 1806'. By this time he was in his thirteenth year and working full-time for the sake of the family. Elsewhere he wrote, 'I have a Superficial Knowledge of the Mathematics which I gained partly by self-Tuition (as I was very fond of them once) and partly by the assistance of a Friend whom I shall ever remember with Gratitude'. A footnote identified the friend as 'Mr John Turnill Late of Helpstone now in the Excise'. The likelihood is that Clare's interest was stimulated by Merrishaw, but that limited attendance at school confined his classroom studies to the basics, and thereafter he taught himself with the assistance of Turnill.

After he left school for good, he 'felt an itching after every thing'. He obtained textbooks on mensuration and practical geometry, arithmetic and algebra. From these he copied rules and problems into his exercise book and 'persevered so far as to solve many of the questions in those books'. For a time he had the ambition to become a teacher himself. Turnill laid out a plan of advanced mathematical study for him, but then left home to work for the Excise, and Clare 'luckily abandoned the project, not without great reluctance'. He remained good with figures and the mental discipline required by mathematics prepared him for his future studies in botanical and ornithological classification.

At home in the Helpston cottage, he would read through mealtimes. On winter evenings, the old table—which was accustomed, Clare writes, to bearing only a barley loaf or dish of potatoes—was covered with pens, ink and papers as the boy worked at his books or calculated on a slate 'a knotty question in Numeration, or Pounds, Shillings, and Pence'. His mother would stop her spinning-wheel or look up from her needlework and express the hope that one day her son's pen would bring a reward to his aged parents for the trouble they had taken in sending him to school. His greatest wish was gratified when they lived to see his poetry in print: 'that pleasure I have witnessed and they have moreover lived to see with astonishment and joy their humble offspring noticed by thousands of friends and among them names of the greatest distinction'.

Clare was always hungry to learn, often obsessively so. He would borrow textbooks on different subjects, or buy them with the few pence he saved. Then he would throw himself headlong into the subject, studying page by page, fancying he could master every detail. He felt physically sick when he came across something he could not understand. The compulsion to pursue knowledge was damaging to his health: 'Study always left a sinking sickening pain in my head otherways unaccountable.' Were these headaches the beginning of his mental difficulties? Or is there a more mundane explanation, such as the strain on the eyes caused by poring over small print in dim cottage rushlight?

He acquainted himself with 'Mathematics Particularly Navigation and Algebra, Dialling, Use of the Globes, Botany, Natural History, Short Hand, with History of all Kinds, Drawing, Music etc etc'. Just about every discipline, that is to say, except formal grammar: 'Grammer I never read a page of in my Life', he noted, 'nor do I believe my master knew any more than I did about the matter'. Merrishaw seems to have taken the sensible view that clear penmanship would be of more value to his pupils than polished grammar. Clare's handwriting in his childhood exercise book is very neat.

The teaching of grammar was intimately linked to the study of Latin. It was the mark of the more advanced education provided by the Grammar Schools—*grammar* in that title refers to Latin, not English grammar. The study of Latin and attendance at grammar school were the road to the professions and to social advancement. This path was not available to Clare. He said that at one time in his youth he wanted to learn Latin, but was prevented by the lack of suitable textbooks. He comforted himself with the thought that this saved him the trouble of many an aching head.

There were other books, which offered pure delight instead of mental strain. 'The romance of "Robinson Crusoe" was the first book of any merit I got hold of after I could read.' Whilst at the Glinton school, perhaps aged around seven, he borrowed *Crusoe* from a boy called Stimson (a cousin on his mother's side?). The condition was that the book had to be returned in the morning. But it snowed heavily overnight, preventing Clare from making the two-mile cross-country walk to school. The book remained his for a week, and on future walks to and from school he dreamed of 'new Crusoes and new Islands of Solitude'. Some time after this, he also got to read the book that had been for a century the most popular classic in humble homes, John Bunyan's *Pilgrim's Progress*. It pleased him 'mightily'.

Clare identified strongly with Crusoe's solitude. His love of books began to isolate him from the other boys. On winter Sundays he would sit at home on his corner stool, poring over a book, while the lads played football on the village green. In summer he walked in the woods and fields alone, a book in his pocket. The villagers found this behaviour very odd: 'some fancying it symptoms of lunacy and that my mother's prophecies would be verified to her sorrow and that my reading of books (they would jeeringly say) was for no other improvement than qualifying an idiot for a workhouse'. For whole days at a time, he would seclude himself in the open air, walking, reading, engaging in makeshift study by drawing squares and triangles in the dust on the walls of barns or writing on scraps of paper in which tea or sugar had been wrapped when his mother brought the shopping home from Stamford or Market Deeping. Embarrassed by the comments of neighbours, Mrs Clare sometimes tried to force her boy into company.

He learnt from books whilst in the fields, but he also learnt from the fields themselves. He observed the habits of birds: the 'sweeing' flight of the woodpecker, the jay's warning chatter, the sound of the cuckoo both far and near, the restless music of the nightingale, the clap of a wood pigeon's wing at dusk. He was anxious to note minute details: the flight of insects, the opening of flowers, a simple bridge or wooden stile with ivy growing round the posts. He would pull his hat down over his eyes to shade them from the sun, then look up 'to watch the rising of the lark or to see the hawk hanging in the summer sky and the kite take its circles round the wood'.

From the age of about seven, his Sunday job tending horses and cows in the fields had been a licence to ignore the bells summoning all to church. When there were other boys around, he played at 'marbles on the smooth-beaten sheep tracks or leap-frog among the thymey molehills'. While the grown-ups were in church, the boys stole peas and took them to the gypsy camp where they could be boiled on the fire. 'The fields were our church and we seemed to feel a religious feeling in our haunts on the sabbath.' It is doubtful, though, whether the other boys shared Clare's intensity of feeling. He was growing so far 'into the quiet love of nature's presence' that he was 'never easy' save when he was in the fields.

In his autobiography, he brought his poet's eye to the memory of a boy's idle Sundays. The sheep-track through the thistly pasture. Hunting for wild flowers, then dropping down on a thyme-covered molehill to survey the summer landscape. The varied tints in a flat field: the green of the ripening grain and the copper of clover in blossom; 'the lighter hues of wheat and barley intermixed with the sunny glare of the yellow charlock and the sunset imitation of the scarlet head-aches [i.e. poppies] with the blue corn bottles'. And the greens of the wood: white poplar, grey willow, mellow lime. Spangled dragonflies, darting swallows, wild geese scudding through the sky in formations that made 'all the letters of the Alphabet'. 'The mysterious spring sound of the land rail that cometh with the green corn.' The 'long purples' at the edge of the meadow lake. The marshy fen, with a solitary heron sweeping across its melancholy sky. The steep edge of the stone quarry. Human figures at labour or at rest in the landscape: woodman, shepherd, milkmaid. Windmills turning slowly in the summer breeze. 'The steeples peeping among the trees round the horizon's circle.'

He would listen 'with raptures' to the sound of hedge crickets. He was alert to tiny things: the cracking of the corn stubs in the sun and the 'bounce' of the grasshopper. 'And I watched with delight on haymaking evenings the setting sun drop behind the brigs and peep again through the half circle of the arches as if he longs to stay.' The location here is Lolham Bridges, to the north of Helpston. Its four ancient arches did not bridge a river, but served as the passageway for a section of the Roman road that was liable to flooding. Nearby there is another single-arched bridge spanning a hollow. It is still just possible to make out among the names carved into the stonework on the underside 'J Clare Helpstone 1811'.

There was a little patch of common land called Tankers Moor, where a spring bubbled up and dribbled its way through the grass. Hundreds of minnows swam in the shallow water. 'When a boy', Clare remembered, 'we used to go on a Sunday in harvest and leck it out with a dish and string the fish on rushes—and thereby thinking ourselves great fishers from the number we had caught, not heeding the size.' From a very early age he also loved fishing alone; Izaac Walton's *Compleat Angler* became one of his favourite books.

His memories of boyhood embrace both company and solitude. There is vigour and playfulness in his recollection of being one of a group of boys who chased squirrels, robbed birds' nests (though in retrospect he felt sorry for the birds), poked their arms down rabbit-holes (running off in fear when someone suggested there might be a snake there), and pulled down 'boughs from the trees to beat a wasps' nest till some of us were stung and then we ran away to other amusements'. Intensity and yearning are reserved for the memory of secluded spots, the bowers where he encloses himself under an old ivy-covered oak in Oxey Wood or at Langley Bush or below Lee Close Oak. As he grew up, he watched with pain as each of these harbours of security disappeared. The bower in Oxey Wood was destroyed by woodmen who 'fancied it a resort for robbers'. Langley Bush was 'broken up by some wanton fellows while kidding furze on the heath'. And Lee Close Oak was felled in the enclosure. The carpenter who bought the wood, hearing it had been a favourite spot of Clare's, gave him two rulers cut from it.

In some autobiographical notes, Clare listed the following as the childhood games he remembered:

> Playing at soldiers—nine peg Morris
> Making cockades etc of corn poppies and bluebottles
> Making house of sticks clay and stones
> Gathering broken pots—getting mallow seeds and calling them
> cheeses when playing at feasts.

The child, wrote Wordsworth, is father to the man. As a young man, the boy who had played at soldiers joined the militia. Nine-peg Morris was an outdoor game, the playing area cut in turf. All his life Clare was happiest out of doors. Is it fanciful to see the other games as prefigurations of a poet's life? They have in common the arts of pretence and of *building*. As both boy and man, Clare used his imagination to turn humble objects into grander things. Like a bird building a nest, he collected fragments and made them into wholes, into homes.

Boys are always having accidents—especially in the country. Here are some of Clare's. He and some other lads were tending cows in a meadow dotted with pools. They tried to outdo each other in successive games. How far into the water dare you go? He didn't realize that the gravel on which he stood was only a ledge. His heels slipped and he was in deep, on his way to the bottom. 'I felt the water choke me and thunder in my ears and I thought all was past'. He was rescued by some of the boys who could swim. On another occasion the boys were floating in a pool on bundles of bulrushes; when 'mine getting to one end suddenly bounced from under me like a cork', Clare nearly went under.

Bird's-nesting was dangerous sport too. On one occasion a group of boys found a buzzard's nest high in a very difficult tree, tied a hook to the end of a long pole, attached it to the collar of the tree, and Clare pulled himself up. But he had to swing himself round an overhang, whilst grasping at a side branch: 'I attempted it and failed so there I hung with my hands and feet dangling in the air—I expected every moment to drop and be pashed to pieces for I was a great height'. Some of the boys had run away, but others pushed him up with the pole and he clambered onto the branch, exhausted. When he was older, gathering acorns in the foliage alone, he fell some fifteen feet to the ground and was badly concussed: 'I lay for a long time and knew nothing . . . I could not catch my breath unless by deep groans'. 'And I got over that', he adds casually. But we cannot rule out the possibility that the concussion had long-term effects.

Like most children, Clare had a more complex imaginative life when alone than when in company. Among his friends, he professed a disbelief in ghosts, witches and rural superstitions—'yet when I was alone in the night my fancies created thousands and my fears was always on the look out every now and then turning around to see if aught was behind me'; 'if I deny their existence in the day I soon recant my opinions at night when I am wandering alone by haunted spots'. He was terrified by his first will-o'-the-wisp, a common sight in the marshy fens. Taking the horses out to the heath on spring evenings, he would suppose the squeal of a badger to be the scream of a woman.

Once he helped with the harvest over in the village of Ashton. The supper to celebrate the harvest home went on till nearly midnight and he had to return across 'Barons Park', where there were ruins of a Roman camp and a Saxon castle. It was a spot renowned for ghosts and goblins. He thought he saw something on the path and his imagination 'magnified it into a horrible figure' with huge ears and shaggy hair. But he returned the following evening and realised that it was only a lost foal. The realisation hardened him in his disbelief of ghosts.

This story recalls 'The Fakenham Ghost', a ballad by one of Clare's favourite poets, Robert Bloomfield. It tells the old and supposedly true story of an old woman at night who thought she encountered a ghostly monster when it was really 'An *Ass's Foal* [that] had lost its Dam / Within the spacious Park'. We must beware of taking Clare at his word, for he was quite capable of viewing his world through his books.

He kept a tame sparrow called Tom. To begin with, he was afraid that the family cat would kill it, so he held the bird in his hand as she approached, then smacked her as she sniffed at it. She thus learnt to take no notice of it. Clare was now ready to let the bird loose in the house. Tom and Puss were initially wary of each other. When he chirruped, she 'would brighten up as if she intended to seize it but she went no further than a look or smell'. Puss then had kittens. When they were taken away from her, presumably to be drowned, she adopted the sparrow. She would caress it, mew to it and even 'lay mice before it the same as she would for her own young'. Tom grew in confidence and eventually took to perching on Puss's back. But after three years, he flew away and disappeared. Clare went out and called to all the sparrows he could find—'for he would come down in a moment to the call and perch upon my hand to be fed'—but without success. He suspected that Tom had made the fatal error of mistaking another cat for his friend.

There was also a robin, recognisable by a white scar on one of its wings, which for three successive winters came into the cottage through a broken window-pane. It would perch on a finger and take crumbs from the hand. Sometimes it seemed to be settling down on the spindle of a chair for the night, ruffling its feathers and putting its head under its wing until 'something or other always molested it when it suddenly sought its old broken pane and departed when it was sure to be the first riser in the morning'. Together with the wren

and the martin, the robin was a bird that did not suffer the maraud-
ings of village boys, for to steal its eggs was always supposed to result
in a broken leg.

Birds and animals were friends for Clare. He kept tame stock doves
well into his adult life. Among human companions, his first close
friend was Richard Turnill, brother of John.

Their father Robert was a tenant farmer in the parish and their
mother was, according to Clare, 'skilled in huswife physic and
Culpepper's Herbal'. Richard was Clare's junior by two years. As
young boys they played house together. When a little older, they
hunted for birds' nests and snail shells. Out on the heath, among the
hedgerows and lying on their backs on the soft grass in summer, gazing up at the blue sky and the changing shapes of the clouds, they
would dream and plan and 'talk in rapture o'er our joys to come'.

At the age of seventeen, Richard died of typhus. One of Clare's
early poems was written in his memory. It has the elaborate title and
abstract diction conventional to eighteenth-century memorial verse:
'Elegy Humbly attempted (from the overflowing effusions of a feeling heart) to pay a small tribute of esteem and gratitude to the memory of my dear friend companion and schoolfellow R T who was
suddenly cut off in his youthful days by the fatal depredations of the
Tipus Fever.' The poem itself is as forced in its language as the title,
but it is an early example of Clare's technique of projecting a sense of
loss into the scenes of his childhood. Years later, Clare wrote that
Richard Turnill was 'the first whose loss accostomd me to the lorn
sorrows and feelings experienced in departed friendship'. He had just
turned twenty when his friend died. The loss of his dearest boyhood
companion marked the end of his own carefree youth.

Richard's older brother John, who helped Clare with his mathematics, went off to London and a career in the Excise that eventually
took him to Manchester. He was intellectually inquiring. He liked to
solve the puzzles that appeared in the almanacs. He made up rhymes,
riddles and rebuses. He constructed a makeshift sun-dial and a
pasteboard telescope, through which he'd study the stars with the

assistance of an astronomical guide bought for a penny from a second-hand bookstall. He drew by perspective and 'made an instrument from a shilling art of painting which he had purchased that was to take landscapes almost by itself—it was a long square shape with a hole at one end to look thro and a number of different colored threads crossed into little squares at the other—from each of these squares different portions of the Landscape was to be taken one after the other and put down in a facsimile of these squares done with a pencil on the paper'. Clare preferred the natural 'instantaneous sketches' made by sunlight and shadow upon the ground.

Like his brother, John Turnill inspired one of Clare's early poems. It was a sonnet of gratitude for the pains taken in helping the younger boy with his book-learning. The Turnills became symbols for Clare of his own double self, one a lover of the fields and the heath, the other ambitious with his books. Richard's death and John's departure from Helpston set him thinking about his own future, his own place. The Turnill family were better off than the Clares—both Parker and John worked for them as casual labourers—but in later years they did not escape the effects of the enclosure of the parish. In March 1811, Robert Turnill's landlord reclaimed his farm and the family was served with a notice to quit.

When Clare's first book appeared in 1820, his publisher John Taylor contributed a biographical introduction, based on notes provided by the poet himself. Taylor made a major point of John Turnill's role in shaping Clare's intellectual development, saying that without this friend 'he would not have been the Poet he is', since 'without writing down his thoughts, he could not have evolved them from his mind ... his vocabulary would have been too scanty to express even what his imagination had strength enough to conceive'. Turnill modestly regarded this as excessive praise for his role.

Another friend was a boy called Tom Porter. He liked flowers and gardening. He and Clare dug up wild orchids and planted them in the garden of the Porters' isolated cottage at Ashton Green, a mile to the west of Helpston. Porter's great-grandfather had been steward at one of the local big houses, Walcott Hall, and the family still possessed some of his old books. Clare went over on Sundays and read them, especially liking a herbal and a travel book. Tom collected second-hand gardening books. He remained a close friend into adulthood. The association between bookishness and gardening was of considerable importance to Clare.

He fell in love for the first time while still at school. The girl's name was Mary. Like the Turnills, she was from a farming family of a higher social standing than the Clares, the Joyces of Glinton. James Joyce lived in the oldest farmhouse in the village and owned many parcels of land in and around the parish. He was a churchwarden. Mary, born in January 1797, was the youngest of his four children.

Clare said that Mary Joyce won his affections not only for her pretty face, but also because she was the quietest and sweetest-tempered girl in school. In his autobiographical 'Sketches' he suggested that she knew nothing of his fondness for her and that he did not know whether she would have been inclined to encourage or reject him. 'It was platonic affection,' he writes, 'nothing else but love in idea'. In short time other girls excited his admiration, so that 'the first creator of my warm passions was lost in a perplexed multitude of names that would fill a vol to Calendar them down ere a bearded chin could make the lawful apology for my entering the lists of Cupid. Thus began and ended my amorous career.'

The way in which Clare writes about Mary here is simultaneously off-hand and wistful. This is typical of his profoundly divided sense of himself as a lover. On the one hand, he is a youthful Don Juan, filling up a book with the names of girls who have taken his fancy before he has even grown any hair on his face. On the other hand, his platonic love for Mary Joyce, which begins and ends in his own imagination, constitutes the whole course of his amorous career. He remained obsessed with the idea—the ideal—of love as something unobtainable. The greater the distance from his classroom crush on Mary, the more it took on the aura of the one great passion of his life. Being associated with the years before puberty, the passion for Mary was kept free from the taint of sexual desire. This in turn meant that Clare's attitude to sex itself was sometimes casual, sometimes filled with disgust.

In his 1824 autobiography, chapter six was called 'Memorys of Love'. He tells of how, as he grew up, he mixed as much as he could in female company, going to dances 'for the sake of meeting with the lasses'. 'For I was,' he says, 'a lover very early in life'. And he goes into more detail about his feelings for Mary: merely to gaze on her face or fancy a smile on her lips would suffice him. In this fuller and more candid recollection, John and Mary are intimate friends at school: 'We played with each other but named nothing of love'. In contradiction to the earlier statement that he had no conception of whether his feelings were reciprocated, Clare says that he thought he read affection in Mary's eyes. They walked together in leisure hours. Their talk was only of play, but when their hands touched John's heart turned chill with excitement. As he gazed intently upon her face, 'a tear would hang in her smiling eye and she would turn to wipe it away'.

Playing one day in the churchyard, he threw an unripe walnut at her. It hit her in the eye and she cried. There must have been other children present, because John did not show any regret, for fear that 'others might laugh it into love'. This memory, recorded nearly thirty years after the event, shows how deeply Clare was affected in retrospect by his feelings for Mary. He is still feeling the cruelty to the girl consequent upon the boy's desire not to be laughed at by his mates. She is lodged fast in his head: 'I cannot forget her little playful fairy form and witching smile even now.'

He wrote songs and ballads in her praise, some of his first attempts at poetry. He fantasised first about making her his own and then that he would be denied her because of his humble station. 'When she grew up to womanhood she felt her station above mine,' he wrote, only to admit in the next sentence that the thought was but his fancy: 'at least I felt that she thought so—for her parents were farmers and Farmers had great pretensions to something—then so my passion cooled with my reason and contented itself with another—though I felt a hopeful tenderness that I might one day renew the acquaintance and disclose the smothered passion'. In one form or another, that hope stayed with him all his life.

Clare returned to his childhood again and again in his poetry.

'Childish Recollections', published in 1821 in his second book, sketches the scenes where he played childhood games. With other boys: a dyke they jumped across, a gate they called their wooden horse. And alone: gathering cowslips ('cowslaps', he calls them) and snail shells ('pooties'), damming a brook with turf and stones, climbing a tree to watch the ploughmen, making imaginary cottages out of pebbly shells, digging little wells with a makeshift wooden knife and filling them with spring-water. In manhood he considers himself to be an 'intruder' upon these 'childish scenes', whose bliss will never be replicated. 'Might I but have my choice of joy below', he concludes, 'I'd only ask to be a boy again'. There is nostalgia here, but nothing approaching anguish.

Ten years later, in a poem called 'Childhood', he is poised between the joy of memory and the grief of loss: 'The past it is a magic word', he begins, 'Too beautiful to last, / It looks back like a lovely face'. Would that be the face of Mary Joyce? Yet this is not only a poem of loss and longing. It is filled with energy and affection for the companionship, the imagination and especially the mischief of youth: playing ball, climbing the church porch to cut names upon the lead, pelting stones at the weathercock, twirling tops and rolling marbles, racing over the broken-railed bridge, hopscotch, stilts, bows and arrows, 'I spy' at dusk, shuttlecocks sent high in the air towards the moon, pockets full of acorns, the search for hips and sloes in winter, pelting a snowman named Bonaparte, robbing all the eggs from an owl's nest and mocking her as she flew, urging a dog 'To chase the cat up weed-green walls / And mossy apple tree; / When her tail stood like a bottle-brush / With fear'. Clare looks back, approaching the age of forty, and sees that the flowers, the birds, the trees, the pond and the weather continue unchanged, whereas his own past survives only in memory and poetry.

When he is fifty-five, in the asylum where he will spend the remainder of his days, the memories are all still vivid in another poem called 'Childhood'. Indeed they are more precise than ever: the heavy old desk at which he sat doing his sums for Merrishaw whilst dreaming of 'the wildwood', the churchyard where he threw the walnut at Mary, the hedge with its glossy red hips and the green-linnet's nest he'd hurry to find before school, the fuss his mother would make when he came home from the heath with torn clothes, the doll's tea-party prepared with Sophy, the stile that he rode a cock-horse, 'The mile-a-minute swee / On creaking gates'. But in the poem's startling final line he writes 'All forget us before we are men'. Clare's sense of rejection and neglect overshadows even his own past. He is in despair not because he has forgotten his childhood, but because his childhood has forgotten him.

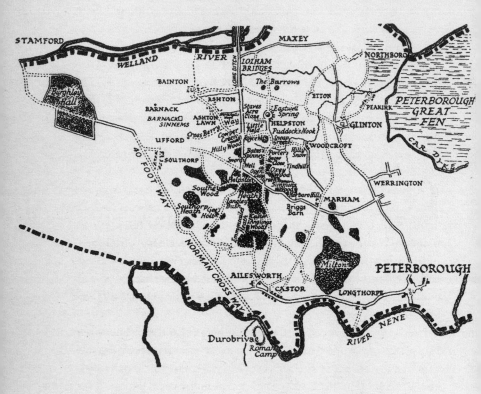

STAMFORD
WELLAND RIVER
MAXEY
NORTHBORO
LOLHAM BRIDGES
BAINTON
The Barrows
PETERBOROUGH GREAT FEN
Burghley Hall
ETTON
ASHTON
Staves Acre Close
Eastwell Spring
PEAKIRK
BARNACK
ASHTON LAWN
Cross Berry Way
Little Field
HELPSTON
Puddock's Nook
GLINTON
CAR DYKE
BARNACK SINNEMS
Cowper Greens
Royce Wd
Snow Green
WOODCROFT
UFFORD
Hilly Wood
Bates Spinney
Porters
Hilly Snow
SOUTHORP
Swordy Well
Open Wood
Oxey Close
Tindhill
WERRINGTON
40 FOOT WAY
Southey Wood
Heath
Open Wood
Simmons Gravel
Narboro Hills
MARHAM
Squthorp Heath
Gee Holt
Langley Bush
Briggs Barn
Lea Anglinus Wood
Milton
PETERBOROUGH
NORMAN CROSS WAY
AILESWORTH
CASTOR
LONGTHORPE
Durobrivae
Roman Camp
RIVER NENE

Scale of Miles
0   1   2   3   4

CLARE'S HOME TERRITORY: STAMFORD AND THE BURGHLEY ESTATE
TO THE NORTHWEST; PETERBOROUGH AND THE MILTON ESTATE TO
THE SOUTHEAST; THE VILLAGE OF HELPSTON NEAR THE CENTRE,
WITH CLARE'S FAVOURITE PLACES TO ITS IMMEDIATE SOUTH (OXEY
WOOD, HELPSTON HEATH, LANGLEY BUSH, EMMONSALES HEATH);
MARKET DEEPING JUST OFF THE MAP TO THE NORTHEAST;
MARY JOYCE'S GLINTON TO THE EAST AND NORTHBOROUGH
TO THE NORTHEAST, ON THE EDGE OF THE GREAT FEN

CHAPTER THREE

HORIZONS

One summer day when Clare was still a child he started off in the morning to gather rotten sticks from the wood, but he 'had a feeling to wander about the fields'. The yellow furze of Emmonsales Heath stretched away into the distance. He had often gazed in that direction. Now his curiosity got the better of him and he set off to explore. 'I had imagined', he recollected later, 'that the world's end was at the edge of the horizon and that a day's journey was able to find it'.

He thought that when he reached the brink of the world he would find a large pit. He would look down and see the secrets of the universe, just as when he gazed into a pool of water he could see the heavens. As he put it in 'Birds Nesting', written many years later,

> To the worlds end I thought I'd go
> And o'er the brink just peep adown
> To see the mighty depths below.

'I eagerly wandered on and rambled among the furze the whole day', he remembered, 'till I got out of my knowledge when the very wild flowers and birds seemed to forget me and I imagined they were the inhabitants of new countries.' On the heath, the sun shone from a different angle and each minute revealed a new world, a new wonder.

He was so absorbed in the scene that before the morning seemed to be over, it was dusk. A white moth fluttered, while snail, frog and mouse went on their evening journeys as 'the hedge cricket whisper[ed] the hour of waking spirits'. The boy found the right track by chance, 'but when I got into my own fields I did not know them— every thing seemed so different'. Not even the church, 'peeping over the woods', could stabilise his sense of where he was. When he got home he found his parents in great distress, and half the village looking for him. That day a woodman had been killed by a falling tree and they feared that the boy had suffered the same fate.

Clare spent many of his happiest days wandering alone on Emmonsales Heath. He grew intimate with the flora and fauna of Helpston and its surrounding parishes. His sense of his own identity was bounded by the horizon of his locality. To leave Helpston was to go out of his knowledge. To return was unsettling: the known and loved place seemed different. In reality, Helpston was the same. It was Clare who was different. Once a native has gone away, he can never fully return.

Clare's self and his poetry were shaped as much by environment as by heredity. To understand him, we need to know his native place. Let us begin with the four corners of his known world.

Helpston is in the center of a square-shaped area known as the Soke of Peterborough, bounded to the south and east by the River Nene, to the north by the River Welland, and to the west by the stretch of the Great North Road that passed from Wansford to Stamford. Wansford, to the southwest of Helpston, was little more than a staging-post, famous for an inn called the Haycock where Lord Byron was fond of staying when travelling between London and his home in Nottinghamshire. There was also a mill for the manufacture of cheap paper, a commodity of which Clare was always in need.

Peterborough, with its ancient cathedral, lies to the southeast of Helpston. It was known for an annual fair and was the meeting place of Northamptonshire, Huntingdonshire and Cambridgeshire.

Though the home of two important people in Clare's story, Dr Skrimshire and Marianne Marsh the Bishop's wife, he did not go there often.

Clare's first journey out of the Soke was eastward across the Cambridgeshire fens to Wisbech. He never visited the city of Cambridge, but was acutely aware of the university. Christ's College owned land in the village of Helpston and appointed its vicar. A more personal contact was established in 1820 when Clare became friendly with Chauncey Hare Townsend, a student at Trinity Hall.

To the east and north of Helpston, in the midst of reclaimed fenland, lie the villages of Glinton and Northborough. And to the northeast, just over the border into Lincolnshire, is Market Deeping. This was the nearest sizeable community to Helpston. There were shops and places of public resort—a weekly market, a small theatre and several inns, including the Bull, where packages from London were usually left for Clare to collect. It was in Deeping that Clare bought his first writing-book and made his first attempt to get his poems published.

When the Clare family moved the three miles from Helpston to Northborough in the early 1830s, their correct postal address became 'Northborough, Market Deeping, Lincolnshire'. Clare had many reasons to feel displaced by the move. One small part of his alienation was a sense that the Northamptonshire poet was in danger of dropping off the edge of his own county. When writing home from the asylum, he doggedly addressed his letters to 'Northborough, near Market Deeping, Northamptonshire'. The people of Helpston thought of Northborough as a place on the margins; they had a phrase for slow-witted workers, 'Send him to Norborrey hedge corner to hear the wooden cuckoo sing'.

Stamford, also just into Lincolnshire, lay to the northwest of Helpston. This was the cultured market town where Clare bought the book that inspired him to become a poet and made the contact that led to the publication of his first volume. The newspapers that Clare avidly read were published there, as were many books. It boasted mu-

sical evenings, both public and private, and a theatre. The Friday
market brought in farmers and shoppers from a wide radius within
Lincolnshire, Rutland and Northamptonshire.

The myth of Clare as pure child of nature depends on an image
of rural ignorance as well as deprivation. But there is London preju-
dice at work here. Stamford was no backwater and even Deeping had
a theatre. Provincial culture radiated out from the market towns,
bringing news and knowledge to the villages, albeit on a weekly
rather than a daily basis. Clare's Stamford publisher explained to his
London one that 'There is no direct communication with Helpstone
of any kind. It is a solitary village and all the intercourse it has with
the world is the once a week market post'. When Clare became published, his mother, wife or sister would walk to Stamford or Deeping
to send and receive post for him.

Stamford was not only a provincial center: being a staging-post on
the Great North Road, it had a direct line of access to London news.
Several local tradesmen, notably the grocer and man of letters Octavius Gilchrist, were well connected in London. The *Stamford Mercury* was one of the country's leading newspapers, the articulate
voice of eastern England. In 1809 John Drakard established a rival
paper, the *Stamford News*. He appointed as editor a radical young
journalist called John Scott, who anticipated Clare in treading the
path from Stamford to London.

Scott attracted widespread attention through his championing of
the oppressed, his vigorous advocacy of parliamentary reform and
his outspoken attacks on the abuses of power. His denunciation of
military flogging in an article entitled 'One Thousand Lashes!'
cost proprietor Drakard an eighteen-month prison sentence. On
Drakard's release in 1813, Scott started a London edition of the paper,
which a year later he renamed the *Champion*. It became one of the
leading liberal journals in the turbulent years after Waterloo, in large
part due to the editor's eye for talented young writers. He created
regular columns for William Hazlitt, J. H. Reynolds and Charles
Lamb. In 1820 they all followed Scott to a new journal, the *London*

Magazine. It in turn became the most exciting literary monthly of the age.

The question of parliamentary reform was an especially sensitive matter in Stamford, for it was a 'pocket borough'—that is to say, the two Members of Parliament returned at each election would be those who served the interest of the local grandee, the Marquess of Exeter. In 1812 a candidate stood against the Exeter interest and duly came bottom of the poll. The local gentry and tradesmen who had the privilege of voting knew on which side their bread was buttered: the Marquess owned a large proportion of the town.

The road from Helpston to Stamford was just under five miles long. It passed through the village of Barnack, where there were stone quarries dating back to Roman times. Charles Kingsley, author of *The Water Babies* and *Alton Locke* (the story of a poet from humble circumstances), spent part of his childhood in the vicarage there during Clare's years as a local celebrity. He always remembered the fenland landscape fondly.

For the last mile before Stamford the road followed the northern edge of Burghley Park. Though the Soke was bounded by road, river and market town, power resided in two great estates. Burghley was the seat of the Exeters, who dominated Stamford and the western half of the Soke; Milton that of the Fitzwilliams, who dominated Peterborough and the eastern half. They were political opponents: the Exeters sat in the House of Lords as Tories, the Fitzwilliams as Whigs. The Fitzwilliams, known to locals as the Miltons, were among the wealthiest and most venerable families in the land. Milton Hall had been their principal seat until 1769, when they inherited the vast Wentworth estate in Yorkshire. Still, as at Burghley, their house in the Soke boasted a magnificent private art collection and library, while the park housed kennels for the hunt. The Milton hounds had a reputation second to none.

Helpston was on the cusp of the two interests. The Fitzwilliams were lords of its two manors, but the most substantial public house in the village was the Exeter Arms. After Clare became famous, each family recognised the value of his name. The juggling of rival patrons would be one of the poet's more delicate tasks, but he was always eager to acknowledge the true nobility of both families. He scribbled a memorandum to this effect in his middle years:

> For so long as the Miltons and the Exeters have been a name in this neighbourhood, there is not one instance that I know of where they have treated success in his willing industry with unkindness in either insulting dependants with oppression or treating poverty with cruelty—not one—and this is a proof to me that nobility is the chief support to industry and that their power is its strongest protection.

In his autobiographical prose Clare often doffed his cap to 'industry', a virtue that all working men were supposed to cultivate. This may have been because he was acutely conscious that poetry was something that could only be cultivated in the opposing state of 'idleness'. His compulsion to write so much that it frequently made him ill is explained in part by the need to make his vocation a form of industry and not an indulgence.

Clare's horizon was set by the parishes surrounding Helpston. These were, counting clockwise from the north, Maxey, Etton (with Glinton just beyond), Ufford and Bainton. Northborough, where he later moved, was to the east of Maxey; Castor, where his mother's family came from, to the south of Ufford. During his childhood most of these parishes had open fields. In 1799 Bainton was enclosed.

Ten years later, when Clare was sixteen, a parliamentary act was passed allowing for 'Inclosing Lands in the Parishes of *Maxey with Deepingate, Northborough, Glinton with Peakirk, Etton, and Helpstone* in the County of *Northampton*'. The principal purpose of the act of enclosure was to maximize the profit available from the land:

> And whereas some Parts of the said Arable, Meadow, and Pasture lands are intermixed, and otherwise inconveniently situated for the respective Owners and Occupiers thereof, and the said Commons and Waste Grounds yield but little Profit, and in

their present State are incapable of any considerable Improvement, and it would be very advantageous if the said Arable, Meadow, and Pasture Lands, and also the said Commons and Waste Grounds, were divided and inclosed, and in specific Shares thereof allotted to the several Persons interested therein, in proportion and according to their respective Estates, Rights, and Interests; But such Division, Allotment, and Inclosure cannot be effected without the Authority of Parliament.

The price of 'Improvement' was the loss of the 'Commons and Waste Grounds'. It took until 1820 to bring the enclosure fully into effect. Nearby Castor, meanwhile, remained as one of the country's longest-surviving open-field parishes, only being enclosed in 1898.

Under the open-field system, the agricultural land around the village of Helpston was divided into three large fields, Lolham Bridge Field to the north, Heath Field to the west and Woodcroft Field to the east. The fields were divided into 'furlongs' and the furlongs into 'lands', strips of ground ploughed into ridges. Each landowner or tenant in the village held a number of lands dispersed around the three fields. To the south, there was woodland—Royce Wood and Oxey (or Oxeye) Wood, favourite haunts of young Clare. And a little further south, the horizon for which the boy had set out that summer morning: the common land, available for rough grazing, of Emmonsales (otherwise known as Ailesworth) Heath.

In Clare's world, there was an intimate relationship between society and environment. The open-field system fostered a sense of community: you could talk to the man working the next strip, you could see the shared ditches, you could tell the time of day by the movement of the common flock and herd from the village pound out to the heath and back. Once a year everyone would gather to 'beat the bounds', that is to say, walk around the perimeter of the parish as a way of marking its boundaries. The fields spread out in a wheel with the village at its hub.

In a brilliant analysis of Clare's 'open-field sense of space', the critic John Barrell has argued that 'the topography and organization of an open-field parish was circular, while the landscape of parliamentary enclosure expressed a more linear sense'. The three large open fields formed a circle, with Helpston at its centre, around which crops were rotated annually. Livestock would be moved 'around the circle of the parish as they grazed in turn the fallows, the commons, the meadows, the stubble, the fallows again'. The countryside of Clare's childhood was in the most literal sense open, and many of his poems both describe and formally enact motions that are circular. But with the enclosure, the parish was divided into rectangular fields which were further subdivided by their owners. The enclosure award map of 1820 is ruled by a sense of linear—and again in the most literal sense—*enclosed* space.

In the years from 1809 to 1820, as Clare grew from adolescence to adulthood, Helpston and its neighbouring parishes were steadily enclosed. New public roads were staked out by 1811, new allotments of land within the next year, minor and private roads the year after that. In 1816 a parish meeting in Helpston drew up new bye-laws in which local rights of way were restricted in accordance with the new disposition of land. The final enclosure, the Award of 1820, enumerated the ownership of every acre, rood and perch, the position of every road, footway and public drain. Fences, gates and No Trespassing signs went up. Trees came down. Streams were stopped in their course so that the line of ditches could be made straight.

The economic effects of enclosure have been hotly debated in the century since 1911, when the socialist historians J. L. and Barbara Hammond published their classic study, *The Village Labourer 1760 – 1832*. According to one view, enclosure was solely for the benefit of the larger landowners. Small owner-occupiers and tenant farmers are supposed to have lost their land, while labourers who were no longer able to benefit from the commons were forced onto poor relief. The counter-argument is that enclosure increased both agricultural productivity and rural employment. Analysis of land-tax assessments and expenditure on parish relief suggest that in the case of Helpston more smallholders and tenant farmers lost their land in the years immediately before the enclosure than in its aftermath, whilst the labouring poor may actually have been marginally better off as a result of enclosure.

But what matters to individual lives is personal experience, not economic statistics. The family of small farmers best known to Clare were the Turnills. They were forced from their home without compensation at the time of the enclosure; as far as Clare was concerned this was proof that the new regime gave unrestricted power to the large landowners. Equally, Clare loved to spend time with the gypsies who camped on the commons and margins: where were they to go once the 'waste' grounds became private property? It was through such eyes as these that he saw enclosure.

For many villagers, enclosure was experienced as an engine of social more than economic alienation. Use of the commons was technically a right restricted to those who occupied certain properties, but psychologically the unenclosed spaces were perceived as belonging to everyone. Enclosure was therefore symbolic of the destruction of an ancient birthright based on co-operation and common rights. The chance of Clare's time and place of birth gave him an exceptional insight into this changed world. An unusually high proportion of Helpston villagers held common rights. An unusually large area of the parish consisted of heathland and 'wastes' from which the commoners could gather fuel. And the open fields survived until an unusually late date. For all these reasons, the effect of enclosure was felt especially strongly in Helpston and by Clare.

Particular resentment was caused by the infringement of ancient customs. Festival days and their attendant rituals marked the high points of a labourer's year. On Whit Sunday, for instance, all the youth of Helpston had, for as many years as anyone could remember, met at Eastwell Fountain to drink sugared water as a good-luck charm. With enclosure, the spring at Eastwell became private property, so the custom was abolished; years later, Clare revisited the deserted spot and wrote an angry poem of loss. Equally, the march towards more intensive production led to the abolition of the annual holiday on Plough Monday. 'The vulgar tyrants of the soil', wrote

Clare in another verse fragment, 'Deem them an hinderance of toil.'

For Clare himself, enclosure infringed the right to roam, which had been one of the joys of his youth. It was an offence against not only community and custom, but also the land itself. In some of the most powerful pages ever written on Clare and enclosure, E. P. Thompson grasped the radical significance of this, discerning that 'Clare may be described, without hindsight, as a poet of ecological protest: he was not writing about man here and nature there, but lamenting a threatened equilibrium in which both were involved'.* The effect of enclosure on both people and landscape, together with a highly personal sense of loss at the disappearance of the open fields of his youth, became the subject of some of Clare's most powerful writing:

> By Langley Bush I roam, but the bush hath left its hill;
> On Cowper Hill I stray, 'tis a desert strange and chill;
> And spreading Lea Close Oak, ere decay had penned its will,
> To the axe of the spoiler and self-interest fell a prey;
> And Crossberry Way and old Round Oak's narrow lane
> With its hollow trees like pulpits, I shall never see again:
> Inclosure like a Bonaparte let not a thing remain,
> It levelled every bush and tree and levelled every hill
> And hung the moles for traitors—though the brook is running still,
> It runs a naked brook, cold and chill.

Many years after Clare had left it, the village of Helpston and its surroundings were described by G. J. De Wilde, a newspaper editor who became interested in the poet during his asylum years:

> A not unpicturesque country lies about it, though its beauty is somewhat of the Dutch character—far-stretching distances,

---

*Strikingly, the earliest piece of explicitly ecological literary criticism (so far as I am aware) was an article called 'Enclosures: the Ecological Significance of a Poem by John Clare', by Robert Waller, published in *Mother Earth: Journal of the Soil Association* in 1964, just two years after the modern environmental movement was born to the cry of Rachel Carson's *Silent Spring*. On Clare and ecology, see further Chapter 6 of my *The Song of the Earth*.

level meadows, intersected with grey willows and sedgy dikes, frequent spires, substantial watermills, and farm houses of white stone, and cottages of white stone also. Southward, a belt of wood, with a gentle rise beyond, redeems it from absolute flatness. Entering the town from the east you come to a cross, standing in the midst of four ways ... Before you, and to the left, stretches the town, consisting of wide streets or roadways, with irregular buildings on either side, interspersed with gardens now lovely with profuse blooms of laburnum and lilac ... The cottage in which John Clare was born is in the main street running south.

It sounds as if De Wilde went there on a fine summer day. Frederick Martin, in accordance with his desire to emphasise Clare's poverty and exclusion, characterised the village rather differently, drawing attention to 'the old Roman road now full of English mud' and 'the low huts of the farm labourers'.

It was a country of great houses and tiny villages. The gap between rich and poor was almost immeasurable. A two-roomed cottage could be rented for two pounds a year and a man could reasonably hope to support a family—without any kind of luxury—on thirty pounds a year, twenty of which would go on food. But in years of poor harvest and consequent high grain prices, he would struggle. And throughout the Revolutionary and Napoleonic Wars, prices were exceptionally high.

A casual labourer such as Parker Clare would have earned about a shilling a day—for which he could buy one large loaf of bread.* The availability of work fluctuated with the seasonal and economic cycles,

---

*A note on money: there were twelve pence (d.) to the shilling (s.), twenty shillings to the pound. The average wage of a Northamptonshire agricultural labourer when Clare was a young man was eight shillings a week (about 40 modern pence, 60 U.S. cents, 0.6 euros) or about £20 per year ($30, 32 euros). It was, however, hard to support a family on less than £30–£40 a year. A pot of ale cost a penny; a loaf of bread varied from 4d. to 1s., according to the price of grain. Since bread is now a lot cheaper than beer, it is pointless to try to convert these sums to modern equivalents.

so Parker's annual wage might sometimes have been little more than ten pounds—which is why he needed to set his son to work as soon as the boy had sufficient strength. A major landowner, by contrast, could expect an annual income of over two thousand pounds from rents alone. The Earl of Fitzwilliam spent over ten thousand pounds in connection with the enclosure of Helpston and Maxey, for which, thanks to increased rents, he gained a thirty per cent return on his outlay.

During Clare's childhood, the county of Northampton introduced the so-called Speenhamland system of poor relief, whereby wages were supplemented from parish funds up to a minimum figure. This was a mixed blessing, since it allowed farmers to keep wages low. The spectre of the poorhouse was ever present, and the Clares became acutely conscious of it when Parker's rheumatism took a turn for the worse and his son had to become the breadwinner. Charitable benefits were available in the village—coal for widows, a clothing club—but malnutrition and disease were commonplace.

There were houses for about sixty families. The population at the beginning of the nineteenth century was three hundred. Almost everyone was employed in agriculture, though there was some limework available. Clare always struggled to obtain paper and was mocked by his fellow-villagers for his attempts at writing. It is a mild irony that shortly before his death employment prospects in Helpston were greatly improved by the establishment in the village of a high-quality paper works.

One of the purposes of the Speenhamland system was to discourage the movement of paupers from parish to parish—the benefit was only available where you had a settlement. There was, however, seasonal movement of migrant labour. In one of his earliest surviving prose sketches, written in his twenty-first year and never published, Clare describes an encounter with 'a Company of miserable Hibernians' (i.e. Irish). 'Weary, fainting and poverty struck', these 'pitiful Emigrants' passed through Helpston on their return from working in the fens—having found little reward, 'it being a very bad Harvest'. One of them, named Parbrick, was muttering to himself:

'By Jesu, though I've got neither money Victuals nor Clothing without shoes and stockings—and scarce a bit of Breeks left to cover my A——s and I don't care for that for I think I have got something in my head that will better all this Presently—Why to be sure I have—I'm certain on't so thou need not doubt on't . . .' this he repeated at least 20 times, bursting out now and then into a loud laugh.

What he had in his head was a plan to beg a penny off each person he met. A penny per person is a trifle, but ' "now let me see," continued he, "suppose there's 20,000 men in England Rich and Poor" '— wouldn't twenty thousand men mean twenty thousand pence, an enormous sum of money? Clare regarded the man as a 'scheming fellow' who did no service to the reputation of his fellow-countrymen, but the encounter seems to have stuck in his own head. Irish immigrants feature in a number of his poems. And his description of Parbrick—'With nothing to eat but a mouldy crust (and that but a very small one) with not a Farthing in his Pocket without a Friend in a strange Country Unknown and Unsupported'—prefigures his description of himself over twenty years later, beside the road to the north on his journey home from the Essex asylum.

A vivid passage in Clare's *Shepherd's Calendar* evokes the Scottish drovers who travelled the Great North Road with their small but sturdy highland cattle, their 'petticoats of banded plad', 'blankets o'er their shoulders slung', blue caps on their heads with scarlet tassels and thistle patterns. His own Scottish blood stirred by the sight of men in kilts, Clare wrote of their 'honest faces frank and free / That breath of mountain liberty'.

The migrants who most fascinated him were the gypsies. Their favoured local camp was at Langley or Langdyke Bush, an old whitethorn tree that became one of the most important landmarks in Clare's poetry. Dating back to Saxon times, it was renowned as the meeting-place of the 'hundred court' of Nassaburgh—that is to say, as the symbolic site of the common law rights of the local people:

O Langley Bush! the shepherd's sacred shade,
   Thy hollow trunk oft gain'd a look from me;
Full many a journey o'er the heath I've made,
   For such-like curious things I love to see.
What truth the story of the swain allows,
   That tells of honours which thy young days knew,
Of 'Langley Court' being kept beneath thy boughs
   I cannot tell—thus much I know is true,
That thou art reverenc'd: even the rude clan
   Of lawless gipsies, driven from stage to stage,
Pilfering the hedges of the husbandman,
   Spare thee, as sacred, in thy withering age.
Both swains and gipsies seem to love thy name,
   Thy spot's a favourite with the sooty crew.

Langley Bush was on King Street, the Roman road (a branch of Ermine Street) which ran in a straight north-south line through the parish to the west of the village. Between the road and the village there was an old Roman quarry called Swordy Well, where Clare tended sheep and cows as a boy, played 'roly poly' on the gentle rise, and botanised when he grew up. On the far side of the road lay Cauper Green. 'I hope [that] is not spelt right, it is so ugly a word. Should it not be *Cooper* or *Cowper?*' asked his publisher. Clare preferred its rough grass to a trim lawn and relished both its wild flowers and its remnants of antiquity—old coins, even a skull and bones. He was fascinated by the relics of ancient times. They inspired him to meditate on time, on mortality and endurance. He was fully aware that *Remains* was a word used not only for archaeological ruins, but also for the posthumously published works of writers.

The gypsies were also associated with an isolated farmstead two miles from the village. 'Disinhabited and in ruins', it was known as the 'heath house'. His mother told him a local legend—at once grisly and funny—about its murderous history, which he turned into a poem. And he wrote evocatively of it in an autobiographical fragment:

I remember with what fearful steps I used to go up the old tottering stairs when I was a boy in the dinner hours at harvest with other companions to examine the haunted ruins—the walls were riddled all over with names and dates of shepherds and herdsmen in their idle hours when they crept under its shelter from showers in summer and storms in winter and there were mysterious stainings on the old rotting floors which were said to be the blood of the murdered inhabitants—it was also the haunt of Gipseys and others who pulled up every thing of wood to burn till they left nothing but the walls—the wild cat used to hide and raise its kittens in the old roof, an animal that used to be common in our woods though rather scarce lately— and the owls used to get from the sun in its chimney and at the fall of evening used to make a horrid hissing noise that was often taken for the waking noise of the haunting spirits that made it a spot shunned desolate and degected.

Degected is one of Clare's many felicitous nonce-spellings, seeming to combine *neglected* with *dejected*. (As for the wild cat—now confined to the Highlands of Scotland—it is a reminder that Clare was surrounded by a more diverse variety of undomesticated animals than we are.)

The principal landmark to the east of the village, into the parish of Etton, was Woodcroft Castle, a mediaeval manor house with a moat and a circular tower. Clare held down a ploughing job there for a month while he was a teenager. 'It is a curious old place', he wrote,

> and was made rather famous in the rebellion of Oliver Cromwell —some years back there was a curious old bow found in one of the chimneys and the vulgar notion was that it was the identical bow that belonged to Robin Hood so readily does that name associate itself in the imagination with such things and places. I had a coin of Cromwell's brought me last year by a neighbour, picked up in the neighbouring field, as large as a crown piece.

Clare told the story of Woodcroft Castle's Cromwellian fame in a 'tale' inserted within his long poem 'The Village Minstrel' (though excluded from the published text). During the Civil War, the house was occupied and defended by a royalist company under the captaincy of Michael Hudson, the King's chaplain. A parliamentary force set out from Stamford, passed through Helpston ('ah Helpstone I ween / Thou ne'er knew a rebel before'), and attacked the stronghold. According to Clare's account, Hudson's men, outnumbered three to one, fought bravely to the last, but ended up being herded to the top of the tower and thrown into the moat. Hudson clung to the parapet, only to have his hand 'slashed off on the tower as he hung / and his body fell bleeding below'.

The locality had other Civil War associations: there had been a skirmish between parliamentary and royalist forces at Cauper Field, while Cromwell's widow was buried in Northborough churchyard (as Clare's widow would be). Clare's respect for nobility meant that he had no time for Cromwell and the regicides: he always wrote of the Civil War as a 'rebellion', the term used by those who opposed the parliamentary side.

He was equally indignant about the killing of the French king in the year of his birth. His autobiographical 'Sketches' end with a strong affirmation of his anti-revolutionary political creed:

> I believe the reading a small pamphlet on the Murder of the French King many years ago with other inhuman butcheries cured me very early from thinking favourably of radicalism— the words 'revolution and reform' so much in fashion with sneering arch infidels thrills me with terror when ever I see them—there was a Robspiere, or something like that name, a most indefatigable butcher in the cause of the French levellers, and if the account of him be true, hell has never reeked juster revenge on a villain since it was first opened for their torture— may the foes of my country ever find their hopes blasted by disappointments and the silent prayers of the honest man to a power that governs with justice for their destruction meet always with success. That's the creed of my conscience—and I care for nobody else's.

It might be thought that Clare is asserting his political orthodoxy here in order to reassure his publisher that his work will always be safely free from sedition, but we should be wary of ascribing such an ulterior motive to him. He invariably made a point of saying what he meant, straight from the heart. Indeed, his bluntness sometimes got him into trouble. He said to people's faces the same that he would say behind their backs. 'I was in earnest always or I was nothing ... if I tried to dissemble my real opinion my innocence would break through and betray me, so I spoke as I thought.'

Should we therefore take him at his word when he says 'with the old dish that was served to my forefathers I am content'? He wrote a poem in praise of his native England, which began with a quotation of some patriotic lines from William Cowper:

> England, with all thy faults, I love thee still—
> My country! and while yet a nook is left,
> Where English minds and manners may be found,
> Shall be constrain'd to love thee.

On copying out his poem for his publisher, Clare joked, 'I think I shall stand a chance for the Laureat Vacancy next time it turns out!!!!' He had the instinctive conservatism and patriotism of the countryman.

His suspicion of the kind of innovation represented by Cromwell in the seventeenth century and the French Revolutionaries in his own time did not, however, mean that he was incapable of political indignation. But his political horizon had the same limits as his physical one. He raged at the injustices of local life. As we will see, he angered at least one of his patrons by publishing poetic lines about 'accursed wealth'; he accused enclosing landlords of tyranny; he spoke for the rights of the common people, the gypsies and even of the common itself (and of trees and badgers and birds). His recollection of Woodcroft Castle combines anti-Cromwellian sentiment with a warm-hearted allusion to Robin Hood. The point about Robin Hood is that he is a hero of the folk tradition. He outwits the Sheriff of Nottingham's 'lawless law' (Clare's term for enclosure). He robs from the rich to give to the poor. He inhabits the greenwood, which Clare always associates with freedom. And all along he is innately noble, an aristocrat in disguise. Anti-Cromwell but pro-Robin, Clare combined allegiance to the ancient rights of the English commoner with distaste for 'revolution and reform'. Among the political commentators of his age, his position was much closer to that of William Cobbett, conservative-radical countryman, than that of William Hazlitt, liberal metropolitan apologist for both Cromwell and the French Revolution.

The historian E. P. Thompson has written of the paradox whereby the popular culture of the eighteenth century was simultaneously rebellious and traditional: 'The conservative culture of the plebs as often as not resists, in the name of custom, those economic rationalizations and innovations (such as enclosure, work-discipline, unregulated "free" markets in grain) which rulers, dealers or employers seek to impose.' Clare conforms to this model. That is why he was deferential to the local grandees—with their sense of *noblesse oblige*—but bitterly satirical towards the newly prosperous, socially aspirant farmers who benefited from the enclosure at the expense of the rights and customs of his own class.

As may be seen from Clare's use of the term *infidels* with respect to reformers, politics was intimately bound up with religion. And here too, Clare regarded himself as a traditionalist. The parish church of St Botolph and the octagonal fourteenth-century cross on the green were the symbolic centres of village life. There was an 'Independent' Non-conformist chapel in Helpston, though Primitive and United Methodist chapels were only built around the time of Clare's death. His brief flirtation with radical religion will be examined later, but his 'Sketches in the Life' includes a strong statement of religious orthodoxy: 'I reverence the church and do from my soul as much as any one curse the hand that's lifted to undermine its constitution—I never did like the runnings and racings after novelty in any thing ... The "free will" of Ranters, "new light" of Methodists, and "Election Lottery" of Calvinism I always heard with disgust and considered their enthusiastic ravings little more intelligible or sensible than the bellowings of Bedlam.'

The tall spire of Glinton Church, visible for miles across the flat landscape, is glimpsed in many of Clare's poems. It was an important landmark for him not because it pointed to Heaven, but because it pinpointed the location of fond recollections—of schooldays and

Richard Turnill and Mary Joyce. Though he professed himself an Anglican, Clare's attendance at church was most irregular. His deepest feelings of a religious kind were reserved for his experience of nature and his memories of childhood innocence and joy.

The spatial horizon of the young Clare was fixed by the boundaries of the Soke of Peterborough. His temporal horizon was determined by the rhythms of the working day and the agricultural year. His fondest memories were of the freedom of Sundays, for the other six days were filled with work in schoolroom, barn or field. Save on holidays: 'When I was a boy a week scarcely came without promise of some fresh delight,' he recollected, 'Hopes were always awake with expectations [and] the year was crowned with holidays.' Hard labour meant that holidays were the year's greatest treat for the villagers.

Christmas was like a week containing two Sundays. Evergreens were placed in the windows and the children fetched ivy branches from the woods. Parker and Ann coloured them with whitening and laundry blue, then stuck the branches behind the pictures on their wall. The morris dancers would perform a mummers' play, for which the actors playing the King of Egypt and Prince George wore wooden swords and hats decorated with carpenter's shavings and cut paper, while the Buffoon had a hunchback, a bell between his legs and a tail trailing behind. A fight, a mock death, the Doctor to make all well, then a song and a dance. Later in life, Clare got old John Billings, one of the regular actors, to recite the text of the play so that he could write it down.

February brought Valentine's Day. Clare saw himself as an eager lover even when he was still a child: 'though young we was not without loves—we had our favourites in the village and we listened the expected noise of creeping feet and the tinkling latch as eagerly as upgrown loves—whether they came or not it made no matter.' The disappointment did not matter: it was the pleasure of anticipation that made the day.

April Fool's was a special favourite, which the children would talk about weeks in advance. They boasted 'how we would make April fools of others and take care not to be catched our selves', but when the day came they were duly tricked into 'such April fool errands' as being sent to fetch pigeon's milk or to find a needle with a glass eye.

At Easter the village cross down the road from the Clares' cottage was 'thronged round with stalls of toys and sweets—horses on wheels with their flowing manes and lambs with their red necklaces, and box cuckoos'. The children had to resist the temptation to steal them before Easter morning, when the boxes of sweets were opened up and, at a penny a time, there was barley sugar, candied lemon and peppermint, coloured sugar plums, tins of lollipops, gingerbread in the shapes of coaches and milkmaids.

On St Mark's Eve (24 April) it was a custom for young maids, and sometimes men, to bake a 'dumb cake'. A party—never to exceed three in number—would meet in silence and make a cake. At midnight they would eat it, still in silence. If anyone spoke, the spell would be broken. Then they would walk up to bed backwards 'and those that are to [be] married see the likeness of their sweethearts hurrying after them as if they wanted to catch them before they get into bed, but the maids being apprised of this beforehand take care nearly to undress themselves before they start [and] are ready to slip into bed before they are caught'. On the same night, 'the more stouthearted' would lay a branch in the church-porch and return at midnight, when those who were to marry or die in the coming year would see a vision of a wedding or a funeral. An 'odd character' called Ben Barr watched the porch every year and thus claimed to know the fate of all the villagers, which he would divulge in return for a small fee.

Clare considered it part of his vocation as a poet to preserve old customs such as this, as he sensed they were in decline with the march of 'progress'. Many of his poems are linked to particular occasions such as Valentine's Day, April Fool's Day and St Mark's Eve. Sometimes they seem to combine village traditions with personal recollections: 'The Dumb Cake Pastoral' features two girls at the Rose and Crown Inn, Oundle, where he lodged during his time in the militia.

On May Day, the first cow that was turned out into the pasture was given a garland on its head, the last a branch of thorn on its tail. This game was turned into a courtship ritual, as Clare explained in a letter on village customs that he sent in 1825 to a magazine that specialised in the documentation of folk traditions, Hone's *Every-Day Book*:

> The young men who wish to claim the favour of their favourites wait on the green till a [late] hour and then drive out the cows of the maiden [whom] the[y] love, who of course wins the garland and in the ev[ening] she is considered the Queen of the May and the man, whether her favourite or not, claims her as his partner for the dance at night, a custom that she dare not refuse to comply with as she would lose her reputation and sweetheart into the bargain and grow into a byword for a shrew and be shunned accordingly.

The sheep-shearing feast—as celebrated in Shakespeare's *Winter's Tale*—came in late June. The youngsters hung around the clipping pens and the old shepherds gave them frumenty, a dish of hulled wheat boiled in milk and seasoned with sugar and plums. Then in September it was the harvest home. In *The Shepherd's Calendar* Clare paints the village boys thronging round the wagons decked with light blue ribbons and garlands of flowers for the homecoming of the last of the harvest:

> Anon the fields are nearly clear
> And happy sounds oft meet the ear
> Of boys who halloo 'There they come!'
> And run to meet the Harvest Home,
> Stuck thick with boughs and thronged with boys
> Who mingle loud a merry noise,
> Glad that the harvest's end is nigh
> And weary labour nearly by,
> Where when they meet the stack-thronged yard
> Cross buns or pence their shouts reward.

The reward for everyone was the knowledge that the harvest was safely gathered in, the seasonal cycle complete.

The next year's Christmas season would be heralded by St Thomas's Eve (20 December), when, as Clare noted, it was 'a common custom for the young girls to lay a red peeled onion under their pillows to dream of their sweethearts'. Once the twelve days of Christmas passed, the first day back at work was known as Plough Monday. Hone's *Every-Day Book* had given an idealistic account of village traditions on this day. Clare responded with what he called 'a dirty reality': where the magazine had pleased its predominantly urban readers with images of ploughboys dressed in white shirts and ribbons, Clare told of how the Helpston boys met at the blacksmith's, blackened their faces with a mixture of soot and grease, attached themselves to a skeletal plough and went round and round the village, tanking themselves up with beer, pulling up shoescrapers outside cottage doors, winding ropes round each other, and finding the dirtiest corners of the farmyards in which to tumble and scrap. Labourers, meanwhile, blacked up their faces and went round the village grotesquely cross-dressed as 'plough witches'. Though Clare always looked back with longing upon his childhood, once he grew in confidence as a writer he refused to poeticise the life of the village. He reinvented the pastoral tradition of poetry in a mode of dirty realism.

The pace of work was slower in the winter, the landscape stiller. Many of Clare's most poised poems are winter scenes. Winter gave him more time for writing, since less employment was available on the farms. In the cold and dark of the year, the milk-boy who had sauntered idly to the pasture in summer would complete his morning work in haste, while 'the shepherd cuts his journeys short and now only visits his flock on necessity—Croodling with his hands in his pockets and his crook under his arm he tramples the frosty plain with dithering haste, glad and eager to return to the warm corner of his cottage fire'.

The only worker, says Clare, who 'sees the beauties and horrors of winter mingled together through the short day' is the woodman. He returned to this figure again and again in his writings. In late 1819 he composed both a prose sketch called 'The Woodman or the Beauties of a Winter Forest' and a poem called 'The Woodman'. To Clare's disappointment, his publisher excluded the beautifully observed prose piece from the collection *The Village Minstrel*, but the poem was included. It gives a vivid sense of the woodman's working day in winter.

He wakes as the bell of the snow-covered village church strikes four o'clock. Shrugging as he sees the frost on the window, he gets up—the rest of the family can lie in till eight, but he must go and earn his wage (the wish to linger in bed recurs several times in Clare's poems). He breakfasts on water-porridge and puts a barley crust into his bag for lunch. It is a long walk from his cottage to the wood where he is working. 'The cemented ground' is 'hard as iron'. The woodman's nailed boots bounce off it and the echo of his tread sounds across the frozen pool. He chops wood through the short day, in the solitary company of a robin, to which he throws crumbs. The sun sinks, 'Round as a football' (as often, Clare takes his simile from village games rather than poetic tradition), and the woodman fills his bag with billet-wood for his cottage fire. He walks home as the frost begins to 'crizzle' (freeze) pond and brook. At home, his family are waiting for him, supper stewing on the hook over the fire. He keeps his leather leggings on as he tells his children about the day. Smoking in his corner chair by the fire, he feels so good he might as well be king of England. He checks the sky for the next day's weather, says his prayers and retires to bed.

The poem and the prose-sketch cover very much the same ground, but the differences between them reveal some of the difficulties Clare faced in looking beyond his locality to the world of print. The poem is often derivative in diction (it was indeed written in conscious imitation of the ballad form of Burns's 'The Cotter's Saturday Night'), whereas the prose is written more in Clare's own distinctive voice. Its principal difference from the poem is its greater degree of botanical exactitude: 'jagged leaves of Lungwort' and, more intricately, 'His eye also catches the straggling privet and the twining brier who (though not evergreens) is still discernible from their leafless neighbours by a few shattered leaves tinged with the decaying colours of russet and purple'. Clare had not yet found a way of making poetry out of the fragile minutiae that animated his love for the richly textured world encircled within the horizon of his knowledge.

CHAPTER FOUR

GARDENER, SOLDIER, LIME-BURNER

A letter that Clare wrote to his son in 1849 gives a poignant sense
of how he was once at the heart of a close-knit working community. Nearly all his peers remained in Helpston throughout their
lives, several with large families. Henry Snow, labourer, and his wife
Martha were typical—they had four girls and two boys. Clare's letter
mentions at least twenty-eight families, almost half the total number
in the village:

> There is William and John Close—do they live at Helpstone
> yet and how are they—how is John Cobbler of Helpstone—I
> worked with him when a single Man and Tom Clare—we used
> to sit in the Fields over a Bottle of Beer and they used to Sing
> capital Songs and we were all merry together—how is John and
> Mary Brown and their Daughter Lucy and John Woodward and
> his Wife and Daughter—William Bradford and his Wife—
> Sally Frisby and James Bain and old Otter the Fiddler and
> Charles Otter and John and Jim Crowson—most of us Boys and
> Girls together—there is also John and James Billings and Will
> Bloodworth and Tom and Sam Ward and John Fell and his Wife
> and John King and Mr and Miss Large and Mr and Miss Bellars
> on the Hill and Mr Bull and all enquiring Friends and Mrs
> Crowson—many are dead and some forgotten—and John and

Mrs Bullimore the Village Schoolmistress and Robin Oliver and his wife and Will Dolby and his Wife and Henry Snow and his Wife and Frank Jackson and his Wife—Richard Royce and his Wife and Daughter and Jonothan Burbidge and his Wife and Daughter and all I have forgotten remember me kindly to—for I have been a long while in Hell—how is Ben Price and Will Dolby—for I liked Helpstone well—and all that lived in it and about it for it was my Native Place.

William Bradford kept the Blue Bell; old Mrs Crowson was the village baker; John Fell and the elder Crowson brother were stonemasons, Ben Price a thatcher, Jonathan Burbidge a carpenter, John Close a gardener. There were the farmers such as Mr Large, Mrs Bellars and Mr Bull. But most of the boys with whom Clare grew up struggled to support their families through casual agricultural labour. Some, such as the Jacksons and Tom Clare and his wife Ann, eventually became paupers.

'Hell is other people', says a character in a play by Jean-Paul Sartre. For Clare it was the opposite: he is 'a long while in Hell' because he has been removed from the other people of his native place. Only in death was he restored to their company. Some of the names in this letter can be matched to those on the graves near Clare's in the churchyard beneath the octagonal tower of St Botolph's. Richard Royce, for instance, 'departed this life September 11 1866 in the 95th year of his age'—sometime weaver and village shopkeeper, he was born before Clare and died after him. He rests with Elizabeth Royce, his wife, who lived a mere seventy-five years. The Helpston churchyard is also a reminder that the village was inhabited by prosperous farmers as well as impoverished labourers: the stonemason could have charged handsomely for the elaborate grave of Clare's contemporary, John Vine Chapman, who died in 1866 in his seventy-third year.

There was a possibility that Clare himself might, like Thomas Hardy's fictional Jude, have become a writer on gravestones rather than paper: 'My scholarship was to extend no farther than to qualify me for the business of a shoemaker or Stone Mason, so I learned cross multiplication for the one and bills of account for the other.' When he left school at the age of about twelve, there was a feeling that his constitution would be too weak for full-time work as a thresher with his father.

Two possible apprenticeships became available, one in Glinton and the other with a Helpston cobbler called Will Farrow, 'a little deformed fellow' who, as a kindness to Parker Clare, proposed to take the boy on for a nominal sum. But Parker did not have the money and John himself 'did not much relish the confinement of apprenticeship'. Farrow was known as a particular character in the village: 'famous for a joke and a droll story', with a knack for thinking up nicknames that stuck.

Farrow's brother Tom was a sailor. He kept a journal and, on returning from sea, got Clare to copy out part of it. Only one passage stuck in Clare's memory: an account of a traveller who once sailed on a ship on which Farrow served, 'an odd young man lame of one foot on which he wore a cloth shoe—who was of a resolute temper, fond of bathing in the sea and going ashore to see ruins in a rough sea when it required six hands to manage the boat'. He was so demanding that 'his name became a bye word in the ship for unnecessary trouble'. The name—and this was the first time that Clare heard it—was Byron.

The ship in question was probably the *Salsette*, which Byron and his friend Hobhouse boarded in the spring of 1810, bound for Constantinople. As the frigate waited at anchor for permission to enter the Dardanelles, a violent storm blew up. The rough weather, which exhilarated Byron, lasted for two weeks, during which there were excursions ashore to inspect the ruins that were believed to be the site of Troy. A few days after this, Byron achieved his legendary feat of swimming the Hellespont. Clare only once saw the sea and never left his native land. Byron was everything that he himself was not, and yet Clare, in time, would feel strangely close to him. It is fitting that the first encounter between the peasant poet and the lordly one should have been by way of a common seaman.

When the offer came of an apprenticeship with shoemaker Farrow, Clare seems to have been in an early teenager's phase of sullenness. He didn't know what he wanted to do with his life. He dreaded leaving the home where he had been 'coddled up so tenderly and so long'. He was by his own admission a 'silly shanny boy'. He also turned down the chance of being apprenticed to George Shelton the stone-mason, shying off on the grounds that he was afraid of heights ('though I had clumb trees in raptures after the nests of Kites and magpies').

'I felt timid and fearful of undertaking the first trial in every thing': he would not commit himself and his parents would not force him against his will. So he stayed at home and picked up casual work as it came along—weeding wheat-fields in the spring, haymaking and bale-stacking in summer. When he was out of work, he collected dried cow-dung and rotten sticks for the cottage fire. He hung around with sheep-tenders and herd-boys, but grew ashamed that he was not able to 'meet manhood' as he would wish.

He dreamed of great things. He wanted to do something that would make him stand out from his peers. There was his love of books, and Turnill was helping him with his studies in the evenings. He worked hard on his handwriting, hoping it might better his prospects.

It was at this point that he was 'sent for to drive plough at Wood-croft Castle of Oliver Cromwell memory'. Mrs Bellars, the mistress of the house, was good to him and he always remembered her fondly. In the summer of 1825 she came to see his garden and he went with his daughter Anna to see hers. He was still asking after her in his letters from the asylum. But in typical teenager fashion he set himself against the job from the start: it meant getting up far too early in the morning and getting his feet far too wet when the moat overflowed onto the causeway that led into the house. After a month he went home to see his parents on a Sunday and did not return to work the next day.

His parents didn't know what to do with him. They 'fancied that I should make nothing but a soldier'. Then an uncle came to the rescue. Morris Stimson was footman to a counsellor-at-law in Wisbech, some forty miles across the fens to the east. On visiting his sister in Helpston, he mentioned that there was a vacancy in his master's office. Parker and Ann thought that this would be the perfect solution for their clerkish son. John doubted his own abilities, but was willing to give it a try. At least there would be the excitement of seeing a new place.

When Clare reached the turnpike road at Glinton, he looked back at the familiar landmark of the church spire. It was as if he were going into another country: 'Wisbeach was a foreign land to me for I had never been above 8 miles from home in my life and I could not fancy England much larger than the part I knew.' He walked to Peterborough, where he boarded the horse-drawn barge that went weekly to Wisbech along the River Nene. He paid his eighteen pence and spent the journey rehearsing the answers he would give when interviewed by the lawyer. He later remembered how his heart burned with hopes of success; he could scarcely contain himself from laughter at the thought of 'the figure I should make afterwards when I went home to see my friends, dressed up as a writer in a lawyer's office'.

His mother had kitted him out in his Sunday best: a white neck-cloth and a pair of gloves to hide the hands that were coarse from labour. But she could not afford a new coat. He felt self-conscious in his old one, which was far too small—the sleeves extended barely below his elbows. When the boat landed at Wisbech Bridge, he was so wrought up with his mental preparation for the interview that he almost forgot how he was supposed to find the right address. Wisbech was a prosperous port and trading centre, intimidating with its grand townhouses along the quayside.

He collected himself and asked for Councillor Bellamy's: 'people stared at me and paused before they pointed down the street as if they thought me mistaken in the name. "And are you sure it is Councillor Bellamy's you want?" said another—"I am sure of it," I said, and they showed me the house in a reluctanty way.' He stood outside the door, afraid to ring, wishing he were back home on his favourite corner stool (again and again at times of stress, he longed for the secure *corner* of his cottage). When he summoned up the courage to ring the bell, he was relieved to find that it was his uncle who answered the door. He was the only manservant. Uncle Morris told the boy that his master was expecting him. He took him to the kitchen for tea and told him not to hang his head, but to 'look up boldly and tell him what you can do'. Clare was too nervous to eat.

Councillor Bellamy appeared and the boy held up his head as well as he could: 'but it was like my hat—almost under my arm' (one thinks of poor Joe Gargery visiting Pip in *Great Expectations*). Clare describes the scene as if it were a little play. Bellamy: 'Aye, aye, so this is your nephew, Morris, is he?' Stimson: 'Yes, Sir.' Bellamy: 'Aye, aye, so this is your nephew?' (then rubbing his hands as he leaves the room) 'Well, I shall see him again.' Out he went, and he never saw the boy again.

Mrs Bellamy told Stimson that the lad could stay until the boat returned to Peterborough on Sunday. So he spent Saturday wandering around Wisbech. He looked in the bookshop windows, and in one of them saw some specimen paintings by a local artist who was 'taking portraits and teaching drawing in the town'. The painter's name was Rippingille. Little did Clare know that they would later become friends. The paintings that Clare remembered were 'genre' scenes: a village alehouse, a letter-carrier—works of art made out of everyday village life.

The next day his uncle put him on the boat and he was home by evening, snug on that corner stool, telling the family about his adventures. The 'melancholy smile' of his parents' welcome 'bespoke their feelings of disappointment'.

Good fortune followed soon after. Francis Gregory, proprietor of the Blue Bell public house next door to the Clares' cottage, owned six or eight acres of land. A single man of about forty, suffering from poor health and living with his mother, he needed a boy to work for him— cleaning pots in the pub, ploughing the land (Clare can't have been as frail as his autobiography implies), tending horses and cows, weeding, running errands. Clare was offered the job, as a favour to his parents. He was happy to accept it. Leaving home would be no ordeal if it simply meant moving into the pub next door.

Both Gregory and his mother treated him 'as well as if I was their own'. He was hired for a year. Gregory liked singing, but only had two songs in his repertoire. As for his jokes, Clare said that they were like a pack of cards—'always the same but told in a different turn'. Young Clare was generally left alone to get on with his work. The solitude gave him 'a habit for thinking'. He muttered and talked to himself, and was then ashamed when passers-by overheard him. His thoughts became so 'active' that he found himself distracted in company and preferred to be alone. On Sundays he hid in the woods instead of going to church. He watched the insects climbing over grass and leaf, or read in a book, bringing the characters alive in his imagination.

Once or twice a week he was sent to fetch flour from a mill in the village of Maxey. The track passed a spot known for ghosts and hobgoblins, arousing fear when he had to make the return journey at dusk in the short days of winter. His eye 'was warily on the watch, glegging under [his] hat at every stir of a leaf or murmur of the wind'. In order to put the ghosts out of his head, he made up stories in which he was the hero: a soldier or a knight errant, travelling heroically in foreign lands until 'a fine lady was found with a great fortune that made me a gentleman'.

Telling stories in his head as he walked, reciting rhymes to himself as he worked in the field: the life of the poet was beginning. 'I always turn to this year's service with F. Gregory as one of the pleasantest occurrences in my existence', he wrote in 'Sketches in the Life', 'I was never hurried in my toils, for he was no task master, or sworn at for committing a fault—a gentle chiding he always deemed sufficient for any thing that I might do wrong—I believe this usage and this place to have been the Nursery for fostering my rustic Song.'

Work for Gregory, however, carried no long-term prospects of betterment. Clare was impressionable. One regular drinker in the Blue Bell was a braggart from Market Deeping called Bill Manton, who took the boy under his wing and told him he would have a fine future as a sign-painter and stone-cutter. But there was the small matter of the apprenticeship fee. The proposal came to nothing. Clare left Gregory's service when the year was up. The pub had introduced him to the manly world of sociability and political debate. His kind employer died of tuberculosis a few years later, in 1811. John Turnill wrote an epitaph for Gregory's simple gravestone.

Soon after Clare left the service of Gregory, his flower-loving friend Tom Porter told him that the master of the kitchen-garden at Burghley needed an apprentice. On a fine Sunday morning Parker Clare took his boy to the great house. The garden-master received them. Since he wore white stockings and a neckcloth, Parker and his son assumed he was 'a gentleman of great consequence himself': 'so with all humiliation to his greatness we met him with our hats in our hands and made a profound Bow even to our knees ere we proceeded in the enquiry'. 'I often thought afterwards', wrote Clare in 'Sketches in the Life', 'how the fellow felt his consequence at the sight, for he was an ignorant proud fellow'. When Clare retold the story three years later in his longer autobiography, the country clown doffs his hat to the gardener 'as if he had been the Marquess himself'. The added dramatic touch may have been inspired by a well-known story about John Abercrombie, the author of several influential gardening manuals, being introduced to the Duke of Leeds's head gardener and finding him 'a gentleman so bepowdered, and so bedaubed with gold lace, that he thought he could be in the presence of no less a personage than the Duke himself'.

Clare was given the post as a temporary kitchen-garden apprentice. The proposed term would be three years—that is to say, he was not formally 'bound' into a full seven-year apprenticeship. His wage would be eight shillings per week for the first year and a shilling more each successive year, 'out of which sum he would have to provide his board and all other necessaries except lodging'.

It would be difficult to exaggerate the contrast between the towering opulence of Burghley and the cramped cottage in which Clare had grown up. He would have seen the servant's quarters inside the house, because his principal job in the kitchen-garden was to take fresh fruit and vegetables down to the Hall for the cook once or twice a day. He saved his money to buy one of Abercrombie's gardening manuals. Later, he recalled his pleasure in the wild flowers that had sown themselves in the vegetable plots, including an unusual yellow poppy. From a distance he saw the son of the Marquess, a boy two years younger than himself: 'I have him in my mind's eye in his clean jerkin and trousers, shooting in the Park or fishing on the river.' He did not yet know that this boy, one of his future patrons, was the child of a peasant, conceived in a cottage almost as humble as his own.

Another of his duties was to run errands into Stamford. The head kitchen-gardener started to take advantage, sending him into town 'at all hours in the night for one thing or other—sometimes for liquors'. When he wasn't drinking at home, Clare's boss was drinking in Stamford. So his wife would send the boy to fetch her husband home. Lacking the courage to do this, Clare would spend the night out in the park, sleeping under a tree. On autumn nights, the frost covered one side of his body 'like a sheet' and left it numb—an affliction that returned every spring and autumn.

He and the other apprentices were locked into the 'garden house' at night to keep them from robbing the fruit. But they climbed out of the window, got over the wall of the park and headed into Stamford. A former Burghley House servant called 'Tant' (short for Antony) Baker ran a pub called the Hole in the Wall, which was accordingly the favourite watering-place of the Marquess's staff. The other lads stood Clare his drinks and his taste for ale was born. He called it by the name made popular from Burns's famous tale of Tam O'Shanter's drunken ride: 'Inspiring bold *John Barleycorn*'.

In retrospect Clare said of the head kitchen-gardener, 'to give him his due, he used me better than he had done others before and even after I left him gave me a good word as a still and willing boy'. At the time, though, he found the demands of his bad-tempered master intolerable. A year into his service, he was taken aside by the foreman, who had also grown weary of being shouted and sworn at. The two of them decided to quit. They made their escape early on an autumn morning.

A day's walk of twenty-one miles brought them to Grantham, where they lodged at an alehouse called The Crown and Anchor.

Clare felt homesick during the night. The next day they inquired after work. Having no success, they moved on to Newark, an important centre for horticulture. There they found employment with a nurseryman named George Withers. They lodged at the house of a lame man whose son was a carpenter celebrated for making fiddles.

Clare felt out of place in the bustling town of Newark. He had never been so far from Helpston; he missed the landmark of Glinton steeple. Such was his disorientation 'in this far land'—all of forty miles from home—that 'I even was foolish enough to think the sun's course was altered and that it rose in the west and set in the east'. At the nursery they had to hoe up the weeds between the young trees, but the ground was baked hard by the September sun. The Nottinghamshire militia was recruiting locally and, possibly emboldened by drunkenness, Clare made an attempt to enlist, but he was found to be too short. Finally, unimpressed by the nurseryman's wages, he and his friend left town with their bill for lodging unpaid. They made it to Stamford in a day, but dared not stay in an inn, so they spent the night under a tree and awoke covered with frost, 'as white as a sheet'.

He returned to a life of casual labour, working sometimes in the gardens of local farmers and sometimes in the fields. He preferred the space and solitude of the open heath, where 'poetry was a troublesome but pleasant companion, annoying and cheering me at my toils'. He describes his writing as a compulsion:

> I could not stop my thoughts and often failed to keep them till night, so when I fancied I had hit upon a good image or natural description I used to steal into a corner of the garden and clap it down, but the appearance of my employers often put my fancies to flight and made me lose the thought and the muse together, for I always felt anxious to conceal my scribbling and would as leave have confessed to be a robber as a rhymer. When I worked in the fields I had more opportunities to set down my thoughts and for this reason I liked to work in the fields and bye and bye forsook gardening altogether till I resumed at Casterton. I used to drop down behind a hedge bush or dyke and write down my

things upon the crown of my hat and when I was more in a hip
for thinking than usual I used to stop later at nights to make up
my lost time in the day.

He always kept a pencil in his pocket, having obtained a dozen for a
shilling from a Jew at Stamford Fair.

Wishing to work in isolation, dropping down behind a hedge and
scribbling on the crown of his hat, dreaming by day, staying on late at
night, spending Sundays in the woods or on the heath alone instead of
going to church: his reputation for oddity had good grounds. Whilst
some of the villagers thought he was soft in the head, others took a
kindlier view of the boy's bookish habits. Deciding that his talents
were wasted in the fields, they persuaded the parish clerk to inter-
vene. Knowing that Lord Milton had shown certain kindnesses to
Parker Clare, he took John to Milton Hall to see if a position could be
found for him.

They saw two crows on the way, a sign of good luck. On their arrival
at the great house they were told that his lordship would see them in
due course. The hours passed and nothing happened. They went
home disappointed. The next day, the clerk had the better idea of
catching Lord Milton as he did the rounds of his estates. They met
him at the Heath Farm, near the village.

The garrulous clerk immediately 'began to descant' on Clare's
merits, causing the boy to hang his head with embarrassment. But
before long, he changed the subject and pulled out an antique box
'which he had found in levelling some headlands near Eastwell
Spring, a spot famous for summer Sunday revels—it was in the form
of an apple pie and contained several farthings of King Charles the
first's or second's reign'. Lord Milton gave the clerk some money for
the box and, on hearing that the youth was Parker Clare's son, promised to do something for him. One suspects, though, that he was just
finding a polite way of stopping the busybody clerk from pestering
him. Nothing further was heard of the promise.

We cannot be exact about the chronology of Clare's early life. He
probably began the apprenticeship at Burghley in 1807 and went to

Newark in the autumn of 1808. In 1809, when he turned sixteen, he seems to have begun his first major poem of rural life and landscape. It took its name from his home village of 'Helpstone'. Very little is known of the next seven years. His memoirs mention various jobs, including fencing and planting hawthorns. Elsewhere, he mentions in passing that for several seasons he had work hoeing in the turnip fields in company with his father's old friend John Cue of Ufford. Cue was renowned for his turnips.

Clare recollects some periods when he wrote poetry in every spare moment, others when he mixed more in the company of 'young chaps of loose habits'. Poetry was 'for a season thrown by' as he fell under the influence of 'partners whose whole study was continual contrivances to get beer'. Despite his weak constitution, he sought to keep up with their drinking, especially on Saturday nights. These were known as 'randy nights', when they all met in the pub to drink and sing 'and every new beginner had to spend a larger portion than the rest, which they called colting'.

It was during this desultory period in Clare's life, from 1809 to 1817, that Helpston and its neighbouring parishes were gradually being enclosed. The fencers and hedge-planters listened out in the pubs for news of where they could find the work that came with enclosure. In solitary labour on the heath Clare had the space in which his imagination could range, whereas when working with a team on the labour of enclosure his poetic freedom was reined in and his taste for ale took over. One night there was a quarrel at a dance and Clare ran off with another man, who took the beer. The two of them spent the night in a rickety old barn, getting so drunk that they did not notice that the gable-end under which they were sitting was on the point of collapse.

Every year in late summer Clare joined the other villagers to gather in the harvest. In August 1811 he witnessed a traumatic accident. In 'Sketches in the Life' he attributes his periodic 'indisposition (for I cannot call it illness)' to 'fainting fits, the cause of which I always imagined came from seeing when I was younger a man named Thomas Drake after he had fell off a load of hay and broke his neck'. This apprehension of death haunted him profoundly:

The ghastly paleness of death struck such a terror on me that I could not forget it for years and my dreams was constantly wanderings in churchyards, digging graves, seeing spirits in charnel houses, etc. etc. In my fits I swooned away without a struggle and felt nothing more than if I'd been in a dreamless sleep after I came to myself, but I was always warned of their coming by a chillness and dithering that seemed to creep from one's toes ends till it got up to one's head, when I turned senseless and fell. Sparks as of fire often flashed from my eyes or seemed to do so when I dropt, which I laid to the fall. These fits was stopped by a Mr Arnold, M.D., of Stamford, of some notoriety as a medical gentleman and one whom I respect with grateful remembrances, for he certainly did me great benefit, though every spring and autumn since the accident my fears are agitated to an extreme degree and the dread of death involves me in a stupor of chilling indisposition as usual, though I have had but one or two swoonings since they first left me.

Dr Arnold owed some of his celebrity to the fact that his father, who kept a private asylum in Leicester, was one of the country's leading experts on madness.

Given the vividness of Clare's imagination, there is nothing surprising about this account of psychological conditions such as bad dreams and seasonal morbidity. But the attribution of extreme physiological symptoms—they sound very like those of non-convulsive epilepsy—to the mere witnessing of a fall seems far-fetched. Clare half-admits as much himself when he says that he *always imagined* his fits were provoked by Drake's death. The self-diagnosis reveals the extreme sensitivity of his disposition, but it could have been his own fifteen-foot drop from a tree whilst gathering nuts that caused the periodic flashing lights and swoons.

'Sketches in the Life' gives the impression that Drake's death occurred soon after Clare left school, whereas in fact it did not happen until he was eighteen. Drake was a respected figure in the village. He was a churchwarden. In view of the manner of his unfortunate death, a certain poignancy attaches to some of the disbursements he recorded in the churchwarden's account book: 'Two Jurneys with my Cart 6s 6d' and 'Jurney to Benton with my Wagin 5s 6d'. If, that is, Clare was not misremembering or exaggerating the incident: the local newspaper merely reported that whilst working in the fields, Drake 'was seized with a fit, and died instantly'.

With his eighteenth birthday that summer, Clare became eligible for military service. The following spring he was sworn into the local militia of the County of Northampton. 'The country was chin deep in the fears of invasion', he wrote when recalling the year 1812, 'and every mouth was filled with the terrors which Buonaparte had spread in other countries'. Clare was a war baby. Throughout his childhood and teenage years, Britain was in arms against Revolutionary and then Napoleonic France.

In the course of the wars, a variety of local defence volunteers— precursors of the Home Guard of the Second World War—were recruited. Shortly after the breakdown of the peace treaty that had been agreed to at Amiens in 1802, Sir Walter Scott was organising a cavalry troop of young Edinburgh gentlemen, while William Wordsworth began exercising with the Grasmere Volunteers. As Napoleon swept across Europe, winning stunning victories over the Russians and Austrians at Austerlitz in 1805, then the Prussians at Jena the following year, there were fears that he would soon be turning his attention to England, perhaps even by building a tunnel under the Channel. In 1808, soon after becoming minister for war, Viscount Castlereagh set about organising the haphazard array of domestic defence forces into a more formal network of local militias which would act as a third line of defence behind the army and the regular militia. Each parish had to provide a certain number of men, either as volunteers or through a compulsory ballot. Those who volunteered would receive a bounty of two guineas, while those enrolled through the luck of the draw would 'go for nothing'. The commitment would be for four years, with an annual training period of up to four weeks.

Clare decided not to take a chance on the ballot. Together with a neighbour, he went to Peterborough to be sworn into the Eastern Regiment of the Northampton militia. 'The morning we left home our mothers parted with us as if we was going to Botany Bay, and people got at their doors to bid us farewell and greet us with a sort of Job's comfort that they doubted we should see Helpstone no more.' 'For a week or longer,' according to Martin, 'their daily business, in the service of King George the Third, was to get drunk, to parade the streets singing and shouting, and to fight with the watchmen of the town.'

They were marched to Oundle for three weeks of basic training. A 'motley multitude of lawless fellows', some thirteen hundred in all, assembled in the fields. They were sorted into companies, known as the Bacon-Bolters ('grenadiers' or tallest men), the Light-Bobs (light brigade) and the Bum-Tools (odds and sods). The companies felt as great an enmity among each other as they did for the French. Being scarcely five feet tall, Clare was a Bum-Tool. According to Frederick Martin, his uniform was far too big for him and his helmet far too small. He got into trouble for not keeping his tunic clean.

He lodged at the Rose and Crown Inn, kept by a kind-hearted widow and her two 'good-natured' daughters. The company Captain was firm but fair—unlike 'a little louse-looking Corporal' who took delight in finding fault with Clare and taunting him with bad jokes about his awkwardness as a soldier. By his own admission, the new recruit often failed to concentrate on his drill because he was too busy writing poems in his head. The little Corporal kept threatening him with the 'black hole' (punishment cell) and the 'awkward squad' (group kept back for further training). He was obviously trying to provoke his man, and eventually he succeeded:

> He was presently at his pert jests and sneering meddling again.
> Madness flushed my cheek in a moment and when he saw it he
> rapt me over my knees in a sneering sort of way and said that he
> would learn me how such fellows as I was dealt with by soldiers.
> I could stand it no longer, but threw my gun aside and seizing
> him by the throat I twisted him down and kicked him when he
> was down.

The Captain investigated the incident and Clare got away with an extra tour of guard duty. The Corporal never troubled him again and the recruits were soon sent home. According to Martin, Clare acquired in Oundle not only a knowledge of the goose step but also, more valuably, a second-hand copy of Milton's *Paradise Lost* and an odd volume (with some leaves torn out) of Shakespeare's *Tempest*.

A year later, Clare received an order signed by the parish constable to the effect that he was to report to Oundle Market Place at nine o'clock on the morning of Friday 28 May 1813, for two weeks of further training and exercise. Then the following February he was ordered to go to Oundle again, so that the local militia could establish which men were willing to sign up for an extension of service. Any man failing to attend would be deemed a deserter and fined twenty pounds; the penalty for non-payment of the fine would be hard labour in the house of correction or confinement without bail in the common gaol. Clare himself explained what the extension of service involved: there was a fresh bounty of two guineas for those who enlisted 'to be sent so many miles out of the county to guard barracks, castles or any other urgencies that might happen'. Five shillings would come as a down payment, the remainder to follow when the men were required. He gladly took the five shillings, but never heard anything more about extended service.

The war was almost over by this time, though the militia was not formally disbanded until the autumn of 1816. Theoretically, militiamen would have been liable to serve in the event of domestic disturbances such as riot and machine-breaking. Although Clare's active military service involved nothing more than a few weeks of training, technically speaking he was an enlisted man, liable to be called up at a moment's notice, for four full years (1812–16). There is some evidence that employers were reluctant to take such men into regular employment. 'No person will hire a servant who may be compelled to leave them at short notice, and, perhaps, when wanted most,' noted a local landowner—'And although the time of training is short, yet militia habits unsettle and vitiate; and I have known many instances where those men return with the itch, and communicate it to their families.'

Clare's employment remained highly irregular throughout this period. For the most part he seems to have been with the fencing and hedging gangs engaged on the work of enclosure. These were years of great hardship for the family. In 1813 the owner of their tenement, Millicent Clark, handed over her financial affairs to her sons. They promptly raised the rent on their properties. The next year, they divided the Helpston tenement from three dwellings into five. The Clares found themselves reduced from four rooms to two. From 1814 to 1820 Parker, Ann, John, Sophy and grandmother Alice were confined to 'a corner of one room on a floor for 3 Guineas a year and a little slip of the garden'. The state of agriculture did not help: the long Napoleonic Wars finally ended in 1815, but the Corn Law kept the price of bread high. The harvest failed in 1816, mainly because of the terrible weather (it became known as 'the year without a summer'). Unemployment rose and there were food riots in eastern England, some twenty miles from Helpston.

Clare recalled that when the cottage was divided, his father's privilege for being a long-standing tenant was first choice as to a share of the garden. Parker was therefore able to retain the portion containing the Golden Russet apple tree whose fruit provided the money to pay the rent. But misfortune followed upon misfortune. Parker Clare had suffered from rheumatism for at least ten years, but around this time his condition (common among labourers who endured poor diet, long hours worked outdoors in all weather, damp cottages, clothes that would not dry after washday) became chronic. Lord Milton generously arranged for Parker to go to the Sea-bathing Infirmary at Scarborough for relief, but the good work was undone when he returned home part of the way on foot to save expenses, and 'his exertions and exposure to the weather brought on the pain again, and reduced him to a more deplorable state than ever'. From 1814 onward, he was in receipt of Parish Poor Relief.

Parker had a proud and independent spirit. He hated the idea of being given something for nothing. As his son put it, it was his 'greatest despair' to think of 'being forced to bend before the frowns of a Parish'. So he 'pottered about the roads putting stones in the ruts', fancying that he was receiving his five shillings a week for this and not as charity. Casual labour of this sort was sometimes a condition of poor relief, but in Parker's case it seems to have been undertaken on his own initiative.

A few years later, the old apple tree failed to bear fruit and the Clares were unable to get up the rent. When John was 'discovered' as a poet late in 1818, the family owed two years' arrears and were going to have to leave the cottage the following year—Parker, Ann and grandmother Alice to the poor-house, John and Sophy into service. John was in a state of despair, to the extent of having suicidal thoughts.

But this is to jump ahead. The family had been dependent on John's earnings for some time. His employment had been irregular, partly because of his own variable health, which he ascribed to his witnessing of Thomas Drake's fatal fall from that hay cart in 1811. There was frequently rent to make up. Shoe bills and baker's bills went unpaid. Late in 1816 John finally seems to have found a more regular job. From December of that year until the following August his name appears in an account book listing weekly payments to 'Extra Labourers in Burghley Park Nursery and Plantations'. His wage of twelve shillings a week was substantially better than that for fieldwork on the farms.

In his first week back at Burghley, Clare worked on the plantation, but thereafter he joined a group of up to a dozen men whose principal task was recorded as 'Scouring out Fish Ponds'—that is to say, clearing out weeds and sludge in order to keep the water fresh for the fish that were farmed for consumption at the great house.* Later in life, he sometimes wrote about fishponds:

> What wonders strike my idle gaze,
> As near the pond I stand!
> What life its stagnant depth displays,
> As varied as the land:
> All forms and sizes swimming there,

---

*It is unlikely that Clare's gang spent all their time scouring the ponds; they also seem to have engaged in general maintenance of the grounds in the area of the ponds, 'digging Earth' and 'mowing weeds'.

> Some, sheath'd in silvery den,
> Oft siling up as if for air,
> Then nimbling down again.

The task of the scouring gang was to keep the waters in the Burghley fishponds clear of the infectious effluvia known as 'den' or 'dain' that Clare observes here.

He was still writing delicately of fishponds in the autumn of 1841, after his journey home from the asylum in Essex:

> Closes of greensward and meadow eaten down by cattle about harvest time and pieces of naked water such as ponds lakes and pools without fish make me melancholly to look over it and if ever so cheerfull I instantly feel low spirited depressed and wretched—on the contrary pieces of greensward where the hay has been cleared off smooth and green as a bowling green with lakes of water well stocked with fish leaping up in the sunshine and leaving rings widening and quavering on the water with the plunge of a Pike in the weeds driving a host of roach into the clear water slanting now and then towards the top their bellies of silver light in the sunshine—these scenes though I am almost wretched quickly animate my feelings and make me happy as if I was rambling in Paradise and perhaps more so than if I was there where there would still be Eves to trouble us.

For Clare even a fishpond is saturated with feeling and memory. Its temper can change his mood and shake off his anxiety about womankind (there were several Eves who troubled him out of his own early paradise). Yet the emotional heat of the writing entails no sacrifice of cool precision in Clare's descriptive art, as when he catches the quavering of the rings on the surface of the water after the plunge of the pike and the slanting motion of the escaping roach.

A name that appears opposite Clare's in the Burghley account book is that of George Cousins. In a scrap of autobiographical recollection, Clare remembered him as one of the most singular and inoffensive men he had ever met. Like old Granny Bains, Cousins was renowned for his ghost stories. Though credulous and easily teased, he had a good memory. The only books he knew were the Bible and Abercrombie's *Gardening*. He liked to wander round village churchyards, reading the epitaphs on graves and committing to memory those he liked best. 'He had an odd taste for gentlemen's coats of arms and collected all the livery buttons he could meet with.' He lived to the age of sixty-five, when he was accidentally poisoned.

We do not know why Clare stopped working at Burghley in August 1817 or how the family survived through the following winter. But in the spring of 1818, the year he would turn twenty-five, Clare left the crowded cottage. He recalled feeling 'utterly cast down' because he could not help his parents enough to keep them from poor relief. He had an especially bitter memory of the 'unfeeling town officer' who had come 'to clap the town brand' on his father's possessions as a mark that he was now formally dependent on the parish. Later, Clare would let loose his revenge in some savage lines in his satirical poem 'The Parish', but for now the best that he could do was seek work away from Helpston.

He departed in the company of an out-of-town labourer named Stephen Gordon, brother of a local man. They found employment in a limeworks a few miles north of Stamford, at Bridge Casterton (now Great Casterton) in the county of Rutland. Lime-burning was choking work that required the heating of chalk or limestone in a kiln in order to make quicklime for mortar and fertiliser.

When the two men arrived in Casterton they were penniless. They began by working from first light until dark, and sometimes continued all night. They lodged in 'a house of scant fame' kept by a Mr and Mrs Cole, who packed in three men to a bed. Casterton was on the Great North Road, so the lodging house gave Clare the opportunity to observe a motley assemblage of travellers from both London and the north.

He and Stephen Gordon worked hard to save money. Within six weeks Clare had put aside about fifty shillings, enough to help his parents with the rent back home and still have something left for the new olive-green coat that he had promised himself. The lime-kilns were owned by a Mr Wilders, who also kept Casterton's principal pub, the New Inn. When his wife heard that Clare had been employed at Burghley, she gave him work in her own garden during the summer.

'It was a pleasant lively town,' wrote Clare, 'consisting of a row of houses on each side the turnpike, about a furlong long.' The River Gwash—barely more than a stream—meandered behind the houses on the south side of the road, then crossed under a modern bridge and 'wound along a sloping meadow northward losing its name and its waters into strangers' streams'. He wrote a sonnet associating the Gwash with inner calm. He liked to walk along the river to the pretty village of Tickencote; as he did so, he planned and wrote what he regarded as some of the best of his early poems.

Then in the autumn, Clare and Gordon went to Pickworth, a few miles further north, where Wilders was establishing another kiln. Pickworth stimulated Clare's interest in the distant past. A solitary Gothic arch was all that remained of a long-ruined church. And the place where they sunk the pit was 'full of foundations and human bones'. One Sunday, after a morning's digging, Clare was inspired into an 'Elegy Hastily composed and Written with a Pencil on the Spot In the Ruins of Pickworth Rutland'. It is a meditation, very much in the eighteenth-century style, on ruin, mortality and the decay of all human things.

The Casterton lime-burners spent their Sundays drinking at the Flower Pot, a little pub at Tickencote. On one occasion when they were walking there, Clare spotted a girl heading across the fields. He climbed to the top of a pollarded tree to get a better look at her and to see which way she was going. 'I was in love at first sight', he remembered. He did not come down until she was out of sight. The reaction of his fellow-labourers to this behaviour is not recorded. Like William Hazlitt, whom he would later meet, Clare had a dangerous propensity for instant infatuation.

On this occasion, luck was on his side. One evening a few weeks later he saw the girl again when he was on his way into Stamford with his fiddle for an evening's drinking and music-making. He dared to speak to her and 'succeeded so far as [to] have the liberty to go home with her to her cottage about 4 miles off'. His poetry helped him to fix in his memory the tree under which they met, the shady spot where she first smiled and the stile over which he helped her step. This encounter, he wrote in his autobiography, 'became the introduction to some of the happiest and unhappiest days my life has met with'. Her name was Martha Turner. He would come to call her Patty—and to court, bed and wed her.

Born at Tickencote on 3 March 1799, Martha was nineteen when she met Clare. He was nearly twenty-five. She lived with her parents, William and Sarah Turner, at Walk Lodge, a secluded cottage in the hollow of a woody dale between Casterton and Pickworth. They were cottage farmers. That is to say, William Turner rented a few acres of land and employed labourers to help him work them. Socially, then, Martha was a cut above the Clares.

Nearly half a century later a visitor to Northborough gallantly described her as 'still a fine, matronly, blooming woman' who must have been 'a very comely girl in her day'. Clare's love poems hint that she was not quite so slender and delicate as Mary Joyce. Whereas the lost ideal was remembered as a sylph, the future wife was built for labour. She sometimes appears in Clare's poetry milking cows or carrying heavy pails.

On that first evening, Clare was so absorbed in 'pleasant shapings' of his future prospects with Martha that he didn't attend to the route they were taking across a large open cow-pasture. It was twilight by the time he returned home and he took a wrong track in crossing the common. Not sure which way to turn, he sat down on an unploughed ridge beside a wheat-field and composed two poems about Martha. One of them describes her as 'artless', an epithet he also used in his autobiography when describing his first impression of her. The word suggests an attractive naïveté and openness, but it was also the case that Martha could not read or write.

The other poem turns their first encounter into a ballad: boy says 'good evening' to girl in order to make her speak. She blushes to the colour of the setting sun and tries to brush him off. He replies that he means no harm. Still she does not speak, but her look is more encouraging. He asks her where she lives. She points towards her cottage and agrees to let him accompany her to the door. He praises her beauty—her eyes especially—and she feels 'Confusion mingling fear and shame / Between the "Yes" and "No" '. Then he

> told her all the open truth,
> 'Bout being a labouring swain,
> With not one groat to boast, forsooth,
> But what hard work did gain.

He apologises for his humble clothes. By this time they are near her cottage and she is afraid of being seen. He snatches a squeeze and a kiss, and vows they will meet again. This poem was included in Clare's second published collection. He says in his autobiography that he wrote it on the very evening when he first spoke to Martha, though the parting kiss in particular sounds more like a poet's fancy than a report of fact.

According to Clare's autobiography, he remained on the spot where he wrote this poem until the moon was up. He then saw something shining brightly on the other side of the common. Thinking it was 'bare ground beaten by the cows and sheep in hot weather', he headed towards it, only to find to his terror that it was water. 'The lengthy silver line' that stretched from him was the River Gwash. He spent the rest of the night under the nearest hedge. As with several of the more colourful recollections in Clare's autobiography, there may be some exaggeration here. The moonstruck lover missing his way and nearly drowning is very much a figure out of ballad and folk-tale.

Throughout the summer months of 1818, when the weather was warmer than it had been during the previous two chilly years, Clare visited Walk Lodge on Sundays and some weekday evenings. He was glad to escape from Cole's crowded lodging and the imposition of extra duties by Mrs Wilders at the inn. There were many secluded spots in which he could walk with Martha. The landscape felt liberating in comparison with the freshly enclosed fields of Helpston: 'heaths and woods swelled their wild and free varieties to the edges of the horizon'. In a large wood he helped Martha gather lilies of the valley for her flower-pots. They threw stones into 'swallow pits' so deep you could count a while before hearing the echo of the impact.

But as in all good love stories, there was a rival. A local shoemaker was courting Martha, though his visits were, according to Clare, 'approved of more by her parents than herself'. Martha was more interested in the flower-gathering lime-burner. Years later she would recall how 'When John came I'd run and get my gingham dress from the hedge where it was airing, and put it on whether dry or not'. But to her parents, who had known better times financially and still had prosperous friends, an association with a casual labourer would have been a stain upon the family name. 'Such', wrote Clare, 'was the tide that bore strongly against us on our first acquaintance'.

A RUSTIC's PASTIME,

IN LEISURE HOURS;

J*CLARE.

Some like to laugh their time away,
To dance while pipes or fiddles play,
And have no sense of ony want
As lang as they can drink or rant:
The rattling drum or trumpets toot
Delight young swankies that are stout:
May I be happy in my lays,

Is all my wish; well pleas'd to sing
Beneath a tree, or by a spring.

RAMSAY.

HELPSTON;
1814.

CHAPTER FIVE

'IN LEISURE HOURS'

In 1798 Samuel Taylor Coleridge and William Hazlitt were staying at a village inn in the west country. In the breakfast parlour
they saw a worn-out copy of James Thomson's poem *The Seasons*
lying on a window-seat. '*That* is true fame!' exclaimed Coleridge.
Though addressed to aristocratic and gentrified patrons, Thomson's
long descriptive poem had genuine popular appeal—it went through
over 250 editions between 1790 and 1830. So it was by no means an
unusual occurrence when in the summer of 1806 a Helpston weaver
showed a fragment of the poem to a bookish thirteen-year-old village boy. What was remarkable was the intensity of Clare's reaction.
The Seasons opened him to his own vocation.

He never forgot the sensation—a 'twitter of joy' in the heart, he
called it—that he felt upon reading the first few lines of 'Spring':

> Come, gentle Spring, ethereal mildness, come;
> And from the bosom of yon dropping cloud,
> While music wakes around, veil'd in a shower
> Of shadowing roses, on our plains descend.

Hitherto, his knowledge of poetry had been confined to ballads, tales
and Pomfret's moralising 'Love triumphant over Reason'. Thomson's
poem, originally published in the 1720s, had a moral and religious

agenda. It was a celebration of the divine order behind the apparent chaos of nature. But for Clare, as for Wordsworth (who regarded it as almost the only worthwhile nature poetry of the eighteenth century), *The Seasons* was memorable above all for its descriptions—of weather, of landscapes, of Nature in all her varied moods and colours.

Clare read as much of the poem as he could before giving it back to its owner. The book was falling apart and most of 'Winter' had gone missing. He was amazed that a work of such beauty could have been handled so carelessly. But the weaver only laughed at him and said that ' 'twas reckoned nothing of by himself or [his] friends'. He was a Methodist, who regarded Wesley's hymns as far superior to Thomson's blank verses.

Determined to obtain a copy for himself, Clare nagged his father until the money was his. The very next Sunday, he walked to Stamford. The bookshop was shut. He contrived a plan to return on a weekday when it would be open. His job that week was tending horses, so he paid one of the other boys a penny to mind his and another penny to keep the secret. As soon as the horses had been taken outdoors, he headed off. He arrived in Stamford so early that the town was almost deserted. At last, though, the bookseller opened his doors. A copy of *The Seasons* was Clare's for the bargain price of a shilling (the weaver had paid half as much again for his).

The sun was now up and it was a beautiful morning. He couldn't wait to delve into his book, but didn't want to be seen reading in public on a working day, so he climbed over the high wall that ran beside the road home. This took him into Burghley Park.

He nestled on a lawn beside the wall: 'and what with reading the book, and beholding the beauties of artful nature in the park, I got into a strain of descriptive rhyming on my journey home'. He composed a poem called 'The Morning Walk', the first that he committed to paper. A companion-piece, 'The Evening Walk', followed soon after.* Clare then tried his hand at 'several descriptions of Local Spots

---

*The influence of Thomson in this period was such that the 'loco-descriptive' genre became a frequent starting-point for a poetic career—as with Wordsworth's first two published works, *An Evening Walk* and *Descriptive Sketches*.

in the fields'—poems on the nooks and corners where he had searched for snail-shells, flowers and nests in his childhood. When he developed a fuller sense of what was involved in the making of poetry, he burnt many of these. Others he polished and rewrote 'perhaps twenty times over till their original form was entirely lost'.

In these early years, Clare was ashamed of his poetry. He wrote in secret and hid his manuscripts in an old unused cupboard. When his mother said that she needed the storage space, he began using a hole in the wall. Mrs Clare found them in her spring-cleaning. Without telling her son, she would use them whenever she needed kettle-holders or firelighters. She assumed that John had merely been copying things out in order to improve his handwriting.

Clare 'humoured her mistake a long time', but eventually half confessed his habit. When his father hummed over an old ballad, Clare would boast that he could beat it, then a few days later declaim his own composition. But his parents were not encouraging. So he tried a trick: he read out poems of his own, but said that he had copied them from books. And then his parents would say, 'Aye boy, if you could write so, you would do'. This went on for two or three years. When Parker returned from work, they all sat round the fire and Clare would recite. He learnt from their raw responses. If they laughed, he was writing in a style that was affected. If they failed to understand, he was being obscure. Eventually he came to trust his own judgement more than theirs.

When he was about sixteen, his mother told him to leave off writing and buy no more books. She gave him a large box, with a lock and key, in which to keep his possessions. She reasoned that if he were careful with his things, he would learn to become thrifty with money. But he didn't listen to her advice: the box made the perfect place of safety for his scraps of paper and the books on which he spent his every spare shilling. On another occasion, his mother gave him a pocket handkerchief from the May fair at Market Deeping, embroidered with a picture of Thomas Chatterton and the text of one of his poems. Years later, when her son was famous, Mrs Clare reminded him of the gift, saying that she had little thought how one day he would be a poet himself. One of his surviving early poems, 'The Resignation', was an imitation of Chatterton written as if by the poet just before he poisoned himself with arsenic, at the age of seventeen, having been reduced to despair by poverty and neglect.

He borrowed books whenever he could. In one of them he came across the remark that 'a person who knew nothing of grammar was not capable of writing a letter nor even a bill of parcels'. At this he was 'quite in the suds'—'For I had hardly h[e]ard the name of grammer while at school'. So he bought a textbook to educate himself. He was not impressed: 'finding a jumble of words classed under this name and that name and this such a figure of speech and that another hard worded figure I turned from further notice of it in instant disgust'. He knew that his speech was understandable, so if he wrote as he spoke, he would have no need of formal grammar. Why shouldn't writing have the ease and informality of speech? 'So in the teeth of grammer I pursued my literary journey as warm as usual, working hard all day and scribbling at night or any leisure hour in any convenient hole or corner I could shove in unseen.' Even as a mature writer, he held fast to the view that to learn 'enough of grammar to write sufficiently plain so as to be understood by others as well as to understand his own consceptions himself' was sufficient for a man to develop 'an enlightened and liberal mind'. After all, 'the correct placing of pauses stops and other trifling' was a matter about which all the authorities were at loggerheads. His own experience was that reading the newspapers had given him all the grammar he needed: 'before I was 20 or knew any thing whatever of the proper construction of sentences—yet I was so far benefited from reading in old newspapers etc. as to write pretty correctly and never any otherwise than to be intelligible.'

Lack of formal grammar was both a blessing and a curse to Clare as a poet. A blessing because it freed him to write in a uniquely authentic vernacular voice. A curse because it meant that others—friends and editors—had to assist his poetry into the shape that would make it acceptable to the reading public, and in so doing they sometimes distorted his voice. This would eventually lead to dispute and disappointment.

Given his proficiency in mathematics and natural history, not to mention the way that his reading ranged from literary classics to local newspapers, it would have been perfectly possible for Clare to master the basics of grammar, spelling and punctuation. But he did not. He left thousands of pages of manuscripts in which there is hardly any punctuation and the spelling is highly irregular. His grammatical forms followed the Northamptonshire dialect of the time rather than the standard English of print. It was Clare's choice to write thus in his manuscripts, and one feels very close to him when reading his words in their original, 'primitive' form. The question inevitably arises: should those idiosyncratic forms be followed when his words are reproduced in print? Or was Clare quite aware that there is a distinction between the freedom that is possible in a personal manuscript and the norms that are required by the conventions of print? These are highly contentious questions, to which we will return.

Clare was troubled by grammar because he was caught between an ambition to become a poet of the printed kind, as represented by Thomson, and an allegiance to that oral tradition which he described in one of his poems as

> The whole of music which his village knows
> Which wild remembrance in each little town
> From mouth to mouth through ages handles down.

He inherited his father's taste for ballads sung over beer. Much of his work grew from the traditions of the village, as is apparent from a poem-title such as 'Song taken from my mother's and father's recitation and completed by an old shepherd'.

He was fascinated not only by the folk songs of the village but also by gypsy culture. His reputation as an oddity, an outsider, a wanderer and a trespasser was compounded from an early age by association with the so-called sooty crew: 'My odd habits did not escape notice—

they [local villagers] fancied I kept aloof from company for some sort of study—others believed me crazed and some put more criminal interpretation to my rambles and said I was night walking associate with the gypsies, robbing the woods of the hares and pheasants, because I was often in their company.'

During the years when he worked with the heavy-drinking fencers and hedge-setters, he became more closely acquainted with the local gypsies. The principal local tribe was known as 'Boswell's Crew'.* They were famous as fiddlers and fortune-tellers. One member of the clan, Tyso Boswell (who came to an unfortunate end when he was struck by lightning), had a daughter called Maria. Her husband taught Clare to play the fiddle 'by the ear'. This accomplished gypsy violinist was John Gray, son of Fowk Gray. The Grays were a vast extended family of eastern county travellers who frequently intermarried with the Boswells and the Smiths.

Clare's continuing interest in gypsy music may be seen from one of his journal entries: 'Finished planting my a[u]riculas—went a botanising after ferns and orchises and caught a cold in the wet grass which has made me as bad as ever—got the tune of "highland Mary" from Wisdom Smith a gipsey and pricked another sweet tune without name as he fiddled it.' Here Clare is seen in his self-appointed role as a mediator between oral and written culture: the gypsy plays folk tunes, while he writes down ('pricks') their musical notation. Wisdom Smith was either a gypsy in his sixties—his daughter Salome and granddaughter Lettice had both got married in Helpston the previous year—or his son, who was about the same age as Clare.

By the time he came to keep a journal in 1824–5, Clare had been writing down song and dance tunes for several years. Two of the most beautiful manuscripts in the Northampton collection of his works are oblong music books, without words, one undated and the other in-

---

*Their leader, 'King Boswell', died in 1824 at a great age, whilst camping on Southorpe Heath. The funeral took place in the village of Wittering, just south of Stamford. The gypsy king's many children and grown-up grandchildren followed him 'in singular pomp to the grave'.

scribed 'John Clare/Helpstone/1818' and which he entitled *A Collection of Songs Airs and Dances For the Violin*. Clare transcribed over 250 tunes into these volumes, carefully noting down their titles. Embracing hornpipes and other nautical tunes, military marches, all manner of dances and such well-known ballads as 'Black-ey'd Susan', they vary from the simplicity of 'Oh dear what can the matter be' to the sophistication of 'Handels Gavott' and 'Mozarts Waltz'. It was probably schoolmaster Merrishaw who had taught him the art of musical notation.

Clare was struck by the warm tempers and strong friendships of the gypsies, intrigued by their distinctive Old Testament names such as Wisdom and Israel. He observed their customs, noting how the men often had a crooked finger on one hand, the means by which gypsy parents would disable their sons from being sentenced to serve in the militia as punishment for petty theft. Tyso Boswell had been press-ganged in his youth, so he had reason to save his children from a life of service in the armed forces.

Clare hated the way that the travellers were denounced by respectable society: 'Everything that is bad is thrown upon the gypsies—their name has grown into an ill omen and when any one of the tribe are guilty of a petty theft the odium is thrown upon the whole tribe.' His wrath was stirred by a newspaper report of a case that came before the January 1819 Quarter-Sessions in Peterborough. Two gypsies, Newcombe Boss and George Young, were charged with having stolen a gelding worth five pounds. They were found guilty and sentenced to death. The following month, on application for pardon made to the Prince Regent, they were reprieved and sentenced instead to transportation for life. The reaction of a local sheep farmer was recorded in that year's *Fireside Magazine*: 'I have heard, with joy mingled with fear, that a couple of gypsies have just been convicted for horse-stealing at Peterborough and condemned, but that their sentence has been commuted to transportation. Thus, thank God, there will be two less in the country. Would I could say two thousand.' Clare took particular note of the words of the sentencing magistrate, the Reverend Samuel Hopkinson:

An ignorant iron-hearted Justice of the Peace at ———— Sessions, whose name may perish with his cruelty, once sitting as judge in the absence of a wise and kinder-hearted associate mixed up this malicious sentence in his condemnation of two gypsies for horse-stealing: 'This atrocious tribe of wandering vagabonds ought to be made outlaws in every civilized kingdom and exterminated from the face of the earth' and this persecuting unfeeling man was a clergyman.

For Clare, who believed in the right to life of even plants and insects, it was shocking that a man of the cloth should speak thus of a human tribe. In view of what happened to the gypsies of Europe just over a hundred years later, the word *exterminated* is horribly prophetic.

As for Boss and Young, they arrived in New South Wales in September 1819. An acquaintance later described Boss (whose real name may well have been Boswell) as polite and well-spoken, not particularly gypsy-looking save for his walk and build and yellow neckerchief. He was one of the very few transported gypsies to pay a return visit to England later in life, following a pardon—he even had his photograph taken, spruced up to look like a gentleman. Boss's stiff pose for the camera parallels Clare's aura of discomfort both when he was painted early in his fame and when he was photographed shortly before his death.

Gypsies were demonised not only for their begging and pilfering, but also because their strange language was suggestive of the black arts. On gaining close acquaintance with the Boswells, Clare 'found that their mystic language was nothing more than things called by slang names like village provincialisms and that no two tribes spoke the same dialect exactly'. It was not until later in the nineteenth century that Romany scholars proposed that gypsies and tinkers possessed a distinct language, 'Shelta', not just a set of distinctive dialects.

In his poetry, Clare mixed a similar cocktail to that of the gypsies: a combination of intimacy with the natural world, local grounding of language and dependence on a long tradition of song and tale-telling. He shared, for instance, the gypsies' detailed knowledge of plants and made notes of their dialect names for various wild flowers: 'Wasp weed is the water betony . . . this is a celebrated plant with the gipseys for the cure and relief of deafness—Buckbane is the bogbean—husk head is the self-heal, a cure for wounds, and furze-bind is the tormentil, a cure for fevers, adder bites etc.'

The other local tribe besides the Boswells were the Smiths, one of the most famous of all nineteenth-century gypsy clans. It would not have been beyond the bounds of possibility for Clare to have gone off and joined them. One of his fellow-workers at Pickworth did just that:

> I had a great desire myself of joining the Smiths Crew and a young fellow that I worked with at a limekiln did join with them and married one of the gipseys. His name was James Mobbs and he's with them still—I used to dislike their cooking, which was done in a slovenly manner, and the dread of winters cold was much against my inclinations—their descriptions of summer revellings, their tales of their yearly journeys to Kent and their rendezvouses at Norwood where they got swarms of money by fiddling or fortune-telling and them that could do neither got a rich harvest by hop-pulling which work they described as being so easy, were tickling temptations to my fancy.

That the thought of bad food and cold winters prevented Clare from going the way of Mobbs was typical of his refusal to romanticise reality.

William Wordsworth wrote a poem in which attraction to the picturesqueness of a gypsy camp was modified by moral disapproval of idleness. Clare's first poem about the gypsies, published in 1820 in his first collection, but apparently written around 1809 when he was just sixteen, also uses the traditional language of the picturesque, but it avoids moralising:

> To me how wildly pleasing is that scene
> Which does present, in evening's dusky hour,
> A group of Gipsies, centred on the green,
> In some warm nook where Boreas has no pow'r;

Where sudden starts the quivering blaze behind
  Short, shrubby bushes, nibbled by the sheep,
  That mostly on these short sward pastures keep;
Now lost, now seen, now bending with the wind:
And now the swarthy Sybil kneels reclin'd;
  With proggling stick she still renews the blaze,
  Forcing bright sparks to twinkle from the flaze.
When this I view, the all-attentive mind
  Will oft exclaim (so strong the scene pervades)
  'Grant me this life, thou spirit of the shades!'

As in many of Clare's early poems, the language of this sonnet awk-wardly mixes the classical ('Boreas' for the north wind and 'swarthy Sybil' for the old woman) with the vernacular—both *proggling* ('med-dling, poking') and *flaze* ('smoky flame', probably a blend of *flash* and *haze*) had to be explained in the glossary to the 1820 edition.

Years later, during his time in Dr Allen's private asylum, Clare stumbled upon a gypsy encampment whilst walking in the Epping Forest in the depth of winter. The sonnet he wrote on this occasion was stylistically very different from the early effort on the same theme. It has the precision and the simplicity, the shafts of beauty and the lack of glamour, that characterise his mature poetic voice:

The snow falls deep; the Forest lies alone;
The boy goes hasty for his load of brakes,
Then thinks upon the fire and hurries back;
The Gipsy knocks his hands and tucks them up,
And seeks his squalid camp, half hid in snow,
Beneath the oak, which breaks away the wind,
And bushes close with snow like hovel warm:
There stinking mutton roasts upon the coals,
And the half-roasted dog squats close and rubs,
Then feels the heat too strong and goes aloof;
He watches well, but none a bit can spare,
And vainly waits the morsel thrown away:
'Tis thus they live—a picture to the place;
A quiet, pilfering, unprotected race.

The camp may still be like a 'picture', but the cold hands, squatting dog and stinking mutton on the fire have the smell of reality upon them.

It was not only with the gypsies that Clare indulged his taste for songs and tales, smoking and drinking. He spent many a Sunday and a winter evening at a cottage just along the street from his own. 'It was a sort of meeting house for the young fellows of the town, where they used to join for ale and tobacco and sing and drink the night away.'

The hosts were two brothers, John and James Billings. Neither had married, so their cottage, with its crumbling walls and threadbare thatch, became known locally as Bachelors' Hall. John, a full thirty years older than Clare, was a great believer in ghosts, which gave him enough stories to fill a whole winter by the fireside. Clare sometimes went fishing with him. James, who was eight years younger than his brother, was the gunner on one occasion when the youthful Clare joined a small poaching party. They started a hare in the woods. James raised his old gun and fired—only for it to explode in his hands, shattering the barrel and half the lock. No one was hurt, but Clare took it as a warning and never went poaching again. He did well not to take the chance: the severity of the game laws was such that an apprehended poacher might face imprisonment, public whipping, hard labour or even transportation.

Clare did not spend all his time with the 'Bachelors'. There was mixed company to enjoy at wakes, weddings, housewarmings and holiday festivities. Sometimes on a Sunday, the village youths would hang out at a remote lodge house on Ashton Green, to the west of Helpston. It was there that an Ashton girl called Elizabeth Newbon laid open her interest in Clare by writing 'an unfinished sentence with chalk on a table'. He guessed that the rest of the sentence was in his favour. She didn't deny it, and a long courtship began. It went on 'for years with petty jealousies on both sides'. Eventually, Betsy made the classic move of a young woman wanting to discover the extent of her boyfriend's commitment. She put it about that he had been unfaithful to her, no doubt hoping for a denial and perhaps even a marriage proposal in compensation. But Clare 'felt the accusations as insults'. His temper mastered his affections and he ended the relationship. This was shortly before he left for Casterton, where he would meet his future wife Patty.

In retrospect, Clare said that Elizabeth Newbon was no beauty but was his 'first love reality'—by which he meant his first real relationship with a girl. For a long time he 'fancied she was everything'. Mary Joyce had been a schoolboy's crush. There were other girls 'I felt a sudden affection for and who on my disclosing it would affect to sneer and despise me'. But with Betsy he progressed from meetings at the lodge house to visits in her home, a sign of serious courtship.

Her father was a wheelwright and something of a religious maniac, who set store by his large personally annotated Bible and a sixteenth-century volume that purported to offer a key to the Book of Revelation. Old Newbon 'believed the explanations there given as the essence of truth and every newspaper occurrence that happened in war and political governments he fancied he could find there'— not to mention Bonaparte and the latest comet. He tested young Clare on his biblical knowledge and found it severely wanting.

Another acquaintance out towards Ashton was childhood friend Thomas Porter. It was with him that Clare shared more refined tastes: searching the woods for wild flowers, poring over stalls of old books at fair time in Deeping or Stamford. He was the first person to whom Clare confided the fact that he wrote poetry. Porter kept the secret, but not being a particular lover of poetry himself, offered little comment. Clare asked him if he understood his work. Porter had a one-word reply: 'yes'. Clare was not to be discouraged. He knew that his friend was 'a strict observer of nature and acquainted with most of her various pictures through the changes of seasons'. If nothing else, the affirmative suggested that he was writing accurately about the natural world around them.

Though Porter knew nothing of poetry, he shared Clare's feelings in the fields. This got Clare thinking. If someone who had never read—perhaps never even heard of—such nature poets as Thomson, Cowper and Wordsworth nevertheless responded to nature in the same way as they, then there must be 'universal feelings' about nature of which poetry was but an echo. Was it not a classic response to 'real poesy' to whisper to oneself, 'Bless me, I've felt this myself and often had such thoughts in my memory'? Clare saw it as his task to write down the poetry that was already there in nature itself.

The two young men walked and talked and fished together, reading the same language in nature, but turning to very different books. Porter stuck to tales and jest-books: 'he felt as happy over these while we wiled away the impatience of a bad fishing day under a green willow or an odd thorn as I did over Thomson and Cowper and Walton which I often took in my pocket to read'. This is one of many passages in Clare's autobiography where one discovers something of the breadth of his reading. We know about his Thomson. He owned an 1815 edition of William Cowper's poems. His patron Lord Radstock would give him another one five years later. During this period, Cowper was greatly admired for his feeling for nature—he was the favourite poet of not only the romantic Marianne Dashwood in *Sense and Sensibility* but also Jane Austen herself. Clare admired dozens of passages of natural description in his long poem *The Task*, as well as such shorter lyrics as 'The Poplar-Field', a lament for trees felled in the name of landscape improvement. It was well known that Cowper was a depressive, a sufferer from that 'despondency' which Wordsworth identified in 'Resolution and Independence' as the fate of the true poet.

Izaak Walton's *Compleat Angler* was a more cheerful book, a much-loved celebration of the peaceful and contemplative joys of fishing in the English countryside. It was a particular favourite of Clare's, though he 'never caught any more fish than usual by its instructions'. He had bought his copy for two shillings at a bookstall kept by a Stamford shoe-knacker called Adams.

Clare said that Thomson's *The Seasons* and Milton's *Paradise Lost* formed his foundation in poetry. He discovered them early in life and read them through again and again until he was at least thirty. Another of his early purchases was Enfield's *Speaker*, an immensely popular anthology of purple passages from a wide array of English poets. His taste in novels was more limited. He said that the only ones he knew were *Robinson Crusoe*, Fielding's *Tom Jones* and Oliver Goldsmith's immensely popular sentimental tale of a kind but naive parson, *The Vicar of Wakefield*. Clare read it through every winter, but was always disappointed by the happy ending.

Hungry for books, he regularly went into Stamford to the book-shop of John Drakard, where he would buy a pennyworth of slate pencils or a few sheets of writing paper. Drakard used old book catalogues as wrapping paper, so Clare greedily devoured the titles and details of books he could never afford to buy. He regarded the catalogues as the most valuable part of his purchase. The memory stayed with him. When he became a literary man, he maintained a ritual on cutting open the pages of a new book or magazine: the first thing he would read was the list at the back advertising the publisher's other titles. Recalling this, he remarked that 'anticipation is the sweetest of earthly pleasures—it is smiling hope standing on tiptoes to look for pleasure—the cutting open a new book, the watching the opening of a new planted flower at spring etc.'

He saved such shillings as he could afford and assembled a motley library, ranging from mathematical textbooks and surveyor's manuals to works of piety and ethical reflection. In his early reading days one favourite was *The Female Shipwright*, which he got from his uncle (the same one who had brought Pomfret's poems to the cottage?). It was 'a true story printed by subscription for the woman whose history it related'—another writer from humble circumstances who set about publishing by subscription a literary work based on personal experience.

Two other books left a lasting impression: 'Bloomfield's Poems was great favourites and Hill's Herbal gave me a taste for wild flowers which I loved to hunt after and collect to plant in my garden which my father let me have in one corner of the garden.' Poetry and wild flowers always remained two of his greatest loves.

Hill's *Family Herbal*, first published in 1754, got Clare interested in the naming and classification of plants. He happened upon a second-hand copy of James Lee's *An Introduction to Botany* (1760), which was intended to introduce its readers to the new system of plant nomenclature that had been developed in the mid-eighteenth century by the Swedish naturalist Linnaeus. Linnaean classification, the so-called sexual system, was based on the number of a flower's parts. It also introduced binomial nomenclature of generic and specific names. This organised, encyclopaedic system was typical of the new classification of knowledge associated with the cultural advance that became known as the Enlightenment, but for Clare it was a 'dark system'. For a time he tried sorting the local plants into Linnaean families and tribes, but he abandoned the project with dissatisfaction. The universalising ambition of the system, with its complex Latin names and 'systematic symbols', did not answer to his perception of the wild flowers peculiar to his own neighbourhood. He saw flowers in their local, living environment. He was not interested in 'a collection of dried specimens class[ed] after Lienneus into tribes and families as a sort of curiosity'. His attitude to the Linnaean system was very similar to his view of grammar-books. Just as he was disgusted by a linguistic system that paid more attention to formal grammatical nomenclature than communicative power, so he despised the classification of flowers according to their formal generic status as opposed to their environmental context and medicinal use.

He collected fossils as well as flowers. His friend John Turnill took specimens to a local gentleman-collector, Dr Dupere of Crowland. In later years, this would be an interest that Clare shared with his friend E. T. Artis, steward at Milton Hall and a renowned archaeologist and antiquarian. But though he was developing varied intellectual interests—'poetry, natural history, Mathematics'—he had little desire to write down anything apart from his own rhymes.

In 1800 Robert Bloomfield, sometime agricultural labourer and shoemaker, published a poem called *The Farmer's Boy*. An astonishing twenty-six thousand copies were sold within three years. For comparison: Wordsworth and Coleridge's two-volume *Lyrical Ballads*, published the same year, struggled to reach a four-figure sale.

Bloomfield was the single most important exemplar for the possibility that an English labouring poet born into a humble home could make his way in the literary world.

The Farmer's Boy revealed to Clare that it was possible to write a poem on the seasons in the manner of Thomson, but to combine descriptions of nature with an account of rural labour. Bloomfield's second book, entitled *Rural Tales, Ballads, and Songs*, showed how the kind of material that Clare knew from pedlars' broadsheets and village tradition could be polished into poetry for a more genteel public. His third volume, *Wild Flowers; or Pastoral and Local Poetry*, struck a chord with both Clare's botanical interests and his strong sense of 'local' attachment.

In the marketplace of publishing, Bloomfield's primary appeal was novelty. Each of his successive volumes of poetry was less successful than the last, and he died in poverty in 1823. By that time, Clare's own poetic career was well under way.

In 1814, the year he turned twenty-one, Clare bought himself a present. In the eight years or so since Thomson's *Seasons* had started him on the road to poetry, he had often thought of collecting his best work in a book. Whilst in Market Deeping on fair day, he went to the shop of J. B. Henson, a local printer and bookseller. Henson knew the young man by sight, because he had brought in books for him to bind and had sometimes attended the chapel at Helpston in which Henson delivered sermons in his other capacity, that of an Independent preacher. Clare asked the price of a blank book: it was eight shillings, a full week's wages. Henson was inquisitive as to his reasons for wanting it. He was puzzled, for the young man's 'ignorant appearance and vulgar habits' made him seem unlikely to be literary. Clare had long kept his poetry habit secret, but his tongue was loosened by the ale he had drunk at the fair: he dropped some hints about dabbling in rhyme. Henson expressed interest in seeing his work, but for four years nothing came of the suggestion.

Clare inscribed an imitation title-page on the second leaf of his book, inking the words thickly to give the appearance of print:

'A Rustic's Pastime, in Leisure Hours; / J * Clare. / Helpston; / 1814'. Between his name and the place he wrote an epigraph, some lines in which the Scottish wig-maker poet Allan Ramsay contrasted the 'young swankies' who laugh and drink and rant away their time with the young poet whose sole ambition is 'to sing / Beneath a tree, or by a spring'. Clare himself was embarking upon manhood, consciously detaching himself from the village roisterers. He was announcing— to himself, though nobody else—that his literary career was about to begin.

Among the most admired poems of the eighteenth century was Thomas Gray's 'Elegy Written in a Country Churchyard'. It expressed feelings, said Dr Johnson, to which every bosom returns an echo. At its heart is the image of the poets who might have been: how are we to know whether some anonymous villager, now lying forgotten in a country graveyard, might not in more favourable circumstances have become another Milton? One can see why the poem would have spoken very personally to the young Clare. When he bought his blank book from Henson and began to write out fair copies of the early works that he wanted to preserve, the first poem that he chose was called 'Lines written while viewing some Remains of an Human Body in Lolham Lane'. It echoes the sentiments of Gray's famous poem: suppose that these bones of a stranger who met an untimely end long ago were those of 'a genius powerful and strong / Well skill'd in all the majesty of song'. Clare's fair-copying of his own poems was an attempt to escape the fate of the bones by the roadside and to reach instead for 'Parnas hill', Mount Parnassus, the traditional home of the Muses.

Another poem that he carefully copied into 'A Rustic's Pastime' turned to the theme of poetic immortality in the form of an address 'To Mrs Anna Adcock, author of "Cottage Poems." ' Adcock was an impoverished schoolmistress from nearby Rutland. In his poem Clare praised her as the 'Sweet Songstress of the Rustic grove'. He would come to regard her work as 'very middling', but she had given him hope that a provincial poet could get into print—in 1808 she had published her *Cottage Poems* by subscription to pay off her creditors.

Clare dreamed that his poetry would bestow immortality not only on himself but also on his native place. In 1813 a poet from Spalding called David Hurn had sung of the River Welland in his *Rural Rhymes*—why should Clare not do the same for his own environment? Scattered through 'A Rustic's Pastime', written in the spaces left after he had given up on his fair copies, there are fragments of 'Helpstone', the long poem that would begin his first published collection. He wanted to preserve the character of the childhood places that were disappearing as enclosure changed the face of the land.

The effect of enclosure is the theme not only of 'Helpstone' but also of the strongest poem in 'A Rustic's Pastime'. Dated 1818 in Clare's own hand and entitled 'The Lamentations of Round-Oak Waters', most of it is written in the voice of the stream that was fed by the natural spring in the open field to the south of Royce Wood.* The 'genius of the brook' laments the loss of the trees and bushes that had sheltered it prior to the enclosure. The surrounding pastures, meadows and fallows are now 'all beset wi' post and rail / And turned upside down', 'There's scarce a greensward spot remains / And scarce a single tree'. The encloser's axe has cut down the willows beside the brook. Blame is attached not to the 'sweating slaves' who did the physical work (Clare himself was one such), but to the law of enclosure and the profiteers who benefited from it.

Clare is here revealed as a poet of protest, but he was at the same time a loyal patriot. Among the other poems copied into 'A Rustic's Pastime' were verses beginning 'Hail England old England my Country and home / Thou pride of thy Sons and thou dread of the world'. He also included lines praising Wellington as a second Nelson,

---

*The stanza and rhyme forms are the same as those of Burns's 'The humble petition of Bruar Water to the Noble Duke of Athole', a poem also written in the voice of a stretch of water. Influence or coincidence? Clare wrote defensively in a fragment: 'The Critics speaks their guesses or opinions with such an authourity of certainty as tho they were the fountain of truth ... several of them complaind at my too frequent imitations of Burns—now the fact is that when my first poems was written I knew nothing of Burns not even by name, for the fens are not a literary part of England ... I had an odd Volume of Ramsay a long while and if I imitated any it shoud be him to which I am ready to acknowledge a great deal.'

a celebration of the victory at Waterloo in 1815, and a poem called 'The Disabled Soldier *or British Loyalty*', in which the speaker is 'A True Blue Britton' rather than the kind of pitiful, neglected figure cut by the discharged soldiers in Wordsworth's poems.

He would have to mature as a poet before developing a confident language of political satire. He did nevertheless experiment with an ironic vein in a few of his early poems. 'On the Death of a Quack' is a brief satire on a quack doctor who gulls 'Village Lout and Farmer's wimsy wife' with his dubious pills and powders. This was based on a man who arrived in Deeping and became known as Doctor Touch, because it was rumoured that he could cure people just by touching them. Will Farrow the shoemaker and Parker Clare went into Deeping to find out the truth of the matter. It turned out that Touch did not use his bare hands, but applied large blisters at half a guinea apiece (the money to be paid down before he began his work). Parker and Will refused to go along with this. Touch 'was very importunate and even abusive at their credulity'. They returned home, told their tale, and Clare wrote his poem. Touch remained in Deeping for some time, finding 'plenty of believers to maintain his hoaxing pretensions'. But when two or three patients died under his care, the tide turned and 'he decamped in the night'.

Unrefined as Clare's art was in 'A Rustic's Pastime', he was clearly establishing his voice and marking out his range of poetic material. The everyday life of his village was one major subject. He even wrote an elegy of over two hundred lines on the death of 'Dobbin', an old cart-horse who 'was in great fame in the Village for his gentleness and strength and readiness at all sorts of jobs'.

His own life also gave him material. Girls, for instance. There is an acrostic for his 'first love reality', Miss Betsy Newbon of Ashton, and a sonnet entitled 'A moment's rapture while bearing the lovely weight of A. S—r—s'. I have not been able to trace the latter in the Helpston records—perhaps, like Mary Joyce and Betsy Newbon, she came from a neighbouring village—but the poem has the feel of a very specific memory: Anna in her Sunday dress ('Robes which half show what modesty conceals') sits for a moment on his knee, her bosom rising, while he puts his hand around her slender waist and wishes to arrest the fleeting moment and 'bear her weight through all eternity'. Another early poem is a ballad about 'The lovely Jeannette the pride of the green'. But before we start looking for her in the parish records, we should note that in a different manuscript Clare wrote out the same poem in praise of 'The lovely Louisa the pride of the green'. Perhaps he knew a Jeannette and a Louisa, but it is more likely that on this occasion he was imagining a generic rustic maid, not remembering or trying to impress a real girl.

Throughout Clare's work, and especially in the early poems that strongly smack of the poetic language he inherited from his reading, there is a complex relationship between personal experience and literary convention. So, for instance, one of the longest and most carefully copied poems in 'A Rustic's Pastime' is called 'The Wish'. Here Clare wishes that he could be free from 'all labouring strife', living in a 'decent house' made of more solid materials than the wattle, daub and thatch of his own cottage ('Of British oak the roofing should be made / And best of slate should be upon them laid'). He asks for a reasonable number of rooms and a cupboard for a library of choice authors, a sizeable and well-ordered garden, a good view, unmarried contentment without a 'noisy wife', a modest and not too ignorant domestic maid, and sufficient income to spare a crust for a passing beggar. At one level, this is Clare's fantasy of escape from poverty into the life of a gentleman-poet such as Thomson or Cowper. But at another, it is merely an exercise in the writing of a particular kind of poem, the praise of rural ease. Abraham Cowley's much-imitated 'The Wish', written in the mid-seventeenth century, had expressed exactly the same desire for a single life of contemplation, with a library and a garden. The tradition goes back to Horace in Roman times.

And what if the wish had been fulfilled? Clare would have been cut off from the social and natural environment that was the very wellspring of his poetry. The voice of 'The Wish' does not feel properly his own. As he later told his publisher, 'I had got the knack of writing smoothly with little sense'. The true poet in Clare could never have sat composing elegant lines in a comfortable parlour. His muse belonged elsewhere: to the fields, the heath, the margins and secret places, to the time of forced unemployment rather than a gentleman's leisure. Once when he was out 'rhyming', he was mistaken for a poacher. The passage where he describes the incident gives a vivid sense of where he really belonged:

> I always wrote my poems in the fields and when I was out of work I used to go out of the village to particular spots which I was fond of from the beauty or secrecy of the scenes or some association and I often went half a day's journey from home on these excursions—in one of these rambles I was in a narrow escape of being taken up as a poacher—it was a fine day and I went to wander on Wittering Heath with the double intention of rhyming and seeking wild plants—I found a beautiful spot on the side of a rivulet that ran crooking and neglected among the yellow furze and misty green sallows that met on both sides—I sat down nearly concealed in the furze and tall downy grass and began to rhyme till I insensibly fell asleep and was awakened by muttering voices on the other side of the thicket— I looked through and saw they were keepers by their guns—one of the dogs came up and peeped at me and the men made a stop as if they suspected something was in it—I felt very fearful but it was soon over for they passed on—I was far away from any road and my account of myself would have seemed but an idle one—it would have only raised their suspicions and I should have been taken up as a poacher undoubtedly so as soon as they were safe off I made the best of my way out of danger for the part I was in was enclosed with a wall and belonged to the Marquis.

CHAPTER SIX

'HOW GREAT ARE

MY EXPECTATIONS!'

Eighteen-eighteen. Clare was lime-burning at Casterton. Desperately short of money, concerned about his parents' poverty and ill health, in love with Patty but without prospects of his own, he decided to try to get his work into print.

His only contact with the publishing world was J. B. Henson, the man from whom he had bought the blank book into which he had been copying the poems he wished to preserve. On the day of Deeping Fair back in 1814, Henson had prised from the tipsy Clare the information that he dabbled in rhyme. Had he not expressed a desire to see his writing?

Henson had arrived in Market Deeping as a schoolmaster. He turned to bookbinding and trade in second-hand books. Then he established a printing press, beginning with auction bills, ballads and broadsheets, before trying his hand at pamphlets and small books: *The History of Joseph and his Brethren*, Bunyan's *Pilgrim's Progress* in a series of sixpenny numbers, a small book of arithmetic by a fellow Deeping schoolmaster, 'a political pamphlet of wooden ingenuity by a Northamptonshire farmer', and some religious volumes for a London publisher called Baines. His religious interests also took the form of preaching and serving as a clerk with the 'congregational dissenters or Independants'—as has been mentioned, Clare had heard him preach in the Independent chapel in Helpston. Henson was eventually found out in 'dirty doings' of a worldly kind (perhaps some sexual or financial misdemeanour), as a result of which he was rejected by the Congregationalists.

Clare plucked up his courage and went to Henson with two of his earliest sonnets, one on 'The Setting Sun' and the other 'To a Primrose', together with his poem on the death of Thomas Chatterton. Preacher Henson would have especially approved of Clare's comparison of the sunset to the Christian soul's departure in death to heaven. As for the Chatterton, he considered it a good subject for a penny broadsheet to sell to hawkers.

Clare wanted a proper book, not a one-off of this kind. Sensing the opportunity to make some money by marketing a new 'peasant poet', Henson agreed to get in touch with his London bookseller. But he claimed that the only viable means of publication would be subscription. That is to say, his own costs would be guaranteed by subscribers giving an advance undertaking that they would purchase the book. Clare had no choice but to go along with this suggestion, though he 'detested the thoughts of Subscription as being little better than begging money from people that knew nothing of their purchase'.

The catch was that Henson would only start printing the book when three hundred subscribers' names had been gathered. In order to get up a subscription list, there would have to be a prospectus, with a specimen of the poetry. Henson proposed that Clare should draw up an 'Address to the Public' himself. He would then print three hundred copies of the proposals on a double sheet of foolscap, for which Clare would be charged a pound. Clare was wary: what kind of a publisher was incapable of writing his own promotional material? Yet he went along with the arrangement, duly saving the pound by dint of hard work day and night at the Pickworth kiln. On 3 November 1818, he wrote to Henson asking him to print the prospectus. He wanted to give the book the modest title 'A Collection of Trifles in Verse'. Henson told him that he should make it clear what kind of trifles they were: 'whether *Religious, moral or Missellaneous*'.

It was a couple of weeks before Clare found himself able to write the prospectus. Mr Cole's noisy lodgings at Bridge Casterton did not give him any privacy. He was, however, doing some extra work at a lime-kiln at Ryhall, about three miles from Pickworth. Walking there and back alone, he took the opportunity to sketch out a draft in his head. On one occasion, his 'prosing thoughts lost themselves in rhyme': sheltering by a hedge, he reflected on his parents' distress at home, his labours to work the family out of debt and his 'still added perplexities of ill-timed love'. He burst out with the question 'What is life?' and instantly realised that this would be a good subject for a poem. He 'hastily scratted down the 2 first verses of it'. 'And what is life?' he asks—it is 'A bubble on the stream / That in the act of seizing shrinks to nought'.*

He continued on his way to work. Unable to take his mind off his poetic plans, he sat down on a lime-scuttle and pencilled out his address to the public. For better or worse, it would have to do. He set off for Stamford immediately, though hesitating on the road and wondering whether he ought to get the opinion of a friend before committing his words to print. Just outside Stamford, he stopped and read his words through again, correcting them as best he could. When he got to the Post Office, he was asked for an extra penny since it was past the normal closing time. 'The man looked a little surprised at the unusual garb of the letter,' Clare recalled. It was 'directed with a pencil, written on a sheet of paper that was crumpled and grizzled with lying in one's pocket so long, and to add to its novelty sealed with shoemaker's wax.' He handed it over and beat a hasty retreat.

Henson replied that he would print the prospectus immediately.

*On 26 June 1818, an anonymous poem called 'Life's Likenesses—Written in imitation of the Poetry of the 17th Century' was published in the *Stamford Mercury*. Its imagery is very similar to that of Clare's 'What is life?': 'Life is—what? / It is a bubble on the main, / Rais'd by a little globe of rain . . .' It has been ascribed to Clare himself, but he said that the first time he saw a poem of his in print was when he received Henson's prospectus, and besides, he did not begin reading and imitating seventeenth-century poetry until some years later. It is much more likely that Clare read the poem in the newspaper and imitated it himself. Tempting as it may be to imagine that all his compositions were spontaneous, his early poetry was often highly derivative.

He would bring some copies over to Stamford. They should meet at the Dolphin in the Beast Market, where they could talk over further details. On Tuesday 1 December 1818, Henson handed over one hundred copies of the *Proposals for Publishing, by Subscription, A Collection of Original Trifles, On Miscellaneous Subjects, Religious and Moral, in Verse.* It laid out the conditions of sale specified by Henson: price three shillings and sixpence; three hundred copies to be subscribed for, or the work would not appear; to be 'printed on a superfine yellow wove foolscap paper, in octavo size, forming a neat pocket volume'; a list of subscribers' names to be included; on completion the book to be delivered to subscribers free of additional charge; payment on delivery. There then followed Clare's address to the public. Its tone was, to say the least, defensive. The poems are described as a mixture of juvenile productions and the 'offsprings of those leisure intervals which the short remittance from hard and manual labour sparingly afforded to compose them'.

> The least touch from the iron hand of *Criticism* is able to crush them to nothing, and sink them at once to utter oblivion. May they be allowed to live their little day and give satisfaction to those who may choose to honour them with a perusal, they will gain the end for which they were designed and their author's wishes will be gratified.

To conclude the prospectus, the sonnet 'To the Setting Sun' was given as a specimen of Clare's work. It was the first of his poems to appear in printed form. Clare recalled his feelings on looking at it as he sat with Henson in the Dolphin: 'I scarcely knew it in its new dress and felt a prouder confidence than I had hitherto done'. But his joy was dampened by Henson's demand for not only the agreed pound, but also a further five shillings for expenses.

While they were drinking together, Henson handed out some copies of the prospectus. The first gentleman who cast an eye over it took one look at Clare and walked out of the bar without saying a word. The second praised the sonnet, offered Clare a drink and asked to be put down as a subscriber. Years later, Clare remembered this man with gratitude. He was the Reverend Thomas Mouncey, second master at the Stamford Free Grammar School. Henson, meanwhile, slipped out of the bar, leaving Clare to pick up the tab.

Clare's elation at his prospects bubbles out from his next letter to Henson. It is the first of his letters to survive:

> Sir
>
> I send you some of the principal Subscribers which I have procured lately: the first of which is a Baronet!!! who speaks very highly of my 'Sonnet' in the prospectus—Good God, how great are my Expectations! what hopes do I cherish! As great as the unfortunate Chatterton's were, on his first entrance into London, which is now pictured in my Mind—and undoubtedly like him I may be building 'Castles in the Air' but Time will prove it—Please do all in your power to procure Subscribers (as your address will be look'd on better than that of a Clown) when 100 is got you may print it if you please so do your best—and if ever it lies in my power to give friendship its due you shall not go unrewarded
>
> yours   John Clare

Clown, a term often applied to Clare (by himself and others), meant 'uneducated rustic', not 'jester'. The Baronet who inspired Clare's awed exclamation was Sir John English Dolben of nearby Finedon Hall. Nearly seventy but sprightly of limb and open in spirit, he was a lover of literature who 'carried so many small volumes about him in his numerous and capacious pockets, that he appeared like a walking library'. He also subscribed to the poems of another Northampton-shire scribbler, John Merry, 'The Bard of Moulton Mill'.

Other known subscribers were the vicar of Helpston, a local Non-conformist minister, and Francis Willis of Greatford, a village to the east of Stamford. Willis was the grandson and namesake of the doc-tor who became famous when he was credited with curing George III from his first attack of madness in 1788. Greatford Hall was a private lunatic asylum maintained by three generations of Willises. Clare visited the younger Francis there in April 1820.

Henson agreed that he would print the book as soon as a hundred subscribers had signed up. Clare had sacrificed a week's wages in Rutland to go home and seek out those first few (seven were found in all), so he felt badly betrayed when Henson then changed his mind and announced that he would not begin printing unless Clare came up with a cash advance of fifteen pounds. Clare 'had not 15 pence nor 15 farthings to call [his] own' at this time. Henson dropped his price to ten pounds, making Clare still more suspicious of his manner of doing business.

Clare was now thoroughly embarrassed. The circulation of his proposals had revealed his poetic ambitions to his fellow-villagers, but now it looked as if the venture would come to nothing. He considered running away from it all. Twice he went to Stamford in order to enlist in the artillery, but he was prevented by a combination of his insufficient height, his own vacillation, the 'love matters' that were now 'a strong tether' to his native region, and a kindly recruiting officer who saw that he had only taken the King's Shilling because he was drunk.

To make financial matters worse, a bill for fifteen shillings arrived from a Mr Thompson who kept the 'New Public Library', a bookshop and lending library in Stamford High Street. He was selling up and wished to close his accounts. Clare sent his friend Thomas Porter to plead for more time on his behalf. Porter took along three copies of the prospectus, to show Thompson that Clare's fortunes might be about to change. He also hoped that there would be potential subscribers among the bookshop's customers. Porter returned with a message: 'the money was what he wanted, and the money he would have'.

The new proprietor was already established in the bookshop. Whereas preacher Henson and churlish Thompson were forbidding figures who did not hesitate to make demands of Clare, Edward ('Ned') Drury was a youth of just twenty-one—someone of Clare's own generation. His father was a printer in Lincoln, who was presumably setting his son up in Stamford to prepare him for taking over the family trade. Young Drury looked at Clare's prospectus and saw an opportunity to make his mark on the literary life of the town. Despite knowing nothing more of Clare than what Porter had told him, and nothing more of Clare's abilities than what he could glean from the prospectus, he paid off Thompson's bill himself.

Clare received this good news from Porter, but was uncertain how to proceed. The very next Sunday Drury went to Helpston, accompanied by Richard Newcomb, the son of the proprietor of the *Stamford Mercury* newspaper. They dined with Mr Clark, the well-to-do farmer who was the Clares' landlord. Inquiries were made as to the poet's character and abilities. Clark knew nothing about Clare's poetic aspirations, so Drury and Newcomb decided to visit the man himself. They found the cottage, but he was not there. He was spending his Sunday with the Billings brothers at Bachelors' Hall. Sister Sophy was sent to fetch him.

According to Frederick Martin's biography, Clare was on the point of leaving Helpston. Martin says that after the failed attempt to join the artillery, Clare and a fellow unemployed labourer named Coblee made a pact to go and seek work elsewhere. Clare wanted to head north to Yorkshire, Coblee east into the fens. They agreed to toss a coin. It fell in Yorkshire's favour, but Coblee procrastinated. They would meet at Bachelors' Hall on Sunday to make a final decision. Word spread of the impending departure of Clare's companion, a popular man in the village, so that Sunday a large number assembled at the Billingses' cottage—together with a large number of bottles of ale. It was then agreed that a stick would be placed firmly in the ground (cottage floors were of bare earth covered with sand), that everybody would dance round until it toppled, and that Clare and Coblee would venture in whichever direction it pointed. As the story goes, at a pause in the dancing (the stick still in the ground) a shrill little voice was heard outside: ' "John Clare must come home at once, there are two gentlemen waiting for him: two real gentlemen." "Shall I go?" inquired John. "Go, by all means," dictated the elder of the bachelor brothers, "we will wait for you." They waited long, but John did not return.'

Although it must be assumed that, as always, Martin embellished this story in the telling, there is circumstantial evidence in support of its underlying truth.* Even if the precise coincidence of timing is exaggerated, the story does not lose its point: if Drury had not intervened, Clare could well have left the parish for points north and never become a published poet.

Clare himself left a record of what happened next. He arrived home with Sophy to find the two gentlemen with his parents. Newcomb did most of the talking. First he said that he and his friend had come to put down their names as subscribers. Clare thanked them. Then they asked to see some of his manuscripts. They seemed pleased with them. Newcomb asked about the status of the arrangement with Henson. Clare explained the terms, hinting at his dissatisfaction with how things were turning out. They would not wish him to break his word, they said. But as they were leaving, Clare was told that if he got his manuscripts back from Henson, Drury would print them without any subvention. Indeed, they would give Clare money for his 'necessities'. Clare was delighted. Newcomb invited him to dinner the following evening and the two gentlemen left the cottage.

A moment later Newcomb reappeared and said: 'If you get the manuscripts from Deeping, Mr Clare, we shall be glad to see you; if not, we can say nothing further about the matter.' Clare was furious at the sudden change of tone. It seemed to imply that they believed that if they gave him an inch he might take an ell. He regretted having bothered to come from Bachelors' Hall. The twist established a precedent for many of Clare's subsequent encounters with patrons and publishers: one moment he would be deeply grateful for their interest in his work, the next he would feel slighted and abused.

He did not go to dinner with Newcomb on the Monday. Instead he wrote to Drury, enclosing some poems and apparently expressing some reservations about Newcomb. Drury replied that he should

---

*Principally the corroboration (from census records and a letter that was not known to Martin) that 'Coblee'—actually John Cobbler—was a fellow-labourer of Clare's in Helpston. Clare himself used the device of the falling stick in his poem and prose story 'The Two Soldiers'.

'place full and undivided confidence' in Newcomb, 'who has both the power and the will of doing every service that can be wished'. He wrote enthusiastically of Clare as potentially 'a second Burns, or Bloomfield', and proposed that he should come over to Stamford the following Sunday, when he would purchase his manuscripts 'on speculation'. He also suggested how Clare might word a letter to Henson: 'Sir, By the Bearer pray return the MSS of Poetry, etc., you have in possession, and I beg to signify that I do not intend to present my writings to the public, *for the present*. I am etc.' 'The above is only a suggestion', he added in a postscript.

Clare ignored the suggestion and sent a more honest letter to Henson. He said that the demand for fifteen pounds was a breach of their agreement and he mentioned the better prospects that he had now found with Drury. His mother delivered the letter to Deeping. She came back with the manuscript materials that Clare had left with Henson. He had been reluctant to hand them over.

Clare went to Drury with the manuscripts and stayed the whole day. Drury promised to pay his debts and gave him a guinea as an earnest of his good intentions. He also showed him Lord Byron's exotically Turkish tale *The Giaour*. This was Clare's introduction to the poetry of the age's most famous writer. No formal agreement was made, but over the next few weeks Drury began sending Clare both money and advice. The former was more welcome than the latter.

The Helpston vicarage was just across the road from Clare's cottage. Some time around Christmas 1818, Clare showed his work to the vicar, Charles Mossop. The poems that Mossop commended would be dismissed by Drury as mere 'bagatelles'. Drury preferred the 'moral and rural subjects' of the poems he had already seen. Never confident in his own judgement, Clare was always eager to show his work to others, but his difficulty in accepting criticism was exacerbated by conflicting advice from different quarters.

Parson Mossop, twenty-five and only recently installed, happily encouraged Clare in his aspirations but was perhaps uneasy at the idea of a village labourer pronouncing on 'moral' subjects. The aged vicar of Little Casterton, Richard Twopenny, to whom Drury had shown the poems, took a stronger view. He 'sent them back with a cold note stating that he had no objection to assist in raising the poor man a small subscription, though the poems appeared to him to possess no merit to be worthy of publication'.

Drury was insufficiently experienced to know that writers need to be protected from such harsh rejections. He read the note to Clare, who was devastated—'as I fancied all men in a station superior to me as learned and wise, especially parsons'. Clare said that his despondency over the dismissive note was almost 'carried too far' and confided to Drury that he had thought of suicide. Drury reminded his charge of the writers who had suffered long before achieving hard-won fame: Milton was only paid ten pounds for *Paradise Lost*; Dr Johnson once wandered all night without a bed; Henry Kirke White 'became an errand boy to a butcher to buy books'. Later, when basking in the success of his first published volume, Clare took pleasure in writing a little squib about how he didn't care twopence for the twopenny wisdom of Reverend Twopenny.

After his failure with the clergy, Drury turned to the gentry. He approached the baronet who had chanced upon Clare's original proposals. Sir English responded with enthusiasm. Greatly cheered, Clare 'rhymed on and became pacified'. As the winter progressed he finished off many of the early poems that he had previously left in fragmentary form. In his draft autobiography he recollected some of the original circumstances of composition. There was an address to a lark 'made one cold winter's morning on returning home from raking stubble as the ground was so froze that I could not work—I frit the lark up while raking and it began to sing'. 'Evening' was altered from a long early poem written after cow-tending on the common, while 'Noon' was composed 'on a hot day in summer while I went to fill my father's water bottle with water at Round Oak spring'. There were also ballads based on village tales and newspaper stories.

The newspapers of the day regularly published poetry (Clare said that he took to writing sonnets on finding in an old paper some 'very pretty' sonnets by Charlotte Smith, who was perhaps the most accomplished female poet of the age). Drury assisted him in trying to get some of his poems published in the *Stamford Mercury*. He corrected a draft letter to the editor, suggesting that the signature should be altered from 'A Northamptonshire Pheasant' [*sic*] to 'A Northamptonshire Rustic'.

Clare had worked at the Pickworth lime-kiln until late in 1818. He had then returned to Casterton until the onset of frost put an end to his work for Mr Wilders. For the rest of the winter he remained at home 'scribbling etc. for the forthcoming book'. Drury's monetary advances were vital to the Clare family's subsistence at this time. As we have seen, the Clares were behind with the rent and on the point of eviction. Drury's faith in the potential of Clare's poetry saved Parker and Ann from the poor-house.

Henson was still badgering Clare, even though many weeks had passed since their abortive negotiations. Drury gave advice on how to handle him, but felt that matters would be exacerbated if he became involved himself. He was busy copying out the poems to send to 'a literary gentleman for his opinion, advice as to the shape, and size of the book, etc.'

Clare, meanwhile, was cheered by a visit from the Congregational minister of Northborough near Deeping. He had seen the Henson proposals and put himself down as a subscriber. His name was Isaiah Knowles Holland. He had asked a local farming family—probably the Clarks—what was known of Clare and been told that he was a 'quiet inoffensive fellow'. He sent a message to the effect that he would like to meet him. Still low in self-confidence after Twopenny's rejection, Clare did not want to show himself. So he sent a note via his mother thanking the 'unknown gentleman' for taking the trouble 'to Enquire after *a Clown* who as yet *Slumbers* in *Obscurity* and perhaps whose *merits* deserves no better *fate*'. Holland asked Ann Clare various questions and said that she should caution her son against publishing his poems with Henson, 'as he thought it would go a great way to ruin the success they might meet with elsewhere'. Since Holland moved in Dissenting circles in Deeping, he is likely to have known about Henson's dodgy reputation.

He visited the Helpston cottage. When he arrived, Clare was copying out a poem to send to Drury. Holland leant over his shoulder to read it, offering words of encouragement. He shared with Clare his enthusiasm for Henry Kirke White, the son of a Nottingham butcher who had gained the patronage of Robert Southey upon publishing a volume of poetry at the age of eighteen. White had gained a coveted place at Cambridge only to overwork himself to a premature death at the age of twenty-two. Southey wrote a memoir that was published together with White's poetic *Remains*.

Holland began to lend Clare books. A copy of Burns inspired Clare to imitation, but the pastorals of the gentleman poet Shenstone were not to his taste: 'Putting the Correct Language of the Gentleman into the mouth of a Simple Shepherd or Vulgar Ploughman is far from Natural'. Coming in time to trust Holland as a 'Gent: of Learning', Clare sent poems to him for comment: 'I ask not for Flattery—Just as you think Sir I wish you to Speak'. In one letter he included his tale 'The Fate of Amy', based on an old village story, explaining that he had given his imagination free scope in altering the narrative, avoiding that 'truth' which in his opinion always 'crampt the Imagination'.

Clare sometimes visited Drury on Sundays. He borrowed books, including the poetry of Kirke White and Bloomfield. He wrote through the winter and into the spring, sending Drury new poems and corrections to old ones. Some of his letters reveal insecurity, for instance when he asks for information as to the quality of a potential rival, Samuel Messing of Exton in Rutland. Drury replied that Messing's volume, entitled *Rural Walks; or Poems on Various Subjects*, was 'most contemptible', but that its impressive list of two hundred subscribers presented a problem: they were exactly the sort of people whom he was intending to approach for Clare and they would be unlikely to want to support a second book of poetry, especially as the first one was so '*very bad*'. This was one reason why he was considering an alternative course.

Drury added, in order to show that he was working hard, that he had arranged for one of Clare's poems to be published in the *Macclesfield Courier*. He claimed that a paper from a distant part of the country had been chosen so that when Clare's book came out there could be no complaint that it consisted of 'old Newspaper Poetry'. But one suspects that his contact in Macclesfield was a fallback after he had failed in various attempts to place Clare in the *Stamford Mercury*. Leaving aside the sample poem circulated locally in the Henson prospectus, the sonnet 'To the Glow-worm' in the *Macclesfield Courier* of 8 April 1819 has the distinction of being the first of Clare's poems to have appeared in print. It was published without attribution, which was perhaps a good thing, given that it was a cumbersome effusion that began with the unpromising line, 'Tasteful Illuminations of the night'.

The appearance in print of a collection by Clare, as opposed to the odd single poem, was still some months away. In the spring, financial need forced him to return to Casterton. He thought of giving up on his poetry. All that summer he was working again for Mr and Mrs Wilders in the garden of the New Inn. He earned nine shillings a week, one and sixpence of which went on lodging. He returned home at weekends, and every Monday morning walked the nine miles to Casterton. On wet days when it was impossible to work, he went into Drury's shop in Stamford to read books and find new tunes for his fiddle.

Mrs Wilders, who had taken an interest in Clare ever since discovering that he had worked at Burghley, asked to see some of his poems. She told visitors to the inn about him. He got out of the way when he could, but on one occasion a gentleman told him that a stanza in his poem 'Evening' closely paralleled a passage in some 'Poems in England by a Native of the West Indias'. Fearing he would be taken for a plagiarist when the poem appeared in print, Clare sent Drury a revision of the lines.

Drury remained mysterious about his plans for publishing Clare's first book. He informed Clare that 'they were in the hands and met the favourable opinion of a gentleman who could and would do them justice'. But he would not reveal the name. He kept assuring Clare that his poems were going to be a great success. A painter of profiles named Gillespie was engaged to take the poet's likeness. 'These things were trifles to remember', wrote Clare later, 'but they were great at their beginnings—they made me all life and spirits and nothing but hope and prosperity was before me'.

The gentleman into whose hands Drury had put the poems was his cousin. An aunt, Sarah Drury of Newark, had married a Yorkshireman called James Taylor, who had become a bookseller in another midland town, East Retford in Nottinghamshire. John Taylor, one of their sons, born in 1781, had been trained up in the family business before moving to London, where he moved into publishing. He got a job with a company called Vernor and Hood. Within a few days of his arrival there, he met their most celebrated author: Robert Bloomfield, who had been paid a staggering four thousand pounds for his *Farmer's Boy*. Taylor realised, as he never would have done in provincial Retford, that there was serious money to be made out of books. In 1806 he set himself up in a bookselling and binding business in Fleet Street, in partnership with a friend named James Augustus Hessey.

They began by publishing conduct books, sermons and other safe but unspectacular titles. They added some poetry to their list. Then early in 1817 they were introduced to the twenty-one-year-old son of a livery-stable keeper from Moorfields. He had abandoned his surgical training and was on the point of publishing his first book of poetry. His name was John Keats. Taylor was convinced of his potential greatness. Keats's first collection of poems sank almost without trace in 1817, but Taylor and Hessey stepped in and published his long poem *Endymion* the following year. It was savaged in the Tory press, mainly because of Keats's friendship with Leigh Hunt, editor of the liberal magazine the *Examiner*. Hunt had been politically notorious since 1813, when he had received a two-year prison sentence for publishing an attack on the Prince Regent.

Drury knew that Taylor and Hessey had some experience in the publication of poetry and had sent them some of Clare's works with the explanation that 'They are written by a laboring man in this neighbourhood, who seems to have a strange taste for poetry, and if *his* compositions are poetry, there cannot be a stronger proof of the art being a *gift*, as it is called'. Making clear that he was eager to get into the business of publishing in conjunction with his bookselling, he asked Taylor's opinion as to the likelihood of Clare's poems being economically viable 'without the midwifery of a list of Subscribers'. He also requested help with corrections: 'In reading the work over your kind alteration of any error, false grammar or rythm will be thankfully acknowledged by me and the poor author,—who has had every disadvantage in respect to education, reading, and advice'.

Taylor expressed strong interest, so Drury wrote again with an account of Clare and the circumstances in which they had met. He embroidered the tale in order to play up both Clare's poverty and his own role in discovering the rustic genius. He did not mention the Henson business, saying only that he had witnessed an altercation about Clare's bookbinding bill and noticed that 'a piece of dirty paper, that had enveloped the letter brought by the man, had writing like verse on it'. Picking it up, he found the sonnet on the subject of the setting sun (thus giving the impression that he had discovered a scrap of unknown handwritten verse, not a printed prospectus). Drury's fanciful account—Clare himself called it a hoax—nevertheless found its way into the introduction to Clare's first book.

Drury also omitted to mention that Newcomb accompanied him to Clare's cottage and that Clare had to be fetched from Bachelors' Hall (whence he would have arrived with alcohol on his breath). Instead, Taylor was given a vivid snapshot in prose:

> I procured a horse and rode over to Helpstone, where in the worst hut of the meanest village I ever saw, I found the poet's father and mother. The man was stiffened with rheumatism to such a degree that he could only move his eyes; the mother was cross in her looks, and gipsey-like in her appearance; and they were sitting against a little bit of a fire of sods and stick. On enquiring after her son, the woman called out 'Jack', when lumping down the steps came the poet from the upper room of the house. He was shy and clownish in his manners, but the restraint wore off a little, and he shewed me 'My Mary' half finished.

This little scene would do very well for publicity purposes.

Drury suggested that it would be best for Taylor to support the publication of a volume, while initially remaining in the background. Clare's genius, he argued, was dependent on his humble status as a gardener. It would be a recipe for disaster to remove him from that environment and take him up to London, though in time it might be advisable to set him up as a village schoolmaster. For this, he would need some more education. Later in the year, Clare expressed his enthusiasm for the idea: 'I hope you have not forgot your promise of sending me to some School—I shall certainly reap great benefit from such an advantage.'

One part of Drury was genuinely concerned for Clare's welfare, while another part was looking to his own fame as the discoverer of a new poet and the proprietor of a goose that had the potential to lay golden eggs. He ended the letter to Taylor by painting Clare as a wild untutored genius, a child of nature:

> Your hopes of good grammar and correct verse, depend on the inspiration of the mind; for Clare cannot *reason*; he writes and can give no reason for his using a fine expression, or a beautiful idea: if you read Poetry to him, he'll exclaim at each delicate expression 'beautiful! fine!' but can give no reason: yet is *always* correct and just in his remarks. He is low in stature—long visage—light hair—coarse features—ungaitly—awkward—is a fiddler—loves ale—likes the *girls*—somewhat idle,—hates work.

There is condescension here, but also terrific enthusiasm. And Drury was right about the *instinctive* quality of Clare's judgement—this is something that comes across in the poet's character-sketches of acquaintances as well as his responses to what he read and saw.

Early in May 1819, Drury sent Taylor some more poems and a brief memoir of Clare. Taylor began the work of editing and correcting. Drury admired his 'judicious alterations' and acknowledged that Clare wrote too much too quickly. But he was as convinced of his man's potential as Taylor had been of Keats's: 'No where do I see that compactness of style that marks mediocrity or maturity, but the in-equality of strength and weakness indicates greater powers than are yet developed: all he writes is the birth of the moment, and therefore is rough and unpolished, but that does not alter the beauty of the thought in Burns's sometimes uncouth and vulgar dialect, then why should it in Clare's native and simple language?'

Burns was a precedent for the publication of poetry in local dialect, but his name was also shorthand for the dangers facing a writer plucked from poverty to celebrity: drink, sexual temptation, early death. Aware of this, Drury defended Clare:

> He is no drunkard, but I know from constantly studying his character that if encouraged foolishly he could not resist the temptations of conviviality; and after sitting for hours silently, and reading the countenances and characters of his compan-ions, he would on a sudden burst out into a flow of festivity and folly, that sober folks would term drunkenness, etc. Again, hav-ing such a relish for what is beautiful, and so little amusement of a robust and active kind, I should think he has been fond of the society of females, and so got into bad name that way: but I will engage that he is wrongly accused there.

Despite making this defence, he added that though Clare was in his mid-twenties, his 'moral age' was eighteen.

Clare queried a few of Taylor's alterations, but took pleasure in most of them. He felt bad that pressure of work at Casterton meant that he had little time to write good new poems. He scolded Drury for sending even his poetic 'rubbish' to the still unidentified 'gentleman-editor'.

The appearance of Messing's *Rural Walks* had put Drury off the idea of publication by subscription. Instead, the publishers decided they themselves would risk the loss if the volume flopped. By August there was a firm understanding whereby the poems would be pub-lished jointly by Drury in Stamford and Taylor and Hessey in Lon-don. Clare would be paid according to Taylor and Hessey's 'Idea of his Deserts', while profits would be shared equally between Drury and the London firm. But no written contract had been drawn up for Clare to sign.

Taylor had been given the materials to write an introduction. He warmed to his task, believing that, having backed a cockney genius in the form of Keats, he had now found a country one. Clare willingly provided the biographical information needed to market him as a 'peasant' phenomenon: 'I am not against having my humble Occupation, mean patronage, and scanty Education—or any thing of the like hinted at in your preface—just what you think suitable so may do.'

Drury prepared advertisements for the newspapers. Taylor began sending poems to his printer for typesetting. Proofs were dispatched for the approval of Drury and Clare. For the most part, they accepted Taylor's judgement as to which poems to include and which to exclude. Drury made it his responsibility to encourage Clare to stick to writing about 'rural subjects', which he and Taylor both regarded as the matter of his best work.

Clare himself was closely involved in the process of preparing his work for publication. Fair copies of the poems were returned to him for comment. He added explanations and judgements in the margin, vigorously scoring through some poems and scrawling above them such comments as 'D——d stuff' and 'Cursed silly. J.C.' He was learning the art of self-criticism. One of his notes reads:

> Those marked ✔ are to be printed   Those X are to be omitted
> Order of the pieces
> 1   Helpstone etc entitled Poems—headed Helpstone
> 2   Songs and Ballads, headed the same
> 3   Sonnets, headed Sonnets
> All markt wi a C. are favorites of mine.

When the book was published, Taylor respected Clare's tripartite division and his desire to give pride of place to the long poem named after his native village. The poems that Clare wanted omitted were omitted, though room was not found for all those he wanted to include.

Taylor was scrupulous in keeping his own interventions to a minimum, as he explained to Drury: 'My Rule has been to leave every thing as Clare wrote it, with such Corrections as I should have suggested to him had he been present'. He said that his emendations were 'always trifling', for instance involving 'grammatical and orthographical amendments which the Printer would have been scarce able to pass by, when they could be effected without altering the sense or the original expressions'. 'But other Things of a doubtful Character, or not glaringly wrong,' he added, 'are suffered to remain as the author wrote them, and better so, as they shew that they belong to the imperfect Education he has received.' Sometimes he corrected a word or phrase, then thought again and returned to Clare's original. Such was his 'Wish to keep to all the original Writing as nearly as may be'. From the start, then, Taylor's principal desire was not to improve Clare's work, but simply to make it publishable. If he had not made some basic corrections to grammar and spelling, the printer would have done.

In the autumn, Clare wrote to the Reverend Isaiah Holland with the news that 'My First Atempts at Poetry are nearly Publishd—They have this Title "Pastoral Sketches in Poems Songs Ballads and Sonnets by John Clare A Northamptonshire Pheasant" Printed for Taylor and Hessey London'. At this time he was writing his poem 'The Woodman', in the style of Burns's 'Cotter's Saturday Night', and he asked Holland for permission to dedicate it to him in gratitude for the support that he had given through the year. He did not send the reverend gentleman another Burns imitation written around the same time, a ballad in praise of ale, from which we learn that Clare was capable of drinking Tant Baker's strong nut-brown liquor a quart at a time (cost: tenpence).

Clare asked Holland to approach Lord Milton on his behalf with a request for permission for the volume to be dedicated to him. 'Inform him that I am the Son of the *Lame man* at helpstone', he added, in allusion to his Lordship's earlier kindness in sending Parker to the sea-bathing infirmary at Scarborough. But Milton was away on a European tour at the time.

In November 1819, Wilders proposed reducing Clare's gardening wage from nine to seven shillings a week, in view of the lighter workload in the winter months. Clare said that he had been promised nine shillings all the year round, so he quit his job. But he remembered Wilders as a good master and Casterton as one of the best places he knew—'I left it with regret and rather wished to return as I liked the town and the fields and solitudes were wild and far better than the fenny flats etc. that I been used [to]'. His eye had often been drawn to 'the horizon sweeping faintly blue / That prickt its bordering circle round the view'. Open and undulating, with sheep nibbling on the heath, the environment had offered a taste of freedom in contrast to enclosed, ploughed-up Helpston.

On leaving Casterton, Clare went to Stamford to see Drury, who had just published some sample poems in the *Stamford Mercury*. Some time during the summer, Drury had at last told Clare that it was Taylor who had been reading and commenting on his work. At Drury's on the morning of 13 November the poet met his editor for the first time. Years later Clare wrote down his impressions of the man who came to play the central role in the unfolding of his career in print. He described him as a fellow of 'very pleasant address' who 'works himself into the good opinions of people in a moment'. Though cautious at heart, he showed 'his sunny side to strangers'—but he would sometimes come at a point indirectly, like a lawyer. Clare came to admire the forensic skill of a book Taylor had written in which he identified the celebrated late eighteenth-century political satirist who signed himself 'Junius'. He noted that Taylor was a fluent talker on all literary, political and scholarly subjects, even those of which his knowledge was but superficial. This pen-portrait was written much later, after a falling out: it does not do justice to the warmth of friendship between the two men in the early years of their relationship.

Taylor was visiting Drury in order to discuss progress on Clare's book, but he was staying in Stamford with an old friend, Octavius Gilchrist. Earlier in the year, Taylor had offered Drury a formal introduction to Gilchrist, but his cousin had declined because of his own association with the Newcombs and the *Stamford Mercury*. Gilchrist was editor of the rival—and politically radical—paper, *Drakard's Stamford News*. In 1812 he had actually fought a duel with young Richard Newcomb. Born in Twickenham in 1779, the son of a gentleman who had served in the dragoon guards, Octavius Gilchrist went to Oxford, but left in order to assist his uncle in the running of a Stamford grocery business. He inherited the business as well as taking on the editorship of Drakard's weekly paper. He was a keen antiquary and a vigorous participant in literary controversies (he knew the noted literary editor William Gifford and contributed to his influential *Quarterly Review*). He had published an *Examination of the Charges maintained by Malone, Chalmers, and others of Ben Jonson's Enmity towards Shakespeare*; in 1820 he would become involved in an acrimonious dispute, to which Lord Byron was also a party, concerning the moral character and poetical merits of Alexander Pope (Clare's name got caught in the crossfire). Taylor realised that, as Stamford's leading literary light, Gilchrist would be bound to take an interest in the new local poetic phenomenon.

For all that had come before, Taylor was not absolutely convinced that Drury had Clare's best interests at heart. His acquaintance with Gilchrist gave him the opportunity to let it be known that he was prepared to commit himself wholeheartedly to Clare. So it was that the day before Taylor met Clare at Drury's, he told Gilchrist that his firm would give Clare a hundred pounds whether or not the forthcoming book was a commercial success. This was a great deal more money than Drury had put up—he had advanced Clare no more than twenty pounds. As Drury had prised Clare away from Henson, now Taylor, with the collusion of Gilchrist, was preparing to prise him away from Drury.

Clare was staying overnight in Stamford, at Drury's. In the evening, a maidservant arrived inviting him to Gilchrist's. Clare did not want to go. Since he had just left Casterton, he had only his work clothes on, not his Sunday best. But Drury persuaded him that it would be diplomatic to put in an appearance. He took Clare to Gilchrist's door. According to Gilchrist, Clare knocked hesitantly and, as soon as he had been brought in and introduced to the company, slumped into a chair, where he sat shyly through the evening. 'Nothing could exceed the meekness, and simplicity, and diffidence with which he answered the various inquiries concerning his life and habits, which we mingled with subjects calculated or designed to put him much at his ease'. Taylor did what he could to stir Clare's interest with London literary talk.

Gilchrist reported that Clare was very moved when one of the party sang 'the pathetic ballad of *Auld Robin Gray*'. The singer may well have been his wife, who had a good voice. Elizabeth Gilchrist had two sisters who had married a pair of Stamford brothers called Simpson. The party that evening may have included some of the Simpsons, who were also very keen on music. Clare must have been acutely conscious of how his life was changing. It was the day on which, in the words of the *Mercury*, 'The lower orders of Stamford had their annual uproar, the bull-running'. Instead of spending the evening in the Hole in the Wall talking over the chase, Clare was in the refined musical company of the higher orders of Stamford.

He remained at Gilchrist's for about two hours. His thank-you letter for the evening took the form of a poem called 'The Invitation', in which he described his tentative knock, Mrs Gilchrist's warm welcome, his bow and mumble, his awe at the finery of the room ('He blinkt, like owls at candle-light, / And vainly wish'd a hole to hide in'), and the way the 'gentry' then showed him kindness and sought to put him at his ease.

After this eventful stop-over in Stamford, Clare went on to Helpston. Taylor soon put his commitment in writing by promising to advise Clare on his poems 'without Emolument or Advantage, on all future Occasions, let who would be his Publishers'. Gilchrist took it upon himself to compose on Clare's behalf a fulsome dedication to Lord Milton. Drury thought that it would be a good idea to have a dedication, but not Gilchrist's. He persuaded Clare to send Taylor a wording of the poet's own, together with a note explaining that Gilchrist's was 'too Refined and Elegant to flow from the pen of a Clown'. Taylor eventually decided that a dedication should be dispensed with altogether. He had written a prefatory memoir describing Clare's 'friendless Case', so it would hardly be consistent to associate the book with a Lord.

Over the next few weeks, Gilchrist extended the hand of friendship to Clare. He offered to help him improve his poems, invited him to a concert in the Stamford Assembly Room, and lent him books: 'I shall send you—uninvited—Wordsworth's poems'. Clare soon sent back the Wordsworth and asked for a Byron instead, but he appreciated the concert, which began with the overture to Mozart's *Magic Flute*. Mr Haydn Corri presided from the piano and Mr Crouch played the cello. Both men were also composers. They would soon set some of Clare's poems to music.

By Christmas, the plan to establish Clare as a schoolmaster had been dropped, though Drury still thought it would be a good idea for him to get some instruction in the improvement of his grammar. Taylor proposed that Clare should be paid a weekly financial allowance, but Drury preferred more *ad hoc* advances for the payment of debts, purchase of 'good clothes', and gifts of necessities for Parker and Ann, whom he sometimes visited.

At the end of the year, the book was very nearly ready for printing. Taylor had finished the introductory memoir and compiled a glossary of Clare's dialect words, which he asked the poet to check ('for I dare say I have not always hit his meaning'). John Scott, Gilchrist's predecessor as editor of *Drakard's Stamford News*, was launching a new literary monthly with the new year. It had been agreed that Gilchrist would use it to introduce Clare's name to the London literary public. Just before going out to dinner on New Year's Eve, he wrote to Clare telling him that a copy of the magazine was expected in the morning.

There were two clouds on the horizon. One was the question of financial arrangements for the publication of the poetry. Taylor and Hessey had a policy of buying the copyright of their authors outright, in return for a flat fee. But Drury did not want to put matters wholly in their hands. He continued to regard Clare as his own discovery. He had fed Clare with promises and small cash sums, but, never having published a book before, had not committed himself to a formal offer for the purchase of copyright. Clare himself was diffident about his worth, grateful to Drury for publishing him at all, and lacking any friend who could offer him informed and disinterested advice. Around this time he wrote a sonnet contrasting his own case with that of Kirke White, whose poems had been helped into print by the well-connected Robert Southey ('A labouring clown, a wild uncul-ter'd stem, / No Southey's hand will lend its help to me').

The Newcombs persuaded Drury that the time was now right for a formal agreement. On 20 December an arrangement was proposed whereby the poet would receive a quarter of the profits of all his fu-ture works, Clare signed on New Year's Day. Taylor only heard about this agreement from Gilchrist, who said that Clare had been bounced into it by the elder Newcomb ('an unhanged rogue') and his son-in-law, a 'knavish Attorney' called Thompson.

Clare remained adamant that he had not actually signed away ownership of his copyright. According to his memorandum of the time, 'Drury has persuaded me to write down in his account book under my accounts with him that I have sold him my first Vol for 20 which is to be deducted from my account as he only wishes to have a check against Taylor and Hessey who he strongly thinks will cheat him'. The twenty pounds was Drury's calculation of the amount he had advanced to Clare. The question of money would return as the cause of bitter disputes.

The second delicate issue was Clare's moral character. Drury was haunted by the way that the Burns publishing bandwagon had been thrown off course as a result of the poet's dissipation. The Newcombs had been making inquiries in relation to the schoolmastering scheme, and it was clear that any prospect in that area would have re-quired very strong character references. Drury seems to have heard some bad rumours about Clare from local Methodists, but he eventu-ally put these down to their pique at his 'secession from their society'. Clare himself left only a brief note of his flirtation with the Metho-dists at this time: 'I found the lower orders of this persuasion with whom I associated so selfish narrow-minded and ignorant of real religion that I soon left them'. He said that they believed every bad opinion, except about themselves. Preacher Henson may well have had something to do with the rumours, given the breakdown of his working relationship with Clare.

Drury also had some first-hand information: Clare had been telling him about his love life. He had become involved with a young girl called Betty Sell, a labourer's daughter from the village of Southorpe. The relationship began in late March with 'a heedless [   ] at Stamford Fair'. Clare's modern editors fill in the blank in his manuscript with 'frolic' or 'flirtation', but the self-censorship suggests that the reality was something rather stronger. Clare accompanied Betty home and soon wrote a ballad about her, in which she has glossy black curly hair and hazel eyes. He seems to have continued to see her through the summer; he speaks of making a 'foolish confidence' with her.

The return to Casterton in April 1819 had, however, taken Clare back to Martha ('Patty') Turner. With the news that his poetry had been taken up in Stamford, her friends, who had initially disapproved of her walking out with a lime-burner, now began to court him. Last autumn's undesirable was this spring's interesting catch. In situations such as this, Clare tended to dig in his heels. Indignant at their former slights, he visited Patty less frequently and was cool in response to her friends' invitations.

He sent the poem called 'Betty Sell' to Drury for possible inclusion in his volume, but later scribbled a note saying 'I don't wish you to print this in the Vol: as it will offend my favourite "Patty of the Vale" '. Drury reported to Taylor—presumably on the basis of what Clare told him about the relationship—that Betty Sell was a *'Cyprian'*, though Clare had not known this when he met her. *Cyprian* was a term for a prostitute, although it may simply have meant that Betty was notoriously promiscuous.

In his autobiographical recollections, Clare himself was ambiguous about the extent of his sexual activity. He says that until he went to Casterton and met Patty, his 'dealings with love was but temporary'. He would see a pretty girl, 'scribble a Song or so in her praise', spend a couple of 'innocent and harmless' Sunday evenings with her, then move on to the new allurement of a fresh face. But in the very next breath he admits that 'temptations were things I rarely resisted—when the partiality of the moment gave no time for reflection I was sure to seize it whatever might be the consequence'. Startlingly, he then goes on to write of how his easy nature, 'either in drinking or anything else', meant that he was easily led into snares by 'profligate companions', who would then laugh at him. At such times as fairs he would be 'coaxed about to bad houses', where 'not only my health but my life has often been on the eve of its sacrifice by an illness too well known and too disgusting to mention'. The clear implication is that he slept with prostitutes on more than one occasion and either contracted—or believed he had contracted—a sexually transmitted disease.

By the end of the summer John Clare and Patty Turner had slept together. Perhaps his sexual self-confidence had grown with the prospects opened up by Drury. Perhaps Patty was growing concerned that she might be losing him to Betty. Whatever their motivation, the result was to change Clare forever: when he left Casterton in November, Patty was pregnant.

He said that his feelings for Betty had grown into an 'affection that made my heart ache to think it must be broken—for Patty was then in a situation that marriage only could remedy'. But it was some time before he was willing to put that remedy into effect. Once she could no longer conceal her pregnancy, Patty told her parents. They were not sympathetic: she had not listened to their advice when they recommended the shoemaker rather than the lime-burner; she had made a hard bed and she must lie on it. Clare's first inclination was a stubborn disposition 'to leave them the risk of her misfortunes'—as the Clares had been left some sixty years before when his grandmother was impregnated and deserted by the roving Scotsman John Donald Parker.

He was, however, too tender-hearted not to respond to Patty's complaint of her parents' coldness towards her. He promised that the prosperity that would come from his poems would allow him to marry her. In the meantime, he gave her money so that she had a degree of independence from her parents. This earnest of his good intentions 'pacified them and left her at peace'.

Yet he was not at all sure that he did want to marry her. Did he want to be tied down with a wife and baby at exactly the time when his poems were giving him a first prospect of new horizons? And Betty Sell was not the only other person on his mind. During the winter back home in Helpston, he renewed his acquaintance 'with a former love'. This was almost certainly Mary Joyce. She was now turning twenty-three and still unmarried. Her father, whom Clare had imagined to be hostile to him on grounds of income and status, had died. 'My long-smothered affections for Mary revived with my hopes and as I expected to be on a level with her bye and bye I thought then I might have a chance of success in renewing my former affections'.

'I felt awkwardly situated and knew not which way to proceed', explained Clare in his autobiography. 'I had a variety of minds about me and all of them unsettled'. His state of mind is strikingly revealed by the poetry he was writing at this time.

We have no way of knowing whether a poem about a mother cautioning her son to 'let these poor stuck-up fine wenches alone' was a flight of fancy or a response to something Ann Clare said about Patty Turner and her snobbish friends. But, as Drury and Taylor recognised, Clare wrote at his best when he worked from experience. In his early work at least, his voice is truest to himself in those poems that are 'the birth of the moment'. There is manifestly an autobiographical origin to a group of poems written while Patty was pregnant and not intended for publication. 'To ———— under a Cloud' is about the sins of the flesh and the withering of a flower that has been 'all despoiled by luckless amorous Johny'. 'An After Repentance' includes such lines as 'Past is the scene of love's delights / Curst bitter dregs the sweet succeed' and

> A sinful sad unruly lout
> I quake I quake at gossip time
> Whose tongue blabs every secret out.

And a song called 'O say not love' has the poet's beloved in tears as she faces slander and reproach.

He poured out love poetry in 1819 and 1820. Sometimes it is tantalising: there is an exquisite two-stanza lyric of love-longing that survives only in a single pencilled manuscript version, headed with the solitary letter 'S'. We have no way of knowing who 'S' might have been, and what real feelings Clare may have had for her—a passing fancy, another of his infatuations, a piece of pure invention?

On other occasions, the poetry is light and playful:

> Bessey's the top wench that walks on a Sunday
> To seek for a sweetheart or show a new dress,
> Once I loved Nelly, a short stump, a grundy,
> But soon left her off when I saw bonny Bess.

Even when the tone is plaintive, the matter is not necessarily autobiographical: he writes a love ballad in the voice of a sailor away from his Jenny, despite the fact that he never went to sea himself. Such a Jenny is clearly imaginary. As for the 'Jenny Young' whose charms are enumerated in another lyric, she might be imaginary or she might have been real. And then there is the Jenny in a ballad on the relative merits of indoor and outdoor courtship, a poem at once comic and erotic:

> How can I kiss my love
> Muffled i' hat and glove ...
> Lay by thy woollen vest
> Rap no cloak o'er thy breast
> There my hand oft hath prest
> Pin nothing there
> There my head drops to rest
> Leave its bed bare.

Here one suspects that something of the experience of courting Patty has been projected onto a fictional Jenny. But is it significant that in one manuscript Clare wrote a song called 'Mary leave thy lowly cot' over the top of this one? And is this Mary a fictional character, or a projection of Mary Joyce, or a blend of Mary and Patty? It was, after all, the Turners and not the Joyces who lived in a 'lowly cot'.

We certainly cannot take it for granted that all Clare's poetic Marys are Mary Joyce. Among the poems written around this time and then published in Clare's collections of 1820 and 1821 were a song to a false Mary, a parody of William Cowper entitled 'My Mary' (in which the eponymous maiden carries pigswill and waddles like a duck), and an address to a city girl called Mary that was written before Clare had ever been to the city. None of these is in any sense 'about' Mary Joyce.

Several poems addressing 'Mary' were, however, pointedly omitted from Clare's published collections. In one the speaker is haunted by Mary's smile and he avers that fond feelings for her will never forsake him, even though 'Fate's bonds are on me, that cruel enslaver, / And love is not lawful to meet as before'. This sounds like the work of a man who is tied to one woman, but still longing for another. In a second, the poet says that he has kissed many girls

> But never o never such 'lectrified feeling
> Ere throbbed through my heart, be as fair as they be,
> When round thy sweet charms my embraces was stealing
> My soul stood spectator in presence of thee.

This is immediately followed in Clare's manuscript by a ballad about a single meeting 'When I prest that soft bosom so white and so warming / and kissed thy cheeks' freshness so luscious and sweet', but then 'I left thee to meet thee no more'. There is an electricity in these pieces which suggests that some time between meeting and marrying Patty, Clare did renew his acquaintance with Mary Joyce—and might once have kissed her. At the very least he was fantasising about kissing her.

Late in December 1819 Clare sent a sheet of songs and ballads to Octavius Gilchrist's wife. It consists of four poems. A song called 'Jewel of All' is about an artless beauty who is 'queen of my heart and the pride of the vale'. Clare called Martha Turner 'Patty of the vale' on account of the secluded dell in which her cottage was located, and 'P——y' is indeed named in the copy of the same poem that Clare sent to Isaiah Holland. So one of the four poems is for the woman who was pregnant with his child. But two other lyrics on the sheet are ballads of unrequited love addressed to 'Mary'. The fourth poem describes a girl at dusk. In the copy sent to Mrs Gilchrist, she is named as Martha. But Clare wrote out this same ballad in three other manuscripts. In one the girl is an unnamed 'lassey', in another she is 'Dolly', and in the third she is 'Mary'. In one version, Clare hedged his bets and gave the poem the title 'To x x x'.

Contrary to the protestations of 'Jewel of All', there was no single 'queen' of Clare's heart on the eve of his appearance in the world of literature. The women in his life were already becoming poetic symbols. He was well acquainted with the Bible and its Martha and Mary: in St Luke's gospel, Jesus comes to a village and enters the house of two sisters. Martha is the practical one, who busies herself serving their guest. Mary, meanwhile, simply sits at the Lord's feet and listens to him. The two sisters reappear, with similar characteristics, in St John's account of the raising of Lazarus from the dead. Martha became the patron saint of good housewives, represented in Christian art as being clad in homely costume and bearing a bunch of keys. Mary symbolised something very different: unadulterated love.

PART TWO

Fame

1820–1827

At length 'twas known his ways by woods and brooks
Were secret walks for making rhymes and books
Which strangers bought and with amazement read
And called him poet when they sought his shed.

CHAPTER SEVEN

PRESENTING THE PEASANT POET

PEASANT: *one whose business is rural labour.*
—DR JOHNSON'S *DICTIONARY*

The first number of the *London Magazine* was published on 1 January 1820. Immediately following an editorial and an opening article by John Scott, the nascent journal's publisher, appeared Octavius Gilchrist's 'Some Account of John Clare, an Agricultural Labourer and Poet'. Clare was launched together with the magazine:

> 'A happy new year,' and the first number of a publication which has for its object to extend the influence of letters, and to aid the inquiries of science, may not be inaptly employed in introducing to the world a name, hitherto altogether unknown to literature, but which, if our estimate of genius be not more than commonly inaccurate, seems to merit a considerable portion of regard, while, at the same time, it stands in need of popular encouragement, and even protection.

Gilchrist went on to present Clare as coming from the most humble circumstances imaginable. He gave an account of his first meeting with the poet, at the evening party in Stamford: 'there was a carpet, upon which it is likely he never previously set foot; and wine, of

POEMS

DESCRIPTIVE OF

RURAL LIFE AND SCENERY.

BY JOHN CLARE,

A NORTHAMPTONSHIRE PEASANT.

" The Summer's Flower is to the Summer sweet,
" Though to itself it only live and die."
Shakspeare.

LONDON:

PRINTED FOR TAYLOR AND HESSEY, FLEET STREET;
AND E. DRURY, STAMFORD.

1820.

which assuredly he had never tasted before'. This is nonsense, not least because Clare went to Gilchrist's from the home of Drury, who would undoubtedly have had a carpet (and wine).

The article then described the poverty and illiteracy of Clare's family, his discovery of poetry ('the *Wild Flowers* of Bloomfield, and the writings of Burns, were sufficient to stimulate his innate genius for poetry'), and his way of writing in the fields with a pencil, using slips of paper laid on the crown of his hat. The encouragement of Dissenting minister Holland was mentioned, but Gilchrist assured his readers that Clare himself remained orthodox within the Church of England. Interspersed in the article were some tasters of Clare's work: the sonnets 'To a Primrose' and 'The Setting Sun', and the thank-you poem he had sent to Gilchrist after their first meeting. Clare did not see the magazine for a few days. He was distracted by the death of his grandmother, who was buried on 4 January.

'Mr G. has *picturesqued* finely in the London Mag.', wrote Drury to Taylor the day after the magazine appeared. But there was no doubt that the article introduced the name of Clare to a large literary public. The first number of the *London* had a substantial sale—it had to be reprinted after a week. John Drakard copied Gilchrist's article into the *Stamford News*, adding to Clare's local celebrity.

In the rival *Stamford Mercury*, Drury printed the first piece of fan-mail that Clare received, a letter from a Norfolk gentleman who saw the article in the *London* and admired the poetry, but wished to advise Clare that he would do well to accept his lowly station, be a good example to his neighbours and not allow himself to be 'taken by the hand for a short time as a novelty, and then dropped' in the manner of the unfortunate Burns. A joiner from a village near Newark saw Drury's article in the *Mercury* and wrote to Clare telling him about his own poetic aspirations. Fame was already beginning to extract a price in the form of unwanted mail. And since it was normal for postage to be paid by the receiver rather than the sender, this cost Clare money as well as the time taken to compose courteous replies.

In publishing the letter from the Norfolk gentleman, Drury had hinted at the centrality of his own role in the discovery and promotion of Clare. Taylor was not pleased: 'The disgusting conceit of Edward Drury much offends me. I have seen the Newspaper in which his letter appears.—When you read the Introduction to Clare's Poems you will see that I have given him (E.D. I mean) sufficient Commendation in all Conscience, and without the Meanness of this attempt to raise him into greater Consequence he might have had his Vanity enough gratified.' The differences between Drury on the one side and Taylor and Gilchrist on the other were growing.

Gilchrist had suggested in the *London* that the real test of Clare would be whether he was capable of writing long poems as opposed to brief lyrics. Since October, Clare had in fact been working on a long autobiographical poem called 'The Peasant Boy'. In the summer he would begin a series of linked narrative poems on village life, called 'Ways of a Village'. 'The Peasant Boy' eventually became 'The Village Minstrel', the title-poem of his second book, which also included a handful of the village stories (more of them appeared in his third book in 1827).

Drury, with his fears about the fate of Burns, told Taylor that Clare was being pushed too hard:

> It is to be greatly feared that the man will be afflicted with insanity if his talent continues to be forced as it has been these 4 months past; he has no other mode of easing the fever that oppresses him after a tremendous fit of rhyming except by getting tipsy. A single pint of ale very often does this, and next morning a stupor with head-ach[e] and pains across the chest afflicts him very severely. Then he is melancholy and completely hypochondriac.
>
> You will easily suppose how true is my account when I assure you he has rhymed & written for 3 days and 3 nights without hardly eating or sleeping. I therefore watch with a degree of fear Mr Gilchrist's proceedings; they are doubtlessly judicious as stimulants;—but sedatives are necessary for the man's welfare as much as stimulants.

Drury was the first person to recognise the delicacy of Clare's mental condition. Learning from his early mistake of showing him the Rev-

erend Twopenny's dismissive letter, he had for some time been stressing to Taylor how sensitive Clare was to criticism: 'A slight word, the
absence of commendation, in short any thing less than praise freely
bestowed gives him a mean opinion of his compositions.' He may also
have taken note of an anxious, depressed remark that Clare had scribbled into the manuscript of the poems that Taylor would soon be
publishing: '[I cannot] think nor compose nothing—my soul is in a
lethargy my warmth for rhyming has left me my poetical spirit is no
more—Get the Book out as soon as you can I long to know my doom
—the sooner the better   John Clare.'

Drury's diagnosis was as good as, if not better than, those of the
doctors who entered the story in later years. He recognised that writing poetry was a kind of compulsion for Clare, but that it over-
stimulated him, leading him to become drunk in order to wind down.
The headaches and chest-pains that followed—a mixture of hang-
overs and psychosomatic reactions?—led to depression and hypochon-
dria. Drury had seen Clare at close quarters for some months. He
knew about such intimate matters as the affair with Betty Sell. He
could see that the poet was already locked into a potentially cata-
strophic circle of symptoms.

Taylor evidently reported these concerns back to Gilchrist, who,
on recovering from a fit of gout, told Clare that 'Taylor is fearful that
you are exerting your mind too much in composition, and he urges
me to use my influence in dissuading you from that course'. 'This I
should very strenuously do,' added Gilchrist, 'if I thought his fears
were well founded, which I trust they are not.'

On Saturday 15 January 1820, Clare's first book was published under
the title *Poems, Descriptive of Rural Life and Scenery. By John Clare,
a Northamptonshire Peasant*. Clare had wanted the title-page to
have an epigraph from the Scottish artisan poet Allan Ramsay, but
Taylor replaced it with some well-known lines from Shakespeare's
sonnets. The quotation was designed to make Clare look like the ar-
chetypal unknown rustic genius, the flower that is born to blush unseen and waste its sweetness on the desert air in the manner of Gray's

'Elegy': 'The Summer's Flower is to the Summer sweet, / Though to itself it only live and die'.

Taylor's introduction to the book began with the claim that Clare was 'the least favoured by circumstances, and the most destitute of friends'—which is to say, friends in high places—'of any [poet] that ever existed'. It then offered a biographical sketch that included the story of Clare saving his shilling to buy Thomson's *Seasons* and writing his first poem as he walked back through Burghley Park. There was no mention of Henson; Taylor repeated Drury's story about finding the 'Setting Sun' sonnet scribbled on a dirty scrap of paper that had been used to wrap a letter.

Clare was then praised for his distinctive use of a vernacular style and regional dialect. The 'indifference with which he regards words as governing each other' was due to 'his evident ignorance of grammar'—but this should not cause 'real embarrassment'. Clare, said Taylor, gave voice to 'the unwritten language of England'. The meanings of his 'provincialisms' were given in a glossary at the back of the book (the model for this was probably Burns's debut volume of 1786).

Above all, Taylor emphasised Clare's responsiveness to nature. He remarked on the originality whereby the poetry was inspired by swamps and flats, not the 'romantic prospects' to which poets were usually attracted. And he presented Clare as a poet of immediate impressions:

> He loves the fields, the flowers, 'the common air, the sun, the skies;' and, therefore, he writes about them. He is happier in the presence of Nature than elsewhere. He looks as anxiously on her face as if she were a living friend, whom he might lose; and hence he has learnt to notice every change in her countenance, and to delineate all the delicate varieties of her character. Most of his poems were composed under the immediate impression of this feeling, in the fields, or on the road-sides. He could not trust his memory, and therefore he wrote them down with a pencil on the spot, his hat serving him for a desk.

In the short term, this image worked wonders. *Poems, Descriptive of Rural Life and Scenery* sold out its edition of a thousand copies within two months. A second edition of two thousand more went before the end of the year and another reprint followed in 1821. But in the longer term, it would prove difficult to shake off the suggestion of naïveté conveyed by Taylor's introduction. To present Clare as a child of nature did no service to his breadth of reading and depth of formal artfulness.

Taylor's introduction set the tone for the critical response to the volume. Within days, an unsigned notice appeared in the *New Times*, saying how the poems provided a rare glimpse of 'the unmixed and unadulterated impression of the loveliness of nature on a man of vivid perception and strong feeling, equally unacquainted with the arts and reserve of the world, and with the riches, rules, and prejudices of literature'. On the same day, a brief account appeared in the *Stamford Mercury*: though the paper was 'much more agricultural and commercial than literary in character', it could not forbear to notice the 'novelty' and 'extraordinary merit' of the new local literary genius.

About seventy poems were included in the collection. As Clare had wished, the volume was divided into three sections. First came a miscellany of poems headed by 'Helpstone'. There followed a selection of 'Songs and Ballads', then a group of sonnets. The subject-matter ranged from seasonal description ('Summer Evening', 'The Harvest Morning', 'A Winter Scene' and so forth) to flora and fauna ('The Robin', 'The Primrose', 'The Ant') to tales of village customs and misadventures ('The Village Funeral', 'The Fate of Amy') to homely philosophising and sentimental moralising (as represented by 'What is Life?', written when Clare was struggling to draft the prospectus for Henson). Early readers and reviewers often singled out the latter poem for high praise. The volume was rounded off with a narrative poem called 'Crazy Nell', which had been added at the last minute to spice up the collection with 'terrific and pathetic Scenery'. Based on a newspaper story, it ends with Nell losing her reason and becoming 'A maniac restless and wild'. Her afflicted parents are unable to help her.

Among the ballads was 'Patty of the Vale', which linked love for a secluded place with love for the woman who lived there. Taylor's introduction had not mentioned Patty Turner, but his decision to present Clare to the public in such a way that the life and the poems were intimately connected meant that questions would soon be asked about her.

As in much of the previous eighty years' poetry of 'sensibility', a major theme throughout the collection was the brevity of life and the consoling thought of eternity in the face of ever-present mortality. The sonnets were as often didactic as descriptive ('To Religion': 'Thou only home the houseless wanderers have; / Thou prop by which the pilgrim's woes are borne . . .'). Throughout, the style was frequently derivative and sometimes overtly imitative. Thus 'Familiar Epistle to a Friend' borrowed both the tone and the stanza form of Burns.

Four collections of Clare's poetry were published in his lifetime, but sales of the later ones came nowhere near those of the first. In retrospect, we may say with confidence that each book was better than the last. The disjunction between sales and quality was unfortunate for Clare's place in the nineteenth-century literary canon. As his work improved, it became less known. Accordingly, his true genius was not widely recognised until a very long time after his death.

Poems, Descriptive of Rural Life and Scenery is peppered with such overblown numbers as 'An Effusion to Poesy on receiving a Damp from a genteel Opinionist in Poetry, of some sway, as I am told, in the Literary World', which begins 'Despis'd, unskill'd, or how I will, / Sweet Poesy! I'll love thee still'. Lines such as these may reveal something about Clare's insecurity, but they are written in a wholly artificial poetic voice.

Even those poems in the collection that came from the territory that Clare would eventually make uniquely his own are weighed down by a compulsion to moralise. Thus 'To an Insignificant Flower obscurely blooming in a lonely wild' has very little to say about the actual flower. It is merely the pretext for an excursion on the hackneyed theme of the rural poet as genius doomed to obscurity. Later, Clare would have the confidence to let the act of intimate observation speak

for itself: 'I love all wild flowers (none are weeds with me) affectionately—there is a little white starry flower with pale green grassy
leaves grows by woodsides and among bushes—I know not its name
but it is a boyish favourite and the same that those stanzas address as
"a nameless flower obscurely blooming in a lonely wild." ' In this passage, written in 1823, he has felicitously misremembered the title of
the poem that was published in 1820: the ponderous 'Insignificant
Flower' has become the plainer 'nameless flower'. It was the development towards simplicity that marked the maturing of his poetic
voice.

'Dawnings of Genius' is a first tentative attempt at a poem on the
great theme that Wordsworth called 'the growth of a poet's mind'.
But Clare is not yet bold enough to write from memory in the first
person. A generic ploughman stands in for him:

> In those low paths which Poverty surrounds,
> The rough, rude ploughman, off his fallow-grounds,
> (That necessary tool of wealth and pride,)*
> While moil'd and sweating by some pasture's side,
> Will often stoop inquisitive to trace
> The opening beauties of a daisy's face;
> Oft will he witness, with admiring eyes,
> The brook's sweet dimples o'er the pebbles rise;
> And often, bent as o'er some magic spell,
> He'll pause, and pick his shaped stone and shell:
> Raptures the while his inward powers inflame,
> And joys delight him which he cannot name.

Clare's poetry improved as it became more personal. He kept returning to the primal scene of inspiration that is sketched here, but in his
mature poems the description of the scene would become much more
conversational. He will write in the first person of how he is out walking in the fields when he suddenly stops and stoops to notice a flower

---

*A line that would get Clare into trouble with his patron, Lord Radstock. See
Chapter 9.

or a bird's nest. He shares his find with the reader, as if speaking to a friend who is standing beside him. The transformation of a seemingly small experience into something magical is facilitated by the matter-of-factness in the language.

Many of the 'provincial' words in *Poems, Descriptive* that were included in the glossary have a wonderfully physical sound: *crumping*, *drowking*, *fluskered*, *kerchup*, *proggling*, *quawking*, *scrigg'd*, *sloomy*, *snifting* and *snufting*, *soodles*, *waterpudge*, *whanged*, *witchen*. But they sit awkwardly beside the Latinate abstractions that Clare's reading had taught him were the appropriate stuff of poetry: *Grandeur*, *Industry*, *Mysterious cause!*, *Extravagance*, *Luxury*, *Contemplation*, *Oblivion*. A poem called 'The Fountain' is typical in its juxtaposition of colloquial freshness ('and with a swish / Whang'd off my hat') with poetic cliché ('Her dusky mantle Eve had spread') and moralising ('Hope bursts cheated into vain extremes').

The poems published in Clare's first book only represent a small proportion of his early work—and not necessarily the best of it. Among the manuscripts he was filling at this time were his old school cipher-book, the blank book bought from Henson, three notebooks of pencil drafts, the principal manuscript sent to Taylor and three manuscript books of further poems. The contents amount to well over three hundred poems. He was already writing lines that anticipate his later manner, but usually in poems that he did not believe were fit or ready for publication. There is an early incomplete sketch called 'A Ramble', in which Clare figures himself as a lover of those simple things of nature that are neglected by the hurrying passer-by:

> How beautiful e'en seems
> This simple twig that steals it from the hedge
> And wavering dipples down to taste the stream.
> I cannot think it how the reason is
> That every trifle nature's bosom wears
> Should seem so lovely and appear so sweet
> And charm so much my soul while heedless passenger
> Soodles me by, an animated post,
> And ne'er so much as turns his head to look

But stalks along as though his eyes were blinded
And as if the witching face of nature
Held but now a dark unmeaning blank.

Here the absence of grandiloquence, the matter-of-fact tone of voice, means that 'dipples' (dips) and 'soodles' (saunters) are well bedded in. They do not leap out from the page as marks of rural quaintness.

Again, the following brief lyric, jotted on a loose sheet of paper sometime in 1819 or 1820, has a quiet perfection in its precision and lack of pretension:

TO THE FOX FERN

Haunter of woods, lone wilds and solitudes
Where none but feet of birds and things as wild
Doth print a foot track near, where summer's light
Buried in boughs forgets its glare and round thy crimpèd leaves
Feints in a quiet dimness fit for musings
And melancholy moods, with here and there
A golden thread of sunshine stealing through
The evening shadowy leaves that seem to creep
Like leisure in the shade.

These two poems were not just passed over for Clare's early collections: neither of them appeared in print until 1989.

For Clare, the most important poem in his first book was the opening one, 'Helpstone', which he had written during the years when the parish was being enclosed. He did not, however, have full confidence in it, continuing to regard it as a fragment despite having reworked it on numerous occasions. In his manuscript, he scribbled a defensive note to his publishers, saying that although they might get the impression that he had plagiarised Oliver Goldsmith's *The Deserted Village*, he had not read more than about a hundred lines of that famous poem. Whatever the direct influence may or may not have been, Clare's twin themes were also Goldsmith's: nostalgia for the village of his youth is mingled with sorrow and anger at the way in which both the landscape and the settled rural way of life have been destroyed by economic 'progress'. Thus Goldsmith:

Sweet smiling village, loveliest of the lawn,
Thy sports are fled and all thy charms withdrawn;
Amidst thy bowers the tyrant's hand is seen,
And desolation saddens all thy green:
One only master grasps the whole domain ...
　　Ill fares the land, to hastening ills a prey,
Where wealth accumulates and men decay:
Princes and lords may flourish or may fade;
A breath can make them, as a breath has made;
But a bold peasantry, their country's pride,
When once destroyed, can never be supplied.

And Clare:

Now all laid waste by desolation's hand,
Whose cursed weapon levels half the land.
Oh! Who could see my dead green willows fall,
What feeling heart, but dropt a tear for all?
Accursed Wealth! O'erbounding human laws,
Of every evil thou remain'st the cause.
Victims of want, those wretches such as me,
Too truly lay their wretchedness to thee:
Thou art the bar that keeps from being fed,
And thine our loss of labour and of bread;
Thou art the cause that levels every tree,
And woods bow down to clear a way for thee.

Though its elevated diction and smooth rhyming couplets were drawn from the common stock of eighteenth-century poetry, 'Helpstone' was nevertheless stamped with Clare's own hallmark insofar as it insisted on the intimate relationship between his own feelings and his native place. It established his 'strong attachment' to every local landmark, right down to the posts and stones by the wayside. And it introduced an image to which he would return again and again, that of the Helpston of his childhood as a lost Eden.

At publication time, Taylor sent a dozen complimentary copies of *Poems, Descriptive* to the author, care of Drury. Clare happened to make one of his Sunday morning calls the next day, unaware that his book had finally appeared, 'so he had a most Agreeable Surprize'. By the time Drury shut his shop on the Monday afternoon, he had sold all but one of the copies that Taylor had sent him. He asked for another twenty-five to be sent urgently by mail-coach, with fifty more to follow by wagon. He also requested half a dozen copies in fine binding for the 'customers in high life' who would want to 'encourage the Peasant-Poet'.

Clare then came down with a bad winter cough, aggravated by anxiety as to the critical reception of his work. He told Drury that his mind was 'unstrung'. His mother worried that he wasn't eating properly. He was unable to go in person to deliver an inscribed copy of his book to Gilchrist. The latter wrote in his usual bantering style with his reaction to the published poems: 'I must tell you candidly, and without a compliment, they have disappointed me,—they have disappointed me agreeably, for they are still better than I looked to find them.' Gilchrist had expected 'tenderness and feeling and a mind awake to the beauties of nature', but not the 'grasp of thought and strength of expression' that the poems sometimes revealed. He invited Clare to dine with him on 1 February, when they could peruse the next month's magazines and reviews for notices of the book. They would, however, have found only one: the *Gentleman's Magazine* reprinted the brief notice that had first appeared in the *New Times*.

The first substantial review came at the beginning of March, in the *New Monthly Magazine*. Here and elsewhere, Clare was praised for his accurate observation of nature and the effective use of provincialisms in his vocabulary. The parallel with Burns was made explicit. Clare's appeal reached across the political spectrum: the *Eclectic Review*—voice of the Dissenting movement—said that he had genius rather than mere talent, whilst the right-wing *Anti-Jacobin Review* lauded him as a second Burns without the 'impurities (and even impieties) which disgrace the latter'. The *London Magazine*, which made a point of its non-partisan politics, had a judicious review by the editor himself, John Scott, singling out for special praise 'the author's ardent attachment to places', the force of his 'recollection of favourite spots'.

Some of the early reviews were lukewarm and some later ones reacted against what was seen as the over-promotion of Clare, but the overall balance was highly encouraging. Clare's name even reached as far as America: when Keats's brother George sailed for New York from Liverpool on 1 February 1820, he had with him a copy of *Poems, Descriptive* destined for Drury's brother Michael, a Philadelphia bookseller who duly arranged for the appearance of a favourable review in a leading literary periodical, the *Analectic Magazine*.

In May there was a discerning, though hardly disinterested, review in the influential *Quarterly Review*, written by Gilchrist and polished up by the editor, his friend William Gifford. Here Clare was presented as being in a far more parlous state of poverty than Burns and Bloomfield ever were. The poetry was praised for its combination of emotion and description: 'He looks abroad with the eye of a poet, and with the minuteness of a naturalist, but the intelligence which he gains is always referred to the heart'.

When Clare was well enough to get out and about at the end of January, he sold his twelve personal copies. Some people paid the published price of five shillings and sixpence, others more (six shillings, eight shillings, even ten shillings and sixpence). Having forgotten to hold back complimentary copies for Patty's uncle, his landlord and Lord Milton, he asked Drury if he could buy some more for that purpose. Drury would not let him pay. He thought Taylor had made a mistake in giving Clare all twelve copies at once, 'for it is not a pleasing thing to see an Authour selling his own books'. But Clare needed the cash in hand.

The Reverend Isaiah Holland called and told him that he had been informed by a literary friend that the poems were already proving a success. According to Frederick Martin, Holland treated the Clare family to a celebratory meal, brought round on trays from the Blue Bell. On another occasion, Clare's elation at being a published author led to an incident when he got 'very drunk indeed', causing Drury 'much inconvenience of a very disgusting nature'. Drury extracted from Clare a vow that he would not get drunk for a year. A local military man had taken an interest in the poet, and was prepared to offer him a job and even a home, so Drury was anxious for Clare to crack his drinking problem.

Clare's mother delivered a copy of his book to Milton Hall. Lord Milton, back from the Italian tour that had prevented him from responding to the request to be the dedicatee, asked for ten more copies to be delivered by Clare himself the following Sunday. Parson Mossop had told him about the poetic phenomenon in the manor of which he was lord. An act of patronage would clearly be appropriate. According to Clare, Milton's enthusiasm converted Mossop from his own initial scepticism about the quality of the poems.

Drury heard about the impending visit. He advised Clare not to wear his Sunday best. The important thing was to have a 'clear clean shirt, clean stockings and shoes'. He sent a shirt of his own, suggesting that Clare should tuck in 'the frippery of the frill' under his clean waistcoat. 'A nice Silk handkerchief will also be useful', he added. Drury also gave Clare the news that a composer called Haydn Corri had set one of his poems to music and that the most exciting new prima donna of the day, Madame Vestris, would be singing it on the London stage. Haydn (named after the composer) was the son of Domenico Corri, a music publisher and operatic composer who was at this time declining into insanity.

Milton Hall, set in a large enclosed park, was the winter home of the Fitzwilliams. In 1820 Lord Fitzwilliam (second Earl in the English peerage, fourth in the Irish) was over seventy years old. From Eton onward, he had been a friend of Charles James Fox, the great opponent of Tory prime minister William Pitt, but though one of the senior Whigs in the House of Lords he remained on the margin of politics. He was dismissed from the post of Lord-Lieutenant of Ireland, perhaps because of his Catholic sympathies. Just a few months before the publication of Clare's book, he was also dismissed from the Lord-Lieutenancy of the West Riding of Yorkshire because he had called a public meeting in York to condemn the magistrates who had provoked the 'Peterloo Massacre' by ordering the mounted militia to charge into a protesting Manchester crowd.

Fitzwilliam had married Lady Charlotte Ponsonby. She was a quiet, settled woman, unlike some of her blood-relations—she was a cousin of the beautiful gambler Lady Georgiana Spencer and the aunt of Lady Caroline Lamb, who was driven to derangement by her infatuation with Byron. The Fitzwilliams had only one child. Born in 1786, he held the title Viscount Milton and grew up to inherit a parliamentary seat in Yorkshire, one of the family's 'pocket boroughs'. He also inherited his father's liberal politics. He was chairman of the committee in support of the Greek War of Independence and eventually became a strong supporter of the 1832 Reform Bill, going so far as to advocate non-payment of taxes in the period when the bill was stalled in the House. Like his father, he opposed the action of the magistrates at Peterloo. He was an early advocate of the repeal of the Corn Laws, even though reduced grain prices would have been detrimental to the family fortune, which was based on the land (though they also had substantial mining interests in Yorkshire).

Lord Milton was a cultivated man, with interests that were curiously similar to Clare's: natural history, mathematics, antiquities. He had married his cousin Mary. They had ten children and were a famously happy family.

Rather too early on the Sunday, Clare arrived at Milton with his parcel of books. He was the object of much teasing whilst he waited in the servants' hall—terms such as 'larned poet' and 'philosopher' were bandied around. He was so nervous that he could not eat or drink anything. Lady Milton then heard of his arrival. The footman showed him to her morning room, saying that Lord Milton would see him in half an hour. Her Ladyship talked easily to him and asked what were his favourite books—and could she give him one as a present? He was on the point of asking for a Shakespeare, but held his tongue 'for fear of seeming overreaching on her kindness'. At various points in their conversation an assortment of her ten children passed through the room as if by accident, but obviously with the purpose of seeing him. 'This is our neighbour the Poet', said her Ladyship. Lord Milton then came out of his dressing room and questioned Clare. He spoke kindly, in 'a slow sententious manner', explaining that it was only because he had been abroad that he had failed to reply to the letter asking him to be the dedicatee of the book. He gave Clare a ten-pound note.

Old Fitzwilliam and his wife then came in. The Earl gave Clare five pounds and a bit of advice: the promises of booksellers were not always to be trusted, so it might not be advisable to give up on manual labour. Lady Fitzwilliam and Lady Milton each chipped in with another pound. Lady Milton then 'enquired minutely respecting his parents and said as she noted down a memorandum or two [in] her book "I shall remember all this"—which it is evident she did do for a good supply of blankets and every thing that can comfort old people were sent next day or two'.

Clare then returned to the servants' hall, where he was plied with ale. He went home with more cash in his pocket than he'd ever had before. According to Drury, his *mind* remained 'quite tipsy' for some time to come. Gilchrist denied this, considering it mischievous gossip on the part of Drury, springing from pique at Clare's reports of the Earl Fitzwilliam's warning against the machinations of booksellers.

A fortnight later Fitzwilliam wrote to Taylor, offering to contribute one hundred pounds towards the purchase of an annuity for the poet. 'His Talents are very extraordinary', he remarked, noting that the absence of grammar revealed the poems to be 'the Effusions of an uneducated Genius'. The Fitzwilliam family would provide Clare with financial assistance throughout the remainder of his life (they also contributed to the fund that Taylor raised on behalf of the dying Keats).

Clare then had a visit from the Honourable Mr Henry Manvers Pierrepont, brother-in-law of the Marquess of Exeter. Would he call on the Marquess at Burghley? When the appointed Sunday came, it snowed. He only had one pair of shoes, and he was afraid that after the walk through the snow they 'would be in a dirty condition for so fine a place'. So he didn't go until the Monday. The porter was annoyed. Why had Clare not come the previous day? The weather was no excuse: 'They expected you and you should stand for no weathers, though it rained knives and forks with the tines downward—we have been suspected of sending you away.'

After a wait, he was sent for. Clare had a vivid memory of his walk to the upper reaches of the great house: '[I] went upstairs and through winding passages after the footman as fast as I could hobble, almost fit to quarrel with my hard-nailed shoes at the noise they made on the marble and boarded floors'. Once again he was kindly received. The Marquess asked to look at Clare's manuscripts, which Pierrepont had asked him to bring along. Like Fitzwilliam, he counselled Clare not to trust the men in the book trade. He apologised on behalf of his sister, Lady Sophia, who had hoped to meet Clare, but was unwell on account of having sat up too long the previous day in the hope of his coming.

The interview lasted half an hour. Clare was 'eyeing the door and now and then looking at my dirty shoes and wishing myself out of the danger of soiling such grandeur'. The Marquess saw his embarrassment and told him to go for some dinner in the servants' hall. Clare remained fixed to the spot—he had no idea how to find his way back through the labyrinthine passages. So the Marquess opened the door himself and accompanied his visitor. They were in one of the long passages when he suddenly stopped.

He told Clare that he had no work available in his gardens, but that he would like to give him fifteen guineas a year for life, which ought to be enough to enable him to pursue his studies for at least two days a week. Clare was astonished. A servant was called, and he 'went off scarcely feeling the ground'. That evening he saw Gilchrist in Stamford—he too scarcely believed it, and Clare wondered if he had misunderstood what was being offered. But it was true: a surviving account ledger at Burghley House, written in a beautiful italic hand, records that from this time on an 'annuity' or 'pension' was paid to Clare every year, in four quarterly instalments, each of three pounds, eighteen shillings and ninepence.

The generosity of the Marquess may be explained by his own extraordinary origins. In 1789 the tenth Earl of Exeter had suffered a humiliating blow when his wife ran off with a clergyman named Sneyd. His response was to close up Burghley and retreat to distant Shropshire, where he bought a cottage and seven acres of land. He promptly fell in love with a farmer's daughter, sixteen-year-old Sarah Hoggins. In April 1790 he obtained a licence to marry her, giving his name as 'John Jones of Great Bolas, yeoman'. The following year, he obtained the Act of Parliament that was necessary for his divorce. A few months later, in a grimy church in the city of London, he married Sarah a second time. She was five months pregnant with the child who would eventually become the Marquess who received Clare that snowy morning in February 1820.

Sarah became known as the 'Cottage' or 'Peasant' Countess. She and Exeter had a second child, Sophia (now married to Pierrepont). The Peasant Countess died during childbirth, aged twenty-three. Three years later, in 1800, Exeter married again, this time to a divorcée. The year after that, his rank was raised from earl to marquess.

The story of the Peasant Countess became a *cause célèbre*. William Hazlitt knew it because the courtship had occurred in the part of Shropshire where he spent his childhood. In a magazine article about the pictures in the Burghley House collection, which he visited in 1822, he told a wonderful, though probably apocryphal, tale of how the Earl married Miss Hoggins without revealing his real identity, then drove her across country in a post-chaise. They arrived at Burghley Park:

> The gates flew open, the chaise entered, and drove down the long avenue of trees that leads up to the front of this fine old mansion. As they drew nearer to it, and she seemed a little surprised where they were going, he said, 'Well, my dear, this is Burleigh-House; it is the home I have promised to bring you to, and you are the Countess of Exeter!' It is said, the shock of this discovery was too much for this young creature, and that she never recovered from it.

Some years later, Tennyson read Hazlitt's account and turned it into his poem, 'The Lord of Burleigh'. The Irish poet Tom Moore had also versified the story, and given it a happy ending, in one of his *Irish Melodies*, published the same year as Clare's first book. Drury told Clare a version of the tale, in which the bride initially imagined she was going to live in the house as a servant, 'until the attendants undeceived her next morning'. He suggested that this would be a good subject for a poem. When Clare eventually took up the story, he had the tact to approach it very indirectly.

The son of the Peasant Countess was about the same age as the Peasant Poet. In their conversation, he might even have discovered that Clare also had a younger sister called Sophia. Was his generosity inspired by some strange feeling of kinship? On seeing Clare shifting uneasily in the fine room, looking anxiously to the door, he would have found it hard not to think of the disorientation his mother must have felt upon her first arrival at Burghley.

Clare took to heart the words of the Marquess about selling himself to his publishers. He went to Drury and asked for the agreement of 1 January to be returned. Drury said he would burn it. He thrust a folded paper between the bars of the fire grate. 'How do I know that is the agreement?' asked Clare. 'Let me see it first'—at which Drury took out the burning paper, extinguished it, put it in his pocket and said that he would not destroy it except in the presence of witnesses. So they parted.

Following his visits to Milton and Burghley, Clare drafted a letter of thanks to Fitzwilliam, Milton and Exeter, intended for publication in the second edition of his book. It did not appear in print, perhaps because Clare was not pleased when news of the generosity of his aristocratic patrons was leaked to a national newspaper, the *Morning Post*. 'Good men don't like their kind actions to be made so public', he wrote to Taylor—who quite agreed.

The source of the leak was a retired admiral. The Honourable William Waldegrave, born in 1753 as the second son of an earl, had a distinguished naval career. As captain of a frigate, he quelled a mutiny and hanged the ringleaders. He edited a collection of accounts of the victories of the fleet in the French wars entitled *The British Flag Triumphant!* A friend of Nelson, he became naval governor of Newfoundland and was given the title first Baron Radstock. During his governorship he dealt uncompromisingly with another mutiny, led by some army deserters whom he claimed were in league with the United Irishmen. Both in Canada and back in London after his retirement he contributed greatly to the relief of the poor. Radstock was a deeply religious man, an Evangelical Anglican who was active in the Society for the Propagation of the Gospel. He wrote a pious tract called *The Cottager's Friend, or a Word in Season to him who is so Fortunate as to possess a Bible or New Testament and a Book of Common Prayer*. It sold so well that it went through twenty editions in just a few years.

Radstock was friendly with a picture dealer named Thomas Emmerson and his wife Eliza, who had a nervous sensibility and a passion for poetry. Two weeks after the publication of *Poems, Descriptive*, Eliza Emmerson presented a copy to Radstock together with some poetic lines of her own, exhorting him to 'take this little volume to thy care— /And be the friend of Genius—and of "Clare!" ' Radstock took up the cause with alacrity. Together with a keen traveller and celebrated mountaineer called Captain Markham Sherwill, he began a campaign for the promotion of Clare. They went to see Taylor, in order to establish contact. Sherwill undertook to mention the poems in a letter to Sir Walter Scott; he also sent money for Clare's parents. Radstock dropped Clare's name in all the best circles in London, even enlisting the support of the prime minister, Lord Liverpool. He also wrote the letter to the *Morning Post* and gave Taylor a volume of sermons to send as a present (those on Prosperity, Adversity and Humility were especially recommended). He even wrote to Lord Milton suggesting that he should find a rent-free cottage and garden for the poet. He told Sherwill that he was afraid that gifts of cash might have a bad effect on Clare. A rent-free cottage, a cow and two pigs would serve much better.

Eliza Emmerson, meanwhile, sent an impassioned letter to Clare, together with a gift of Edward Young's gloomy *Night Thoughts*, the book that had first inspired her love for poetry. 'Of your Poems', she wrote, 'I am almost at a loss how to express my admiration of them:

they are at once, simply beautiful—affecting—and occasionally sub-lime! You prove yourself in your scenes from Nature to be truly Na-ture's child!' She addressed the package care of Drury, who failed to forward it to Clare for several weeks.

Sherwill also sent a book which Clare had chosen: the *Remains* (posthumous works) of Henry Kirke White, that poet of humble cir-cumstances about whom the Reverend Holland had enthused. Sher-will continued to correspond for some months, saying of Clare's letters that 'They flow from the heart, and from a heart without guile, without ostentation'. He also placed promotional material in the *Morning Post*, but the plan to interest the great Sir Walter in Clare's poetry did not come to much. Scott sent a presentation copy of his poem *The Lady of the Lake*, but declined to sign it. Sherwill ex-plained that 'Sir W.S. seemed bound hand and head, not from any dis-approbation of your talent or taste, but occasioned by the high path in which He strides in the literary field of the present day'. Clare was disappointed—and then offended when Taylor suggested in print that the reason he wanted a signed copy was to increase the cash value of the book.

Radstock's support came with a price. In his letter to the *Morning Post* he suggested that in the forthcoming second edition of *Poems, Descriptive* 'some two or three poems might be expunged, in order to make room for others of riper and purer growth'. The key word here is *purer*. Radstock was particularly offended by a stanza in the farm-yard poem, 'My Mary'. In Clare's manuscript we read that this Mary is not afraid of muck: 'when the baby's all besh-t', Mary—wishing to please the mother—'kisses it / And vows no rose on earth's so sweet'. Taylor had replaced the rude word with a blank, but the rhyme on 'kisses it' left little to the imagination. Equally offensive to Radstock's deeply religious frame of mind was 'Dolly's Mistake', a comic ballad about extra-marital sex.

Taylor wrote to Clare, saying that, though he was not fastidious himself, several notable personages including Radstock had objected to these two poems. Exeter's brother-in-law, the Honourable Mr Pierrepont, was also to draw Gilchrist's attention to the same poems.

Drury was more relaxed, noting that Burns had got away with many obscenities and that Clare prized his 'dirty verse' and was particularly fond of 'My Mary'. Clare objected to any changes, but reluctantly agreed to a compromise whereby the offensive blank would be replaced by the word *unfit*. The question of censorship would blow up again later in the year.

Taylor, a Non-conformist in religion and a professional middle-class literary man who despised the old traditions of aristocratic patronage, revealed his concerns about Radstock's interference in a letter to his father:

> Lord Radstock still exerts his utmost Interest to sell the Book and did I not hate Patronage for its *selfishness* (for such it is too frequently), I could not but admire the pains he takes.—He is now proposing by broad Hints a better Bargain as he thinks for Clare's next vol. viz. For us to publish, and divide the Profits with the author.—This I would willingly consent to, if anybody would do the Office of Editor *gratis*.—It is amusing to think how different our estimate would have been formed of these poems in any other person's hands. I should be entertained to see Gifford and Murray attempt to decypher and publish them, and should have no objection at all if the latter should make an offer of 500£ or 1000£ for the next volume.

He went on to suggest that Radstock and the rest of the fashionable world would treat Clare as a nine days' wonder, then forget him. His point about the 'Office of Editor' is just: he had to spend an immense amount of time on Clare's manuscripts to get them into a fit state for publication. John Murray, Byron's publisher, would not have been likely to take such trouble for an unknown poet.

Octavius Gilchrist often asked Clare if he would like to see London. Clare was too nervous to travel alone, so Gilchrist said that they should go together. So it was that, as Burns had been paraded in Edinburgh after the publication of his first book, Clare spent the first week of March 1820 in London.

They went on the Regent, the early-morning four-horse coach

from Stamford that undertook to do the hundred-mile journey in a mere thirteen or fourteen hours. Clare felt awkward in his humble clothes. Full of anticipation at the prospect of seeing a place known only from fireside tales, he looked out from the coach at the labourers ploughing and ditching in the fields: 'the novelty created such strange feelings that I could almost fancy that my identity as well as my occupations had changed—that I was not the same John Clare but that some stranger soul had jumped into my skin.'

They passed through Stilton, Huntingdon, St Neot's, Tempsford and Biggleswade. In Huntingdon, Gilchrist pointed out the birth-place of Oliver Cromwell and the home of the poet Cowper. The latter interested Clare more than the former. At dusk they saw the glow of the great city on the horizon. Soon 'the road was lined with lamps that diminished in the distance to stars'. 'This is London,' said Clare. Gilchrist laughed at his ignorance and told him that there were still several miles to go. It was night by the time the coach drew up outside the George and Blue Boar in Holborn. They walked the short distance to the Strand, where Gilchrist's German brother-in-law kept a jewellery and watch-maker's shop.

They learnt that Madame Vestris was singing Haydn Corri's arrangement of Clare's poem 'The Meeting'* at the Theatre Royal Drury Lane that very evening. But they had arrived too late to hear her, so they took a moonlit walk through the streets instead. The Thames from Westminster Bridge was less imposing than Clare had expected. He was 'uncommonly astonished' to see so many finely dressed ladies walking the streets at night. He had to be told that they were prostitutes. Gilchrist's brother-in-law—who liked a joke and made excellent punch—also scared him with Londoners' stories of pickpockets and kidnappers. It did not take much to intimidate the countryman: 'I felt often when walking behind Gilchrist almost fit to take hold of his coat laps'. When they saw anything out of the ordinary Clare would murmur 'Oh Christ'.

*This poem had been printed in Taylor's introduction to *Poems, Descriptive*, together with a defensive acknowledgement of its resemblance to a lyric by Burns.

He was kept busy for a week. There were visits to Poets' Corner in Westminster Abbey and both the main theatres, Drury Lane and Covent Garden. The two houses were staging rival adaptations of Sir Walter Scott's recent bestseller, *Ivanhoe*. In one version, Ivanhoe chose the fair Saxon Rowena as his love, in the other the dark Jew Rebecca. We do not know whether Clare was provoked into reflection on his own choice of love. He thought that both plays were bad, but enjoyed the accompanying farces.

Gilchrist's brother-in-law also took him to the Vauxhall pleasure gardens. Vauxhall offered wooded groves, picturesque walks, covered colonnades, classical alcoves and temples. Coloured lights were hung in the trees and an orchestra played. Clare's host made him shut his eyes until he was in the heart of the gardens: 'and when I opened them I almost fancied myself in fairyland, but the repetition of the roundabout walk soon put the Romance out of my head and made it a faded reality'. The landscape of Vauxhall provided an artificial and well-ordered version of nature for the benefit of the gentry. Clare preferred the real thing.

According to Frederick Martin's biography, Gilchrist wanted to introduce Clare to all sorts of fine people, but Clare was 'unwilling to play the part of a newly-discovered monkey or hippopotamus'. He did, of course, go to see his publishers. Martin claimed that Taylor saw that one reason for Clare's reluctance to show himself in company was his poor wardrobe. With characteristic frankness, Taylor mentioned the matter and offered Clare clothes: 'But Clare refused to take anything, except an ancient overcoat somewhat too large for him, but useful as hiding his whole figure from the top of the head down to the heels. In this brigand-like mantle he henceforth made all his visits, unwilling to take it off even at dinner, and in rooms hot to suffocation.' As often, Martin is likely to be exaggerating on the basis of a kernel of truth.

One gift of clothing that Clare certainly did accept was a fine silk cravat, which he wore when sitting for his portrait. Taylor had stayed in touch with a Lincoln school-friend called William Hilton, who had become a painter (his talent was acknowledged when he was elected to the Royal Academy in 1819). Whilst training as an artist, Hilton became very close to Peter de Wint, a fellow-pupil. De Wint married Hilton's sister, Harriet, and the three of them lodged together in London (later, Hilton would complete the circle by marrying de Wint's sister). Hilton specialised in historical subjects and portraits, de Wint in watercolour landscapes. Hilton had sketched John Keats, with a possible view to a frontispiece for the volume of his poetry that Taylor was about to publish. Taylor now wanted a portrait of Clare, for which he paid Hilton fifteen guineas.

Hilton's painting is the iconic image of Clare in his prime. There is a visionary gleam in the poet's piercing blue eyes. His light-brown hair is unkempt, his cheeks flushed, lips parted as if about to breathe out some exquisite line of verse. He looks hot and uncomfortable in wing-collar, carefully folded neckerchief and tightly buttoned yellow waistcoat. Hilton's original oil canvas was hung in 'the back shop' at Taylor and Hessey's Fleet Street premises. After Taylor's death it was bought at auction by Frederick Martin, Clare's first biographer. It is now in the National Portrait Gallery off Trafalgar Square in London, only a few hundred yards from Waterloo Place, where Taylor took it when he moved from Fleet Street in 1823. Copies in watercolour were undertaken for Lord Radstock and Mrs Emmerson, and for Clare himself as a gift to his father.

Clare warmed to Hilton. The writers in the *London Magazine* circle warmed to the painting. 'C in alt', Thomas Hood called it: Clare in a moment of high inspiration. An engraved copy was used as frontispiece to Clare's second book. It elicited some purple prose from Thomas Wainewright, the *London*'s art critic:

> Did you ever see a thing copied so accurately, and with so much feeling, as this brilliant little print by Scriven, after Hilton's natural and characteristic portrait of Clare?—what life in the eyes! What ardent thirst for excellence and what flexibility and susceptibility to outward impressions in the quivering lips! Observe the thigh caught up unconsciously by the hand! It does Hilton's penetration credit to have arrested that most unsophisticated and speaking action.

The hand nervously catching the thigh is not actually visible in the original painting: it seems to have been an expressive innovation on the part of the engraver.

At Taylor's, Clare met his publisher's partner for the first time. He liked him very much, but in this case we do not have a pen-portrait by Clare himself. Taylor must provide one instead:

> James Augustus Hessey is thin, dresses principally in black, his face is round and good-humoured when he does not frown— when he does, *it has the contrary expression* ... He has a readiness of droll quotation, and humorous allusion—is somewhat witty but had rather be considered a man of strong sense. His enunciation is not very distinct, but rapid, and when he wishes to utter his opinion in a serious manner, he hesitates or stutters a little, as if in doubt what words to select next ... His knowledge of the flute qualifies him to play an accompaniment to the piano ... In a word, he has wit and accomplishments sufficient to please everybody, and sense enough to make *them* the subordinate part of his character.

Taylor and Hessey held a dinner party in Clare's honour. It gave him the chance to meet some of the firm's other writers, whom he would get to know better when he returned to London two years later. Keats was ill, but his witty friend J. H. Reynolds was there, as was Henry Cary, the translator of Dante into English. Cary recorded his impression of Clare in a letter to his brother-in-law: 'He has the appearance rather of a big boy who has never been used to company, than of a clown, though his dialect is clownish enough; and like *all true geniuses*, he was longing to be at home again'.

Taylor said that Clare 'pleased us all with his simple manly sensible Conduct and Conversation'. At the dinner party the Peasant Poet sat next to Lord Radstock, the old admiral who had taken up his cause with such enthusiasm. This is how Clare described him:

> A large man of a commanding figure ... Lord Radstock at first sight appears to be of a stern and haughty character, but the moment he speaks his countenance kindles up into a free blunt

good-hearted man, one whom you expect to hear speak exactly
as he thinks—he has no notion of either offending or pleasing
by his talk and care[s] as little for the consequences of either—
there is a good deal of bluntness and openheartedness about
him and there is nothing of pride or fashion—he is as plain in
manner and dress as the old country squire.

Clare liked the bluntness of address and the fact that Radstock did not
behave like a lord. In the country, Milton and Exeter had received
him kindly but then sent him off to eat in the servants' hall. In the
city, he was sitting round a table conversing informally with a member of one of the noblest families in England.

Clare spent more time with Radstock towards the end of his week.
The Admiral introduced him to Eliza Emmerson. According to Martin, 'Clare at the first interview was not at all favourably impressed by
this lady; for she assumed what he fancied to be a theatrical air; burst
out in bitter laments about what she termed the "desolate appearance" of her visitor, and wept that "so much genius and so much
poverty" should go together'.

Clare's own impression was that Emmerson 'has been a very pretty
woman and is not amiss still'. He felt that her youthful beauty must
have had the unfortunate effect of making her continue to think that
all her male friends were 'admirers of her person as a matter of
course'. This tendency made her behave in ways that at first sight
seemed ridiculous. Her 'tastes, feelings and manners' were 'almost
romantic'. But once he knew her better, qualities of true friendship
would be revealed. He later acknowledged that she was the 'best
friend' he ever found.

The coach home to Helpston stopped off at the Bull Inn, Ware.
Clare had a drink and eyed up the pretty serving maid. Once on the
road again, he composed a lyric about the peculiar pleasure of such
fleeting encounters with sexual desire. The poem is, however, tinged
with wistfulness and mild guilt. He was, after all, on his way home to
the woman who was heavy with his child.

Clare also wrote a sonnet 'On Leaving London', in which he expressed his joy at seeing again the cottages and farms of the country.

1 (TOP) John Clare's cottage in Helpston, as it is today

2 (BOTTOM) Glinton Church, from a drawing by George Clark.
Clare went to school in the vestry and met Mary Joyce there

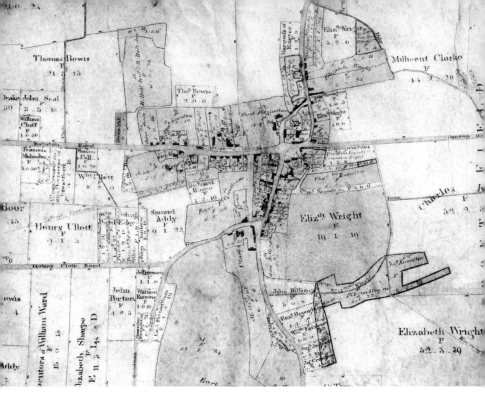

3 (TOP) Enclosure award map for the parish of Helpston

4 (BOTTOM) Burghley House, where Clare worked in the kitchen-garden

5 (TOP) Milton Hall, where
Clare found friends
in the servants' quarters

6 (LEFT) Newcombe Boss,
a gypsy from a tribe known by
Clare, dressed as a gentleman

7 (ABOVE) Octavius Gilchrist,
Stamford grocer and
man of letters

8 (TOP) John Taylor, Clare's publisher

9 (BOTTOM) James Augustus Hessey,
Taylor's publishing partner

10 (ABOVE LEFT) The Marquess of Exeter,
who gave Clare an annuity of fifteen guineas

11 (ABOVE RIGHT) Lord Milton, patron and reformer

12 (RIGHT) Admiral Lord Radstock,
who established a trust fund for Clare

13 (OPPOSITE TOP) Helpston, drawn by William Cowen, with Clare's cottage made to look more picturesque than it was, published as the frontispiece to volume two in the second issue of *The Village Minstrel*

14 (OPPOSITE BOTTOM) E. V. Rippingille's oil painting *The Stage-Coach Breakfast*, 1824: Charles Lamb is handing the bill to 'Rip' himself, who sits beside Wordsworth, Coleridge, Dorothy Wordsworth; C. A. Elton by the fireplace, one of his daughters pouring tea; possibly Clare looking at clock by the window; possibly Eliza Emmerson gazing in mirror to the right

(BELOW RIGHT) Detail from *The Stage-Coach Breakfast*

A SPARRING MATCH AT THE FIVES COURT.

ROMAN REMAINS

15 (TOP) *A Sparring Match at the Fives Court*, drawn
by Robert Cruikshank and engraved by his brother
George. Clare visited this arena with 'Rip' in 1824

16 (ABOVE) E. A. Artis (in top hat) conducting Roman
excavations, in an engraving from *The Durobrivae of
Antoninus*. Labourers' clothes and tools of this kind
were familiar to Clare from his work as a lime-burner

17 (RIGHT) Roman pavement reconstructed from
a fragment discovered by Clare near Oxey Wood

Their 'simply pleasing charms' were 'far superior to the city's noise'. 'I've seen the world, found nought that I could wish / And fly contented to thy peace again'; 'I'll eat my crust and fancy I am blest', he concludes. He wrote and told Taylor how glad he was to be at home again. But another poem written around this time acknowledges that he would 'take it mighty hard' if 'neglect' were to follow after the 'fussed regard' and 'promised great reward' of having been 'stilted up' as 'a rustic bard' and 'strutted' above his station.

After his exposure to fame and London, he could never fully return to his old life. In this sense, his consciousness of a new identity as he sat in the Stamford coach was prophetic.

The London trip had been a success. The second edition of the poems, with double the print run of the first, was imminent. The Peasant Poet was making a splash. With Burns it had all gone wrong due to drink and womanising. The shine had been taken off his literary debut by adverse publicity surrounding his adultery with Jean Armour, her pregnancy and eventual delivery of twins. Conscious of this and of the religious sensibilities of patrons such as Radstock, Clare's friends had been persuading him to make an honest woman of the pregnant 'Patty of the Vale'.

A week after returning to Helpston, Clare got married. The banns had been read in church before his departure. He arrived home to find eighteen letters waiting for him, among them one from the local vicar telling him that Radstock had sent twenty-five guineas—but also warning him against 'pride and presumption' and stressing that continued patronage would depend on his good conduct. He was a public figure now, and therefore obliged to live up to his responsibilities.

Patty was given away in Great Casterton Church by her uncle, not her father. It is not clear whether her pregnancy was the reason for this—possibly not, given that there was a family dinner at Walk Lodge on the day of the wedding. Clare's instructions for that morning were to walk the nine miles to the uncle's house, arriving 'at Half past Eight or Nine o'clock at farthest, then go immediately to church and breakfast afterward'. He was accompanied by his sister Sophy, who served as the second witness. Patty's gown was a gift from Mrs Emmerson. When Clare and his bride turned from the altar after pronouncing their vows, they would have seen the royal coat-of-arms high on the wall at the far end of the nave, together with a painted inscription that read FEAR GOD. HONOUR Y^e KING.

Parson Mossop wrote to Lord Radstock with news of the marriage and Gilchrist ensured that an announcement of it was inserted in the *London Magazine*. Hessey sent Clare a Cremona violin. For a time, Clare was anxious because it seemed to have got lost in the process of carriage, but it turned up after a fortnight and always remained a highly valued present. Clare sent a piece of wedding cake to Drury and two to Taylor (sufficient for him to give portions to Mrs Hessey and Mrs de Wint). There was no honeymoon. And it was not felt appropriate that the pregnant Patty should be seen in Clare's cottage. She stayed at her parents' home near Casterton until her confinement. He remained deeply fond of Walk Lodge and its secluded vale, writing a poem of fond farewell when Patty's parents left the family home a couple of years later.

The effusive Eliza Emmerson wrote Clare a letter the day before he married the illiterate Patty. She thanked him for a poem he had sent: 'I shall *treasure* it in *my heart*, where it shall be kept *secret and secure from the world*—as I shall *also, your letters to me*, and *every thing* you may acquaint me with concerning yourself.' She asked him to sign his letters to her with his name, not his initials. And she reassured him that 'Your "dear Patty" must not be *jealous* that I write thus to you, I do it, for her sake in part, for in *comforting*, and *cheering your drooping spirits*, with the warm language of true friendship, I am at the same time securing *her future happiness in you*!' He was going to have to get used to the very different ways—and very different words—of his new wife and his new friend.

CHAPTER EIGHT

THE PRICE OF FAME

Clare saw little of his wife in the first three months of their marriage. In April and May 1820 there was further talk of the proposal that Lord Milton should have a cottage built for them. On one occasion, his Lordship sent a message that the poet should meet him in the fields, possibly to 'choose a bit of ground' for it, but Clare was in Stamford with Octavius Gilchrist, so failed to turn up. He wrote a letter to Milton stressing that he was 'independant' and did not wish to put his Lordship to any trouble. Nothing more was heard of the new cottage.

On 2 June 1820, John and Patty's first daughter was born. She was named Anna Maria. Anna was for Clare's mother, but Maria was not for Patty's (Mrs Turner was called Sarah). Was it a sign that somewhere in his heart Clare still longed for his Mary?

On 1 July Clare brought his wife and baby daughter home to Helpston. Octavius Gilchrist wrote to him a few days later saying, 'Do you find yourself more comfortable now the Spouse is with you? You must be "very throng," as they say in Lincolnshire, with so many in your house'. Parker, Ann, John, Patty, sister Sophy and the baby would indeed have been a 'throng' in one room upstairs and one down, but by good fortune the tenant next door had just moved out, so John was able to take on the tenement adjacent to his father's. In effect, then, the Clares were now back in the situation that they had been in before 1813: they had two rooms upstairs and two down. Sophy married a Northborough labourer called William Kettle in 1821, but there is evidence to suggest that she continued to live with the family until at least 1824. As Patty bore children, the house became more and more crowded. Neither of Clare's parents died until after the family's move to Northborough in 1832.

Clare had not entered into his marriage with wholehearted enthusiasm. 'I held out as long as I could and then married her', he later wrote. When Patty and baby Anna moved to Helpston he felt more positive. He told his publisher that he thought Patty would 'prove a better bargain than I expected'. But within a month he was writing to Eliza Emmerson of 'domestic troubles'. His feelings continued to fluctuate. The following spring he wrote that 'Patt and myself now begin to know each other and live happly and I deem it a fortunate erra in my life that I met with her ... the cut of her face always delighted me more than any other and had I never seen her my attempts at poetry woud never have been resumd after my removal at Casterton'. But later in the same letter, we learn that at this moment Patty was six months pregnant and dangerously ill. Clare was perhaps talking up his marriage out of guilt at his previous complaints about Patty and fear at the prospect of losing her.

His love for his children is beyond doubt. When Anna was six weeks old, Clare sent Hessey a poem 'To an Infant Daughter', in which he wrote of the special sense of tenderness felt by a first-time father as he says 'Thou'rt mine'. But the poem is also filled with fear. It expresses the wish that Anna should 'Be ignorant as is thy mother' and grow up 'unknown to rhyming bother'. Poetry is an affliction he does not wish upon his daughter:

> L——d help thee in thy coming years
> If thy mad father's picture 'pears
> Predominant——his feeling fears
>   And gingling starts.
> I'd freely now gi' vent to tears
>   To ease my heart.

This is one of the most revealing stanzas of poetry that Clare ever wrote. The intensity of his hopes and fears for his baby daughter has made him conscious of the price that is being exacted by his own compulsion to rhyme. The primary meaning of *mad* in this context is 'overrun with strong feeling', but one detects the shadow of deeper disorder.

Hessey liked the poem, but judged that it would be inappropriate to publish it immediately, since it would reveal to the public that Clare had become a father only a few months after getting married. When it was published in the poet's second collection just over a year later, the stanza about the mad father's 'feeling fears / And gingling starts' was omitted.

A family brought financial responsibility. Clare now needed to support not only his parents, but also his wife and child. By early summer, there was good news about the trust fund that was being set up in his name. Taylor and Hessey contributed one hundred pounds to match the sum provided by Earl Fitzwilliam. Lord Radstock added a further hundred in the form of smaller donations solicited from an assortment of other peers and gentlemen. In April, Taylor purchased £250 of five per cent Navy Stock in order to establish the fund. In June, the total was topped up to £375, courtesy of more donations collected by Radstock, whose solicitations on Clare's behalf were only temporarily suspended by an awkward fall down a stone staircase. The fund yielded an annual dividend of just under nineteen pounds, though this went down to fifteen guineas per year in 1823 when the interest rate was reduced to four per cent. There was also Exeter's promise of fifteen guineas a year for life and a ten-pound annuity from Earl Spencer (discussed below). Clare would therefore have an assured annual income of about forty pounds, a sum comfortably in excess of an average labouring wage.

Radstock proposed that in the short term, while the trust was being set up, Clare should be paid a pound a fortnight out of the money he had collected. But Taylor stressed the importance of not eating into the capital. Instead, he sent Clare 'occasional Remittances' of small sums resulting from people charitably paying in excess of the cover price for their copies of *Poems, Descriptive*.

This measure was insufficient to save Clare from the necessity of manual labour during the summer of 1820. In August, Taylor suggested that outdoor work at harvest time would be good for his health and give him a 'Sense of Superiority to the Slavish Favours of the rich'. He added that Clare was in a much more fortunate position than Keats, whose latest book had sold fewer than five hundred copies and whose tuberculosis was likely to prove fatal. Taylor worried, however, about the company Clare kept in the fields. More than once he sent a stern letter about the perils of drink. Drury had reported to him that 'John Clare has been to see me this day, and I asked what to insert [by way of a message]—"tell them" quoth he, "I am at harvest work, but went a frolicking yesterday at Mr Simpson's of Casterton—got too much of Barleycorn broth—fell down, and got a black eye" '.

Though Clare was always sure to express due gratitude for the patronage of Lord Radstock and the Fitzwilliam family, it was to Exeter that he felt a special debt. The Fitzwilliams acted partly from a sense of *noblesse oblige*, since they were lords of the manor in which Clare lived. Radstock's patronage was never without the appendage of tiresome homilies along the lines laid out in his first surviving letter to Clare: 'I think too highly both of your understanding and heart— and above all of your Gratitude to God, to suppose you will neglect the serious study of our holy religion according to the *Established Church*, and that you will let its laws and its principles serve you as an unerring guide through life.' He was always sending Clare morally and spiritually improving books, inscribed with exhortations to rectitude and comformity: 'Beware, beware, beware *Enthusiasm*, it being the most dangerous enemy that true Religion has to encounter'.

Exeter's patronage, by contrast, 'was not sought for by a soul'. The Marquess knew nothing of Clare prior to the appearance of *Poems, Descriptive*. In February 1821 he called at Clare's cottage in person to inquire after the progress towards publication of the poet's second book. 'What a contrast between Lord R and this gentle nobleman, aye chucky', wrote Clare to Taylor (*chucky* was his term of affection for his publisher).

The cynical interpretation of Exeter's patronage is that he wanted to outdo the Fitzwilliams, his political rivals, in generosity. But his visit to the Helpston cottage belies this. It suggests a genuine personal interest on the part of the Peasant Countess's son. Clare was tongue-tied in front of his grand visitor, and could not bring himself to apologise, as he wished to, for a faux pas he had made in Drury's shop the previous autumn. On that occasion,

> A gentleman came in and asked me how I did—I very bluntly answered 'very well thank you Sir'—he stared me very hard and asked the prentice if it was not Clare and told me that he came to hear if my book was out—'no Sir'—with my hat on—was the answer—he went out without saying a word more—and he had not gone 2 minutes when the disclosure of the secret came out—d-m it—'twas a thunderbolt to my ignorance and I stood gauping like an idiot to hear the man say it was no worse a person than the marquis—what the marquis will think of me I don't know but I wish very much I had been the length of London out of the matter.

On his way home after this incident, Clare sat down on every stile and 'repeated it over to my self how I had acted which every repetition made more rediculous'. An apology was eventually conveyed via Pierrepont. The Marquess said that no offence had been taken.

One Sunday morning over breakfast at Drury's back in 1819, Clare had met a former army doctor who on a posting in the West Indies had become acquainted with the satirical poet 'Peter Pindar'. Clare remembered this man, Dr J. G. Bell, as a droll fellow who 'used to cut all the curious and odd paragraphs out of the newspapers and paste them on sheets of pasteboard'.

Late in 1819 Bell noticed a magazine article about the second Earl Spencer. It told of his great library at Althorp and his munificent patronage of literature. Bell took the liberty of writing to the Earl with information about Clare and a request for financial support. Spencer was wintering in Naples, but he replied in February, saying that if Clare's friends were to establish a fund to save him from a life of hard labour, he would contribute to it. Bell wrote again, telling of the success of Clare's volume and of the transformation whereby 'his cottage at Helpstone is not unfrequently graced by the splendid equipage of opulence stopping, where nought but dung carts and wheel barrows stopped before'. Spencer decided not to make a capital contribution to the fund, but to give Clare an annual payment of ten pounds, in half-yearly instalments (he sometimes forgot to pay, and embarrassing reminder letters had to be sent).

In his unfinished autobiography Clare gave his own account of the splendid equipages that began drawing up at his door. His fame lasted for a good two years after the appearance of his first book. In September 1821 we find him positively looking forward to the time when he could expect to be left alone:

> I am sought after very much agen now 3 days scarcely pass off but sombody calls—some rather entertaining people and some d——d knowing fools—surely the vanity woud have kill'd me 4 years ago if I had known then how I shoud have been hunted up—and extolld by personal flattery—but let me wait another year or two and the peep show will be over—and my vanity if I have any will end in its proper mortification to know that obscurity is happiness and that John Clare the thresher in the onset and neglected ryhmer in the end are the only two comfortable periods of his life.

Mostly, the gentry came to gawp. They offered gifts of books, but then failed to send them: 'I had the works of Lord Byron promised by 6 different people and never got them from none of them.' The books' failure to appear was a relief to Clare's mother, who was worried that there wouldn't be room for them in the house (eventually, Clare built up a library of over four hundred books, many of them presentation copies). Clare hated the visits, and got out of the way when he could, leaving his wife and mother in a bad temper when they were caught with a dirty house.

One dandified visitor made a pretence of great learning, but knew nothing. He asked for Clare's walking stick as a souvenir (complete with autograph on the crook). 'He then asked me some insulting liberties respecting my first acquaintance with Patty and said he understood that in this country the lower orders made their courtships in barns and pigsties and asked whether I did.' His wife, who was accompanying him, said that he was fond of a joke and she hoped that Clare was not offended. But the remark did not sound like a joke to Clare. He later discovered that the man 'was but a scant remove from the low order himself as his wife was a grocer's daughter'.

After wasting an hour of Clare's time, the dandy said that he would have liked to give him a book, but that it was obvious from his unexpectedly good library that he didn't need any. He added, 'still I should make you an offer of something—have you got a Bible?' Clare said nothing, but Parker Clare piped up: 'We have a Bible, sir, but I cannot read it, the print is so small, so I should thank you for one'. The man looked very confused. It was clear from his manner that he had mentioned the one book which he could be sure they possessed, so as to avoid giving them anything.

Another visitor, named Edward Baily Preston, announced that he was a very great poet who knew everybody who was anybody in the literary world. 'He had a vast quantity of manuscripts, he said, by him—but had not published much at present, though he had two rather important works in the press at that time, whose publication he anxiously awaited ... he was for ever quoting beauties from his own poetry.' Preston had paid a similar visit to Bloomfield, and spoke of him 'as familiar as if he had been his neighbour half a life time— he called him "brother Bob" '. He asked lots of questions and answered them himself with guesses before Clare had a chance to reply. Preston also claimed intimate knowledge of painters and Royal Academicians. He could 'criticize their various excellences and defects with great dexterity of tongue'. He praised Hilton as 'the top of the tree'. As he did so, he 'stood abusing a sketch of my head that hung by the wall and finding a thousand faults with it'. Clare let him go on, then told him that the water-colour was by Hilton. 'He turned himself round on his heel, blamed his eyesight, and discovered nothing but beauties afterward.'

Preston stayed the whole day and wore Clare out. The flavour of his conversation may be tasted from a letter that he wrote to Clare some time later:

> Dear Bardie ... I now take the guid grey goose quill to scrap ye down a weak thing or two—In primus then I am as dull as a drone beetle; for the very unfavourable state of the atmosphere tears or rather melts my poor sensitive nerves all, to nothing ... Were it not for a kindly visit from my, almost, ever-propitious muse now and then; a bit of scrat, (as you Northampton lads ha it) from some one like ourselves, spleen would soon kill me out right. ... It has been my joy and crown of rejoicing, all my complicated journey through life's waste howling wilderness, to meet with now and then a bright gem of intellect blazing from an uncouth and shapeless rock; or a spring of pure feeling's water bubbling from the uncultivated waste, and diffusing verdeur and flowers over my path. On such phenomina I have gazed with unutterable extacy, and counted the discovery of them one of the sunshiny days of my dark journey—such my dear sir I esteem the commencement of my correspondence with you.

And so on, ad nauseam. Preston announced that he was going to be in Peterborough and would call on Clare again. Like many other unwanted letters, this one came without the postage prepaid.* Clare did not reply and, to his immense relief, Preston did not reappear on his doorstep.

Other fans with over-blown literary pretensions of their own included Thomas Roberts, a schoolmaster from a village near Spalding, who sent an eight-page epistle full of such phrases as 'your brilliant ophthalmic organs', 'the feathered songsters are warbling their evening adorations from each umbrageous retreat' and 'serenely segregated from the malapert and hypochondriachal vapours

---

*Thus, for example, Clare's journal for 27 February 1825: 'Recieved a letter in ryhme from a John Pooley a very dull Fooley who ran me 10ᵈ further in debt as I had not money to pay the postage—I have often been botherd with these poet pretenders.'

of myopic Criticks'. He seems to have missed the point that plainness of natural description was Clare's distinctive innovation in poetry.

Visitors often arrived when Clare was out working in the fields. He would be called in, and lose his day's wage. One day in the summer of 1820 when he was out reaping wheat, a message came from the Reverend Samuel Hopkinson, vicar of Morton in Lincolnshire, a village about ten miles north of Stamford: a horse would be at Clare's door 'on such a morning at such a time of the clock'. There was 'no option whether I chused to go or not'.

Mrs Hopkinson duly paraded him around her husband's parish. The local women knew her well: 'they would scarcely wait to hear her speak ere the wheel was started into a quicker twirl or the pots and pans scoured with a more bustling hand'. Back at the vicarage, the good lady showed Clare to a writing desk in an upstairs room, laid out with paper, pen, ink and sealing wax. She hoped he would write something every day during his stay. She also proposed going through his poems page by page, making observations and suggesting improvements for the next edition. 'She read in a loud confident voice', Clare remembered, 'like the head boy in a school who is reckoned a good reader and whose conceit thinks he is so good'—though she often jarred and muttered over words that she didn't understand.

Old Hoppy, as Drury called him, took Clare to see such local sights as Grimsthorpe Castle and Folkingham Gaol. Everywhere they went, 'he would question those that appeared his inferiors as if they were undergoing an examination in a court of justice'. This was a man who had 'written a book with a design of instructing his parishioners in a pompous and long-winded style'. He was also the magistrate who at the Peterborough courthouse in 1819 had advocated the extermination of the gypsies from the face of the earth.

On one sightseeing trip, they heard a labourer breaking into a whistle by a plantation. Hopkinson swore that it was a poacher and told Clare to investigate. Clare knew that 'the whistle was a song tune, but it was no use'—Hopkinson forced a confrontation, only to discover that the man was merely doing his fencing work.

The Hopkinsons had two daughters. Ann and Elizabeth were well read, quiet and amiable, but they had quarrelled with their mother and did not come downstairs for the duration of Clare's stay. He paid a second visit to Morton a year later, when the girls each presented him with a volume of poetry.

Patty does not seem to have been pleased that Clare went off to Morton when the baby was still less than three months old. To judge from a letter written shortly after his return, she gave him a hard time: he complained that she was proving herself a 'termagant' and 'one of the most ignorant and I fear will turn out the most obstinate of woman creation'. Cramped, noisy and fraught conditions at home were probably what made Clare accept the second invitation to the Hopkinson vicarage. Old Hoppy and his busybody wife were not Clare's idea of good company, but their house was a place of quiet refuge.

Another visit north of Stamford was to Holywell Hall, the house of General Birch Reynardson, one of Drury's customers, who took an interest in the poet. Clare went on a beautiful April day. The General showed him his library, the largest he had yet seen. They strolled in the grounds, which were undergoing fashionable improvement: 'A little river ran sweeping along and in one place he was forming a connection with it to form an Island'. In one sunny spot there was a large sun-dial 'and near it under the shadows of some evergreens was a bird house built in the form of a cage, glass all round and full of canaries that were fluttering about busily employed in building their nests'. Clare met the children's governess here and mistook her for the General's wife. The mistake was not 'unriddled' till Clare worked it out for himself, whereupon he felt 'ashamed and vexed'.

The governess, a Birmingham girl, took a fancy to him. She asked him to write out some of his verses for her. After Clare had been given dinner in the servants' hall—where he recognized 'an old enemy in a letter-boy who had often annoyed me while passing to Stamford by our kiln at Ryhall'—the housekeeper invited him to her room. The governess came in and chatted. Pretty, impertinent and over-familiar, she gave Clare her address and asked him to write. When he left the Holywell estate that evening, he found her lingering on the path. She said she would walk some of the way home with him, and went on talking about his poems and her desire to establish a correspondence. He tried to get rid of her when they reached the edge of the heath that overlooked Patty's cottage. But she lingered and chattered on till it grew very late. Then a man on horseback suddenly came up and asked which road they had come from; thinking it was the General, she hastily retreated, but on finding her mistake she returned and talked on at Clare for half the night. When he eventually got away, he didn't have the courage to shake her by the hand.

He did, however, write to her. His first intention was to be 'very warm and very gallant', but on second thoughts he made the letter 'a very cold one' in which he told her he would not see her again. He feared 'that she only wanted me to write love-letters to have the pleasure to talk about them and laugh at them'. But he enclosed a poem for her. The thought of her advances made him 'rather conceited'.

An unwelcome visitor was Henry Ryde, agent of the Burghley estate. An ill-tempered man, he was rude to Clare, perhaps because he resented the patronage his master was bestowing on a mere labourer. Equally unwelcome was the reappearance of Henson of Market Deeping. He seems to have fallen on bad times as good ones came to Clare; now he wrote with a grovelling request to have some printing work put his way.

Others were more welcome, none more than Chauncey Hare Townsend, an undergraduate from Trinity Hall, Cambridge. He had won the Chancellor's Medal for a poem of his own and he admired Clare's work so much that he felt inspired to write a sonnet in his honour:

> There is a vivid lightning of the breast,
> Flash'd from a spark of kindred poesy,
> Which poets only know . . .
> O Clare, such answering electricity
> Darts, from thy numbers to my soul addresst!
> Thou hast read Nature with a Poet's eye,
> Thou hast felt Nature with a Poet's heart . . .

One fine evening in April 1820, he turned up at the Helpston cottage to deliver his poem in person. He asked if John Clare lived there: 'I told him I was he and he seemed surprised and asked again to be satisfied, for I was shabby and dirty.' Clare had little to say for himself. He had what he called 'a natural depression of spirits in the presence of strangers'. This made him 'dull and silent'; if he attempted to say anything he 'could not recollect it and made so many hums and hahs in the story' that he was 'obliged to leave it unfinished at last'.

Clare considered Townsend to be somewhat infected with the dandyism that was endemic among the Cambridge undergraduates of the time. 'He mimicked a lisp in his speech which he owed to affectation rather than habit, otherwise he was a feeling and sensible young man.' Townsend talked about poets and poetry and the fine scenery of the Lake District. Then he put a folded paper into Clare's hand. After he left, Clare found the sonnet and a pound note.

They struck up a correspondence. Clare apologised for his apparent sullenness during the visit: 'I am defiled with the old silence of rusticity that always characterized me among my neighbours before I was known to the world—I was reckoned a "glumpy half sort of fool" amongst 'em.' Townsend replied that there was no need to apologise: true poets were always moody. He had genuine respect for Clare and concern for his well-being—which led him to deliver a warning against the evils of alcohol and the fate of Burns. He also sent a rheumatic application for Parker, which was gratefully received. Townsend feared that Clare had taken offence at his advice, but this was not the case:

> The plasters you sent my father has succeeded beyond our expectation and he is able to potter about with one stick and put a few stones in the rutts on the road for amusement—I can assure you your advice is no offence in the least tho I like yourself hate sermonizing but in giving a person hints for amendment I cant think that sermonizing not in the least—so I heartily thank you for it and will reap the benefit it contains if I possibly can—but as blunt I think is best—I will not assure you if it be possible—

> still you have my grateful acknowledgement for the present and
> future hints for my happiness—all else is a fault with me.

'Blunt I think is best': this is true Clare. He was glad to be given advice, both personal and literary, but he liked to be given it straight, without 'sermonizing'.

Townsend paid his respects while *Poems, Descriptive of Rural Life and Scenery* was still in its first flush of success. A year on, visitors were still turning up every few days. Frederick Martin told of two elderly bespectacled schoolmasters from Peterborough who subjected Clare to a rigorous cross-examination, causing him to lose half a day's work in the fields, and of three old ladies from Market Deeping who said they had bought his poems and could not rest till they saw him face to face. One of them was somewhat deaf, so Clare had to answer all their questions twice, the second time at a shout. They didn't know the way home, so Clare showed them the first couple of miles and then adjourned to the pub instead of returning to work. Another morning, 'the inmates of a whole boarding-school, located at Stamford, visited the unhappy poet, and a shower coming on, the fluttering damsels with their grave monitors crowded every room in the little hut, preventing the baby from sleeping and Mrs Clare from doing her weekly washing'. Other well-wishers took Clare to the pub and got him drunk.

Although Martin's details are not to be trusted, there is no question that Clare was annoyed by many of his callers. He was accordingly very pleased whenever a 'sensible Gent' arrived. In April 1821, there was Dr Noehden of the British Museum, who 'talked civily and unasuming'. Clare said in a letter that he 'felt the loss of his company after he left'. Noehden seems to have been accompanied by E. T. Artis, the house steward at Milton Hall, who would soon become one of Clare's most important friends in the locality.

In November 1820 Hessey proposed to Taylor that Clare should be brought back to London, so that they could work on getting his chaotic manuscripts into shape for a second published collection: 'I never expected you would do any thing with Clare's MSS and I think it would be the best way to have him in London that you may go thro' his MSS together and get them finished at once—it will be very awkward going to that comfortless Village in this damp cold weather.' But Clare was unwell that winter, so the detailed editorial work was done through the post.

Taylor did make his way to 'that comfortless Village' the following autumn. He published an account of his visit in the *London Magazine*. It tells of how he met Clare on the road, about a mile from home. The poet was with his wife and Patty's sister (of whom we know almost nothing). They were on their way to a Turner family reunion in Casterton: 'I was very unwilling to disturb the arrangement,' says Taylor, 'but Clare insisted on remaining with me, and the two cheerful girls left their companion with a "good bye, John!" which made the plains echo again, and woke in my old-bachelor heart the reflection "John Clare, thou art a very happy fellow." ' It sounds as if at this time relations were good between John and Patty, and Patty and her family.

Taylor and Clare spent the morning out in the fields, looking at the sites that had inspired the poems: Lolham Bridges, Langley Bush, the village itself. Then they went to his cottage, which Taylor knew from the adjacent elm trees that had been mentioned lovingly in one of the poems. He talked to Parker—now needing two sticks to get about—in the garden, while Clare prepared bread and cheese and got beer in from the Blue Bell. Once inside, Taylor noticed Clare's pictures: 'On a projecting wall, which is white-washed, are hung some well engraved portraits, in gilt frames, with a neat drawing of Helpstone Church, and a sketch of Clare's Head which Hilton copied in water colours, from the large painting, and sent as a present to Clare's father.' The drawing of the church was by Clare's Stamford friend, Frank Simpson, a keen draughtsman who had recently sketched his cottage as an intended (though unused) frontispiece for the second volume of *The Village Minstrel*.

Little Anna, now sixteen months, woke up and 'tottered along the floor', Clare looking on affectionately. After lunch, Clare opened up his old oak bookcase—a gift from Octavius Gilchrist—and showed Taylor his library. His 'very good collection of modern poems' was especially noted, among them works by Burns, Cowper, Wordsworth, Coleridge, Keats, Crabbe (a gift from Lord Milton that had arrived that very day) and Allan Cunningham (another Taylor and Hessey author, whom Clare wanted to meet). After another walk, the two men parted on the road to Barnack.

Clare was a discerning reader of his fellow-poets. He kept an ear open to contemporary critical opinion, whilst holding fast to his own views. His thoughts on Wordsworth were given in a letter to Captain Sherwill:

> Do you know personaly Wordsworth and Colridge, they are two favourites with me—have you seen Wordsworths last production 'Sonnets to the River Duddon'—they call 'em good—how like you his Sonnet on 'Westminster Bridge'—I think it (and woud say it to the teeth of the critic in spite of his rule and compass) that it owns no equal in the English language.

Clare disliked Milton's sonnets because they were too rule-bound. By contrast, he said, Wordsworth 'defies all art and in all the lunatic Enthuseism of nature he negligently sets down his thoughts from the tongue of his inspirer'—a judgement that makes Wordsworth's method of composition sound more like Clare's own than it really was. Clare thought that there were 'affected fooleries' in some of Wordsworth's longer poems, but that 'still with his faults and abilities he is a poet with whom for origionallity of description the present day has few if any equals'. He then added, after a dash, 'for the present'—as if in hope that one day soon he himself would surpass Wordsworth in originality of natural description. Which in time he perhaps did.

Clare thought that the Suffolk parson-poet George Crabbe 'writes about the peasantry as much like the Magistrate as the Poet—He is determined to show you their worst side'. In a letter to John Taylor, he expressed his preference for Wordsworth over Crabbe, whilst also ridiculing Wordsworth's 'Nursery rhyme' manner. Taylor read out part of the letter at one of his literary dinner parties. Thomas De Quincey, the 'opium-eater' and devoted Wordsworthian, was there. He expressed surprise that Clare should even have made the comparison, since Wordsworth 'sought to hallow and ennoble every subject on which he touched', whilst Crabbe—a deeply unromantic writer—did all he could to make his poetic world 'flat, prosaic and commonplace'. De Quincey went on to defend Wordsworth's ballad 'We are seven'. Despite De Quincey's protestations, Clare was right to say that poems such as this were easily parodied. He himself wrote a brilliant parody of the sonnet on Westminster Bridge. But Wordsworth at his best could lift Clare from his depressions: 'even in this season of dejection', noted De Quincey, 'he would uniformly become animated when anybody spoke to him of Wordsworth—animated with the most hearty and almost rapturous spirit of admiration'.

Among Coleridge's poems, Clare had a particular admiration for 'The Eolian Harp', a hymn of praise to the spirit of divine poetry in nature. (He would have been interested to know that for a time Bloomfield manufactured Aeolian harps, stringed instruments that produced a haunting sound when exposed to the wind.) Wordsworth and Coleridge were, however, past their poetic prime by 1820. Clare was more curious about younger writers, above all Taylor and Hessey's other protégé, John Keats.

He was sorry that they had not met up in London. 'Give my sincere Respects to Keats and tell him I had a great desire to see him and that I like his first vol of Poems much', he wrote to Taylor on returning home to Helpston. Taylor also gave him a copy of Keats's second book, the long poem *Endymion*. He did not get into it for a while, but he eventually liked it very much and found its language 'warm'. He later cited the poem's opening lines, beginning 'A thing of beauty is a joy for ever', as the finest imaginable example of 'the beautiful in poetry'. At the end of June 1820, Taylor sent Keats's new volume, his third and last book, which included the odes, 'The Eve of St Agnes' and the unfinished 'Hyperion'. Clare immediately began picking out 'striking' images, such as the lines in 'To Autumn', 'Season of mists and mellow fruitfulness' and 'Then in a wailful choir the small gnats mourn'.

Clare's one reservation about Keats was the way that he kept up 'a constant allusion or illusion to the Grecian Mythology'. He felt that, like other urban poets, Keats did not know nature at first hand: 'his descriptions of scenery are often very fine but as it is the case with other inhabitants of great cities he often described nature as she appeared to his fancies and not as he would have described her had he witnessed the things he described'. The nightingale of Keats's ode is in a long tradition of poetic nightingales, going back to the ancient Greek myth of Philomel, whereas Clare's 'The Nightingale's Nest' is grounded in natural history.

Just after Clare left London, Taylor showed his poem 'Solitude' to Keats, who observed that 'the Description too much prevailed over the Sentiment'. That summer, Clare was distressed to hear from his publishers that Keats's tuberculosis was approaching its final stages. A blood vessel had burst in his lungs. Taylor and Hessey arranged for the dying poet to go to the warmer climate of Italy for the winter. Despite his terminal illness, Keats was reading Clare and eager to offer advice. At the end of September, Taylor reported that

> Keats is on the Water going to Naples, and has been for nearly a Fortnight ... If he recovers his Strength he will write to you. I think he wishes to say to you that your Images from Nature are too much introduced without being called for by a particular Sentiment.—To meddle with this Subject is bad policy when I am in haste, but perhaps you conceive what it is he means: his Remark is only applicable now and then when he feels as if the Description overlaid and stifled that which ought to be the prevailing Idea.—He likes your first pastoral which ED [i.e. Drury] copied and sent very much indeed.

Clare replied that Keats's advice would not be 'thrown away' if he could help it, 'tho you are well aware of my stubborness'. Keats's criticism was just: the greatest fault in Clare's poetry is an excess of description. He was so eager to do justice to every detail of his environment that he often went on for too long and failed in the art of self-selection.

'I hope poor Keats will return to England as he coud wish', wrote Clare. He did not. On 19 March 1821, Taylor heard that Keats had died in Rome just over three weeks before. 'One of the very few Poets of this Day is gone', he wrote to Clare. '——Let another beware of Stamford', he added, taking the opportunity to give another of his warnings against the town's drinking establishments. Clare responded with a rather conventional sonnet 'To the Memory of Keats'. He felt the poem's inadequacy, the inadequacy of any words. The fate of Keats made him think of his own fate and 'the apathy of mellancholly' descended on him. 'But dear Taylor', he wrote, 'with the affection that one brother feels at the loss of another do I lament the end of poor Keats'. He later asked Taylor for a Keats sonnet in manuscript, so that he could have a specimen of his handwriting as a talisman.

Keats and Clare never met or corresponded directly, though they wished each other well. One day in June 1820, Keats went into Taylor and Hessey's office with some corrections for his new volume of poetry. He scribbled down some revised lines for 'Lamia' on the first piece of paper that came to hand. It was the back of a letter from Clare. Thus their paths crossed like ships in the night. For a while, Clare was much the more famous of the two poets. In 1835 Taylor said that he would have liked to bring out an edition of Keats's poems and letters, but he could not because he would not be able to sell even 250 copies. Then, as Clare fell into neglect in the Victorian era, Keats rose to posthumous fame.

Clare was sorry that he didn't get the chance to correspond with Keats. He was exasperated by some of the self-proclaimed poets who did write to him. He received many letters that began as fan-mail, then modulated into requests for comment on the writer's own work (which was usually hackneyed). Correspondents of a higher class were generous with moralistic advice. Thus James Plumptre, a Cambridgeshire parson with decided opinions on the correct principles for poetry: 'there are many things in your Poems which do not accord with my ideas, as your use of *Fate* and *Fortune*, and some *curses*. I am pleased, however, to see occasional marks of a love for religion . . . You will probably write and publish much more, and I hope you will turn your thoughts towards some instructive popular Songs for the lower classes.' To assist with this prescription, the Reverend Plumptre kindly sent Clare some tracts published by the Society for Promoting Christian Knowledge. Clare told his publisher about Plumptre's interference, and got exactly the right reply: 'Keep as you are: your Education has better fitted you for a Poet than all School Learning in the World would be able to do.'

When real poets wrote, Clare was delighted. He had asked Drury to send a copy of his book to his admired Robert Bloomfield, and in July 1820 he received a letter addressed 'To Mr Clare / Brother Bard, and fellow labourer'. 'Nothing upon the great theatre of what is called the world (our English world)', wrote Bloomfield, 'can give me half the pleasure I feel at seeing a man start up from the humble walks of life and show himself to be what I think you are.' When Clare's second poetry collection was published the following year, he asked Taylor to send Bloomfield a complimentary copy. Bloomfield did not reply for some time, since he was in very poor health by then. 'Neighbour John', he eventually wrote,

> If we were still nearer neighbours I would see you, and thank you personally for the two vollms of your poems sent me so long ago. I write with such labour and difficulty that I cannot venture to praise or discriminate like a critic, but must only say that you have given us great pleasure.
>
> I beg your acceptance of my just published little vollumn; and, sick and ill as I continually feel, I can join you heartily in your exclamation—'What is Life?'

Bloomfield died in pain and poverty a year later.

As with Keats, the two poets hoped to meet but never did. When Clare returned from his second trip to London, the coach passed close to Bloomfield's village of Shefford in Bedfordshire. Clare was drunk on this journey. He wondered afterwards whether, had he been sober, he would have stopped off and called on his fellow-poet. On his third visit to London, in 1824, he met Thomas Inskip, a literary-minded Shefford watchmaker who had known Bloomfield. 'Why did not you come, Clare, before he died?' asked Inskip (who, years later, would correspond with Clare in the Northampton asylum). Clare composed a trio of fine sonnets in Bloomfield's memory and even contemplated writing his biography. 'In my opinion', he told Inskip,

> he is the most original poet of the age and the greatest Pastoral Poet England ever gave birth too—I am no Critic but I always feel and judge for myself—I shall never forget the pleasures which I felt in first reading his poems—little did I think then that I should live to become so near an acquaintance with the Enthusiastic Giles* and miss the gratification of seeing him at last—I am grievd to hear of his familys misfortunes—w[h]ere are the icy hearted pretenders that came forward once as his friends—but it is no use talking—this is always the case—neglect is the only touchstone by which true genius is proved.

*The protagonist of Bloomfield's *Farmer's Boy*.

CHAPTER NINE

'EXPUNGE EXPUNGE!'

Towards the end of March 1820, Clare received a letter from Taylor congratulating him on his marriage. It was sent together with eight complimentary copies of the second edition of *Poems, Descriptive of Rural Life and Scenery* and some morally high-fibre books that were a gift from Lord Radstock. The letter also contained the news that Taylor's correspondence with Edward Drury was 'not as amicable' as he could wish. 'Have you any Letters of his,' Taylor asked Clare, 'wherein he speaks of the Share I took in bringing out the Poems?—or any later Letters referring to the Agreement?' The price was being paid for the lack of a formal agreement laying out the rights and benefits of all three parties.

The chief bone of contention was the agreement with Drury that Clare had signed on 1 January, whereby the poet received a quarter-share of the profits from his works. Taylor thought that this was not only exploitative but presumptuous, in that his firm had done all the work of printing and promoting Clare. Drury was hurt by the accusation. He was the one who had 'discovered' Clare, shown the poems to Taylor, and assisted the poet with his day-to-day financial needs. Taylor and Hessey had sold the complete run of the first edition of the poems, and yet they had not been forthcoming with a substantial cash payment for its author. Taylor threatened to have no further dealings with Drury; he complained that his cousin simply refused to see how badly he had treated Clare by making him sign the agreement. From Drury's point of view, it was Taylor who was being unreasonable:

> I humbly conceive that I have made every reasonable concession that can be expected of me: I know my power too well to be bullied out of it and it is of very little import to me what the world chooses to say of me; *I* am like the insect on a falling tree, too small and insignificant to be injured. Do not an injustice to Clare or me by any ill-advised proceeding, but consider well whether you have any cause to be angry before writing your next letter to me; for if after this plain answer to your prejudices you still continue disaffected towards me I can of course feel no confidence in you and our intercourse ceases.

Taylor regarded this as a 'very unsatisfactory' answer, but he despaired of getting any other. It looked for a time as if the Stamford-London partnership would break up. Where would that leave Clare?

A few weeks later Drury backed down. He saw that the dispute was hurting Clare, and he did not want to get on the wrong side of the mighty Marquess of Exeter, who had been advising the poet against enslaving himself to his booksellers. He gave the ill-conceived written agreement to his brother, who took it to London. Richard Woodhouse, lawyer to the firm of Taylor and Hessey, read it, made a memorandum and destroyed it. 'So you are again a free Man', Taylor told Clare.

Taylor and Hessey proposed a new arrangement whereby they would give Clare 'at least *half* of all the Profits that may arise from the present or future Works' and that they would take 'all Responsibility of publishing upon themselves alone'. Though the 'published and unpublished Works of John Clare' would remain 'under the Management of T & H', Drury would be given a half-share in all residual profits after the deduction of expenses and of sums given to the author. Certain ambiguities did, however, remain. In particular, it was not made explicit whether the hundred pounds contributed by Taylor and Hessey to Clare's trust fund was an independent gift or a payment out of his share of the profits. Clare assumed that it was a gift.

Despite Drury's humiliation over the publishing agreement, he remained a loyal supporter. He stressed the need for Clare to write in his own voice and from his own experience rather than literary convention: 'One great thing is the identifying *yourself* with the subject ... You always excel when you write as you would have spoken and acted in the reality ... infuse more *reality* into your songs ... you have a talent within you of which you are scarcely aware as yet'. On the cover of the letter in which he gave this excellent advice, he added an encouraging postscript: 'You are as good as Hogg!' (a reference to another much-admired labouring-class poet, James Hogg, 'the Ettrick Shepherd'). Drury's good judgement is also apparent in his letters to Taylor about the new poems that Clare was working on in 1820: 'If I am not mistaken Clare's talent is shown stronger in the present collection than in that printed:—but it ... should be left as much as possible in its native roughness:—all polishing of words & numbers lessens the interest his writings excite.'

Drury suggested subjects for poetry, proposing for instance that Clare should try his hand at a pastoral drama. He advised on financial affairs and kept Clare up to date with gossip ('Earl Spencer has lost his youngest son the Hon. Capt Spencer, who has been killed in a duel with his Lieutenant'). He also offered practical help. Early in 1820, Clare's mother had injured the middle finger of her right hand. The wound was not properly treated. By July it had turned badly septic. Drury went in a gig to fetch the old woman. He took her to Stamford's best surgeon, who got to work with his knife. But the wound did not heal well, so Ann Clare had to remain in Stamford. Drury arranged lodgings close to the surgeon's house. He visited her twice a day. Clare himself visited on alternate days, his wife or sister on the intermediate ones. Mrs Gilchrist and the Simpsons rallied round. Drury reported the prognosis to Hessey in London:

> The surgeon can hardly pronounce how the case may turn out, as the dropsical tendency of the patient and her age in a manner defy the usual mode of treating the cancer: but as far as my own

judgment extends I think the poor woman very bad. Her hand
is lifeless, and there are severe shooting pains through the dead
fingers which occasionally shoot up the arm to the shoulder.
The old woman is very weak also and with no appetite though
we get every kind of delicacy to tempt her to eat. John is very
careful and attentive.

He was unduly pessimistic. Three weeks later Ann Clare was well
enough for Drury to take her home to Helpston. He paid the surgeon's bill and all other expenses in Stamford.

Passing through Huntingdon on his first journey to London, Clare
had been more moved by the poet Cowper's house than Lord Protec-
tor Cromwell's. Similarly, his letters of these years reveal a far deeper
interest in poetry than in politics.

He could not, however, avoid the great public question of 1820: the
problem of the royal marriage. The Prince of Wales had been estranged from his wife Caroline for many years. Now he had come to
the throne as King George IV and wanted her out of the way. Caroline
was offered a substantial annuity in return for renouncing the title of
queen and going to live permanently abroad. She refused, so the government instituted proceedings against her for adultery. 'Are you "St
Caroline" or "George 4th"?' Clare asked Hessey, 'I am as far as my
politics reaches "King and Country"—no Inovations in Religion and
government say I.' Allegiance to the King or the Queen became a
political test, with liberals rallying to the Queen's cause and tradi-
tionalists standing by the monarchy.

Drakard's radical *Stamford News* was pro-Queen, Newcomb's conservative *Stamford Mercury* pro-King. Clare's position pleased Lord
Radstock and Mrs Emmerson, but he was going against the grain of
popular opinion and he had to keep his head down in December when
there was a great local celebration in response to the news that parliament had abandoned the bill that would have deprived the Queen
of her rights. When she died eight months later, Clare looked back on
the whole business with disgust: 'I'm of no party but I never saw such
farcical humbug carried on in my life before and I never wish to see

it agen for its lanched me head over ears in politics for this last twelvemonth and made me very violent when John Barleycorn inspird me.' Clare was for king and country, rather than the martyred Queen. Yet he was also acutely conscious of the gap between the rich and the poor and of the double standard by which their sins were judged. In July 1821 he published a poem on this theme in the pro-radical paper, *Drakard's Stamford News*.

The violence of local politics in this period is brought vividly alive in a letter from Clare to Taylor, written in February 1821: 'Drakard the Editor of the *Stamford News* has been severly beaten this week in a rather cowardly way by a person coming in with the excuse of buying a book who while D. turnd to look [for] it cudgeld him with a stick and rid off'. The man with the horsewhip, and a footman for company, was no less a personage than Lord Cardigan, a local Tory grandee who had made a modest contribution to Clare's trust fund (years later his son would lead the ill-fated charge of the light brigade, immortalised by Tennyson).

The political temperature had been raised nationally by the 'Peterloo massacre' of September 1819, when armed militia had charged into the crowd during a peaceful demonstration in Manchester. A new word entered the political lexicon and was much bandied around in pamphlets and caricatures: 'radical'. For a 'church and king' traditionalist such as Lord Radstock, it was essential that Clare's work should in no way smack of radicalism. He used his influence to interest the Bishop of Peterborough in the new poet within his diocese. Emmerson reported to Clare that 'Lord R——, to convince the Bishop of the purity of your political principals, read some extracts from a letter which you wrote me on the subject of the Q——'s conduct, and your sentiments of Loyalty and attachment to your King and Constitution; with which, the Bishop expressed himself much pleased'.

Early in May 1820 Radstock wrote to Eliza Emmerson, referring to his efforts to persuade his fellow-noblemen to contribute to the poet's trust fund: 'How truly dear Clare is to me, let my every days exertions in his favor tell.' But he then gave her some firm instructions:

If you are determined to serve poor Clare——you *must do your duty*! You must tell him to expunge certain highly objectionable passages in his 1st Volume before the 3rd Edition appears, passages, wherein, his then depressed state hurried him not only into error, but into the most flagrant acts of injustice; by accusing those of pride, cruelty, vices, and ill directed passions——who are the very persons by whose truly generous and noble exertions he has been raised from misery and despondency.

He went on, warming to his theme:

It has been my anxious desire of late, to establish our poet's character, as that of an honest and upright man——as a man feeling the strongest sense of gratitude for the encouragement he has received——but how is it possible I can continue to do this if he suffers another Edition of his poems to appear with those vile, unjust, and now would be ungrateful passages in them?—— no, he must cut them out, or I cannot be satisfied that Clare is really as honest and upright as I could wish him!——tell Clare if he has still a recollection of what I have done, and am still doing for him, he must give me unquestionable *proofs*, of being that Man I would have him to be——*he must expunge expunge*!

Eliza copied this letter to Clare. Much as it grieved her, she felt duty-bound to urge him to comply with his Lordship's wishes. She had herself already expressed her concern about the lines in question:

Let me now entreat you, as a true friend, as a Sister——to write immediatly to Mr Taylor, and desire him *from yourself*, to expunge the objectionable lines——you have them *marked* in the vol^m I sent you——for alas! they were named to me but too soon after your poems were published——as conveying '*Radical* and ungrateful sentiments', and I in consequence ventured to *note* them so pointedly in the margin, hoping you would withdraw them of your own accord, after the 1st Edition:——It is *not* now too late, to undo all the mischief——And it will be honorable in you, now that you enjoy blessings before unknown to you, and the severe privation of which, alone induced you to exclaim against the higher classes of society! *freely* then, my friend, withdraw every offending line, it will be *worthy* of your *honest, noble Nature*. There are 10 lines in the 'Helpstone' beginning with 'Accursed wealth'—and also one sadly disliked in your beautiful poem on 'Genius'—'That necessary tool to wealth and pride'. I ventured to write a line on the margin to substitute this—and I thought it connected the subject very well—if you will indulge me by adopting this line, no person can ever know it, or indeed any other alteration I presumed to suggest in my marginal notes:—I would be your friend!

She then went on to tell Clare that he would be pleased to hear that Lord Radstock had sufficiently recovered from his fall downstairs to be able to get out in his carriage. A postscript added insult to injury: Eliza informed Clare that Lord Radstock would send him *Walker's Dictionary* so that he could improve his language. 'And he wishes you to study the principals—viz—spelling, pronunciation, and grammatical sense—these, are very essential to you as a poet'. (It has to be said that her own spelling and grammatical sense were not always perfect.)

The same day as Mrs Emmerson, Captain Sherwill, also under pressure from Lord Radstock, wrote to Clare with a similar request to remove the offending lines. Clare immediately capitulated, though not to the extent of adopting Eliza's proposed alternative line in 'Dawnings of Genius':

Dear Taylor
Being very much botherd latley I must trouble you to leave out the 8 lines in 'helpstone' beginning 'Accursed wealth' and two under 'When ease and plenty'—and one in 'Dawnings of Genius' 'That nessesary tool'—leave it out and put ***** to fill up the blank—this will let em see I do it as negligent as possible—d—n that canting way of being forcd to please I say—I can't abide it and one day or other I will show my Independance more stron[g]ly than ever—you know who's the promoter of the scheme I dare say—I have told you to order and therefore the fault rests not with me while you are left to act as you please
                              Yours   John Clare

Eliza's letter had suggested that to make up for the folly of the lines on 'Accursed wealth', Clare should write a poem for Radstock on the subject of 'Gratitude'. He told her that he would. In her next letter she said, 'I like *your idea* of a poem on Gratitude'.

Taylor did not bow to pressure so quickly. 'I am inclined to remain obstinate', he told Clare, 'and if any Objection is made to my Judgment for so doing I am willing to abide the Consequences'. He saw Mrs Emmerson and told her—no doubt with some pleasure—that two thousand copies of the third edition of *Poems, Descriptive* had already been printed off, so it was too late for any alterations. And he was scornful of the idea of a forced poem on gratitude: 'I like your Independence, Clare, and am sorry that any persons should be so ill judging as to try to screw you up to the Squeak of Flattery.—Take your own Course; write what you like.'

Radstock's attempt at censorship inevitably strained Clare's relationship with Eliza Emmerson. Impulsive and depressive herself, she was quick to take offence (even when no offence was meant) but equally quick to make up. In one letter she says how upset she has been to hear that Clare has told Drury that he is 'oppressed and harrassed by the *laborious correspondence*' he is obliged to keep up. That Clare confided this to a *man* has made the implied offence to her much worse. But with her next letter she sends half a dozen silver teaspoons and a pair of sugar-tongs with her name engraved on them, together with a portrait miniature of herself which she wants Clare to keep in his '*own private drawer*'. In the next, she becomes the spokeswoman for Radstock's discontent. Yet in the one after that she offers to counsel Clare with respect to his 'domestic troubles'. Then she becomes flirtatious: 'Would to God I could do that, for you, which my heart dictates ... I will as "unblushingly" add, pray let me enjoy my share of your kindest ~~feelings~~ regard.' The striking-through is suggestive, especially as she quickly goes on to say that Patty must always remain in 'the warmest corner' of his heart and that she only wants to be the 'second best inmate' of his bosom.

When the third edition of *Poems, Descriptive* arrived in Stamford in July, Octavius Gilchrist could not discover any changes in it. But when Clare looked at it, he found to his intense annoyance that 'Dolly's Mistake' and 'My Mary' had been removed. 'The Country Girl' had already been taken out in the second edition. Taylor was standing firm on the question of political censorship, but had already acted on the concern that had come from several quarters with regard to the indelicacy of these poems. Two of them were about extramarital sex and the third was written in a ribald style.

Clare wrote to Hessey, 'cursed mad'. Taylor's judgement had gone 'a button hole lower' in his opinion: 'it is good—but too subject to be tainted by medlars' *false delicacy*—damn it I hate it beyond every thing those primpt up misses brought up in those seminaries of mysterious wickedness (Boarding Schools)'. One is reminded of Keats's reported comment the previous year when Woodhouse, acting on behalf of Taylor and Hessey, objected to a sexually explicit stanza in 'The Eve of St Agnes': 'He says he does not want ladies to read his poetry: that he writes for men'.

Clare wrote for 'the multitude' and he thought that his ordinary readers particularly liked 'Dolly's Mistake' and 'My Mary'. 'I know his taste and know his embaresments', Clare continued in his letter to Hessey about Taylor. 'I often picture him in the midst of a circle of "blue stockings" offering this and that opinion for emprovement or omision—I think to please all and offend [none] we shoud put out 215 pages of blank leaves and call it "Clare in fashion".' Hessey tried to reply diplomatically, saying that it wasn't really worth inquiring whether Taylor's delicacy in making the omission was 'false or true'. For him, the important point was that the continual objection to the offending poems in such prominent places as the *Morning Post* might have the effect of damaging the book's sale. Taylor and Hessey knew that genteel female readers constituted the prime market for poetry such as Clare's. It was of paramount importance not to offend their sensibilities. The decision was a commercial one, in no way comparable to interference of Radstock's kind.

By the autumn of 1820, *Poems, Descriptive* was heading towards a fourth edition. Radstock remained insistent about 'Accursed wealth'. Taylor told Clare that it was time to back down: 'Lord R. had expressed his Intention of disowning you in such strong Terms, unless the radical Lines as he calls them were left out, that I conceived it would be deemed improper in me as your Friend to hold out any longer'. The cut was duly made. Taylor reassured Clare: 'When the Follies of the Day are past, with all the Fears they have engendered, we can restore the Poems according to the earlier Editions'. But there was no fifth edition.

The differences between Taylor and Hessey on the one hand, and Radstock and Emmerson on the other, blew up again in December 1820 when planning began in earnest for the publication of Clare's second collection of poetry. The lord and the gentlewoman took it upon themselves to stand up for Clare in the matter of his finances. He should not commit his next book to Taylor and Hessey without a written agreement in advance. Radstock asked to be consulted about the terms. He took it as a snub when Taylor declined a dinner invitation (to include haunch of venison), pleading pressure of work. There was a sharp exchange of letters, which Taylor concluded frostily: 'I will write to Clare to know whether we are to treat with him, or your Lordship, for the Copyright of his next volume; and upon his answer will depend whether I shall again have the honour of addressing your Lordship.' The next day he did indeed write to Clare: 'Unless you commission Lord R. to interfere in this Matter I know of no Right that he has to write to me on the Subject.' Mrs Emmerson, meanwhile, attempted to ease the situation, but only aggravated it, by sending Clare copies of the curt letters that had passed between his publisher and his patron. In her view, Radstock was Clare's 'literary Parent', a person to be valued above his mere publisher. Clare replied to her the day after Christmas, in a letter revealing his 'extreme agitation of mind'.

The quarrel was a storm in a teacup and caused unnecessary stress to Clare. Radstock's proposal was exactly the same as Taylor and Hessey's, namely that Clare should have a full half-share of the profits from his work. The animosity had more to do with nuances of respect than questions of money. Radstock was an old man whose first contacts with literature had come at a time when aristocratic patronage was still a plausible means of subsistence for poets. Taylor belonged to a new generation. He was a Non-conformist businessman for whom publishing was a commercial affair that had nothing to do with deference to the whims of blue-blooded patrons. In becoming a celebrated author, Clare found himself not only torn from his own world of rural labour, but also torn between the very different assumptions and manners of the aristocracy and the middle classes.

He realized that his first loyalty was to his publisher. He agreed that Lord Radstock was interfering unnecessarily, and suggested that Woodhouse should draw up an agreement that gave copyright to Taylor and Hessey in all his work, past and future, in return for a half-share in the profits. Taylor replied graciously, saying that he could not possibly enter into an arrangement so potentially detrimental to the poet. Taylor and Hessey's usual policy was to buy the copyright of a work outright, in return for a single lump-sum payment. They would take the loss if a book failed and the profit if it succeeded. The offer of a half-share of profits and the refusal to let Clare bind himself to them in perpetuity show how exceptionally well disposed they were towards him.

All the parties in these publishing disputes meant well, but their unseemly squabbling put Clare in a very awkward position. He needed Drury as his local contact, but he also needed Taylor and Hessey as his means of access to the London publishing scene. And he also needed the assured income that could only be provided by the trust fund, towards which Radstock had contributed so much. He showed considerable tact—not a quality that came to him naturally—in managing to remain on terms of warm friendship with one and all.

On 2 April 1820 Clare wrote to James Hessey, thanking him for the fiddle sent as a wedding present. 'I am a blunt fellow', he remarked as he went on to reflect upon his encounters with the 'Celebrated London Writers and Painters'. 'You will readily excuse my silly remarks', he added, 'it is only for your own eye—I shall never get that polish which some recomends to me I cant abide it—I write to you and

T[aylor] as I shoud to a Country friend—I tell you my most simple opinions of things that strike me in my own rude way as I should have done 3 or 4 years back.' Towards the end of the letter, Clare told Hessey that he had written a good many sonnets. He gave the titles of the two he liked best, but added in parenthesis that 'Taylor has took all the pride away that I had in the poetical line of judging'.

Publishers, who are businessmen as well as book lovers, have always found it difficult to handle writers tactfully—poets especially. For Taylor and Hessey, the handling of Clare was probably the most delicate and time-consuming literary task of their publishing partnership. Clare's country bluntness and lack of polish—his 'own rude way'—had to be nurtured. These were the qualities that enabled them to market him as the peasant phenomenon; furthermore, the more poems he wrote, the clearer it was becoming that his plain style produced his most original work. At the same time, for Clare to make a national impact he had to be brought to London and introduced to influential figures in both the literary world and polite society. There was a danger that a taste of this world would cut him off from the sources of his poetic power.

The presentation of the poems was as much of a problem as the handling of the man. Clare needed encouragement to keep on writing, but once he began writing he could not stop, so there was an equal need to select and to edit his outpourings. As is revealed by the parenthesis in the letter to Hessey, the acts of selecting and editing took away Clare's confidence in his ability to judge his own work. Had it not been for Drury, Taylor and Hessey, Clare's poems would have been unpublishable, but in order to make them publishable compromises had to be made on the characteristics that were the essence of Clare.

Particular difficulties arose at those moments when necessary correction passed over into outright censorship, as with the removal of 'all besh-t' from 'My Mary'. In the early years of his career, Clare remained good-humoured about such interventions, as may be seen from his affectionate mockery of Taylor in a comic verse-letter to Captain Sherwill, written in May 1820:

Theres T[aylo]r muses good old chuckey
That like a carful hen or duckey
Brought off her brood that long unlucky
Unhatchd had lain
And where bad words their plumes did muckey
Washt out the stain.

Eventually, however, Clare's working relationship with his publishers broke down. Neglect and mental collapse soon followed. Biographers and critics have therefore been easily tempted to blame Taylor and his colleagues for the catastrophes that befell the poet.

The orthodox view in the second half of the twentieth century was that Clare was a perpetual 'victim'—first of interfering editors, then of ignorant doctors. A belated attempt was made by modern scholars to 'free' him from the control of Taylor. It was proposed that the best way of doing justice to the 'rude way' of his poetry was to publish it in the unpolished form in which it appeared in his original manuscripts—unpunctuated, unedited, highly irregular in spelling and punctuation. Yet it would never have occurred to Clare that his poetry could be published in this form. He expected his editors to insert punctuation and to correct his spelling.* And he actively sought advice with regard to every aspect of his writing. Even as a boy, he had tested out his first poetic efforts on his parents and his friend Tom Porter. The 'restoration' of his poems to their original manuscript form buys into what has been called 'the myth of solitary genius'. It erases the enormous contribution to Clare's poetic development that was made by such friends as Drury, Taylor, Hessey, Eliza Emmerson and Joseph Henderson (head gardener at Milton Hall, whom we will meet later).

The correspondents most valued by Clare were those with whom he could discuss his work, often in considerable technical detail. His poetic gift cut him off from his fellow-labourers in Helpston, so it was all the more important to him that he should become part of what may properly be called a community of letters. He kept his incoming

*See further, Appendix: Clare's Text.

correspondence, carefully ordering the letters and stitching them together into hand-made books.

Drury and Taylor were his most important collaborators, but his lost letters to Eliza Emmerson were packed with musings and debates about the art of poetry. Tantalising fragments, such as a discussion of the importance of '*breaks and pauses*' in poetic writing, can be reconstructed from her surviving replies. Difficult as it was for Clare to accept criticism, he wanted his poems to be read critically before they were committed to print. He wanted to improve the technical mastery of his work.

Sometimes one senses that he deliberately played up to the image of peasant 'rudeness' in order to elicit the response that his work was not rude at all, but highly sophisticated. In May 1820 he told Taylor that 'I have been trying songs and want your judgment only either to stop me or to set me off at full gallop which your disaproval or applause has as much power to effect as if spoken by a magijian—the rod of critiscism in your hand has as much power over your poor sinful ryhmer as the rod of Aaron in the Land of Egypt'. He then wrote out a song beginning 'Swamps of wild rush beds and sloughs squashy traces' and explained that 'I measured this ballad today wi the thrumming of my mothers wheel—if it be tincturd wi the drone of that domestic music you will excuse it after this confession'. Yet the three-stanza song is beautifully accomplished in rhyme, rhythmic variation, controlled alliteration and vivid imagery. You would never know that it had been composed to the steady click of a spinning-wheel.

Ned Drury sensed that the more famous Clare became, the more control his London publisher would take. Whereas his own input had been vital to the preparation of *Poems, Descriptive of Rural Life and Scenery*, he had much less to do with the editing of Clare's second collection. In July 1820 he asked if he could keep the poet's earliest manuscript-book, 'A Rustic's Pastime, in Leisure Hours', as a memento of their collaboration. Clare gave it to him with a generous inscription: 'These leaves of scribbling that only deserve and certainly woud have been obliterated by the flames had not friendships warm atachments interposed to retrieve them from so just a fate are left to E. Drury as desired. Helpstone July 1820 John Clare.' There is no reason to doubt that, had it not been for Drury, Clare might have burnt all his poems and abandoned his vocation. But one gets the feeling that Clare is now moving on and leaving Drury behind. Despite being marginalised by Taylor, Drury continued to read and comment on Clare's writing. Nearly two years after ceding control of publication to his cousin, he was still copying out poems. He professed himself struck mute with admiration for one called 'The Last of Autumn', in which he found 'a sweet strain of reflexion, pensiveness, and regret'.

His father's acute rheumatism, his mother's hand injury, the novelty of marriage and Patty's move to Helpston, the new baby, the physical effort of working in the fields as well as writing and polishing poems for a second collection, the quarrel between Drury and Taylor, Radstock's demands, fan-mail (some desired, some not) to answer, the need to respond to the suggestions for poetic revisions and new subjects that came from Drury, Taylor and Emmerson: within a few months of the publication of his first book, Clare was under strain of a kind for which he had scarcely been prepared by life as a gardener and lime-burner.

In April 1820 he paid a courtesy visit to one of his early supporters, Dr Francis Willis, owner of the private lunatic asylum at the nearby village of Greatford. Passing over Lolham Bridges on the way home, he collapsed in a quasi-epileptic fit. 'Wether I lay down or fell down I cant tell but when I came to my self my hat was lying at a distance frome me and my coat was rather dirtied.' He was afflicted with shiverings for the next few weeks. Taylor suggested that he should be bled and purged and have a pitch-plaster placed on his chest; he was also concerned that Clare was overworking. Maybe it was not a coincidence that in a letter of this time Clare referred to his periods of rapid, prolific poetic composition as being 'in the fit'. A Peterborough doctor, Fenwick Skrimshire, was called in. Drury was concerned: 'Follow Dr Skrimshire's directions *particularly*; but I could wish that your Mother would tell him how little you eat; for I fancy he is not aware of that.' Skrimshire was a man of varied accomplishments, not all of them medical. He shared Clare's interest in natural history and the study of birds' eggs in particular.

Captain Sherwill thought that he was suffering 'some effect of mind' as a result of his success—and Clare's health did indeed improve when he began spending more time in the down-to-earth company of his fellow-villagers. But from this period onward, ill health of one sort or another recurred every few months. In November, he told Eliza Emmerson of 'depressions' and 'phantasies of the brain' in which his imagination was taken over by 'demons'. Hessey sent a barrel of oysters, saying that he would find them very nourishing and good for his health. Both early and late in 1821, he was again confiding to Emmerson that he had 'nervous fears', a sense of being 'mentally afflicted' and recurring visions of 'blue devils'. He wrote to her of his 'dread of Death' and fear of 'dropping-off'. She empathised, having had her own experience of what she called 'nervous depression'.

Sometimes he would write poetry with manic energy, but on other occasions he was unable to raise his pen. He often needed the stimulus of his publisher's urgings: 'the fact is if I cannot hear from John Taylor now and then I cannot rhyme—I dont know the reason but so it is.' Taylor's support was not always forthcoming, due to pressure of business and the fragility of his own health.

It was a time of great turmoil on the London literary scene. In March 1821 Taylor wrote to Clare in considerable distress with news that John Scott, editor of the *London Magazine*—the journal that had launched Clare's career the previous year—had died as a result of a wound inflicted in a duel with a representative of the editor of a rival magazine. Taylor and Hessey soon took over publication of the *London*; poems by Clare frequently appeared in its pages.

At exactly the time when Scott was gunned down, and whilst the news that Keats had coughed his last blood was on its way back to England, Clare was preoccupied with another death sentence:

> My two favourite Elm trees at the back of the hut are con-
> demned to dye——it shocks me to relate it but tis true——the sav-
> age who owns them thinks they have done their best and now he
> wants to make use of the benefits he can get from selling them
> ... I have been several mornings to bid them farewell——had I
> £100 to spare I woud buy their reprieves——but they must dye——
> yet this mourning over trees is all foolishness they feel no pain
> they are but wood cut up or not——a second thought tells me I am
> a fool ... this is my indisposition and you will laugh at it.

Far from laughing at Clare's 'indisposition', Taylor told the story
about his care for the elms in the introduction to the poet's second
book, as a way of revealing his extraordinary sensitivity to nature.
Clare was not well at this time, but the very fact that he recognised
as much shows that he was by no means out of his mind: 'I am in that
muddy melancholy again——my ideas keep swimming and shifting in
sleepy drowsiness from one thing to another——this letter will denote
the crazy crackd braind fellow it has left behind.' The 'savage' who
had condemned the trees at the bottom of Clare's garden was a prosperous local landowner named Mr Addy. Drury interceded with him
on Clare's behalf and won a reprieve for the elms.

The letter bringing this news was tarnished by the less welcome
information that Drury had reason to believe that Clare's local supporters, such as General Birch Reynardson and Dr Willis, disliked his
'connexions' and considered him 'a radical man' in consequence of
his intimacy with Gilchrist (whom Taylor had proposed as a buyer
for the trees). Drury was concerned about any association with the
world of religious Dissent; he hoped that the poetry of nature would
restore Clare to more orthodox piety: 'I am glad the rhyming fit is
on again, for if you rightly direct your views it will lead you from
"Nature to Nature's God." ' Once again, Clare's anxieties were aggravated as he was torn between different factions.

In May 1821 his eleven-month-old daughter was very ill and
Patty's difficult second pregnancy was far advanced——Drury noted
that her bump was 'monstrous'. In early June, Clare wrote that 'Ex-

pectation is at its height'. He had two births in mind, those of his second child and his long-delayed second book.* But he was in a state of great agitation about the prospects of both. It was at this time that he wrote his sonnet in memory of his own twin sister, who had died in early infancy.

Perhaps he had a premonition. Eleven days later Patty gave birth to 'a fine Boy'. But the baby died within twenty-four hours. Clare immediately wrote Taylor with the sad news: 'Its gone home agen—I am very nervous, that is to say very crazey.'

His friends offered all the support they could. The Simpsons of Stamford sent practical comfort in the form of ale and potatoes, together with a condolence letter: 'We all Sympathise in the loss of the little anonomous but dry up your tears you may have occasion for them from an opposite Cause for who knows how soon it may be followed by his Brother or a plurality of them … Regards also to Mrs Clare—the Survivor.' Hessey wrote on behalf of Clare's publishers. He sent an immediate payment of the half-yearly dividend on the trust fund, together with 'the deep and sincere Sympathy of all your friends' and an apology that the money was 'so poor a remedy for such Affliction as you have met with'.

A high-spirited letter arrived from Eliza Emmerson, who had not heard of the birth and death of the new baby. Clare wrote and told her his news, quoting Jesus's words about how God numbers the fall of every single sparrow. Emmerson responded with a letter full of Christian consolation and exhortations to submit to the divine will. She commended Clare's reference to the sparrow and said—with her characteristically extreme sensibility—that whenever she plucked a flower she regretted depriving one of nature's lovely objects of its vegetable existence. She then suggested that if his next child were to be a girl, he should give it her own names, Eliza Louisa.

Her letters were becoming increasingly intimate. By the end of the year she was asking whether her little namesake was on the way and

---

*The final sheet of proofs (bar the introduction) had at last been sent by Taylor.

telling Clare that she wanted to invite him to London for Christmas, but could not because her husband was abroad and '*cold decorum*' would not allow her to entertain another man whilst she was home alone. Mr Emmerson was often away in Paris, dealing in art. Eliza was now thirty-nine, eleven years older than Clare. She was lonely and childless.

With the death of his first son, Clare lost interest in the progress of his second collection of poetry. When its two volumes were once again delayed in the press, he grimly joked to his publisher that he would wear his black waistcoat in mourning 'for the last twin childern which I fancy are still born and gone hom agen'—that last phrase being the very one he had used when telling Taylor about the real dead baby a few weeks before.

Around this time he wrote an unpublished poem on his favourite theme of childhood joy. It includes a pair of stanzas in which he comforts himself with the thought that his baby has gone to heaven, escaping the troubles and the doubts that come with growing up:

> I can't repine
> Though thou art now another's, blest above
> With better joys and better love than mine
> And mix'd with nature that is all divine.
> Creeds disagree: no matter, thou'rt at rest.
> No sin, no care on this vain earth was thine.
> If thou art not, religion's all a jest.
> But why should parents doubt, my cherub, thou art blest?
>
> Thou scaped all anguish that grows up with man,
> All doubts and fears and terrors that ensue
> When reason gains on thought a mighty span
> And stretches round the mind a boundless view
> That ends in mist where truth however true
> Must have its doubt to shadow at its side.

This is a poem that suggests that Clare's religious faith was shaken by his baby's death. 'Creeds disagree' reveals his impatience with doctrinal differences between the churches. What matters to him is the fundamental belief that the child is at rest. But where? With 'nature that is all divine', as Clare originally wrote, or in heaven 'with cherubs that are all divine', as he later revised the line? Clare seems torn between a sense of the divinity of nature and a more orthodox belief in Christian salvation. And he cannot suppress the darker thought that his baby might not have found peace, in which case religion would be nothing but a cruel joke.

Many times in Clare's life, thoughts of what might have been and a sense of loss turned his mind to Mary Joyce. It was therefore a cruel irony that a few weeks after the loss of the baby he had a chance encounter with her. 'I have had the horrors agen upon me by once again seeing devoted Mary', he informed Taylor in a letter that included a poem called 'Farewell to Mary' ('We met—we loved—we've met the last / The farewell word is spoken . . .'). He told Taylor that he was going to give up writing love poetry and that this 'crazy reverie' would be 'the last doggerel that shall ever sully her name and her remembrance any more'. As far as we know, Clare never did see Mary Joyce again. But the 'Farewell' poem was far from the last thing he would write about her. Some time later he composed a 'Dedication' to her, in which she returned to him like 'beauty floating in a dream' and her 'sweet face' became the symbol or 'type' of the vanished past. A vision of Mary was lodged permanently in his imagination.

CHAPTER TEN

LUBIN'S DREAMS

C lare's main task in 1820 and early 1821 was the preparation for the press of a second major collection of poems. In May 1820 Drury sent Taylor a manuscript book containing copies of what he considered to be the best of the poems written in the course of the previous twelve months. Taylor was amazed at the quantity. Even a quick dip into them, the reading of 'one here and there', revealed that the second volume would 'contain much better things' than the first.

Clare responded to Taylor's surprise: 'you are blind in my manners and plans of writing—when I am in the fit I write as much in one week as woud knock ye up a fair size Vol—and when I lay down the pen I lay it down for a good long while—reccolect the subjects are roughly sketchd in the fields at all seasons with a pencil'. He told Taylor that the poems sent by Drury were not the only ones he had been writing; others had been passed to Octavius Gilchrist. As the months went by, more and more material was forwarded to London. Clare often enclosed new work with his letters to Taylor and Hessey. By the end of 1821 he had written over seven hundred poems, some of great length. Only about two hundred appeared in his first two collections. Others remained in manuscript, many of them unpublished for well over a century.

If Clare were alive today and receiving psychiatric treatment, he would probably be diagnosed as suffering from manic depression, which is technically known as bipolar disorder. Whatever the validity of such a diagnosis in strictly medical terms, judging from Clare's account of how he could write enough poems to fill a book in a week but would then dry up altogether for 'a good long while', *bipolar* and *manic* are fitting terms for his habits of writing.

The sheer quantity of poems meant that Taylor needed several months to select and edit the material for the new volume. He was also slowed by his own poor health, both physical and mental. Much to Clare's frustration, advertisements for his new book began to appear in November 1820 but publication did not take place until September 1821. His poetic style was developing at great speed, with the result that by the time the book was published much of it seemed to its author to be old hat.

One of his new projects was an idea of Drury's. At the very time he released Clare from the publishing agreement that had so angered Taylor, Drury collected a new 'Garland' of songs from Clare's manuscripts. That summer he informed Hessey that he was going to publish a collection of one hundred Clare songs, set to music. He gave an assurance that Clare's writing of these songs did not 'interfere with other compositions', claiming on the contrary that they would be 'no mean embellishment' to the 'newly coming volumes' of more substantial and varied poetry. Hessey had his doubts: there might be copyright difficulties and Taylor really ought to have the chance to exercise his editorial prerogative.

Lord Radstock and Eliza Emmerson were adamant that Clare should not proceed with this project. 'What is the importance of a 100 Songs compared with your 2nd Vol^m of Poems?' asked Emmerson. Radstock said that writing songs for public performance would be bad for Clare's reputation as a man of honour. The theatre was a disreputable institution, and all association with it should be avoided.

After the success of Madame Vestris's rendition of 'The Meeting' at Drury Lane, the Covent Garden soprano Miss Stephens had performed the same poem to the tune of a popular aria from Rossini's latest opera. Clare was again being taken up by rival factions. The publication of a large collection of songs would make more material available to both playhouses—and perhaps the down-market 'illegitimate' theatres would get in on the act as well. This was not the sort of arena in which the pious Radstock wanted Clare's works to circulate. What is more, Drury had enlisted the services of the London music publisher who had given the public Tom Moore's highly popular but distinctly risqué *Irish Melodies*. As he so often did, Clare found himself caught between the conflicting views of his various friends, patrons and publishers.

Drury sent the London publisher, James Power of the Strand, sixty-two of the proposed one hundred Clare songs. Some of them were set up in type. 'I should have protested against them had I seen the Music', objected Taylor. The plan then petered out. No collection appeared, though the following year a number of individual songs were published by the Royal Harmonic Institution with music by the composer and celebrated cellist Frederick Crouch, who had played at the Stamford concert that Clare had attended.

Songs were a pleasant diversion. What Clare really wanted at this time was to develop his narrative art. He craved advice, but was frustrated when presented with conflicting opinions. In earlier poems such as 'The Lodge House' and 'Rob's Terrors of Night or Courting on Ass Back', he had tried turning into verse the 'gossips' tales' of Granny Clare and the other old village women. Now he wanted to produce a whole sequence of narrative poems. Taylor had reservations:

> You must not mind my Criticisms, Clare, but *write away*—Only if you tell a Story again, like the Lodge House, don't let the Circumstances occupy so much of your Attention to the Exclusion of that which is more truly poetical.—I have not Time today to tell you exactly what I mean—But I can conceive that as a Story this of Lodge House may appear to all your Hearers capitally told, and yet that it has not the Superiority about it which makes Good Poetry.—Poets do not tell Stories like other people; they draw together beautiful and uncommon but very happy Illustrations, and adorn their Subject, making as much Difference as there is between a common Etching and a full painted Picture.—But I am sure you know very well [what Po]etry is.

Drury, meanwhile, despite some hesitation over the 'painting of Nature's deformity', was enthusiastic about Clare's plan for a series of linked narratives and sketches of village life:

> My cousin John must give his opinion on the Pastoral I have here sent, which is a specimen of what Clare intends writing to illustrate The Ways of the Village, or Village Scenes: the next topicks he employs his pen upon are Angling, Nutting, Wading, and some Love Adventures to give identity to the plan. He has it in view to make Maggy (the naughty damsel of the above piece) sorry for her misdoings and seeking after Robin again; the same characters will appear very often in the different poems so that when the book is formed the most prominent personages will become old acquaintance with the reader ... I like his taste for my own part but I doubt the public and posterity will not admire his 'breeks' 'shock-head' and shaving soliloquy which are really burlesque. At the same time they form a new order of English Pastorals and it is worth consideration whether that is not a recommendation for him to go on as he has begun.

Taylor's instinct was that Clare's readers wanted lyrical description of natural scenery. Drury took the bolder view that their man should take the risk of persevering with a new kind of pastoral that refused to gloss over what Clare later called 'dirty reality'.

The poem that Drury sent Taylor was Clare's 'first pastoral' in the new mode—the piece that was read and admired by the dying Keats just before he set sail for Italy. This was the first work in which Clare revealed the extent of his gifts in the arts of narrative and characterisation. It established a model for a kind of poetry to which he devoted considerable time and energy. The eventual fruit would be his two major long poems, 'The Parish' and *The Shepherd's Calendar*.

In the summer of 1820 Clare bought a new manuscript book and headed it with one of his hand-inscribed title-pages: 'Village Scenes / and / Subjects on Rural Occupations / By John Clare / the Northamptonshire / Peasant Author of / "Poems on life and Senery" & "Rural Poems & Songs" / Helpstone / August 21 1820'. In the autumn, using his fairest writing hand, he copied into his new manuscript book the 'village scenes' on which he had been working: 'Rural Morning', 'The Crossroads or Haymakers Story', a revision of his old elegy on the cart-horse ('Death of Dobbin'), 'Rural Evening', 'Rustic Fishing', and 'Sunday Walks'. Other pieces in a similar vein were added over the ensuing months, including 'The Widow or Cress Gatherer', 'Jockey and Jinney or First Love', 'The Workhouse Orphan', and 'Maggy's Repentance'. The last of these was the promised sequel to 'Love's Soliloquy', in which Robin's beloved regrets her flirtation with a flashy and fashionable but unreliable footman called Tim instead of the loyal labourer.

Clare was over-optimistic in his assumption that a selection of 'Rural Poems and Songs' would soon be published and that 'Village Scenes' could follow as a third book. A lot of editorial work was still required. Taylor proposed instead to publish a two-volume collection; the sequence of narrative poems together with a selection of songs would form one volume, while the other would be made up of descriptive pieces, sonnets and other poems.

Towards the end of 1820 Clare became disillusioned with his narratives of humble rural life. 'I get on cursed bad with "Ways in a Village"—I find the thing too circumscribd and narrow for ones thinking—always dinging at rural things wornt do'. He wanted to give himself more stylistic 'liberty'. Taylor told him that there was no need to go on adding poems; there were now quite enough 'to make a respectable Volume'.

Just as Clare was expressing his satisfaction with the proposal for a pair of volumes ('your plan cannot be improvd—a second reading of it has pleasd me mightily'), Taylor changed his mind about the structure and emphasis. On 5 January 1821 he sent an account of his editorial work to his brother Jem in the north country:

> This Evening I have completed my Selection of Clare's MS Poems for the next 2 Volumes. There is sufficient for that quantity, all truly good, and therefore we had better publish them at once prefixing his Head to the 1st volume to give Purchasers an additional spur.—It is no light task you are aware to read over *so*

many times as Duty requires I should this poor fellow's cramp Handwriting, and to weigh and consider what he means, and whether he can express it better some other way which I would hint to him, and whether any alteration could make that good which is at present middling—All this is happily so far done that, on the absolute Merit of each piece I am not likely to differ henceforth from my present judgment, tho' on *lines* and *words* there is a good deal of Room yet for Emendation.

The next day he informed Clare that his printer was laying in new type to begin work on the volumes. Proofs would be sent as soon as they were ready. He had, however, looked in more detail than before at Clare's long autobiographical poem, 'The Peasant Boy'. Originally, he had failed to pay much attention to it because Drury had sent it with a pencil-note saying 'let it pass in Oblivion'. Now Taylor had found, to his surprise and satisfaction, that 'it would constitute the greatest Ornament of the new Work'. The poem should appear first, with a new title that would also be the title of the two-volume collection: 'The Village Minstrel, and other Poems'.

On receiving Taylor's letter, Clare went back over his 'hasty scribbld' long poem. He agreed with his publisher: though he had not thought especially well of the poem at the time of writing, on rereading it he found 'some of the best rural descriptions I have yet written'. Once the editorial pencil of Taylor had 'gone over it here and there', it would 'take'.

Taylor must have thought that a lead poem linked to Clare's life-story would be the best way of continuing to hold public attention. The inclusion of the long autobiographical poem meant that there would have to be fewer 'ways of the village' pieces. He chose six of them. The rest were set aside. One called 'The Vicar' was incorporated into Clare's satire 'The Parish'. Others eventually appeared in Clare's third collection, *The Shepherd's Calendar*. Still others remained unpublished until the 1990s.

There was one problem with the new plan of giving prominence to 'The Peasant Boy', or 'The Village Minstrel', as it was now to be called.

Lord Radstock had read the manuscript and put a mark indicating 'This is radical Slang'* beside two of the best stanzas:

> There once were lanes in nature's freedom dropt,
> There once were paths that every valley wound,—
> Inclosure came, and every path was stopt;
> Each tyrant fix'd his sign where paths were found,
> To hint a trespass now who cross'd the ground:
> Justice is made to speak as they command;
> The high road now must be each stinted bound:
> —Inclosure, thou'rt a curse upon the land,
> And tasteless was the wretch who thy existence plann'd.

> O England! Boasted land of liberty,
> With strangers still thou mayst thy title own,
> But thy poor slaves the alteration see,
> With many a loss to them the truth is known:
> Like emigrating birds thy freedom's flown;
> While mongrel clowns, low as their rooting plough,
> Disdain thy laws to put in force their own;
> And every village owns its tyrants now,
> And parish-slaves must live as parish-kings allow.

Taylor told both his brother and Clare that he did not want to cut these lines. He had had enough of Radstock's interference and the lines could not be removed 'without spoiling good poetry'. Besides, it would be the thin end of the wedge to start censoring on political grounds—cut these stanzas and Radstock would then find something else to be unhappy about.

Taylor did, however, propose some cuts to 'The Village Minstrel' for the sake of aesthetic economy. Clare had embedded some self-contained narratives within the poem, a 'Pauper's Story' and a tale of

---

*Just as the use of *radical* in a political sense was new in the early nineteenth century, so was the word *slang*: Radstock's very choice of phrase reeks of disapproval for anything newfangled.

Woodcroft Castle. Taylor regarded these as unnecessary digressions. He also regularised some of Clare's metrical variations and asked him to look again at certain lines. And he queried certain 'Provincialisms':

> We have but few Provincialisms in the poem, and I should be glad if we could get rid of one that is left *himsen*; but if it cannot be easily done never mind.—Real English Country Words are different in my mind and should be judged differently from those which are only peculiar to a district, and perhaps *himsen* and *shanny* are of the latter Class.—Shanny is not used beyond the Trent, tho' himsen is common enough I know.

This comment suggests that he wanted to present Clare's poetry as the authentic voice of the English countryman, whilst avoiding words that could only be understood by Northamptonshire readers.

The title was also a matter for discussion. Taylor did not like Clare's original 'Peasant Boy' because it was too close to Bloomfield's celebrated *Farmer's Boy*. But it was pointed out to him that 'The Village Minstrel' might be thought too close to James Beattie's popular poem of the 1770s, *The Minstrel*, which narrated the poetic growth of a rural 'primitive' in a manner that bore considerable resemblance to Clare's work. Furthermore, both poems used the stanza form that had been pioneered by Edmund Spenser. Drury got involved in this debate. He proposed 'Village Minstrelsy' for the title of the collection, but the retention of 'The Village Minstrel' for the lead poem. He noted that the basis and outline of the poem did resemble *The Minstrel* and that it would therefore be best to present Clare's work as a 'bold challenge' to Beattie's. To reject the title would risk the charge that Clare really had 'secretly and disguisedly' taken Beattie as his model. An alternative 'romantic designation' for the whole book would be 'Lubin—the Village Minstrel'. *Lubin* was the name of the protagonist of the lead poem. Or perhaps 'Wood Notes Wild', an allusion to a famous line of Milton's about Shakespeare singing his native wood-notes wild. 'I am taken with the pleasant sound of Clare's Wood Notes Wild!' said Drury.

Taylor rejected 'Village Minstrelsy' as being 'too like "English Minstrelsy"—a Compilation of Sir Walter Scott's which *did not sell*, and that is another bad Sign'. Having considered other alternatives such as 'The Minstrel Villager' and 'The Village Muse', Taylor decided that the best option was to revert to Clare's original 'The Peasant Boy'. That phrase *did not sell* was enough to make Clare himself reject 'Minstrelsy'. He didn't like the new suggestions either. He thought that Taylor's original title of 'Village Minstrel' stuck in the memory best of all.

This discussion about titles is characteristic of Clare's relationship with his publisher. A selective reading of the evidence would tempt one to suppose that control of Clare's work was wrested from him, but the reality was a process of frank and courteous exchange of views. Taylor preferred Clare's title and Clare preferred Taylor's, whilst Drury was nudged aside: this was symptomatic of how affairs had developed. Early in 1822 Drury left Stamford for Lincoln. He did not, however, lose contact with Clare altogether.

Clare valued and respected Taylor's editing. He agreed with him about the cutting of the 'Woodcroft Castle' digression and was grateful for many local improvements: 'I think your ending of the Minstrel closes capital ... dont alter your mind in adding the verses already omitted for you will certainly spoil it—your alterations of the last lines of each verse cannot be better so I left them untouched.' And in another letter: 'do as you have done for you cant do better—we must as you justly observe have it as free from faults as possible.' Taylor was often diffident about his changes: 'Here the change is decidedly for the worse', he wrote on seeing how one of his revised stanzas looked once set up in proof. It was sometimes Clare who had to insist that the alterations should stand.

At its best, the relationship was one of highly constructive collaborative dialogue. Thus Taylor: 'Perhaps you like the word dropped in two Syll[ables]—if so I will restore it'; 'I did not like your line nor my own first Correction—Can you better this?' And Clare: 'your assistance in such things I find very nessesary and I in fact will not do without it—so in future when you want any alterations youll know how to get them—your omissions in the other poems are capital—I saw their defects and wondered I never saw them before you crossd them out'. Or, in playful but still grateful mood: 'you rogue you, the pruning hook has been over me agen I see in the vols, but vain as I am of my abilities I must own your loppings off have bravely amended them ... friend I believe you are a caterer of profound wisdom in these matters'.

The success of *Poems, Descriptive of Rural Life* had been due as much to the image of Clare as to the poems themselves. In order to sustain that success in the second collection, Taylor asked Clare for a sketch of his life-story, which would enable him to write an introduction that filled in some of the gaps that had been left by the account of the peasant poet in the introduction to his first book. In February and March 1821 Clare wrote his 'Sketches in the Life of John Clare written by himself and addressed to his friend John Taylor Esqr'. He dispatched the manuscript on 3 April. Unlike his later unfinished autobiography, the 'Sketches' were intended as raw material for Taylor's introduction, not for publication in their own right.

Clare's concern through the summer was not the way in which Taylor was dealing with his material, but the slowness of the process. At one point, Drury stirred the pot by saying that he had heard that Taylor and Hessey had been sitting on a set of proofs for a month, without bothering to send them to Clare. Hessey wrote encouragingly in May to say that both he and Taylor were convinced of the superiority of *The Village Minstrel* to *Poems, Descriptive*. A few poems were placed in the *London Magazine* as tasters, though Clare was not sent the extra money he had been promised for this.

By early summer, everything was ready in proof except for the introduction. In August, Gilchrist was in London, telling Taylor that Clare was so upset at the delay that he had taken up drinking again. Taylor dispatched a tetchy letter to Helpston: 'I had thought you felt more Regard for me than to plunge into old Excesses and lay the Sin at my Door'. He said that the whole process of preparing the book would have been a great deal quicker if he had been able to find someone to assist him with the editing. He would gladly have paid for this, but no one apart from himself was able to cope with the poor state of Clare's manuscripts. He reminded Clare that he had suffered from illness and overwork himself, but pointedly stressed his own temperance. The voice of the non-drinking Non-conformist speaks here.

Clare, in turn, was upset at the accusation that he had been complaining about Taylor. He would sooner the volumes were delayed till the Christmas after next than have anyone other than Taylor himself do the editing. When he at last saw the introduction in early September, he thought that it could not have been done better.

On 22 September 1821, James Augustus Hessey finally had the pleasure of sending John Clare a dozen finished copies of his new book. The title-page of each of the two volumes had a quotation from Spenser's *Shepheardes Calender*. Volume one carried a frontispiece: Edward Scriven's engraving of the Hilton portrait. Two thousand copies were printed, with complimentary ones going to Clare's various patrons (Exeter, Milton, Radstock). Eliza Emmerson wrote to congratulate him, describing the book as his second child. This was somewhat tactless in view of the death of his real second child only a few months before.

John Taylor's introduction to *The Village Minstrel, and Other Poems. By John Clare, The Northamptonshire Peasant; Author of 'Poems on Rural Life and Scenery'* included substantial quotation from the poet's autobiographical 'Sketches'. It made public the story of his dealings with Henson, the benefactions of the Fitzwilliams, Exeter and Spencer, and the role of Radstock in establishing the trust fund. A footnote listed the names of the principal contributors to the fund, in order of rank. Prince Leopold* was at the head of the list, followed by three dukes, six earls, four lords, two knights and two gentlemen.

Taylor also mentioned Clare's marriage to 'Patty of the Vale', whose 'portion consisted of nothing beyond the virtues of industry, frugality, neatness, good-temper, and a sincere love for her husband'.

---

*Princess Charlotte, daughter of the Regent, had died in 1817, shortly after being delivered of a stillborn daughter. Leopold was her disconsolate widower.

There is some reason to doubt that she was in truth always characterised by neatness and good temper.

The introduction then explained the origins of the poems in the book: some were up to ten or twelve years old, whilst others had been written since the publication of *Poems, Descriptive*. To show that memory and loss were among Clare's key themes, Taylor then quoted from the letter on the condemnation of the two favourite elm trees. And to stress the grounding of the poems in 'country sports and customs', he reproduced Clare's own explanations of various allusions in 'The Village Minstrel', such as Dusty Miller (a mumming ritual), Fiery Parrot (a flirtation game involving a candle and a tub of water) and Booted Hog (a whipping game at the expense of boys who neglected their duty in the harvest or allowed the pounding of the cattle they were minding). The introduction concluded with Taylor reiterating the claim that Clare's greatest quality was his capacity to make the reader see flowers and trees and inanimate things with new eyes.

The 130 or so poems in *The Village Minstrel* reveal Clare as a far more versatile and accomplished writer than had been apparent from his first book. The main body of the first volume was dominated by the title-poem, which occupied sixty pages. It was followed by a miscellany of poems, with songs and ballads interspersed among descriptive and reflective pieces. The miscellany continued in the second volume, though here the emphasis was on longer poems, including the run of narratives in rhyming couplets that had been intended for the 'Ways of the Village' project. The second volume was rounded off with sixty sonnets and a glossary that Taylor had compiled from information provided by Clare.

Most of the glossary entries consisted of one- or two-word explanations—'Drowk, dropping'; 'Flitting, departing'; 'Hurkles, crouches'; 'Pooty, a snail shell'; 'Water-blobs, the meadow-bught, or marsh-marigold'—but some provided the occasion for little explanatory essays, signed 'J.C.':

> Wood seers.—Insects that lie in little white knots of spittle on
> the backs of leaves and flowers. How they come I don't know, but
> they are always seen plentiful in moist weather, and are one of

the shepherd's weather-glasses. When the head of the insect is seen turned upward, it is said to betoken fine weather; when downward, on the contrary, wet may be expected. I think they turn to grasshoppers, and am almost certain, for I have watched them minutely.

In the next few years Clare would perfect this art of watching minute things minutely and writing of them in exact and evocative prose.

The title-poem was Clare's first attempt at a sustained autobiographical meditation in verse. It tells the story of a 'humble rustic' called Lubin, a thresher's son. He is inspired by 'The charms that rise from rural scenery' and 'the sports, the feelings of his infancy'. A solitary child, he delights in watching animals specking the fields and the church-steeple peeping over the edge of the wood. He is fascinated by rural superstitions, fairy tales and old women's gossip—he regards storytelling as the key to a sense of community and the endurance of village traditions. He has a child's fear of graveyards at night, a love of sequestered places in the day. Youthful hours are filled with the search for snail-shells ('pooty-shells'), the imitation of thrush-song, and a first stumbling attempt to write a poem based on the close observation of a primrose.

Nature seems to sing and Lubin finds a response in his heart. As in the long tradition of eighteenth-century landscape poetry, he loves to view a 'prospect'. But whereas a poet such as Thomson would look down from a hill, Lubin looks up from the ground. His only eminence is a molehill,* where

> oft he dropt him down,
> To take a prospect of the circling scene,
> Marking how much the cottage roof's-thatch brown
> Did add its beauty to the budding green

*The poet (and other characters in many of Clare's poems) frequently sits or lies on what he calls a 'molehill'. Children play on them and in one poem boys light a fire on one. They are also covered with vegetation, notably thyme. These features suggest that Clare was thinking not of molehills but of the dome-shaped grassy mounds, which could be a metre in diameter and half a metre in height, built by the yellow meadow ant (*Lasius flavus*), which was common around Helpston.

> Of sheltering trees it humbly peeped between—
> The stone-rocked wagon with its rumbling sound;
> The windmill's sweeping sails at distance seen,
> And every form that crowds the circling round,
> Where the sky stooping seems to kiss the meeting ground.

Clare positions himself at the centre of a 'circling' landscape. He is fascinated by the horizon because it is the point where the sky meets the earth and completes the circle.

The price of Lubin's absorption in nature is alienation from his fellow-villagers. He watches but does not participate in May Day sports on the green. His love of reading sets him apart. 'Crusoe's lonely isle' is singled out as a favourite story. He is aware that it is a matter for wonder that an ambition in poetry should be developed by someone who has been 'Bred in a village full of strife and noise' among 'Old senseless gossips, and blackguarding boys, / Ploughmen and threshers'. Lubin, dressed in old clothes patched by his mother, feels sympathy for the poor cottagers and 'every woe of workhouse-misery', but the inspiration for his poetry comes from the minutiae of the natural world, right down to the midges that torment the milk-maids during their evening work. His sympathy for all living things makes him hate badger-baiting and cock-fighting.

At the climax of 'The Village Minstrel' comes the protest against enclosure, including the stanzas that Radstock had censured as 'radical Slang'. Lubin laments the nakedness of the landscape after enclosure, then mourns for his own lost youth and innocence. Political anger is subordinated to the affective and the aesthetic. The main focus is the ploughing over of the heath—'not a cowslip on its lap remain; / The rush-tuft gone that hid the skylark's nest'. The sky falls silent as the bird is rendered homeless.

In almost every particular of experience and attitude, 'Lubin' is Clare. But the language and form of the poem are inherited and for the most part conventional. 'The Village Minstrel' marks out the terrain of Clare's later poetry, but he has not yet found a voice that is true to both himself and that terrain. Later, he made the shrewd self-criticism that the problem with the poem was that it did not 'describe the feelings of a ryhming peasant strongly or localy enough'. As Clare matured, his poems became more *local*. Paradoxically, it is through the very quality of locality that he achieves his universality.

After 'The Village Minstrel' comes an 'Effusion', written in the first person and partly addressed to his 'corner-chair', in which Clare expresses surprise at his new-found poetic fame. He adds that he needs to earn money from his work in order to support his aged parents. The impression of humility, quaintness and poverty squares with the image of Clare put forward in Taylor's introduction. The following poem is an 'Address to my Father, on his receiving an easy chair from the Right Hon. Lady ————'. Having borne his rheumatism with resignation, Parker Clare is rewarded by a present from Lady Fitzwilliam. The poem is a public thank-you letter, with the name of the donor discreetly blanked out in deference to the aristocratic desire for private acts of patronage not to be vaunted too vulgarly. Then follows 'Holywell', which traces the walk to the home of General Reynardson. Again, the patron is not named, but the prominent position of the poem is a way of acknowledging his interest in Clare.

The second volume of the collection includes a similar gesture of gratitude to the Earl of Exeter. A poem entitled 'Narrative Verses, written after an excursion from Helpstone to Burghley Park' traces an actual walk whilst at the same time serving as a metaphor for the poet's career as he passes from village to great estate. This device of writing walking poems that serve indirectly as thank-you poems to patrons serves Clare better than the direct expression of humble gratitude. A poem addressed 'To the Right Honorable Admiral Lord Radstock' is embarrassingly deferential:

> And, hour by hour,
> Reflection muses on the good and great,
> That lent a portion of their wealthy power,
> And sav'd a wormling from destruction's fate.
> Oft to the patron of her first essays
> The rural muse, O Radstock, turns her eye,
> Not with the fulsome noise of fawning praise,
> But soul's deep gushings in a silent sigh.

These lines protest too much. Their fulsomeness rings the exact note of 'fawning praise' that they are attempting to avoid.

One turns the page with relief to find a quieter poem, 'The Wild-Flower Nosegay'. Here Clare accurately and unpretentiously enumerates the flowers that he has observed in fields and hedgerows. The poem's final stanza, on the remembrance of 'childish scenes', was one with which he was especially pleased. He told Hessey that it was 'such a favourite of mine that it is the only one I can repeat of any of my poems and my selfish consiet is constantly repeating it'.

The most characteristic poems in *The Village Minstrel* are those where Clare describes himself walking or sitting alone in the countryside, watching and recording the processes of nature. They are written in a variety of different forms. 'The Last of March, written at Lolham Brigs' has an eight-line stanza with intricately woven rhymes. Most of the longer pieces are in couplets with a firm, sometimes monotonous beat and often predictable rhymes. It is in some of the sonnets at the end of volume two that Clare's miniaturist art begins to mature. The following example was first sent to Taylor in a letter dated 14 December 1820, with the comment 'this cold morning has produced a Sonnet for you such as it is':

> The small wind whispers through the leafless hedge
>   Most sharp and chill, where the light snowy flakes
> Rest on each twig and spike of wither'd sedge,
>   Resembling scatter'd feathers;—vainly breaks
> The pale split sunbeam through the frowning cloud,
>   On Winter's frowns below—from day to day
> Unmelted still he spreads his hoary shroud,
>   In dithering pride on the pale traveller's way,
> Who, croodling, hastens from the storm behind
> Fast gathering deep and black, again to find
>   His cottage-fire and corner's sheltering bounds;
> Where, haply, such uncomfortable days
>   Make musical the wood-sap's frizzling sounds,
> And hoarse loud bellows puffing up the blaze.

Many of Clare's early poems are constrained by the bounds of regular metre and strong rhyme, whereas here he begins to find fluidity within the shell of the sonnet form. He is developing the confidence to set up a creative tension between the movement of his verse-lines and the construction of his sentences. Crucially, he allows subject and verb to be separated by the line-endings: 'The light snowy flakes / Rest'; 'vainly breaks / The pale split sunbeam'. There is still an incongruous mix of traditional high poetic diction ('Winter's frowns') and homely vernacular dialect ('croodling', 'frizzling'), but this fault does not detract from the skill whereby the stillness of the winter scene is rendered with a precision and an attention to light that create the verbal equivalent of a water-colour by Peter de Wint.

The reviewers of Clare's first book had spent much of their time expressing amazement that anyone from such impoverished circumstances could write poetry at all. Some of the reviews of *The Village Minstrel*, such as that in the *Gentleman's Magazine*, discussed the improvement in the poet's financial position, but most of the monthly magazines now paid more attention to the strengths and limitations of his work.

The *Literary Gazette* thought that the quality of the collection was mixed, but that several of the poems would 'raise the reputation of the rustic bard above his former fame'. Clare's descriptive powers were praised above his lyrical art. He was compared to George Morland, the painter of humble rustic scenes. The reviewer noted Clare's love of the distinctive landscape around Helpston: 'The rushes, the sedges, the "willow groves," and the sluggish rivulets of a marshy part of Northamptonshire, are to him what the forest, the mountain, the lake, and the ocean, are to other poets.' The title-poem was assumed to be modelled on Beattie's *The Minstrel* but at the same time manifestly autobiographical: 'In the person of Lubin, Clare draws his own portrait, and largely insists on his love of Nature—the grand fountain of all his emotions and of all his writings.' The reviewer was careful to note, though, that Clare was no mere child of nature, but a studious and well-read writer: 'The variety of verse which Clare has tried, shows that he has read a good deal, and studied both our ancient and modern bards.'

The *Literary Chronicle* said that the title-poem alone was enough to 'justify all the praise that has been bestowed on John Clare, who, in vivid descriptions of rural scenery, in originality of observation and strength of feeling, richness of style and delicacy of sentiment, may rank with the best poets of the day, though a humble and untutored peasant.' The *Monthly Magazine*, by contrast, found some things to praise, notably the sonnets, but generally took a loftily condescending view:

> We are willing to give full credit to the motives of those, whose benevolence has prompted them to introduce the effusions of the Northamptonshire peasant to general notice, but we may reasonably doubt how far they have been the means of enriching, in any great degree, our stores of national poetry, or are likely to bind a wreath more permanent than that woven by the caprice of fashion, or the prevailing appetite for novelty, round the brows of the object of their patronage.

This is the voice of a reviewer in love with the sound of his own orotund prose. His judgement reeks of snobbery: he is unhappy at the way that 'Ploughmen, milkmaids, and other similar prodigies have acquired an ephemeral celebrity'. The more encouragement such upstarts receive, the more danger there will be of 'the evil of incompetent intruders into the walks of literature'.

These first reviews appeared in October. The following month the *European Magazine* apologised for not having noticed the volumes earlier and went on to offer high praise of Clare's naturalness. The *New Monthly Magazine*, also in November, emphasised the moral and social worth of Clare's poems: 'he can teach us to feel for his poverty, and for the privations of that large class of society to which he belongs; he can teach us to rejoice in the pleasures and enjoyments, scanty as they may be, that fall to their lot; he can teach us to value their labours, and to extend our charities beyond the cold and calculating limits of parish dues.'

Two months later, the *Eclectic* published a long review, with ex-

tensive quotations. The poems were described as 'perfect in their
kind', despite their 'modest pretensions'. The comparison with the
paintings of Morland, first gestured at in the *Literary Gazette*, was
developed more extensively:

> These poems breathe of Nature in every line. They are, like
> Morland's inimitable drawings, not studies from nature, but
> transcripts of her works: his cattle, his birds, his trees and
> bushes are all portraits. There is a literal fidelity in the sketches,
> which only true genius could keep from sinking into vulgarity;
> while the rural feeling which pervades and characterizes them,
> gives meaning and animation to the tameness of the rural
> scene. The best substitute for a walk in the country—we do not
> mean Hampstead—to those who are immured in the metropo-
> lis, would be, so far as the mind is concerned, the perusal of some
> of the poems of John Clare.

The *London Magazine* ran Taylor's article on his visit to Clare, but no
review—the poet J. H. Reynolds drafted one, but Taylor was not
satisfied with it. Radstock, meanwhile, sent Clare some remarks on
the new poems by an anonymous critic. Clare considered them a mixture of just criticism and 'humbug'.

The Village Minstrel thus benefited from serious attention and a
solidly favourable, if less than ecstatic, consensus of opinion. Sales
were, however, much slower than those of *Poems, Descriptive*. By December, only eight hundred of the two thousand copies had been sold.
Six months after publication Clare told Taylor that he felt 'hipt' (annoyed) at the book's comparatively poor performance. Its predecessor
had sold out two editions in the comparable period of time. He suggested that Taylor should publish a notice in the *London* announcing
another new volume 'as a stimulant to revive the flatness of these'.

Taylor replied that many people had bought the first book because
it was the talk of the town and out of sympathy for Clare's circumstances. This time, the purchasers were 'the real Admirers of Poetry',
whose 'numbers are very few'. He reminded Clare that sales of
Keats's poems still had not reached five hundred. *The Village Minstrel* did eventually achieve sufficient sales to merit a reissue within

a couple of years. On this occasion, the second volume was given an engraved frontispiece in the form of a picturesque drawing of Clare's cottage, giving the false impression that it stood alone rather than in a row of tenements.

Late in 1821, Clare added to his collection of 'Village Scenes' a tale called 'The Fate of Genius'. It was a kind of sequel to 'The Village Minstrel', telling of a rustic poet who, like Lubin (and Clare himself), begins as a solitary child and grows into a poet of nature. His fellow-villagers call him 'the crazy man' because of his lonely wanderings in the fields.

> At length 'twas known his ways by woods and brooks
> Were secret walks for making rhymes and books,
> Which strangers bought and with amazement read
> And called him 'poet' when they sought his shed.

But, filled with envy, the local people turn to slandering him. Stung by criticism, he decays and dies. His 'learned friends' imagine that he has been killed by the malice of the envious. The poem suggests that at this time Clare was insecure about the effect of his poetic fame on his place in village life. Perhaps remembering the rumours that had circulated some months earlier to the effect that Keats was killed by the harshness of his critics, he gloomily imagines his own impending decline. Thoughts such as these have an uncanny way of being self-fulfilling. Clare is almost making himself into 'the crazy man'.

That December he was plagued with bad dreams. He had read Thomas De Quincey's *Confessions of an English Opium-Eater*, which had appeared in two recent numbers of the *London Magazine*. The combination of his own nightmares and De Quincey's surreal visions inspired him to write a poem called 'Superstition's Dream'. He sent copies to Taylor and Mrs Emmerson. She told him that it was the finest thing he had written (and suggested a few improvements). A vision of the Last Judgement, it smacks to the modern reader of 'Gothic' excess, but it reveals that Clare's state of mind was becoming deeply disturbed:

And 'midst the dreads of horror's mad extreme
I lost all notion of its being a dream:
Sinking, I fell through depths that seem'd to be
As far from fathom as Eternity;
While dismal faces on the darkness came,
With wings of dragons, and with fangs of flame,
Writhing in agonies of wild despairs,
And giving tidings of a doom like theirs.
I felt all terrors of the damn'd, and fell
With conscious horror that my doom was hell:
And Memory mock'd me, like a haunting ghost,
With light and life and pleasures that were lost.

This poem was published in the *London Magazine* the following February, then reprinted in the volume of Clare's poetry that was published in 1827.

A closely related piece, 'The Night Mare', was written at the same time but remained unpublished until long after Clare's death. This dream begins with a blissful vision of heaven. A figure with 'blue eyes and face divine' steps out from the crowd of angels. She seems familiar but the dreamer cannot remember her earthly name. She takes him by the hand and they watch the end of the world together. Then she draws back in fear as a demon takes her place and drags him down to hell—but not before her parting words allow him to recognise her voice:

'Twas Mary's voice that hung in her farewell;
The sound that moment on my memory fell—
A sound that held the music of the past;
But she was blest and I alone was cast.

Clare claimed that the poem was both the record of an actual dream and the product of his reading of De Quincey. At the climax of the *Confessions* the opium-eater has a dream of paradise in which he is restored to his lost ideal love, Ann of Oxford Street, a kind-hearted prostitute. Clare gives a similar role to Mary Joyce, despite the fact that, far from being lost in the London crowd or among the angels in paradise, she was alive and unmarried across the fields in Glinton.

It was a hard winter. On 1 January 1822 Eliza Emmerson wrote from London, asking whether Helpston had been affected by the floods she had been reading about in the newspaper. Like many depressives, both she and Clare suffered from mood swings related to the weather. Dark February days brought torpor, apathy and 'leaden interaction of mind and body'. Clare had written to her of 'domestic troubles'; she hoped that he was referring to nothing more than his mother's long-term affliction with dropsy.

The weather meant that no labouring work was available. Clare had time on his hands. He went on working at his narrative poems and began planning a novel, which was to be called 'Uncle Barnaby's Family' or 'Cares and Comforts'. Eliza gave good advice: knowing that most novel-readers were women such as herself, she recommended plenty of *pathos* and particular attention to the 'exquisite sensibilities of the sex' (i.e. of females).

The novel never progressed beyond a few fragments. Taylor thought that it was a bad idea and Clare had other things on his plate. In January he was invited to stay at Milton Hall for a few days—not to visit Lord Milton, but to spend time with the servants. Clare found them to be 'well informed men, not unacquainted with books'. He said that he 'never met with a party of more happy and heartier fellows in my life'. There was Frederic Roberts, an admirer of Tom Moore's *Irish Melodies*, Monsieur Grilliot the French cook (familiarly known as Grill, he was full of good humour and had a face like a caricature) and 'Hague the wine butler, whose library consisted of one solitary book, *Brown's Reflections on a Summer's Day*'. Clare gave Roberts manuscripts of some of his songs, both comic and lyrical, but it was the senior staff who would become his closest friends: Edmund Tyrell Artis, the household steward, and Joseph Henderson, the head-gardener. He remembered them fondly in his autobiography: 'There was Artis up to the neck in the old Norman Coins and broken pots of the Romans; and Henderson, never wearied with hunting after the

Emperor Butterfly and the Hornet Sphinx in the Hanglands wood and the Orchises on the Heath.'

Artis was four years older than Clare. Born in Suffolk, he became a confectioner in London before being hired by the Fitzwilliam family in 1813. As house steward he earned a hundred pounds a year. He was a keen antiquarian and archaeologist. In the spring of 1821, whilst searching for fossils, he unearthed a beautiful mosaicked Roman pavement near the manor house at Castor, just outside Peterborough. So began a project, which filled his spare time until his death in 1847, to discover and map the many Roman remains in the area. Artis established that there had been a major settlement called Durobrivae between Castor and Wansford, joined to London by Ermine Street. A skilled draughtsman, he drew plans of the Roman city and got up a subscription for a collection of magnificent engraved plates illustrating his discoveries. It was published in parts between 1823 and 1828, under the title *The Durobrivae of Antoninus*. He also produced a collection of illustrations of fossil remains of plants, very knowledgeably classified. Both the Geological Society and the Society of Antiquaries honoured him with fellowships.

Within a few days of the visit to Milton Hall, Artis sent a letter addressed to 'Friend Clare', making an arrangement for them to go to Stamford together. Soon after, he took a life-mask of the poet's head. Clare did not enjoy the experience of having his head covered in plaster, and he opened his eyes before the oil was removed, causing them to smart and go bloodshot. To his disappointment, Artis's handiwork fell to pieces after eighteen months. But the friendship flourished. Clare even got Lord Radstock, via Mrs Emmerson, to make inquiries—albeit unsuccessful ones—as to possible funding for Artis's research.

Henderson was a man of the same generation as Artis. Like many other head-gardeners of the great English estates, he was a well-educated Scotsman. His accomplishments were considerable, as his obituary would record in 1866:

> He was a man of a very high tone of mind, and acquired a surprising stock of knowledge on various subjects, notwithstanding the constant demands on his time as superintendent

of the Gardens, first at Milton, and afterwards at Wentworth. He had a fair knowledge of Latin and French, was an admirable draftsman, and besides possessing very extensive botanical information, he was a good ornithologist and entomologist.

He too became a good friend. 'J Henderson will be happy to see Mr Clare at any time that he can make a call at Milton convenient', he soon wrote. By April, Clare was sharing manuscripts of his poems with Henderson, seeking advice for improvements, particularly in the area of grammar. Artis, despite his accomplishments as archaeologist and palaeobotanist, was as deficient as Clare when it came to grammar and spelling: 'I should been over fore this but I realy have been so busey that I could not spare time I have mad sum new discoverys since you where at Milton but shall say nothing of them, *cum and see*.' Henderson, on the other hand, with his rigorous Scottish education, could be relied upon to provide sensible corrections. Roberts, the Milton servant who was a fan of Tom Moore's poetry, also chipped in with advice.

With Artis and Henderson, Clare felt that he was part of an intellectual community. They lent each other books and exchanged literary opinion and gossip. They shared each new issue of the *London Magazine*; most months it included a poem or two by Clare. Henderson was especially impressed by the essays of Hazlitt and Lamb. Artis's excavations inspired Clare to write a poem on 'Antiquity', published in the *London* in April 1823. The steward's ornithological and botanical knowledge made him a potential collaborator on Clare's 1825 project to write a 'Natural History of Helpstone' or 'History of favorite Birds and Flowers'. The same year, Clare found some fragments of Roman pottery in his beloved Oxey Wood. Some time later, Artis dug extensively around the site and discovered that there had once been a fine Roman villa just outside Helpston. Clare himself wrote a report of the discovery for the *Stamford Mercury*.

Henderson, meanwhile, sent Clare the seeds of florists' flowers and asked him for assistance in building up his collection of birds' eggs. He promised to call when pressure of work diminished with the

Fitzwilliams' departure to their summer estate in Yorkshire: 'Should leasure permit when the family are gone I intend to set apart an whole day for an excursion among your heaths and commons a' bird nesting, Botanizing and Butterfly catching, so I would have you keep a sharp look out, for I shall beat up your quarters.' He invited Clare to join a group of friends on a field-trip to Whittlesea Mere. Like Clare, he was a man as happy with a butterfly-trap as a book.

Stimulated as he was by this new company, Clare did not forget his old village companions. The Billings brothers were in grave financial difficulty. In order to stay on at 'Bachelors' Hall' after the implementation of the Enclosure Act, they had to raise a two hundred—pound mortgage on their property. They had got behind with their payments and were now facing legal action and possible eviction. Clare had the idea of taking on the mortgage himself. Bachelors' Hall would become 'Poets Hall'. In order to raise the money, he would dash out a new volume of poems under a feigned name. Or perhaps Taylor could give him two hundred pounds in return for the absolute right to publish all his poetry for the next five years. Taylor was sceptical. Clare's future works might be worth more than two hundred pounds, so the deal would be an injury to the poet and a discredit to the publisher; or they might be worth less, in which case there would be a loss that Taylor and Hessey could ill afford. Besides, if the original mortgage had been for two hundred pounds, the sum required for its redemption would be far higher. He strongly advised Clare against getting involved, especially given the lack of proper legal advice. He did, however, send five pounds in gold to help with the Clare family's winter needs. Fortunately, Lord Milton stepped in and lent old Billings twenty pounds to pay off his arrears.

The Billings brothers were Clare's oldest friends in the village. By now, he told Taylor, they had become his only ones. This was an exaggeration, but Clare did feel increasingly isolated by his reputation as a poet:

> I live here among the ignorant like a lost man in fact like one
> whom the rest seems careless of having anything to do with—

> they hardly dare talk in my company for fear I shoud mention
> them in my writings and I find more pleasure in wandering the
> fields than in musing among my silent neighbours who are in-
> sensible to every thing but toiling and talking of it and that to
> no purpose.

This feeling of alienation explains why Clare delighted in the more sophisticated company of Artis and Henderson at Milton.

His ability to write was intimately linked to both the weather and his mental state. He always felt worst in spring and autumn. March 1822 was an especially bad month: a 'confounded lethargy of low spir-its' pressed so hard upon him that at times he felt 'as if my senses had a mind to leave me'. His fickle muse would 'stilt' him 'up to madness', then reduce him to exhaustion and a sense of being 'nearly extin-guished by melancholy forebodings'. His dark mood was reflected in a poem called 'A Shadow of Life, Death and Eternity', which he shared with Taylor, Hessey and Henderson. Sometimes, though, the best course seemed to be to avoid poetry altogether: 'I take a great deal of Exerscise and try to write nothing which I do as the best way to mend and get better.'

At the end of April, Clare's health improved with the weather. His spirits were raised by the receipt of that letter from his admired Bloomfield. He also responded enthusiastically to the poems of an-other *London Magazine* author, Allan Cunningham, which were sent by Hessey. Although Patty was well advanced in another pregnancy, it was agreed that he would pay a second visit to London. Hessey sent him five pounds for the journey and told him that he was welcome to stay in Fleet Street—though Eliza Emmerson also put in a claim, saying that she had set aside an attic room for him in her new house in Stratford Place, just off Oxford Street. Octavius Gilchrist was in very poor health, so this time Clare travelled alone.

CHAPTER ELEVEN

THE GREEN MAN IN LONDON

It was a rough coach-trip, as he reported in a letter home to his family: 'My journey up ended very bad indeed—we went 20 miles and upwards in the most dreadfull thunder storm I ever witness'd and the rain was very heavy and lashing but as I am safe thats satisfaction enough—my respects to all and a kiss for Anna.' He would be away for his daughter's second birthday. He promised to do some clothes-shopping on behalf of Patty and sister Sophy, but could not guarantee when he would have the opportunity. A second letter, written a fortnight later, reported that he had managed to buy some lengths of fabric—which turned out to be over-priced and of poorer quality than could have been obtained back in Stamford. Clare's letters home say nothing about Patty's pregnancy, but express concern about the well-being of his tame doves.

The visit lasted three and a half weeks. Clare still viewed London very much as an outsider. He sat for hours in the window of Taylor and Hessey's Fleet Street premises, watching the passers-by. When walking out alone, he peered with fascination in the bookshop windows, but was fleeced by shopkeepers and embarrassed at how little money he was able to give to an African beggar outside St Paul's. He found a good companion in Thomas Bennion, head porter and factotum at the publishing house. They went to raree-shows together and

Bennion introduced him to the booksellers he was visiting on behalf of his employers, though more often than not these men were too busy to take much interest in Clare. The Peasant Poet was no longer the talk of the town.

He was, however, a *London Magazine* author. Taylor had by now gathered a loyal group of contributors, who met regularly for literary dinners. Five days after his arrival in town, Clare attended one of these events for the first time. It was hosted by Thomas Griffiths Wainewright and his wife Eliza in their palatial rooms in Great Marlborough Street, commencing 'at half-past six *precisely*'. The other guests were Taylor and Hessey, the Reverend Henry Cary, Allan Cunningham, Charles Lamb and Thomas Hood. Shy as ever, Clare was the last up the stairs and Wainewright's 'gentleman's gentleman' was on the point of refusing to admit him (though he made up for this by being especially attentive for the rest of the evening).

Clare described Wainewright, who was just a year younger than himself, as 'a very comical sort of chap' who 'wears a quizzing glass and makes an excuse for the ornament by complaining of bad eyes'. He was the Oscar Wilde of his day: an aesthete and a connoisseur, a stylist in both dress and prose, famous for his yellow kid gloves, a wearer of many masks, a man for whom social life was a performance. He wrote for the *London Magazine* under the pseudonyms Janus Weathercock and Cornelius Van Vinckbooms. His minor celebrity as an artist and essayist turned to major notoriety in the 1830s, when rumours circulated concerning the sudden deaths of his uncle, his mother-in-law and his wife's half-sister. Poisoning was suspected though never proved, but in the year of Clare's first committal to a lunatic asylum Wainewright was found guilty of forging legal documents in a life-insurance scam and sentenced to transportation to Van Dieman's Land (Tasmania). Clare never heard about these later dramas, but he didn't know quite what to make of Wainewright. In the words of Thomas Hood, the kind and sensitive deputy editor of the *London*, Clare's 'previous experience of life' was 'staggered' when he found himself sitting 'on the satin damask of the drawing room of his exquisitely scented and lisping master'. Hood's *Literary*

Reminiscences included an affectionate account of Clare as 'our Green Man', with 'his bright, grass-coloured coat and yellow waist-coat'. So slight he was in frame, so delicate in complexion and sensibilities, that Hood considered him insufficiently rough to seem like a true rustic—he was more cowslip than cowherd.

Henry Cary could hardly have been more different from the dandyish Wainewright. Clare described him as 'A tallish spare man with a longish face and a good forehead—his eyes are the heavy-lidded sort whose easiest look seems to meet you half closed'. Amiable, unassuming, always smiling, he was a clergyman in his fiftieth year, educated at Rugby and Oxford, now a parson in Chiswick, living in a house once owned by William Hogarth. He had published his translation of Dante's *Divine Comedy*—the first complete English version—at his own expense, and it had then been highly acclaimed when republished in three handsome volumes by Taylor and Hessey. Clare considered him 'one of those men which have my best opinions and of whom I feel happy with every opportunity to praise'.

Charles Lamb, whose 'Elia' essays—comic, poignant, whimsical—were for many readers the high-point of the *London Magazine*, is brought to vivid life in Clare's pen-portrait:

> He is very fond of snuff, which seems to sharpen up his wit every time he dips his plentiful finger into his large bronze-coloured box, and then he sharpens up his head, throws himself backward in his chair and stammers at a joke or pun with an inward sort of utterance ere he can give it speech, till his tongue becomes a sort of Packman's strop turning it over and over till at last it comes out whetted as keen as a razor—and expectation when she knows him wakens into a sort of danger as bad as cutting your throat. But he is a good sort of fellow and if he offends it is innocently done. Who is not acquainted with Elia and who would believe him otherwise?

Wainewright remembered how Lamb teased Clare and punned at his expense, making his ears tingle and his cheeks glow. Lamb bantered about certain 'Clare-obscurities' in the peasant poet's verses, arising from his lack of grammar; Clare responded by vehemently denouncing 'all Philology as nothing but a sort of man-trap for authors'. It was all in the best of spirits. 'Princely Clare,' Elia called him, and 'Clarissimus'. Neither the London essayist nor the Northamptonshire poet was much above five feet tall. When they walked down the Strand arm in arm, people said 'there go Tom and Jerry', an ironic allusion to the brawny roisterer Corinthian Tom and his country cousin Jerry Hawthorne in Pierce Egan's immensely popular novel *Life in London*.

The one person in the group whose background was similar to Clare's was the Scotsman Allan Cunningham. A former stonemason, so big that the playful Reynolds called him 'dwarf', he habitually dressed in black. He had walked in the funeral procession of Burns and become friendly with James Hogg, the 'Ettrick Shepherd'. Among the Londoners, he threw himself with ardour into conversation about poetry but could not keep up with the punning in which the rest of the company indulged themselves. Non-stop punning of dazzling creativity was the calling card of the Regency literary wit. When puns were up, said Clare, Cunningham's head went down 'over his glass, musing and silent'.

Clare had the same reaction. He liked to joke but did not have the gift of the instant pun. He would never be a real insider. Taylor, nevertheless, praised him for holding his ground with the best of the literati. Though 'a little too much elated with a Glass of Ale if you indulged him in it', he had 'a Fund of Good Taste and so many shrewd Remarks to make on what any one said,—besides his Judgment of Books was so very sound,—that let what would be the Subject of Conversation he was always well worth listening to'.

To judge from Clare's accounts, the life and soul of the dinner parties held in Taylor's rooms in Fleet Street was John Hamilton Reynolds, the best punster of them all, a friend of Keats who squandered his considerable literary gifts in light verse and occasional reviewing, but did not seem to care about his reputation. 'He sits,' remembered Clare,

> as a careless listener at table, looking on with quick knapping
> sort of eye that turns towards you as quick as lightning when he
> has a pun, joke or story to give you—they are never made up or

studied, they are the flashes of the moment and mostly happy. He is a slim sort of ... unpretending sort of fashionable fellow without the desire of being one——he has a plump round face, a nose something puggish and a forehead that betrays more of fun than poetry——his teeth are always looking through a laugh that sits as easy on his unpuckered lips as if he were born laughing. He is a man of genius and if his talents was properly applied he would do something——I verily believe that he might win the favours of fame with a pun.

After a dinner in honour of Clare on 7 June, Taylor sat down at midnight and wrote to his family in the country: 'I have had my Company and they are gone again, and Clare is gone to bed.' It had obviously been a successful evening and Reynolds was always to thank for that. Reynolds himself was alert to the paradoxes of Clare's personality: he described him as quiet but enthusiastic, 'guileless yet suspicious', a true observer of nature but a man alive to higher things.

There were other claims on Clare's company besides those of the *London Magazine* set. On the very evening of Wainewright's party, Eliza Emmerson was sitting up late in her new house in Stratford Place, writing to Clare in a hurt tone. Why has he not been to see her? Has Patty's health required him to turn round and go straight back to Helpston? 'How anxious I am to have you under my roof', she pleads. Her husband is out of town, but she wants to introduce him to another of her protégés, a young painter. She has got a cold, so has lost her ability to taste and smell. She feels as if she is losing all her senses, 'except *feeling*!——*that* is as sensitive as ever.' Clare cried off with 'pains both of the body and mind'——the after-effects of Wainewright's wine?——but agreed to call on Eliza at the end of the week. 'Come to me as early on friday as you can', she scrawled in a postscript to her response. He may have gone early, but he did not stay late, because he had a dinner engagement that night at the house of a family friend of Taylor's, where he seems to have enjoyed the quiet of an evening away from the literati.

After Clare returned home, Emmerson wrote in fond memory of their 'alas! *too short interviews*'. For a couple of nights he appears to have stayed in a little room with a skylight at the top of her house. She christened it 'Clare's Room'. She also cherished the memory of an evening when she read to him and he began writing a 'little but *powerful* Poem'. Though she regretted the brevity of his visit, she was pleased to have brought him together with the painter Edward Villiers Rippingille. Known to his friends as 'Rip', he was about the same age as Clare. The son of a farmer from King's Lynn in Norfolk, he began his career by exhibiting locally—it was his paintings that Clare had seen in the shop window in Wisbech—and then had mild success in London when examples of his work were included in the 1814 and 1819 shows at the Royal Academy. He moved to Bristol and became part of a lively circle of artists known to Mrs Emmerson, whose family came from the area.

Rip was another punster and liked to project the image of a man of the world. He had a reputation as a drinker, a spendthrift, a political radical and a womaniser. Clare, with his usual astute eye, called him 'a rattling sort of odd fellow with a desire to be thought one'. They went drinking together, on one occasion spending the whole night at a tavern called Offley's, famous for its Burton ale. This seems to have put Rippingille 'in great disgrace at Stratford Place'. He soon headed back to Bristol, inviting Clare to visit him there. Clare greatly enjoyed Rip's company, though he was later warned by Bennion that he should be careful what he said around him, because he was a gossip who liked to regale Mrs Emmerson with exaggerated tales of Clare's misadventures.

Some way through Clare's stay, Gilchrist had arrived in London. He introduced Clare to the opinion-forming literary editor William Gifford, who told him that *The Village Minstrel* was vastly superior to his first volume, whilst warning him to beware of publishers. The next day Gilchrist took Clare to Albemarle Street to see John Murray, Byron's publisher. As they were leaving Gifford arrived: so much for avoiding publishers. Murray was cordial, but if Gilchrist was angling for an offer from Murray to take over as Clare's publisher, he was deluded.

Clare firmly intended to remain loyal to his friends in Fleet Street,

as he made clear when telling Taylor of his reaction to Lord Radstock's boast that he could set him up with Murray. Radstock had told
Clare that he would introduce him to Murray, who would give up to
a thousand pounds for his poems—he was 'the fashionable Bookseller', whereas Taylor and Hessey 'only published Children's Books'.
Clare had replied that he owed everything to Taylor and Hessey, and,
as for the character of their publications, they could hardly be classed
as 'Juvenile Booksellers' when they had published 'Cary's Dante,
Cunningham's Play, Keats's Poems and besides the London Magazine'. Taylor was not on speaking terms with Radstock at this time, so
Clare once again found himself being quarrelled over. He divided his
time between Fleet Street and Stratford Place in full knowledge of
the opposition between their respective occupants.

Clare also went with Taylor and Hessey to visit Henry Cary in rural Chiswick. He accepted an invitation to spend two days there. He
seems to have been glad to get away from Mrs Emmerson, with
whom he had had a tiff—possibly over the carousing with Rip.
Whilst he was in Richmond, she wrote telling him that they must put
certain 'unpleasant recollections' behind them.

At dinner with Cary, a jug of ale was provided for his particular use.
He relished the house's Hogarthian associations, but took even
greater pleasure in going to nearby Richmond to see the grave of
James Thomson, whose *Seasons* had inspired him to become a poet.
Cary had a much younger wife, whom Clare claims to have 'a long
while' mistaken for his daughter. In his autobiographical recollections he did, however, like to present an image of himself as a country clown getting into embarrassing muddles, so there is probably
some exaggeration here. There is certainly no warrant for a story in
Frederick Martin's biography in which Clare offends his hosts by
writing a flirtatious poem to the wife on the assumption that she was
one of the daughters of the house (Cary didn't actually have any living daughters).

Clare departed from London in a hurry, leaving a silk handkerchief behind at Mrs Emmerson's. She forwarded it to him, with another one as a remembrance. The reason for the hasty departure was

the news from Helpston. Patty was 'in a dangerous State'. Taylor's helpful porter was given the job of making sure Clare caught the overnight coach. They spent the day together and got drunk. Bennion accompanied Clare—on the cheap seats on top of the coach—as far as the Angel at Islington, where a fellow-traveller called for brandy and water to toast the poet. Clare was still drunk when the coach reached Peterborough. He staggered home in the morning to find that he had a three-day-old daughter.

The child was named Eliza Louisa, after Mrs Emmerson, to whom Clare was soon writing a confessional letter that described Patty as 'a faded flower' and told of how he had been resorting to drink 'to stifle recollections of the past'. Eliza sent a silver christening cup for the baby and a gown, contributed by Lord Radstock, for Patty to wear at the baptism. Clare's parents stood as proxy god-parents on behalf of Emmerson and Radstock. Ned Drury was also invited to the christening, but was unable to come down from Lincoln.

Clare was by no means glad to be home. In his thank-you letter to Taylor he said that his heart had ached as he lost sight of London, 'at the thought of being forced away perhaps for ever from the merriest set of fellows I ever met with'. His glimpse of a different world had been all too brief, though some compensation was to be found over at Milton Hall. Henderson was delighted that he was home and longed to hear him 'analyze the legions of London Literati'. Henderson's own analyses of the writings of the Londoners were extremely astute. He thought that Lamb was a much better prose-writer than poet, which indeed he was, and when Clare lent him William Hazlitt's *Lectures on the English Poets* he responded with a brilliant account of the critical art of that book: 'He cross examines a character, and then patches his sentences together, until he makes the poor fellow tell more of his mind than the author himself was acquainted with.'

Letters were also a life-line. They came from friends old and new. His old school-friend John Turnill sent a rhyming letter from Manchester, full of nostalgia for Helpston and the days before the enclosure. Drury wrote with his usual sensible advice on Clare's latest poetic project, a volume to be called 'Walks in Summer'; his opinion was that the market for 'purely rustic manners and scenery' was now saturated and that Clare should try something more sophisticated. Charles Lamb said that he should avoid 'rustick Cockneyism' and elevate his pastoral to greater refinement: 'Transplant Arcadia to Helpstone.' Lamb had just been to Paris, on his only trip abroad, and he offered some comic culinary advice in addition to his more serious prescription for Clare's poetry:

> Since I saw you I have been in France, and have eaten frogs. The nicest little rabbity things you ever tasted. Do look about for them. Make Mrs Clare pick off the hind quarters, boil them plain, with parsly and butter. The forequarters are not so good. She may let them hop off by themselves.

Patty was in no state to do anything of the kind. A few weeks after she recovered from her labour, an epidemic of fen-fever descended on the locality. It worked its way through Clare's family, affecting his old mother and the two little ones most severely. Just when it seemed that everyone was better, sister Sophy came down badly and Clare feared for her life. She survived, but her new baby—named John after Clare himself—did not.

He was also concerned about the very poor health of Gilchrist, who kindly sent a cap for Patty and a doll for little Anna. In December, Clare wrote to Emmerson of his 'mental sufferings' and complained to Hessey that, save for a few local visits, he had done nothing for the past few months except 'pay almost a daily worship' to strong beer. He got drunk to make solitude less irksome, but found it made it worse. A gloomy letter early in the new year makes much the same point:

> Many miles stretch their weary lengths between present miseries and former comforts. I am wind-bound in my sultry corner, drinking now and then a pot of misnamed Medley, as nigh Ale as shadow is to substance—small beer's sad reality—or now and then seeking the 'Bell' to be cheered with the [?——] of company who sleep all day with their eyes open and only [wake] to howl about the times. Books and Authors are dark and

unknown things, as if they inhabited the bottom of the sea—
this is a fine part of the country for blue devils and low spirits,
but a damned bad place to cure them.

For the first time since his success, Clare was declining into a sustained period of depression and ill health. His letters again and again told of 'blue devils'. Tom Bennion replied that he knew nothing of that 'infernal tribe', probably because his mind was always too occupied with business. He was among the most well-meaning of Clare's correspondents, but the worst possible thing you can say to a depressive is to imply that the problem is the result of indolence and that it will be solved by getting on with business.

For several weeks in March and April 1823 Clare felt ill every morning as soon as he got up. The doctor prescribed a 'vomit'. Then the two little girls fell ill again. He was made desperately anxious by the fate of a neighbouring family who 'lost a son and a daughter both in one day when they thought they was recovering'. Clare's account of the symptoms in this case makes it sound like tuberculosis. His fear that his own children's coughs would prove fatal was not realised. But within weeks of recovery from one illness, Anna Maria came down with another, as measles brought her close to death. 'Had I know the trouble that come with childern in spite of the pleasures I woud have had none', wrote her father.

His love for his first daughter is exquisitely expressed in some short poems he wrote about her that summer. In 'To Anna three years old' he looks at her on her sickbed and remembers how her 'little hand' would 'Catch at each object passing by' as they walked in the fields together.

> In sudden shout and wild surprise
> I hear thy simple wonderment
> As new things meet thy childish eyes
> And wake some innocent intent.

In some other verses, the sight of her neglected doll is the 'trifle' that stirs his tenderness. He voices the thought of every parent of a sick child:

> I think I never felt before
> The love I bear thee now
> And wish I'd shown my feelings more
> My child could I know how
> If thought could move the pain away
> I'd think the very wind
> To calms that it might hurt thee not.

Strain at home may, however, have made him look elsewhere for comfort. A letter from Emmerson reveals that he had confided to her that he had been '*love-sick* of late'. 'What says your Patty to this?' she asked in reply. In one of her most percipient observations, Eliza suggested that the tendency to fall in love at the drop of a hat was the inevitable consequence of Clare's poetic sensibility. Patty would have to accept that her husband 'must have his idols of the mind as well as of the heart':

> Besides, first impressions will linger about us even after the spell be broken:—and thus it is, we remain the slaves of feeling, tho' but in degree; for there are shades in love as there are in colours. You tell me you are now 'recovering apace'—I am happy to hear it and pray do be content with one fair she—and leave all the rest of our sex to wander where they will except it be the loves of your imagination.

Eliza catches a key truth about Clare with her remarks about the lingering power of first impressions and the intimate relationship between his poetic imagination and his erotic desires. There was a recurring pattern in his life whereby the advent of domestic difficulty would cause him to fall in love with someone new and simultaneously to return in imagination to his idealized first love. In 1823 he was 'lovesick' for an unknown girl, and he also wrote a series of new poems for the *London Magazine* suggesting that he was still in love with the angelic form of Mary Joyce.

We do not know how far, if at all, he indulged his new passion. But he was gaining a reputation as someone who had an eye for the girls: a comic paragraph by Reynolds in the *London* hinted at Samuel Taylor Coleridge's opium addiction and John Clare's promiscuity. In each case, it might be observed that there is no smoke without fire.

In the summer of 1823 he was anxious to see a new pamphlet on the subject of his poems. Entitled *Four Letters from the Revd W. Allen, to the Right Hon. Admiral Lord Radstock, on the Poems of John Clare, the Northamptonshire Peasant*, its publication was financed by Radstock and Mrs Emmerson. Taylor and Hessey had refused to have anything to do with this attempt to reinvigorate the publicity campaign on Clare's behalf. In their view, it smacked of old-style patronage and puffing of a kind that would prove counter-productive. Clare himself was afraid the pamphlet would be full of empty praise that his enemies would take for mere flattery.

Allen's little book was the most detailed analysis yet of *Poems, Descriptive* and *The Village Minstrel*. It argued perfectly reasonably, with judicious supporting quotations, that Clare's poetry was distinguished for taking the reader's imagination to the fields and woods, where all the beauties of nature were pointed out 'in a way that enables you to see them with the same eyes that he does'. It was by no means an outrageous puff to suggest that Clare was unequalled in offering 'a faithful and distinct portraiture of rural life in England'. Mrs Emmerson sent him a copy, complete with marginal annotations highlighting references to the special contribution that she and Lord Radstock had made to his success.

Clare himself preferred disinterested support of the kind that appeared around the same time in *Flora Domestica*, a volume of botanical lore illustrated from the works of the English poets, by Elizabeth Kent, sister-in-law to the poet and editor Leigh Hunt. About eight lines of Clare were quoted in the main text and a further sixty in the preface. 'None have better understood the language of flowers than the simple-minded peasant-poet, Clare', wrote Elizabeth Kent— though she added that he was mainly concerned with wild flowers, whereas her interest was domestic ones (in fact Clare did cultivate 'florists' flowers' in his garden).

In addition to worries about his literary reputation, there were the usual money problems. These were briefly alleviated in the autumn of 1823 when Hessey forwarded a gift of five guineas from a wealthy West Indian gentleman who happened to be called Sir Michael Clare. The trust fund was by now in operation and the annuities from Spencer and Exeter were being paid regularly—Clare wanted to thank Exeter by dedicating his next volume to him—but Taylor and Hessey had been slow in making up the accounts on his literary earnings. Hardly a month passed without at least one poem by Clare being included in the *London*, but he was receiving no extra payment for these.

Octavius Gilchrist, who had taken Clare up with such enthusiasm when he was still unknown, died on 30 June 1823, aged only forty-four. Some weeks later Robert Bloomfield, who had shown that it was possible for a humble rural poet from the eastern counties of England to make his way in print, died in poverty. Clare's thoughts had been dark for some time. He had freshly copied out his poem 'Edmund and Hellen', giving it the alternative title 'The Suicide'. Bloomfield's death inspired him to write three fine memorial sonnets, but Gilchrist's made him confront the thought of oblivion: 'I have apathy about me that looks on the powers of hells and heavens as mysterious riddles and Death as an animal consequence—I hope its not heathenism.'

In the autumn he wrote to Emmerson of being haunted by a 'troublesome nothing' and of the 'abiding shadow' of 'visionary miseries'. In the dark days of winter he described 'fiery torments' and 'enduring a Hell for the last fortnight'. Patty was about to have another baby, but Hessey was over-optimistic in writing at Christmas with the hope that 'the addition to your family will prove an addition to your Happiness'. The birth of a first son, Frederick, in early January 1824 was not followed by the dispatch of cheerful letters to London. Clare's severe depression endured from the autumn of 1823 until at least the following summer. Never again did he fully succeed in banishing his 'blue devils'.

Taylor, who was himself suffering from depression and debilitation, went north in November 1823 to attend the funeral of an old family friend. On the way up he paid his respects to Gilchrist's widow in Stamford. On the way back he changed coaches in Stamford. Hessey proposed that Clare should take this opportunity to walk in from Helpston and cheer Taylor up. They do not seem to have met, but Taylor was somehow alerted to the seriousness of Clare's condition. He appears to have engaged Dr Skrimshire to visit Clare. The relevant correspondence is now lost, but Frederick Martin saw it when preparing his biography of Clare:

> The medical gentleman, while carefully watching all the symptoms of the disease, now began to fear that he would be unable to master it, and wrote to this effect to Mr Taylor, entreating him to use his influence to get Clare removed to some hospital, or other house where he might have the necessary attention. In the letter it was stated without disguise that the illness of the poet was mainly the effect of poverty. His dwelling, the Peterborough physician argued, was altogether unfit for a human habitation, being dark, damp, and ill ventilated, with a space so circumscribed as to be worse than a prison for two families. He insisted, therefore, that to make recovery possible a better home should be found for Clare himself, and, if possible, for his wife and child, pending the removal of his aged and suffering parents. A copy of this note the writer sent to Lord Radstock, knowing that his lordship had taken, from the beginning, a deep interest in Clare's welfare.

Radstock responded with two letters to Lord Milton, 'soliciting his Lordship's benevolent grant of a cottage and a piece of garden'.

Just as Clare was subject to the competing claims of several patrons, so he had to cope with the different prescriptions of different doctors. In February 1824 Lady Milton asked her personal apothecary, Mr Walker, to call on him. He prescribed bleeding and various medicaments. But Clare became unhappy about both Walker's billing procedures and his 'quackery'. He had more faith in a figure from his past: Dr Arnold of Stamford, who had treated him many years back for the symptoms that were supposedly provoked by his witnessing of Thomas Drake's fall from a hay-cart. In March, Taylor wrote on his behalf to Arnold, requesting a visit; a few weeks later he sent Clare a five-pound note with the instruction that two guineas of it should be used to pay Arnold's fee. Arnold and Skrimshire seem to have agreed that Clare needed fresh air and exercise. There may be some basis in fact for this fanciful encounter described in Martin's biography:

> One day he stayed out longer than usual, and, the doctor arriving, a search was made after him. It was fruitless for some time; at last, however, he was found in his favourite hollow oak, sitting as in a trace, his face illumined by the setting sun. Enraptured joy seemed to pervade his whole being; unutterable bliss to fill his mind. The doctor looked serious, and made an attempt to upbraid his patient, but which was entirely unsuccessful. 'If you loved the sun and flowers as I do,' quietly said Clare, 'you would not blame me.'

Even during his depression at this time Clare was still 'delighted with the *Muse of Nature*' and pursuing his 'old favourite track' in verse. Arnold encouraged him in his resolution to get out of the house and start earning some money by doing 'a little work on the Milton Estates'.

One of Clare's doctors also suggested that he should drink coffee instead of tea. His Stamford friend Frank Simpson provided a supply. Taylor, meanwhile, also consulted his own physician, Dr George Darling, who sent some pills: one lot to keep the bowels open and another to act as an analgesic. It was proposed that Clare should come to London to see Darling in person.

During this period Clare sought solace not only in what Mrs Emmerson somewhat disapprovingly called his 'religion of nature' but also in a renewed interest in Non-conformity. For all the good offices of Parson Mossop, orthodox Anglicanism did not satisfy him. Fearful of lapsing towards heathenism, he turned for a time to the congregations of 'Enthusiasts' that were thriving in the area at this time. A decade after he had first met Henson at the 'Independent' chapel, only to secede from 'Methodistical' company in 1819, he flirted once again with religious Dissent.

His thoughts of death led him to meditate on the afterlife and to draw up a will. In February 1824 he wrote to Hessey with 'a question about Faith and Works'. A reading of the New Testament Epistle of James had led him to doubt his former notion—an essentially Calvinist one—that faith alone guaranteed salvation. Hessey agreed that good works were also important: the true Christian will show his faith *by* his works. He added, however, that a man on his deathbed would have no opportunity to do further good works, so such a person would have to rely on faith alone. In the depths of his depression, Clare was worrying that he might be damned for his sins of idleness, drunkenness and lechery. Hessey replied with the hope that he would live a long life of 'Piety and Virtue', but reassured him that at his current point of extremity faith in God was what really mattered. He encouraged him to go on reading his Bible and sent some exhortatory religious tracts.

By the end of March Clare had decided to join the 'Primitive Methodists' or 'Ranters'. He had hesitated because of their ideas of 'Free Grace', 'Election' and 'Predestination', which had made him think that they paid insufficient attention to amendment of life, but—with the assistance of Hessey's letters and tracts—he now saw through their 'vulgar errors'. Perhaps remembering his dealings with Henson, he acknowledged that there were 'dangerous characters' and 'religious hypocrites' amongst the Dissenters, but he had convinced himself that such unhealthy influences could be disregarded. The Ranters would provide him with what Taylor approvingly called 'real practical Religion'. Taylor, who had Non-conformist instincts himself, had no fear of Clare 'plunging into the excesses of Enthusiasm'. Religious passion, he thought, was 'far better than Coldheartedness'.

A few weeks later Clare sent Hessey his impressions of the Ranters. They were 'a set of simple sincere and communing Christians with more zeal than knowledge, earnest and happy in their devotions'. His own 'dark unsettled conscience' was put to shame by their 'earnest though simple extempore prayers'. The 'enthusiasm' in their preaching, prayers and manners was utterly without affectation. He then described how they spent their Sundays: 'at 7 o'clock they meet to pray, at 9 they join the Class, at half past 10 they hear preaching, at half past 2 they meet again to pray and at 7 in the evening preaching again.' The 'Class' was devoted to reading and discussion of the Scriptures.

The Primitive Methodist movement had emerged in the early nineteenth century as an offshoot from Wesley's Methodist church. The Primitives had the democratic passion of true evangelism; they believed that lay people as well as ordained clergy, and women as well as men, were qualified to preach. They appealed especially to the labouring classes and were prominent in Northamptonshire from about 1818. They would walk through the streets of a village, singing their hymns to the accompaniment of popular folk tunes, then announce a service of preaching and prayer. This would usually take place in the open air in a field. Both the music and the setting would have especially appealed to Clare. They placed a special emphasis on the Old Testament Psalms, texts that always remained close to his heart.

He drew a striking contrast between his passionate reaction to the Ranters' open-air prayer meetings and the uninspiring tedium of Parson Mossop's orthodox Anglican church services: 'my feelings are so unstrung in their company that I can scarcely refrain from shedding tears and when I went church I could scarcely refrain from sleep.' He attended services of the Wesleyan Methodists as well as the Ranters. He was especially impressed by a Wesleyan preacher called William Blackley, whose voice reminded him uncannily of John Taylor's. Blackley's 'persuasive tenderness of speech' was, however, too mild-mannered for the bulk of the congregation, who preferred 'shouting and ranting'. Clare was too private and restrained—ultimately too intelligent and introspective—for the excesses of religious enthusiasm.

Then as now, the enthusiasm of an evangelical community had the potential to cheer the spirits of a depressive, but also ran the risk of making him feel even more of a worthless misfit than he had before. The letter to Hessey describes some classic symptoms of clinical depression: 'my insides feels sinking and dead and my memory is worse and worse nearly lost ... I cannot reconcile my own mind what to do, for I think my disorder incurable because I feel as I never felt before in my life and further I cannot feel much better—if I do it's only for a day or two and then I am as bad as ever.' He always felt worst in the evenings. He said that it was as if cold water were creeping all about his head.

Taylor and Hessey continued to advocate a visit to London to see Dr Darling. They were convinced that the illness was 'what the doctors (or rather the ladies) call nervous, that is, occasioned by over-excitement of mind'. Darling, they said, had the right combination of good sense and medical ability to treat this condition. In particular, he had 'much experience of the diseases of literary men, and will know better than most practitioners how to treat your case'. He had not, of course, been able to do anything about Keats's consumption, but the prospect of being treated by Keats's doctor was a straw at which Clare was now glad to clutch. He struggled to summon the energy to leave home, but by mid-May he had grown impatient with his local doctors. Hessey sent money for the journey, urging him not to scrimp by travelling on the outside of the coach, and Clare duly boarded the London coach on 20 May 1824. He stayed for eleven weeks.

He would walk among the city crowds trying to catch the eye of the most beautiful women. But at night he was nervous in the streets. When he called on Mrs Emmerson, he often stayed very late because he was afraid to walk back to Hessey's* for fear of meeting with supernatural apparitions: 'thin death-like shadows and gobblings [sic] with sorcerer eyes were continually shaping in the darkness from my haunted imagination and when I saw any one of a spare figure in the

*Hessey and his wife still lodged over the business premises in Fleet Street, but Taylor had moved earlier that year to elegant rooms in Waterloo Place, Pall Mall (much closer to Mrs Emmerson's house in Stratford Place, just off Oxford Street). On this visit Clare seems to have stayed first with the Hessey family, then with Taylor.

dark passing or going on by my side my blood has curdled cold at the foolish apprehension of his being a supernatural agent whose errand might be to carry me away.' He had a particular fear of dark alleys and the narrow, poorly lit Chancery Lane. One evening he could not pluck up the courage to go down there, so he tried to find another route to Fleet Street, got lost, offered a watchman a shilling to show him the right way, and ended up paying half a crown.

Dr Darling, who looked rather like a Methodist parson, was 'of the old school of blue pill and black draught'. His advice was, however, eminently sensible: rest, not too much reading and writing, no over-excitement. The mere change of scene seems to have improved Clare's health. A series of visits brought him out of himself. Hessey took him to see a poetry fanatic called Mr Vowler, who lived near St Paul's; there they met a painter called William Etty, a friend of Hilton whose work Clare came to admire. He took a liking to Vowler's sister, who had a vocal impediment and could only speak in a whisper. Later, Taylor and Hessey took him to have tea with Charles and Mary Lamb, who had moved out to a house by the New River in Islington. Charles was always good company, but the figure of Mary cast a shadow. She had been consigned to her brother's care after stabbing their mother to death with a kitchen-knife. Her fits of violence sometimes returned and she would have to be temporarily removed to an asylum.

At the end of May, Clare saw Eliza Emmerson for the first time since his arrival in town. She wrote to Patty, telling her that her husband's health was improving day by day. The fact that Clare had not written himself caused some consternation at Helpston. Patty got a neighbour to write back on her behalf: 'we Received Mrs Heammissons, Letter, but was Afraid you was wors as you did not writ your self.' The news at home was that sister Sophy had given birth to a fine boy, again called John.

Mrs Emmerson had been suffering from nervous debility herself. She had often shared accounts of her symptoms with Clare: 'the wandering pains—the cold chills—the nervous weeping . . . perspirations and cracking of the joints.' But his presence in London cheered her no end. She was soon sending him a flirtatious dinner invitation: 'I shall be "Joan all alone"——my good man having started this morning for Bath to bring up my eldest niece to visit me.' Being childless, she greatly valued the company of her niece, just as she took great interest in the welfare of Clare's children.

By mid-June she was able to report to Patty that Clare's spirits had improved, as had his appetite and digestion. He was sleeping better and not complaining so much of headaches. She sent the London papers for Parker's amusement and asked Patty to perform a special duty:

> I am requested by your dear Husband, to beg of you to go to the *drawers* upstairs and get my Portrait in the red morocco case, if you do not find it in the drawers, you must open the *Bookcase* to look for it, as Clare is not certain in which of them he has put it:——you will be so good as let the Portrait be very *carefully packed up* in brown paper and get some friend to direct it to *my address as below*——as I am going to have it *framed* by your Husband's request, that it may hang-up, in your cottage.

There is no record of Patty's reaction to the information that her husband kept a portrait of Eliza shut away in a red morocco case, or of whether it was indeed framed and then hung on the wall of the cottage. The picture is lost, so we do not know what Mrs Emmerson looked like.

Eliza was demanding of Clare's time. If he did not see her for a few days, she would accuse him of cruelly deserting her. She tried to drag him into tea parties with her niece Henrietta. One Monday evening he left her house feeling ill and she wrote first thing the next day asking him to return the following morning and stay through until dinner. There is a cryptic reference in a letter to Clare from William Sharp, a friend whose family lived near Helpston but who was himself employed at the London office that dealt with undeliverable mail: 'I am glad at length to hear you are alive and wish you were better——I had almost despaired of any further intelligence of you——but 'twas foolish of me to think of competing with "quality" especially the *Ladies*——I wish their friendly tenderness had proved a more salutary balm.' It sounds from this as though Clare may have told Sharp that Emmerson had taken responsibility for looking after him, but that her solicitations were something of an imposition. When he finally left town on 8 August, he disappointed her by not going to say goodbye.

Some way into Clare's visit, Emmerson's other protégé, Rippingille, had arrived from Bristol. He was accompanied by Charles Abraham Elton, translator of Greek and Roman classics, poet, politician and *London Magazine* contributor—a man whom the diarist of literary life Henry Crabb Robinson described as a sturdy fellow who looked more like a huntsman than a scholar. The son of a wealthy Bristol baronet, he was estranged from his family on account of an unacceptable marriage to a famous local beauty. When Clare left town in August, Elton wrote a verse-epistle in his honour, describing him as 'cockney Clare', with the implication that the Northamptonshire poet had become one of the literary lads about town. The epistle pleased Clare very much and was published in the *London*, though it is hard to know what ordinary readers would have made of it, given that it is full of in-jokes and private nicknames.

Together with Rippingille and Elton, Clare visited the celebrated phrenologist Jean Deville, who kept a gallery of plaster-cast heads, which he used to demonstrate his belief that the characteristics of murderers, poets, painters and mathematicians could be inferred from the shape and bumpiness of the brain, felt through the skull. Deville took a cast of Clare's head. He announced that the bumps proved that Clare was a poet. 'Are you a poet, Sir?' he asked. 'Yes'. 'Aye, aye, the system's right', he continued—and then, as Clare wryly put it, 'in smiling silence waits your decision of his remarkable prophecy.' Clare agreed to let Deville take his bust in plaster because his friends wanted a copy. The experience was stifling and he vowed not to undergo it again.

Clare gave the cast to Mrs Emmerson. She put it on top of her bookcase, but a few weeks later it fell off, cut her head and 'was shivered to atoms by the fall'. Elton also took home a cast of Clare's head. His famously beautiful wife and daughters fell quite in love with it.

Rippingille told the ticket-keeper at the Royal Academy who Clare was, so he was allowed to go there whenever he wanted. When Taylor and Hessey were busy at work and Rip otherwise engaged, Clare spent the day alone looking at the paintings. He would have passed Burlington House, the magnificent premises of the Academy, each time he made the fifteen-minute walk from Taylor's new home in Waterloo Place to Eliza Emmerson's house just off Oxford Street—a walk that also passed within a stone's throw of John Murray's house in Albemarle Street, with all its Byronic associations.

Rip sometimes took him along as he networked in the art world. They called on Sir Thomas Lawrence, the society portraitist. As they got to his door they saw Prince Leopold going in to sit for his picture, so they took a turn round the square. Clare would never have had the courage to introduce himself and thank the Prince for his generous donation to the trust fund. Once they saw him leave, Rip sent in his card and they were shown into Lawrence's painting gallery. When Sir Thomas himself appeared, he shook Clare by the hand and inquired after his well-being. They chatted for some time and just as they were about to leave Lawrence said that he could not let Clare go without showing him a 'brother poet': he led them into another room, where 'a fine head of Walter Scott' stood before them.

Lawrence congratulated Rip on his recently exhibited oil painting *The Stage-Coach Breakfast*, telling him that at the private view before the opening of that year's Academy show, the royal family had taken more notice of it than any other painting. It is an imaginary scene depicting Rippingille's literary acquaintances: the Lake Poets, who had Bristol connections, and members of the *London Magazine* circle. Coleridge is holding out a boiled egg for Wordsworth to sniff, while Southey ogles one of Elton's lovely daughters and Dorothy Wordsworth sits glumly with her hands folded. Elton looks on indulgently. Rippingille himself is in the foreground, having his boots pulled on as a footman—Charles Lamb, no less—hands him the bill. Standing in profile at the back of the group there is a short, delicate figure, hat on head, resting his hand on a grandfather clock. He seems to be a misfit among the literati, eager for the coach to arrive. It may possibly be a representation of Clare. And to the extreme right, an elegant lady with fading good looks adjusts her travel-wear in a mirror: could this be the only surviving image of Eliza Emmerson?

Clare's excursions with Rip were not all so elevated as the visit to Sir Thomas. They went to Astley's, an 'illegitimate' theatre just off the Strand, specializing in raucous circus-like entertainments. Clare especially remembered the tumbling. On two or three occasions they also went to the New Royal West London Theatre, on Tottenham Street in Soho. Popularly known as the French Theatre, because of the nationality of the company who played there, it was the smallest and raciest theatre in town. The repertory consisted of bawdy farces with titles such as *La Leçon singulière* and plots involving bad-tempered old husbands, beautiful young wives, a music or dancing master, and all sorts of hanky-panky. What was going on—and coming off—on stage was perfectly obvious even though, like most of the audience, Rip and Johnny did not know a word of French. Rip conjured up the atmosphere in a letter recalling their nights out together: 'smoke, smocks, smirks, smells and smutty doings'. They took a special fancy to the leading actress, the one who always ended up cuckolding her husband. She appeared under the name Mademoiselle Delia. Rip drew a pencil sketch of her for Clare to keep, and later teased him about his obsession with her.

The Tottenham Court Road—like Oxford Street, Regent Street and the Strand—teemed with prostitutes. The French actresses supplemented their income in the time-honoured way. Mademoiselle Delia herself was probably out of Clare's league, but a letter from Rip, sent shortly after his own return to Bristol, is ripe with punning suggestiveness: 'Why will you stay roasting your soles on the hot pavement of Regent Street and the Strand and leave the muses sitting on the green moss weeping and perhaps getting the pip, to be sighed to only by the winds and the long grass—o Johnny Johnny, and you swallowing the crab juice of another Darling.' The weather was hot in London that summer, but Rip is playfully implying that Clare may be risking roasting his soul as well as his soles by consorting with street-walkers. He reiterates Reynolds's jokey accusation in the *Lon-*

don Magazine that whilst in town Clare has been unfaithful to his rural muse. Since several of his published poems explicitly identified that muse with 'Patty of the Vale', there may be a hint that Mrs Clare, stuck at home with the children, had good cause for annoyance ('getting the pip'). 'You take care of yourself, no *pleughing* I trust, the *Delia* fever is abated I hope, or perhaps has given place to another'. *Ploughing* is slang for having sex. And, in the light of Rip's equal relish for puns and what he called 'carnal luxuriating',* 'swallowing the crab juice of another Darling' may refer to something else in addition to Dr Darling's medications. When Clare wrote 'Don Juan' in Dr Allen's asylum, his troubled mind returned persistently and guiltily to playhouses and prostitutes, sexual perversion and disease.

Rip also introduced Clare to another form of low-life that would return to haunt him in the asylum:

> The first jaunt that we took together was to see the 'Art of Self-Defence' practiced at the fives court. It was for the benefit of Oliver and I caught the mania so much from Rip for such things that I soon became far more eager for the fancy than himself, and I watched the appearance of every new Hero on the stage with as eager curiosity to see what sort of a fellow he was as I had done before the Poets—and I left the place with one wish strongly in uppermost and that was that I was but a Lord to patronize Jones the Sailor Boy who took my fancy as being the finest fellow in the Ring.

It was the age of 'boximania'. Benefits and exhibition matches at the Fives Court, for which there was a three-shilling entrance charge, were the showpieces of the sport. Pugilists such as Tom Oliver were national heroes, the living embodiment of the John Bull toughness that had put Napoleon to rout. Harry 'Sailor Boy' Jones had served in the navy in the time of Nelson. He was so ardent for a fight that he or-

---

*Rippingille's two mistresses bore him at least seven children. His letters are the ripest that Clare received: 'it is now eleven at night for the last 3 hours I have been standing over a half naked beautiful Girl whose knees and thighs I have been imitating in clay and have every now and then caught glimpses that have given an odd twinge and an odd kind of twist to my vision'.

ganized a bout on his wedding day, going straight from the church to the ring, where he polished off his opponent in twelve minutes flat.

Clare's fantasy was to be a lord offering patronage to a humble boxer, just as various lords had offered him patronage. The idea of Clare watching for new stars in the world of prize-fighting as avidly as he kept his eyes open for new poets now seems curious. We think of poetry as something gentle and sedentary, not to say effeminate, as far removed as imaginable from bare-knuckle fisticuffs with a baying crowd in attendance and big bets at stake. But in Regency culture there was an extraordinary symbiosis between boxing and literature. Byron sparred with 'Gentleman' John Jackson and employed him as a minder. Some have even supposed greater intimacy between them. J. H. Reynolds was both theatre critic and boxing correspondent for the *London*. His poetry collection of 1820, a book owned and admired by Clare, was called *The Fancy*, the generic term for the world of prize-fighting. It included two sonnets in praise of Jack Randall, known as the Nonpareil. 'Randall, John—Irish parents—age not known / Good with both hands, and only ten stone four.' In drawing together poetry, philosophy and pugilism, Reynolds explicitly compared Randall to Lord Byron. Years later, in Dr Allen's asylum, Clare fused the two figures into his own impersonation of 'Boxer Byron'.

Randall, a champion lightweight, had become a boxing promoter. His pub, the Hole in the Wall in Chancery Lane, was the heaving heart of the Fancy. It was there that you went to find out the venue of the next big outdoor fight: the Fancy moved from place to place, relying on word of mouth, always keeping one step ahead of the law. William Hazlitt walked into the Hole on the evening of 11 December 1821. He was told that Bill Neate would encounter Tom 'the Gasman' Hickman down at Hungerford the next day. Hazlitt hitched a ride, saw the Gas-man fall to a mighty left-hook, and a couple of months later published 'The Fight', one of the greatest essays in the English language. Coleridge had famously distinguished between 'the fancy' and 'the imagination', but in the circle of the *London Magazine* the two were not so far apart.

The Fancy referred both to the art of boxing and those who followed it. Enthusiasts came from all classes, right up to the entourage of the Prince Regent, who at his coronation as George IV in 1821 was attended by eighteen prize-fighters, led by 'Gentleman' Jackson and including the formidable four Toms—Oliver, Cribb, Spring and Belcher. They were notionally 'pages' but actually served as the unpopular new King's security guards.

At the bottom end of the social scale, the swagger of the Fancy was embodied in the world of Pierce Egan's *Life in London*. A vaudeville dramatisation of this novel, entitled *Tom and Jerry*, was playing to packed houses at Astley's whilst Clare was in town. Soon after returning home to Helpston, Clare himself made the link between boxing and poetry, referring to Byron's Don Juan as 'a fit partner for Tom and Jerry fond of getting into scrapes and always finding means to get out agen'.

London Magazine dinners were becoming less frequent, but Clare attended a memorable one in Fleet Street in early July. Samuel Taylor Coleridge, though not a contributor to the magazine, was the guest of honour. By this time he had 'a venerable white head' and a severe drug problem. As was his wont, he dominated the conversation. Clare observed that 'his words hung in their places at a quiet pace from a drawl in good set marching order, so that you would suppose he had learnt what he intended to say before he came'. He sensed that Coleridge was repeating material from his public lectures.

This was also the occasion on which Clare first met Hazlitt, whose prose style he admired more than that of any other living writer. He left a brilliant pen-portrait of Hazlitt's edginess—which was habitual, but would have been aggravated by the presence of Coleridge, whom he had once worshipped but now despised as a political turncoat:

> He sits a silent picture of severity—if you was to watch his face
> for a month you would not catch a smile there—his eyes were
> always turned towards the ground except when one is turned up
> now and then with a sneer that cuts a bad pun and a young au-
> thor's maiden table-talk to atoms wherever it is directed ...

when he enters a room he comes stooping with his eyes in his hands as if it were throwing under gazes round at every corner as if he smelt a dun or thief ready to seize him by the collar and demand his money or his life. He is a middle-sized dark-looking man and his face is deeply lined with a satirical character. His eyes are bright but they are rather turned under his brows. He is a walking satire and you would wonder where the poetry came from that is scattered so thickly over his writings. For the blood of me I could not find him out, that is I should have had no guess at him of his ever being a scribbler much more a genius.

There was another brilliant essayist but social misfit in the company that night. Again, Clare observed with an unerring eye: 'A little artless simple-seeming body, something of a child overgrown, in a blue coat and black neckerchief—for his dress is singular—with his hat in his hand, steals gently among the company with a smile, turning timidly round the room—it is De Quincey the Opium Eater.' If Hazlitt was uncomfortable because of Coleridge's presence, De Quincey may have been uneasy because of Hazlitt's: they had fallen out the previous autumn over a question of plagiarism. More generally, a number of the *London* authors felt that both they and the paper were suffering because of the preferential treatment given to De Quincey. The *Confessions of an English Opium-Eater* had been a stunning success for Taylor and Hessey, but De Quincey had failed to produce the promised sequel and was instead filling the pages of the *London* with dull articles on the economic theories that were obsessing him. Thomas Lovell Beddoes noted acutely and, as it proved, prophetically that 'Taylor has lately refused a paper of Procter's and one of Reynolds and kept back Darley's* ... for the purpose of introducing that thrice-double demoniac the oeconomical Opium-eater. Exit London.'

*On this London visit Clare became acquainted with the Irish poet George Darley, two years his junior and Taylor's latest discovery. They shared a skill in the writing of lyrics in the style of the seventeenth century. Darley was a manic-depressive. B. W. Procter, who wrote plays and poems under the name 'Barry Cornwall', was another *London* author, who often attended the dinners; Clare found his work amusing, though lightweight. He eventually became a commissioner in lunacy.

Taylor's nerves were bad. The literary end of the publishing business was in trouble: the bottom was dropping out of the poetry market. One event above all others signalled that a golden age of poetry had suddenly come to an end. Clare arrived in London that May some two weeks after a dispatch from Greece: Lord Byron was dead. As Cunningham wrote in the *London Magazine*, the news came 'like an earthquake'. Everyone of a literary disposition remembered where they were when they heard: 'Byron is dead! I was told it all at once in a roomful of people. My God, if they had said that the sun or the moon had gone out of the heavens, it could not have struck me with the idea of a more awful and dreary blank in the creation.'

The body was brought back to England. The Dean of Westminster refused burial in the Abbey. On Monday 12 July the hearse set off from Great George's Street on the journey to the village church in Nottinghamshire where Byron would be laid in the family vault. It led a procession of coaches, many of them gilded with the arms of the aristocracy, but empty of passengers. Scandal was following him to the grave.

Clare was wandering up Oxford Street on his way to Mrs Emmerson's when he saw 'straggling groups of the common people collected together and talking about a funeral'. He joined the crowd, not knowing whose funeral they were waiting for. A hundred or more people had gathered by the time the hearse appeared. It seemed 'small and rather mean'. Immediately behind it came a coach with an open window, through which one could see a pall draped over an urn containing the poet's heart and brain, which had been removed at autopsy. A young girl standing beside Clare gave a deep sigh and said 'Poor Lord Byron'. Clare looked into her face: 'it was dark and beautiful and I could almost feel in love with her for the sigh she had uttered for the poet.' She counted the carriages as they passed and told him that there were sixty-three or sixty-four in all.

He was deeply affected by this moment. The 'quality' watched from windows above, 'but they wore smiles on their faces and thought more of the spectacle than the poet'. It was the ordinary people who were doing Byron honour. This meant more than all the newspaper puffs and magazine mournings put together. High society and all the moralisers could say as they would about Byron's fame:

> He has gained the path of its eternity without them and lives above the blight of their mildewing censures to do him damage—the common people felt his merits and his power and the common people of a country are the best feelings of a prophecy of futurity . . . they are the feelings of nature's sympathies unadulterated with the pretensions of art and pride. They are the veins and arteries that feed and quicken the heart of living fame ... They did not stand gaping with surprise on the trappings of gaudy show or look on with apathised indifference like the hired mutes in the spectacle, but they felt it—I could see it in their faces.

That was the night he left Eliza's house, feeling ill. The memory of Byron, and all its associations, would long stay with him. His notebook fragments on the subject of poetic fame keep returning to the example of Byron, as when he writes apropos of the question of whether there should be a monument to him in Westminster Abbey, 'Time is his monument on whose scroll the name of Byron and the Muse shall be legible characters when the walls and tombs of Westminster shall mingle with the refuse of ruins'.

By the end of July, Clare's overall health had improved sufficiently for him to go home. Hessey sent word to Patty in advance, together with a bank draft for fifteen pounds to clear off all unpaid bills. Dr Darling, perhaps aware of the looming financial difficulties facing Taylor and Hessey, seems to have taken Clare aside and suggested that he should make alternative plans to a career in poetry. There just wasn't going to be enough money in it. England had been through a period of poetical fever—witness the phenomenal sales of Burns, Scott and Byron—but now a reaction was setting in.

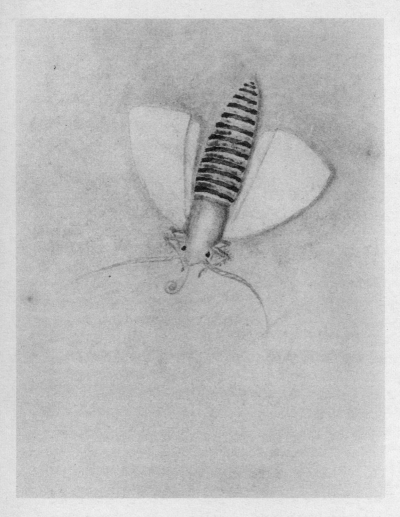

SKETCH OF HORNET MOTH IN CLARE'S JOURNAL

CHAPTER TWELVE

BIOGRAPHIES, BIRDS

AND FLOWERS

A month after going home Clare decided to start keeping a journal. He had brought back from Taylor and Hessey a printed diary called The Student's Journal, designed so that it could be started at any time, not just in January. A quotation from Gibbon on the title-page explained the book's purpose: 'I propose from this day to keep an exact Journal of my Actions and Studies, both to assist my Memory, and to accustom me to set due value on my Time.' Sundays were given double space, since the day of rest left extra time for reading and meditation. At the back of the volume there was room for an 'Annual Retrospect' in which users could assess how well they had spent their time in the course of the year.

Clare was still in a dark mood. Opposite the title-page of his new journal he drew a tombstone inscribed with the names of Chatterton, Keats and Bloomfield. He was placing himself firmly in the Prematurely Dead Lower-Class Poets' Society. But he began his diary-keeping with the firm intention of making the most of whatever time was left to him: 'I have determind this day of beginning a sort of journal to give my opinion of things I may read or see and set down any thoughts that may arise either in my reading at home or my musings in the Fields.' For the first few months he crammed as much writing as he could into the available space. As the twelve-month period progressed, his enthusiasm waned. More and more days were left blank. The journal is, however, the closest we ever come to the feel of Clare's day-to-day existence. It records the things that were dearest to him: reading, writing, walking, natural history observations, the health of his family, his literary friendships. He also copied curiosities from the *Stamford Mercury*—a 105-year-old woman cutting new teeth (to the great surprise of her family); a seven-foot-long, fifty-seven-pound eel caught in Essex—and he recorded observations on village life, ranging from gypsy weddings to changes in the land: 'Took a walk in the fields saw an old woodstile taken away from a favourite spot which it had occupied all my life.' He even tells of the noise of the rats scuttling in his roof at night.

When he spent most of a day reading, his evening journal entry would consist of a brief observation on the book in question. On Tuesday 7 September 1824 he read in Foxe's *Book of Martyrs* and concluded that 'Tyrany and Cruelty appear to be the inseperable companions of Religion's Power and the Aphorism is not far from truth that says "All priests are the same" '. Given this sentiment, it is not surprising that Clare's return to Helpston was not accompanied by a return to the Methodists. The journal shows that on Sundays Clare often read the Bible or a religious treatise, but there is no mention of attendance at any religious service.* He preferred to go for a walk. As an antidote to the militant religiosity of Foxe, and to occupy a rainy day, he turned to one of his best-loved books, Walton's *Angler*: 'one may almost hear the water of the river Lea ripple along and the grass and flags grow and rustle in the pages that speak of it'.

The compressed format of the journal allowed Clare to express his opinions of his reading matter in crisp, decisive terms. The *London Magazine* came early each month. Verdict: generally going

*The only possible exception is Sunday 3 October 1824, when he gave Parson Mossop his new will to examine: this *may* have been handed over at church. But on Christmas day there is no mention of going to church, only of how as a boy he was eager to attend the church 'to see it stuck with evergreens (symbols of Eternity)'. On Palm Sunday 1825 he notes going to the woods to seek 'sallow palms' (*salix*) for the children, but says nothing of church.

downhill, save for Lamb's essays. He revisited Chatterton's poems: old favourites, wonderful for natural descriptions (thunder-storms, flowers). Byron's *Don Juan* was brought over by Henderson: '2 verses of the Shipwreck very fine and the character of Haidee is the best I have yet met'—he was presumably attracted by the way that Haidee is the embodiment of female youth, beauty, innocence, sexual availability and premature mortality, all rolled into one. The latter part of *Don Juan*, in which the hero visits England, he found tiresome.

Shakespeare's sonnets were 'great favourites', as *Henry V* had been since his boyhood; he now read *A Midsummer Night's Dream*, which made him hope he would have the chance to read all the other plays before he died. He thought that Shakespeare's masterpiece was *Macbeth*: 'what a soul-thrilling power hovers about this tradegy—I have read it over about twenty times and it chains my feelings still to its perusal like a new thing'. His judgements on other celebrated poets were more mixed. Alexander Pope: some fine passages, but 'the uninterrupted flow of the verses wearys the ear'. Wordsworth: 'natural and beautiful'. Robert Blair's poem *The Grave*: morbidly beautiful, with Shakespearean touches. Bishop Percy's collection of ballads, *Relics of Ancient Poetry*: 'the essence and simplicity of true poetry'—he wished he had encountered the book at the start of his poetic career because it would have formed his taste and laid the foundation of his judgement in thinking and writing poetically.

The odes of William Collins? Lusciously sweet, lacking in pomp, better than those of Gray. Milton: *Paradise Lost* sublime, especially the beginning and the ending; *Paradise Regained* unreadable; *Comus* graced with a beautiful description of an ox and a hedger at evening. Josiah Conder, a poet published by Taylor and Hessey: good imitations of the Psalms (something Clare would later try himself) and a fine bird poem spoilt by the unnatural personification 'Sir Nightingale'. J. H. Reynolds's 'Romance of Youth' in his collection *The Garden of Florence*, sent with the author's compliments: 'several beautys' but some natural descriptions marked by artificial 'conseits'.

He read prose as well as poetry. He wondered why Dr Johnson had omitted the Elizabethans, his own favourites, from the lives of the English poets. And he praised Hazlitt as 'one of the very best prose writers of the present day', singling out the *Lectures on the English Poets* as his best work, whereas 'his political writings are heated and empty full of sound and fury—I hate polotics and therefore I may be but a poor judge'.

All these entries were written between September and December 1824. In the new year, Clare changed tack and used his diary primarily for natural history field observations and to keep a record of letters sent and received. After his autumnal fit of reading he had sated his book-appetite for a while.

Although the first four months of Clare's journal are dominated by his reports of reading, there are many entries that give a vivid sense of other dimensions of his life at this time. There is no mention of any labouring employment, though he had helped gather in the harvest (and then got drunk) at the end of August. Despite the ministrations of Dr Darling, he was still fragile. When health and weather permitted, he worked in his garden. He transplanted flowers from the woods, and exchanged seeds and cuttings with friends, sometimes by post ('Recieved a Letter from Mrs Emmerson with a Parcel containing a present of a Waiscoat and some fine Polyanthus, Brompton Stock and Geranium Seed').

The journal records many walks, the first of them on 9 September, the opening day of the shooting season. Clare sympathised with the hares and the pheasants as they ran from the dogs; he returned home early for fear of being 'shot under the hedges'. Walking in the fields and woods could be hazardous. Keepers were suspicious of men who looked like labourers but were not labouring:

> Took a walk in the field a birds nesting and botanising and had like to have been taken up as a poacher in Hilly Wood by a meddlesome conseited keeper belonging to Sir John Trollop—he swore that he had seen me in act more than once of shooting game when I never shot even so much as a sparrow in my life— what terryfying rascals these wood keepers and gamekeepers are—they make a prison of the forrests and are its joalers.

A few weeks after being mistaken for a poacher, Clare had a dangerous encounter of another kind:

> Met with an extrodinary incident to day while Walking in Open Wood to hunt a Nightingales nest—I popt unawares on an old Fox and her four young Cubs that were playing about—she saw me and instantly approachd towards me growling like an angry dog—I had no stick and tryd all I coud to fright her by imitating the bark of a foxhound which only irritated her the more and if I had not retreated a few paces back she woud have seized me—when I set up an haloo she started.

It did not, however, come naturally to Clare to impersonate a hunter. More usually, his attitude to animals of all kinds was characterised by exceptional tenderness:

> Found the old Frog in my garden that has been there this four years—I know it by a mark which it recieved from my spade 4 years ago—I thought it woud dye of the wound so I turnd it up on a bed of flowers at the end of the garden which is thickly covered with ferns and bluebells and am glad to see it has recoverd—in Winter it gets into some straw in a corner of the garden and never ventures out till the beginning of May when it hides among the flowers and keeps its old bed never venturing further up the garden.

He kept two live specimens of the small hawk known as a hobby. The larger and tamer one flew after him when he went walking in the fields and came when he whistled. When he was away from home for four days, it sat in his empty chair and refused food. The family thought it was fretting itself to death in his absence, but Clare took the view that it wasn't well anyway and that the meat he had given it was too strong. When he came home to find it dead he felt 'heartily sorry' for his 'poor faithful and affectionat hawk'.

He sought to add a new string to his bow as a natural historian by improving his draughtsmanship. Hessey agreed that 'a little drawing of landscapes, of cattle, birds, flowers etc. will add greatly to your amusements and will give nature a new beauty in your eye'. Many of the poetic manuscripts on which he was working in this period are embellished with delicate sketches in the margins. He found a hornet moth in Royce Wood and made a particularly fine drawing of it on the final leaf of The Student's Journal.

Clare's diary reveals the ups and downs of the depressive life. On the day of the Michaelmas holiday, known as the Helpstone Statute, he was well enough to go out and look at the girls, despite the pouring rain: 'the lasses do not lift up their gowns to show taper ancles and white stockings, but on the contrary drop them to hide dirty ones'. But the next day he was 'Very ill and did nothing but ponder over a future existance'. The black thoughts continued for two further days: 'A wet day, did nothing but nurse my illness—Coud not have walkd out had it been fine—very disturbd in conscence about the troubles of being forcd to endure life and dye by inches and the anguish of leaving my children and the dark porch of eternity whence none returns to tell the tale of their reception'. And again, 'Tryd to walk out coud not—have read nothing this week—my mind almost over-weights me with its upbraidings and miserys—my childern very ill night and morning with a fever.' Then the weekend came and he felt able to do some reading and take a walk in the fields, where his heart was lifted by the thin sounds of the cricket and the shrew. Within a fortnight, however, the gloom was back: 'Very ill to day and very unhappy—my three Childern are all unwell—had a dismal dream of being in hell—this is the third time I have had such a dream.'

Fen fever, ague and influenza flourished in the damp autumn weather. Clare's illness was physical, not merely psychological. Nor did he have the utter self-absorption that is brought by depression in its severe form: his anxiety rested on his children as much as his own immortal soul. He was unselfish enough to take the trouble to start teaching some basic arithmetic to a lame pauper boy in the village. His worries about money and career were wholly understandable. When someone told him that poor Bloomfield had supported a family of six on a mere hundred pounds a year, he noted that he himself had to support eight people on less than fifty: 'this is a hungry difference'.* Despite the family's poverty, Clare continued to spend considerable sums on books and occasional indulgences.

Hunger and poor diet undoubtedly contributed to his decline. According to his first biographer, Clare once fainted when walking with Artis in the fields: 'he had eaten nothing but a few potatoes with milk for twenty-four hours, having left his home in the morning without taking any food whatever.' Frederick Martin goes on to tell a delightful story of Monsieur Grilliot the Milton chef arriving at the Helpston cottage with a stone bottle full of broth, heating it on the fire and reviving poor Clare.

The physical symptoms were real, yet his fragile mental state led him to exaggerate small rebuffs. He discovered that an almanac called *Time's Telescope* had referred to him as 'Robert' rather than 'John' Clare: 'There went the left wing of my fame', he ripostes. The editorial work on his next volume of poems was proceeding slowly and this led him to feel that Taylor and Hessey were not giving him the support he needed: 'the worlds friendships are counterfits and forgerys ... my affections are sickend unto death and my memorys are broken while my confidence is grown to a shadow—in the bringing out a second Edit of the Minstrel they was a twelvmonth in printing a title page'. This entry seems a little harsh, given that it was written on receiving a letter from Hessey explaining that all but essential business had been halted by a terrible fire in Fleet Street which had destroyed six or seven houses—the firm's own premises had only been saved by a strong party wall and a drop in the wind. Hessey had been forced to remove his family, his account books, papers and the most valuable part of the stock across the street to a neighbour's house.

The conviviality of the Londoners was quickly becoming a distant memory. Clare felt isolated. Walking in Lea Close, he noticed an old

---

*'Eight people': himself, his mother, father, wife, three young children—but who is the eighth? Perhaps sister Sophy, if her husband, William Kettle, was unable fully to support her.

hazelnut tree that he had climbed as a boy. It still stood but 'the Inclosure has left it desolate, its companions of oak and ash being gone'. Irrationally, he felt he was in the same position as that tree. The changes in the land wrought by enclosure were by now symbolic of his own narrowing prospects and the loss of the familiar landmarks of his childhood. Nor did the march of progress end with the enclosure. On one of his walks in Royce Wood he encountered three men surveying the potential route of a proposed London-to-Manchester railway. 'I little thought', he wrote, 'that fresh intrusions woud interrupt and spoil my solitudes after the Inclosure.'

He wanted solitude in which to walk and write, but he also needed intellectual stimulation. For this reason, the companionship of Henderson and Artis was especially important to him. His spirits were cheered when Henderson came with the news that he had discovered a new species of fern out on Whittlesea Mere. Clare began a fern collection of his own, explaining in a letter that he 'love[d] wild things almost to foolishness'.

In December he spent four nights at Milton, where he enjoyed looking at Henderson's collection of ferns and some of the handsomely illustrated botanical and entomological volumes in Artis's library. He liked a good argument about plants: 'Took a Walk to "Simons Wood" found 3 distinct species of the "Bramble" or mulberry—Henderson will have it there is but 2 but I am certain he is wrong and believe there is 4.' And a few days later: 'the authoress (Miss Kent) of the "Flora Domestica" says the snow drop is the first spring flower—she is mistaken—the yellow winter aconite is always earlier and the first on the list of spring.'

Natural history was much on his mind. In the autumn of 1824 he was working on two new books, both in prose rather than verse. One was the autobiography, which he intended to be more candid than the sketch of his early life that he had sent to Taylor three and a half years before. The other was to be ' "A Natural History of Helpstone" in a Series of Letters to Hessey' (for which he drafted some brief technical essays, 'On the sexual system of plants' and on 'the Fungus tribe and on Mildew Blight etc.'). Gilbert White's *Natural History of Selborne* was his precedent for a volume of parish-based natural history observations structured in epistolary form.

The first seed of the natural history letters was sown by Clare's response to Elizabeth Kent's *Flora Domestica*. On reading that book in the summer of 1823, he wrote to Hessey with an extensive commentary on it, offering corrections and additional information. His principle in plant lore was that 'the vulgar are always the best glossary to such things'. Countrymen were to be trusted more than poets. It was an error of judgement for Kent's brother-in-law Leigh Hunt to have called 'heart's-ease' (the wild pansy, *Viola tricolor*) 'the Sparkler': the name was more fitting for a liqueur than a flower. Some of Clare's comments on *Flora Domestica* were published in the *London Magazine*. For instance: 'The Author is mistaken about the Cowslip, as it is a very favoured flower, and no cottager's garden is without it'. A year later, on his return from London, Clare wrote to Hessey about the habits of swallows. Hessey responded enthusiastically and Clare began to put together his proposed volume.

Over the next six months he filled two notebooks with a wealth of natural history notes. In March he came up with a new title for his proposed book: 'Intend to call my Natural History of Helpstone "Biographys of Birds and Flowers" with an Appendix on Animals and Insects.' A month later, however, he was flagging: 'Resumed my letters on Natural History in good earnest and intend to get them finished with this year if I can get out into the fields, for I will insert nothing but what comes or has come under my notice.' He completed about a dozen letters, a large number of fragmentary notes, and a remarkable list of birds, but he never put the book into a final shape. Some of the letters were sent to Hessey and desultory notes were added in the late 1820s and early 1830s, but the project to publish his natural history prose works in their own right lay dormant for a century and a half.* In the spring of 1825 there were also various related

---

*In 1983 Margaret Grainger published a wonderfully full edition of *The Natural History Prose Writings of John Clare*.

plans, none of which came to fruition: to collaborate with Artis on a 'History of Birds', with Henderson on a book of annotated flower poems, and with Miss Kent on a volume that did for birds what her *Flora Domestica* had done for flowers—that is to say, to combine a poetry anthology with a collection of field notes and folklore.

Clare and Miss Kent exchanged several lengthy letters about birds and their habits. In one of these he told her that he had long since stopped taking eggs from nests, as he had done as a boy. 'You need not have told me that you had ceased to deprive the birds of their brood', she replied,

> I could not have believed you, had you even *told* me that you were capable of such a thing. I cannot suppose that a poet *ever did* such a thing; for a man who has the sensibility he must have to *be* a poet, cannot well be a brute; and what but brutality is it, after the thoughtlessness of boyhood has passed away, to inflict unnecessary pain upon any living creature. Had any one put your poems in my hands, and said to me, the author of those poems, took bird's-nests. I should have answered,—"Not *after* he wrote these poems; I am certain."

For the adult Clare, 'Birds Nesting' meant observing nests, not stealing from them. He wrote a 600-line poem of this title, describing the nests of an array of birds: the 'redcap' (goldfinch), blackcap (which sang so sweetly in Open Wood that he mistook it for the nightingale), mavis (mistle) thrush, blackbird, 'willowbiter' (pettichap), skylark, kingfisher, swallow, 'firetail' (redstart), 'Egypt bird' (spotted flycatcher), wren, green woodpecker, wryneck, and several others. Like the natural history letters, this exquisite poem remained in manuscript for over a century and a half. Clare did, however, go on to write a large number of shorter poems on particular nests, some of which were included in his 1835 collection.

Had 'Biographies of Birds and Flowers' been published, it would have made Clare's gift for natural observation and description apparent to a readership beyond the consumers of poetry. The letters are written with a relaxed combination of scientific precision and lyrical affection. They are not without humour. Noting how Londoners were very fond of talking about nightingales, Clare remembered how during his recent visit he had been walking in the fields of Shacklewell with a friend (William Sharp, the Helpston man who worked in the Dead Letter Office). They saw a gentleman and a lady listening very attentively beside a shrubbery: 'and when we came up we heard them lavishing praises on the beautiful song of the nightingale which happened to be a thrush—but it did for them.' The thrush sang on, as if proud to be mistaken for its more famously musical cousin.

The letters begin with birds, evoking the characteristics of a wide array of species: Clare moves easily from the nesting habits of the bullfinch to the darting movement of the flycatcher to the piercing cry of the nightjar (remembered from when he worked on the kilns at Casterton). Later, he turns to snakes, wild flowers, the classification of snail-shells, the spawning of frogs and the perseverance of the green tiger beetle. But he keeps being drawn back to birds, and their nests in particular. They would soon become the subject-matter of some of his very greatest poetry.

The majority of the extant natural history letters are in one manuscript, a selection of further notes in another. Some of the latter fragments are mini-essays with titles such as 'Animal Instinct', 'Signs of the weather by animals—wet', and 'On Ants'. Others are more like the journal entries, written with the immediacy of the moment:

> March 25th The woods covered with anemonies or ladysmocks ... a little nameless bird with a black head and olive green back and wings—not known—seems to feed on the Ivy berry—comes when they are ripe and disappears when they are gone—said to have a sweet song—the blue anemonie or anemonie pulsitilla haunts the roman road—the bumbarrel featherpoke or longtaild titmouse its nest—the craunking noise of the woodpecker boring new holes a token of spring.

The bird list, compiled in April and May 1825, enumerates the habits of over a hundred species with which Clare was familiar from personal observation, local lore and the information of Artis. It has some wonderful autobiographical touches, such as an account of a tame magpie that he kept 'till it got drownd in a well' where it liked to look at itself in the water.

The list remains valuable as a record not only of ornithological distribution in the 1820s, but also of bird-related customs:

> Martin—
> Martins do not come till after the swallow and seldom make their appearance till May—they make their nests under the eaves of houses where some people deem them sacred and reckon the appearance of a Martins nest under their eaves as a good Omen and as a charm against thunder and lighting ... Childern are cautioned not to destroy them in the fear of incurring therebye almost an unforgiven offence to their maker and if a hardend boy happens to destroy one his parents consider that something serious will befall him—thus they gain an asylum under most cottages by this tender and praiseworthy superstition.

Clare was acutely conscious of change in the countryside. He feared that the old customs and superstitions were disappearing, as were the songs and tunes of the folk tradition. He made it his business to preserve them in writing. So too with the characteristics and distribution of birds and flowers. In one of his manuscript books he inscribed a title-page: 'English Orchises copied from *English Botany*, with his own marginal notes'. Henderson did the copying from a botanical handbook (which had beautiful plates by James Sowerby) and Clare inserted notes telling of where orchids could be seen locally. Or once seen, but no longer: the early marsh-orchid 'was very plentiful before the Enclosure on a Spot called Parkers Moor near Peasfield-hedge and on Deadmoor near Sneep Green and Rotten Moor by Moorclose but these places are now all under plough'.

A fragment in a different notebook, dating from the same period, lists some of Clare's pleasures: waiting in a favourite spot to hear the song of the nightingale, gardening, cutting open a new book on a spring morning, waiting for a lover, pressing a primrose as both a pledge of spring and a bookmark. Gardening, birding and botanising were as central to his life as reading, writing and loving.

By the middle of January 1825 Clare had drafted nine chapters of his autobiography, reaching from his childhood to the publication of his first book. He went over the same ground as that covered in the memoir sent to Taylor, but with more detail and some altogether new material, such as the story of his experiences in the militia. Some of the chapters were given titles: 'My First Feelings and Attempts at Poetry', 'Memorys of Love'. By May he had brought his narrative more or less up to date, with accounts of his three visits to London. It was here that he wrote his vivid pen-portraits of the *London Magazine* authors.

In this period of physical illness, depression and even suicidal thoughts, Clare was taking stock. He was deeply troubled about both the fate of his immortal soul and the wording of his will—he drew up several different drafts, one of which survives. It reveals his concern for the future well-being of his parents, sister and children, and his desire for appropriate mementos to be given to those who had stood by him. A precious four-volume edition of Byron would go to Eliza Emmerson and Hilton's water-colour portrait to Lord Radstock. He also began drafting a letter of advice for his children to read after his death.

The aim of the autobiography was to ensure that his own record of his life would survive him. We have seen that the deaths of Bloomfield and Byron were very much on his mind. It was a sure bet that biographers would be queuing up to expose the scandalous life of Byron. He was in touch with Bloomfield's literary executor, and even briefly contemplated writing his biography. Though it might have looked like vanity for a country 'clown' to write his autobiography, he was anxious not to suffer the fate of Bloomfield and Byron: he wanted to pre-empt the envious and the gossips, who might otherwise have attributed his early death to his being a drunkard or having ambitions above his station.

Clare drafted his autobiographical sketches in several different notebooks. The marks of work in progress are readily apparent: a note saying 'for the next Chapter', a jotting that reads 'Heads: / Beginning with the world / chusing friends / opinions in religion'. Many of the fragments are scored through and marked 'done with'. This shows that they had been written up in a fair copy. He wanted to show his memoir to someone he could trust. Though he had no qualms about exposing his own faults and failings, he was less sure of his tone in writing about other people. He would not flatter, but did not wish to offend. He decided that the Reverend Henry Cary would be the right reader. Not only was Cary much respected by everyone in the circle of Taylor and Hessey, he was also a good judge in matters biographical—Clare remembered that he had contributed a fine *London Magazine* article on the life of Chatterton.

So he wrote to Cary, asking him to read the autobiography. Cary assented gladly: 'I will read the memoirs of yourself which you propose sending me; and not fail to tell you, if I think you have spoken of others with more acrimony than you ought.' Unfortunately, the surviving correspondence between Clare and Cary lapses for a period of three years hereafter, so we do not know whether the fair copy was indeed sent. The likelihood is that it was and that Cary at some point gave it into the safekeeping of Taylor. Circumstantial evidence suggests that this lost manuscript was among the Taylor papers seen by Frederick Martin when preparing his biography of Clare. Had it been published in or immediately after the poet's lifetime, *The Autobiography of John Clare* could have become a classic of the genre.

In a fragment intended for the book's conclusion Clare apologised to his imagined readers for some of his anecdotes being 'very trifling' and his expressions 'impertinent'. He asked for indulgence on the grounds that 'most of the naritive was written in severe illness'. And it is illness that dominates his correspondence in the year following his return from London.

'I am getting worse and worse and what my complaint is I cannot tell', he informed Cary in September 1824. 'You must excuse this scrawl for I am ill able to write or do anything else—I thought I was getting well once but I've not a hope left me now.' Dr Darling sent some new pills, but—much to Hessey's consternation—Clare stopped taking them after a few weeks. His constitution was also upset by an over-rich pie and pudding, but then in later months he failed to nourish himself sufficiently. He lost the will-power to reply promptly to his letters. This worried Hessey, who was having to handle all the publishing business and correspondence himself since Taylor was also suffering from a severe nervous disorder.

Dr Skrimshire was engaged again. He called on Hessey in London and told him that there had been little improvement in Clare's health. In January 1825 Henderson invited his friend to a birthday ball at Milton, even having the forethought to send over an umbrella so that he would not get wet on the way. Clare seems to have been unable to rouse himself to the task of going. The next month, his elder daughter fell seriously ill. He feared smallpox. Dr Darling suggested that leeches should be applied to the little girl's temples, to abate her fever. Mrs Emmerson wondered whether the combination of fever and wasting suggested that the illness had its origin in worms. She also sent her annual Valentine's Day poem, which on this occasion Clare dismissed as a trifling distraction from serious concerns.

Darling sent more advice: keep strictly to the diet prescribed, 'keep the bowels freely open', take the powders that have been provided, exercise moderately, and if possible 'get your limbs and back rubbed for an hour morning and evening with a blacking brush'. One would like to know Patty's reaction to the idea that she should spend her time occupied thus, in addition to coping with three frequently sick children under the age of five, a sister-in-law with a new baby, and her husband's two aged parents.

Clare was brought especially close to his elder daughter Anna by her illness. During her convalescence he read her Mrs Barbauld's *Lessons for Children*—a book recommended by Cary—over and over again. She loved books. Clare must have been especially delighted when one day she ran out of the house to meet Mrs Gilchrist (Octavius's widow), holding in her hand a copy of Thomson's *Seasons*, the poem that had so inspired him.

Only a few months after her recovery, Anna was ill again, this time

catching a fever from her sister Eliza. On 'Darling Anna's' fifth birthday, 2 June 1825, Clare described her as his 'weakling flower fast fading in the bud'. His own restless anxiety is apparent from a journal
entry of a few weeks earlier: 'Coud not sleep all night—got up at
three oclock in the morning and walkd about the fields'. The intense
love he felt for his young children is clear from a prose fragment written a few years later: 'My family has increased and my affections also
grow with them . . . whenever I am surrounded by my family there is
my comfort and if I was in the wilds of America with them for my
companions there would my home be.'

The worries about money were piling up and there were the usual
incidental annoyances such as the shortage of affordable paper. One
morning he tried scraping thin layers of bark from a birch tree and
splitting them into sheets. He found that they received the ink very
readily. Later, he would manufacture his own ink, a mix of bruised
nut galls, green copper and stone blue soaked in a pint and a half of
rain-water and shaken every day until fit for use. Holding some of his
manuscripts today, you may see how the home-made ink has eaten its
way into the paper.

Late in August 1825 he learnt of old Lord Radstock's death. Whatever the disputes over 'radical Slang' and poems of dubious morals, he
had been one of Clare's most energetic patrons and promoters. His
passing marked the end of an era. Clare wrote a brief poem in the Admiral's memory, calling him 'the poor man's friend on earth'. Mrs
Emmerson was upset, not least because his Lordship had been struck
by his final fit of apoplexy under her very own roof. She persuaded
her husband to take her into the country to recover her spirits. They
would stay at the Bull Inn in Market Deeping, and she would at last
have the chance to meet Clare's family.

The visit was a great success. The Emmersons arrived at Helpston in
a chaise and took the children for a ride out to Langley Bush. Clare
showed them all the sights in the neighbourhood. Eliza thought that
Maxey was an especially pretty village. They discussed Clare's future
as an author in the light of the growing difficulties in his relationship

with John Taylor. From this time onward the Emmersons would take an increasingly active part in managing his literary affairs. Eliza also left some money with Patty, to provide for the schooling of the two girls. Anna was five by now. Eliza Louisa was only three, but her god-mother was determined that her little namesake's education should be paid for by no one but herself. Further sums of money were duly sent in later years.

Old Parker gave the guests some hazelnuts and, on returning to London after their four-day visit, Eliza reciprocated by sending Spanish onions for his garden. Clare picked roses for his patroness before accompanying her and her husband back to Deeping. He walked home with gifts of dolls and gingerbread for the children.

A few weeks later Eliza added a postscript to one of her letters, in which she playfully warned against 'Billings and Cooings'—code for drinking bouts and amorous dalliance ('Billings' because the brothers of that name were Clare's chief drinking companions). In one of Clare's manuscripts of this period there are some cryptic fragments concerning the female sex: some lines about trusting 'an harlots smile'; a prose scribbling headed 'Woman' and beginning 'Hasty decisions are like flowers coming in flower out of season'; a variation on the theme of *carpe diem*:

> Dost think that beautys power
> Lifes sweetest pleasure gives
> Go pluck the summer flower
> And see how long it lives.

Towards the end of the year Clare informed Dr Darling of an inflammation on an unidentified part of his body. He also seems to have expressed worries about somehow infecting his children. 'Make your conscience easy respecting your children for however much they may suffer it will not be from any voluntary fault of yours', the doctor reassured him.

Eliza's fears were realised. Shortly before Christmas 1825 Clare confessed to her that he was having an affair. Early in January, he wrote with a fuller account of it. The letter is lost, like nearly all the others he sent to Emmerson, but her reply leaves no room for doubt:

> You have been *wandering* from home,—from *yourself* and alas! from happiness:—And much do I fear, that *my influence* as your attached and *true friend*, will have little power to win you back to tranquility and to domestic peace—and above all, to *your dear Children*, for it is them I *feel* the *most for*, on the present occasion! I deeply regret 'the *cause* of your late out-breakings from propriety'—but why my dear Clare, will you allow the temper or injudicious conduct of others, to harry you away from your own reason,—and induce you to do such things as can only bring upon you, the loss of health the expendature of money, and that wretchedly *disturbed mind*, of which you complain so forcably and with so much *just reasoning* . . . I am not a 'prude', nor a 'moralist'—but I would be enough of the philosopher and friend—to prevail on you by every gentle, kind, and reasonable entreaty, to give up your acquaintance with ———— it is an unworthy connexion, and can only bring you a train of miseries! . . . I hope ———— will do all in her power to make your mind more contented, and enable you to pursue your Literary labours . . . God bless you, my dear Clare—write to me, of your return to home, and to the perfect return to *domestic comfort* with *your family*! Adieu Ever Yours Eliza.

The first blank indicates an unnamed lover, while the second must be a reference to Patty, whose 'temper or injudicious conduct' Clare appears to have blamed for his '*wandering* from home'. Eliza's talk of possible financial consequences suggests that the affair must have been quite serious—a woman to pay off, potentially even an illegitimate child to support?

We do not know exactly when the affair began or when it ended. In March Mrs Emmerson was still writing of his 'present infatuated, "tortured" and, I will add, besotted and inactive state'. In April she taunted him that he had failed to come to London to finalise his will and sort out his business affairs with Taylor because 'some *loadstone* binds you—something more attractive than green fields, and birds, and flowers'. She again stressed the necessity of his giving up the liaison, assuring him that in saying this she was being cruel to be kind. Clare then spent some time away from home, visiting the Simpsons in Stamford and Henderson at Milton Park. Emmerson expressed the hope that the change of scene would help him to make the break from his lover.

Rippingille had written after a long period of silence. Clare replied in the middle of May, inviting him to stay and giving the impression that domestic harmony had been restored: 'I am sure Patty will be as happy to see you as my self—my Study is not thronged with the Muses but with the melodious mischief of 3 Childern and my Pastoral Mistress is on the eve of bringing another into the world to add to the Band.' The new baby was born on 16 June 1826. It was a boy and they named him John after his father. Conscious of the need to feed his ever-growing family, Clare spent the rest of the summer engaged in hard manual labour in the fields.

His affair appears to have endured for most of Patty's pregnancy and to have come to an end shortly before the birth. The possible consequences of an extra-marital liaison were brought vividly home to him a couple of months later when his friend Artis departed from his post as steward at Milton, on account of having impregnated a milkmaid. The girl seems to have died, possibly in childbirth. Clare told Mrs Emmerson, who was shocked that a man of such accomplishments should sacrifice his job and abnegate his familial responsibilities merely 'for the gratification of a few inconsiderate hours of sensual pleasure'.

For Clare, though, the biggest problem was the perennial one of money. Shortly after the birth of the new baby, there came a voice from the past: Ned Drury. It was years since he had ceased to be involved in the publishing of Clare, but now Taylor and Hessey, who were settling accounts following the dissolution of their partnership, had demanded from him over a hundred pounds in connection with their collaboration on the production of the early poems. Drury accordingly wrote to ask Clare for reimbursement for cash advanced during the writing of *The Village Minstrel*, together with other expenses, 'viz. supplying you with Goods, procuring Medical advice for your Mother, Binding your Books, and other particulars.' Clare was furious. There had never been any understanding that Drury required payment for such things as the assistance with his mother's medical needs. Taylor and Hessey paid the forty pounds that Drury was demanding from Clare, but the financial dispute between them would flare up again three years later.

Little work was available in the fields once the harvest was gathered in. In the autumn Clare's health took its habitual seasonal turn for the worse. As the year 1826 came to an end the children were ill again. Patty's father died and she had an uncharacteristic period of illness herself. Eliza Emmerson sent a guinea so that the family could have a decent Christmas dinner of roast beef and plum pudding (and good ale for Clare himself). She also gave him two silk handkerchiefs as a present, together with more guineas for the girls' schooling. The Earl of Exeter provided a pheasant at New Year. All this was a welcome change from the usual diet of bread, cheese, potatoes, porridge and tea, but the outlook for the future was bleak—especially since Clare's relationship with his publishers had become increasingly fraught.

CHAPTER THIRTEEN

STAND-CARTS AND GO-CARTS

At the beginning of February 1822 John Taylor sent John Clare two new quarto-sized exercise books. They would serve as 'a Stand-Cart and a Go-Cart': one could be returned for editing while the other was being filled with new material. Stand-cart and go-cart are admirable metaphors for Clare's manuscripts, which all through these years went backwards and forwards between Helpston, Waterloo Place and Fleet Street (the premises of Taylor and Hessey)—not to mention Stratford Place (Mrs Emmerson's home) and Milton Park, where Henderson became a valued reader. The poems were drafted at great speed, but then underwent an elaborate process of revision and correction, expansion and contraction. A major part in that process was carried out by hands other than the poet's own.

Clare sent his poems to Taylor. Taylor corrected them and posted them back. Clare revised them and Taylor then published a selection, individually in the *London Magazine* or as a collection in book form. This arrangement lasted for several years. Although *The Village Minstrel* did not create the same splash as *Poems, Descriptive of Rural Life and Scenery*, there was a mutual understanding that a third collection would soon follow. As time went on, however, the collaboration became less congenial.

At the same time as sending the two new notebooks, Taylor asked for help in correcting the poem that was to be published in the next issue of the *London*: 'The first Verse of "I've met the Winter's biting breath" is not equal to the rest of that little Poem—the false Rhyme of *warm* and *calm*,—and the bad Grammar of bore for *borne* rendering some change in that Rhyme also necessary, impose on the Corrector a Task in which I should be glad to have your Assistance'. A couple of weeks later he objected to some lines that Clare had added to the beginning of the poem. They consisted of an address to the spring:

> And fairest daughter of the year
> Thrice welcome here anew
> Tho gentle storms tis thine to fear
> The roughest blast has blew.

'I cannot mend this Verse', replied Taylor, 'pray help me out with it. *Blew* ought to be *blown*.'

Something in Clare snapped:

> Your verse is a develish puzzle—I may alter but I cannot mend—grammer in learning is like Tyranny in government—confound the bitch I'll never be her slave and have a vast good mind not to alter the verse in question—by g-d I've tryd an hour and cannot do a syllable so do your best or let it pass.

He offered the alternative line 'The worst has bade adieu', but acknowledged that this was 'd——d lame'.

The poem, entitled 'The Approach of Spring', was published a few days later, with the lines rewritten altogether:

> The winds, that late with chiding voice
> Would fain thy stay prolong,
> Relent, while little birds rejoice,
> And mingle into song.

Taylor scribbled a hasty apology: 'The first Stanza was attempted to be mended by a Friend, but, I fear you will think he has marred it.' Clare's reaction is not recorded, but the exchange presaged problems that grew increasingly severe as author and publisher worked towards their next big project.

'The *Months* are a capital Idea', wrote Taylor in a postscript to his note about the revision of the 'Spring' poem. The idea was to produce a sequence of poems, one for each month of the year. The initial intention seems to have been to publish each poem in the relevant monthly number of the *London*, but soon there was talk of a new volume based on the plan. Over the next year and a half, Clare drafted January, February, June, October and December in one of his exercise books, April and some sketches towards September in the other one, and March, May, July, August and November in a third manuscript volume. He was also working on a wide range of other poems: sonnets and short lyrics, a lengthy satire called 'The Parish', and a variety of narrative poems. His letters of 1822 and 1823 tell of several different plans: a sequel to the autobiographical 'Village Minstrel', a volume to be entitled 'Summer Walks', a selection of stories for children, a collection of poems to be published under the pseudonym Percy Green with the title 'Edmund and Helen or the Suicide / A Story of Love / with other Poems'.

The most significant of these other works was 'The Parish', a satire of nearly two thousand lines. Early in January 1823 Clare told Hessey that it was finished, but he went on tinkering with it for several more years. The very idea of a satire, with its strong political connotations, alarmed Mrs Emmerson: 'How goes on your "Satire" "the Parish"— is it in verse or prose? Though, in any form, I almost hate the name of Satire, however ably indulged, it is an *unamicable* use of abilities, and often serves to destroy our better faculties and feelings—Pardon me, for thus pre-judging your "Parish".' When she read it, her fears were confirmed: she admired its force but told Clare that it was '*not* for *present* publication'. Though she did not say so, she was clearly thinking that the poem's savage portrayal of the hypocrisy of clerics and other authority figures would be wholly unacceptable to Lord Radstock.

Clare also gave a manuscript of 'The Parish' to Henderson. With his habitual generosity and acuity, the learned gardener spent every evening for a week working through it in detail, making comments and suggestions. The poem took the form of a series of sketches of village 'characters'. Henderson liked this as a general plan, but considered its tone 'reather too severe—too pointed, and perhaps too personal.—not that I think you have overdrawn any character or thrown his delinquencies into broader light than they deserve,—but that I think the poem would be equally effectual, gain more readers, and more admirers, if it were less pointed and less severe.' The poem had a motto from England's greatest poetic satirist, Alexander Pope: 'No injury can possibly be done, as a nameless character can never be found out but by its truth and likeness.' Henderson, who knew Helpston, seems to imply that, on the contrary, some elements of 'personal' insult might well be detected.

William Sharp of the Dead Letter Office gave similar advice. As a specimen of the poem, Clare sent him the section concerning the parish overseer. 'My Dear Sir', he replied, 'do you not fear to provoke these potentates and entail upon yourself a portion of their cruel tyrany?' Sharp thought that Clare was at his best when at his most tender and delicate: vindictiveness did not beseem him. Clare himself acknowledged that the portrayal of the overseer was an act of revenge on the man who had come to 'clap the town brand' on his father's goods when Parker went onto poor relief:

> Having no credit which he fears to lose
> He does whatever dirty jobs they choose:
> Tasking the pauper his labours to stand
> Or clapping on his goods the parish brand
> Lest he should sell them for the want of bread,
> On parish bounty rather pinned than fed,
> Or carrying the parish book from door to door
> Claiming fresh taxes from the needy poor,
> And if one's hunger overcomes his hate
> And buys a loaf with what should pay the rate,
> He instant sets his tyrant laws to work
> In heart and deed the essence of a Turk,
> Brings summons for an eighteen penny rate
> And gains the praises of the parish state,
> Or seizes goods and from the burthened clown
> Extorts for extra trouble half a crown.

Like Byron, Clare had immense admiration for Pope. He could not see why men of taste such as Hazlitt held his poetry in such low esteem. 'The Parish' is his most sustained attempt at robustness in the manner of Pope's rhyming couplets, though the verse has a roughness that one would never find in Pope.

The poem has many memorable vignettes: the fashionable Miss Peevish Scornful who ends up running off with a serving man instead of the squire; the braying rattle, Young Headlong Racket; Proud Farmer Cheetum with his horses, dogs and whore; the Ranter priests more interested in sectarian railing than true religion; Dr Urine the quack; Young Brag, the 'village politician' who is a patriot one moment and a radical the next. Henderson shrewdly observed that the transitions from one character-portrait to the next were too abrupt. Like many of Clare's long poems, 'The Parish' offers a series of sketches rather than a unified whole. Insofar as there is a unifying theme, it is a favourite of both Clare himself and the satirical tradition in which he was working: the idea that 'The past and present always disagree / The claims of ruin is what used to be / Old customs usage daily disappears'.

Satire is often a conservative form. It looks back to a lost golden age as a way of castigating the corruptions of the present. Early in 'The Parish', Clare praises the farmers of yore, with their sense of community and *noblesse oblige*, their old oak table at which 'master, son and serving man and clown / Without distinction daily sat them down'. Then in the middle of the poem, there is a long sequence in praise of the 'True Patriot', a passage later published independently in *Drakard's Stamford News* with the heading 'To Lord Fitzwilliam'. And near the end, there is a portrait of a 'good old Vicar' from the previous century, a man who cared daily for his flock, in sharp contrast to the 'hunting parsons' who succeeded him. In these three passages, as so often, Clare's politics are close to those of William Cobbett: nostalgia for the supposedly settled rural order of the past is played off against the cruelty, selfishness, hypocrisy and avarice of improvers and 'new men'.

In February 1825 Clare was informed that 'The Parish' was not suitable for inclusion in his volume of poems structured around the months of the rural year. He thought of it as the best thing he had ever written, so he was determined to find another outlet for it. He told Eliza Emmerson that he was considering publishing it together with his narrative poem 'Edmund and Helen'. She again warned him against bringing into print a piece that smacked of 'political opinions'. This may have led him to decide that it would be less risky if he approached a provincial as opposed to a London publisher. Perhaps he would be able to publish it without Radstock ever knowing.

Some time before, he had been sent a prospectus for a new periodical, emanating from the Lincolnshire town of Holbeach, called the *Scientific Receptacle: A Literary, Mathematical, and Philosophical Repository*. Despite having some understandable reservations about its 'crabbed name', he submitted some short poems to this journal. In August 1825 he received a personal visit from the editor, Henry Clay. They must have talked over publication possibilities, because the following month Clay showed 'The Parish' to the bookseller who printed the *Receptacle* and it was agreed that the poem would be published independently in an edition of a thousand copies. Clay proposed to Clare an arrangement of '*half profit, half loss*'. He said that he thought highly of the poem as a satire and that he was confident 'there would not be much danger of loss from its publication'. Clare was paid an advance. After some delay, the bookseller, Mr Pitman, calculated that it would make a book of eighty-two pages, which he would publish at the price of half a crown. In August 1826, Clare told Mrs Emmerson that the book was ready for publication, but nothing further is heard of it. We do not know why the arrangement fell through. The poem was not published for over a hundred years.*

In August 1823 Taylor told Clare that he would be glad to publish a new volume the following winter. The poems that had appeared in

---

*It appeared in J. W. Tibble's 1935 edition of *The Poems of John Clare*, in an inaccurate and incomplete text. A fuller text was published by Eric Robinson in a Penguin edition in 1985 and a further corrected one in Carcanet Press's *John Clare: A Champion for the Poor* (2000).

the *London Magazine* could be reprinted together with the 'long and good' ones that Clare had been working on. Talking the idea over with Hessey, Taylor had the idea of calling the volume 'The Shepherd's Calendar', 'a Name which Spenser took for a Poem or rather Collection of Poems of his.—It might be like his divided into Months, and under each might be given a descriptive Poem and a Narrative Poem'. Thus verse-tales such as 'Jockey and Jenny' would be placed under the month in which the story was set. Clare thought that 'The Shepherd's Calendar' was a better working-title than the one he himself had in mind, which was 'The Wilderness or Pastorals, Summer Walks and Sonnets'. He was confident that he could soon 'daub' some new pictures for the descriptive pieces, but felt that Taylor was over-optimistic in assuming that there would be a narrative poem for every month.

He sent one of his manuscript volumes down to Hessey, who responded with a mixed report. Some of the poems he liked very much, but others were too similar to what Clare had done before. They were 'too general to excite much Interest'; they lacked the necessary human touches. 'The Shepherds Calendar', Hessey explained, 'should consist of delineations of the face of Nature, the operations of the husbandman, the amusements, festivals, superstitions, customs etc. of the Country, and little stories introduced to illustrate these more accurately and to fix an Interest on them.' He mapped out a rough plan, assigning the material he had seen to particular months, though also warning Clare that one of his tales, featuring carousal and seduction on the autumnal festival-day of the 'Helpstone Statute', was too coarse for publication.*

Despite these strictures, Clare was delighted with Hessey's response to his manuscript. He seems, however, to have struggled with the plan. In a lost letter to Hessey, written just before Christmas 1823,

---

*Otherwise known as 'The Recruiting Party', this poem was begun back in December 1820 as part of Clare's 'Ways in a Village' project. It survives in seven different drafts and was eventually published in the *Stamford Champion* newspaper in 1830.

he said that he was thinking of giving up on the calendar idea. Hessey urged him to persevere, but advised against the inclusion of a verse-tale based on the story of the Marquess of Exeter and his Cottage Countess. He would do better to concentrate on his own village: 'The distresses of some classes of the poor in Winter may be finely and pathetically delineated—what is more painful than abject Poverty and disease in times of general Merriment such as Christmas?' Clare did, however, continue with his poem based loosely on the story of the Cottage Countess. He called it 'Valentine's Eve' and sent it to Taylor, who read part of it, then put it aside and admitted a year later that he had lost it. Clare hoped to give it a prominent place in the collection he put together in the early 1830s, but it was not published until the 1960s.

Early in 1824 Clare sent the second of the quarto manuscript books to his publishers. He gave notice that after completing the 'Calendar' he would take a long sabbatical from publication, whilst attempting various new forms, in particular the drama and 'one hundred sonnets as a set of pictures on the scenes and objects that appear in the different seasons'.

The New Shepherd's Calendar had been advertised in Taylor and Hessey's catalogue of forthcoming books. But ill health and business difficulties then intervened. Taylor simply could not face the work of putting another collection of Clare's poems into shape. The visit to London in the summer of 1824 did nothing to speed the process of preparing the new book for publication. Hessey's conscience was struck by the lack of progress. On Clare's departure from London, he suggested to Taylor that it was time to have the poems copied.

They agreed on the man for the job. Harry Stoe Van Dyk was a journalist, poet and all-round man of letters who assisted in the editing of the *London Magazine*. He met Clare at Taylor's and they got on very well. Clare described him as 'of a very timid and retreating disposition before strangers' but 'very warm-hearted' to his friends. Van Dyk offered to undertake the copying and immediately struck up a cheerful correspondence with Clare, in which he deprecated his own work: 'Your opinion of my verses perfectly corresponds with my own. The Sketch that you particularly object to is devilish bad indeed, the only excuse I can make is that it was written in little more than an hour in a noisy room.' In order to earn his living, Van Dyk had to continue with his own journalistic and editing commitments, so the copying of Clare's poorly written manuscripts proceeded very slowly. He soon regretted taking on the job, and at the end of October it was handed over to an amanuensis called Fleetwood. Van Dyk continued to offer constructive criticism.

Hessey, meanwhile, informed Clare that the poems were 'by no means fit for the public eye at present'. They had been written too hastily and would require extensive revision of a kind that only Clare himself could carry out. His early works had 'already described in admirable colours the Morning and the Noon and the Evening, and the Summer and the Winter, and the Sheep and Cattle and Poultry and Pigs and Milking Maids and Foddering Boys'. Readers would now expect something more: 'Let your Descriptions apply to the states of Nature in the various seasons of the year—make them as rich and as true as possible, but let them be *select*'. Greater depth was needed: 'Life', 'human Feelings', 'reflection', in short, a subordination of description to 'higher objects'.

Clare's response was to write to his friends in exasperation: 'the MSS they have in their hands for the new book will I believe never be revised or published and this perplexity when I am well enough to think almost makes me ill agen.' Whether or not it made him ill, the frustration was certainly enough to cause him to go on a drinking binge with the Billings brothers early in 1825. By February, though, Fleetwood had copied nearly all the poems and Van Dyk was promising Clare that printer's proofs would soon be with him. When the first sheet was sent, it revealed Van Dyk's heavy editorial hand:

> I have taken great liberties with your text *in omissions* which I hope you will pardon for I feel that it is a very delicate task and one on which I often doubt my own capability of judging. Here and there I have ventured a line also and have thus secured a pilfered passage to posterity. Do not, however, scruple to reject my alterations, which are not made thro' vanity but to prevent a re-

currence of rhyme—or obviate some trifling defect in Grammar etc etc. Whenever any portions are sent down to you please to look at them with attention, as I am not sure of particular words being rightly copied.

As well as offering improvements and taking liberties in this way, Van Dyk found himself mediating between Clare and 'T and H' as they debated which poems to include and how to structure the volume. There seems to have been considerable chaos in Waterloo Place: Van Dyk learnt very late in the production process that Taylor had further manuscripts of which he was not aware. Clare's own thoughts about the prospect of his book ever seeing the light of day are vividly revealed by a dream recorded in his journal: 'I thought I had one of the proofs of the new poems from London and after looking at it awhile it shrank thro my hands like sand and crumbled into dust.'

Mrs Emmerson became involved. She invited Van Dyk round for dinner and reported back to Clare, indignant at Taylor's long silence and apparent inattention to the poems. Clare wrote to Taylor, who replied that he would willingly wash his hands of the volume if Emmerson thought she could find a different publisher who would have more confidence in it: 'It is better to terminate the Connection at once, than to continue in Distrust.' He assured Clare that he was working closely with Van Dyk, not leaving everything to his editor's discretion. The particular problem was 'January'. The poem had to be good because it was the first in the series, but it seemed to everyone at Taylor and Hessey's that it was one of the weakest. They had worked on it for hours without being able to improve it.

In April Clare wrote to Hessey, complaining about Taylor: what did he mean by employing Van Dyk as editor and not even making him aware of all the manuscripts? Why had Van Dyk written saying that more proofs would arrive within three days when nothing had then come for three weeks? He did not know that a sudden decline in Van Dyk's own health, both physical and financial, was creating further distractions. Emmerson then reported that Taylor was unhappy with Van Dyk's excessive cutting. She was moving strongly to the view that Clare should edit and even publish himself. This was indeed the course he would eventually seek to take. Around this time he obtained from Drakard, the Stamford stationer, a folio blank book in which to make fair copies of his best poems: this was the beginning of the self-publishing project that would be called 'The Midsummer Cushion'. The book cost nine shillings and sixpence, the equivalent of a week's wages for fieldwork.

Despite telling Henderson that he intended to 'close with Taylor and Hessey', Clare decided that his only short-term course was to patch up the relationship. 'I know that my temper is hasty', he wrote to Taylor,

> and with that knowledge of my self I always strive to choke it and soften hard opinions with reasonable interpretations—but put yourself in my place for a minute and see how you would have felt and written yourself ... I have no desire to seek another publisher, neither do I believe any other would do so well for me as you may do, much less better.

Then on 2 June 1825 he received a parcel containing the latest *London Magazine*, a new batch of proofs, a much-cut version of 'January', a note from Hessey and a letter from Taylor containing a bombshell: 'When Midsummer comes, my old Friend Hessey and I shall have dissolved Partnership.—He retains the Retail Trade and the House in Fleet Street—and I shall keep the Publishing business and manage it here [in Waterloo Place] myself.' He assured Clare that the arrangement would have no adverse effect on his work, but it could not have seemed like that. Clare had always relied equally on the good counsel of both men. The end of their partnership, and the demise of the *London* that would be one of its inevitable consequences, did not bode well for his own future prospects. It could hardly have been a surprise when Hessey wrote in July with the news that they were indeed concluding negotiations to sell the *London Magazine*.

One of Clare's greatest misfortunes was that he began writing his best poetry at a time of severe commercial recession. In the latter part of 1825 nearly eighty banks went out of business. Eighteen twenty-six became known as the year of the Great Panic. Publishing was especially badly hit: the spectacular bankruptcy of the houses of Constable in Edinburgh and Hurst, Robinson in London ruined Sir Walter Scott, the man who had hitherto been the very epitome of the best-selling author.

Another unwelcome letter arrived just over two weeks after news of the formal demise of Taylor and Hessey. Taylor, presumably conscious of the need for cost-cutting, announced that they had twice as much material as was needed for a book. He suggested abandoning the plan of both a descriptive and a narrative poem for each month: 'Shall we insert the Descriptions alone and leave the Tales for another Volume? "Clare's Cottage Stories" would not make a bad title.' He admitted, though, that a volume consisting only of descriptive pieces would suffer from 'sameness' and 'diminished Interest'.

For Clare, it was more than a little ironic that despite all Hessey's earlier admonitions to cut down on natural description and spice up the human interest, Taylor was now proposing something that would have exactly the opposite effect. He agreed that cutting was needed—'there is nothing in the Description for Feby that is worth preserving'—but he also knew that his very best writing was in the descriptive sections: 'I think the one for March is better as there are images in it not noticed before by me or anyone else as I am acquainted with'. As an example of his noticing, he singled out 'the description of Droves of Wild Geese that are very characteristic companions of this Month':

> He hears the wild geese gabble o'er his head
> And pleased wi fancies in his musings bred
> He marks the figured forms in which they fly
> And pausing follows wi a wondering eye
> Likening their curious march in curves or rows
> To every letter which his memory knows.

The flying geese were duly retained in the published text, though over a quarter of the 'March' poem was cut.

The art of noticing was one of Clare's principal poetic gifts. He had astonishingly sharp eyesight and an intuitive responsiveness to minute particulars. Among the little things noticed at random in 'March' are the first half-open cowslip of spring, the mud knocked from a herd-boy's boot, couch-grass tangled in a plough, and a single slow-moving bird specking the wide arch of the fenland sky:

> While, far above, the solitary crane
> Swings lonely to unfrozen dykes again,
> Cranking a jarring melancholy cry
> Through the wild journey of the cheerless sky.

Little progress was made in the autumn and winter of 1825. Taylor, deeply distressed by the collapse of the partnership, was severely ill with 'brain-fever'. His mind wandered with delirium and the feeling of 'pressure and tightness upon his brain'. The symptoms were remarkably similar to those of Clare at the same time: 'this last five or six days I have been alarumd with fresh symptoms of that numbness and stupidness in the head and tightness of the skull as if it was hooped round like a barrel.' In December there was talk of bringing the collection out in two volumes, one with the calendar and the other with the tales. The Emmersons, following their visit to Market Deeping, began badgering Taylor in a way that did not altogether please Clare. Sympathising with his old friend's illness, he was conscious that the slow progress of the book was as much of a burden to his publisher as to himself.

The end of Taylor and Hessey led Clare to step up his efforts to find other outlets for his work. In the course of 1825 he had some success with William Hone's weekly journal the *Every-Day Book*: he managed to place his letter on rural customs and a lyric he pretended had been written by the seventeenth-century poet Andrew Marvell. He also struck up a correspondence with the poet and hymn-writer James Montgomery, editor of a liberal paper, the *Sheffield Iris*. Montgomery published more of Clare's 'imitations' of seventeenth-century poets. Unlike Hone, Montgomery suspected that Clare had really written the lyrics himself. In confessing to his fraud—for which he had a venerable precedent in Chatterton's pseudo-mediaeval poetry—Clare explained that it was merely his lack of confidence in his own judgement of the quality of his imitations that had led him, albeit deviously, to seek the opinion of someone on whose literary taste he could rely.

He responded to various requests to contribute to literary annuals. These productions were bucking the trend of decline in literary publishing. Whereas ordinary volumes of poetry languished unsold, anthologies such as the *Literary Souvenir; or, Cabinet of Poetry and Romance* sold thousands of copies. Aimed at the Christmas and New Year gift market, they were lavishly produced with decorated boards, silk bindings, steel-engraved illustrations and gilt-edged paper. In August 1825 Clare was asked to submit poems to the *Amulet* and the *Literary Souvenir*, both of which were to be published the following January. The editor of the *Souvenir* assured him that 'the most celebrated writers of the day' would be numbered among his fellow contributors. He sent a lyric called 'First Love's Recollections', in which he conjured up the memory of Mary Joyce:

> Mary! I dare not call thee dear,
> I've lost that right so long;
> Yet once again I vex thine ear
> With memory's idle song.

His copy of the volume eventually arrived with a covering note from the editor. Once again, he had come under the tyranny of grammar:

> I hope you will approve of the alterations I have felt it incumbent to make in your Poem 'First Love's Recollections'. It was full of beauties but occasionally very incorrect as to construction and versification but in its present state it may I think vie with the very best things in the book. I assure you I made the poem just what I considered it should be, and if I had half an hours conversation with you I could easily convince that I have materially improved the poem.

'As to the Poetical Almanacks', he wrote to Hessey, 'they may all go to Hell next year.' His contributions were so altered that he did not know them. To add insult to injury, the editors sometimes tried to fob him with a complimentary copy instead of a fee for his work.

Since the poetry market was drying up, Clare—acting on the advice of Eliza Emmerson—turned his thoughts to prose publication. With the example of Hazlitt in mind, he began to write essays on 'common every day matters and things of life'. It was an opportunity to vent some spleen by exposing 'the cant and humbug' of the fashions and opinions that were spreading through society. Van Dyk wrote regularly for the *European Magazine*. Taking advantage of this contact, Clare managed to get an essay published there in November 1825. Entitled 'Popularity in Authorship', it had originally been drafted for the section of his autobiography where he reflected on the fame of Lord Byron. The essay's argument is that short-term popularity is not synonymous with true fame. Byron 'looked down as a free-booter on the world below, scorning with seeming derision the praise that his labour had gained him, and scarcely returning a compliment for the laurels which fashion so eagerly bound around his brow'. Clare concludes, with hope for a posthumous reputation of his own, that whereas 'fashionable popularity changes like the summer clouds', the best 'living shadow of true fame' is 'the quiet progress of a name gaining ground by gentle degrees'. His friends thought well of the essay and he began to think of others in a similar vein, with such titles as 'On Superstition' and 'Hasty Decisions'. Hessey, however, warned him against too much exposure in print as a prose writer. The next volume of poetry was what really mattered. Not that there was any sign of Taylor getting that into print.

Towards the end of January 1826 Clare wrote to tell Taylor that he could not cope with further delays and cross-purposes. Taylor immediately scribbled back a very short note informing him that no progress could be made because the 'July' poem was 'unfit for Insertion'. A fuller, and very harsh, explanation followed the next day:

> Heretofore I have submitted, and apologized, and taken Blame to myself,—because I was resolved, if possible, to complete my Undertaking, whatever Pains it cost me: but your frank Censure has at last relieved me from my irksome Situation, and I must now as frankly tell you, that for the principal part of the Delay

and for the present total Stop again, you are alone responsible—
Look at the Vol. of MS. Poems which I now send you, and show
it where you will, and let any of your Friends say whether they
can even read it.—I can find *no one* here who can perform the
Task besides myself. Copying it therefore is a Farce for not three
Words in a Line on the Average are put down right, and the
number omitted, by those whom I have got to transcribe it, are
so great, that it is easier for me at once to sit down and write it
fairly out myself—But suppose I attempt to do this; here I encounter another Difficulty:—The Poems are not only slovenly
written, but as slovenly *composed*, and to make Good Poems out
of some of them is a greater Difficulty than I ever had to engage
with in your former Works,—while in others it is a complete
Impossibility.

Taylor went on to tell Clare that he must do his own editing. As far as
he was concerned, the only way to deal with 'July' was not to cut out
what was bad but to make an earnest search for the tiny number of
lines that were good. A 'descriptive Catalogue in *rhyming Prose*' did
not in his view make a publishable poem. 'You can write better when
you choose', he added, 'not a better hand only, but better poetry'. The
letter ends with a sense of considerable relief: 'Farewell, dear Clare. I
am not the less your Friend for speaking so freely.' Taylor's outburst
was the product not only of his own strained nerves, but also of the
frustration of his seven years' struggle with Clare's crabbed hand and
incoherent grammar.

Five days later he sent another letter, apologising for his tone. Clare
told Eliza Emmerson how hurt he felt, but he declined to enter into a
'paper war' with Taylor. He simply wrote a new and much shorter
poem for 'July', and got on with the business of revising the other poems. It was as if a festering boil had been burst. Taylor professed himself delighted with the new 'July'—he said that not a single word of
it needed alteration (though he did make a few changes). And he
went on pruning the other poems: he was particularly concerned
about prosaic passages, feeling that Clare wanted to make the calendar pieces a 'complete Record of Country Affairs' whereas he was

looking for 'a Selection of the Circumstances that will best tell in Poetry'.

By this time, Clare was happy to let Taylor edit the poems in any
way he saw fit. He just wanted the book to be in print, not least so that
he could get on with other projects such as the pseudo-Elizabethan
tragedy that he hoped to pass off as the work of Christopher Marlowe.
He remained remarkably patient even as Taylor confessed to losing
some of his manuscripts. The revised calendar poems were finally in
shape by the end of March 1826. Clare acknowledged that the 'severe
discipline' of self-editing had greatly improved them: 'if a first copy
consists of a hundred lines its second corrections generally dwindle
down to half the number and I heartily wish I had done so at first'.

In April they turned to the revision of the 'village stories'. Taylor
found these easier to cut. By July the collection that had once looked
far too long was now coming in under two hundred pages. Taylor
therefore asked Clare if he could fill it out by reprinting some of the
poems that had been published in the *London Magazine*. Alterna-
tively, the 'very clever Imitations of the old poets' might be included
at the end—or perhaps these should form the basis of another book
called 'Visits of the earlier Muses'. But, absorbed as he was with the
winding up of his partnership with Hessey, Taylor remained pessimistic about the future financial prospects of any kind of poetry: 'in
these hard Times when no Books are selling, you must do all you can
to keep your Expenses down'. In the end, *The Shepherd's Calendar*
was made up to a respectable 240 pages by the inclusion of nine poems that had been published in the *London* back in 1822 and 1823,
among them the much-admired 'Superstition's Dream' (now called
simply 'The Dream').

Clare reported to Mrs Emmerson that he was happily reunited
with Taylor, and that the new book would finally be out in October.
She had grand ideas of Clare producing 'a *set* of *modern antiques*':
the *Calendar* would follow in the footsteps of Spenser; 'Visits of the
Early Muses' would collect Clare's imitations of the Elizabethan and
seventeenth-century lyric poets, together with the mock-Marlovian
tragedy; his 'old songs' would form a 'New Robin-Hood's Garland';

and his new-found skill as a prose writer could be put to good use in a series of 'Biographical Criticisms of the Poets of last Century'. His Robin Hood would show the world that he was '*not "little* John"!'

Despite Taylor and Hessey's formal separation of their publishing and retailing operations, they still worked closely together. In September it was Hessey who wrote with the news that the title-page of the new book, together with its dedication addressed to the Marquess of Exeter, was now set up in type. The only things lacking were a preface, which Clare should write himself, and a drawing for the frontispiece, for which they were going to approach William Hilton or Peter de Wint.

Clare dashed off the preface. As instructed by Hessey, he attributed the long delay in the book's publication to his 'long illness'. He also thanked Taylor for his 'kind assistance' in ushering the poems into notice and his critical exertions in correcting them for publication. Taylor felt that it would not be wise to publish an admission that Clare's poems required extensive correction before becoming publishable, so this acknowledgement disappeared under his 'Slashing' pen, as did various other parts of the preface, including an expression of thanks to the Sir Michael Clare who had sent his namesake a donation from the West Indies.

At the end of November six copies of the new book were at last dispatched to Clare. The bad news was that de Wint had not yet found a subject for the frontispiece, so actual publication would be delayed still further. Clare gave one of the copies to his friends the Simpsons in Stamford. The family listened in rapt attention as Frank read aloud one of the village stories called 'The Memory of Love'. Simpson cheeringly told Clare that every reader of taste, feeling and sense would admire the 'unaffected Narrative' of the tales, the 'Simplicity and Nature' of the calendar, and the 'Sublimity' of 'The Dream'. Eliza Emmerson agreed with this judgement: the new volume confirmed that Clare's mind was a '*Crucible*' that received, analysed and purified all the forms of nature, while at the same time—thanks to the grandeur of 'The Dream' and 'Life, Death, and Eternity'—it showed that he was capable of 'higher subjects than talking about birds and flowers'.

De Wint did not produce a drawing until the new year. His first attempt satisfied neither Taylor nor the artist himself. A further delay was caused by the slowness of the engraver. *The Shepherd's Calendar; with Village Stories, and Other Poems* was finally published at the end of April 1827. Joseph Henderson considered that de Wint had taken a long time to produce 'a meagre piece for the frontispiece': it was hardly a preparation for the rural realism of the poems to begin the volume with an engraving that showed a peasant drinking from a barrel rather than a bottle.

The best water-colours of Peter de Wint re-create the atmosphere of the Lincolnshire flatlands in a spirit remarkably close to that of Clare's poems. Clare himself regarded him as the absolute modern master in the art of landscape. In 1829 he wrote to de Wint, requesting a sketch to hang on the wall of his cottage beside his water-colour copy of the Hilton portrait: 'nothing would appear so valuable to me as one of those rough sketches taken in the fields that breathe with the living freshness of open air and sunshine where the blending and harmony of earth air and sky are in such a happy unison of greens and greys that a flat bit of scenery on a few inches of paper appear so many miles'. The drawing that caused the final delay of the *Calendar* is not, however, a landscape but a very conventional rustic genre painting. When it came to what Clare called the 'pastoral poesy of painting'—'the grouping of peasantry', the shadowing of 'story' on canvas, and 'a true english consception of real pastoral life and reality of english manners and english beauty'—he admired Rippingille more than any other artist. A frontispiece by 'Rip' might have been truer to the earthy spirit of the collection. Still, de Wint did at least provide his sketch for free.

On 1 May 1827 Taylor was finally able to dispatch to Clare twenty-four copies (carriage paid) of the new book, complete with frontispiece. Twelve of them were for him to pass on to the Marquess of Exeter, to whom the poems were dedicated 'in grateful remembrance of unmerited favours'. Mrs Emmerson wrote a few days later to say that she had received her dozen copies and that Taylor had reported a very encouraging initial sales figure of 400. There must be some exaggeration here, because two years later the book had only sold 425 copies.

Within a few months of publication, Taylor was complaining what a poor season it was for new books, that the *Calendar* 'has had comparatively no Sale', and how 'the Time has passed away in which Poetry will answer'. Clare blamed 'Novels and such rubbish' for taking over the literary marketplace. His friend Henderson was puzzled at the poor sales because his sense was that locally the *Calendar* had done better than Clare's previous books. The Sheffield poet and editor James Montgomery, by contrast, was not surprised: 'poetry has had its day in the present age, and two more generations must go by before there is such another revival in its favour, as was excited by the agitation of human minds of every degree and order, by the events of the French Revolution'. Despite this gloomy prognosis, he told Clare not to be discouraged and to go on '*writing your best*'.

A brief but favourable advance notice of the new collection had appeared in the *Literary Gazette*. The first substantial reviews followed in July in the *Eclectic Review* and the *Monthly Magazine*. That in the *Eclectic* was written by the magazine's editor, Josiah Conder, a long-time admirer of Clare. 'Nothing', he wrote on quoting some lines from 'July', 'can be more perfect than this summer picture of still life, with its entomological embellishments. While we dwell upon the scene, we seem to become boys again, and long to have a pelt at that same squirrel.' Clare was especially pleased to be praised heartily by a reviewer who was himself one of Taylor's small stable of poets.

In October a review in the *Literary Chronicle* (unsigned, but by a friend of Van Dyk's) claimed that Clare had now made good his early promise to be the English equal of Burns. He was as good as any living poet 'in accurate pictures of rural scenery, in depth of feeling, and originality of observation'. This reviewer especially liked the narrative poems. One line from 'The Sorrows of Love', 'While anguish rush'd for freedom to her eyes', was given the ultimate accolade: it was said to have 'Shakspearian splendour'. Two of the shorter poems, 'Antiquity' and the visionary 'Dream', were praised for having 'an almost Byronic strength and originality'. Several reviewers noted the similarity of 'The Dream' to Byron's apocalyptic poem 'Darkness'.

Van Dyk himself was delighted with the volume that he had helped to edit. He praised Clare for simplicity and naturalness of expression: 'I like thoughts as I like pretty women—the less dress upon them the better'. Most critics agreed that Clare had fully found his own voice, but there was less coverage of this third book than there had been of the first two. The reviews were scarcer, briefer and—if generally respectful—less enthusiastic than Clare and Taylor had hoped for or the book deserved. Poetry was on the wane and Clare himself was no longer a phenomenon. Editors no longer considered him worth the column-space that had been devoted to his previous works and, more particularly, to the story of his early life.

More than five years passed between the conception and the publication of the poems on 'the *Months*'. *The Shepherd's Calendar* was advertised by Taylor and Hessey over three years before it could be purchased. One sympathises with Clare. But if one actually looks at the three principal manuscripts from which Taylor and his associates had to work, one sympathises with them. The descriptive and narrative poems amount to more than five thousand lines. There are frequent insertions, alterations and sequences of near illegibility. A two-volume collection would not have been a commercial proposition, yet the twelve monthly descriptions left uncut would have amounted to nearly two hundred printed pages. What Taylor needed for them, and what he eventually got, was about a hundred. As we have seen, Clare himself recognised that his verses were often improved when correction 'dwindled them down' to half their original length.

The clutter, insertions and erasures in Clare's manuscripts are an editor's nightmare. Even when clean copies were made, they did not last long. The manuscript in which first Van Dyk and then Fleetwood copied poems for the new collection was sent to Clare. He inserted his own emendations and comments in pencil. But since the transcriptions were only written on the right-hand pages, he took the opportunity to draft revised versions and new material on the left-hand ones. For reasons of this sort it took Clare's modern editors forty years to decipher, transcribe and publish the full body of his surviving poetic manuscripts. Scholarly conditions and conventions enabled them to respect the poet's every line. Taylor and Hessey, by contrast, were struggling to keep their business afloat, seeing a host of other books through the press and publishing a monthly magazine. Taylor, like Clare, suffered from severe ailments of both stomach and mind; Hessey was bringing up a young family of six children. Sales of *The Village Minstrel* had been disappointing and poetry publishing— save for the luxury annuals—appeared to be in terminal decline. Any other house would, one suspects, have pulled the plug on Clare's project altogether.

We now value Clare's poetry, *The Shepherd's Calendar* especially, for its intimately detailed evocation of an ancient rural way of life that is lost. In manuscript, the 'January' poem has a leisurely five hundred lines, moving from the labours of 'A Winters Day' to the fireside storytelling of 'A Cottage Evening'. Taylor knew that what he called Clare's 'complete Record of Country Affairs' would not make a viable publication. He had to judge which sections would 'best tell in Poetry'. In 'January', as in many other cases, those judgements were very good. The 'Winters Day' section goes over ground that Clare had already trodden in poems such as 'The Woodman'. Over half of it was cut from the published version. The 'Cottage Evening', by contrast, was new and extraordinarily vivid: it was only trimmed by about ten per cent.

In 'May' Clare wrote,

> My wild field catalogue of flowers
> Grows in my rhymes as thick as showers
> Tedious and long as they may be
> To some they never weary me.

This almost reads like an invitation to his editors to trim some of the tedium. Clare had an obsessive desire to enumerate every flower and every bird that he knew. The wild field catalogues of his verse and prose were a psychological necessity to him. Years later, in the asylum, he developed an analogous compulsion to list women's names. A catalogue was not, however, a work of art, let alone a poem that could make its way in a crowded and diminishing marketplace. The catalogue of flowers inevitably disappeared from the published 'May', as did an exquisite sequence of bird observations later in the same poem.

First impressions of Taylor's editing can be misleading. The main focus of 'June' is the sheep-shearing festival. Clare's perennial sense of the fragility of the old way of life, in which masters and men came together at holiday time, led him to end the poem as follows:

> All this is past—and soon may pass away
> The time torn remnant of the holiday
> As proud distinction makes a wider space
> Between the genteel and the vulgar race
> Then must they fade as pride o'er custom showers
> Its blighting mildew on her feeble flowers.

Taylor's published text omitted the last four lines. This might be construed as an act of censorship provoked by discomfort at the implied politics of Clare's castigation of the widening class division in rural society. Yet in 'December' there is a similar attack on 'pride' and defence of 'custom'. If Taylor were engaged in active censorship, one would have expected him to cut this too. He did not. Instead, he gave it special prominence by moving the stanza in question from the middle of the poem to the very end, so that it serves as a summary of not only 'December' but the whole calendar:

> Old customs! Oh! I love the sound,
>   However simple they may be:
> Whate'er with time hath sanction found,
>   Is welcome, and is dear to me.

> Pride grows above simplicity,
>   And spurns them from her haughty mind,
>   And soon the poet's song will be
>   The only refuge they can find.

It is possible, then, to make Taylor's motives for alteration seem more sinister than they were.

Many of the distinctive excellences of *The Shepherd's Calendar*— its range of verse forms, its attunement to seasonal change and the dependence of rural life on the vagaries of the English weather, its acknowledgement of women as repositories of the oral traditions of a community—are as apparent from the published text of 1827 as from modern editions based on Clare's original manuscripts.* At the same time, Clare's bad handwriting and the insensitivity of Taylor and his colleagues to some of the idiosyncrasies of the Northampton-shire dialect meant that the published text contained many mis-prints and misrepresentations of Clare's original meaning. So for instance in 'May', 'dreaming joys' become 'dreary joys' and 'A high blue bird is seen to swim / Along the wheat'—the latter because Fleetwood mistook *hugh* (Clare's spelling of *huge*) for *high* and Tay-lor did not spot the anomaly.

The principal difference between Clare and his publishers was over the nature of the 'human interest' in the collection. Taylor and Hessey wanted picturesque scenes in the descriptive poems and lively romance in the narrative ones. In the revised 'July' that so pleased Taylor, a shepherd sleeps in the sunshine, a cow-boy plays with his dog by a pond, and at evening a mower sits on a bench out-side his house, smoking and watching his children as the birds sing. Clare, by contrast, wanted to go beyond the traditional association between pastoral verse and leisured ease. He knew from hard experi-

---

*Clare's original manuscript text of the twelve poems on the months was re-stored by Eric Robinson and Geoffrey Summerfield in their edition of *The Shep-herd's Calendar* (Oxford University Press, 1964); the *Cottage Tales* manuscripts were published in full by Eric Robinson, David Powell and P. M. S. Dawson in 1993 (Carcanet Press). On the editorial question, see further discussion in the Ap-pendix.

ence that all through the day and all through the year labour was the real lot of the countryman. As he made clear in a letter to the ex-stonemason Allan Cunningham, he placed himself in the company of other labouring poets, such as James Hogg (who had himself written a prose 'shepherd's calendar') and above all Bloomfield. They might be looked on as 'intruders and stray cattle in the fields of the Muses', but their very lack of an Oxford or Cambridge education meant that they could write pastoral that was true to the real life of the peasantry as opposed to the elegant fancies of classical tradition. The original 'July' was an overlong and messy manuscript, dissolving without a clear transition from daytime labour to evening leisure. It does, however, evoke the real work of haymaking. For centuries, well-to-do poets had played the role of swain and made pretty love to imaginary shepherdesses. Clare gives the feel of what it was really like to sweat in the fields. In so doing, he introduces an earthy eroticism that was not to his publishers' taste:

> Wi smutty song and story gay
> They cart the witherd smelling hay
> Boys loading on the wagon stand
> And men below wi sturdy hand
> Heave up the shocks on lathy prong
> While horse-boys lead the team along
> And maidens drag the rake behind
> Wi light dress shaping to the wind
> And trembling locks of curly hair
> And snow white bosoms nearly bare
> That charms one's sight amid the hay
> Like lingering blossoms of the may.
> From clowns' rude jokes they often turn
> And oft their cheeks wi blushes burn
> From talk which to escape a sneer
> They oft affect as not to hear.

Those snow-white bosoms might appear to be a mere poeticism, but they are actually grounded in the rhythm of the rural year. Come 'August' the gleaners following the harvest will be sunburned: haymaking in July would have been the first occasion in the summer during which the village women would have rolled up their sleeves and assisted in the fields.

The narrative poems are also in the tradition of labourers' verse. The poetic 'tales' that had made serious money in the previous decade were the oriental romances of Byron and the mediaeval stories of Scott, but the models for Clare's 'cottage tales' were the robust idiom of Burns and the specific example of poems by Bloomfield with such titles as 'Walter and Jane; or, The Poor Blacksmith. A Country Tale' and 'The Broken Crutch: A Tale'. In a fragment of an essay intended for the *London Magazine*, Clare complained that because 'college poets' loved to show off their reading, the literature of the age was full of such commodities as gods, goddesses, shepherdesses, Goths, Vandals, monsters, witches of Atlas, black dwarves and Scottish superstitions, whilst the 'true pastorals' of Bloomfield, 'our English Theocritus', lay neglected.

The Simpson family's particular enthusiasm for 'The Memory of Love' was shared by other readers, such as the poet George Darley and Gilchrist's widow Elizabeth. It is among the most effective of Clare's narratives because, albeit indirectly, it is among the most personal. The poem begins with an old labourer called Robin sitting under a walnut tree at sheep-shearing time. He tells his young fellow-workers of how he had once fallen in love with a dark-haired beauty. After various clumsy overtures, he got to dance with her during an evening of gypsy revelry:

> Oh! The first time I touch'd her gentle hand,
> I felt a joy you'll never understand,
> Unless ye chill 'neath true love's ecstasy,
> And then you'll own the pleasant pain with me.

But she was engaged to another. When the banns were read in church, he shut his prayer book and walked out, not knowing where he was going. He has never forgotten her:

> Her face to me was Memory for life.
> Her looks, her ways, in winning forms would steal,

> Leaving a pain I never ceased to feel;
> Her very voice would Memory's partner be,
> And music linger'd in the sound with me.

Isolated by his obsessive memory, Robin ends up in a second childhood, playing nine-peg Morris and other games with the children on the moor.

Although Robin is an invented character, a lot of Clare is projected into him. Robin meets his love when working away from home, as Clare met Patty—and she too had a rival suitor. At the same time, the girl's dark ringlets and her way of stepping over a stile, together with an evocation of Stamford Fair, are suggestive of Betty Sell. And the sense of love lost, the power of memory and the retreat into childhood inevitably conjure up Clare's feelings for Mary Joyce.

There was an audience for Clare's tales of the loves and woes of ordinary village folk, especially when read aloud. But narrative poetry was on the wane: Sir Walter Scott's abandonment of verse for prose fiction had led the way towards an age in which the novel took hold as the dominant form for storytelling. The realm of poetry was becoming increasingly confined: the only substantial demand was for brief lyrical effusions of the kind that filled the pages of the annuals and monthly magazines. Some of the most admired poems in Clare's 1827 collection were the short ones, the 'fillers' at the back, reprinted from the *London Magazine*.

These are mood poems, in which the mind of the poet is tuned to the seasons of the year and the textures of the natural world. The feelings they evoke are what came naturally to Clare, but their diction is over-exclamatory, their rhythm, rhyme and stanzaic form somewhat constrained and artificial. He needed the looser, more capacious form of the calendar poems to exercise his eye for minute particulars. And in order to achieve a voice that was fully his own he also needed to find a place for the kind of social commentary that had driven 'The Parish'. Of all the hundreds of poems that he wrote during the mid-1820s, one stands out as combining all these qualities. And yet he did not have the confidence to send it to Taylor for consideration for *The Shepherd's Calendar* volume. Quintessential Clare, it is one of the great poems of the nineteenth century—though it languished unknown well into the twentieth.

It began as an autumnal moorland landscape evoked at the close of the first draft of 'October'. Omitting it from the fair copy of the calendar poems that he sent to Taylor, Clare revised and expanded it as a discrete piece in another manuscript, giving it the title 'The Mores'. The revised version begins with the openness and freedom, both literal and metaphorical, of the pre-enclosure landscape:

> Far spread the moory ground, a level scene
> Bespread with rush and one eternal green
> That never felt the rage of blundering plough
> Though centuries wreathed spring's blossoms on its brow,
> Still meeting plains that stretched them far away
> In unchecked shadows of green, brown and grey.
> Unbounded freedom ruled the wandering scene
> Nor fence of ownership crept in between
> To hide the prospect of the following eye—
> Its only bondage was the circling sky.
> One mighty flat undwarfed by bush and tree
> Spread its faint shadow of immensity
> And lost itself, which seemed to eke its bounds,
> In the blue mist the horizon's edge surrounds.

This was the 'sweet vision' of Clare's 'boyish hours'. But now it has faded:

> —a hope that blossomed free
> And hath been once, no more shall ever be:
> Enclosure came and trampled on the grave
> Of labour's rights and left the poor a slave.

All have vanished: the poet's youth, the rights and freedoms of the poor, the moors and commons. Each element is now bound in: 'Fence now meets fence in owners' little bounds ... In little parcels little minds to please.' Footpaths have been closed off, the right to roam suspended:

Each little tyrant with his little sign
Shows where man claims earth glows no more divine;
On paths to freedom and to childhood dear
A board sticks up to notice 'no road here'.

William Wordsworth had written of how recollections of childhood give us intimations of immortality even as 'Shades of the
prison-house begin to close / Upon the growing Boy'. Clare attached
the trauma of lost innocence very specifically to the enclosure of
Helpston. His poetry held his sense of personal loss together with indignation at the curtailment of ancient rights within his community.
Save in memory and poetry, there was no road back to childhood, to
the unenclosed commons, to Eden. As his depression closed in upon
him, the only future was alienation.

PART THREE

Alienation

1827–1837

I've left mine own old home of homes

Green fields and every pleasant place

The summer like a stranger comes

I pause and hardly know her face

CHAPTER FOURTEEN

FRIENDSHIP'S OFFERINGS

Some time near the end of the 1820s, John Clare scribbled a draft letter in one of his notebooks. He compared himself to 'the poor purgatorial convict of the Grecian mythology':

> I have for these nine years been rolling hopes to that mountain of promise pointed out to me in the beginning by friendly intefer-ences and often I have seemed as if I had accomplised to the very top when down went hopes and all together to the bottom again—in the shape of broken promises stinging impositions and other trouble unaccounted for and unknown till they made their appearance—and as yet I am but as an alien in a strange land.*

Everyone who struggles to overcome depression has moments when they feel like Sisyphus in the ancient myth. You have struggled to push your rock up to the crest of the mountain and then it goes rolling back down to the depths. For Clare, this was the pattern not only of his mental state but also of his literary career. He would be promised great things, but then helpful assistance would turn to painful impo-sition and unexpected twists or delays would make him despair of ever seeing progress beyond that first flush of short-lived fame.

---

*'I have been an alien in a strange land' (Exodus 18:3): one of Clare's many bib-lical quotations.

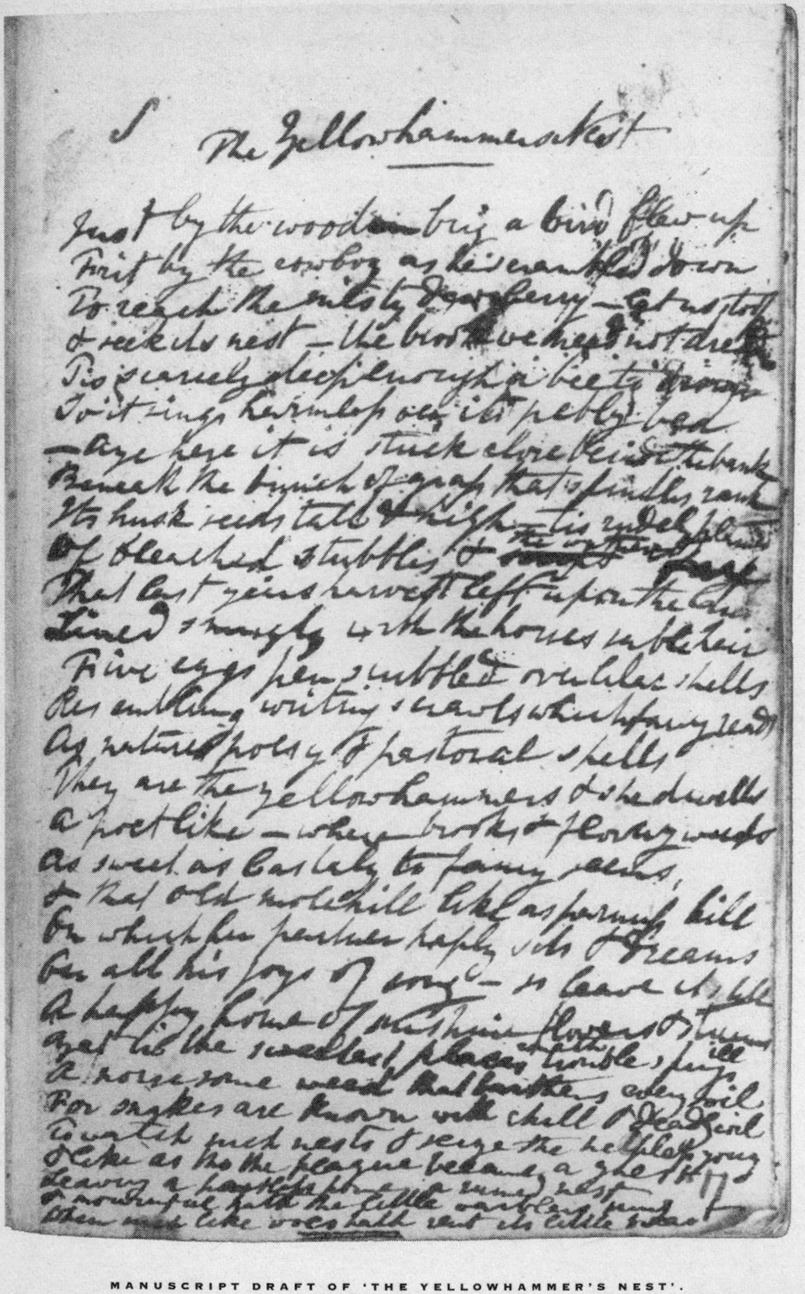

The phrase 'friendly inteferences' sums up his dilemma. From Drury in the early days, to Taylor and Hessey through the 1820s, to Henderson at Milton Hall and Mrs Emmerson in her letters, to the editors of the annuals on whom he increasingly relied for publication: they all meant the best for Clare and his work, but they all interfered with advice of one kind or another. He must often have wanted to scream, Why don't you all just leave me alone? But then he would realise that, though surrounded by his growing family, he often felt profoundly alone. Sometimes he was glad of that, but at other times he was in anguish at his state. He had both a 'passionate fondness for Solitude' and a deep need for belonging. He built his garden of Eden in his poems, idealising his memories of childhood, of Helpston before the enclosure, of young Mary Joyce.

Clare brooded more and more on the Old Testament, turning to the sublime agony of Job, the laments of the Psalmist and the figure of Ruth amid the alien corn. 'And as yet I am but as an alien in a strange land': his fame had made him feel estranged from his neighbours, yet he was never at ease in literary London; the landscape in which he found peace as he walked seemed estranged from itself; and in 1832 he would leave the cottage that had always been his home.

It was not as if he lacked friends. There were the Simpsons in Stamford, cheerful and solicitous, reminding him of the importance of regular bowel movements: 'If you have no other medicine for that purpose take say Tea Spoonsful of *Epsom salt* dissolvd in about a Cup ful of Water early in the Morning'. Octavius Gilchrist's widow kept in touch. Artis went to London and discussed Clare's business affairs with Mrs Emmerson's husband. Henderson shared books, conversation, plants and natural history discoveries. In the summer of 1827 he and Clare went orchid-hunting together. Scattered among Clare's surviving correspondence there are many letters from Henderson that must have heartened him greatly, hungry as he was for interesting company: 'If the weather is fine on Monday I intend to take a turn among the Stone pits and commons in the direction of Helpstone, Barnack, and Southorpe—will you join me? I mean to make out the day between entomology and botany'. On this particular occasion, though, Clare was left waiting to no avail. Henderson was detained on business for his masters at Milton.

The *London Magazine* circle had broken up. In December 1827 John Taylor was appointed bookseller to the new University of London. He would hereafter be an academic publisher, not a literary one. Upon his new appointment, he promptly fell ill. 'Perhaps the honor is too great for him to support and has overcome his Nervous System', wrote his former partner Hessey in a letter to Clare. For a time there was the prospect of a *London* author becoming England's first professor of English literature: London was the earliest university to establish such a post, and both Harry Stoe Van Dyk and George Darley were considered for it. Van Dyk, however, died in 1828.

As the years passed, Clare's contacts with the London literary world became fewer and further between. Darley proved the best at keeping in touch. His long and lively epistles were written in a spirit of true poetic brotherhood. As an Irishman he sympathised with Clare's sense of being an outsider; Clare in turn admired the manner in which Darley combined the vocation of poet with a gift for mathematics. In wrestling with his hopes and fears about posthumous fame, Clare hitched his own star to that of his brother in poetic labour. The name of Darley, he assured the younger man, would one day be 'among the many that shall be elected as true Poets of the 19th century'. Then he added that he was doing his utmost to make the name of Clare one of that same number.

With the narrowing of his London acquaintance, Clare increasingly depended on local contacts for literary conversation. A Mr Gouger of Oakham, whom he had met briefly at Gilchrist's, asked him over for some informal 'bachelor's fare'. The vicar of Market Deeping invited him to dinner and took the trouble to send a horse, so that he would not have to walk along the dirty lanes in the wet spring weather. Clare replied that he was such a bad horseman, he would prefer to walk whatever the conditions underfoot. The literary gentlemen of both Holbeach and Boston regarded him as something of a local hero. Several requests came for visits of a kind that may be thought of as the nineteenth-century equivalent of the modern author's promotional tour of speaking engagements and book signings.

In one of his more desperate letters, Clare complained that what he needed to go on writing, and indeed living, was 'a stimulus, an encouraging aspiration that refreshes the heart like a shower in summer'. Instead of this, he had faced 'nothing but drawbacks and dissapointments', not least because he lived 'in a land overflowing with obscurity and vulgarity far away from taste and books and friends—poor Gilchrist was the only man of letters in this neighbourhood and now he has left it a desert'. Gilchrist's premature death in 1823 had been a terrible blow, but the complaint is unfair to friends of later years: not only Artis and Henderson, but also Frank Simpson, Gilchrist's nephew by marriage.

The Simpsons were a family of soap-boilers, prominent among the businessmen of Stamford. Alderman Simpson was mayor in 1824. His children contributed greatly to the cultural life of the town. His sons Frank and Octave were talented amateur draughtsmen, whilst his daughters Eleanor and Eliza were musical. Frank prepared an illustrated book on ancient baptismal fonts; like Clare's *Shepherd's Calendar*, its progress was uneasy in the poor publishing climate of the 1820s, but it did eventually get into print. As part of his research for this project Frank travelled around the neighbouring countries, sketching churches and their fittings. Clare accompanied him on at least one such trip, which inspired a sonnet on Crowland Abbey. Frank also made various trips—some for business, some artistic—to London. He built up a network of acquaintances among artists and antiquarians. So it was that the Simpson brothers became friendly with another pair of artists, Henry and William Behnes, brothers who were both specialists in the sculpting of portrait busts. Clare duly met them on one of his visits to the Simpsons.

In July 1827, Henry (Harry) Behnes stopped off in Stamford whilst travelling back to London after executing a commission at Louth in northern Lincolnshire. He poked around the town's antiquities, and then Frank Simpson offered him the choice of either a visit to the picture gallery at Burghley House or a drive over to Helpston to visit

Clare. He chose the latter. 'This was the first time I had seen Johnny Clare in the country', he informed a correspondent a few days later, 'and my description of my interview with This extraordinary Being This real *Genius* in every sense of the word will form the subject of a very interesting chat at our next meeting.' After the visit, Behnes returned to the Simpsons' for dinner and stayed up drinking till one o'-clock in the morning, when he boarded the night coach, taking with him a packet of letters from Clare to his London friends.

On delivering one of them to Mrs Emmerson, she invited him in for tea and he told her of the welcome he had received from Clare, of the poet's '*Botanical* pursuits', his '*delightfully* rustic attire', his unshaven chin 'and all the other etcetera that are so peculiarly the attributes and habits of the genius of solitude'. As a gesture of thanks for the visit, Behnes sent a model village for Anna and Eliza (who had just turned seven and five) and toy hussars for Frederick (now three and a half). Eliza Emmerson swiftly added the name of Behnes to those of Clare, Rippingille and Derwent Coleridge on the list of young male artists in whom she took an interest. 'I have twice paid my adoration at the *Shrine* in *Stratford Place*', Harry soon reported.

That summer Clare also sat at the grandest dinner table he had ever encountered. His meals at Burghley and Milton had been confined to the servants' hall, whereas on this occasion he found himself dining as a guest of honour in the Bishop's palace in Peterborough. His host the Bishop was Herbert Marsh, Lady Margaret Professor of Divinity at the University of Cambridge and the foremost mind in the early nineteenth-century Anglican church.

Now in his early seventies, Marsh was nearing the end of an exceptionally controversial ecclesiastical career. As a young Cambridge college fellow, he had been close to William Frend, the university's leading radical don. When Frend was prosecuted for sedition, Marsh went to study in Germany. He translated into English the work of J. D. Michaelis on the origin and composition of the gospels, one of the foundational texts of modern biblical criticism. He also wrote a book in German arguing that France was the aggressor in the wars of the 1790s. For this he was proscribed by Bonaparte. He hid in the house of a merchant named Lecarrière. In 1807 he returned to England, accompanied by the merchant's daughter, Marianne, whom he married as soon as they landed at Harwich. As Lady Margaret Professor, he introduced his students to scientific biblical criticism. He became Bishop of Peterborough in 1819, and fought fiercely against evangelical infiltration of his diocese. Though renowned as a polemicist, he also had a reputation for generosity to local people. He, and especially his German wife, took a particular interest in the Helpston poet. Clare praised Mrs Marsh for her 'sterling good sense and sweet condescending behaviour'. By *condescending* he meant 'acting on terms of equality, regardless of rank'.

In October 1827 the Bishop himself called at the Helpston cottage. To Clare's acute embarrassment, he could not invite his illustrious visitor to step indoors, since the door was locked against him. Could Patty have thrown him out of the house in a fit of pique at his drunkenness or philandering? It is more likely that there was simply a muddle. Patty's mother had just died, and it is possible that she had gone to sort out family affairs, taking the children with her.* Whatever the cause, there is something bizarre in the image of the nation's foremost theologian sitting in his carriage or on his horse in a muddy village street, making small talk with a peasant who can't get into his own cottage. But no offence was taken, and a few months later Clare was invited to spend a day and a night at the Bishop's palace, where he inspected Mrs Marsh's mineral collection. She also lent him a collection of poetic epitaphs and gave him a pocket microscope for his botanical and entomological pursuits. Her companion Miss Mortlock gave him a steel pen, telling him that it would serve him much better than quills (provided it was always wiped carefully after use). In later years, Miss Mortlock sent such helpful commodities as tea, camphor lozenges and gingerbread for the children.

*Little is known about the fate of Patty's family, though in 1829 Henderson tried to get her sister a job as a servant at Milton.

There was a plan for Taylor and Darley to come to Helpston over Christmas 1827, but the proposed visit was postponed till the following spring, then abandoned altogether. Eliza sent her usual Christmas gifts: a box of books, a waistcoat piece for Patty to make up, two neckerchiefs of Indian silk (one in yellow and both 'of the *newest fashion*'), money for school fees and a guinea for roast beef and plum pudding. Among the books was Captain Medwin's *Conversations of Lord Byron*, which Clare devoured. The voice of the lordly poet was entering his head. Behnes, meanwhile, sent a box of toys for each of the children and a glass bottle of eau de cologne for Patty, which broke in the post, giving a sweet smell to everything else in the package.

Clare's seasonal ailments—ague, headaches and lethargy—returned in the autumn of 1827. He was ill for the remainder of the year. In his thank-you letter to Behnes for the Christmas presents he complained, 'I am very unwell and what ails me I know not but my head is horribly afflicted with a stupid vacancy and numbness that is worse than hell itself . . . the horrors are upon me and will have their will or humour out before they leave me.' His psychological condition was worse than ever before; he suffered from persistent nightmares and a sense of being persecuted by 'blue devils'. On being told of Clare's symptoms, Dr Darling's initial instinct was to blame overeating, under-work and 'the excitable and consequently depressible nature of the Poet's feelings'. He prescribed bicarbonate of soda, exercise and plenty of bowel movements. Marianne Marsh thought it was rheumatism and suggested that Patty should make some flannel shirts; she also sent a sheet of anti-rheumatic plaster.

Around this time, Clare scribbled a number of rough sketches in the margins of one of his notebooks, among them a devil and a woman's torso scratched out with a heavy blot blacking the genital area. Above, a neat rectangle has been cut from the manuscript, suggesting that someone has removed an even more offensive image. In January 1828, a confession was made to Hessey: Clare admitted that he feared his illness was something far worse than rheumatism. The relevant letter is lost, but Hessey's reply reveals that Clare was assuming he had contracted a sexually transmitted disease:

As there is reason for the suspicion you entertained, from the character of the Person concerned with you, I think you should not be content without taking the Opinion of a Medical man on the case unless you actually find that all the symptoms have entirely disappeared. On your wife's Account (whose name I am ashamed to couple with yours in speaking on such a subject) this is proper and your duty, and I trust you will think with me and act accordingly. No respectable medical man would betray your confidence, and the assurance of such a man would put your mind at ease.

Spiritual advice was mingled with medical. Clare had asked how he should best make his peace with God. Hessey told him to respond as David had done in the Old Testament, upon committing the double crime of adultery and murder: 'You have sinned like him in the first instance, and in intention have been guilty of the second'. The 'intention' to which Hessey refers was presumably something Clare had said about contemplating self-murder. The darkness of his mood at this time is visible in some lines of poetry written on the address leaf of a letter from Dr Darling:

> For him the whole wide world contain no Friend
> His griefs to sooth or weakness to defend
> Look where he might all he possesd had fled
> and he himself tho living seemed as dead.

Several imitations of penitential psalms, together with 'Stanzas written after sickness', a poem including such guilt-ridden lines as 'I pawned my heart to sin who still / On me for pay did call', may also belong to this period.

Following Hessey's advice, he told Darling of an 'eruption' in the area of his groin. Even if in reality it was only something like stress-related eczema, Clare firmly believed that it was the mark of his sexual transgression. His sense of guilt is further revealed by an entry he added to his old journal at this time, in which he admitted that his 'foolish follys' had caused him to lose his health again, perhaps permanently. *Folly* was the term he used for sexual dalliance.

It is not clear whether Clare was engaged in a new adulterous relationship or whether he believed he was experiencing a fresh eruption of disease caught as a result of his affair in 1825–6. Either way, his writings in this period smack of both guilt and sorrow in matters of the heart. In a gap between poems in a notebook he was filling in 1828, he drew a rectangle round the words 'Jealous goodness' beside a marginal sketch of a shrewish, long-nosed woman. Then in the same manuscript beside a stanza that begins 'Wast thou a tyrant that disdained though clay', he wrote the name of his wife: 'Martha Turner / Walk Lodge'. On the other hand, he wrote a poem that is explicit in its gratitude for Patty's forbearance of his 'folly'.

Early in November 1827 he sent Henderson a poem in memory of a former lover who had died at a young age. His friend regarded it as one of the best elegies he had ever written, if not the very best. 'Thou art gone the dark journey', it begins,

> That leaves no returning
> 'Tis fruitless to mourn thee
> But who can help mourning
> To think of the life
> That did laugh on thy brow
> In the beautiful past
> Left so desolate now.

Tantalisingly, the woman memorialised thus is referred to only as 'Miss ++++'. Many of Clare's love poems are about imaginary or idealised females, but there is no reason to doubt that this one was inspired by the death of someone whom he once loved deeply. When Clare wrote asterisks or crosses in place of a name, he was usually careful about their number (always five for Patty). This poem survives in several manuscripts, with marks indicating that the subject had a first name of six letters and a surname of four. Could it have been Betsey Sell, with whom he strayed from Patty just before his marriage? A search of the (incomplete) parish records of the period has not, alas, yielded the date of her death or the name of any other plausible candidate. Whatever the identity of the lover in question, this poem, together with the letters about sexually transmitted disease, confirms that there were more than two women in Clare's life. As Patty Turner was not the only one with whom he made love physically, so Mary Joyce was not the only one whose love he idealised spiritually.

In the summer of 1831 Clare sent Eliza Emmerson a draft of a ballad in praise of a girl called Mary Lee. Eliza expressed the hope that the girl in question was a worthy recipient of such a good poem. She clearly believed that there was an original for this particular Mary. But when Clare used the ballad form he was working in an oral tradition rather than recording his own feelings. Another manuscript of the same poem calls the girl 'Bonny Rosalie'. It is most unlikely that she was based on a real person. In lyric mode, though, Clare often wrote with a high degree of specificity. Thus 'Valentine to Mary', published in the *London* in May 1823, unquestionably draws on the memory of his youthful love for Mary Joyce, and 'To ++++ on Newyears Day' is a title that only makes sense as an address to a particular person on a particular occasion.

To Clare's annoyance, 'Thou art gone the dark journey' was rejected by the first literary editor to whom he sent it. The poem was, however, accepted by Thomas Hood, former sub-editor of the *London Magazine*, who had become editor of an annual called the *Gem*. Clare sent it to him in response to a request for 'one of your Songs to Mary,—or suchlike'. It is important to realise that Clare's poems of love and memory were not all inspired specifically by Mary Joyce. In his imagination, she developed into a symbolic figure that incorporated other lost girls whom he may have know much more intimately than he ever knew her. Because Mary was always elusive, she served as a screen for more down-to-earth memories that would have been painful to articulate directly. Later, in the Northampton asylum, Clare began to make lists of every Mary—and ultimately every girl—he had ever known. The notion of Miss Joyce as his one true desire was a convenient fiction of his poetry and his first biographers. He eventually gave 'Thou art gone the dark journey' a title that sums up his two great themes: 'Love and Memory'. This little poem is as strongly felt as any he wrote on the subject, but the one thing we can say for sure about the deceased young woman it salutes is that she was not Mary Joyce—who lived on for another decade.

It was agreed that he should go back to London to see Dr Darling in person. Mrs Emmerson readied his '*sky chamber*' on the top floor of her elegant townhouse in Stratford Place. She even considered putting him up in the '*Blue*-room' on the main floor, though this would have meant moving the niece who was staying with her. She sent her annual Valentine's Day poem, with a flirtatious inscription on the address panel: 'I wish that I could transport myself to thy chimney corner, and wisper in thine ear—soft soothing strains of Holy friendship, and sweet Poesy'. She suggested that he should bring his manuscripts to town and they would work together on his next volume of poetry. That would take his mind off his health troubles.

Clare's final visit to London lasted from 23 February to the end of March 1828. This time he stayed with Eliza throughout. He saw a good deal of Henry Behnes, who took his bust. Over the coming months, Behnes proved himself an excellent friend. He went in pursuit of literary editors who owed Clare money and sent cheery letters with gifts for the children. At Christmas he dispatched two bottles of wine for Patty and one of brandy for Clare.

The bust shows a Clare of fuller face than in the Hilton portrait, though his hairline has receded and his high brow is furrowed. An open-necked smock makes him look more robust and less uncomfortable than in the painting, with its stiff wing-collar and elegantly tied cravat. The visionary gleam in the eye is still there, though one suspects that it owes as much to Behnes's observation of Hilton's painting as to the subject himself. What the bust does not suggest is the way that Clare was putting on weight with middle age. 'He was short and thick,' wrote a literary editor who met him in London at this time, 'yet not ungraceful in person. His countenance was plain but agreeable; he had a look and manner so dreamy, as to have appeared sullen—but for a peculiarly winning smile; and his forehead was so broad and high, as to have bordered on deformity.' According to the phrenological theory then in vogue, that high forehead was characteristic of both the genius and the madman—and thus symptomatic of the close kinship between the two conditions.

Mrs Emmerson was delighted with the bust. She said that it made Clare seem like a modern Shakespeare. 'Too bad Eliza' was his wry response. Though mocking her excessive claims for his genius, Clare came to rely more and more on Emmerson for poetic advice. It was clear that Taylor was no longer in the business of publishing poetry. Clare determined to make the break from his old mentor as gently as he could, and Eliza would take on the role of unofficial editor. After returning home to Helpston, he posted down to her a precious 'little manuscript book' containing the best of his new work.

Clare was missing his old friends. He went to see Henry Cary, who was now working at the British Museum, but felt nervous of intruding and overawed by the quantity of books. The magic of the evening parties of the 'Londoners' could not be reproduced. There was a new crowd at Taylor's. When Clare praised the draughtsmanship of his Stamford friend Frank Simpson, some 'coxcomb' laughed at him for his provinciality—though Taylor himself came to the defence and said that Simpson's works were worth their place in the Royal Academy.

One evening Clare attended a party of literary men and painters at the home of Alaric Watts, editor of one of the poetic annuals. He sensed himself out of place: he knew no one and was still feeling unwell. His host's personal kindness on this particular occasion was some small compensation for his rejection of various poems that Clare himself valued especially highly. 'I have no objection to make you some pecuniary return if you send me any poem worthy of yourself', Watts informed him in one letter, 'but really those you have sent me of late are so very inferior—with the excepting of a little drinking song which I shall probably print—that it would do you no service to insert them'.

Clare wrote home, anxious about Patty's health. Not for the first time, he was away from Helpston as she was progressing through the latter stages of a difficult pregnancy. As if to compensate, he told her with pleasure of the books and toys he would be bringing home for the children. His health showed some sign of improvement, whether due to the sulphur baths he was taking, the ministrations of Dr Darling or simply the change of scene. Then he left town in a hurry, failing to pack his books and leaving his great-coat behind. Behnes saw him off and returned to tell Eliza that he was safely on the coach. The romanticising Frederick Martin claimed in his biography of Clare that the hasty departure from London was precipitated by homesickness brought on by the sight of some early spring violets during a walk on Hampstead Heath. It is more likely that he was summoned home by concern over Patty and her unborn baby. Eliza sent on his things, together with some verses entitled 'Lines to a Poet and Friend, on his Leaving my Residence' and the information that she was 'intellectually lost' without him.

The baby was born on 29 April 1828. It was a boy. They called him William Parker, after his grandfathers, William Turner and Parker Clare. In the fifth month of the infant's life, his father spent another three weeks away from home, this time among the literary gentlemen of Boston, Lincolnshire. It was the furthest north he ever travelled, and the only occasion on which he saw the sea. 'You cannot conceive the invigorating effects of the sea breezes', his prospective host had written earlier in the year, when trying to entice him to visit: 'they must have a happy effect upon your nerves'. This invitation came from Henry Brooke, editor of the *Boston Gazette* newspaper. On Clare's arrival, Brooke duly took his visitor to see the sea at high tide. Clare picked up a sea serpent and various seaweeds, which he sent down to Henderson. On hearing of the visit, Frank Simpson was keen to know what he thought of the sea and whether he had witnessed the recent 'Magnificent Lunar Rainbow'.

Clare was introduced to the Mayor of Boston, who lent him Leigh Hunt's memoir of Byron and asked for two sets of his poems. A letter was dispatched to Patty, requesting that copies should be sent up as a matter of urgency. There was a plan for Clare to make a speech at a literary soirée, but he was too shy to do so. Instead, he got drunk at the Mayor's dinner: 'a lady at the table talked so ladily of the Poets that I drank off my glass very often almost without knowing it and he [the Mayor] as quickly filled it.' The combination of the resultant hangover and a cold confined him to his bed for a couple of days after this.

He was ill again on his return home. The ague had made its autumnal return to the fens. Clare cursed himself for bringing sickness back with him from Boston. He was barely able to leave the cottage for six weeks. The fever went all round the family and the new baby was especially poorly.

In July 1830 he was invited to dine at the Bishop's palace before going to the theatre in Peterborough. He accompanied Mrs Marsh, her companion Miss Mortlock and some young clergymen to a performance of *The Merchant of Venice*. Something untoward happened that evening. Frederick Martin's account of Clare's behaviour seems to be only mildly exaggerated:

> At the commencement of the fourth act, he got restless and evidently excited, and in the scene where Portia delivers judgment, he suddenly sprang up on his seat, and began addressing the actor who performed the part of Shylock. Great was the astonishment of all the good citizens of Peterborough, when a shrill voice, coming from the box reserved to the wife of the Lord Bishop, exclaimed, 'You villain, you murderous villain!'

Clare was escorted from the theatre. In retrospect he was deeply embarrassed. Frank Simpson heard about the 'unfortunate Affair' and suggested that an immediate letter of apology was in order. 'It was your frailty not your Viciousness which was uppermost', he added, 'and the (tho warm yet unwise) Conduct of your Companions which hurried you into Error'. Presumably in saying this he was reassuring Clare that he believed the incident was caused by mental confusion rather than alcoholic intoxication. It is not clear in what way the conduct of Clare's companions aggravated the situation. Anyway, Marianne Marsh accepted the apology and sent grapes for convalescence and gingerbread for the children.

Although Frederick Martin misdated the incident in Peterborough, his account of it is unusually reliable because it was based on his correspondence with Charles Mossop, the vicar of Helpston. The day after the theatrical outburst, Mossop invited Clare over the road to the vicarage to meet a friend who was staying with him. His recollection to Martin, albeit over thirty years after the event, was that Clare 'had not been long seated in the room ere he showed aberrations of intellect by variety of fancies; among the most prominent was that of appearing to see spirits of a hideous description moving about in the ceiling of the room'. Mossop reported that he had communicated his alarm to Lord Milton, who sent for Dr Skrimshire.

Clare's hallucinations at the time of the theatre-trip and its aftermath were more severe than anything he had suffered before. He had just turned thirty-seven. On hearing what had happened (from Harry Behnes, who had the news from Frank Simpson), Eliza Emmerson wrote to Patty with a note of alarm that was new to her letters: 'I hope in God! the account of his illness and the *mental* part of it is without foundation.' By early September, Clare was on the mend, but later in the autumn of 1830 he was 'dreadfully ill' again and had to be blistered, cupped and fitted with a seaton in his neck (a length of thread or horse-hair drawn through the skin to allow a discharge of 'bad blood'). He was imagining unreal sights and sounds and, in a further alarming development, showing signs of paranoid suspicion of those around him. He also complained that it was hard for Patty to sympathise with his condition: 'she is never or so seldom ill that she forgets from time to time what illness is'.

Patty had plenty to cope with as it was. On 24 July 1830, just over a week after the incident in the theatre, she gave birth to another child. A girl, she was named Sophie after Clare's sister. Behnes agreed to be godfather and one of the Simpson sisters came for a while to help with the children. She may have stayed at the vicarage—Parson Mossop and his sister offered the Clares a great deal of practical assistance at this time. Old Parker and Ann Clare had moved out of the cottage earlier in the summer, creating more space for the growing family: there would now be only two adults and six children to share the two bedrooms, instead of four adults and five children. Clare's parents remained in the village, possibly in a neighbouring cottage.

There was also a plan for the eldest boy, Frederick, now six, to be enrolled at Christ's Hospital, the charitable school in London where Coleridge and Lamb had met. Mrs Emmerson was going to assist with the costs. But, like so many other plans for the improvement of Clare's condition, this scheme came to nothing.

The first year of the new decade initiated a period of rapidly fluctuating moods for Clare, of new hopes and old disappointments. Small setbacks affected him deeply, as when 'The last of my Poor Stock Doves got murdered in the cage under the Eldern Tree in the Garden by a Dog after I had kept it seven years'. One week he would write a letter complaining of terrible health, the next he would take a positive view of his suffering. In October, John Taylor told his brother Jem that 'Clare sent me a beautiful letter today, describing his Illness and its Effects, which are a Conviction of his Soul's Immortality and of the Truth of the Bible which he reads almost constantly. I never read a letter of his with more pleasure.' And in December, Eliza Emmerson received a letter that gave 'a charming picture of *real* comfort, of chimney-corner enjoyment, of winter delight, of social and sweet Cottage love'.

As the years passed, however, the depressions became far more frequent than the elations. In January 1831 little William Parker was unwell and, much to Clare's distress, his eldest niece died. He himself was unwell the whole year, suffering from stomach pains and a burning sensation in the groin and 'fundament'. His headaches were growing unbearable: 'I awoke in dreadful irritation thinking that the Italian liberators were kicking my head about for a foot ball' (the reference to the Risorgimento movement led by Giuseppe Mazzini shows that he was still reading his newspaper). He beat his pillow and complained of sleeplessness, of general debility, apathy, fear of madness and death, a 'prickly feel about the face and temples'. His head was 'stupid' and his 'nerves disordered'; he again had the delusion of being under the influence of 'evil spirits'. He sobbed and—something he said had never happened before—lost his appetite. This time he did not improve with the summer weather. He wondered whether he should return to London and in particular to the steam baths in Great Marlborough Street that had helped him on his last visit. If nothing else, London would be a change from his own fenland backwater. By the autumn of 1831, when illness struck yet again, it was clear to Clare's friends that some major change was needed in order to improve his spirits.

'My family increases and my income diminishes', he complained. No book royalties were coming in and there had been a drop in the interest rate on the annuity from the trust fund. The annuals and the newspapers were the only potential sources of literary income. So it was that through the late 1820s Clare found homes for his poems in such outlets as the *Literary Souvenir*, the *Pledge of Friendship* and the *Amulet*.

The editor who served him best was Thomas Pringle of the aptly named *Friendship's Offering*. A poet and anti-slavery campaigner, Pringle was a friend of Allan Cunningham and James Hogg, the 'Ettrick Shepherd', poets whom Clare regarded as kindred spirits north of the border. Pringle first solicited work from Clare in July 1828, telling him that he had admired his poems ever since seeing some of them in the *London Magazine* whilst he was living in South Africa. Clare appreciated directness in financial matters, so Pringle established the right footing by immediately stating that he would match the rate of pay offered by other publications such as the *Amulet* and the *Forget Me Not*. He gave straight opinions of the poems that were sent to him, while asking practical questions such as whether the preferable designation in print was 'Mr John Clare' or 'John Clare the Northamptonshire peasant': 'though it be a trifling matter it is one in in which your own wishes ought to be consulted'. He acknowledged that his publication contained indifferent as well as good work, and he sent Clare his own poems for comment, saying, 'I like a man who "calls a spade a spade"—and who will tell a friend his faults and a brother poet his failures'. This was a man with whom Clare could do business. He wrote back to Pringle, saying that he was all too aware of the faults in his own poems and eager for suggested improvements.

He would especially appreciate advice on a long poem that he was just starting to write.

Most of Clare's poems for the annuals were published between 1827 and 1830. Thereafter the majority of the editors lost interest in him. Pringle was the exception: he continued to publish Clare until 1835. He made a particular request for the '*bird-nesting descriptions*' that are among Clare's most beautifully crafted works. In theory Pringle could have taken over the role of publishing mentor that Taylor had performed for so long, but in practice his poetic and editorial activities were but the occupation of his leisure hours. The bulk of his time was devoted to his duties as secretary to the Anti-Slavery Society. Clare himself took an interest in the anti-slavery campaign and on one occasion promised to write a poem for an anthology on the subject. 'Slavery is an abominable traffic', he wrote, 'and they who sanction it cannot be Christians for it is utterly at variance with religion and nature'.

The annuals, several of which were highly profitable operations, had the potential to offer a tidy income. Rudolph Ackermann's *Forget Me Not* paid twenty guineas a sheet and the *Spirit of the Age* a pound a page. L. T. Ventouillac's *Iris: A Literary and Religious Offering* (which had a strong moral and religious agenda) offered 'ten pounds per sheet for poetry, a sheet consisting of thirty two pages the size of the *Bijou*, or a very little larger than the *Amulet*'. Sometimes, however, Clare would send a batch of poems and only one would be accepted, and in that case payment consisted solely of a complimentary copy of the book. Samuel Carter Hall, editor first of the *Amulet* and then of the *Spirit and Manners of the Age*, had a tendency to pay only part of his promised fee—or indeed not to pay at all. 'I am at the world's end, Harry,' wrote Clare to Behnes early in 1831, 'and if you could get Mr Hall to pay me ever so little of what he promised me, I shall be set up and satisfied.' But William Sharp, another friend who helped with the London end of Clare's business affairs, found Hall 'as hard to catch as a little Eel'.

Hall was more neglectful than exploitative. He did make the effort to seek a publisher for a new volume of Clare's work even though he must have known that there was no money to be had for poetry outside the gift-book anthologies. The editors of the annuals did not consciously set out to take advantage of Clare's humble and provincial circumstances. They gave him encouragement and constructive advice: 'Nothing you write can possibly be too long for me or any of your readers but I think you do yourself injustice in a pecuniary point of view by writing so much at length.—Briefer pieces and such consequently as demand less time and labour would well satisfy me and I am sure our Paymasters also.' Clare's perception, however, was that he was getting a raw deal: he remarked that some of the editors paid him 'by promises and promises only' and that others turned down his submissions 'without any reasons at all', whilst publishing far worse things in their place.

In short, his literary earnings did not provide enough to sustain his growing family. Early in 1827 he had the idea of setting up a smallholding. He would rent a cottage and 'as much land as will find me employment the year round'. As a self-sufficient farmer he would be able to escape the humiliation of begging for casual employment. But all he seems to have managed was to rent a patch of ground on which he grew potatoes. He continued to rely on income from short-term paid labour. Harvest in August and September was the best season of the year for this—that was when the whole village turned out to work. In September 1828 he told Eliza Emmerson that he had been harvesting and 'revelling afterwards' in Stamford. We do not know what proportion of his earnings went straight into the hands of the publicans. That winter, his name appears against a twelve-shilling wage in a Burghley farm account, and the following April he reported that he had been 'head over ears at hard work for the last three weeks in the field'. On 18 April 1829 the Burghley steward noted a variety of activity on the estate: the shepherd and his boy had gone to Boro Fen, the farmer was sowing small seeds with Spriggs and Harriss harrowing behind, Ford and Trigg were thrashing, Stangar minding the pigs, Henson and Isaac bringing in malt, and 'Clare cutting a hedge'.

The man who arranged this employment was probably Henry Ryde, the Marquess of Exeter's agent. Clare did not like him or his son. 'I have my antipathys and I cannot get over them', he confessed to Frank Simpson, a friend of the Rydes: 'I am often vext at myself but its no use, my likes and dislikes remain in me and upon that system I cannot like the Rydes I cannot by G— and the more I know of them the more it increases—their ways are so d——d insulting and their word stands for nothing'. He could not abide people who failed to keep their word, whatever their class. He was grateful to the Rydes for bringing the occasional hare or pheasant for the pot, and for arranging work on the Burghley estate, but he thought that they were overstepping the mark when they began attempting to further his literary career. Father and son set themselves up as rival patrons. Ryde Junior took it upon himself to seek a new publisher for the poems and then his father turned up and asked for Mrs Emmerson's address: he was going to London and wanted to do something on Clare's behalf there. To Clare, all this was but 'pomposity and fudge'. 'I can see thro this Farce of Folly and mock patronage', he fumed to Simpson, 'this play at chuck ball and catch it between Mr R and Mr R the son and egad I'll be a ball no longer so here the Farce ends.'

When, however, Ryde Senior and his wife did dine with the Emmersons in London in May 1828, they announced that Clare would soon be provided with a comfortable cottage and an acre or two of land at Barnack. That would have been a real reward for the dedication to the Marquess that had been prefixed to *The Shepherd's Calendar*. Behnes told Clare that he needed to butter up Mr Ryde ('*soap him*', as the idiom of the time had it). Frank Simpson liaised. In November Clare was invited to dine with the Rydes, though he was still suffering the after-effects of the fever he had caught in Boston. The plan for a cottage at Barnack was still alive in March 1829 when Clare paid a visit to Burghley Cottage, the agent's house, but nothing more was heard of it after that.

While Ryde acted on behalf of the Exeters, Clare also looked to the Fitzwilliams at Milton. To Henderson he expressed his disappointment that there had been no formal thanks for the copies of *The*

Shepherd's Calendar that he had sent to the Hall, though he was assured that this was no deliberate snub. The lines from 'The Parish' praising Fitzwilliam as a 'True Patriot' appeared in the *Stamford News* in August 1827 and the following July Henderson spoke to Lord Milton with a view to gaining some assistance in sorting out Clare's complicated financial dealings with his former publisher. In a quiet way, the rivalry that had marked the patronage of Clare from the outset was still in place. From 1829 onwards, there was renewed talk of the Fitzwilliams being the ones who would provide a cottage and some land.

In addition to casual labour in the fields and piecework income from the annuals, Clare also sought to augment his earnings by selling his own books. In April 1828, directly after returning home from his fourth visit to London, he asked Taylor for half a dozen sets of each of his books and an extra half-dozen of the latest one, *The Shepherd's Calendar*. Frederick Martin has a characteristically colourful but unsubstantiated account of this venture, in which the itinerant bookseller is turned away by a clergyman who considers it unbecoming for him to promote himself in this way, but then sells all his wares, at full price or above, to a group of lively and literary horse-dealers, who ply him with hot brandy for good measure. In reality, by July he had sold just two sets and only been paid for one of those. Though it brought illness, the Boston trip was worthwhile if only because it gave Clare the opportunity to sell his stock.

In August 1829 Clare received from Taylor and Hessey the financial accounts that he had long been agitating to see. He was busy working on the harvest, so it was not until November that he looked at them in detail. They did not make for happy reading. There were six accounts, lettered A, B, C, D, E and F.

A was the 'Cash Account'. It credited Clare with the profits on his books together with the dividends and annuities paid through Taylor each year. Its debit side consisted of cash payments made to Clare by Taylor and to others on his behalf (including the bill that Drury had sent in 1826), as well as a charge for books supplied (carried over from a detailed listing in Account F). The net result showed that Clare was in debt to Taylor and Hessey to the tune of just over £141, the equivalent of three and a half years' worth of his regular annuity and dividend payments or nearly six years' income for agricultural labour.

Account B gave details of the trust fund established by Lord Radstock. Account C dealt with Clare's first book, *Poems, Descriptive of Rural Life and Scenery*. Despite indicating that over 3,500 copies had been sold, it showed no profit for Clare. Profits were divided between Drury on the one hand, Taylor and Hessey on the other. To add insult to injury, Taylor had charged five per cent commission for his editorial work and £20 was entered as having been paid to Clare for Drury's purchase of the copyright.

Account D, for *The Village Minstrel*, was healthier: 1,250 copies sold, profit £56, half of which was credited to Clare. But there were several questionable deductions before the figure of £56 was reached, among them fifteen guineas to cover the cost of Hilton's portrait, which had been commissioned by Taylor. Finally, Account E told the sorry story of *The Shepherd's Calendar*: 425 copies sold, meaning that Taylor was out of pocket by some £63 for production costs.

Clare was good at arithmetic. When he scrutinised the accounts carefully, he quickly saw that, by negligence or design, he was the victim of several sleights of hand. He made various notes on the documents, his good memory serving him well:

> In this cash account there is nothing allowed me for my three years writing for London Magazine. I was to have £12 a year and this with £7 given to them for me by a Duchess and never sent makes viz.
>
> 3 years writing for Mag _____ £36
> Duchess Subscription _____ 7
> _____
> £43 never yet
> accounted for

He had several other complaints, all well justified. A debit for paper in the Book Account was especially galling in view of his perpetual shortage of that commodity. The Book Account also charged him more than the sum that had been agreed on for the copies of his own works that he had purchased in order to sell himself. As for *Poems, Descriptive*, he denied selling his copyright to Drury, from whom he had never received the purported twenty pounds. The Hilton portrait was Taylor's idea and had remained in his possession. Whilst it was fair to debit Account D for the fee for the engraving of it that had appeared in *The Village Minstrel*, it was unjust to charge Clare for the painting itself.

When Clare told Mrs Emmerson about the accounts she remarked with some sharpness, 'of course, this Picture is, in such case, your *own property* and you will claim it!' She also dug out an old letter from Drury to Radstock that supported Clare's claim that he had never sold his copyright: 'I consider that the published work, and those that are forthcoming, are bona fide John Clare's property', Drury had written.

Deeply hurt, Clare got in touch with Drury: '*you know* that I never recieved a farthing extra from you beyond the debt which you claimed and was paid for and that the selling of the copy right was all fudge which you desired me to accord with merely as you said to prevent Mr Taylor from depriving you of your share as you feared he would do'. Drury stood his ground and added a further indignity by claiming that he had incurred a financial loss on his printing of Clare's songs because the frequency of his appearances in the *London Magazine* had cheapened the worth of his writings. No longer in any mood to compromise, Clare drafted a furious reply denouncing Drury's 'pathetic pretensions' of caring for his welfare and 'whining commendations' of his own past actions. It was a bitter end to the friendship that had launched his literary career.

He handled Taylor with more circumspection, laying out his case in a long letter that was prepared in several careful drafts. The tone was both cordial and restrained. Good wishes were sent not only to Taylor himself, but also to Hessey, who—to Clare's astonishment— had recently gone bankrupt. In sharp contrast to Drury, Taylor responded with respect and a spirit of compromise. He said that he would have to discuss Clare's 'Corrections' with Hessey, but that some of them deserved to be allowed, and would be, and that he was much pleased with the manner in which they were stated: 'You need never expect any Difference of Feeling in me from the candid Declaration of your own Views and Opinions.'

At the beginning of January 1830, Taylor sent Clare a ten-pound note, which overpaid the half-yearly annuity due to him by more than two pounds. This was a gesture of reconciliation. In effect, the question of the accounts was quietly dropped. Clare continued to receive his income from the trust fund—further diminished, as the government reduced the interest rate still further—and his regular payments from his noble patrons. Taylor did not request any repayments for books, paper or cash previously advanced. At the same time, Clare did not see the benefit of such further income from book sales as there might have been—but that was hardly a loss, since sales had almost completely dried up.

'I am no publisher of poet[ry] now', wrote Taylor: he had moved into the business of university textbooks. Hessey, meanwhile, set himself up as an auctioneer. Clare told Cary, the Londoner in whom he placed a special trust, that he regarded his financial affairs with Taylor as settled, although he was disappointed with the outcome. In particular, he was disillusioned with the 'half-profits' arrangement into which he had entered. The one thing the accounts revealed for certain was how easy it was for a publisher to find expenses—the cost of copying, engraving and so forth—to deduct from his profits before sharing them. For this reason, when Clare finally placed his fourth book with a new publisher, he sold it outright for £40 instead of seeking half-profits.

Although the whole affair left a bitter aftertaste, Clare did not let it affect his friendship with Taylor. He dismissed Drury as 'a trafficing hugster [huckster] after self interest', but, despite his initial impression on receiving the accounts that he had mistaken 'Collins' Ready Reckoner for a Treatise on Friendship', he acknowledged that Taylor had remained true to him. Inevitably, though, they drifted apart with the end of their business dealings. Taylor wrote every six months, when sending the annuity money. 'In this *half yearly* correspondence', replied Clare in July 1830, 'there is always somthing very gloomy and melancholly stirred up with former reccolections.' He looked back on the years of their closest partnership, 1820–4, as the happiest in his life. The memory brought sadness at the dispersal of his old friends. He asked after Lamb and Wainewright, told of his sorrow at Mary Lamb's recurrent mental illness and his incredulity on hearing the news that Hazlitt had died, 'neglected and forgotten'. Such, he said, was the usual fate of genius.

In January 1831 Taylor lent Clare the copy of Chaucer's poems that had belonged to Keats. Of such small but telling acts is enduring friendship made. Clare especially admired Chaucer's natural descriptions, which he thought had not dated through the passing of the centuries; he was also intrigued that some of Chaucer's vernacular vocabulary was still in use among his own people. The example of Chaucer gave a much-needed boost to his commitment to both local dialect and the robust, earthy idiom of his own verse.

One of the enduring myths about Clare is that he was the victim of both editorial high-handedness and sharp financial practice on Taylor's part. In reality, there was never an absolute break between them. The accounts were a mess not because Taylor was trying to dupe Clare but because all Taylor and Hessey's finances were a mess. The reason Taylor did not publish another book of Clare's poetry after *The Shepherd's Calendar* was that he did not publish any books of poetry after *The Shepherd's Calendar*.

CHAPTER FIFTEEN

'I NEVER MEDDLE WITH POLITICS'

John Clare was a poet of the people. We have seen that his creative aspirations had their origin in the folk tradition, his earliest inspiration coming from the ballads sung to him by his parents and the tales told by his grandmother and the old village women such as 'Granny' Bains. Throughout his writing career, he collected songs, pricked out gypsy tunes and wrote down the words of ballads known to his acquaintances in the village, among the servants at Milton, and elsewhere.

His Scottish friend Allan Cunningham also had a particular interest in vernacular culture. As a token of esteem from their common publisher, John Taylor, Clare had been given Cunningham's *Songs of Scotland*. Over the years he had acquired a number of other printed collections, such as *Remains of Nithsdale and Galloway Song* (given by Rippingille), Joseph Ritson's *Select Collection of English Songs*, and *Robin Hood: a Collection of all the ancient Poems, Songs, and Ballads, now extant, relative to that celebrated English Outlaw*. Robert Burns remained his great exemplar for the combination of traditional material and original invention.

In the mid-1820s, his reading of—and contributions to—the *Every-Day Book* of the radical publisher William Hone had shown him that there was a market for what we would now call folk culture.

Clare's fifteen minutes of metropolitan literary fame now over, perhaps it was time to take the long view: in the essay published in the *European Magazine* in 1825 he had distinguished between ephemeral 'popularity in authorship' and the more enduring 'common fame' of 'those things and names that are familiar among the common people'. The mark of Chatterton's fame was his presence in penny ballads and on pocket handkerchiefs such as the one that Clare's mother had bought him at Deeping Fair. And the most venerable poetry of all was the oral tradition of legends and stories in rhyme that was 'as old as England' itself.

As the ancient landscape had been irredeemably changed by enclosure, so too the old ballads were being forgotten. Not even the folk tradition was immune from the taste for brash new fashions. 'I commenced sometime ago with an intention of making a collection of old Ballads', he explained in a draft preface to his planned collection of folk poetry,

> but when I had sought after them in places where I expected [to] find them, viz. the hay field and the shepherds hut on the pasture—I found that nearly all those old and beautiful reccolections had vanished as so many old fashions and those who knew fragments seemed ashamed to acknowledge it as old people who sing old songs only sung to be laughed at—and those who were proud of their knowledge of such things knew nothing but the sensless balderdash that is brawled over and sung at County Feasts Statutes and Fairs where the most sensless jargon passes for the greatest excellence and rudest indecency for the finest wit.

The fragility of the oral tradition in an era that was branding itself 'the age of progress' made Clare all the more determined to write down every scrap of old verse that he could find. In so doing, he was not only repaying a personal debt to his father and the memory of his childhood, but also making a polemical case for the value of inherited popular culture. He was intrigued by the paradox that 'the lower orders of England' were perfectly capable of treating public executions as holiday entertainment, and yet the very same people 'will stand around an old ballad singer and with all the romantic enthusiasm of pity shed tears over the doggerel tales of imaginary distress': the ballad tradition was proof that rural working people were not, as was sometimes claimed, 'destitute of the finer feelings of humanity and taste'.

Clare carefully drew up a title-page for his collection, emphasising the value of the material to the culture of both region and nation:

> National and Provincial Melodies
> Selected from the Singing
> and Recitations
> of
> the Peasantry in and about
> Helpstone and its neighbourhood
> with some alterations and corrections
> necessarily required

Just as he accepted that his own work required some necessary corrections on the part of his editors, so as a folk-song collector he set about rendering oral material fit for print. In August 1827 Harry Stoe Van Dyk inquired whether he had found a publisher for the collection, whilst also offering to ensure that the metre of the poetry corresponded with the metre of the music. But the 'National and Provincial Melodies' remained another of Clare's unfinished projects.

In the light of the collapse of the market for poetry, he also considered remaking himself as a prose writer. He made various fresh attempts at story-writing. A tale of 'The "old farmer" and his neighbour the Vicar' evoked the way of life of fifty years before, in which traditional customs and mutual obligations still held good. 'The two Soldiers' and 'The Stage Coach' were attempts at narrative. For a time Clare considered stitching his stories together into a prose 'Parish Register' under the possible title 'Memoirs of Uncle Barnaby'. As in novels such as Goldsmith's *Vicar of Wakefield*, there would have been a mixture of sentimentalism, satire and adventure; the solid worthiness of simple folk from an earlier generation would have been contrasted with the selfishness of the present.

Despite his success at verse-narrative, Clare found himself unable to sustain or structure his prose tales in such a way as to produce a complete novel. He realised that shorter forms were his strength, so he devoted considerable effort to a proposed collection of essays along the lines of Charles Lamb's *Elia* and William Hazlitt's *Table Talk*. When he was in London in early 1828, Allan Cunningham, who was now a literary editor, asked him for 'a prose tale'. After considerable procrastination, and with the stimulus of some sensational newspaper stories sent by Cunningham, he eventually obliged with a lively essay 'On the Wonders of inventions curiositys strange sights and other remarkables "of the last forty days" in the Metropolis in a Letter to A Friend'. The essay's combination of energised astonishment and wry detachment nicely catches the countryman's response to the bustle and innovation of London life, where 'the strides towards the perfection of wonderment of the imperial city' were so rapid that merely to think about them was like 'going in a new patent Gurney steam carriage'.

Draft passages for about thirty essays are to be found in Clare's various notebooks of this time. He made out various lists of titles for inclusion in the proposed volume. Among his subjects were prayer, resolution, pretension, thinking, self-conceit, station in life, honour, false appearances, money-catching and pleasure. In the manner of the *London Magazine* essayists, he moved easily between, on the one hand, personal reminiscence and opinion, and on the other, maxims, general truths, and reflection on proverbial wisdom and well-known quotations.

One of these essays, entitled 'On Political Religion', contains some notably robust writing: 'Politics may be defined as the struggles of opposition to act in unison where the greatest evils ever canvassed find some base enough to support them and the best good ever offered for the countrys benefit and the peoples happiness is never aimed at but there is some mean enough to opposite it—thus "Party is the madness of many for the gain of a few." ' Religion, Clare argues here, does not have to be explicitly connected to oppressive government in order to serve the rich at the expense of the poor: it is 'forced down the throats of the people to teach them patience only to bear unjust burdens the better in the shape of taxes etc. for the sole benefit of luxury and extravagance'. But the people are not as stupid as authority imagines them to be: sermons on patience may sometimes make them stubborn for their rights rather than reconciled to their impoverished lot.

Clare is at his most forceful on the hypocrisy of the prosperous: 'Every discontented tradesman declares the poor peasant's lot to be the happiest in the world and the hardest labour as the best exercise, yet he would sooner chuse any lot than that of poor man and any labour but that of hard work'. Almost without realising it, he was becoming a more overtly political writer than he had been before.

The draft essays are also very funny, especially at the expense of those who have pretensions to social status. One piece consists of a series of letters written in the style of a greengrocer's wife telling her daughter how important it is to master the art of correct spelling: 'to be wyse is to be larneyd our Paa paa yur furthor wishes mee yur maa maa to introduce you into the hart off sphellin correctedly as that is the rutt hend of the tree of nowlege'. Given this mockery of bad spelling, it is difficult to imagine that Clare would have wanted his own deficiencies in that art to have been reproduced in print as they have in various modern editions of his works.*

Perhaps the best of the essays is that 'On Affectation'. Here Clare uses personal experience to make his case that affectation is the most ridiculous of all human follies:

> I was once invited to join a tea party at the house of a friend's acquaintance where the good people possessed a pretty daughter in the shape of a pert forward girl who said and did every thing with the greatest self-possession imaginable—she was considered pretty by her acquaintance and very handsome by her par-

*See Appendix.

ents and herself. I observed she laughed at every thing and often at nothing ... she seemed determined to keep laughing, which she did in a very mechanical and unfeeling manner as if something more than happiness was the cause, for she rather grinned than laughed and when any thing occurred that caused the rest to laugh heartily she only forced the cold smile and grin as usual, but I discovered that these smiles or lip drillings discovered a beautiful set of teeth and I soon found that the gummy smiles was for the purpose of showing them and not from the accident of being suddenly pleased or delighted with any thing that occurred in her hearing.

Even before the guests sat down, their hosts were telling them that their daughter was a genius in everything she did, whether playing the piano or spouting Shakespeare ('superior even to Kean', said the mother, referring to Edmund Kean, the most celebrated actor of the age). The girl then showed off her needlework designs for a firescreen, in the form of a picture of Chinese mandarins. Clare spilt his tea all over it, the girl fled to the next room in a fit of pique, and the mother had hysterics. When Miss returned, she sneered that Clare was a boor who handled paintings in the same way that a clown handled a soap-wrapper. The only way of making it up to her was to admire her other artwork and then—agony for a true poet—to praise her efforts in verse. By using humour, Clare succeeds in satirising those who think themselves his betters, while also gently mocking his own persona of country bumpkin.

In December 1829 he told Eliza Emmerson of his plan for a volume of essays on 'every day matters'. Had he completed the book and found a publisher for it, his public image would have taken a new turn. Instead of being praised only for simplicity, accuracy of description and closeness to nature, he would have been revealed to have not only the personal touch, but also the sententiousness and insight, together with the humour and the gift of irony, that characterise the essays of Hazlitt and Lamb.

There were various other unfulfilled projects in this phase of Clare's career, among them a disquisition on the somewhat hackneyed aesthetic theme of 'the sublime and the beautiful'. He also discussed with Taylor a plan to write the biographies of the Elizabethan and Jacobean poets, as a 'prequel' to Dr Johnson's *Lives of the English Poets*,* which did not extend back beyond the mid-seventeenth century. But as his health declined in the early 1830s, his prose writing petered out. We have only a jigsaw of fragments in his later notebooks.

In 1830 Clare began to fall into arrears with his rent. The following year he received a bill for the purchase of books that was *four years* overdue. Interest rates were going down and down, reducing the half-yearly dividend on his trust fund. The cobbler had to be paid for mending the children's shoes and the cost of schooling was a constant drain, despite assistance from Mrs Emmerson. He was determined that the children should remain in school for as long as possible, whatever the necessary sacrifices at home. In a notebook fragment he argued from personal experience for the value of state-supported education: 'I should like to see the effect of schools established by government in every village—I should think they would put human life and commonsense into that dull and obdurate class from whence I struggled into light like one struggling from the night mare in his sleep and now I only see the wretched ignorance I have left behind me in more vivid lights.' All three of his daughters and three of his four sons became literate.

Whatever hardships John and Patty had to endure, they ensured that their children had sixpenny chapbooks for Christmas. Among the chaotic fragments of Clare's papers we find the following touching little note:

Christmas Boxes promised my childern
Anna   Valentine and Ornson
Eliza   Cock Robin
Frederic   Peacock at Home and Butterflyes Ball

---

*A copy of which was among the many books presented to him by Lord Radstock in the early days of his fame.

John	Dame Trott and her Cat
William	Mother Hubard and her Dog
Sophy	House that Jack Built

Remembering his own boyhood joy at the arrival of the itinerant 'bookman', Clare did all he could to develop both the reading skills and the imagination of his children.

The cost of books, pens and paper made it hard to sustain a literate, let alone a literary, life. There was never enough paper in the Clare household. Every scrap was saved; some of the poetic manuscripts consist of stitched-together letter covers. The sheer incongruity of Clare's situation is apparent when you handle his raw materials. 'Shadows of Taste', one of his most characteristic nature poems, was drafted on the back of a handbill addressed to the electors of Stamford—'Vote for *those* who will promote the *Interests* of *True* Religion ... It is the *present* form of our Constitution alone which provides for the *Instruction of the Poor*.' It was also the present form of the constitution that poor men should not have a vote. Clare's only political voice was his published writing.

The severity of the family's financial difficulties in the early 1830s was a sign of the times. The talk in Helpston was of sales and bankrupts, of 'bustle and bother'. There was, in Clare's words, 'country meeting mania', in which 'every village is metamorphosed into a Forum and every Giles into an Orator—but the strangest metamorphose of all is these out-of-place tory folks becoming radicals and brawling in every corner of the country about reform'.* How it would all end he could not imagine.

His correspondence in 1830 and 1831 dwelt more on political affairs than his own money troubles. 'Thus the Country goes staggering on,' wrote Taylor, 'first one Class then another getting a Blow, till at last either all will be exasperated and bear it no longer, or John Bull will be content to lie down like a Brute and ruminate on the Glory

---

*From a letter to William Robertson, the region's leading theatre manager, who had visited Clare and invited him to Grantham. Clare didn't go, but he met Robertson again at the theatre in Peterborough in the summer of 1830.

that has been and is departed for ever'. It was a time of severe national unrest. The economy was in crisis. Taylor, who was busy writing economic tracts with such titles as *An Essay on Money* and *Currency Fallacies Refuted*, blamed 'that foolish Currency Bill of Peel's'. Agitation for political reform was growing to a crescendo, spurred on by the election victory of the progressive Whigs under Earl Grey and Lord John Russell, and the accession to the throne of William IV, who was perceived to be more liberal-minded than his brother George IV. Throughout the rural south, meanwhile, there were arson attacks and other signs of severe discontent among agricultural labourers. In 1832 the government narrowly succeeded in introducing the great parliamentary reform act, but the extension of the franchise was principally for the benefit of urban property-owners. It achieved nothing for the rural poor. Riots in the countryside were brutally suppressed. There were about twenty executions and hundreds of men were sentenced to imprisonment or transportation to Australia.

Back in 1820 Clare had been all for king and country. He had dissociated himself from the radicals who exploited George IV's ill-treatment of his queen as a pretext for the furtherance of their own ends. In this new crisis, his position was more complicated, despite his continued claim 'I never meddle with politics'. He dismissed the business of political parties and electioneering as 'nothing more or less than a game at hide and seek for self-interest', in which Whig and Tory were almost interchangeable terms. And yet his reply to Taylor on the subject of the 'bad times' cut through the cant of false radicalism whilst simultaneously pinpointing the real grievances of the poor. A party man he was not, but political opinions he certainly had.

In his letter to Taylor, as in several major poems such as 'The Parish', 'The Fallen Elm' and 'The Hue and Cry', he was sceptical about those who took up the cause of reform when their real motivation was self-interest:

> The Farmer as usual is on the look out for 'high prices' and 'better markets' as he stiles them altho these markets are always known to be curses to the cottager, the labourer and the poor mechanic.

> The Parson is now stirring up to radicalism (which some years ago he cryed down as infidelity) for a reduction of taxes merely because he sees that somthing must be done and as he wishes to keep his tythes and his immense livings untouched he throws the burthen on government.
>
> The Speculator is looking out for a new paper currency which placed a false value on every species of his trafic and thereby enabled the cunning to cheat the honest . . . so long will a few build their prosperity on the ruin of thousands.

At the same time, Clare recognised that a properly regulated system of paper currency would be a great deal more efficient than trafficking in gold. With characteristic modesty, he proclaimed himself no politician in comparison with Taylor. But he proved himself an astute analyst of the contemporary scene, arguing forcefully that the first response to the economic and social problems of the nation should be greater 'equality' of taxation, a reduction of tithes paid to the church, and reform of placements, clerical livings and corrupt government 'pensions'. Such sentiments might once have been 'considered as proceeding from a Leveller and a Radical', he went on— but now the label 'Radical' had become as meaningless as 'Whig' and 'Tory'. He claimed not to be a leveller, because he did not want 'a farthing of that which belongs to another', but he stood by a 'political creed' that said it was the government's duty to foster 'the general good of the community rather than to encourage the knavery of individuals'. No just government could justify taking heavy taxation from the poor while leaving the rich untouched.

As so often, Clare found himself pulled between conflicting factions. His habitual response was to dig in his heels and stand his own ground. Just before Christmas 1829, Stamford's veteran radical publisher John Drakard told him that in the new year he would be launching a new paper—the *Stamford Champion*—and that he would be delighted to include anything by Clare if he should happen to have 'a politically inspired thought'. In the course of the following year, Clare sent Drakard a number of poems, some of which were published in the *Champion* and others in *Drakard's Stamford News*. The most substantial of these was 'The Hue and Cry: A Tale of the Times'. Perhaps because of its political content, it appeared without Clare's name. It is a vigorous satire on the moral panic provoked by the bogeyman of the shadowy radical who advocates what we now call political 'direct action'. There were local tales of mysterious horsemen riding through the night and stirring up discontent. The mythical figure of 'Captain Swing' was blamed for many a riot or arson attack. Clare's poem swipes at the propaganda work achieved by rumour and wild accusation:

> Some said it was Cobbett, some said it was Paine,
> Some went into France to Voltaire
> And when they got there, why they got back again
> To discover that nothing was there.
> Some rummaged old sermons, some printed new tracts
> And handbills like messengers ran.
> Conjectures were many, but few were the facts
> As to who was the crooked old man.

This is a very different voice from the Clare who examines birds' nests or yearns for the lost Eden of his childhood, but in its own register it has the unencumbered vigour that is his hallmark.

Although in this poem Clare mocked the paranoia of the anti-radical camp, he had no time for mob violence. In December 1830 he was especially horrified by an arson attack on a large farm out in Deeping Fen. The fire lasted for six hours, destroying the stables, a barn, a granary and a threshing machine. Even the pro-radical *Stamford Champion* had condemned this 'most terrific and destructive fire which has been lighted in our neighbourhood in these days—or rather nights—of horrible incendiarism'. It chilled Clare's blood to think of what had happened, not least because his humanitarian instincts recoiled from the suffering of the cows, pigs and horses burnt to death in the blaze. There had been many rick-burnings in the months before, but this event struck home because of the loss of animal life—and the fact that the owners of the farm that had been attacked were the Clark family, his own landlords, with whom he had maintained good relations over the years.

'God forbid that I should live to see a revolution', he wrote to Taylor. In a letter to Marianne Marsh he attacked the 'mob impulse' and the 'threatening of revolutionary forebodings' in the 'machine breaking and grain destroying mania' of the winter of 1830–1. It would be an injustice to say that here he was voicing a conservative thought simply because he was writing to a bishop's wife. The woman who had met her husband when her father hid him from Napoleon's agents was no apologist for political tyranny and the Bishop himself was a friend to the poor, even though it was in his church's interest to advocate the maintenance of tithes. Marianne Marsh openly discussed politics with Clare and sent him '3 Numbers of Cobbett's penny tracts'. He responded with a coolly measured judgement on both the writings of the great rural agitator and the need for the right sort of political reform:

> I look upon Cobbett as one of the most powerful prose writers of the age—with no principles to make those powers commendable to honest praise—the Letters to farmers contain some very sensible arguments and some things that appeared to be too much of party colouring—there is no medium in party matters—where there is excess it is always on one side—and that is the worst of it—I am no politician but I think a reform is wanted—not the reform of mobs where the bettering of the many is only an apology for injuring the few—nor the reform of partys where the benefits of one is the destruction of the other—but a reform that would do good and hurt none.

To Clare's eyes, Cobbett was essentially right in his analysis of the state of rural England—and in particular the sufferings of the rural poor at the hands of self-interested improvers and representatives of new money—but essentially wrong in pursuing 'present grievances, piques and self-interested animosities' as opposed to the underlying principles of social justice. Ultimately, he thought, Cobbett would go down in history as a time-serving politician rather than the 'great philosopher of domestic life' that he might have been.

It is the clarity of Clare's thought and the independence of his spirit that stand out in his political writings. He advocated neither the reform of mobs nor the reform of parties, because he saw that both came with their own destructive agendas. In a single prose fragment, he can observe on the one hand that 'Nothing can equal in history the fanatical cruelty and barbarity of some of Charles 1ˢᵗ's enemys' and on the other that 'truth often finds king and tyrant synonymous'. Violence was what he hated more than anything else; it must therefore have been intensely traumatic when his own psychiatric condition seemed to take a violent turn a few years later.

He refused to call himself a radical or a leveller, and yet he cared so deeply about his newspaper contribution entitled 'Apology for the Poor' that he returned to it in more than a dozen different drafts. Here he wrote unashamedly in 'the voice of a poor man' and cried out for someone to become a 'Champion for the poor not in his speeches but his actions—for speeches are nowadays nothing but words and sounds'.* 'Is it common sense or radicalism', he asked, 'when the many express their disapprobation of the tyranny and domineering of the few?' There is evidence that this essay did appear in print, probably in the *Stamford Champion*, but the published text is lost.

In exactly the period when he was writing for Drakard's radical *Champion*, Clare was also contributing poems to another new Stamford paper, the *Bee*, which was founded in the autumn of 1830 specifically to resist the cause of reform. Both Frank Simpson's father and the Rydes, father and son, were among this paper's sponsors. Ryde Senior invited Clare to contribute to the first number, just as Drakard had invited him to write on the other side of the political question

---

*He worked around this time on a prose satire of the 'Cant, humbug and hypocrisy' of empty-headed political posturing and speechifying. The intention of this sketch, entitled 'The Bone and Cleaver Club', was to show that 'Truth is always asserted with the fewest words and falsehood with the most protestations'. The 'Club' is a parody of the 'friendly societies' that held monthly debates in pubs.

some months before. Clare was forced to perform his usual balancing act, remaining on good terms with both the Tory faction associated with his patron the Marquess of Exeter, and the Whigs and reformers for whom his other patrons, Lord Milton and the Earl Spencer, were the local standard-bearers. The pro-reform John Taylor quite understood his willingness to contribute to an anti-reform paper: 'Its Principles, I agree with you in thinking, are not those which you are likely to advocate, but the Poet is happily not required to be a Politician'.

When Clare fell out with the editors of the *Bee* and stopped contributing poems to it, the reason was not the paper's politics but its failure to pay him. He was also annoyed by what he perceived as an attempt by Ryde to enlist Eliza Emmerson into the political fray in Stamford. Clare had done her a good turn by being the contact that led the *Bee* to publish some of her own poems, but he did not want her to gain the impression that she would have to pay a party political price for this. 'I wish success heartily to my friends wether wigs tories or radicals', he explained to her, 'but between such matters I am as a blank leaf between two pages of letter-press, ready to receive all impressions that coincide with my opinions or refute them and never caring to take any note of those that do not ... I hate party feuds and can never become a party man, but where I have friends on both sides there I am on both sides as far as my opinions can find it right but no further, not an inch.'

A message came from Milton Hall in July 1831. Henderson the gardener had heard that a cottage would shortly be available for rent in the village of Northborough. It came with a small portion of land. He proposed that Clare should ask the Reverend Mossop to write immediately to Lord Milton on his behalf with regard to his having it. Several applications were in, but the property had not yet been promised to anybody.

That October, Mossop wrote to Eliza Emmerson in London with the good news that the cottage would be Clare's with effect from January—though the rent of about £13 a year, several times what he was paying in Helpston, would stretch his resources. It was a comfortable dwelling with 'an Acre of Orchard and Garden, inclusive of a Common for two Cows, with a meadow sufficient to produce fodder for the Winter'. Clare hoped for a time that income from a new volume of poetry would help finance the move and give him the wherewithal to establish himself as a cottage gardener, but the reports of Pringle, Taylor and Emmerson on the demise of the poetry market swiftly disabused him of any such expectation. Eliza sought to tide the family through the winter by sending second-hand clothes for the children, with the suggestion that the brown paper in which they were folded might serve as a scrubbing apron for Patty. Together with Taylor, she also chipped in towards Clare's doctors' bills, in the hope that he would be able to leave Helpston free from debt. Dr Skrimshire halved his overdue bill for drugs and services rendered.

The impending change of environment led Clare to brood on time and loss. He wrote to Sir John Trollope, a local gentleman, agitating for the preservation of some fragments of a ruined manor house in Torpel Wood from the depredations of road menders in pursuit of stone. He lamented the felling of the last of the row of elm trees that had stood outside his cottage for as long as anyone could remember. 'The old plum tree at the corner is blown down', he also observed, 'and all the old associations are going before me'.

Henderson wrote on 1 January 1832 to welcome the year of the 'emigration' by means of which his friend would achieve 'a more independent condition'. Clare came up with another idea for the payment of his debts and the funding of his cottage garden: he asked Taylor if he could cash in the trust fund, which was performing poorly as a result of the cut in interest rates. Taylor told him that nothing could be done while the co-trustee with legal expertise, flame-haired Richard Woodhouse, was away in Italy. When the trust deeds were consulted, it became clear that the terms would not allow such a course: the interest was for present use, but the principal was to be retained and divided among Clare's children after his death. Clare was angry to learn that he had no control over what he considered his own. The law, he wrote, 'is a rogue'.

In March, Henderson and the agent of the Milton estate met Clare at Northborough to inspect the cottage. It had undergone considerable refurbishment, possibly even complete rebuilding, since being vacated by the previous tenant. Clare wrote to Emmerson with the news that it was 'finished, and beautifully finished'. He was delighted to become a tenant of the Fitzwilliams, who had the reputation of being good landlords. Henderson offered assurance that a water-pump would be ordered. And his advice on landscaping reveals that Clare was about to move to a domain considerably larger than the Helpston cottage with its mere strip of garden:

> I would begin by laying out a walk along the front of the house broad enough to allow your children room to ramble without running on the borders—at right angles with this and fronting the door I would lay out another walk so as to divide the piece into two, I would then measure off borders about 5 or 6 feet wide on the outside next to (and within) the hedge and pails, then run narrow walks or footpaths within these which would give you a line of narrow borders on the east, south & west sides—there would then be two large spaces on each side of the middle walk which you could lay out according to the vagaries of your own fancy ... You propose planting private from some heath but that will shade its leaves in winter—I have plenty of young plants of evergreen private which you are welcome to if an opportunity offers of sending it over.

A large garden of his own, not to mention an established orchard and a grazing pasture, was a better prospect than Clare had ever known before. Yet Northborough was an isolated, inward-looking community. There would be gossips complaining from the start that he had been given preferential treatment. Why should a man who had never been in the regular employ of the Milton estate be entitled to a commodious, well-furbished cottage and a substantial plot of land? Henderson said that such carping should be ignored. All that mattered was that Clare would at last have a comfortable home and the means to provide for his family.

There were apprehensions. His parents—rheumatic Parker in his late sixties, dropsied Ann in her seventies—would still be in Helpston, though the intention was that they should visit as often as possible.* And it would be hard to say goodbye to the cottage in which he had spent all his life. Frank Simpson came over and began a sketch of the fireside for Clare to have as a keepsake, but he did not have time to finish it before the move.

The change in physical environment was a serious concern for a man who had derived his profoundest sense of personal identity from his immediate surroundings. He was leaving the woods and heaths and favourite spots that had known him for so long. This was how he put it: not that he had known the environs of Helpston, but that the place *had known him*. 'The very molehills on the heath and the old trees in the hedges' seemed to bid him farewell. By contrast to Helpston, with its woods and lanes and secure nooks, Northborough was out on the fen. His first impressions had been of a place of bleakness and exposure: 'there is neither wood nor heath, furzebush, molehill or oak tree about it, and a nightingale never reaches so far in her summer excursions'.

On Saturday 28 April 1832 John Clare wrote a farewell note to Parson Mossop and his sister, who had given so much help through all the hard years. Then early on the Monday morning, the family made the walk of just over three miles to Northborough. The weather was cloudy but dry. The move would have been a considerable undertaking, with six children aged between one and eleven, at least one cat, a large oak bookcase and some three hundred books—not to mention all Clare's manuscripts, which he had gathered from various nooks and crannies around the old cottage. 'On flitting from my native place', he later recalled, 'I hunted over my bundles of paper intending to save the trouble of carriage by destroying those I set least store by

---

*According to a visitor in the autumn of 1832, Clare's mother (and by inference father) 'still lived' in the family home in Helpston after the poet moved to Northborough. Did they move back in after the young family left? Or perhaps when the parents moved out in 1830, it was merely to a different tenement in the same row? The visitor reported that Ann Clare was out gleaning when he called—so her health must have been robust.

... but I read them and paused, thinking of old days and old feelings and, excuse my vanity, gentle reader——if I did not think them worthy of your praise, I felt I could not burn them.'

'There are some things that I shall regret leaving', he told Eliza Emmerson, 'and some journeys that I shall make yearly——to see the flood at Lolham Briggs——to gather primroses in Hilly Wood and hunt the nightingale's nest in Royce Wood and go to see the furze in flower on Emmonsails Heath.'

CHAPTER SIXTEEN

FROM MIDSUMMER CUSHION

TO RURAL MUSE

D espite the tortured progress into print of *The Shepherd's Cal-endar* and the lukewarm response when it was finally pub-lished, Clare was determined to go on writing poetry. As with his prose works, several projects failed to come to fruition. He returned to the imitations of Elizabethan and seventeenth-century poets that he intended to gather under the title 'Visits of the Earlier Muses'. His friend Henry Cary, now working at the British Museum, advised him against trying to pass them off as original lost manuscripts in the manner of Thomas Chatterton's pseudo-mediaeval poems. In the event, a decision about how the poems should be presented did not have to be made, for the collection never appeared. Nor did an in-tended volume for children that would have begun with 'The Grasshopper', a narrative poem written when Anna had been a tod-dler and published in 1829 in one of the annuals aimed at the family market.

The frequency with which Clare lapsed into depression and torpor was such that his patterns of writing had become very disjointed. His notebooks of the years from 1827 to 1837 are full of fragments, false starts and erasures. Sometimes, though, he found the energy to drive

MANUSCRIPT DRAFT OF 'THE FLITTING', WITH SKETCH
OF THE BUST OF A WOMAN (PATTY? MARY?)

himself forward. He must have been on a high when he confidently proclaimed that he would soon be writing something that would beat all his previous performances hollow.

This seems to be a reference to a long poem on which he worked in the second half of 1828. In a letter to Harry Behnes, who had become an important confidant, he mentioned that it was called 'The Pleasures of Spring'—and that its progress was stuck. He was satisfied with the descriptive writing, but could not find an 'action' appropriate to the subject. As Taylor told him, this was the old problem with his 'nature' writing: however good the description, unless there was another element, he would just be producing the same kind of work as before. Fellow-poet George Darley made the same point:

> There have been so many 'Pleasures of So-and-so', that I should almost counsel you against baptizing your Poem on Spring—the 'Pleasures' of anything. Besides, when a poem is so designated, it is almost assuredly prejudged as deficient in *action* (about which you appear solicitous). 'The Pleasures of Spring', from you, identified as you are with *Descriptive* Poesy, would, almost without doubt, sound in the public ear as the announcement of a series of literary scene-paintings. Beautiful as these may be, and certainly would be from your pencil, there is a deadness about them which tends to chill the reader: he must be animated with something of a livelier prospect.

'The Pleasures of Spring' was a revised version of 'Spring', written back in 1823. Among the revisions was a considerable expansion of a passage in which a human figure, suggestive of Clare himself, is placed in the landscape. Just as the prose essays were at their best when Clare spiced them with anecdote, so his poetry achieved its distinction when it was at its most personal. He would never solve the problem of the long poem to his full satisfaction, but his finest poems of the later 1820s and early 1830s overcame the 'deadness' of mere description through the particular life of emotion and experience with which they were infused.

Back in 1825, Clare had recorded in his journal the purchase of a blank book in which 'to insert the best of my poems'. Over the following years, using his very best handwriting, he copied into it his long satire 'The Parish', the narrative poem 'Edmund and Hellen', and a large selection of shorter works, divided chronologically into 'Early Poems', 'Poems of a later date' (with an added pencil note, 'Such as are crossed out in this part are intended to be kept out of sight and not to be published'), 'Poems that have been published under various Signatures in different Periodicals', and 'Poems written in 1824 and later'. As a reminder to himself, he jotted above many of the poems the name of the magazine, newspaper or annual in which they had found their way into print.

Then in March 1831, Fanny, cousin of his Stamford friend Frank Simpson, gave him a new blank book. It had over six hundred pages, but was a curious oblong shape; Fanny apologised for its not being exactly what he wanted. Clare was convinced that the best things he had written were among what he called his 'fugitives', the poems that were scattered in a wide array of different periodicals. He wanted Taylor's opinion with a view to a new selection of his work. Maximising the available space for his lines of verse by turning Fanny's oblong book vertically, he started on fresh fair copies. By July he had done enough to tell Thomas Pringle at *Friendship's Offering* that he was 'making some preparation for getting out another vol'. As ever, his plan went through many vicissitudes: this fourth collection did not appear in print for another four years.

In the interim, some new poems were published, notably in Pringle's annual and the Stamford newspaper, the *Bee*. 'The Nightingale's Nest', which appeared in both *Friendship's Offering* and the *Bee* in late 1832, was especially admired by his friends. Frank Simpson called it 'the most exquisite *bit* I ever read' and Eliza Emmerson was so inspired that she wrote a poem of her own entitled 'On reading the Nightingale's Nest by John Clare'. Where was the nest? Was it 'Up the green woodland', as Clare said? No, wrote Eliza, ' 'tis in the *Poet's brest*'—' "Clare" and the "Nightingale" are one!'

'The Nightingale's Nest' begins from a sense of intimacy not only with the bird, the nest and its environment, but also with the reader.

It is written in the present tense. We are immediately drawn into the poem as Clare makes us imagine that we are walking with him:

> Up this green woodland ride let's softly rove
> And list the nightingale—she dwelleth here,
> Hush, let the wood-gate softly clap—for fear
> The noise might drive her from her home of love ...

This was a device that he had pioneered in some other as yet unpublished nest poems written back in 1825–6. Thus 'The Yellowhammer's Nest':

> Just by the wooden brig a bird flew up,
> Frit by the cowboy as he scrambled down
> To reach the misty dewberry—let us stoop
> And seek its nest ...

And 'The Pettichap's Nest':

> and you and I
> Had surely passed it in our walk today
> Had chance not led us by it ...
> Stop, here's the bird—that woodman at the gap
> Hath frit it from the hedge—'tis olive green,
> Well I declare it is the pettichap's.

The early nest poems were written around the same time as the 'Natural History of Helpston', when Clare was spending time with his Milton friends. It is very probable that the poems were inspired by particular walks: 'us' and 'you and I' would originally have referred to Clare and Henderson, or Clare and Artis. By the time of 'The Nightingale's Nest', Clare was in Northborough and hardly seeing his old friends. But by retaining the present tense and the figure of the walking companion, he achieved the element of 'animation' that Darley said was lacking in his merely descriptive writing.

The other animating presence in the nest poems is Clare's own children. In a long poem of the later 1820s, entitled 'A Walk in the Fields' and revised as 'The Holiday Walk', he takes Eliza, Anna and

Freddy away from their toys and books, guiding them through the fields in a walk that serves as both recreation and education in the intricacies of the natural world. So too, in the nest poems Clare takes his urban readers by the imaginary hand and gives them a field lesson in natural history.

By the early 1830s it had become almost impossible to find any major publisher who would make a commitment to poetry. John Murray refused all verse manuscripts after Byron's death and Longman suggested that authors would have more success writing cookbooks. Taylor continued to do what he could for Clare. In April 1831 he passed the proposal for a new volume to Smith, Elder (the publisher of *Friendship's Offering*). There was no response, so Thomas Pringle tried again on Clare's behalf the following winter. He had no success either: 'I regret to say that after all the inquiry I can make among the Trade, I can get little or no encouragement for you at present. Poetry they say is quite unsaleable—and even Wordsworth and other well known writers cannot find a purchaser for their MSS. Smith Elder & Co. will publish Poetry on no terms but the Author's own risk.' Clare neither desired nor could afford an 'own risk' arrangement. Eliza Emmerson had been right when she had reported to him a few months earlier that 'Poetry is in a Consumption, that it languishes upon the shelf and pines away from want of patronage'. In these circumstances, Clare had little choice but to attempt the alternative course of self-publication by subscription. The decline in the market had taken him full circle to where he had started with Henson in Market Deeping fourteen years before.

In 1832 he drafted and distributed various versions of some 'Proposals for publishing in 1 volume, The Midsummer Cushion, or Cottage Poems, by John Clare'. No money was to be paid until delivery (which would be free of charge), the price would not be above seven shillings and sixpence (perhaps less, depending on the number of pages), and the collection would consist of 'a number of fugitive trifles, some of which have appeared in different periodicals, and of others that have never been published'.

Lord Milton gave permission for the book to be dedicated to him.

Clare wrote to thank him, saying that his gratitude went back beyond their personal acquaintance to his Lordship's 'kindness to my lame Father'—he had not forgotten Parker's trip to Scarborough or Lady Milton's provision of winter woollens for his aged parents. He may have visited the Hall in person at this time: an American visitor recalled meeting him in the drawing room at Milton, looking sadly out of his element and sporting 'a beard of a week's growth and neglected apparel'. The visitor walked with Clare in the gardens and was told of his gratitude to the Fitzwilliams for their financial support and the use of their library. 'The poet conversed with me freely', remembered the American, 'but there was a peculiarity in his manner, and an incoherence in his speech, which involuntarily made me say to myself, "Thank God I am not a poet." '

Early in September 1832 a Peterborough printer produced a hundred copies of the prospectus. Clare's friends and patrons set about signing up subscribers. The Reverend Mossop's sister came up with orders for twenty-five copies. The Simpsons, Elizabeth Gilchrist and Henderson all sent lists of names. Clare went to the palace in Peterborough and Mrs Marsh authorised him to put the Bishop down for six copies, herself for two and her companion Miss Mortlock one; she also persuaded the Dean and several others to put down their names. By December well over a hundred subscribers had been found, many of them committing themselves to the purchase of several copies. Most were local, but some were from London, and others from as far away as Scotland (where a Glaswegian accountant called George Reid had taken up Clare's cause), Yorkshire (a correspondent in Halifax wrote that he would do his best even though 'a manufacturing district is but an ungenial soil to foster so rare and so tender a plant as Poesy'), and the west country. A Bath newspaperman promised to send five pounds forthwith. If the book failed to appear, no matter, the money could be given to the children in his name for the purchase of tops and dolls.

Clare wanted the best quality of paper and type, not to mention the prospect of wide distribution. He did not entirely trust the capacities of his Peterborough printer in this respect, so he asked John Taylor if he would like to take over the subscription list. A sense of desperation entered into his attempts to get the book published. The size of his family had broken his 'staff of independence' and he was haunted by his father's words, 'John I should like to see another volume printed before we die'.

Taylor was too busy with his academic publishing to produce the book himself, but better news came at the end of October 1832. Jeremiah How, a relative of the Peterborough printer whom Clare had first approached, worked for the publishing house of Whittaker and Company in Ave Maria Lane. He offered to publish the subscription edition. Around the same time, George Elder, partner in the house of Smith, Elder, said that he would circulate copies of the prospectus and do anything else he could to assist. Harry Behnes and the Emmersons conducted negotiations on Clare's behalf. After consultation with Taylor, they came to the conclusion that How would be the best man for the job. His offer for the purchase of the manuscript would be made via Behnes; a further sum would be paid in the event of a second edition. It would be the responsibility of Clare to set up distribution and payment arrangements with respect to 'the country subscribers'. Behnes thought that this was a fair arrangement, which would save Clare the trouble of handling the entire publishing process himself. He tried to persuade Clare to come to London to help promote the new book.

It was clear that there was no question of How publishing the entire collection (over 350 poems) that Clare had now copied neatly into the book that Fanny Simpson had given him. Behnes added a postcript on the address leaf of the letter to Clare that laid out the publishing deal: 'let your selection for this Publication be the result of unbiased consideration, let it be the wisest act of your life, for on it will depend most of your Future success and most probably a new edition of *all* your works. *Mark that.*'

The collection of poems copied into the blank book given by Fanny Simpson begins with one of Clare's handwritten title-pages. 'The Midsummer Cushion / Or Cottage Poems' is followed by an epigraph from a favourite seventeenth-century poem, Andrew Marvell's 'The Garden': 'How can such sweet and lovely hours / Be reckoned but with herbs and flowers'. The meaning of the title was explained in a draft preface:

> It is a very old custom among villagers in summer time to stick a piece of greensward full of field flowers and place it as an ornament in their cottages, which ornaments are called Midsummer Cushions—And as these trifles are field flowers of humble pretentions and of various hues I thought the above cottage custom gave me the oppertunity to select a title that was not inapplicable to the contents of the Volume.

Eliza Emmerson had initially expressed puzzlement at the title, but she liked this explanation. She probably did not remember as much, but she may have sown the seed for the 'cushion' herself many years earlier, when she told Clare of her admiration for a volume of poetry entitled *The Basket of Wild Flowers* by a Bath hairdresser who had no patron and seven children to support.

Eliza played a vital role in the editing of what was to be Clare's last published volume. For many years he had corresponded with her about his poetry and sent her drafts of work in progress. He was always glad of her advice, even when he did not follow it. They were in full accord that the collection should begin with 'To the Rural Muse', a kind of calling card that was originally begun nearly ten years before as a continuation of 'The Village Minstrel'. Drafts and fragments of it are to be found in no fewer than fourteen different manuscripts. The poem is about Clare's persistent failure to say farewell to his rural muse: however often he tries to turn his mind to other subjects, or to give up poetry altogether, he is always drawn back to his song of the fields, the brooks, the flowers and the cottage hearth. It was, said Mrs Emmerson, 'the *key* to all the poetic gems which will follow'.

As she thought more about the practicalities of publication, Eliza began to have fresh doubts about the title. Was 'The Midsummer Cushion' too quaint? Might it not be a mistake to give a book a title that needed an explanation? She suggested that it would be better to name the book after the lead-poem. This had worked well with *The Village Minstrel* and *The Shepherd's Calendar*. Though lacking the charm and specificity of 'The Midsummer Cushion', a safer title would be 'the Rural Muse, with other Poems and Sonnets'.

Clare spent several months making his selection, copying what he took to be the best of the 'Cushion' poems into a different blank book and adding a few new poems as he went. In August 1833 he sent this fresh manuscript to Eliza. She was thrilled at the manner in which the collection revealed his heart more fully than any of his previous work. He had found a voice that was entirely his own. But there were still well over two hundred poems. Taylor, with his long experience of pruning Clare's works, suggested that she should be prepared to undertake a further cull. So before showing the material to How, Eliza marked the poems that she thought were the best. The manuscript still survives, with her scribbled judgements clearly visible: 'beautiful', 'fine', 'very powerful'.

Jeremiah How procrastinated. One of the partners at Whittaker's had died, so all publication was at a standstill. He was hoping to become a partner himself, and he promised to push Clare's book forward in the new year. There was then a further delay as he devoted all his energy to the costly production of a pair of handsomely illustrated volumes called *Mudie's British Birds*. Eliza's husband Thomas tried to force his hand by saying that Clare was in desperate need of fifty pounds to pay his debts.

In March 1834 Thomas Emmerson concluded the sale. For the consideration of forty pounds, How would have the copyright of the first edition, which would be run to 750 or 1,000 copies. The book would be published under the Whittaker imprint and good production values were guaranteed. How would choose sufficient poems to make up a single volume that could be sold for six or seven shillings. The idea of a list of advance subscribers had been quietly dropped: there would no special provision for delivery to the hundred or more people who had put their names down for copies. The title would be 'The Rural Muse'. Poems omitted from the selection would be returned to Clare, who would retain his rights in them. At the behest of Eliza, a dozen complimentary author's copies were included in the deal.

Taylor was astonished that How agreed to pay as much as forty pounds, given the state of the publishing trade. It was indeed the most lucrative deal of Clare's career, though the lump sum was not quite enough to clear his debts. In June 1834 Clare wrote to How, apologising for not being in touch sooner—he had been unwell. By this time he had dashed off a brief new preface, which said that he had written the poems for his own pleasure but that he would still be glad of praise, even though ill health had rendered him almost incapable of doing anything.

He told How that he wanted the proofs to be corrected by his old friend Taylor: 'I shall be quite satisfied in any thing he wishes or thinks should be altered or ommitted'. In July a reply came with a story that was all too familiar: circumstances beyond the publisher's control had caused a delay, but the book would be in the printer's hands in August, with November pencilled in for publication. Clare's correspondents in Glasgow and Halifax were agitating for news. The proofs, not the finished copy, came in November, at a time when Clare was too ill to work on them. The book consisted of Eliza's selection of just over half the total number of poems in the manuscript that Clare had sent her. She chose forty-two lyrics of varying form and length, together with eighty-six sonnets.

A second set of proofs went to Taylor. As ever, he sought to improve: the amendment of a religious sentiment here, the improvement of a grammatical sequence there. 'My chief Corrections', he explained, 'have been in the Way of making the Verses run along without so often commencing with "And"—or in avoiding the too frequent Repetition of the same Word in the Compass of a Line or two'. His instincts remained good: excessive repetition and the accumulation of conjunctions were the price of Clare's fertility of invention and openness to all impressions.

Thomas Emmerson was concerned that nothing had been heard from Jeremiah How for some time. He called at Whittaker's, only to learn that How had left the company. This was a matter for some alarm, alleviated only when How turned up on the Emmersons' doorstep in December and explained that the book was progressing. He also helpfully suggested that an application should be made on Clare's behalf for financial support from the Royal Literary Fund.

More delay followed in the new year as Taylor did some rearranging of the material. Illustrations were commissioned: an artist was dispatched to Northborough to draw the poet's cottage and the village. An engraving of the former appeared as the book's frontispiece and the latter as a title-page embellishment. Another engraving, based on Frank Simpson's drawing of the Helpston cottage (intended for but not used in *The Village Minstrel*), was also included near the end of the book, and Clare was asked at the last minute for a poem to accompany it. He was unable to write a sonnet on demand, so Eliza Emmerson suggested using a version of 'The Flitting' that he had sent her in the summer of 1832. It was given the explanatory title 'On Leaving the Cottage of my Birth'. Another late addition, to round off the volume, was 'To an Early Friend', a poem of gratitude to Eliza, without whom the book would never have reached print.

On 14 July 1835 Whittaker sent the author four complimentary copies of *The Rural Muse, Poems by John Clare*, dedicated to the Earl Fitzwilliam (the title inherited by Lord Milton following his octogenarian father's death in 1833). A reminder had to be sent to the effect that eight further author's copies were due. Eliza Emmerson thought the volume was a little thin, given its price of seven shillings, but she was convinced that it made up in quality for what it lacked in quantity. She reported an astute remark from her other literary protégé, Coleridge's son Derwent: 'If this little volume of Clare's had come out *twenty* years *ago*—it would have made a great sensation in the poetic world—and it is certain to greatly increase his reputation as a Poet *now* and *hereafter*.' John Taylor agreed: everyone who read it considered this to be Clare's best book. James Montgomery, radical activist, supporter of Clare and editor of the *Sheffield Iris*, himself an accomplished poet, was ecstatic in his praise.

There was even brave talk of a possible American edition that would have established Clare's name across the Atlantic for the first time. But nothing came of this, and sales at home were very slow despite the uniformly strong reviews. First came brief but favourable notices in the *Athenaeum* and *Literary Gazette*, then a long review by the influential Scots professor John Wilson, who wrote under the pen-name 'Christopher North' in *Blackwood's Edinburgh Magazine*. He considered the new book equal to or better than the best of Clare's earlier poems. It was admirable for the clarity of the poet's eye, his 'rich and various imagery of nature', his lack of affectation, his closeness to his surroundings, and his innovative combination of the high and the low: 'We do not believe that any bard before Clare ever mentioned the frog and the lark in the same stanza'. Wilson especially admired the sonnets and the bird poems—a judgement in which most modern readers will concur. He concluded by saying that the book was worth ten times what the reader had to pay for it and that the purchase of it would have the added benefit of assisting Clare and his family out of their poverty.

The reviewer in the *New Monthly Magazine* was of the view that Clare had improved book by book. These poems had a finished quality that had been lacking in the earlier work. And the nephew of the editor of the *Stamford Bee* wrote at some length in a periodical called the *Druids' Monthly Magazine* (which had previously published some individual poems by Clare). He said that the richness and profusion of imagery, the art of acute observation, made Clare's poems 'entirely distinguishable from all others'. Like so many of Clare's reviewers, he could not then resist a move from literary analysis to biographical reminiscence. He told of how he had gone with his uncle to see Clare and Patty, surrounded by their six children. What struck him most forcefully was the poet's eye: 'light-blue, and flashing with the fire of genius: the peculiar character of his eyes are always remarked by people when they first see him'. He also noted Clare's shortness and the distinctiveness of his conversation: 'animated, striking, and full of imagination, yet his dialect is purely provincial'. They had walked round his garden and the poet had pointed to a spot in the hedge of his orchard where a nightingale had built her nest, which, to his indignation, had been destroyed. The implication here is that the damage was done by a marauding human hand, but a different story was told by Clare himself in a sonnet: it was a magpie that killed the fledgling nightingales. 'There is a cruelty in all', he wrote, 'From tyrant man to meaner things / And nature holds inhuman thrall / Against herself'.

The experience of reading *The Rural Muse* is akin to such a walk with Clare through wood and field: you think that you are encountering commonplaces, but suddenly the sharp eye of the poet draws your attention to a little thing hidden in a secret place. And he finds the words to transform the ordinary into something magical.

A casual glance will not reveal the full extent of his technical advance. His matter is much as it ever was. There are celebrations of favourite places such as Emmonsales Heath with its 'wide and common sky', seasonal poems ('Impulses of Spring', 'On May Morning', 'Summer Images', 'Autumn'), reflections on mortality in the eighteenth-century mould ('Thoughts in a Church-yard', 'On an Infant killed by Lightning', 'On Seeing a Skull on Cowper Green'). There are ballads and love poems, pastoral fancies and rural songs. The prevailing mood is elegiac, with several references to the past as a lost Eden (notably in a lyric called 'The Backward Spring'). But look more closely and you find the magic: as some of those reviewers noticed, the nest poems and sonnets have an immediacy unprecedented in Clare—perhaps in any prior English poet.

Again, among the volume's many religious poems there are several in a vein no different from that of, say, Joseph Addison writing a century earlier: 'All Nature owns, with one accord, / The great and universal Lord'. Around this time Clare wrote 'A Confession of Faith' in which he claimed that his religious belief was fundamentally orthodox: 'My creed may be different from other creeds but the difference is nothing when the end is the same—if I did not expect and hope for eternal happiness I should be very miserable.' Yet that creed was uniquely grounded in minute particulars. One of the key poems in *The Rural Muse*, 'The Eternity of Nature', gave Clare's own spin to the conventional idea of the endurance of natural forms. You may trample a daisy but it will 'strike its little root / Into the lap of time' and there will be another daisy in two thousand years for a child to pluck with a delighted cry. Or consider the 'five crimson spots' of the cowslip. Time never makes a mistake in counting: 'look within / Each pip, and five, nor more nor less, are seen'. In a poem such as this Clare succeeds in combining his characteristic descriptive art with more elevated and philosophical insight.

If one had to pick out a single poem to represent *The Rural Muse* at its best, it would be 'The Nightingale's Nest', with its sense of stumbling upon a secret, gaining access to something magical and precious but also fragile and vulnerable. The poem is about not only finding the nest but also leaving it alone and walking onward. 'All seemed as hidden as a thought unborn', Clare writes in a very Keatsian simile, but then in the following lines he uses a language that is wholly his own:

> And where those crimping fern-leaves ramp among
> The hazel's under-boughs, I've nestled down
> And watched her while she sung.

Here words are made to do things they had never done before: *crimp* is a verb (meaning 'to wrinkle') but Clare uses it as an adjective, whilst *ramping* is an adjective (meaning 'wild and luxuriant') but Clare uses it as a verb. 'Nestled down', meanwhile, establishes intimacy between the poet and the nest.

Together with the three nest poems (the pettichap and the yellowhammer were included as well as the nightingale), Clare's other supreme achievement in *The Rural Muse* was his run of eighty-six sonnets. One of them is addressed to Peter de Wint, who found his ideal medium for the visual representation of the eastern flatlands in the art of rapid water-colour sketches. In a similar way, Clare found in the sonnet the place where he could sketch the glimpses and glancing recollections that meant so much to him: footpaths, fishing, a sudden shower, the flood meadows at Lolham, the smell of beans in blossom, stepping stones over a stream, the needle-point of Glinton spire, early morning in spring, the ruin of Crowland Abbey seen by moonlight, a wren (why do poets always write about the nightingale or the cuckoo, never the wren or the robin? he asks).

The fourteen lines of the sonnet constitute one of the most disciplined of poetic forms. According to long tradition, it should be divided into units of eight and six or four, four, four and two. Clare nearly always worked within the essential form, but frequently broke the internal rules. Open the sonnet section of *The Rural Muse* at random and you are almost certain to find a hitherto unattempted rhyme scheme.* Throughout his career Clare challenged the conventions of poetic diction by using the vocabulary of his region; in his poems of the 1830s he challenged the conventions of form, revealing that the sonnet could be divided up in new ways—such as with the rhyming couplet at the beginning instead of the end, or with a seven-seven split instead of the customary asymmetry.

The traditional matter for the sonnet is erotic desire. One might therefore have expected Clare to write a sequence in praise of his lost love. He did not: the sonnets are about his beloved places and his experience of nature. 'Mary' does, however, figure in a number of other poems in *The Rural Muse*. She is the subject of 'First Love's Recollections'; 'The Milking Hour' recalls a final evening conversation with her, walking in a wheat field; and in 'Nutting' Clare compares her auburn hair to the colour of ripe hazels, they shell nuts together, she flirtatiously throws the shells at him and then blushes when he pockets the husks as a keepsake.

In the original 'Midsummer Cushion' manuscript, Clare gathered his most intimate pieces under the rubric 'Poems', but also included a substantial section of 'Ballads and Songs'—forms that are more traditional than personal. A ballad of 'Robin's' love for 'Kitty Fell', songs in praise of 'Sally Green' and 'Peggy Band': these are 'folk' materials,

---

*On trying this exercise, my copy fell open at no. V, 'Evening Schoolboys' (quoted in Chapter 2), which rhymes *abababcbcbcdcd*; I then flicked forward and my eye fell on no. XXV, 'The Crab-Tree', which rhymes *ababacdcdefeff*. I know of no precedent for either scheme.

not reminiscences of real girls and real feelings. Strikingly, Clare placed most of his 'Mary' poems in this section, not among the poems where the 'I' is a clear representation of his own voice. By doing so, he may have been disguising—screening, one might say—the depth of his retrospective feelings for the real Mary Joyce, but he may equally have been signalling that 'Mary' had by this time become a fiction, a symbol of the condition of lost love rather than a real person remembered from his youth.

Only three poems in the more personal section of 'The Midsummer Cushion' refer to Mary. One was the 'Valentine' that had been published in the *London Magazine* back in 1823, another a daydreaming meander of the same vintage, haunted by the memory of the blush, the blue eyes and the press of the delicate hand of the thirteen-year-old girl. Clare omitted both these from the shorter selection of work—238 poems instead of 361—that he sent down to Eliza Emmerson in London.

Among his other omissions was a leisured family poem of some three hundred lines called 'The Holiday Walk':

> Come Eliza and Anna, lay by top and ball
> And Freddy boy, throw away cart and toys all,
> Look about for your hats and dispense with your play,
> We'll seek for the fields and be happy today . . .

This was probably left out for reasons of space. A more surprising omission was 'The Fallen Elm', a poem on the destruction of the elm tree by the Helpston cottage, about which Clare had written so sadly in a letter of autumn 1831. Perhaps he left it out for fear that its angry political voice would have scared off potential publishers. It is one of his starkest attacks on the hypocrisy whereby 'improvement' and enclosure are embarked upon in the name of 'freedom' but bring only oppression:

> With axe at root he felled thee to the ground
> And barked of freedom . . .
> It grows the cant term of enslaving tools

To wrong another by the name of right ...
—Such was thy ruin, music-making elm,
The rights of freedom was to injure thine;
As thou wert served so would they overwhelm
In freedom's name the little that is mine,
And there are knaves that brawl for better laws
And cant of tyranny in stronger powers
Who glut their vile unsatiated maws
And freedom's birthright from the weak devours.

This magnificent lyric, at once elegy and protest poem, lay unknown and unpublished in the Peterborough Museum until well into the twentieth century.

The necessity to reduce the number of pieces in the collection meant that readers of *The Rural Muse* did not get a sense of Clare's ability to sustain his art. So, for instance, the 'Midsummer Cushion' manuscript included several short sequences of linked sonnets— three in memory of Bloomfield, five on 'Footpaths' that are themselves like a series of criss-crossing paths through wood and by hedge- row—but the published selection included far fewer instances where the same subject was continued from one sonnet to the next. The slimming down of the number of poems meant the loss of many lovely noticings—ragwort, field cricket and hedge woodbine—but more than enough was left in the published sonnets to demonstrate the continuing prodigality of Clare's imagery and the unfailing ac- curacy of his eye.

In making her selection from Clare's selection, Eliza Emmerson left out more sonnets. Among the delights she removed were 'Hares at Play' and a series of seasonal 'Wood Pictures'. She also dispensed with various short poems of delicate imagery ('The white-nosed bee that bores its little hole / In mortared walls') and some powerful evo- cations of 'sweet spots that memory makes divine'. Eliza also reduced the number of birds' nests, choosing neither 'The Moorhen's Nest' nor 'The Pewit's'. In the former of these, Clare makes one of his clear- est statements of the need for bonding and belonging that drove his art of finding poetry in the fields:

> I pick out pictures round the fields that lie
> In my mind's heart like things that cannot die
> Like picking hopes and making friends with all.

And in the latter he mimics the bird's 'chewsit' cry and offers a wonderfully accurate description of its 'four eggs of dingy dirty green / Deep blotched with plashy spots of jockolate stain'.

Perhaps the most unfortunate loss among the mid-length poems that had remained in Clare's own selection was 'Shadows of Taste'. First published in the *Stamford Bee* in the summer of 1831, this was a piece that showed him becoming more self-conscious about the art of poetry and its power to intensify impressions and feelings:

> In poesy's spells some all their raptures find
> And revel in the melodies of mind;
> There nature o'er the soul her beauty flings
> In all the sweets and essences of things—
> A face of beauty in a city crowd
> Met, passed, and vanished like a summer cloud,
> In poesy's vision more refined and fair
> Taste reads o'erjoyed and greets her image there.

Eliza's decision to leave it out deprived readers of *The Rural Muse* of a prime piece of evidence that Clare was no naive peasant but rather a thinker deeply concerned with such Wordsworthian questions as the evanescence of beauty, the history of poetic fashion and the distinction between man of taste and man of science.

The most damaging, if inevitable, aspect of the further work of selection undertaken by Mrs Emmerson was its diminution of Clare's range and variety. Faced with the need to reduce a manuscript of nearly two hundred closely written folio pages, many of them in double column, to a small octavo volume of fewer than two hundred pages in good-size print, she took the obvious course of removing all the long poems. Out went the 500-line 'Pleasures of Spring' and the narrative poems 'Valentine Eve' and 'Going to the Fair'. The only 'Tale' retained was the charming 'Adventures of a Grasshopper' that Clare had written for his children; together with 'Summer Images' and 'To the Rural Muse', this was one of the few poems in the published volume to approach two hundred lines. It seems to have been Eliza's rule that there should be no poems longer than this. That meant the loss of 'Childhood', a marvellous memory poem of 440 lines, and the omission of 'The Progress of Rhyme'.

To a much greater extent than 'To the Rural Muse', the latter—a poem of some 350 lines—was the manifesto of the mature Clare. Written in four-stress quickstep couplets, it tells of how poetry has been his joy in sadness, his health in sickness, his wealth in poverty, his hope in labour. 'For everything I felt a love', he writes, 'The weeds below, the birds above'. The poem is both personal and political. It asserts the inalienable 'right to song' of the humble as well as the great, whilst also describing his own compulsion to write: 'Until the vision waked with time / And left me itching after rhyme'. And it reaches to the essentials of his vision: the way in which his poems served as 'dream-songs', the life of the fields as the 'essence' of those songs, the inspiration found in beauty and in youth. This was the third piece in the 'Poems' section of 'The Midsummer Cushion' to invoke 'Mary' as early muse.

The most astonishing sequence in 'The Progress of Rhyme' is one in which Clare seeks to unite his song with that of nature itself by imitating the very voice of the nightingale:

> —'Chew-chew chew-chew' and higher still
> 'Cheer-cheer cheer-cheer' more loud and shrill
> 'Cheer-up cheer-up cheer-up'—and dropt
> Low 'Tweet tweet jug jug jug' and stopt
> One moment just to drink the sound
> Her music made and then a round
> Of stranger witching notes was heard
> As if it was a stranger bird
> 'Wew-wew wew-wew chur-chur chur-chur
> 'Woo-it woo-it'—could this be her
> 'Tee-rew tee-rew tee-rew tee-rew
> 'Chew-rit chew-rit'—and ever new
> 'Will-will will-will grig-grig grig-grig'.

In one sense, this is poetry of the highest order of invention, but in another it is nonsense that reveals the insufficiency of language to convey the 'poesy' that Clare found in the fields. In 'Pastoral Poesy', another of the 'Midsummer Cushion' poems that did not reach print until the twentieth century, Clare argued that 'true poesy' was to be found not in words but in what he called the 'language that is ever green': nature itself. Poetry was the place where he found his dwelling and reconciled himself to his own deprivation in the material world. Poetry gave him peace and blessed him:

> So would I my own mind employ
> And my own heart impress
> That poesy's self's a dwelling joy
> Of humble quietness.

Yet if 'poesy's self' was really nature, then Clare could not dwell there. He was a creature of language: though found in the fields, his poetry existed on the page. In 'The Progress of Rhyme' he tells how the first glimmerings of poetic sensibility came upon him when he was a small boy threshing in the dusty barn with his father. Perhaps from that moment onward he was always doomed to alienation, to a life split between the two worlds of nature and art, of dwelling and writing. Perhaps it was inevitable that the time would come when his mind could no longer hold in balance the contradictions of his being.

ON LEAVING THE COTTAGE OF MY BIRTH.

I'VE left my own old Home of Homes,
    Green fields, and every pleasant place :
The Summer, like a stranger comes,
    I pause—and hardly know her face.
I miss the hazel's happy green,
    The blue-bell's quiet hanging blooms,
Where envy's eye is never seen,
    Where tongue of malice never comes.

I miss the heath, its yellow furze,
    Mole-hills, and rabbit-tracks, that lead
Through besom-ling and teasel burrs,
    That spread a wilderness indeed :

CHAPTER SEVENTEEN

THE FLITTING

When Clare was in the asylum, a Northampton newspaper-man who was enthusiastic about his poetry retraced the family's steps from Helpston to Northborough. He described the journey as 'a pleasant three miles; along a road level and far-stretching; with the tall slender spire of Glinton in the distance; through the pretty village of Etton; and along "the bank", one of those works peculiar to the country, constructed for the purpose of directing and governing the flood waters.' He noticed yellowhammer and wagtail flitting above the ditch of clear water below the dyke, like specks of sunshine and silver light.

For Clare, the three miles might as well have been three hundred. He was going out of his knowledge, away from the parish of Helpston that had mapped the contours of his very being. The dyke signalled that they were entering a different environment, that of the deep fen. In Helpston, Clare had looked west and south to the gently sloping wood and heath; in Northborough, everything seemed to point to the flatlands of the east.

At the centre of the village were an ancient church and a solid manor-house that had once been the home of Oliver Cromwell's daughter. Most of the cottages had sizeable gardens and often an orchard or paddock. The width of the road and the wealth of trees and flowers made it look a more picturesque and prosperous place than Helpston. The cottage that had been refurbished for Clare faced south, with the front turned away from the road. The steep roof was thatched; there were casement windows and a seat outside. Old yews grew in the garden. Once the family were settled, Clare would sit on the seat and give his sons instruction in the art of topiary. Flowers were mingled with vegetables and the orchard provided a good crop of apples.

Inside, Clare set about making the house feel like a home. He hung his treasured pictures on the walls: the water-colour that Hilton had copied from the oil portrait done for Taylor, the original Indian ink drawing by de Wint from which the frontispiece to *The Shepherd's Calendar* had been engraved, Frank Simpson's drawing of Helpston Church, and engraved portraits of Clare's patrons, the Marquess of Exeter, Lord Milton, Admiral Lord Radstock and Earl Spencer (who had provided an engraving in 1830—there had been some confusion and embarrassment when he sent a different image from the one requested).

The accomodation was much more spacious than at Helpston: the cottage had a sitting room, which Clare could use as a study, a kitchen and back-kitchen. Upstairs there were three bedrooms, one of them tiny. Such conditions made washing and cooking easier for Patty, and with separate bedrooms for the children there was a better prospect of sleep at night.

But the village never became home. It felt like a closed community, hostile to newcomers. The surviving letters of Clare's asylum years contain many inquiries after old Helpston friends, but only mention a handful of Northborough neighbours. His poems of this period frequently speak of envy and malice. A large part of the problem was his special relationship with Lord Milton, which was manifest from the improvement of the cottage before his arrival. A rumour spread that the property was being provided rent free. In fact, there was a rent of thirteen or fifteen pounds a year, a sum far greater than that for the Helpston cottage. Henry Ryde, presuming to speak on behalf of Clare's rival patron at Burghley, said that this was far too much and that he would try to find something cheaper on the Exeter estate (he did not). Milton's agent seems, however, to have taken a relaxed view in the matter of rent arrears.

Clare wrote some of his most powerful poems of alienation in the immediate aftermath of the move. Foremost among them was 'The Flitting'. The partial version published in *The Rural Muse* was called 'On leaving the cottage of my birth' and dated 20 June 1832. It begins with the departure or 'flitting':

> I've left my own old Home of Homes,
>   Green fields, and pleasant place:
> The Summer, like a stranger comes,
>   I pause—and hardly know her face.
> I miss the hazel's happy green,
>   The blue-bell's quiet hanging blooms,
> Where envy's eye is never seen,
>   Where tongue of malice never comes.
>
> I miss the heath, its yellow furze,
>   Mole-hills, and rabbit-tracks, that lead
> Through besom-ling and teasel burrs,
>   That spread a wilderness indeed:
> The woodland oaks, and all below,
>   That their white powder'd branches shield,
> The mossy paths—the very crow
>   Croaks music in my native field.

Clare goes on to imagine that the nightingale, like him, is lost and pining for the old haunt of Royce Wood. And even the old 'corner chair' that he has brought with him 'seems to feel itself from home'. In the full text of the poem, the 'strange scenes' of Clare's new parish appear to him as 'mere shadows' and, in an astonishing phrase, 'Vague unpersonifying things'. Whereas in Helpston everything had taken on a personal quality, the Northborough environment has an aura of blankness. It does not share its being with the poet's own identity.

Two closely related works, also written soon after the move, were

'Decay: A Ballad', in which Clare imagines the waning of both his own powers and the natural world around him, and 'Remembrances', a recollection of favourite places and pastimes, written in a fluent six-stress line that belies the poem's own claim that 'words are poor receipts for what time hath stole away'. His remembrance is not just of his old home, but specifically of the pre-enclosure landscape. It was also at this time that he wrote another of his great enclosure elegies, a vigorous poem of political complaint spoken in the very voice of a piece of land, 'Swordy Well'. In Clare's childhood, gypsies had camped in this ancient Roman stone quarry; he had gone there to look for wild flowers, lizards and a lovely copper-hued butterfly. With the enclosure, it was taken by the parish overseers as a source of stone for road-mending. In the poem, the land speaks out against its own enclosure in the same terms that a labourer would have used to complain about his loss of ancient rights. 'I ha'n't a friend in all the place', sings the desecrated earth, 'Save one and he's away'. That 'one' is Clare himself, both physically away from Helpston and mentally distant from his own unenclosed youth.

In a contrasting early Northborough poem, Clare sought to embed himself in his new environment by identifying with a bird that found its home among the dykes, marshy flats and stagnant floods. 'Lover of swamps', he begins 'To the Snipe', 'The quagmire over grown / With hassock tufts of sedge'. By the end of the poem the snipe has taught him that Northborough might afford some sense of shelter and security:

> I see the sky
> Smile on the meanest spot
> Giving to all that creep or walk or fly
> A calm and cordial lot
>
> Thine teaches me
> Right feelings to employ
> That in the dreariest places peace will be
> A dweller and a joy.

He also wrote a poem to the secretive landrail, a bird that was frequently heard but never seen. In a sense this was Clare's own ambition: for his poetic voice to continue to be heard, but for himself to be left alone. He took solitary walks, in places where he felt that he was the only person treading the earth, where 'One unembodied thought / Thinks the heart into stillness as the world / Was left behind for something green and new'. There was, after all, some inspiration to be found in the dreary landscape of dykes and reed-beds.

And there were times when the new cottage began to feel more like a home. 'Like a bird in the forest, whose world is its nest,' he wrote in a poem called 'Home Happiness', 'My home is my all, and the centre of rest'. Here he describes himself sitting by the fire as the cat cleans her face with her foot; he then takes an evening walk around the orchard, rubs perfume from the blackcurrant leaves and remembers the scent left on his hand when he touches a geranium. He could not but be grateful for a garden and orchard that he could call his own.

Northborough was closer to Glinton than his previous home. The tall spire was visible across the fields. For Clare, it was like a spiritual compass, magnetically drawing him to the memory of Mary Joyce. One of the first poems that he copied out after his move was a dialogue called 'Opening of the Pasture—Love and Flattery' (a tale planned for, but excluded from, the *Shepherd's Calendar* volume). The object of love in this poem is called Mary; on making the copy, Clare sketched Glinton Church in the margin at the point where the character speaks for the first time. The marginal drawings in Clare's manuscripts are intriguing and enigmatic: some are idle doodles, whilst others seem to carry deep significance. In one manuscript of 'The Flitting' there is a sketch of a woman on a pedestal: is this an image of woman in the abstract? Or is it Patty, complaining about the effort of the move? Or Eliza, on whose efforts he had come to rely? Or could it be Mary, near whose home he passed as he flitted from Helpston with his family?

> I love to see the slender spire
> For there the maid of beauty dwells,

And stand agen' the hollow tree
And hear the sound of Glinton Bells.

I love to see the boys at play,
The music o'er the summer swells,
I stand among the new-mown hay
And hear the sound of Glinton Bells.

I love the slender spire to see
For there the maid of beauty dwells,
I think she hears the sound with me
And love to listen Glinton Bells.

And when with songs I used to talk
I often thought where Mary dwells,
And often took a sabbath walk
And lay and listened Glinton Bells.

I think where Mary's memory stays,
I think where pleasant memory dwells,
I think of happy schoolboy days
And lie and listen Glinton Bells.

This simple and lucid song was among the last poems Clare wrote before he was taken to Dr Allen's asylum. Glinton spire and the imagined figure of Mary stayed with him all through the Northborough years.

His mood swings were becoming more extreme. Symptomatically, he copied a pair of radically contrasting sonnets onto the same page of his manuscript book: one celebrated the 'reccompence' offered by the 'Pleasures of Poesy' whilst the other evoked the numbing dullness brought by 'Black melancholly'.

He was unwell for much of the first summer in Northborough. This made him reluctant to leave the cottage, though on a number of occasions the Mossops invited him back to Helpston for dinner, always offering a well-aired bed in which he could stay the night. Jane

Mossop forwarded post and served as a contact with Stamford. Clare passed on to her some of Eliza Emmerson's verses for publication in the *Bee*. He endorsed Miss Mossop's judgement upon his friend's talent: 'your opinion of it is right ... she writes too much and that much too hasty, but my task is not that of the critics and therefore I pass them as I received them—she often writes well'. Clare himself knew all about the phenomenon of writing too much and that much too hastily, but for many months in Northborough he was unable to write at all.

His friend Henderson invited him to dinner with Artis, who now had a cottage in Castor, but he was prevented by the weather. Visits to Milton Hall became far less frequent, though on one occasion he was inspired to write a sonnet about its gravel walks, smooth lawns and the heronry on the island in the middle of its fishponds. He began grasping at tokens of past happiness, asking Henderson for a sketch of a favourite willow-tree that drooped over the Milton lake.

Financially speaking, it was not enough to have the orchard and adjoining field. Capital investment was needed to give Clare the wherewithal to work the land. In July 1832 the Emmersons and Taylor proposed to get up a subscription to establish Clare as a smallholder. Eliza herself would give ten pounds on condition that it was spent on the purchase of a cow to be called by the poetic name of Rose, Blossom or May. Taylor would give five pounds for the purchase of two pigs and another five pounds would be found for a butter-churn and 'a few useful tools for husbandry'. Milk, butter and bacon would have greatly enriched the family's meagre diet.

Through the summer, Clare wrote gloomy letters to Harry Behnes (who had now changed his surname to Burlowe so as to distinguish himself from his brother William, a better-known artist but also a man of notorious dissipation). Harry said that he wished he could visit—he would 'give the Blue devils a Kick that would make them "*vomit their cruppers*" '. He tried to cheer Clare up with London gossip, telling of how he had been introduced to the widow and daughter of Lord Byron.

Later, Clare would start having delusions about himself and Byron. At this time, he was not yet showing any signs of what we would now call personality disorder, but he was having visions or hallucinations. His blue devils had ceased to be merely metaphorical. Conversely, he imagined a guardian angel watching over him in his sickness. He told Harry about this spirit in a letter that is lost, but that can be imagined from the reply: 'your vivid description of that kind angel who watched over you in your *heavy Hour* does I have no doubt, as much credit to your *judgement* as to your grateful heart ... such a woman is a "*Diamond of the desert*" '.

Clare returned to his guardian angel in several fragments of writing that we could call a 'dream-diary'. She was like an attendant deity, nursing him, putting her hand under his head to lift it out of pain's way, cheering him with pictures of past happiness, placing herself in the shadows so that he could enjoy the sunshine, giving him faith and wisdom. He recorded a dream that came to him on 13 October 1832. His guardian spirit 'in the shape of a soul-stirring beauty' came to him, looking exactly as she had done in a dream of many years before 'and in which she has since appeared at intervals and moved my ideas into extacy'. In the dream, he was in a strange place in fine company. Despite the solicitude of the person who was apparently the host, he was in low spirits until 'on a sudden a lovely creature in the shape of a young woman with dark and rather disordered hair and eyes that spoke more beauty than earth inherits came up to me in a familiar way and leaning her witching face over my shoulder spoke in a witching voice and cherishing smile sentences that I cannot reccolect'. He did, however, recollect her appearance: he was in no doubt that it was the same figure that had come to him in two earlier dreams.

The first of these was before he had published a word. The female figure came to him in the old Helpston cottage and led him hurriedly out to a nearby hill, from where he looked down on a crowd. Soldiers were exercising on horseback and there was a fair with many ladies in splendid dresses, but none so fine as the lady at his side. 'Shamed into insignificance at the sight', he demanded of her—in his thoughts—why he had been brought so suddenly into such a vast company when all he wanted was solitude. To which she replied, 'you are the only one of the crowd now'. Then she hurried him back and the scene turned to a city. She led him into a bookseller's shop, where 'on a shelf among a vast crowd of books were three vols lettered with my own name—I see them now'. Astonished, he turned to look the beautiful woman in the face, only to awake. 'But the impression never left me and I see her still—she is my good genius and I believe in her ideality almost as fresh as reality'. It is impossible to know whether Clare really did have this exact dream before he became a successful writer, but there can be little doubt that it crystallises his insecurities and ambitions with regard to class, company and poetic fame.

In the second dream, Clare and all his fellow-villagers are gathered into the church for the Last Judgement. He shrinks backwards, wanting to return to his 'reccolections of home', and at this moment 'somthing of a delightful impulse took me seemingly by the arm and led me forward'. The impulse takes the form of the same female figure, 'in white garments beautifully disordered but sorrowful in her countenance'. When his name is called to Judgement, she smiles and speaks. He knows that all will be well. She leads him into the open air, where he awakes to the sound of soft music. This dream closely parallels the poem 'The Night Mare', written under the influence of De Quincey's opium confessions eleven years before: in that poem, as we have seen, the voice of the guardian spirit is identified as Mary's.

In his brief dream-diary, Clare stresses that he has no doubt of the existence of his lovely guardian angel. This does not mean her physical existence: her 'ideality' is as real to him as everyday reality. He is not mad here, but merely speaking of the power of imagination and the *ideal* of beauty. In her presence he is happy, so he has every reason to go on believing in her. Given that Clare met Mary Joyce at the vestry school of Glinton Church, it can hardly be a coincidence that in the second dream his guardian angel comes to him 'just at the school door'. But the meaning of the image is moving further and further away from its autobiographical origin. She represents the muse of poetry, the memory of past joy and a straw of hope clutched for the future. She is no longer—if she ever has been—a real person.

A lucid little lyric, scribbled on the back of a letter draft soon after the move to Northborough, catches the process whereby Clare projected the figure of Mary onto his later feelings:

> I loved thee, though I told thee not,
> Right earlily and long,
> Thou wert my joy in every spot,
> My theme in every song.
>
> And when I saw a stranger face
> Where beauty held the claim,
> I gave it like a secret grace
> The being of thy name.
>
> And all the charms of face or voice
> Which I in others see
> Are but the recollected choice
> Of what I felt for thee.

The commonest noun in Clare's mature poetry—he used it over a hundred times in *The Rural Muse*—was *joy*. 'Mary' had her origins in Mary Joyce, but she also served him as another name for joy.

Clare's increasing emotional volatility caused him to be upset by 'trifles'. His spirits were 'either elevated to extacy or depressed to nothings'. He was especially sensitive to his public image. In August 1832 the gossip column of the London *Athenaeum* carried a story to the effect that Lord Milton had bestowed on Clare 'a handsome house, with a garden and large orchard, amounting in all to six or seven acres, and when this is considered, in addition to a small annuity—some thirty pounds per year or so—we are bound not only to praise Lord Milton, but put his name down among the public benefactors to the muse'. The story was picked up by another paper, the *Alfred*, and by the local press. The appearance of the paragraph in the

Stamford Bee was especially upsetting, given the involvement with that paper of his friends the Simpson family.

He was in a quandary about how to respond: he hated the idea of living on charity and the reports of the extent of Milton's generosity were grossly exaggerated. He turned to his old vicar for advice. Mossop suggested that he should seek to publish a letter laying out the true state of affairs. Clare made several drafts of one, complaining that 'Officious interferences as to my adversity add nothing to my prosperity' and objecting to the way in which his affairs were being 'bandied from pillar to post by every one who has a place in a paper to put forth his individual opinion'. 'I wish to live in quietness', he wrote in another draft, 'but they will not let me.' He did not want to be the beneficiary of patronage; his only desire was to achieve independence.

At the end of September, the *Alfred* published a correction, explaining that, far from having been showered with favours, Clare was 'labouring, with a wife and six children, under very distressing privations'. To stress his poverty still further, the report added that Clare had not gained 'a farthing of his profits from any of his publications' and that when he had applied to his publishers for a copy of their accounts the balance was 'on the wrong side'. The *Bee* repeated this story and added a dig at Lord Milton, who was prominent in the cause of parliamentary reform (which its editors vigorously opposed): 'the Whigs are not of those who delight in doing good, and blush to find fame'. The implication was that Lord Milton's supporters had placed the original story in order to make him seem more generous than he really was.

The follow-up story thus aggravated the affair. Clare had, as his friend Harry Burlowe put it, been made 'a *political cats paw*'. Now there was a possibility of Milton taking offence. And the reference to Clare's financial dealings with Taylor and Hessey—based on information given by Jeremiah How of Whittaker's—was potential dynamite. Taylor duly exploded. On seeing the offending article, he commenced libel actions against both the *Bee* and the *Alfred*. Ironically, he informed Clare of this in the very letter in which he also told him of How's offer of £40 for publication of the new volume under the Whittaker imprint. 'It will give me sincere Pleasure', he wrote through what must have been gritted teeth, 'to find it succeeds better than those which have preceded it which I was so unfortunate as to bring out.—I have been much hurt at finding that my Endeavours to do you Service have ended no better than they have.'

How had used the affair as an opportunity to publicise 'The Midsummer Cushion or Cottage Poems', which he was intending to publish by subscription on Clare's behalf. The *Athenaeum* also printed Clare's 'Proposals' for the new volume, in a carefully worded article by Allan Cunningham that corrected the original story without causing any further offence. Taylor eventually dropped the libel action and another of the many spats between poet and publisher ended in a full reconciliation. But the whole business could not have been better calculated to depress Clare's spirits.

Still he had no cow or pigs, despite Eliza's having composed for him some 'Lines on presenting a Milch Cow to my friend John Clare'. He was worse off than when he had arrived in Northborough. A sub-let of the field that had come with the cottage brought in less rent than was being paid for it. 'I now stop', he wrote to Harry Burlowe in November, 'just like a packhorse tied to the gate of an hedge alehouse on a winter's day with nothing before him, about him, or above, but hard fare and bad weather.' When May the cow did eventually arrive, she proved to be a very poor milker and Clare got rid of her within a year. His efforts to become a smallholder did not reach beyond selling the apples from the orchard and planting up his vegetable garden. Henderson provided him with spinach, lettuce, carrot and turnip seed.

His symptoms grew more severe. 'Last night my very brains seemed to boil up almost into madness and my arms and legs burnt as if it were a listless feebleness that almost rendered them useless.' His doctors were trying various treatments: leeches attached to the temples every third day, a blister on the neck, morning showers, brandy-vinegar and rainwater on a cloth applied to the head. He was seeing evil spirits again, though Taylor assured him that such things did not exist. Frank Simpson, perhaps wishing to make amends for the business in the *Bee*, sent a new doctor called Jackson, who offered his services free of charge and recommended abstention from the strain of reading and writing. But Clare remained ill for much of the year 1833. That January, Patty gave birth to another boy, named Charles.

However bad his own state, Clare never stopped caring for his children. He drafted a letter of advice to them, perhaps with the intention of its being opened in the event of his death: 'In the first place set a resolution down and keep it as you would an oath never to mix or associate in bad company.' He wrote to Dr Darling in London, seeking advice about smallpox inoculation for the youngsters. And he asked Taylor to send school exercise books. He could not bear to see the little ones punished. When a frustrated Patty started wielding the rod, Clare supposedly said that he would rather take the beating himself.

His health continued to decline in 1834. Despondent letters were periodically dispatched to Eliza Emmerson, with strange talk of witches and supernatural beliefs. To the incredulity of the rational Taylor, he announced his firm belief that the family was bewitched. Frank Simpson's mother suggested a dosage of soda and rhubarb. Clare contemplated the more radical step of going back to London to see Dr Darling, but he could not face the journey. He tried describing his own symptoms in the hope that Darling might be able to offer treatment without examining him in person: 'sound affects me very much and things evil as well [as] good thoughts are continually rising in my mind—I cannot sleep for I am asleep as it were with my eyes open and a sort of nightmare awake ... there is a sort of numbing through my private parts'. He felt such a sinking feeling that he thought he was going to submerge through his bed. His only source of comfort was the health of his wife and children. Freddy, now ten, was keen on drawing. He had a paint-box and was hoping that Harry Burlowe might come up and give him some lessons.

Late in the year Lord Lindsay, a young aristocrat who lived in the region, rode over to call at the cottage. Clare was too ill to speak to him. In January 1835 he complained that he was scarcely able to move around the house and that he had not been back to Helpston for two years. Patty gave birth to another baby that did not survive. It was

the first such loss for fourteen years. Seven surviving children out of
nine is a high proportion, given the conditions in which the Clares
lived: testimony to Patty's toughness.

It was a bleak month. Old Parker Clare had been ill much of the
winter. Taylor wrote with news of other deaths: Lamb, Reynolds,
Woodhouse. The only members of the old London circles still in
touch were Cary and Cunningham. News had also come of Earl
Spencer's death and now Clare was worrying about whether his patron's son would continue to pay the annuity. He did: a letter arrived
with the reassurance that 'In a Memorandum which was given to me
by my Father I find a request that I would pay you an Annuity of £10
by half Yearly Payments'. A further fillip came in the form of the £50
grant from the Royal Literary Fund, for which he had applied at the
behest of Jeremiah How. Eliza Emmerson advised him on the wording of a letter of thanks; in composing it, he began with her words but
then went his own way.

Patty and some of the children traipsed over to Peterborough. Mrs
Marsh tried to entertain the boys by showing them a portrait of the
Bishop, who was now an invalid. She sent her visitors home with
cough mixture and a pound of tea. Such gestures were well meant,
but had no effect on Clare. Not even the good reviews of *The Rural
Muse*, which began appearing in July, succeeded in lifting him from
his gloom. The depression lasted all year. In a draft letter of November 1835, he wrote, 'My dear Sir, I am very glad to hear from you but
I am scarcely able to write having done nothing this three year—I
have got a great orchard and garden but I am not able to do any thing
in it'.

The following month his mother died, aged seventy-eight. Parker
left Helpston and joined the family in Northborough. When spring
arrived, Clare had a period of improved health. He started writing
again and set to work in the garden, requesting Henderson to send
shrubs and chrysanthemums. But the financial outlook was still
bleak. A plan on the part of the Marquess of Northampton to raise a
subscription among the local gentry, in recognition of the honour
that Clare had brought to the county, soon fizzled out.

In June 1836 there came a voice from long-vanished nights of adventure in London: a letter from Rippingille. He told of his own sufferings: the loss of two children, both of whom had died at the age of seven—children whom he 'loved as nothing in this world ought to be loved'—and long separation from his family, who were abroad while he remained 'waiting on Fortune, sitting at the step of her door, in hopes she would look out upon me, but God knows to little purpose.' Eliza Emmerson had filled him in on the comparable decline in Clare's fortunes during the last few years. In the spirit of a fellow-artist, 'Rip' let rip on the fate of the true poet in an unrewarding age:

> I hear you are suffering in health and not over-abundant in spirits; alas, alas is this the result of thought, is this the wages of labouring with that mighty engine the brain? Is man so weakly organized, that if he suffer his mind too often to awaken his feelings he sinks, sickens and dies: and is he who has the power to rouse the minds of others, stir their languid natures, and beat out a path to their hearts, to be the victim—to be the sacrifice for the millions? When I look at the 'Rural Muse' which I do often, and think of 40£ as the poet's reward I feel ashamed of the age in which I live and of the world of which I constitute a unit!

The following year, there was talk of a visit. But Rippingille failed to make the journey and Clare never saw him again. He died in 1859 of a sudden heart attack at a village railway station in the northwest. By coincidence, one of Clare's sons was a construction worker on a line nearby.

Clare's most reliable correspondents were fast disappearing. Eliza Emmerson was an almost perpetual invalid, sometimes taking to her bed for months at a time. Harry Burlowe had gone to Italy, where he died in a cholera epidemic. The other Behnes brother, whose surname Harry had forsaken, lived on until the year of Clare's death, when he was found wandering the streets of London, bankrupt and deranged. He was taken to the Middlesex hospital for the insane, where he died.

CHAPTER EIGHTEEN

'AND SO IN SPITE OF
MYSELF I RYHME ON'

There were still occasional requests to submit poems to magazines and anthologies. 'I am sorry to say', Clare wrote in response to one such inquiry,

> that my writings are in such a disordered state that I am not able
> to do any thing with them—when I was well and a thought
> struck me I wrote it down on a scrap of paper and when I wished
> to correct them I stitched these scraps together and found the
> beginning of even a Sonnet at one end of the book and the end
> at the other and I was soon so ill that I could do nothing with
> them though I have been most anxious to do so because I feel
> they are among the best I have written.

The principal manuscripts of this period are indeed Clare's most
scrappy and chaotic, but it is possible to piece together nearly three
hundred new poems, of which over two hundred were sonnets. The
bulk of them were composed when he had a great burst of creative
energy in 1836, after having written barely a line for three years.

By the late autumn of 1836 he had burnt himself out again. In November he told George Reid, his Scottish correspondent who was

sending him books and newspapers, that he was ill again but hoping to put together a new volume when he was better. His working title was 'The Fields, a poem; Tales of the Farm; Autumn, and Sonnets'. 'But I can do nothing', he added. He managed to write a little more in the spring of 1837, though these were months in which his headaches and lethargy caused him to withdraw from the world outside. A sonnet praising the Bishop of Peterborough as scholar, patron and friend was enclosed in one of his last letters to Eliza Emmerson. Had Clare completed a new volume of poetry, this might well have been at its head as a dedicatory verse.

His notebooks are full of false starts, fragments and drafts that peter out. Yet he was still composing pastorals, narrative verses in lively rhyming couplets, lyrics based on old songs, and above all sonnets. Nearly all his Northborough work consists of what he called 'little things' rather than long poems. He revisited his old territory. Birds' nests, favourite haunts, a holding fast to 'common things', the memory of lost boyhood pleasures:

> Oh could I feel my spirits beat
> As once they did when life, a boy,
> Went everywhere with dancing feet
> Met everything with joy.

And he remains a great weather poet, as in 'Snow Storm':

> What a night: the wind howls, hisses and but stops
> To howl more loud while the snow volley keeps
> Incessant batter at the window pane,
> Making our comfort feel as sweet again.

Other lyrics burn with heartsickness or longing for seclusion, even a desire for death: 'Oh take this world away from me / Its strife I cannot bear to see'. A 'Clown's Lament' begins with the familiar complaint, 'O love, what is love but a trouble at best?' He is retreating into his own troubled self: 'Free from the world I would a prisoner be / And my own shadow all my company'.

Sometimes, though, he finds religious comfort. In one poem, the image of Christ as a stranger, an outcast and a fugitive leads him to feel that he should not despair at his own condition. Elsewhere he meditates on the afterlife of his poetry. He is no longer interested in the 'idle fame' of passing fashion and literary celebrity; he wishes instead for 'after fame'. His poetry will be joined with nature in what he calls 'the eternity of song'.

Though he made new song out of fen, reed-bed and kingfisher, he was writing fewer landscape poems. The Northborough environment lacked spinney and copse in which to find shelter. He missed the heath-furze of Emmonsales. The 'treeless fens of many miles' with 'not a hill in all the view' did not answer to his habitual rhythm of walking and gazing, of soodle and pause. The skies were a dull grey and it always seemed to be drizzling. In Helpston he had written scores of crisp, bright winter poems. Now he felt hemmed in by dark days and perpetual damp.

He continued to innovate within the form of the sonnet and to broaden the range of his subject-matter. Though there are some sonnets of memory—one on Casterton where he wooed Patty, another on his childhood friend Richard Turnill—the majority of them have an objectivity of voice that is new to Clare. Rather than pressing his feelings into his surroundings, he seems to be standing back and watching. The first-person voice becomes the exception instead of the rule. Critics have justly compared these mature sonnets to the woodcut vignettes of Thomas Bewick, in which rural life and labour are etched in minute detail with an unsentimental precision. Though Clare did not complete his 'Tales of the Farm', the sonnets provide a full cast of characters for such an enterprise: ploughboys, milkmaids, labourers, a passing tramp, a fowler bent on bird-slaughter, a group of unromantic gypsies.

The most characteristic work of the Northborough years is that which evokes the secretive, the shy and the downtrodden. Spotted flycatcher, darting nuthatch, barred woodpecker, the kicked-out nest of a ground lark, a displaced French girl, fox and pine marten. Above

all, there is a magnificent sequence of five sonnets on a badger that is
hunted, sacked and baited with dogs until

> He falls as dead and kicked by boys and men
> Then starts and grins and drives the crowd agen
> Till kicked and torn and beaten out he lies
> And leaves his hold and cackles, groans and dies.

Clare can speak for the badger because by now he feels kicked and
torn and beaten himself. This sonnet is truncated to twelve lines, cut
off with the badger's death. In an early letter, Clare had complained
about the 'rule and compass' of critics who insisted that a sonnet
should always have fourteen lines precisely.

Because so many of the Northborough poems have an eerily detached tone, those that are in a first-person voice take on an additional urgency. Clare's sense of his own status as a perpetual outsider,
a man who did not fully belong in either the world of landed property
or that of literary propriety, is nowhere better caught than in a sonnet
on his fear of trespassing:

> I dreaded walking where there was no path
> And prest with cautious tread the meadow swath
> And always turned to look with wary eye
> And always feared the owner coming bye
> Yet everything about where I had gone
> Appeared so beautiful I ventured on
> And when I gained the road where all are free
> I fancied every stranger frowned at me
> And every kinder look appeared to say
> You've been on trespass in your walk to day
> I've often thought the day appeared so fine
> How beautiful if such a place where mine
> But having nought I never feel alone
> And cannot use another's as my own.

He wrote over fifty poems that begin 'I love'. Typically: I love to roam, I
love to stroll, I love to wander. But here he begins with *dread*. Every-

where he walks, he is looking over his shoulder. However beautiful a wood or meadow may seem, he never fully finds the ease and solitude he seeks there. He is shadowed by his dread of gamekeeper and magistrate.

In November 1835 John Taylor wrote to his brother in the midlands with the news that he had promised to go to Northborough to see Clare, 'who is very ill, and I fear will require Confinement in a public Asylum before long unless some neighbouring Surgeon should have the skill to understand how to treat him so as to prevent so undesirable a Catastrophe'. He made the visit early in December. Afterwards, he sent a detailed report to his sister:

> I set off to see Clare in a Chaise accompanied by a Medical Gentleman of Stamford, who was to give me his opinion respecting poor Clare's health.—We found him sitting in the Corner Chair, looking much as usual—He talked properly to me in Reply to all my Questions—knew all the people of whom I spoke, and smiled at my Reminding him of the Events of past Days—but his Mind is sadly enfeebled.—He is constantly speaking to himself and when I listened I heard such words as these pronounced a great many times over, and with great Rapidity—'God bless them all'—'Keep them from Evil'—'Doctors'—But who it was of whom he spoke I could not tell—whether his Children—or Doctors—or anybody. But I think the latter—His Children 7 in no. are a very fine Family, strongly resembling him—the youngest, a Boy of 3 or 4 years old—the eldest, a Girl 16—there are 3 Boys and 4 Girls [actually 4 and 3]—The Medical Man's opinion was that Clare should go to some Asylum—His Wife is a very clever active woman and keeps them all very respectable and comfortable, but she cannot manage to control her Husband at times—He is very violent, I dare say, occasionally—His old Father is still living with them.—We went to see a Clergyman who has been always kind to Clare for 20 years and he has promised to see Earl Fitzwilliam about an Asylum.

This is the fullest account we have of the condition into which Clare had deteriorated. He is not out of his mind; he knows who he is, he can answer questions clearly and his memory is well intact. But he is haunted by his inner demons: that repeated phrase 'Keep them from Evil' seems to be related to his fear of the family being be-witched and perhaps even to suggest he was afraid that he himself might harm his loved ones.

Taylor's darkest hint comes towards the end of the passage, when Patty is commended for her good sense and her labours on behalf of the family, but pitied because she cannot always keep her husband un-der control. 'He is very violent, I dare say, occasionally'. We do not know whether that violence extended beyond words to actions, though there are a handful of disturbing fragments in Clare's note-books of this time—stray lines on betrayal, abuse of female fickle-ness, acknowledgement of how 'Passion may a moment cloud / The kindest bosom breathing', a verse couplet that suggests at the very least an imagination in which sexual play spills over into violence ('He throws the thorns about to tear her gown / And tyes the wheat to make her tumble down').

The main reason for putting Clare in an asylum seems to have been that Patty could no longer be expected to go on coping with him. Family tradition corroborates Taylor's sense that she was struggling: in the 1920s one of Clare's grandchildren reported that sometimes the only way of calming him down was for one of the older children to take him aside and talk quietly of country things.

When he wrote to Clare some weeks after his visit, Taylor under-stated his concern: 'I was much pleased to see your Wife and Chil-dren, and your Father, all looking so well.—I thought you too were to all Appearances in good Health'. But these were merely words in-tended to cheer. He went ahead with arrangements based on his knowledge that Clare's health was anything but good.

Taylor approached a highly regarded mad-doctor: Matthew Allen, owner of a private asylum in the Epping Forest, just northeast of London. On 8 July 1837, Clare's Peterborough doctors—Fenwick Skrimshire and Thomas Walker—signed the necessary certificate of insanity. Seven days later he was admitted to Dr Allen's asylum 'by authority of his wife'. We do not know whether he was taken there directly or via London. The man who escorted him had arrived in Northborough with a note from Taylor and the half-yearly annuity from the poet's trust fund. Taylor wrote that 'the Bearer' would look after him on the road and assured him that he would be going to a place where he would receive 'Medical Care' effectual to his recovery. He was taken from home on or around his forty-fourth birthday.

How much did the doctors know? And what exactly did they mean when they certified that John Clare was mad?

Skrimshire's letters and case-notes do not survive, but we may perhaps find an answer in a book that he was working on at the time. A medical guide for village pastors, it has a section on mental disorders. Here Skrimshire distinguishes between '*mania*, or *madness*', which he considers to be in most cases an hereditary disease, and *delirium tremens*, which is usually the result of excessive drinking. A fit of insanity, he explains, is something that comes on suddenly, often during the night. The patient will suddenly jump out of bed under some imaginary alarm, disturbing his family. He will threaten, and perhaps effect, some 'serious mischief' to himself or others, or he may seek refuge from some imaginary danger or dwell with horror on 'some supposed dreadful risk incurred, or injury sustained'. Once restrained, the patient will crouch and submit, 'moodiness succeeding to violence'. He will watch every movement of those about him with suspicion as he broods over his supposed wrongs.

Although such symptoms are sudden, a watchful and practised eye could, according to Skrimshire, notice an unusual appearance or altered manner in the patient for days or even weeks before the outbreak. Among the 'premonitory symptoms' are 'an acknowledgment that he cannot command his thoughts, but that strange and unaccountable fancies present themselves in an incontrollable manner; also, that he hears various noises, particularly of persons talking; that he can distinguish their conversation, which is almost always in reference to himself'. In diagnosing insanity, the key thing to consider is the change in the subject's behaviour. Incoherent speech and strange behaviour are not diagnostic in themselves; what is telling is 'their incongruity and incoherency in regard to, and in relation to, the former deportment of the individual in question'. If a habitually placid man becomes violent, it may be a case of mania.

Skrimshire probably had other patients who suffered from mental illness, but Clare was his best known. He had been treating him for nearly twenty years. There are very close parallels between the symptoms described by Clare in his letters, those observed by Taylor in 1836, and the pattern of behaviour outlined in this contemporaneously written account of the nature of 'mania'. Skrimshire's emphasis on sudden outbursts of violence strongly suggests why he agreed to sign Clare over into the care of Dr Allen.

It would be a mistake to suppose that there was just one thing wrong with John Clare. He suffered from a distressing array of physical and mental symptoms. Different conditions and different levels of severity can be detected at different times in his life. It would also be a mistake to suppose that his problems had a single cause. A century and a half after his death, all we can do is identify a range of possible causes and conditions, and offer some reflections on the various diagnoses made during his lifetime.

When Clare was recertified, prior to his admission to the second asylum in 1841, Skrimshire answered the query 'What are the supposed causes of Insanity?' by writing 'hereditary'. Patty Clare informed her husband's first biographer that there was no family history of insanity, but she may have been speaking defensively or in ignorance. Skrimshire was an educated and conscientious doctor, intimately acquainted with Clare, so he may have had information that is lost to us. We know little about Clare's mother's family: it is not beyond the bounds of possibility that a Stimson sibling or other relative was at some time certified. Equally, we have no knowledge what aberrations the mysterious wanderer John Donald Parker may have contributed to the Clare gene pool.

Doctors often say that they can predict from an early age which of a group of children will have mental health problems later in life. It is usually the one who feels different: the misfit, the loner. Clare's autobiographical writings reveal that he fell into this category. The hostility aroused by such a character in a small close-knit community led to village gossip that marked him out as too clever by half and likely to prove a lunatic. The sense of being a marked man made him feel more of an outsider and an oddity: the village prophecy that he would one day go mad contributed to its own fulfilment.

Specific environmental conditions also played a part. Clare records cyclical episodes of ague and feverishness, traced back to nights spent out of doors. There is a strong possibility that he suffered from malaria, which was endemic in the mosquito-ridden fens of his home territory. This could account for some of his night-sweats, vivid dreams and hallucinations.

His diet consisted principally of bread, potatoes, root vegetables from the garden, tea, ale and tobacco. The family could afford very little in the way of meat and dairy products. He was stunted in growth and his friends often worried that he did not eat enough. Poor diet can have all sorts of effects. Vitamin deficiency may affect the brain and nervous system, in serious cases causing anything from numbness and burning pains to progressive dementia characterised by apprehension, confusion, derangement and maniacal outbursts— the very symptoms experienced by Clare. Though of course there were thousands of other labourers of his class who had equally bad diets and no such symptoms.

Certain specific events may also have been factors. Clare himself ascribed his falling attacks to his witnessing of Thomas Drake's fatal tumble from a hay-cart. In modern America he might thus be diagnosed as having post-traumatic stress disorder. His own fall from a tree is a more likely influence in this regard. The frequent headaches of which he complained may have been the result of stress, but may equally have been caused by a clot or some other long-term after-effect of his concussion.

Dr Nesbitt of the Northampton asylum told Clare's first biographer that he had always been led to believe that the poet's mental affliction 'had its origin in dissipation'. Drink was often blamed for madness in the early nineteenth century. Clare's friends and doctors may sometimes sound moralistic when writing of their concerns about his drinking, but they may also have intuited that it was intimately linked to his depression. He himself noted with some relish that the colloquialism for becoming helplessly drunk was *got his rock off*—a phrase suggestive of losing one's head. Alcohol dependence is another plausible explanation for many of his mental and physical symptoms, though it is noteworthy that Skrimshire carefully distinguished between the *mania* with which he diagnosed Clare and the *delirium tremens* of the alcoholic.

The word *dissipation* also has sexual connotations. We have seen that Clare himself believed he was suffering from a sexually transmitted disease. Syphilis can certainly cause derangement, but Clare's illness did not follow its characteristic pattern. Mercury-poisoning resulting from attempted treatment for syphilis is, however, an intriguing possibility.

In sum, then, Clare's 'mania' is unlikely to have had a single origin. Whatever genetic element there may or may not have been, there were also a variety of possible organic and environmental causes. A book entitled *On Nervous and Mental Conditions*, published when Clare was in Dr Allen's asylum, listed the following among the many possible causes of madness: domestic disturbances and quarrels, disappointed love, sexual indulgence, love of admiration, fear, blows on the head, the witnessing of a sudden death, sudden and unexpected changes of fortune. Clare suffered from all these. Etiologies of this kind had an admonitory as much as a medical purpose, but they were not idiotic: they spoke in the language of Clare's time about the causes of what we now call 'stress'. Similar lists, albeit in more technical language, are to be found in today's diagnostic handbooks for psychiatrists.

Dr Thomas Arnold, father of the Stamford physician whom Clare especially valued, said that insanity could be caused by 'intense application to study' and 'too great activity of imagination'. Ned Drury, one of the men who discovered Clare, noted very early in the poet's career that the manic intensity of his writing might have disastrous consequences. The stress of poverty combined with the drive to be a writer—and the alienation felt by a poet in a non-literary rural community—are quite sufficient explanations for what Taylor called the enfeeblement of Clare's mind.

In the asylum years his symptoms grew more florid. His descent from poetic fame into delusive rambling made it all too easy to invoke the traditional association between genius and madness. Because Clare was perceived as an anomaly within his culture, there was always a tendency to attach labels to him: *mad poet* took over where *peasant poet* left off. Then in the first half of the twentieth century, when there was a particular fascination with schizophrenia, he was posthumously diagnosed as schizophrenic. The idea of a split identity seemed to answer to the sense of dislocation that characterised his later writings.

Posthumous psychiatric diagnosis is a dubious activity. Madness is of an age, not for all time. It is experienced and witnessed in history. Medical disorders, especially those of a psychosomatic nature, are influenced by the ways in which they are conceptualized and treated. Clare's belief in demons and his doctors' faith in the practice of blood-letting are a world away from the modern thinking that divides functional psychosis into two basic types, schizophrenic and manic-depressive, then seeks to control those conditions with drugs.

With this caveat in mind, it may be said with some confidence that Clare is most unlikely to have been schizophrenic. Schizophrenia classically comes on in early adulthood, whereas Clare's first truly 'mad' episode, involving delusions and the hearing of strange voices, seems to have occurred around his thirty-seventh birthday at the time of the episode in the Peterborough theatre. The term *mid-life crisis* is vulgar but useful: Clare was struggling to support his ever-growing family, his relationship with his publisher had collapsed and there was no clear way forward for his vocation. His condition is better described as a 'nervous breakdown' than an eruption of 'lunacy'.

I have said earlier that Clare conforms to the classic pattern not of schizophrenia but of manic depression or 'bipolar affective disorder'. He had phases of depression that sometimes lasted several months, alternating with periods of normality and episodes of mania. Intensive work on his poetry was often followed by collapse into a long period of torpor. The most frequent complaints in Clare's letters are aches, numbness and above all stomach pains—all classic symptoms of depression. There is wisdom in the ancient idea that the seat of melancholy is the digestive system.

The term *depression* was indeed used in the early nineteenth century. Eliza Emmerson was a woman of intense sensibility who was acutely conscious of her own 'nervous depression' and she had no doubt that her friend suffered from the same condition. The standard nosology of insanity proposed that it took two forms, a 'depression of mind' known as melancholia and the maniacal paroxysms or violent fits known as mania. At root, this is the same bipolar model that occurs in modern accounts of depression, with the difference that *manic* is now used for the 'high' phase more generally, not just for 'fits' of violent or irrational behaviour.

Clare was conscious of the seasonal cycle of his illness. In temperate climates depressive symptoms peak in spring and autumn: these were the times of year when he said that the blue devils most often came upon him. Spring and autumn are also the peak times for suicides, a fact noted by Clare's doctor Matthew Allen, who was a great believer in the influence of atmospheric conditions on mental health. Modern surveys suggest that over two-thirds of all people who take their own lives have been previously diagnosed with an affective disorder and that nearly a quarter of all bipolar patients commit suicide. We do not know whether Clare ever attempted to take his own life, but suicidal thoughts and a sense of his own impending death dominated his thinking during many of his most severe bouts of depression, such as that of 1823–4. The depressive feels isolated and undervalued; in Clare's case, these feelings were exacerbated by the vicissitudes in his relationships with his publishers and editors.

In depression he felt unloved, whereas in manic phases he lived with passion. We expect poets to fall in love with exceptional frequency and intensity, but manic-depressives often do so too—Shakespeare's imaginative compacting of lunatic, lover and poet is not without empirical support. As will be seen, an obsession with women grew to be one of his most striking symptoms during the 1840s in the Northampton asylum.

Another common characteristic of mania is binge spending. Clare frequently went on book-buying binges that he could ill afford. Among the fragments in his manuscripts is a note of 'little expenses occurred' including a guinea for a new hat and thirteen shillings and fivepence for 'washing'. We may imagine the marital exchange: Patty accuses him of spending money they haven't got on his new hat and the constant stream of books, while she slaves away at the household chores. Washing would have involved fetching water from the parish pump, heating it over the fire, soaking clothes and linens in a tub by the back door and scrubbing by hand with poor-quality yellow soap. So he makes it up to her by spending more money they haven't got sending everything out to a washerwoman.

In schizophrenia, thought is disordered. Clare was periodically subject to intrusive thoughts of a violent nature, but his disorder was essentially *affective*. Schizophrenia classically produces emotional coldness and volitional impairment, whereas depression brings powerful emotions of the kind on which Clare dwelt in his descriptions of his own illnesses: sadness, tears, gloom, feelings of worthlessness, lethargy, pessimism; sometimes anxiety, anger, fear. If Clare were alive today, he would be diagnosed with manic depression and prescribed Prozac or lithium to even out his ups and downs. It is worth wondering whether such a prescription would have saved him from the asylum at the cost of killing his poetic muse.

Severe depression can become psychotic. Feelings of guilt or inadequacy may spread out into deluded beliefs. So too with mania, the flipside of depression. Elation spills over into delusion. A poet throws himself into an imaginary persona: at what point does he start really believing that he *is* that persona? In the mid-1820s Clare wrote carefully controlled poems in the voice of such seventeenth-century writers as Andrew Marvell and Henry Wotton. He played the literary game of trying to make magazine editors believe that the poems were authentic lost manuscripts, but he did not for a moment believe that he *was* Marvell or Wotton. In Dr Allen's asylum in the early 1840s he wrote less carefully controlled—though still intricately crafted—poems in the voice of Lord Byron. Perhaps he began by playing at being Byron, but as his affective disorder grew more severe he came to believe that he was Lord Byron—or Lord Nelson, or Jack Randall the boxer. These later episodes probably deserve the classification 'psychotic'. But they all occurred *after* Clare was admitted to the asylum. He may have become psychotic because he was surrounded by psychosis—a fellow-patient at Allen's who announced that he was Jesus Christ is likely to have been a genuine schizophrenic.

Taylor selected Dr Allen's asylum for the treatment of Clare because he knew about the regime there: he had published Allen's *Essay on the Classification of the Insane*.* The nineteenth century was an age when there were many attempts to understand madness, to rationalise the irrational, through the work of classification. There will always be commentators willing to suggest that any classification—whether past ('lunatic', 'monomaniac') or present ('schizophrenic', 'psychotic')—is merely part of the restraining apparatus of medical and social control. In response to this, one might say that the advantage of classifying Clare as 'manic-depressive' is to make him something other than the freak of nature which he has all too frequently been presented as. Depression is a darkness known to millions. Clare's genius was exceptional, but his 'madness' was not.

Ultimately, though, a redescription of Clare's condition in the language of twenty-first-century psychiatry tells us no more than what we already know from his own writings and the observations of those who knew him. There is no evidence that he was taken to the asylum because he was 'mad' in the sense of having lost consciousness of his own identity; on the contrary, most of his writings remained wholly attuned to what he called, in a remarkably modern phrase, 'self-identity'. He was taken to the asylum because he needed better care than could be provided by his family.

Clare was deeply impressionable. His poetry is an answering to the

*Discussed in Chapter 19.

world around him. He was also deeply influenced by his reading. Early in his career, he was an avid consumer of the *London Magazine*, the journal that had launched him into the literary world. He would not have missed an article in the March 1820 edition, entitled 'The phenomena of diseased imagination'. Here Coleridge was quoted on the subject of Martin Luther: 'he suffered under great irritability of his nervous system, the common effect of derangement of digestion in men of sedentary habits, who are at the same time intense thinkers'. Deranged digestion, it was claimed, could then lead to apparitions and delusions. The article also discussed Rousseau's paranoia, the poet Tasso's belief that he was 'surrounded by persecuting enemies, even devils and wild spirits', and the diary of a writer named Walderstein who recorded that 'when I am ill, I can think nothing, feel nothing, without bringing it home to myself. It seems as if the whole world were nothing but a machine expressly formed to make me feel my sufferings and inconveniences in every possible manner'. Clare subsequently experienced all the symptoms of dangerously strong imagination described in this article; we should not rule out the possibility that his own derangement was partially shaped by his reading about the mental sufferings of other writers.

The compulsion to be a poet may have made it inevitable that the man from the asylum would one day come knocking on his door. But if he had not been a poet, he would have had no joy and he would not have been John Clare:

> I became fond of scribbling from down right pleasure in giving vent to my feelings and long and pleasing and painful were my struggles to acquire a sufficient knowledge of the written english before I could put down my ideas on paper even so as to understand myself but I mastered it in time sufficiently to be understood by others and then I became an author by accident and felt astonished when the critics became my friends that they should have noticed me at all—and no less supprised at the mistakes they uttered—that one should imagine I had read the old poets when such were as far from my access as earth from heaven and that others should imagine I had coined words

which were as common around me as the grass under my feet—
and all these were burning encouragments that made me work
on—as to profits—the greatest profits most congenial to my
feelings were the friends it brought me and the names that it
rendered familiar to my fireside—scraps of whose melodys I
had heard and read in my corner—but had I only imagined for
a moment that I should hold communion with such hereafter
that would have then been to me 'as music in mourning'—but I
wrote because it pleased me in sorrow—and when I am happy it
makes me more happy and so I go on.

So he wrote in a magnificent letter to his friend Thomas Pringle. We
do justice to Clare not by making him into a victim of either his circumstances or his brain chemistry, but by hearing him speak thus of
the freedom that he found in poetry. His writing is the best diagnosis
of him that we have. He knew that his poetry was at once a losing and
a finding of his true self. A cause of alienation: 'I shrank from myself
with extacy and have never been myself since', he wrote in his rough
draft of this letter. And yet his greatest solace: 'I wrote because it
pleased me in sorrow—and when I am happy it makes me more
happy and so I go on'.

In 1832, when he was most troubled by the business of the newspaper reports about Lord Milton's patronage, he told his friend Henry
Cary of this need to 'write on'. He is urged forward by the 'ambition
to be happy in sadness'; writing poetry is his only way of fulfilling
that ambition. 'If I have merit', he continues, 'summer insects'
(meaning gossips and interferers) 'may annoy but cannot destroy me'.
Then he reflects on his vocation in a manner that is at once self-
deprecatory and defiant:

If you laugh at my ambitions I am ready to laugh with you at my
own vanity for I sit sometimes and wonder over the little noise I
have made in the world until I think I have written nothing as
yet to deserve any praise at all—so the spirit of fame, of living a
little after life like a name on a conspicuous place, urges my
blood upward into unconscious melodys and striding down my
orchard and homestead I hum and sing inwardly those little

madrigals and then go in and pen them down, thinking them much better things than they are until I look over them again and then the charm vanishes into the vanity that I shall do something better ere I die and so in spite of myself I ryhme on.

He rhymed in spite of himself: Dr Skrimshire was doing no more than telling the truth when he wrote on the second certification document, in answer to the question whether insanity had been preceded by any long period of mental exertion, that Clare's outpouring of poetry had been an addiction of many years' standing. But whereas most addictions are there to be kicked, Clare's is to be celebrated. The appropriate word for the self-analysis in his letter to Cary comes not from modern psychiatry but from ancient Greek epic. That word is *heroic*.

· ·

PART FOUR

The Asylum Years

1837–1864

Northampton Asylum July 19th 1848

My dear wife,

I have not written to you a long while but here I am in the Land of sodom where all the peoples brains are turned the wrong way . . .

CHAPTER NINETEEN

DR BOTTLE-IMP AND BOXER BYRON

The city of York was well known for its enlightened, peaceable Quaker community. It was also known for a hell-house of a lunatic asylum: a vast building in which the inmates were confined behind bars in tiny cells, covered with their own excrement, often restrained in 'strait-waistcoats' and subjected to such punishments as the rotating chair and the cold douche. In 1796, to save their own people from such a place, the York Quakers opened 'the Retreat': 'an Institution for Insane Persons of the Society of Friends'.

It stood on a hill, with a fine prospect of woodland and moor. Warm baths were offered and each room was heated by a guarded fire. There were no iron bars on the windows and the use of straitjackets was kept to a minimum. A healthy diet was provided and exercise encouraged; the less severely afflicted patients worked in the garden or on the adjoining farm. And there was a new philosophy of care: 'Moral Treatment'.

According to Samuel Tuke, one of the intellectual architects of the Retreat, insanity had its origin in the mind (not a belief universally shared in the eighteenth century) and therefore the training of the mind was the best way of managing derangement. The 'intellectual, active, and moral powers, are usually rather perverted than obliterated'; the correct term is *mental alienation*, meaning that the mind is suppressed rather than destroyed. Symptoms will be aggravated by the resentment felt at restraint, so the key to treatment is kindness: help patients to help themselves, use coercion only when absolutely necessary, promote the general comfort of the insane, above all avoid fear. Allow visiting and emphasise such activities as gardening, reading, writing, ball games and chess.

The Retreat was made possible not only by the enlightenment of the Quakers but also by a broad change in attitudes to madness at the end of the eighteenth century. In 1788 King George III had gone mad. His recovery was credited to the intervention of Francis Willis, the doctor who ran a private asylum in his house near Stamford, where Clare would make a social call thirty years later. Willis used harsh methods and it is doubtful that his treatment really had much effect on the King's condition, which we now know to have been organic (porphyria). But the public perception was that Willis had proved that insanity could be cured. Equally, perceptions were altered by the very fact that it was the King who had been mad: insanity could no longer be attributed to ignorance, sin or superstition.

In the years immediately after the King's temporary derangement, insanity was reported more widely throughout society and there was accordingly a huge growth in the business of private madhouses. More public institutions were also opened, though nearly half a century passed before a parliamentary act made it compulsory for every county to have an asylum. Clare's lifetime was, then, a transitional period during which insanity came increasingly to be seen as a condition that could be diagnosed, certified and treated within a legally monitored regime. The associated vocabulary began to change: from madhouse to asylum, mad-doctor to 'alienist' or 'medical superintendent', madman (or -woman) to patient.

In 1813, following the damning report of a public inquiry, the management of the York asylum were dismissed and the governors brought in new staff with the intention of applying the very different methods that had proved so successful at the Retreat. Six years later, the asylum apothecary was sacked for taking improper liberties with a female patient. The vacancy was filled by Matthew Allen. Born in

1783 of Yorkshire Dissenting stock, he was the black sheep of his family, twice married before he was thirty, a sometime itinerant preacher and phrenological lecturer who had failed in various business ventures—he was once imprisoned in Edinburgh for selling soda-water without paying stamp duty.

During his time at the York asylum, Allen obtained a doctorate of medicine from Aberdeen—a qualification that could be purchased without attendance. Though without formal training, he held the additional post of curator of the York Medical Library, so he was well read in the relevant literature. He became an apostle of the methods of moral management of the insane that had been pioneered at the Retreat. 'I was the first who carried out a system of kindness', he later claimed, somewhat exaggerating his part in the reforms at York. In fact, he left the asylum after five years, apparently under a cloud due to dereliction of his duties.

Allen moved south and set about establishing a private institution of his own. He had plans drawn up and produced letters of reference attesting to his work in York. In 1829, a licence was granted for him to open an asylum at High Beech* in the Epping Forest to the northeast of London. At first there were two houses: Fair Mead, with room for up to twelve patients, and Leopard's Hill Lodge, housing twenty-four. Allen and his family moved between the two houses; there was always a resident physician in whichever one he was not actually living in himself.

Private asylums were carefully regulated by local court officials, with a system of licensing and visitation, so Allen's plans were duly submitted to the authorities with a full explanatory guide. The houses had good ventilation, with warmth provided by Sylvester's patent heated Air Stove. There were hot and cold baths in the bath houses, Medical Vapour Baths and 'many Water Closets' beyond the outhouses (reached by a covered passage). Patients whose cases were 'of a decided nature' (i.e. the more severely ill) were kept at Leopard's Hill Lodge, where the sexes were segregated; those who were 'more

*Now spelt *Beach*.

correct' lived at Fair Mead, where the sexes shared 'occasional intercourse (especially at Meals and some amusements—Music—Lectures—Cards etc.)'. Allen considered this 'highly advantageous'
because 'it preserves that mutual restraint and softening influence
which the Sexes so powerfully exercise on each other'. As patients
convalesced, they would move from Leopard's Hill Lodge to Fair
Mead. Within each house there was movement between the 'galleries' at the back and the more domestic quarters at the front. Patients in the front rooms were encouraged to think of themselves as
house-guests.

Allen must have obtained considerable financial backing for his
enterprise: the asylum boasted gardens, pleasure grounds and sixteen
acres of fields in which inmates could walk with their attendants.
Like the Retreat, Allen's asylum was in an elevated setting with 'extensive view of Forest, cultivated and distant scenery'. The mature
broad wood of Epping, one of the ancient Royal Forests, provided
'abundant variety of scenery' and 'perfect retirement'. Inmates 'of a
decided nature' went about in the company of attendants, but convalescent patients were given a key and allowed to walk in the forest un-
attended. Allen recorded that there were few escape attempts. Fair
Mead and Leopard's Hill Lodge were made to sound more like a
place of pastoral ease than a lunatic asylum: 'the retirement—pure
air—and sweet scenery around, afford ample scope for walks, without annoyance and apparently without restraint'.

Following the exact model of the Retreat, Allen promised to offer
'domestic comfort, diversity of occupations and amusements' suited
to the various states of his patients, who would all be sufficiently genteel to pay—no paupers were allowed. A close examination of the
ground-plans of the houses reveals a rather less rosy picture than that
offered by Allen himself. Whereas some of the well-to-do and only
mildly insane patients had their own suite of sitting-room and bedroom (which cost them five to seven guineas per week), others lived
in dormitories. At the back of Leopard's Hill Lodge there were small
cell-like rooms for more severely afflicted inmates. And even at Fair

Mead there was a separate cottage 'to be used occasionally for noisy patients'.

To begin with, there were twenty patients, fifteen at Leopard's Hill and five at Fair Mead. Among them was a former surgeon from the York asylum, together with his sister. Both had been certified around the time of Allen's move. He may have taken them south and looked after them privately before opening his doors to others. Allen also suggested to an old Edinburgh acquaintance, Thomas Carlyle, that he might like to live permanently at Fair Mead, at an annual cost of forty pounds for board, lodging and a horse. Carlyle declined, but when his wife Jane visited Allen's asylum in 1831 she said that it was a place to which any sane person would be delighted to be admitted. Roses and grapes grew around the houses, while the gardens and grounds created an air of freedom.

The visiting magistrates concurred. Their annual reports on Allen's establishment were uniformly complimentary: 'This asylum is in every respect calculated to promote the cure of patients placed in it'; 'all are treated with care, kindness and attention'. Particular praise was given to the emphasis on religious practice: convalescents would go to the parish church on Sundays and others attended a service conducted by Allen himself.

The good reputation of a private asylum was crucial to its financial viability. A whiff of scandal and potential clients would look elsewhere. Potential disaster struck Allen late in 1832 after he went to the Court of Exchequer to recover the balance of an unpaid bill. He won his case, but an *ex parte* statement appeared the next day in *The Times*, making public some highly damaging 'false charges and insinuations'. Allen sued for libel, but—as every libel plaintiff knows—the very act of doing so meant that he was running the risk of adverse publicity. He therefore published an extended pamphlet, *Allen versus Dutton*, laying out the full story and printing an array of affidavits and character references. The case revolved around the removal of a female patient from Fair Mead to Leopard's Hill Lodge. To justify his action, Allen needed to explain the system whereby he classified the relative severity of the conditions afflicting his patients. So it was that his defence grew into a much larger book called *An Essay on the Classification of the Insane*, which was published by John Taylor: this is how the latter came to know about Allen's institution and to select it for the treatment of John Clare.

The *Essay* outlined Allen's 'mild system' of moral management, summarised some of his successes, and told of his reluctance to use physical restraint. His aim was to treat his patients as house-guests, 'unless their own conduct should oblige me to act otherwise towards them'. The book also reprinted a series of case-studies from an earlier work by Allen, several of them illustrated with engravings accompanied by diagrams of the patient's brain. Allen was a prominent advocate of phrenology, the art of reading the constitution of the mind from the shape of the cranium. As we have seen, Clare himself was intrigued by the popular phrenologist Deville. Strange as it may seem, this 'science' was of crucial importance in the development of the understanding of the mind. Franz Joseph Gall, the inventor of phrenology, had been the first to convince the medical community that the brain is the organ of the mind, and so observing the brain would enable one to understand the structure and functions of the mind. Gall's theories were as influential in the early nineteenth century as Freud's were in the early twentieth. With its localisation of particular faculties in specific areas of the cerebrum, phrenology might be reclaimed as the grandparent of twenty-first-century neurophysiology. After centuries in which dysfunctional behaviour had been attributed to an imbalance of bodily humours, with melancholia and hypochondriasis being located in the liver, gall-bladder or spleen, theorists such as Allen turned attention specifically to *mental* functions. He defined *insanity* as 'the uncontrolled over-excitement, imbecility, suspended or paralysed state of one or more of the mental functions, arising from some previous faulty state of action'.

Allen versus Dutton, the pamphlet that preceded Allen's *Essay*, is doubly interesting in that it provides a detailed inside story of the asylum whilst also being the first link in the chain of associations that led to Clare's being committed there. The problem began when Mrs

Louise Dutton was transferred from Fair Mead to Leopard's Hill 'in consequence of very dirty habits'. Her husband claimed that Allen had undertaken a contractual obligation to keep her at Fair Mead; he was insulted that she had been removed to what he considered to be the house for 'incurables'. He therefore refused to pay her fees— hence the case in the Court of Exchequer. Mr Dutton then tried to strengthen his case with some very serious allegations of violent mistreatment and, it seems, sexual abuse of his wife on the part of the Allens.

According to Allen, Dutton had failed to appreciate that transfer between the two houses was part of his system of 'moral management'. Leopard's Hill Lodge was not for 'incurables', but merely for patients who required more intensive care. Evidence was also produced in defence against other allegations: Mrs Dutton's room was devoid of linens and curtains not as punishment but because she had smeared them with excrement; the reason there was no fire in the grate when her husband visited was that it was a warm summer day; and as for a claim made by Dutton that he saw his wife being forcibly restrained by a keeper, the reason she had gone into a fit of mania was the very arrival of her husband, for whom she had expressed bitter loathing. Allen also produced an earlier letter from Dutton in which he admitted that he had failed in his own attempts to 'correct' his wife. Her condition always deteriorated when her husband visited.

Allen tells of how Mrs Dutton would be washed and dressed after she had dirtied herself, only to tear off her clothes and dirty herself again. She seems to have been massively incontinent, soiling every room in the house, including recently decorated ones. *Dirtying* was, however, also a euphemism for masturbation. Allen claimed that Dutton was trying to ruin him with 'the dreadful nature' of his charges; the documentation surrounding the court case has dark allusions to 'the xxxxx attempt' and 'the xxxxx attack'. It is unlikely that Allen did rape or beat Mrs Dutton, though one could imagine her making such a claim in a fit of derangement. One gets the strong sense that Dutton was projecting his own violent tendencies onto Allen. But the whole sordid story hints at the dark underside of sex and violence that afflicts every asylum. There was more to life at High Beech than the occupational therapy of musical parties, billiards, cricket, gardening and a patient-produced weekly newspaper.

In 1834, perhaps with half an eye to Dutton's complaint about the mixed company at Leopard's Hill Lodge, Allen added to his establishment a third house, Springfield, for female patients only. At the time of Clare's admission three years later, there were forty patients in all: seven men and four women at Fair Mead, fourteen men at Leopard's Hill and fifteen women at Springfield. Seventeen were classified as curable and twenty-three incurable. Clare was one of six admissions that year. There were seven discharges in the same period (five cured, two improved). The visiting magistrates expressed every satisfaction with the conditions, noting that only one patient, a Mr Best, was kept under restraint. Among Clare's fellow-inmates were several gentlemen, a clergyman, a merchant, a naval man, a student of medicine, many spinsters, two farmers and a governess. During his four years there, the number of patients increased to more than fifty. It is not clear to which house he was initially taken, but in the year of his escape he was in Leopard's Hill Lodge.

Two months after Clare's admission to the asylum, Patty heard via Miss Mortlock at the Bishop's palace in Peterborough that Dr Allen had written to say that his general health had greatly improved. Two months after that, Clare was well enough to write a letter himself:

> My dear Wife
> I write to tell you I am getting better—I can't write a long letter but wish to know how you all are—the place here is beautiful and I meet with great kindness—the country is the finest I have seen—write and tell me how you all are—I can't write a long letter but I shall do better—God bless you all—kiss them all for me
>
> Yours ever my dear wife   John Clare

The rest cure seemed to be working.

Patty also received a letter from Eliza Emmerson. She had written to Clare at his home address in the summer, asking him what he thought about the fact that there was now a young queen (Victoria) on the throne. After more than three months without a reply, she heard a rumour that he was in the York asylum—an understandable error, given Allen's previous connection with that institution. Frederick replied on behalf of the family, with the news that his father's health was improving and that he was particularly benefiting from his walks in the forest. Eliza's own health was so poor that several months passed before she wrote again. When she did, in April 1838, she said that Taylor had told her that Clare was continuing to improve and that she had donated five pounds towards a subscription that was being raised to pay for medical care. This is the last we hear from Clare's most intimate and indefatigable correspondent. She probably died soon afterwards.

At the end of 1839, Matthew Allen certified that his patient was still insane, but reported to his publishers that he was 'improved and improving—In appearance wonderfully stout and Rosy—and in Spirits the very reverse—all life and fun—He now works'. An entry in Clare's notebook makes it clear that in his latter years at Allen's he did indeed undertake gardening and fieldwork, for which he was paid a few shillings per week.

A further report was sent to Taylor and his new partner, James Walton, in the summer of 1840. Clare, now three years into his confinement, was 'in his best State', 'looking very well', 'his mind is not worse'. Around this time, due to some mix-up, a newspaper report announced the death of John Clare in the York asylum. Allen responded with a letter of correction that gives us the fullest picture we have of Clare's state of mind at High Beech:

> Sir,—I observe in *The Times* of yesterday that it is stated in the *Halifax Express* that the poet Clare died some months ago in the Lunatic Asylum at York.
>
> The Northamptonshire peasant poet, John Clare, is a patient in my establishment at Highbeach, and has been so since July, 1837. He is at present in excellent health, and looks very well, and is in mind, though full of very strange delusions, in a much more comfortable and happy state than he was when he first

came. He was then exceedingly miserable, every instant bemoaning his poverty, and his mind did not appear so much lost and deranged as suspended in its movements by the oppressive and permanent state of anxiety, and fear, and vexation, produced by the excitement of excessive flattery at one time and neglect at another, his extreme poverty and over-exertion of body and mind, and no wonder that his feeble bodily frame, with his wonderful native powers of mind, was overcome.

I had then not the slightest hesitation in saying that if a small pension could be obtained for him, he would have recovered instantly, and most probably remained well for life. I did all I could to obtain it for him, but without the slightest success. Indeed, some noblemen have withdrawn the pittance they allowed him, his wife, and family, and most are in arrears.

It is most singular that ever since he came, and even now at almost all times, the moment he gets pen or pencil in hand he begins to write most beautiful poetic effusions. Yet he has never been able to obtain in conversation, nor even in writing prose, the appearance of sanity for two minutes or two lines together, and yet there is no indication whatever of insanity in any of his poetry.

Whether a fickle public could be induced to subscribe to the publication of a selection of it, for the purpose of raising a sum to be sunk as a small annuity for himself and family, is a question that seems right for some one now to ask, and who can do it better than you! It might only require a small leaf of a tree of charity to heal his mind.

I shall feel obliged by your timely insertion of this, and remain,

Sir, yours obediently,   M. ALLEN, M.D.

Given his history, Dr Allen is not always to be trusted on financial matters. The purpose of the subscription to which Mrs Emmerson had contributed five pounds was to raise sufficient money to pay for Clare's maintenance at High Beech, not to provide an annuity for his family. Allen's proposal for a subscription edition of the asylum poetry was probably made with half an eye to his own fees. But the diagnosis of Clare's condition as, effectively, stress caused by poverty was both enlightened and astute.

The *Athenaeum* picked up on Allen's letter in *The Times* and put its weight behind 'a renewed appeal in behalf of the stricken poet'. A published selection of Clare's recent poems would be 'psychologically interesting'. With some tact, it also suggested that any arrears in payment on the part of his patrons was likely to be due to 'forgetfulness rather than unkindness'. In all probability, 'the malady by which the poet is lost to himself has caused him to pass from the memory of others'.

A new subscription scheme was duly launched, though not linked to a prospective volume of poetry. A leaflet was circulated with details of Clare's financial position: since interest rates were down to three and a half per cent, the trust fund now provided less than fourteen pounds a year, while the Marquis of Exeter was still paying fifteen pounds a year and Earl Spencer ten. The aim of the new subscription was to increase Clare's total annual income to sixty pounds a year. A capital sum of five hundred pounds would be needed. If this were to be found, 'it is confidently expected that the happy event of Clare's restoration to health, and to the society of his beloved wife and children, would soon be accomplished'. Despite a generous contribution from the Earl Fitzwilliam, fifty pounds from no less a personage than Adelaide the Queen Dowager, and a number of smaller contributions (including one from de Wint the painter), the donations fell far short of the required total.

Nothing was added to the trust fund. The money that had been raised disappeared into the hands of Dr Allen. He was busy with a new scheme. A month or two before Clare was escorted to Essex, a melancholy young poet called Alfred Tennyson had left his home in Lincolnshire and taken a house in the village of High Beech, a stone's throw from Allen's asylum. He brought several siblings with him, including his brother Septimus, who suffered from more severe depression and was soon admitted to Allen's as a voluntary patient (another Tennyson brother languished permanently in the York asylum). During the years of Clare's confinement, Alfred Tennyson himself spent several extended periods at Fair Mead, occupying a status somewhere between patient and house-guest. On one occasion when he was having lunch with Allen and some of the other patients, the doctor was called from the room. One of the patients brandished a dinner knife at Tennyson, stared at his monocle and asked, 'Why do you wear that glass thing in your eye?' To which Tennyson replied, 'Vanity, my dear Sir, sheer vanity', an answer that apparently defused the situation. We do not know whether Clare and Tennyson met within the confines of the asylum, but they were both regular walkers in the forest, so they are almost certain to have encountered each other—especially since they were both particular friends of another inmate, Thomas Campbell, son of the well-known poet of the same name.

In the autumn of 1840, at exactly the time when Allen was soliciting for money on behalf of Clare, he persuaded Tennyson to give him a thousand pounds, with the promise of a further two thousand on the winding up of grandfather Tennyson's estate, as capital investment in a scheme to develop a steam-powered wood-carving machine for the purposes of home decoration. Allen initially christened his device a 'Pyroglyph', but later changed the name to 'The Patent Method of Carving in Solid Wood'. The security on Tennyson's investment consisted of an insurance policy on Allen's life, a bond and the mortgage of Fair Mead. Matthew Allen was so persuasive a salesman—or Alfred so gullible in his depression—that three of the Tennyson sisters put up a further four thousand pounds between them. The scheme was, needless to say, a disaster that bankrupted both Dr Allen and almost the entire Tennyson family. Clare had left the asylum by the time of the financial collapse, which no doubt hastened Allen's death (he had a sudden heart attack in 1845), but there is little doubt that the money which the Queen Dowager and others intended for the Northamptonshire Peasant Poet was swallowed up by his doctor's doomed entrepreneurial venture.

Dr Allen's letter to *The Times* describes Clare's condition at the time of entering the asylum as more akin to mental exhaustion than actual derangement. The implication seems to be that during his three years at High Beech his morale had improved even as his delusions had become more severe. Allen's most curious claim is that, in contrast to the beauty and clarity of the poetry that he was still writing, Clare could not maintain 'the appearance of sanity for two minutes or two lines together' in his conversation or his prose.

Yet in a letter to Patty, probably belonging to 1840, Clare asserts his own sanity: 'I can prove that I am sensible', he says, before continuing with absolute cogency and deep feeling:

> You can claim me away from this place as your husband, the same as I was when I left you, with honest and good intention to return to my home and family in a day or two. Since then, months have elapsed, and I am still here, away from them, enduring all the miseries of solitude—which every married man must feel, through years of absence and confinement from his own home and family. Take every kind wish from me for your health and happiness, and for a father's love to your children, who ever wishes them well and happy.

This letter has a special poignancy because it offers the only hint we have of Clare's feelings as he was taken from home back in 1837. He honestly thought that he would not be away for long.

Though Allen was wrong about the insanity of the prose, he was right about the sanity of Clare's verse at this time. Few poems survive from the years 1838 to 1840, but those that do bear out Allen's assertion of its clarity and beauty. Allen himself preserved a delicate lyric about a cottage on his estate and 'a sweet Nurse' whom Clare 'used to admire'. A young artist who went sketching in the forest met the poet on his rambles 'and formed such an intimacy with him that Clare would often hand him bits of his pencilings'. He emigrated to California, taking the fragments with him. They were published in a magazine out there in 1873, though the original manuscripts subsequently perished in a house fire. The best of them aches with loss but bears no trace of derangement:

> I long to forget them—the love of my life—
> To forget them, and keep this lorn being my own;

The honey is cell'd in such changeable strife,
   I long to keep sorrow and trouble my own—
To live in myself, and to be what I am,
   And to leave earth's delusions and shadows behind,
Where love may not cheat, nor its happiness damn:
   The shadows of hope I with nature may find.

O, bear me away from this changeable strife,
   To the childhood of nature, the linnet and bee!
Let her flowers be my children, her freedom my wife,
   Where God, my Creator, is constant and free.
The flower on the white bush, the nest in the ground,
   Which my own happy childhood once shouted to find;
Let me live in those scenes, with the wind blowing round,
   And I shall be happy to bear it in mind,

To think of the joys of that once-happy spot
   Where I lived with my children the whole summer long—
The mother, the garden, the books and the cot,
   The theme and affection of many a song . . .

A further twenty lyrics were published in a magazine called the *English Journal*, among them a poem in honour of Wordsworth and several fine sonnets on Clare's forest walks in the company of his fellow-inmates (including 'friendly CAMPBELL', the poet's son).

In both poetry and prose, the few writings that survive from Clare's first three years at Allen's exude a surprising calmness. They constitute the lull before the storm of 1841.

For a period of several weeks that spring, he capitalised every word he wrote. This oddity of orthography is one of only two signs of mental disturbance in a letter to Patty written in March. Clare acknowledged receipt of a letter from the family, written by one of his boys (probably the oldest, Frederick, now seventeen). The incoming letter had contained an affectionate reference to the 'brothers and sisters'. Clare took this as an assurance that all his children continued to 'Love One Another As They Ever Have Done'. He then described Essex as

'A Very Pleasant County' but complained that, as the old saying had it, 'There Is No Place Like Home'. 'For What Reason They Keep Me Here', he continued, 'I Cannot Tell For I Have Been No Otherwise Than Well A Couple Of Years At The Least And Never Was Very Ill Only Harrassed By Perpetual Bother'. He had been well so long that he professed to have forgotten he was ever otherwise. The thought of his confinement led him to mention 'Mock Friends And Real Enemies'—in the circumstances, hardly a statement suggestive of wild paranoia. He longs to be home; he has had three separate dreams about his three boys. In one of them he was 'In A Wrack' with William (who always remained the most difficult son).

The second mark of strangeness is the twist in the letter's tail: Clare sends his love to the dear boy who wrote to him and also 'To Her Who Is Never Forgotten'.

Around the same time, he drafted in his notebook a letter to her who is never forgotten: 'My Dearest Mary / As This Will Be My Last Letter To You Or Any One Else—Let My Stay In Prison Be As Long Or As Short As It May—I Will Write To You And My Dear Patty In The Same Letter'. In May or June, he did as promised and wrote to both Mary and Patty in the same letter. He has been gripped by the belief that he has two wives:

> My dear Wife Mary
>
> I might have said my first wife and first love and first every thing—but I shall never forget my second wife and second love for I loved her once as dearly as yourself—and almost do so now so I determined to keep you both forever—and when I write to you I am writing to her at the same time and in the same letter—God bless you both and forever and both your familys also—I still keep writing though you do not write to me for if a man has a wife and I have two—but I tell it in a couplet with variations as my poetry has been the worlds Horn book for many years—so here it is
>
> > 'For if a husband will not let us know
> > 'That he's alive—he's dead—or may be so'

No one knows how sick I am of this confinement possessing two wives that ought to be my own and cannot see either one or the other—if I was in prison for felony I could not be served worse than I am—wives used to be alowed to see their husbands any-where—religion forbids their being parted but I have not even religion on my side and more's the pity—I have been rather poorly I might say ill for 8 or 9 days before haymaking and to get my self better I went a few evenings on Fern hill and wrote a new Canto of 'Child Harold' and now I am better I sat under the Elm trees in old Mathews Homestead Leppits hill where I now am— 2 or 3 evenings and wrote a new canto of Don Juan—merely to pass the time away but nothing seems to shorten it in the least and I fear I shall not be able to wear it away—nature to me seems dead and her very pulse seems frozen to an iceicle in the summer sun—what is the use of shutting me up from women in a petty paltry place as this merely because I am a married man and I dare say though I have two wives if I got away I should soon have a third and I think I should serve you both right in the bargain by doing so for I dont care a damn about comeing home now—so you need not flatter yourselves with many expections of seeing [me] nor do I expect you want to see me or you would have con-trived to have done it before now

—My dear Mary take all the good wishes from me as your heart can feel for your own husband and kiss all your dear fam-ily for their abscent father and Pattys childern also and tell Patty that her husband is the same man as he was when she married him 20 years ago in heart and good intentions—God bless you both and your familys also—I wish you both to keep in good health and be happy as I shall soon be when I have the good luck to be with you all at home once again—the love I have for you my dear Mary was never altered by time but always increased by abscence

I am my dear Mary your affectionate husband   John Clare

Mary is no longer just a symbol of the past, a muse of creativity and an imagined guardian angel. When Clare writes of 'possessing two wives' and when he tells Mary to kiss her children 'for their abscent father', he has passed into the realm of delusion.

Or has he? We cannot be certain that he wrote the letter with the intention of sending it. It is in his notebook, woven in among the poems that make up his 'Child Harold'. There are two drafts. Is it perhaps a literary composition, even a self-conscious trying on of the role of madman? In what Clare calls his 'confinement' he is equally in love with, and equally cut off from, both Patty and Mary, his real wife and his imaginary one, so there is a sense in which the fiction of the two wives is a way of telling a deep truth.

Whether fiction or delusion, the letter is full of authentic passion: pain of absence from his family, the sense that his beloved nature seems dead, understandable sexual frustration—the defiant talk of taking a third wife is the voice of a man of strong sex drive who has not lain with a woman for four years. Clare says that he has started writing 'Child Harold' and 'Don Juan' to get himself better. Fantasy, like poetry, may be therapeutic: like the Byronic poems, the letters to his long-lost Mary may have been not so much symptoms of delusion as forms of self-treatment.

On several occasions during his time at Dr Allen's, Clare would see a girl and write a poem about her. On Easter Monday 1841, he scribbled down a 'Note for "Child Harold" '. 'At The Easter Hunt I Saw A Stout Tall Young Woman Dressed In A Darkish Flowerd Cotton Gown As A Milkmaid Or Farm Servant And Stood Agen Her For Some Minutes Near A Small Clump Of Furze—I Did Not Speak To Her But I Now Wish I Had And Cannot Forget Her—Then I Saw Another Get Out Of A Gig With A Large Scotch Shawl On And A Pretty Face.' He is watching and desiring. Sex is on his brain and that is one reason why he begins identifying with Lord Byron. Another note to himself, written the previous day, is signed 'Byron' and between the two notes he writes, then crosses out, a cryptic fragment linking the name of Byron to Springfield, the house where Dr Allen's female patients lived:

Boxer Byron
made of Iron, alias
Box-iron
At Spring-field.

Boxing was also on his brain. For all the liberality of Dr Allen's regime, the asylum was inevitably a violent place; we have seen hints of this in the matter of Allen versus Dutton and when the patient raised his knife to Tennyson. The persona of the pugilist became Clare's stance of defiance in this tough milieu. On May Day he wrote into his notebook 'Jack Randalls Challange To All The World':

> Jack Randall The Champion Of The Prize Ring Begs Leave To Inform The Sporting World That He Is Ready To Meet Any Customer In The Ring Or On The Stage To Fight For The Sum Of £500 Or £1000 Aside A Fair Stand Up Fight half Minute Time Win Or Loose—he Is Not Particular As To Weight Colour Or Country—All He Wishes Is To Meet With A Customer Who Has Pluck Enough To Come To The Scratch   Jack Randall

Randall was only five feet six inches tall, tiny for a boxer. Born within a year of Clare, he was renowned as 'The architect of his own fame—he is a pugilist from nature, perfectly self-taught': a fitting role-model for Clare the self-taught poet.

A few days after Clare penned Jack Randall's challenge, he was visited by Cyrus Redding, a literary editor, wine connoisseur and friend of the poet Thomas Campbell. On arriving at the asylum, Redding and a fellow-visitor were informed that Clare was working in an adjacent field, accompanied by four or five other patients. They saw him standing slightly apart from the others, busy with a hoe, and smoking. Redding's companion had met Clare before, possibly on one of his trips to London. He was surprised how much weight Clare had put on and how he was no longer 'attenuated and pale of complexion'. No longer the image of the rarefied poet, he was now 'a little man, of muscular frame and firmly set, his complexion fresh and forehead high, a nose somewhat aquiline, and long full chin'.

Clare answered all the questions put to him 'in a manner perfectly unembarrassed'. He smiled as he remarked upon the quality of the ground he was hoeing. Then he talked about the difference between the wooded hills of Epping and the flatlands of the fen. He 'spoke of his loneliness away from his wife, expressing a great desire to go home, and to have the society of women'. He said that his only solace was his pipe and that he wanted books. 'On being asked what books, he said BYRON.' His visitors promised to send him the works of the noble poet.

'The principal token of his mental eccentricity', Redding continued his report of the visit,

> was the introduction of prize-fighting, in which he seemed to imagine he was to engage; but the allusion was made to it in the way of interpolation in the middle of the subject on which he was discoursing, brought in abruptly, and abandoned with equal suddenness, and an utter want of connection with any association of ideas which it could be thought might lead to the subject at the time; as if the machinery of thought were dislocated, so that one part of it got off its pivot, and protruded into the regular workings; or as if a note had got into a piece of music which had no business there.

The delusion about prize-fighting is presented here as a momentary aberration, almost an endearing eccentricity, rather than a mark of deep-seated madness. Later, back in London, Cyrus Redding spoke to Dr Allen about Clare. Allen expressed the view that 'Clare's mind was so slightly affected that he thought it might be as well if he were at home with his friends, and perhaps better for him'. Redding himself was convinced that if only Clare had financial stability, he would be relieved of the 'care for his subsistence' that was 'the main cause of his present mental hallucination'.

If Allen really believed that Clare might have been better off at home, he probably did not take too much trouble to tell his staff to keep an eye on this particular inmate during his walks in the forest. One Sunday, a couple of months after Redding's visit, Clare was feeling very melancholy. He went for an afternoon walk in the forest, where he met some gypsies who offered to help him escape from the madhouse by hiding him in their camp. He almost accepted, explaining that he had no money to start with, but that he could promise a future payment of fifty pounds. The gypsies—perhaps from the

Smith tribe, who regularly camped in the forest—agreed that they would expect him within a week.

Clare walked to the encampment again the following Friday. The gypsies seemed less keen, so he said little about the plan. Two days later Clare went again. The gypsies had gone. All they had left behind was 'an old wide awake hat and an old straw bonnet of the plum-pudding sort'. He put the hat in his pocket, thinking it might come in handy.

On the Monday he did nothing. Then on Tuesday 20 July 1841 he reconnoitred the route out of the forest that the gypsies had indicated. He set off through Ponders Green, but missed the lane that led into Enfield town. He walked on down the public highway, past a pub called The Labour in Vain. Someone he knew (possibly the publican, a Mrs King) happened to be coming out of the door. Clare asked the way and was pointed towards Enfield. From there, he could pick up the Great York Road where it would be 'all plain sailing and steering ahead, meeting no enemy and fearing none'.

In his pocket he carried a little notebook inscribed 'John Clare's Poems / Feby 1841'. It contained the extraordinary poems that he had been drafting in the months immediately prior to his escape: 'Child Harold', 'Don Juan', 'Hebrew Melodies' and a variety of fragments.

'I awoke', Lord Byron supposedly said with regard to the publication of his *Childe Harold's Pilgrimage* in 1812, 'to find myself famous'. The subject of the poem itself was, among many other things, immortality: 'I twine / My hopes of being remembered in my line / With my land's language.' For Clare, Byron was always the incarnation of poetic fame—and the glamour of *amour*.

At first sight, the life of Byron appears to be an inverse parallel to that of Clare: the lord versus the peasant, the short life versus the long, the cynical versus the romantic, the sane versus the mad, the promiscuous versus the one great love, the cosmopolitan versus the local, the famous versus the neglected. Look deeper, though, and strange similarities become apparent: they both loathed cant and hypocrisy in all forms; Byron was a depressive; Clare was more

promiscuous than the vision of Mary seems to allow; Clare was sometimes a satirist and Byron often a poet of the romantic sublime; Clare
was grounded in his locality but he occasionally dreamed of elsewhere—in particular of Scotland, Byron's childhood home and the
origin of Clare's paternal grandfather. Clare spoke of poetry as his
place of freedom. Freedom-fighter Byron was *the* poet of the age. Is
it any wonder, then, that impersonation of Byron became Clare's
spiritual way out of what he called the 'prison' of the asylum?

He seems to have devoured the package of books sent to him by
Cyrus Redding, and then set about lending copies of Byron's poems to
various women he met on his wanderings around the Epping Forest.
He scribbled a list of 'Books Lent' in the margin of a newspaper: Mrs
Pratt, wife of one of Allen's labourers, had his *Childe Harold*, Mrs
Fish's daughter at a nearby pub called the Owl had *Don Juan* and
English Bards and Scotch Reviewers, while *Hours of Idleness* was in
the hands of Mrs King at the pub on the Enfield highway. Did he
press *Don Juan* upon Miss Fish at the Owl with the intention of softening her up for seduction? Clare knew, not least from a *London
Magazine* article called 'Personal Character of Lord Byron', that Byron was assumed to have gone into exile abroad due to either 'the licentiousness of *Don Juan* or for vices either practised or suspected . . .
there was scarcely a passion which he had not tried'. Byron and sex
had become synonymous.

Clare's 'Child Harold' and 'Don Juan' are carefully contrived imitations of their respective Byronic originals. The former follows Byron's use of the nine-line stanza-form of Spenser's *Faerie Queene*,*
whilst the latter is in *Don Juan*'s rapid *ottava rima* replete with outrageous rhymes. Clare's 'Child Harold' is predominantly lyrical, as
was *Childe Harold's Pilgrimage*, whereas his 'Don Juan' is wholly
satirical and so true to just one dimension of Byron's multi-faceted
mock epic. In both poems, Byron interspersed lyrical songs among
his stanzas of narrative verse. Clare developed this technique and

---

*Though, unlike Spenser and Byron, Clare does not always lengthen the final
line of each stanza to an alexandrine.

made his 'Child Harold' into a veritable compendium of songs. The poem kept on growing and he never finished organising it into a coherent structure.

Whereas Byron's Mediterranean journeys gave shape to his 'pilgrimage', the directionlessness of Clare's life in the asylum dissolved his response into fragments. The stanzas of 'Child Harold' are despairing one moment:

> My Mind Is Dark And Fathomless And Wears
> The Hues Of Hopeless Agony And Hell ...

And defiant the next:

> Plain Honesty Still Is The Truth Of My Song
> And I'll Still Stick For Right To Be Out Of The Wrong
> The Honest And True My Example Shall Be
> For While A Man's Honest His Conscience Is Free.

The poem is a set of loose variations on Clare's great theme of 'love and home'. 'First love's dream' and 'memories of love' bring him freedom from the bondage of his High Beech 'prison'. The figure of Mary is invoked as the 'Essence' of the poet's 'hopes and fears and joys'. 'Love is the main spring of existance', writes Clare,

> —It
> Becomes a soul wherebye I live to love
> On all I see that dearest name is writ.

And yet in the very next stanza, there is a radical change of tone:

> My life hath been one love—no blot it out
> My life hath been one chain of contradictions
> Madhouses Prisons wh-re shops.

At this point, it is as if a stanza from Clare's 'Don Juan' has jumped over into his 'Child Harold'. His mind moves and his moods change at lightning speed.

Several of Clare's 'Child Harold' songs are lovely lyrics to Mary:

> Say What Is Love—What E'er It be
> It Center's Mary Still With Thee ...

and

> I saw her in my boyish hours
> A Girl as fair as heaven above
> When all the world seemed strewn with flowers
> And every pulse and look was love ...

She is the one great love and yet 'I have had many loves'. Mary's status as 'my dear first Love and early wife' does not stop 'Sweet Bessey' (Elizabeth Newbon?) being named shortly afterwards as the object of the first love and fond memory, or another sequence being included on the subject of Clare's courtship of Patty and his joy as he lay on the ground in her arms.

The 'two wives' theme of the draft letter to Mary Joyce is carried over into the poem: 'Where are my friends and childern where are they / The childern of two mothers born in joy / One roof has held them'. But the two wives are also made into symbolic figures: 'Mary and Martha once my daily guests / And still as mine both wedded love and blest'. In the Bible, of course, Mary represents untrammelled love while Martha is the dutiful housewife.

Probably the last addition made to 'Child Harold' before Clare's departure from the asylum was a lyric written in a thunderstorm on 15 July 1841. It captures the contradictions of his mental state. On the one hand, the desolation of depression:

> My soul is apathy—a ruin vast
> Time cannot clear the ruined mass away
> My life is hell—the hopeless die is cast
> And manhoods prime is premature decay ...

And on the other, the endurance of love ('I live in love, sun of undying light') and the freedom of poetic creation:

> Smile on ye elements of earth and sky
> Or frown in thunders as ye frown on me
> Bid earth and its delusions pass away
> But leave the mind as its creator free.

He is moving here towards the vein that would characterise the best poems of his final period.

Byron's *Childe Harold* had also been a poem that evolved over a number of years: the first two cantos were published in 1812, the third four years later and the last two years after that. In the interim, Byron published a number of other works, including *Hebrew Melodies*. A young Jewish composer named Isaac Nathan had asked if he could set some of his poems to music. Byron was prompted to write some lyrics 'on the sacred model—partly from Job etc. and partly my own imagination'. Nathan's settings were, Byron told his wife, '*real old undisputed Hebrew melodies*, which are beautiful and to which David and the prophets actually sang the "songs of Zion" '. The lavishly produced *Hebrew Melodies*, containing both words and music, was highly successful; Clare knew the lyrics from the reprinted text in his various editions of Byron's complete works. Some of the poems are indeed versifications of Old Testament laments such as 'By the Rivers of Babylon We Sat Down and Wept', whilst others are entirely secular—the collection opened with the famous 'She Walks in Beauty like the Night', a song inspired by the sight of Byron's lovely cousin wearing a black mourning gown covered in spangles.

Biblical lamentations appealed to Byron's own depressive tendency as well as to his fascination with the culture of ordinary people in ancient times. The *Hebrew Melodies* were a model for Clare not only because of his obsession with Byron but also because in the asylum he felt that he was himself in captivity like the Jews in Babylon. He was probably also aware of another precedent for the creation of such a work at such a time. When he opened his *London Magazine* back in March 1820, he would have found that John Scott's review of his *Poems Descriptive of Rural Life and Scenery* was the second of the 'Critical Notices of New Books'. The first was a review, also by Scott, of a new edition of *Song to David*, 'by the late Christopher Smart'. This poem, Scott explained, was composed by Smart

> while mental derangement rendered it necessary to confine him in a mad-house; and it is [said] that, being denied materials for writing, he scratched the words on the wainscot with the end of a key ... It bears, however, internal evidence of its birthplace; or at least, that its author was 'of imagination all com-

pact.' Shakespeare describes the quality as the characteristic of three classes of men and we take it that Smart's claim to be ranked in two of these (that of the lunatic and the poet), is established by this work.

Like many of Clare's works, Smart's poem was temporarily lost and only recovered after his death through the efforts of dedicated editors. The *Song to David* anticipates Clare in its allegiance to the Psalmist's vision in which 'all created things redound to the glory of God, and by displaying their beauty and perfection may figuratively be said to *adore* him'. Though it was with a nod to Byron that Clare described his biblical paraphrases of 1841 as 'Hebrew Melodies', their spirit is closer to Smart than Byron. He began with 'David's Lament' at the end of April, then wrote a 'Song of Deborah' based on a passage in the Book of Judges, and continued with the project over several months, adopting a variety of voices ranging from the despair of Job to the vision of the New Jerusalem in the Book of Revelation.

During the very same weeks that he was writing in this spiritual vein, Clare was also composing his most down-to-earth, angry, cynical, sexually charged poem: 'Don Juan'. ' "Poets are born" ', he begins, and then immediately undercuts himself in the exact manner of his Byronic original,

> —and so are whores—the trade is
> Grown universal—in these canting days
> Women of fashion must of course be ladies
> And whoreing is the business—that still pays
> Playhouses Ball rooms—there the masquerade is ...

Clare tells of frisky young married dames and of sex in both high society and low. He moves swiftly from 'there's such putting in—in whores crim con' to Prince Albert's departure for Germany, leaving behind Whig politicians such as Lord Melbourne to strum the 'snuff box' of 'little Vicky', the recently crowned Queen.

One stanza plays on oral sex in an explicit manner that not even Byron would have dared:

> Children are fond of sucking sugar candy
> And maids of sausages—larger the better
> Shopmen are fond of good sigars and brandy
> And I of blunt—and if you change the letter
> To C or K it would be quite as handy
> And throw the next away—but I'm your debtor
> For modesty—yet wishing nought between us
> I'd hawl close to a she as Vulcan did to venus.

Hawl close to means 'have sex with', whilst *blunt* is Regency slang for 'ready money', perhaps suggestive of cash to pay a whore—the effect of changing the *b* to a *c* and taking out the *l* does not need glossing. Throughout his 'Don Juan', Clare keeps returning to playhouses and prostitution. He seems to be guiltily remembering his nocturnal wanderings with Rippingille amongst 'the French actresses in Tottenham Court Road'.* The references to unorthodox sexual practices unavoidably summon up Rip's dirty recollections of Clare '*pleughing*' and 'swallowing the crab juice of another Darling'.

'I really can't tell what this poem will be / About', he continues, adopting the *I'm making it up as I go along* pose of Byron's *Don Juan*. Like its original, Clare's 'Don Juan' is partly a political poem. There is a running gag about 'old wigs', in punning reference to the Whig government, who were defeated in a parliamentary vote of no confidence at the beginning of June 1841 and roundly defeated in a general election at the end of the month. The poem also reflects newspaper gossip of the time concerning licentious goings-on in the court of the unpopular young Queen Victoria. Clare's frustration in the asylum is such that his writing moves vertiginously between sex and politics:

> But I have seen full many a bonny lass
> And wish I had one now beneath the cool
> Of these high elms—Muse tell me where I was
> O—talk of turning I've seen Whig and Tory
> Turn imps of hell—and all for Englands glory.

*Thomas De Quincey's phrase, with regard to Clare's taste for prostitutes (which he himself shared).

Whereas Byron's Don Juan is offered more sex than he knows what to do with, Johnny Clare can only fantasise that 'I have two wives and I should like to see them / Both by my side before another hour'.

Sometimes Clare sets up a contrast between himself and Byron: 'Though laurel wreaths my brows did ne'er environ / I think myself as great a bard as Byron'—a couplet that endorses its own argument through its wittily Byronic rhyme. At other times, the sexually triumphant Byron seems to enter Clare's disturbed mind and become his alter ego:

> Lord Byron poh—the man wot rites the werses
> And is just what he is and nothing more
> Who with his pen lies like the mist disperses
> And makes all nothing as it was before
> Who wed two wives and oft the truth rehearses
> And might have had some twenty thousand more
> Who has been dead so fools their lies are giving
> And still in Allens madhouse caged and living.

Parts of the poem are grounded in real time—'Now this day is the eleventh of July'—whilst also in the grip of a fantasy of double identity: 'Next tuesday used to be Lord Byron's birthday'. The following Tuesday, 13 July, was in reality John Clare's birthday. Exactly a week later he walked out of 'Allens madhouse' for the last time.

In the middle of this disturbing and misogynistic poem, Clare toasts the health of a certain 'sweet Eliza Phillips' and then inserts a lovely song in which he invites Eliza to wander through the summer forest with him. At the end of the poem he writes a letter to 'My dear Eliza Phillips', telling her that he has taken the liberty of dedicating his 'Don Juan' to her 'in remembrance of Days gone bye'. He says that it is well known that he is a prize-fighter by profession, but that since he is 'cooped up in this Hell of a Madhouse' there is nobody to accept his challenges. 'I am almost mad in waiting for a better place and better company and all to no purpose', he adds. 'I do not much like to write love letters but this which I am now writing to you is a true one—you know that we have met before and the first oppertunity that offers we will meet again'.

Like the address to his 'two wives' in the same notebook, the letter to Eliza Phillips may best be read not as a letter intended for posting but as part of the poem, a formal dedication analogous to the stanzas addressed to 'Ianthe' (thirteen-year-old Charlotte Harley) that Byron prefixed to his *Childe Harold*. Who, then, was the sweet Eliza to whom Clare wished to dedicate his sour 'Don Juan'? She may have been one of the local girls he met whilst out on his forest walks, but the main thrust of the poem is disgust at the darker side of life *within* the asylum:

> Theres Docter Bottle imp who deals in urine
> A keeper of state prisons for the queen
> As great a man as is the Doge of Turin
> And save in London is but seldom seen
> Yclept old A-ll-n——mad brained ladies curing
> Some p-x-d like Flora and but seldom clean
> The new road oer the forest is the right one
> To see red hell and further on the white one
>
> Earth hells or b-gg-r sh-ps or what you please
> Where men close prisoners are and women ravished
> I've often seen such dirty sights as these ...

Allen is called 'Dr Bottle-Imp' (a sprite who lives in a bottle) because of his practice of checking the colour and clarity of his patients' urine for diagnostic purposes: he believed that certain forms of insanity were related to kidney dysfunction.* 'Red hell' seems to be a reference to Springfield, the redbrick house for women patients; 'the white one' would then be stuccoed Leopard's Hill Lodge, where Clare himself was residing. The images of ladies driven mad by the pox, of 'dirty sights', 'women ravished' and 'b-gg-r sh-ps' suggest that—perhaps because Allen himself was 'seldom seen' in the summer of 1841, since he was frequently away in London, raising capital for his woodcarving scheme—some of the inmates were getting quite out of hand.

Bottle-Imp was sometimes used with reference to alcohol, so Clare may also be alluding to Allen's heavy drinking.

Could Eliza then have been a fellow-patient to whom Clare took a fancy? There was no Eliza Phillips among Allen's patients in 1841, but there was an Eliza Roberts (a young teacher from Caen in France, admitted a year after Clare), an Eliza Palmer (in her early thirties) and an Eliza Rackshaw (a former governess). A Mary Jane Frances Phillips was admitted on 30 June, at exactly the time when Clare was writing 'Don Juan'. Could it be that, rather as he fantasised about Mary and Martha as his 'two wives', he conflated this Miss Phillips with one of the asylum's three Elizas?

However enlightened the ideals of Dr Bottle-Imp may have been, by the summer of 1841 the asylum had become John Clare's hell. Among the fragments in his High Beech notebook is a poem that begins in disgust at the sexual perversion practised in the asylum and—no small matter for a tobacco addict—anger at the theft of some snuff. The poem ends with a turn from bad company to a prayer for the two women and the beloved children to whom Clare longed to return:

> Nigh Leopards hill stand All-ns hells
> The public know the same
> Where lady sods and buggers dwell
> To play the dirty game
>
> A man there is a prisoner there
> Locked up from week to week
> He's very fond they do declare
> To play at hide and seek
>
> With sweethearts so they seem to say
> And such like sort of stuff
> Well—one did come the other day
> With half a pound of snuff
>
> The snuff went here the snuff went there
> And is not that a bad house
> To cheat a prisoner of his fare
> In a well ordered madhouse

They'll cheat you of your money friend
By takeing too much care o't
And if your wives their cun-ys send
They're sure to have a share o't

Now where this snuff could chance to stop
Perhaps gifts hurded are up
Till Mat and steward open shop
And have a jolly flare up

God almighty bless Mary Joyce Clare and her family
now and forever—Amen
God almighty bless Martha Turner Clare and her family
now and forever—Amen
Our Father etc.

CHAPTER TWENTY

JOURNEY FROM ESSEX

Walking west from Enfield Town, Clare joined the Great York Road, on which the mail-coaches thundered north and south at regular intervals. A brisk walk of about twenty-five miles took him without incident to Stevenage by nightfall. He climbed over a gate into a paddock. His legs were so 'knocked up' that he was afraid he might collapse into the pond in the corner of the field. By scaling some old rotten palings he made his way into a shed where he slept on a pile of clover trusses.

He slept deeply but had a disturbing dream: 'I thought my first wife lay on my left arm and somebody took her away from my side which made me wake up rather unhappy—I thought as I awoke somebody said "Mary" but nobody was near.' All that night he lay with his head towards the north so that he would know in which direction to walk in the morning.

Afraid of being discovered in the shed, he moved on at first light. Back on the road, he continued north. He hailed a man and a boy who were sleeping under a bank at the verge; they woke and told him that the next village was Baldock. A man on horseback in a loose slop-coat passed him and said, 'Here's another of the broken down haymakers', throwing him a penny for a half-pint of beer. Clare picked it up, thanked him, and went into a roadside pub called the Plough. The

DRAFT OF 'CHILD HAROLD' IN POCKET NOTEBOOK

TAKEN ON THE JOURNEY FROM ESSEX

drink and the shelter saved him from a heavy shower of rain. He was fairly lucky with the weather: on the first two days of his walk there were just occasional showers and on the latter two it was dry and not too hot.

On leaving the Plough he thought of begging another penny off two drovers, but they were 'very saucey' so he decided not to beg any more. As he walked through the morning, he seemed to pass the mileposts very quickly, but by evening each seemed further apart than the last. Somewhere beyond Baldock he paused for half an hour in a shady spot, but had nothing to eat.

Late in the evening he took a detour from the main road and passed through the village of Potton. He knocked on a door to ask for a light for his pipe. The occupants—an old woman, a young man and a 'young country wench making lace on a cushion as round as a globe'—received him with civility, but either did not hear properly or were unwilling to answer when he inquired after the whereabouts of the clergyman and the parish overseer. After setting off, he fell into conversation with a countryman who told him that the parson (or perhaps it was the overseer) lived some distance away. So he gave up on the idea of going to a figure in authority, giving his name and begging for a shilling that would buy him a ride home. He was hobbling now: the gravel had got into his old shoes, one of which had nearly lost its sole.

He asked the countryman whether there might be a shed with dry straw nearby, where he could spend the night. The man suggested the yard of a pub called the Ram, and offered to accompany him there. Clare's feet were so painful that he needed to rest before moving on. His companion lingered for a while, 'and then suddenly reccolecting that he had a hamper on his shoulder and a lock-up bag in his hand cram full to meet the coach which he feared missing—he started hastily and was soon out of sight'.

Clare couldn't find the straw bed, so he lay down to spend the second night of the journey in the open air, nestling in a gap between the wall of a shed and a row of elms. But the wind whipped between the trees and he was too cold to sleep. He hobbled on in search of the Ram, night falling fast, candles through windows making the tenants inside seem cosy. When he got to the pub, its lighted windows looked very cheering but, having no money, he dared not go in. And with people still around he decided not to risk the shed. So he walked on along the empty road. At times it was pitch black, overshadowed by trees. He came to a place where there were two turnpike roads, one to the right and the other straight on. Having glimpsed a milestone under a hedge, he turned back to read it, in order to see where the other road led. It said 'London'. Suddenly he was confused: he had forgotten which way was north and which south. In the dark he was no longer sure of any landmarks that he had passed; he walked on for miles, half thinking that he was merely retracing his steps, now in the wrong direction. The thought almost paralysed him, but he made himself shuffle on.

At last he saw 'a lamp shining as bright as the moon'. It marked the tollgate at Temsford, a village about four miles beyond Potton. The toll-keeper came out with a candle and eyed him suspiciously. Without fear, Clare asked whether he was heading northward. 'When you get through the gate you are', said the man. Cheered, he picked up his pace and began humming the tune of 'Highland Mary' as he went. It was very late now. He came to a big house, isolated near a wood. He thought he could hear the occupants creaking in their bed. He crept into the porch and slept there till daylight. Last thing before sleeping and first thing on waking he blessed his 'two wives' and their families. He had covered another twenty-five miles and was now close to St Neots.

On the Thursday, he took a morning rest, sitting on a flint heap just south of Buckden. It was here that he took out his notebook and wrote in an unsteady hand, describing himself as 'The man whose daughter is the queen of England'. His sense of time was becoming confused: he noted that he had been without food 'since yesterday morning—when he was offerd a bit of Bread and cheese at Enfield', but that had been two mornings ago. A full forty-eight hours had passed since he had eaten, so it is hardly surprising that his mind was wandering. The reference to the Queen may have been animated by misogynistic distaste for the royal succession having gone through the female line (an objection noted by someone who visited him a few years later). It may also allude at some level to the salacious gossip about Victoria that he had been reading in the newspaper and working into his poem 'Don Juan'—he had an old *Morning Chronicle* in his pocket. Or perhaps there is some confused memory of the donation that the Queen Dowager had made to the appeal on his behalf: some weeks later, he would write to Matthew Allen about the latter: 'you told me somthing before haytime about the Queen alowing me a yearly sallary of £100 and that the first quarter had then commenced or else I dreamed so',

A gypsy girl came past as he sat on his stone heap by the roadside. They exchanged a few words 'with evident good humour' and then walked together to the next village. She cautioned Clare to put something in his hat 'to keep the crown up', then said in a lower tone, 'You'll be noticed'. He didn't know what she meant. Presumably he was wearing the gypsy hat that he had found in the Epping Forest; it was probably too big for him. She pointed out a short cut along a footpath towards Offord Church (in writing up his journey, Clare misremembered the name as 'Shefford', which was Bloomfield's village). He trusted her but did not trust himself to find the main road again, so didn't take the path.

The remainder of the third day passed in a daze of hunger and dehydration. From Buckden it was about fifteen miles to Stilton. Clare remembered almost nothing of this part of the journey. Once when he was resting a coach stopped in the hollow just behind him, but he had no recollection of its restarting and going past. He satisfied his hunger 'by eating the grass by the road side which seemed to taste something like bread'. It felt like the best meal he had ever had. He seems to have spent some of the third night lying in the ditch at the bottom of a roadside dyke, though when he awoke and found himself soaked to the skin he decided that the best thing was to walk on through the darkness.

On the fourth and final day, he remembered that he had his pipe. But his box of 'lucifers' was exhausted, so he could not light it. He took to chewing the tobacco and then swallowing it. This also helped with his hunger.

In Stilton, he nearly fell asleep on a gravel causeway. He heard a young woman say 'poor creature' and an older one reply that he was probably shamming—though when he got up, he was so lame from walking that she changed her mind. He did not look back. A little further on, at Norman Cross, the road divided. He met two young women and asked them whether the way to the right led to Peterborough. They told him it did, and he felt himself on home territory. He 'went on rather more cheerfull', but needed to take frequent rests.

Just before he got to Peterborough, a couple drove past in a cart. They hailed him. By happy coincidence they were former neighbours from Helpston. He told them that he had not eaten or drunk anything since leaving Essex. They clubbed together and threw him five pence from the cart. He picked up the money and went straight to the nearest pub, where he had 'two half pints of ale and twopenn-'oth of bread and cheese'. Refreshed, though more foot-foundered than ever, he headed on the last few miles through the villages of Walton and Werrington, where he saw a cart carrying a man, a woman and a boy. The woman jumped out and caught fast hold of his hands, telling him to get into the cart. He refused, thinking her either drunk or mad. But then he was told it was Patty. (Was her appearance a coincidence or had the people in the earlier cart sent word that Clare was on his way home?) He got in and they were soon at Northborough.

He did not, of course, find Mary waiting for him. Nor could he get any information about her other than an old newspaper story that she had died some years ago: 'but I took no notice of the blarney having seen her myself about a twelvemonth ago alive and well and as young as ever—so here I am homeless at home and half gratified to feel that I can be happy any where.'

He had not seen her. And she was dead. The newspaper report does not survive, but a death certificate does. Mary Joyce, forty-one years of age, 'Single Woman'. Died 14 July 1838 at Glinton (the day after

Clare's forty-fifth birthday, the first anniversary of his commitment to the asylum). Cause of death: 'Accidentally Burnt'. The coroner's inquest is lost, so we do not know the exact circumstances of the fire, but such disasters were very common in an age of candles, rushlights and open hearths. The local papers are full of stories such as the following account of the death of a Miss Dannatt in the nearby village of Caistor, a few months before Mary's equally fatal accident:

> She was up early in the morning of that day with another sister somewhat her senior to prepare for brewing; while doing something near the fire, a spark or cinder fell upon her dress, which being of cotton, was speedily in a flame. The poor girl in her fright ran upstairs—her sister ran for water—her friends from their beds almost in a state of nudity, and so completely horror-stricken were they all, that the proper measures, that of rolling or wrapping in some carpet, coat or rag, was not resorted to and the flames increased in violence, whilst her afflicted relatives in their said astonishment knew not what to do. The unfortunate young woman was so severely burnt that she died on the following day. She was 16 years of age. A coroner's inquest was held on the body and a verdict returned of 'accidental death'.

Clare may have been told about a similar report to this, describing Mary's death. But he resolutely refused to believe that she was gone.

After four years in the asylum, then a four-day walk of nearly a hundred miles, with three nights in the open air and more than seventy-two hours without anything to eat but grass, one would have expected Clare to spend his first evening back home having a good meal, cuddling his children, talking to his wife, and going to bed early. Yet such was his dedication to writing that on the very night of his homecoming he took out his little notebook once more. He wrote two songs for Mary, the first of which alludes specifically to his journey:

> I've wandered many a weary mile
> Love in my heart was burning

To seek a home in Mary's smile
But cold is love's returning
The cold ground was a feather bed
Truth never acts contrary
I had no home above my head
My home was love and Mary ...

And on the blank leaf over the page from the prayer 'God almighty bless Mary Joyce Clare and her family', he began an account of the journey itself, getting as far as the encounter with the countryman near Potton: 'July 23rd 41 Returned home out of Essex and found no Mary—her and her family are as nothing to me now though she herself was once the dearest of all—and how can I forget'.

The next day he started a fair copy of what he had written and tried to recollect what he could of the latter part of the journey. By the following Tuesday he had finished. As with the 'two wives' letter that accompanied 'Child Harold' and the address to 'Eliza Phillips' that went with 'Don Juan', he added a dedicatory epistle at the end:

To Mary Clare—Glinton
Northborough July 27 1841

My dear wife

    I have written an account of my journey or rather escape from Essex for your amusement and hope it may divert your leisure hours—I would have told you before now that I got here to Northborough last friday night but not being able to see you or to hear where you was I soon began to feel homeless at home and shall bye and bye feel nearly hopeless but not so lonely as I did in Essex—for here I can see Glinton church and feeling that Mary is safe if not happy, I shall be the same—I am gratified to believe so—though my home is no home to me my hopes are not entirely hopeless while even the memory of Mary lives so near me—God bless you My dear Mary—Give my love to your dear and beautiful family and to your Mother—and believe me as I ever have been and shall be

My dearest Mary
your affectionate Husband
John Clare

18 (ABOVE) Peter de Wint's frontispiece for
The Shepherd's Calendar, 1827, with a peasant
incongruously drinking from a barrel

19 (RIGHT) Bust of John Clare by Henry Behnes

20 (RIGHT) Allan Cunningham,
Scotsman, poet, editor and friend

21 (BELOW) The Northborough
cottage, with its garden:
frontispiece to *The Rural Muse*

THE POET'S COTTAGE.
NORTHBOROUGH.

View of Fair Mead House.

View of Leopard's Hill Lodge.

22 (TOP) Dr Allen's asylum at High Beech, Essex: Fair Mead,
which housed both male and female patients

23 (BOTTOM) Dr Allen's asylum: Leopard's Hill Lodge, which
housed more severely afflicted and 'incurable' patients

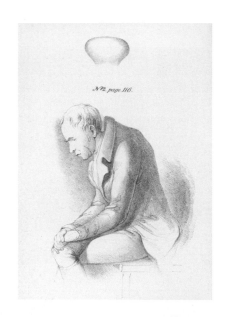

JACK RANDALL

24 (ABOVE LEFT) Elderly patient in an asylum, with a sketch of enlarged cranium thought to be characteristic of lunacy. Dr Allen noted that this patient's mind had 'sunk into a torpid state' but that when provoked he 'used indecent language': Clare had similar symptoms

25 (ABOVE RIGHT) The boxer: Jack Randall. From Pierce Egan's *Boxiana*

26 (LEFT) The poet: Lord Byron, 'the man wot rites the verses'. An engraving from a portrait by Richard Westall

27 (ABOVE) The Northampton
General Lunatic Asylum

28 (RIGHT) Clare at fifty,
in the asylum. A portrait
by Thomas Grimshaw

29 (ABOVE) Clare at fifty-five, in the portico of All Saints' Church, Northampton. A drawing by George Maine

30 (LEFT) Sketch of Clare in old age, by fellow patient G. D. Berry

31 (OPPOSITE) The only photograph of Clare, aged nearly seventy. Taken in 1862 by W. W. Law and Son; published in 1864 with the poet's signature

John Clare

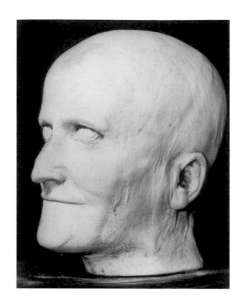

32 (TOP) Clare's death-mask

33 (BOTTOM) 'A poet is born not made':
the lichen-dappled grave in Helpston churchyard

The stubborn belief that Mary was still alive and still in some sense his wife could not have made the reunion with Patty at all easy. Clare's feelings about his real wife may perhaps be inferred from some stanzas that he added to his 'Don Juan' when he copied it into the new manuscript book that he had begun with the 'Journey from Essex':

> Marriage is nothing but a drivelling hoax
> To please old codgers when they're turned of forty
> I wed and left my wife like other folks
> But not until I found her false and faulty
> O woman fair—the man must pay thy jokes
> Such makes a husband very often naughty
> Who falls in love will seek his own undoing
> The road to marriage is—'the road to ruin'
>
> Love worse than debt or drink or any fate
> It is the damnest smart of matrimony
> A hell incarnate is a woman-mate
> The knot is tied—and then we lose the honey
> A wife is just the protetype to hate
> Commons for stock and warrens for the coney
> Are not more tresspassed over in rights plan
> Than this incumberance on the rights of man.

This is calumny and self-exculpation: there is no evidence that Patty was ever 'false', and what spouse is not sometimes 'faulty'? If Clare really did believe that a wife was just the prototype to hate, an incumbrance on the right of man to find sexual 'honey' wherever he can, then Patty would have had some justification in sending him away again.

At first, though, she seemed glad to have her husband home. Allen dispatched a man to try to persuade him to return to High Beech, 'but his Wife thought him so much better that she wished to try him for a while'. Allen informed John Taylor's business partner of this, adding, 'Should he not remain well I hope his friends will send him here rather than elsewhere, as I should feel hurt after the interest I have felt and do feel for him'. Dr Darling in London took the view that Clare might as well stay at home.

Whatever the exact nature of the split in Clare's mind, there is no doubt that by this time he had embodied his double attitude towards women into the split between damned Patty and divine Mary—for whom he dashed off two exquisite songs of love and loss at exactly the same time that he was inserting those vicious extra stanzas in 'Don Juan'. Over the next few months he continued to idealise the memory of Mary and the beauties of nature in extensive additions to 'Child Harold'. In variation upon variation he returned to the same theme: 'A lonely man I roam / And absent Mary long hath left / My heart without a home'; 'My heart my dear Mary from thee cannot part / But the sweetest of pleasure that joy can impart / Is nought to the memory of thee.' He also salved his soul with further biblical paraphrases. But Patty remained excluded from his writing world. When he wrote of 'thou partner of my life', he was addressing 'sweet solitude', not his wife.

For Clare, as for all poets in the Romantic tradition, writing was the place of remembering, of preserving what was lost: childhood, first love, moments of vision, glimpses of ordinary things made extraordinary by virtue of the attention bestowed upon them. Without the loss, there would have been no reason for the poetry. As Clare's admired Hazlitt wrote in one of his essays, it is 'distant objects' that please. Clare himself remarked in an early poetic 'simile' that women are like mushrooms in that they begin to lose their goodness the moment they peep out above the soil: 'they Seldom Get better by Keeping'. The likelihood is that if he had married Mary—or Betty or Susan or Eliza—his later poetry would have idealised his lost Patty. One of his last Northborough pencil jottings reads

> To live with others is not half so sweet
> as to remember thee
>   Mary

The sweetness belongs more to the very act of remembering than to Mary Joyce herself. So too, Clare's bitterness came as much from the very nature of marriage as from Patty's personal failings.

■

In the early autumn Clare wrote to Dr Allen. The actual letter is lost, but to judge from the draft—written round the margins and between the columns of a copy of the *Lincolnshire Chronicle and General Advertiser*—it was not exactly the kind of communication one would have expected an escaped 'lunatic' to send his former keeper. 'My dear Sir', he cordially begins, 'Having left the Forest in a hurry I had not time to take my leave of you and your family but I intended to write, and that before now, but dullness and dissapointment prevented me'. He gave some account of his journey and asked Allen to collect and forward the books (sent to him by Cyrus Redding) that he had left behind; apparently he had carried five volumes with him on the road, leaving six others—all Byrons—in the hands of his lady friends around the forest.

The letter ends with 'best respects' to Allen's family, to the other doctor in the establishment and to Clare's friends among his fellow-inmates at Leopard's Hill, including Thomas Campbell the poet's son. There is no animosity towards Allen, only resentment at the behaviour of certain members of his staff:

> I can be miserably happy in any situation and any place and could have staid in yours on the forest if any of my friends had noticed me or come to see me—but the greatest annoyance in such places as yours are those servants styled keepers who often assumed as much authority over me as if I had been their prisoner and not likeing to quarrel I put up with it till I was weary of the place altogether so I heard the voice of freedom and started.

The implication is that if Allen had moderated his more authoritarian 'keepers' and arranged for some visits from old friends, Clare might happily have remained in the Epping Forest, much as he missed his children.

The most revealing aspect of the letter to Allen is what Clare says about the women in his life. He refers to Patty as 'one of my fancys' and to Mary as 'my poetical fancy'. Clearly he had told Allen about his 'two wives': this suggests that there was considerable confidence between them, because the figure of 'Mary' was strikingly absent from Clare's conversation—whether as himself, as Byron, or as prize-fighter—with other people. Though he still wishes for Mary, and almost every song he writes has some sighs for her, he now seems reconciled to her death, about which he has heard from 'people in the neighbourhood'. He considers himself to have become 'a widow or bachellor I don't know which'. Astonishingly, he asks Allen to send his allowance from the Queen Dowager so that he can 'be independant and pay for board and lodging while I remain here'. He thus appears to be regarding Patty as landlady more than wife. 'Woman has long sickened me', he announces: all wives are 'faithless and deceitfull', the worst are the 'road to ruin' (the same proverbial phrase as in 'Don Juan') and even the best are less useful than 'a good Cow'. He wants only 'to be to myself a few years and lead the life of a hermit'.

Allen did not formally report Clare's escape to the asylum inspectors, as he should have done. When they met with him in October 1841, he recorded Clare as having been 'discharged' in a 'much improved' condition on 23 September. Then in November he replied to the letter, offering a mixture of solicitude, homily and self-justification: 'I am glad to find you think that I ever wished you to be made happy as possible and that it was not my fault if you were not always so, for wherever you are, you will find that this is not always in your own, still less in the power of another—much more depends on our selves than we are willing to admit'. 'Your account of your weary journey is painfully interesting', he added. 'Although hopes and some delicious feelings about freedom made you start and led you on, I am sorry to find all these dreams are not realized, but that you find something wrong where you are as well as here.' As for Clare's desire to 'lead the life of a Hermit', if he cared to return to High Beech, he would be given every facility to do so. There would be no charge for bed and board, and he would be free to go home whenever he chose; the only condition would be that he must do nothing to make himself 'unpleasant as a Visitor'. This sounds like a sincere offer of similar treatment to that which Allen provided for Tennyson.

■

Clare's solitary walks were still yielding him good poems. His eye for landscape and bird life remained as sharp as ever. A stroll through the late autumnal fens on St Martin's Day (11 November) was captured in two perfectly crafted stanzas:

> 'Tis martinmass from rig to rig
> Ploughed fields and meadow lands are blea
> In hedge and field each restless twig
> Is dancing on the naked tree
> Flags in the dykes are bleached and brown
> Docks by its sides are dry and dead
> All but the ivy bows are brown
> Upon each leaning dotterel's head
>
> Crimsoned with awes the awthorns bend
> O'er meadow dykes and rising floods
> The wild geese seek the reedy fen
> And dark the storm comes o'er the woods
> The crowd of lapwings load the air
> With buzzes of a thousand wings
> There flocks of starnels too repair
> When morning o'er the valley springs.

Blea is Northamptonshire dialect for *exposed*, an apt word for both the Northborough environment and Clare's own mental state. In the 'bleached' landscape, there is no place for him to nest; he is as 'restless' as the twigs on the naked branches of late autumn. One expects the poem to end with the birds making wing to the security of the wood at nightfall, like the crow watched by Macbeth as light thickens. But this is a breezy morning poem, in which the birds are taking to the air rather than returning to their nests. Everything is in flight.

His work in these months was fragmentary and disorganised. He added to 'Child Harold' without finding a shape for it. His notebooks are studded with isolated gems, in both verse and prose: 'Nature says "Mary" but my pen denies / To write the truth and so it lives in lies'; 'O would it were my lot / To be forgetfull as I am forgot' (acknowledged as a quotation from Byron); 'immense flock of starnels settled on an ash tree in the orchard and when they took wing it was like a roll of thunder'. His most sustained piece was a prose description of 'Autumn', written with the precision of observation that is his perpetual hallmark:

> solitary persons are sideing up the hedges and thrusting the brushwood in the thin places and creeps which the swine made from one ground or field into another and stopping gaps made in harvest by gleaners and labourers—the larks start up from the brown grass in the meadows where a couple of flutters and flights and drops out of sight as suddenly again into the grass . . . The rawky mornings now are often frosty—and the grass and wild herbs are often covered with rime as white as a shower of snow . . . there is a pair of harrows painted red standing on end against the thorn hedge and in another ground an old plough stands on its beam ends against a dotterel tree.

It was not until the twentieth century that other writers started noticing such ordinary things for their own sake. Those red harrows and the old plough could as well have been observed and valued by one of the great twentieth-century poets of what Gerard Manley Hopkins would call 'thisness'. One thinks of Edward Thomas's 'tall nettles' covering rusty harrow and 'plough long worn out', and indeed of William Carlos Williams's red wheelbarrow, upon which 'so much / depends'.

He felt isolated from the literary world. No one wrote, apart from kindly George Reid in Scotland. The dream of lost love was still haunting him: a poem called 'Anxiety' is juxtaposed to one that begins 'I love the name of woman', together with a letter draft addressed to 'My dear Mary Joyce Clare'.

The last entry in one of his pocket notebooks consists of an observation dated 12 December 1841, 'Found a Cowslip in Flower',* and

---

*This little notebook began with one of the few indications that Clare was sometimes accompanied by his children on his walks in these months: 'Oct' 19 1841—William found a Cowslip in flower' (William was thirteen by this time).

then three stanzas for Mary ending 'Thou'rt my own love for ever'. Another notebook comes to an abrupt halt with an incomplete fair copy of his versification of Isaiah, chapter 47, addressed to the daughters of Babylon. The rough draft from which he was working ends with the lines 'Though slave dealers take thee, though bondsmen enslave thee / There's none shall be able to shield thee or save thee'. His copying was interrupted by the summons to his own Babylon.

Parson Mossop had visited on a number of occasions during Clare's five months back home in Northborough. To begin with, he found Clare 'conversing agreeably', but 'the want of restraint soon generated conduct which became so alarming to his wife and family as to induce them to ask the aid of Earl Fitzwilliam'. Clare had become, in Mossop's words, 'a stranger to his own family'. The reference to 'want of restraint' and 'alarming' conduct suggests that he may well have become violent. His noble patron accordingly took matters in hand. The superintendent of the newly built public asylum in Northampton had in fact written to Fitzwilliam the previous year with the suggestion that Clare could be maintained there at less expense and with greater ease of access than at Allen's private institution down in Essex. Now Fitzwilliam made the necessary arrangements.

On 28 December 1841, Fenwick Skrimshire, this time together with William Page, surgeon of Market Deeping, certified Clare's insanity for the second time. The following day he was admitted to the Northampton General Lunatic Asylum.

CHAPTER TWENTY-ONE

AMONG THE BABYLONIANS

The asylum admission papers included a series of questions in-tended to assist in the 'endeavour to elucidate the nature and causes of Insanity'. Skrimshire provided the answers to most of them. Age? Forty-nine. Usual employment? Gardening. Married? Twenty-two years. Children? Seven. Supposed causes of insanity? Hereditary. Was the insanity preceded by any severe or long-continued mental emotion or exertion? 'After years addicted to poetical prosing.'* Did it succeed any serious illness or accident affecting the nervous system? No. How long since symptoms of aberration were first detected? Fourteen years. Was this the first distinct attack? 'Has had several.' When was the existing attack first noticed? Four years ago. Does any constitutional or hereditary predisposition exist in the family of the Patient to maniacal, nervous or scrofulous affections? 'Yes, as above.' Does the Patient labour under any epileptic, paralytic, contagious or other bodily disorders? No. Has the patient attempted or threatened violence to self or others? No. Is the patient idiotic, mischievous or

---

*Skrimshire's spelling was *prossing*. 'To talk or write in a tedious manner, to chat or gossip' was a new (late eighteenth-century) sense of the verb *to prose*; Skrimshire seems to be emphasising Clare's prolixity. A practical man, he probably found all poetry tedious.

dirty? No. Any previous confinement? 'Allens Asylum High Beach Essex <u>Escaped</u> in July last.'

A few questions were left unanswered. It is especially tantalising that there was no answer to the follow-up on the question of hereditary predisposition to insanity: was it on the mother's or the father's side of the family, and how close a relative was the person suffering from it? This may suggest that Skrimshire was merely hazarding a guess with regard to 'hereditary predisposition'.

Two other answers are especially interesting. 'Fourteen years' suggests that Skrimshire saw continuity from Clare's illness of 1827–8—the period of his final visit to Dr Darling in London—but not as far back as the occasions when he himself provided treatment in 1820 and 1824. The symptoms in those early years were presumably insufficiently severe to be classed as attacks of 'insanity'. The negative to the question about violence, meanwhile, may have been an act of good will to ensure that Clare would not be subjected to restraint. Or it may suggest that Taylor's fears of violence in 1836 and Mossop's hint of it in 1841 were exaggerated.

Frederick Martin alighted on the phrase about addiction to poetry. He assumed that Skrimshire was an ignorant provincial quack who imagined that anyone who wrote verses must be mad and that Clare was confined for the very fact of being a poet:

> On the ground of this new crime, punishable, according to the wise men of Market Deeping, with life-long imprisonment, Clare was torn away from his wife and children, and carried off to the madhouse. He struggled hard when the keepers came to fetch him, imploring them, with tears in his eyes, to leave him at his little cottage, and seeing all resistance fruitless, declaring his intention to die rather than to go to such another prison as that from which he had escaped. Of course, it was all in vain. The magic handwriting of Messrs Fenwick Skrimshaw [*sic*] and William Page, backed by all the power of English law, soon got the upper hand, and the criminal 'addicted to poetical prosings' was led away, and thrust into the gaol for insane at Northampton.

The image of Clare struggling as the keepers came to fetch him is pure fancy. We know nothing about the precise circumstances in which he and his family were told about the decision to certify him, or who accompanied him on the journey to Northampton.

Nor is it the case that Skrimshire proposed addiction to poetry as the *cause* of Clare's lunacy. He said that the cause was hereditary and that Clare's obsessive writing was a form of long-continued mental emotion or exertion that preceded his decline into an acute condition. As we have seen, this is no more than an accurate observation. It is of a piece with Ned Drury's warning over twenty years before that the manic intensity of Clare's writing habit could tip him into insanity.

What is striking about Skrimshire's answers is their implication that Clare's condition was relatively mild. He is not violent. He is not idiotic, mischievous or dirty. He does not have fits; there is no mention of those apparently epileptiform symptoms of earlier years. Patients at the Northampton Asylum were divided into five classes, according to the severity of their condition. The weekly fee for 'Board, Washing, Medical advice, and Medicines' varied according to class; the more care required, the greater the fee. Throughout his confinement, Clare appeared in the 'List of Private Patients, whose payment for Maintenance are in the lowest remunerative rate.' As a 'fifth class' patient he was regarded as needing very little special attention. The rate was nine shillings per week at the time he was admitted. Over the years to his death, it rose to twenty-one shillings, just over half of which was paid by Lord Fitzwilliam, the remainder being defrayed from the hospital's own Charitable Fund.

The Northampton General Lunatic Asylum was a substantial new building that had received its first inmates in the summer of 1838, while Clare was at High Beech. It stood in an elevated position about a mile to the east of the town, looking out over the park and woodland of Delapre Abbey, the vale of the River Nene, and Hunsbury Hill beyond. Built as a quadrangle in fine white stone, it was much the grandest building that Clare ever lived in. Initially housing about seventy patients, it quickly became overcrowded and was enlarged in the mid-1840s. There were galleries for promenading in wet weather and day rooms furnished to look as ordinary as possible. Hot water was accessible in all parts of the building, a luxury previously unknown to Clare. Baths and showers were provided and there was a state-of-the-art laundry.

Paupers were admitted, but Clare was among the paying patients, many of whom had been in trade. When the nationwide census was taken in 1851, Clare's name appeared on the same page as a needlewoman, a stone merchant, a baker, a draper, an ironmonger, a druggist, a chandler, a surgeon, a farmer, two grocers and two 'students'. He was listed as a 'limeburner', though in the next census a decade later he was recorded as 'poet'.

The asylum superintendent was Dr Thomas Prichard. The local newspaper editor described him as 'not mad, but just on the other side of that thin partition by which madness is said to be bounded'. Tall, athletic, handsome, impulsive, energetic, daring, he was said to have a peculiar power of influencing his patients even when they were far from his presence. He was strongly in sympathy with the new methods of 'moral management' that had been pioneered at the Retreat as opposed to the old techniques of coercion. Indeed, he banished all mechanical means of restraint from his regime. Dr Prichard left in unfortunate circumstances in 1845, accused (somewhat unfairly) of drunkenness and neglect of the pauper patients. His liberal regime continued under his successor, Dr Nesbitt. The asylum's annual reports spoke of sports in the grounds, rural walks in summer, board games in winter (bagatelle, chess, dominoes), country dancing and 'occasional musical parties in the centre of the house'. The wards were brightened up with flowering plants and singing birds. Occupational therapy was provided in the form of basket-making, strawplaiting and so forth.

'Fifth class' or 'harmless' patients were given considerable freedom. Clare was allowed to walk the mile into Northampton alone. He quickly became a well-known figure in the town, sitting for hours at a time in the portico of All Saints' Church, always with his tobacco, sometimes with his notebook. In a number of sketches and paintings

by a local artist called George Maine he is seen comfortably en-
sconced in a niche of smooth stone. When the Assizes (criminal trials
in the county court-room) were on, Clare liked to sit in court. Back at
the asylum, he regaled his fellow-patients with lively and exact accounts of the trials.

A fortnight after Clare's admission, Earl Spencer—who happened
to be the asylum's principal benefactor—sent his usual half-yearly
payment of five pounds to Patty. He added a note of praise for the
management of the asylum and an assurance that Dr Prichard was
particularly concerned for Clare's well-being. Prichard himself
wrote to the curate at Northborough the following year, with the
news that

> Poor Clare is in good health but the state of his mind has not im-
> proved. It rather appears to become more and more impaired,
> he used at one time to write many and very good pieces tho' he
> scarcely ever finished them, he now writes but little and in a
> coarse style very unlike his former compositions. I much fear
> that the disease will gradually terminate in dementia.

Many of Clare's asylum poems are lost: we do not have any
Northampton writings in the 'coarse style' that characterised his
'Don Juan'. As the years passed, Clare's language—and possibly his
behaviour—did become more violent, which was distressing to those
who associated him with sweet poetry of nature and the almost ethe-
real look of the Hilton portrait.

He was growing into a portly figure, as middle-aged spread combined with an improved diet. His physical health was better in the
asylum than it had been for years before. A portrait painted in 1844
by the Northampton artist Thomas Grimshaw shows him solidly
built and balding, still with a twinkle in his eye. 'His gait was a
ploughman's', one observer noted, 'one leg seeming to be always in
the furrow. He usually had one hand in his breeches pocket and the
other in the breast of his waistcoat.'

'John Clare is in excellent health,' Prichard wrote to the Northborough curate in 1845, 'but his mind is becoming more and more ob-

scured by his distressing malady—He enjoys perfect liberty here, and passes all his time out of doors in the fields or the Town returning home only for his meals and bed.' Occasionally—once in 1844 and again in 1846 and 1848—he was confined to the asylum after getting drunk in town.

A number of visitors and local people recorded their impressions of Clare. The wording of the various published interviews must be treated with caution, since reminiscences were often published long after the event, and the people writing them may at various points have misremembered, invented, projected, or incorporated details from other reports. But the record is for the most part consistent.

Spencer Hall was a phrenologist, mesmerist, homeopathic doctor and co-editor of the *Sheffield Iris* newspaper, to which Clare had contributed several poems, including his imitations of seventeenth-century lyrics. He called on Clare several times and gained the impression that the staff and management, as well as many of the inmates and an array of local people, 'delighted in showing him all possible consideration and kindness'. On his first visit, in May 1843, Hall spoke to Clare in the grounds of the asylum. Clare was initially shy, but grew more cordial as they talked. Hall found him 'rather burly, florid, with light hair and somewhat shaggy eyebrows, and dressed as a plain but respectable farmer, in drab or stone-coloured coat and smalls, with gaiters, and altogether as clean and brushed up for market or fair'—very much the image presented in the near-contemporaneous Grimshaw portrait. He had been into Northampton to visit a friend or buy tobacco (perhaps both at the same time, since the local tobacconist had become a good friend). On being asked how he was, he replied, 'Why, I'm very well, and stout, but I'm getting tired of waiting here so long, and want to be off home. They won't let me go, however; for, you see, they're feeding me up for a fight; but they can get nobody able to strip me; so they might as well have done with it, and let me go.' Hall suggested that he was surely more proud of his fame as a poet than a prize-fighter. To which Clare replied, 'Oh, poetry, ah, I know, I once had something to do with poetry, a long while ago: but it was no good. I wish, though, they could get a man with courage enough to fight me.'

Hall thought that the identification with prize-fighters stemmed from the way that such men were 'petted and nourished', in contrast to the neglect suffered by poets. He also noted that the talk of having given up poetry long ago came very shortly after Clare had written 'a beautiful and logical poem' for Joseph Stenson, iron-master of the local Patent Iron Scrap Forge Works, a friend of William Knight, the member of staff at the asylum to whom Clare had grown closest.

He asked Clare whether he remembered the *Sheffield Iris*. The reply was startling: Clare said that he knew all about it because he used to edit it. He spoke of having been imprisoned in York. James Montgomery, one of Hall's predecessors on the *Iris*, had indeed been sent to jail in York for publishing a political libel. Whilst there, he wrote a collection of poems called 'Prison Amusements', a title that Clare borrowed when referring to his own asylum poems (Montgomery also wrote a collection of psalm paraphrases called *Songs of Zion* that were precedents for Clare's work in this genre). A further delusion or act of identification followed when London was mentioned: Clare said that he had once been there and had not liked it, but asked to be remembered to Tom Spring the boxer.

On another occasion, Clare was greeted by Hall after he had just returned from 'a long and favourite ramble in the fields'. He began by describing his walk with great accuracy and delight, in beautiful language, but then broke off into foul-mouthed obscenities. Later, they met one last time, in the street near All Saints' Church. Clare's face lit up with a smile and Hall congratulated him on looking so well, but before they parted 'he talked again of wanting to go home, as though all his thoughts centred there'.

Here are some other snapshots from his first decade in the Northampton asylum.

1844. He is given a special seat for Queen Victoria's royal progress through the town. This would presumably not have been the case had anyone known about the stanza in his unpublished 'Don Juan' concerning Lord Melbourne and the Queen's 'snuff box'. Back at the asylum, over tea, the Keeper asks him whether he has seen the Queen. 'Yes,' he replies. 'What did she say to you?' 'O she nodded at me.' 'But what did she say to you?' 'O she said "I'm John Clare".'

That same year, and again subsequently, he is visited by William and Mary Howitt, writers and Quaker philanthropists. They give him William's *Book of the Seasons*, which commended and quoted his work; he writes a poem in gratitude. William remembers Clare's graphically detailed eyewitness accounts of the execution of Charles I, the battle of the Nile and the death of Nelson. Though he has never been on a ship and only once seen the sea, he deals out 'nautical phrases with admirable exactness and accuracy'.

Around 1847. A clergyman on a visit to Northampton is walking with a friend along the road that leads from the town towards the asylum. A man of middling stature walks past in neat rustic attire, apparently lost in thought, muttering to himself in broken sentences. 'That was poor Clare', says the clergyman's friend, a local. 'He is quite harmless, and is permitted to take daily walks into the town. He imagines that an army of soldiers is stationed within a certain circumference of his present abode; and that, therefore, even if he desired to acquire more freedom than he at present enjoys, his efforts to attain it would be frustrated at the outset.' He is said to be content with his lot, enjoying a degree of comfort that he never had in his impoverished early life. 'And has he no lucid intervals?' asks the clergyman. 'I have been informed', comes the reply, 'by those who enjoy his confidence (and his good-will may be purchased at a very small cost, namely, the present of a little tobacco), that he occasionally brings forth some fine thoughts in these perambulatory improvisations. But they must be caught the moment they are uttered, or they are gone for ever.' By adopting the method suggested—liberal gifts of tobacco—the clergyman befriends the poet and wins from him a selection of musings delivered in a 'rapid and peculiar' tone. They talk of politics and Clare is fired into a 'Song to Liberty'.

■

A local custom. Anybody who wants a poem, perhaps as a birthday
gift for a wife or daughter, may go to the man sitting on the stone
ledge in the portico of the church in the middle of Northampton and
purchase some lines for the price of a screw of tobacco or a glass of ale.
Acrostics, in which the name of the lady in question is spelt out vertically down the page in the first letter of each line of verse, are especially popular. One suspects that Clare's tobacco supply is most fully
stocked around Valentine's Day. Many poems of this kind are lost, but
a handful survive.

A report from the editor of the local newspaper:

> We walked side by side towards Kingsthorpe, and at last he star-
> tled me with a quotation from *Childe Harold* and then one from
> Shakespeare. I do not recall what the passages were, but I was
> still more startled when he said they were his own. 'Yours!' I ex-
> claimed, 'Who are you? These are Byron's and Shakespeare's
> verses, not yours!' 'It's all the same' he answered, changing a
> quid from one cheek to the other, 'I'm John Clare now. I was
> Byron and Shakespeare formerly. At different times you know
> I'm different people—that is the same person with different
> names.'

A similar account from the same journalist, given in answer to an inquiry from Clare's first biographer:

> I saw Clare frequently during his residence at the Asylum here.
> At first he was allowed to come into the Town (the Asylum is a
> mile out of it) unattended, and his favourite resort was beneath
> the portico of All Saints Church where in summer time he
> would sit for hours together. He was moody and taciturn and
> rather avoided society. He would talk rationally enough at
> times, about poetry especially, but on one occasion in the midst
> of a conversation in which he had betrayed no signs of insanity,
> he suddenly quoted passages from *Don Juan* as his own. I sug-
> gested, gently, that they were usually attributed to Byron, upon

which he said that was true; but he and Byron were one; so with Shakespeare; Shakespeare's plays were his composition when he was Shakespeare; and turning round upon me suddenly he said: 'Perhaps you don't know that I am Jan Burns and Tom Spring?' In fact he was any celebrity whom you might mention. 'I'm the same man,' he said, 'but sometimes they called me Shakespeare and sometimes Byron and sometimes Clare.'

If the newspaperman is to be believed, Clare was once invited by two fellow-patients to join in a plan to abscond. He declined, supposedly because of his belief in the mesmeric power of control exercised by Dr Prichard. The men got as far as Hertfordshire, but Prichard, who spared no pains in his efforts to recover runaways, got them back. Clare was present when they were brought in. 'I told you how it would be, you fools,' he said.

Another visitor finds him at work in the kitchen-garden behind one of the wings of the asylum. They fall into conversation, walk round the grounds and then go into Clare's room. 'It was an apartment pleasantly situated, having a garden beneath the windows. There was a birdcage, with a skylark in it, near the window; and pointing to the iron bars in his apartment, he smiled gloomily, and said, in a strong provincial accent, "We are both of us bound birds, you see." '

The fullest account of Clare in the asylum was written from behind the bars. It presents a rather different picture from that of the visitors and Northampton locals. William Jerom was a Derbyshire man, about twenty years younger than Clare; described as a 'student', he was a long-term inmate of the asylum. Shortly after the death of his fellow-patient, he recorded his reminiscences, perhaps for the benefit of Dr Wing, the superintendent at that time, who intended to write up the case of John Clare at some length.

According to Jerom, Clare had an 'agreeableness of disposition' that contrasted with the aggressiveness of many of the other inmates. He smoked a clay pipe or chewed tobacco all the time, sometimes roasting the quid in the fire and risking burnt fingers when removing it. The lump of tobacco in his cheek made his face look deformed. He was muscular and thick-set, admired by fellow-patients for his 'witticisms and crank sayings'. The prowess in his limbs and the majesty in his eye led Jerom to christen him 'the King of the Forest'. He sang songs while impersonating Nelson: 'Fight on, my boys, he said, / Till I die, till I die.' Jerom was touched by the way that he never omitted the repeat of *Till I die*. Though tough, he was also docile: 'he always knew his place whether at mealtimes or otherwise and always kept in it'.

He was bald on top, his remaining hair light flaxen at the time of his commitment. It turned to a silvery white, and in his last years it grew long over his shoulders, giving him a venerable appearance. This is apparent from some sketches of him drawn by another fellow-patient, G. D. Berry.

Clare usually walked about in a light fustian coat or jacket, his deep outer pockets stuffed with books, newspapers and notebook. He nearly always had a Byron to hand, sometimes also a copy of Burns. Beneath the outer coat he wore a double-breasted waistcoat, favouring dark olive for colour. 'Also Kerseymere breeches with gaiters, shoes with one tie (he had very handsome feet and hands).' On Sundays he wore a better suit. Jerom's account refers principally to Clare's earlier years in the asylum; subsequently, he favoured a black 'sur-tout' coat with breeches, and in his last years he took to wearing very fashionable trousers.

Jerom saw Clare almost daily for twenty years. He had a different view of the 'delusions' from that of the visitors who only spoke to the poet occasionally: 'Clare had a great knack of personating those in whom he was particularly interested. He almost considered himself to represent the idiosyncrasy of them of whom he spake, as I was Lord Byron, or I was the Marquis of Exeter, etc.' By this account, Clare was *playing at* multiple identities, not really believing in them. The statement that he *almost* considered himself to represent the famous men he impersonated is carefully calibrated to keep Clare just on the near side of madness. It may be that Jerom was defending his friend's sanity as a way of affirming his own, but we cannot rule out the possibility that Clare—admired by his fellow-patients for his sense of humour—was pulling the leg of his interlocutors when he suddenly put on the personae of such heroes as Nelson, Byron and the prize-fighters. It is touching to read Jerom on Clare: both men were classified as lunatics, but in this document each sounds damaged yet fundamentally sane. 'Clare had "a song in the night" ', remembers Jerom, 'he knew his affliction and felt it'. In the fragment on 'self-identity', written during the few months back at Northborough between the two madhouses, Clare affirmed the importance of holding on to the self and suggested that the person who denies his self must be either a madman or a coward. In an asylum letter of 1849, he spoke of being 'quite lost in reveries and false hums'. Can a man who knows and feels both his self-identity and his aberrations in this way really be described as mad?

Unlike fellow-patient Jerom, the asylum superintendents—Prichard, then Nesbitt, then his successor Wing—had no doubt about Clare's mental incapacity. Their reports tell of progressive deterioration and occasional outbursts of violence (certainly verbal, possibly physical). Fewer than twenty letters home survive from the more than twenty asylum years, so it is difficult to trace the progression of Clare's own thinking about his confinement.

These were difficult years for the family back in Northborough. In 1843 Clare's oldest son Frederick—the 'Freddy' of his poems for children—died at the age of nineteen. The following year, his oldest daughter, Anna Maria, also died; she was twenty-four. The cause of both deaths was tuberculosis.

There was also a sexual scandal in the family. Shortly before Clare's escape from the Essex asylum, Anna Maria had married a local labourer, John Sefton. They had a baby the next year. This little girl died of hydrocephalus (fluid on the brain), aged two, some months before her mother. Some time after the loss of his daughter but before the death of his wife, John Sefton began an affair with his sister-in-law, Eliza Louisa Clare (the girl who was Mrs Emmerson's god-daughter). Eliza Louisa gave birth to a daughter shortly after her sister Anna Maria's death. In 1845, pregnant with a second child, Eliza Louisa married John Sefton. It was quite common for a bereaved man to marry his dead wife's sister, but less acceptable for him to impregnate the younger girl before the older one was in the grave (and then to wait for a second pregnancy before legalizing the union).

Clare does not seem to have known about these goings-on involving his daughters. He never met any of his many grandchildren. From a purely practical point of view, it would have been extremely difficult for Patty to make the journey to Northampton to visit him (though the asylum steward encouraged her to do so, even offering to accommodate her if she came). As far as we know, she never went to the asylum during Clare's twenty-three years' residence there.

Old Parker Clare died late in 1846, aged eighty-one. He had taken great pride in his son's success. During the years of fame, Clare had written that it was 'a thrilling pleasure to hear a crippled father seated in his easy armchair comparing the past with the present, saying "Boy, who could have thought, when we was threshing together some years back, thou wouldst be thus noticed and be enabled to make us all thus happy" '. It is moving to find in Clare's library a copy of Wordsworth's *Miscellaneous Poems* of 1820, presented to him by his father, a sometime pauper, with the inscription 'Wordsworths Works 4 Vols are for my Dear Boy John Clare'. One can barely imagine the pain that Parker must have felt on witnessing his admired and cherished son being taken away to the asylum.

Clare's first extant letter home from Northampton postdates all these changes in the Northborough household. The youngest boy Charles had taken over the role of family scribe. He wrote with news of Parker's death, but to judge from his father's reply appears not to have mentioned the loss of Frederick. 'My dear Boy', Clare began his answer,

> I am very happy to have a letter from you in your own handwriting and to see you write so well—I am also glad that your Brothers and Sisters are all in good health and your Mother also—be sure to give my love to her but I am very sorry to hear the News about your Grandfather but we must all die—and I

must [say] that Frederic and John had better not come unless they wish to do so for it's a *bad Place* and I have fears that they may get trapped as prisoners as I hear some have been and I may not see them nor even hear they have been here—I only tell them and leave them to do as they like best—its called the Bastile by some and not with[out] reasons—how does the Flowers get on I often wish to see them—and are the young Children at home I understand there are some I have not yet seen—kiss them and give my love to them and to your Mother and Brothers and Sisters ... I have never been ill since I have been here, save a cold now and then of which I take no notice.

Charles's letter must have spoken of Eliza Louisa's little children and of a plan for his two older brothers to visit Northampton. He would have meant John and William, but Clare assumed he was referring to Frederick and John.

There was another exchange of letters eight months later, by which time John and William had not yet come. Clare gets the names right this time, saying that he doesn't mind the lack of a visit. The boys shouldn't take the trouble to come 'unless it would give them pleasure to do so'. The asylum steward added a note: 'Your Father in this letter tells you that you may not see him if you come—I know not why he should say this, for he is allowed to see anyone he wishes—and he is at liberty to walk out for his pleasure ... if any of you think well to come and see him, I am sure he will be pleased to see you.'

Much of this second letter is given over to a response to Charles's mention of his enthusiasm for fishing:

Angling is a Recreation I was fond of myself and there is no harm in it if your taste is the same—for in those things I have often broke the Sabbath when a boy and perhaps it was better then keeping it in the village hearing Scandal and learning tipplers frothy conversation—'The fields his study, nature was his book'—I seldom succeeded in Angling but I wrote or rather thought Poems, made botanical arrangements when a little Boy which men read and admired—I loved nature and painted her both in words and colours better than many Poets and Painters

and by Preseverance and attention you may all do the same—
in my boyhood Solitude was the most talkative vision I met
with—Birds bees trees flowers all talked to me incessantly
louder than the busy hum of men and who so wise as nature out
of doors on the green grass by woods and streams under the
beautiful sunny sky—daily communings with God and not a
word spoken.

Here the long-term memory is fully intact. Indeed, Clare remains
acutely aware of the gifts that had made him such a good poet of nature: perseverance and attention. His short-term memory is another
matter: 'you never mentioned your Grandfather—give my love to
him', he writes, forgetting the report of Parker's passing in the earlier
letter.

John Clare Junior ('Johnny' or 'Jack') did visit in July 1848. The following day, Clare drafted a letter to Patty:

> My dear wife,
> I have not written to you a long while but here I am in the Land
> of sodom where all the peoples brains are turned the wrong
> way—I was glad to see John yesterday and should like to have
> gone back with him for I am very weary of being here—You
> might come and fetch me away for I think I have been here long
> enough.

He has had enough. He feels 'cheated'. Patty's brother-in-law has also
visited, leading Clare to assume that the purpose was to take him
home from what he calls 'the purgatoriall hell and French Bastile of
English liberty'. He says that he is not allowed 'to go out of the gates'
of the hellish place. This is a slightly exaggerated claim, given that
the letter in which it is made was written as he sat in a green meadow
by the river on a beautiful summer evening.

The letter ends with a cryptic reference that suggests either that
Clare had recently been in a delusional phase or that Patty had relatives living in Northampton: 'I see many of your little Brothers and
Sisters [meaning nephews and nieces?] at Northampton—weary and
dirty with hard work—some of them with red hands but all in ruddy

good health—some of them are along with your Sister—Ruth Dakker who went from Helpstone a little girl'. There must be at least an element of delusion here, since Patty's surname was Turner not Dakker and she was a Casterton girl, not a Helpston one.

The language of imprisonment recurs in another letter to Charles, written nearly a year later: 'I am now in the ninth year of Captivity among the Babylonians and any news from Home is a Godsend or blessing'. Six months later he asked when his son Johnny was coming 'to fetch me away from this Bastile'. Given the relatively open regime at the asylum, at least as far as 'fifth class' patients were concerned, the comparison with the Bastille may not be entirely just, but anger, bitterness and loneliness are the feelings we would expect of anyone who has been committed to a mental institution.

For the most part, though, the letters home contain more longing than fury: 'I very much want to get back and see after the garden and hunt in the Woods for yellow hyacinths, Polyanthuses and blue Primroses as usual'. Feelings of isolation, enclosure and persecution are more prominent in some letter drafts that may not actually have been sent. To his children: 'I should hope you think of and behave well to your poor Mother for I myself am rendered incapable of assisting or behaving well to any one even of my nearest relations—I am in a Prison on all hands that ever numbs Common sense—I can be civil to none but enemies here as friends are not alowd to see me at all'. And to 'My dear Wife':

> I have wrote some few times to enquire about yourself and the Family and thought about yourself and them a thousand other things that I use[d] to think of the children—Freddy when I led him by the hand in his childhood—I see him now in his little pink frock—sealskin cap—and gold band—with his little face as round as a apple and as red as a rose—and now a stout Man both strangers to each other, the father a prisoner under a bad . government so bad in fact that it's no government at all but prison disapline where every body is forced to act contrary to their own wishes 'the mother against the daughter in law and the daughter against the mother in law' 'the father against the

son and the son against the Father'—in fact I am in Prison because I won't leave my family and tell a falshood—this is the
English Bastile, a government Prison where harmless people
are trapped and tortured till they die.

For all the talk of imprisonment and estrangement, the power of
memory is what leaps from the page here: little Freddy in his Sunday
best, not yet breeched, walking hand in hand with his father. It is
merciful that Clare seems not to have known that both Freddy his
firstborn son and Anna Maria his eldest child lay beneath the ground
in Northborough churchyard.

Two further images of this period. A minor versifier called John
Dalby was present on one of the occasions when Thomas Inskip,
whom we will meet in the next chapter, took Clare to tea with G. J. De
Wilde, editor of the *Northampton Mercury*. The occasion inspired
Dalby to pen a poem that is indifferently written but warmly in-
tended:

> A life of dreams! the first, and the most real,
>> Began in boyhood, when his spirit went,
>> Mate of birds, trees, and flowers, glad and content;
> 'Mong sylvan haunts, embracing the ideal,
> Which is the poet's workshop . . .
>> Then came the last of dream, in our sight how sad! . . .
>
> Let me recall him when kind Inskip led
>> The unconscious poet to your home, De Wilde,
>> And we sat listening as to some fond child,
> The wayward unconnected words he said—
> Prattle by confused recollections fed,
>> Of famous times gone by—how Byron piled
>> Praise on him in the *Quarterly*, and styled
> Him of all poets the very head!
> Still dreaming! Happy dreamer! . . .

It is impossible to know how earnestly Clare spoke as he sat taking tea
in town, reminiscing about the long and glowing review of his first

book in the *Quarterly*—a piece that had been written by his friend Gilchrist, not by Byron (whose sole mention of the Northamptonshire Peasant Poet actually came in a passage concerning Gilchrist in one of his contributions to the pamphlet war concerning the merits of Alexander Pope).

And then, more prosaically but more movingly, the vivid and acutely sensitive account of an American called Dean Dudley, who visited Clare at the asylum in March 1850:

> He is a short, stout man, of light complexion and blue eyes. The expression of his countenance is very child-like. His head is uncommonly large, long and deep, resembling that of Horace Greeley. His hair is grey, but his beard red. A person would suppose his age to be about 35, but he says he is 56. He has been in the asylum ten years. His insanity consists in believing his fancyings to be realities, and what he reads to be his own experience.
>
> I told him I lived in America; but I had read his poems and admired them. He said he had been in America, at a place called Albania [Albany], on the Hudson river, and saw Irving and Bryant there. He also saw Corduroy, and was delighted with him. 'Corduroy,' said he, 'dwelt in a beautiful cottage—a poet's cottage, encircled by trees and flower-gardens. Hundreds of gentlemen and ladies, in their splendid carriages, came to see the poet's cottage.'
>
> 'I saw Whittier and Dana,' said he. 'Dana was formerly a clerk in some office, but he became a poet.'
>
> I referred to the British and Scotch poets. He spoke of Burns as of a brother, assuring me he had been in Scotland and seen his grave at Dumfries church.
>
> He said the monument he saw was about as high as the table before us, but now a higher one has been raised. These stories are all fiction: for he never went further from home than London.
>
> When I mentioned Byron, he drew a volume from his pocket, saying he had borrowed it of some one to read. It was half of Byron's poems.
>
> I asked him about his farm at home. 'Oh! dear,' said he, 'I don't

know how things go on there now. I want to go home and be free.' 'Why,' said I, 'this seems to be a pleasant place.' 'O yes, but its a *mad-house*, and nothing less. They won't let me go; I'm a *prisoner* here. Oh! I want to be a free man again, and go where I please. I am sick of this place, where I have no companions but mad-men.' ...

He said he had forgotten all his poems, and wrote none now. He could not repeat a single line to me.

Unable to go beyond Northampton, Clare was travelling in his imagination: to Scotland when he read Burns, to New York and New England when he read Washington Irving, William Cullen Bryant, Richard Henry Dana and J. G. Whittier. Irving's *Salmagundi* was in Clare's personal book collection back in Northborough; his knowledge of the other writers was derived from his recent perusal of an anthology of American poetry that had been recommended to him. He was rarely short of reading matter in the asylum.

It would seem that the now-forgotten New England poet Corduroy, visited in his cottage by genteel admirers in splendid carriages, has become conflated with Clare's memory of his own early fame.* But this is hardly a severe delusion. The act of living vicariously through the writers whose works one admires is a mild form of madness, little more than an extreme version of the imaginative empathy that is at the heart of all good reading.

Contrary to what he said on this occasion, Clare was still writing. A few weeks later Dudley sent a letter from London, and he replied, wishing him well for his journey back to New England and enclosing a song written as a memento of the visit. Here Clare quoted a variation on a line in one of his other recent sonnets: 'Where flowers are, God is, and I am free.' Nature, memory and, increasingly, the thought of God and eternity meant that his mind continued to soar beyond his humdrum life among the Babylonians.

*Dean Dudley did not question this poet's existence, but I have not been able to trace any record of Corduroy—unless Clare was misremembering the name of John Cordingley, whose poems were published in Ipswich, Massachusetts.

CHAPTER TWENTY-TWO

'I AM'

Four years after his commitment to the Northampton General Lunatic Asylum, Clare obtained a pocket notebook with limp green covers. Inside the front he wrote 'John Clare / Northborough / Northamptonshire / Novr 1845'. The naming of his home village was a defiant assertion that he still belonged to a place outside the asylum. Working mainly in pencil, he filled the notebook with letter drafts, quotations, lists of books and girls' names, and about seventy new poems. He began by quoting from Cowper's *Task* a passage of intense longing for seclusion. Later quotations included sequences from the Book of Revelation. Death was on his mind: his reading matter included morbid fare from the eighteenth century, such as James Hervey's *Meditations among the Tombs* and Edward Young's *Night Thoughts*.

In the poems he dreamed of places and people beyond the confines of the asylum. He wrote many lyrics—some in this notebook, more among the works transcribed for him—in Scottish dialect. Burns had been his inspiration, Allan Cunningham his friend. In his imagination he now joined them in the wide-open spaces and fresh air north of the border. Perhaps he was also longing for reconnection with the heritage that had been brought to Helpston by his Scottish grandfather, John Donald Parker.

Several of the 'songs' in the notebook are addressed to particular girls, some of whom have been identified as acquaintances in the locality of the asylum, such as a fifteen-year-old laundress with 'glossy raven hair' called Susannah Chaplin, Ann Sharp of the Flying Horse Inn on the market square, and another Northampton lass called Mary Ann Abbott. Others were distant memories, such as fair-haired Mary King of Helpston and 'Oundle Phebe' from his militia days. 'Sally Frisby' may have been a Helpston girl who died in 1819 aged twenty-two or she may have been the sister of Elizabeth Frisby, a nurse in the asylum. The mix of names suggests that Clare was veering between reality, memory and fantasy. The longest lyric in the notebook was a love poem for a fictitious beauty, the Haidee of Byron's *Don Juan*.

Another forty or so poems from the early Northampton years are scattered in a variety of manuscripts. Many of these were written at the request of people who met Clare as he sat in his stone niche outside the church in town. Again, the majority are love songs, often written for named subjects. As we have seen, it was by writing such poems that Clare earned his tobacco money. The lists of girls' names in his notebooks may have begun as an *aide mémoire* in relation to these commissions. Increasingly, though, he mingled the names of Northampton girls with those of villagers from Helpston, Maxey, Barnack and Glinton. 'Mary Roddis' of the Crow and Horseshoe Inn and 'Hellen of the Plough' are one thing, 'Mary Poppe—Maxey' and 'Ann Hetherley—Glinton' quite another. 'Queen Adelaide' is incongruously placed between 'Bess Gimlie' and 'Mary Ann Collingwood'.

The notebook poems are all short, some fragmentary. Often there is a stunningly powerful first line—'Infants are but cradles for the grave' or 'There is a chasm in the heart of man' or 'The present is the funeral of the past'—but then a lack of direction and a falling away. Yet Clare was still producing poems at a remarkable rate. It was also in 1845 that a young staff member who had taken a particular interest in him, William Knight, was promoted to the post of house steward at the asylum. The previous year, Knight, who dabbled in poetry himself, had begun putting together a collection of 'Poetry by John

Clare written by him while an Inmate of the Northampton General Lunatic Asylum',

> Copied from the Manuscripts as presented to me by Clare—and favoured with others by some Ladies and Gentlemen, that Clare had presented them to—the whole of them faithfully transcribed to the best of my knowledge from the pencil originals many of which were so obliterated that without referring to the Author I could not decipher.

In addition to noting the difficulty of his task due to Clare's pencil work and erasures, Knight also recorded that some pieces were left unfinished because when Clare was interrupted in the middle of a poem he would simply stop—and he was no longer interested in the work of revision.

The two volumes of carefully written Knight transcripts are our principal record of Clare's output in the Northampton years. Knight's own letters reveal his admiration for Clare and his pride in the task of preserving the asylum poems:

> Thus John keeps joging on from theme to theme—from passion to calm nature—from solitude to bustling life—I have not yet seen him this morning but I have no doubt he has something for me—early as it is—for he is up most mornings at six o'clock—and his mind must be employed in writing poetry or Clare will be Clare no longer.

Clare's identity depended on his poetry: to stop writing was to cease to be himself. Knight saw it as his job to help keep the poems coming.

We have seen that Clare always required copyists, editors, advisers and friends in order to sustain his creativity. Drury was the first to play the necessary part, John Taylor and Eliza Emmerson the most significant, but there were plenty of others, including Hessey, Van Dyk, Henderson and Pringle. Within the asylum, Knight took on the role. For a time, Clare also had an outside adviser, Thomas Inskip, the elderly watch- and clockmaker from Shefford in Bedfordshire who years before had tried to set up a meeting with that other 'peasant poet', Robert Bloomfield. Clare once startled his fellow-inmate William Jerom by announcing that he himself was a watch- and clockmaker: in so doing, he was identifying with someone who had become an important correspondent.

Inskip's letters to Knight and Clare survive, but Clare's to Inskip are lost. They would have given us valuable information about his mental state in the late 1840s. His fluctuating moods may be reconstructed from Inskip's replies: one letter was written 'under a paroxysm of insanity', another careered 'through the boundless fields of imagination' and yet was 'disciplined to rationality'. Sometimes Clare shared enthusiasm in both his compositions and his reading— he was dipping into the female poets, greatly preferring the local writer Eliza Cook to the celebrated Mrs Hemans—but late in 1848 he complained that he was growing tired of writing poetry. Around the same time he described the asylum as a hell. The following year one letter was, to Inskip's eyes, quite excellent and 'only a little mad with alliteration', while another was distinctly 'moody'.

Inskip had met Clare back in the 1820s. 'I have often reflected with pleasure', he recalled, 'on the happy Evening we spent in London amongst the *Cockneys*, whom *we both* equally *admire*!' They had stayed out drinking until three in the morning, when Clare returned to Fleet Street to find that Taylor had stayed up for him, ready with a moral lecture. Inskip always regretted that Clare had failed to make the journey to Shefford before Bloomfield died; he would have loved to have been instrumental in bringing together the two men he regarded as the nation's great poets of humble life.

Just before Christmas 1846, Knight wrote to Inskip with the information that Clare had written over 150 new poems in the asylum. He enclosed some examples: 'Graves of Infants', the lines 'I am' ('exquisitely beautiful' was Inskip's response), and some 'Stanzas' in which Inskip found marks of 'a disjointed intellect' but also proofs of a poetic power he did not know Clare possessed.

The following month Clare himself wrote to Inskip, requesting a collection of Bloomfield's poems for the small personal library he was building up in the asylum. In the same letter, he claimed that he had known 'Lucy', the love-object of Bloomfield's poems. He seems to have boasted that he had favoured her with something more than his *sweet heart*: 'I guess that was not the only *sweet meat* you gave her!' replied Inskip. 'O the days when we were young! And the arms-full of Petticoats we rumpled!' With some frankness, he confided to Clare that, despite his age, his 'foreman' was still capable of rising to the memory of past rumpling. Sexual desire, he suggested, was 'the secret of poetic inspiration'. In subsequent letters that are now lost, Clare seems to have told Inskip of his own deep sexual frustration in the asylum.

There can be no denying that, like many creative people, Clare had a vigorous sex drive—especially in his 'manic' periods—so he would have suffered greatly from the fact that from the age of forty-eight onwards he was deprived of the opportunity to sleep with a woman. The periodic violence of his language, and possibly his behaviour, may be attributable to the need to release his sexual energy. Pent-up aggression fuelled by sexual starvation may also account for the obsessive identification with prize-fighters that recurred in some of his letters to Inskip.

Inskip played along with the fantasy about making love to Bloomfield's Lucy. In all his letters he treated Clare with respect and without condescension. They exchanged praise of Shakespeare, whose works Clare had been reading in the asylum, and they discussed Byron. It was through Inskip's good offices that some of Clare's recent poems were published in the *Bedford Times* newspaper between 1847 and 1849. Inskip told Knight to collect 'every scrap of Clare's Muse', even though some of the new poems had an unfinished feel. Upon the suggestion that some polishing might be appropriate, Knight responded with sharp words in Clare's defence: 'do you consider where Clare is when you ask him to correct and revise his pieces?'

Inskip did not desist from offering advice. He told Clare that he admired a poem concerning a 'broad Oak Tree' but that its workmanship had been left 'in one or two places rather slovenly'. No offence should be taken at this comment, he added: a few minutes' reflection would have tightened up the poem. In another letter he described Clare's muse as a slut whose dress he needed to tidy. Inskip offered what Clare always craved from his correspondence with editors: a mixture of practical advice and confidence-building encouragement. He said that it had taken a thousand years for English literature to produce a true pastoral poet of the kind constituted by Clare and Bloomfield—'all the attempts made previously were as much like pastoral, as Diplomacy is like common honesty'—and that it would be another thousand years before there was another such poet, not least because 'there is in fact hardly such a thing left as an English peasantry'. Inskip was also very good at defusing delusions: Clare had complained, bizarrely and disturbingly, that he had no pupils in his eyes; Inskip merely responded with a complaint about his own failing eyesight in old age.

Seventy years old and troubled by various ailments, Inskip kept being forestalled in his intention to visit Northampton and see Clare in person. In addition to his health problems, he had to cope with a daughter in an unhappy marriage. She was regularly beaten up by her husband, who eventually pulled a knife and threatened to kill her and the children, so Inskip took them into his own home. Despite these distractions, he did eventually find time to make a visit to the asylum.

Inskip was an acute critic. He considered the poetry in Clare's first two books unexceptional, but almost every piece in *The Rural Muse* 'above mediocrity'. 'Even the Rural Muse', he went on, 'must give way to many of the pieces he has written in the precincts of the Asylum'. He singled out 'An Invite to Eternity' as 'bordering on the sublime'. In 1848 Clare gave a copy of the same poem to another visitor, who described it as 'weird and mysterious, and it requires an effort to grasp its full meaning'. It is one of his most haunting poems:

> Wilt thou go with me, sweet maid
> Say, maiden, wilt thou go with me
> Through the valley depths of shade,
> Of night and dark obscurity,
> Where the path hath lost its way,

Where the sun forgets the day,
Where there's nor life nor light to see,
Sweet maiden, wilt thou go with me?

Where stones will turn to flooding streams,
Where plains will rise like ocean waves,
Where life will fade like visioned dreams
And mountains darken into caves,
Say, maiden, wilt thou go with me
Through this sad non-identity,
Where parents live and are forgot
And sisters live and know us not?

Say, maiden, wilt thou go with me
In this strange death of life to be,
To live in death and be the same
Without this life, or home, or name,
At once to be and not to be,
That was and is not, yet to see
Things pass like shadows, and the sky
Above, below, around us lie?

The land of shadows wilt thou trace
And look—nor know each other's face,
The present mixed with reasons gone
And past and present all as one,
Say, maiden, can thy life be led
To join the living with the dead?
Then trace thy footsteps on with me,
We're wed to one eternity.

In that prose fragment written at Northborough during his few
months back home, Clare had coined the term *self-identity*. Now he
coins its opposite: *sad non-identity*. The absence of home and family
has stripped Clare of his sense of self. At the same time, the very act
of writing is a defiant assertion of the self. 'At once to be and not to be'
is a breathtaking riposte to Hamlet's question. The asylum is a place

of living death, but the poem creates its own space outside of time where past and present become as one and the living are restored to the company of the dead.

A poem such as this is written in a voice that is uniquely Clare's: the combination of joy and sorrow, diffidence and visionary confidence, is instantly recognisable. Yet Inskip also noted that much of Clare's writing was still under the influence of the poets he admired: 'I find his poetry is an echo (though a fine one) of his readings'. Throughout his career, Clare was engaged—as all true poets are—in the work of imitation and emulation as well as that of original creation. He began with the emulation of Thomson's *Seasons* and the act of poetic identification reached its height with his Byronic 'Child Harold' and 'Don Juan', but there were dozens of other influences at work, ranging from Bloomfield and Burns to the seventeenth-century lyric poets to contemporaries such as James Montgomery and Tom Moore. Even a work as distinctive as 'An Invite to Eternity' has its provenance in the literary tradition: there is a genre of 'invitation' poems (often written in the lilting iambic tetrameter that Clare deploys but subtly varies) of which Christopher Marlowe's 'Come live with me and be my love' is the most famous. Although Clare's asylum poetry lacked the bold formal innovation that characterised the best work of his middle period—his variations upon the sonnet are the best example—it always remained technically accomplished. Only a craftsman still in full possession of his skills could have written, say, the self-conscious imitation of a Shelley lyric that was published in the *Northampton Mercury* soon after his admission to the asylum.

If Inskip stood in for Eliza Emmerson in the role of confidential correspondent, Knight played the part of John Taylor, copying and ordering the poems with an eye on posterity.

When Clare's son Jack visited the asylum in 1848, Knight raised the possibility of publishing a selection of the later poems. In a letter home, Clare confirmed that he had given his consent for a volume of manuscript poems that was in the Northborough cottage to be lent to Knight for this purpose. His youngest son, Charles, searched in his father's papers and found 'three or four Volumes of M.S. Poems that have not been Published'. Clare was a little confused as to which these might be: the only new work he could remember were the scraps he had carried in his pockets on the walk home from Essex and the manuscript book in which he had made fair copies of 'Child Harold', 'Don Juan' and other material back in Northborough.

Whatever the precise nature of the available material, Knight was extremely keen to see it: 'I will pay all expence both up and down,' he wrote to Charles Clare, 'and will see that they are safely returned to you'. He said that if the Clare family could provide a sufficient number of poems written at High Beech, he would add his own transcripts of the Northampton lyrics and thus make up an edition of worthwhile size. The idea was still under consideration two years later. 'I have many pieces that are very choice and do think would be appreciated by the world', wrote Knight to Charles, suggesting that the boy should approach Clare's trustees about the possibility of a new volume. A gathering of the fugitive poems published in magazines and newspapers in the 1830s and 1840s, the High Beech material, and a substantial selection from the Knight transcripts would have profoundly enhanced Clare's reputation.

But nothing further was heard of the project. The key player was Charles Clare: he was the person corresponding with Knight on the one hand and the trustees on the other. He was the only member of the household in Northborough who was sufficiently literary to carry forward the project, and in particular to discover what was publishable among the papers that remained in the cottage. Charles was the child who seemed most like his father. Late in 1849 he had obtained a post as clerk to a lawyer named Sharp in Market Deeping—the kind of position that his father had failed to gain in Wisbech. Soon after this, his handwriting improved markedly. It was commended by John Taylor. For practice in penmanship Charles copied out 'The Laws of Cricket Revised by the Marylebone Club in the year 1823', complete with headings and a title-page designed with the same care as his father's handwritten 'Rustic's Pastime, in Leisure Hours'.

But his health was rapidly declining. The year 1851 was a very dark one for the Clare family: Jack left home to work on the railways, Eliza Louisa's husband John Sefton was in trouble with the Inland Revenue, Patty and Charles were both ill. The man who was supposed to come and buy the apples from the trees in the garden failed to turn up, so they rotted away and there wasn't enough money for a fire in the living room. Damp severely affected the furniture, books and papers. Charles died of tuberculosis the following year. This was yet another of Clare's tragedies: where Shelley left a widow to edit his works, Crabbe a son and Coleridge a daughter, the death of Charles at the age of nineteen deprived Clare of a similar act of filial piety.

The body of work assembled in the Knight transcripts includes a considerable number of routine lyrics, but also some poems of astonishing originality. The old themes of love and joy are played out in a new key. Though there are references to childhood as a lost paradise, instead of always longing for the past in these poems Clare increasingly seeks his freedom in a vision of otherworldliness, as in the 'Invite to Eternity'. For the most part, he reveals little of his inner torment. If he was still writing poems of bitterness and obscenity in the manner of 'Don Juan' and some of the other work written at Allen's asylum, then he did not show them to Knight—or Knight may conceivably have suppressed them.

There are some psychologically revealing lines, such as 'My hopeless nerves are all unstrung', and occasional poems of yearning for release, notably some poignant 'Recolections of Home' that break off with an unfinished stanza,

> I always see a bit of home in every likely thing
> A white-thorn hedge, or bramble bush or pollard willow tree
> Brings me my own snug homestead, and the budding of the spring.

But poems such as this are exceptional: the customary voice of the asylum poems is more impersonal, almost disembodied. Clare was withdrawing into non-identity. In a poem written for Inskip, he describes himself as the bard of cottage, field, wild flower and sheep-pen, but he does not sustain his self-image as bard of nature in his day-to-day poetic practice. Perhaps because he is no longer taking walks in his own fields, a sonnet about a crow flying in the thin blue sky over the level fen is one of the very few bird poems of the asylum years. The most intricate 'nature' writing in the Knight collection is to be found in fragments that are best described as prose-poems: on 'House or Window Flies', 'Pleasant Sounds' ('The crumping of cat-ice and snow down wood rides ... The flirt of the ground-larks wing from the stubbles'), and 'The dew drops on every blade of grass' that 'are so much like silver drops that I am obliged to stoop down as I walk to see if they are pearls'. When he did attempt a longer poem of natural observation (there is one entitled 'A Raphsody'), he was unable to sustain his usual control of rhythm and rhyme.

Fellow-patient Jerom noted that Clare 'always sang with a repeat'. As Taylor and others often complained, repetitiousness was the principal weakness of his poetry. It was a vice that became more severe in the asylum poems—if vice it be, for there is a sense in which the repetitions and refrains that run through Clare's lyrics serve as a ground-bass to keep him tuned to the folk tradition out of which his imagination grew.

Love songs are the very essence of that tradition, and this raises the question of whether Clare's hundreds of asylum love lyrics should be regarded as poetic exercises or expressions of personal feeling. A random glance into the Knight transcripts will immediately turn up a 'bonny Ann', 'sweet Mary', 'dearest Susan' or 'fair Sukey'. In many cases, especially when a poem is called simply 'Song' or 'Ballad', Clare was merely composing in the time-honoured fashion of the folk tradition. At the opposite extreme, there are affectionate poems addressed specifically to Patty and a number of lyrics that reactivate the fantasy about Mary Joyce being his wife. An intriguing piece called 'Love' plays on the biblical motif of paired women (Adah and Zillah, Ruth and Naomi, Kezia and Jemima): the conjunction of Mary and Martha must lie just below the surface of this text. The twinning of female figures allows Clare to reconcile his conflicting emotions, as in a fragment headed 'sorrow is my joy', where he brings together 'Rebecca's faith' and 'the love of Ruth' and then conjoins opposite colours in an extraordinary image of a white snowdrop glowing in a girl's raven hair.

In a song that begins 'True love lives in absence', memory and desire seem to fade together:

> Black absence hides upon the past
> I quite forget thy face
> And memory like the angry blast
> Will love's last smile erace
> I try to think of what has been
> But all is blank to me
> And other faces pass between
> My early love and thee.

And again:

> I sleep with thee, and wake with thee,
> And yet thou art not there:—
> I fill my arms with thoughts of thee,
> And press the common air.

Such lines are of a piece with many pre-asylum lyrics inspired by the memory of Mary Joyce.

The poems that present the biographer with the most difficulty are those that lie between the traditional or generic songs and ballads on the one hand, and the lyrics that name Patty or Mary on the other. In the Knight transcripts, as in the notebooks, there are many love poems that were manifestly written for particular girls, among them Mary Ludgate, Hannah Rolph, Eliza Dadford, Hellen Wright, Arabella Seymour, Mary Beal, Susannah Wells, Ellen Tree, Mary Collingwood and a dozen more who can be traced to either Northampton or the vicinity of Helpston. A certain Jane Wilson is the object of attention on several occasions. One possibility is that the poems of this kind were simply commissions from boyfriends, fathers, brothers or husbands, undertaken in return for tobacco or beer. Another is that Clare saw, took a fancy to, then fantasised about these girls. He seems to have had an especial partiality to breasts and ankles. A third is that he actually presented the girls with their poems, perhaps in a vain attempt to seduce them.

We have no evidence that he entered into any sexual relationship during the asylum years, despite what is suggested by a poem such as the following:

> On the seventeenth of April I' the good year forty nine
> I met a pleasant maiden And I wished the maid was mine
> She'd cowslips in her basket She'd sweet briar in her hand
> Her love I would have ask'd But she would not understand
>
> I touched her gown in passing And she looked in strange surprise
> The meadow pool spread glassing In the beautiful sunrise
> Her shawl was of the flags so green Her gown was brown and red
> Her stockings white as snow was seen And lightsome was her tread
>
> The linnet chirrupt in the thorn The lark sung in the sky
> And bonny was the sunny morn And every road was dry
> I took her by the waist so small All in a pleasant place
> She no denial made at all But smiled upon my face
>
> I cuddled her in the green grass And sat among the hay
> Till sunshine o'er the hill did pass And day light went away
> I kissed her o'er her bonny face So tender and so true
> And left my blessing on the place Among the foggy dew.

I would guess that the first two stanzas of this are based on a real encounter whilst out on a walk, but that the latter two are fantasy. But this can only be a guess. Maybe the whole thing was made up and the poem should merely be read as a romping ballad ('foggy dew' is the traditional language of the form). If, on the other hand, Clare did manage to extract a cuddle and a kiss in the green grass in the dewy early morning of 17 April 1849, we can hardly blame him.

There is firm evidence of Clare's interest in a number of local girls. He drafted a number of love letters in his notebooks. The following is to a Mary Collingwood, for whom he also composed a poem: 'I long to see you and have Loved you from the first Night of my capture here'. And to Eliza Dadford (again, there is a poem for her among the Knight transcripts): 'How I long to see you and kiss that pretty Face—I mean "Eliza Dadford" how I should like to walk with you in the snow where I helped to shake your carpets and take the oppertunity we neglected then to kiss on the green grass and Love you even better than before'. We do not know whether Clare sent these letters or how well he was actually acquainted with the young ladies in question.

In his notebook, immediately under the draft letter to Mary Collingwood, there is one to a Mary Ann Averey. At the end of that, he began listing other names: Sally Mason, Betsey Ashby, Mary Bolland of Maxey. Then he stops himself with the words 'gently John gently John.' His train of thought seems to have run from the girls around Northampton to those of the villages of his youth, from the present to the past. Did he seek to calm himself because the name of Mary Bolland stirred memories of young love—or even of his infidelity to Patty?

A second draft letter to Mary Collingwood, in a different notebook, was written in a code that involved the removal of all the vowels and the letter *y*:

> M Drst Mr Cllngwd
>
> M nrl wrn t & wnt t hr frm Nbd wll wn M r hv m t n prc & wht hv dn D knw wht r n m Dbt—kss's fr tn yrs & lngr stll & lngr thn tht whn ppl mk sch mstks s t cll m Gds bstrd & whrs p m b sh ttng m p frm Gds ppl t f th w f cmmn snse & thn tk m hd ff bcs th cnt fnd m t t hrds hrd
>
> Drst Mr r fthfll r d thnk f m knw wht w sd tgthr—dd vst m n hll sm tm bck bt dnt cm hr gn fr t s ntrs bd pic wrs nd wrs nd w r ll trnd Frnchmn flsh ppl tll m hv gt n hm n ths wrld nd s dnt believe n th thr nrt t mk mslf hvn wth m drst Mr nd sbscrb mslf rs fr vr & vr
>
> Jhn Clr

The letter is hardly less strange once decoded:

My Dearest Mary Collingwood

I am nearly worn out and want to hear from you—Nobody will own me or have me at any price and what have I done—Do you know what you are in my Debt—kisses for ten years and longer still and longer than that—when people make such mistakes as to call me God's bastard and whores pay me by shutting me up from God's people out of the way of common sense and then take my head off because they can't find me—it out-Herods Herod

Dearest Mary are you faithful or do you think of me—you know what we said together—you did visit me in hell sometime back but don't come here again for it is a notorious bad place worse and worse and we are all turned Frenchmen—foolish people tell me I have got no home in this world and as I don't believe in the other [? undertake] to make myself heaven with my dearest Mary and subscribe myself yours for ever and ever

John Clare

This is among the most disturbing letters that Clare ever wrote. It takes us inside his head during a phase of derangement. Even once one has broken the code, it is impossible to decipher the sub-text, especially as we know nothing about the identity of Mary Collingwood beyond the fact that in another of his lists of names Clare identified her as a Northampton girl.

Clare may have used code for fear that an asylum official might have seen his notebook and objected to his corresponding with a woman outside. Or the disappearance of the vowels may have been a step on the road to the later mental degeneration that led him to speak of how his head had been cut off and all the vowels and consonants taken out one by one. Psychoanalysts who see significance in tiny details would no doubt attend to the way that the code slips on the word *believe*. To continue in self-belief was his perpetual struggle in the asylum.

Clare drafted letters to two other girls, using the same code. They are both much lighter and more casually flirtatious in tone. One was to a Hellen Maria Gardiner, who lived in a cottage by a paper mill near the asylum, and the other to Mary Ludgate, daughter of the proprietor of the White Hart Inn in Northampton. All three coded letters are in a notebook that Clare was using in 1850. After the one to Hellen Gardiner, he made a calmer note: '1850 May 12th Plumbs Pears and Apple Trees are in bloom and the Orchards are all blossoms'. In the same notebook he listed nine other girls' names. Six of them were Marys.

He was also filling an old pocket diary with more names. It was as if, having begun by listing the local girls for whom he wrote poems in return for tobacco, he felt compelled to go on and write down the names of every female he had ever met. We cannot know what drove that compulsion: sexual frustration must have played a part, but there was a deeper sense in which he was recording names in order to hold on to his past, his identity. It was around this time that he wrote to his family and reeled off the names of half the Helpston villagers of his youth. More mundanely, he may have been inspired to define himself through a list of names because the old diary that he was using began and ended with printed lists—of bankers and tax rates, duties of servants, ambassadors, coaching routes and times, of Bishops and Deans, Lords, and Members of Parliament with their constituencies.

This notebook contains the names of women from almost every phase of John Clare's life. From Helpston: Elizabeth Burbadge, wife of the village carpenter, and her two daughters Mary and Betsey. From Ashton Green, Ann and Elizabeth Porter, sisters of his schoolfriend Tom. And Betsey Newbon, his 'first love reality' (she was also conjured up in a late poem in the Knight transcripts). From Glinton: Mary Hand. From Stamford: Sally and Sophy, daughters of Drakard the bookseller. From a mill near Peterborough: the Miss Rolphs. From Northampton: Mary Ludgate, Julia Wigginton, and many more.

At times the names become mingled with delusions, including a recurrence of the Byronic impersonation. In reading the following

passage, one must remember that it was John Clare who courted
Martha Turner in 1818, at the age of twenty-five:

Lord Byron was 16 yrs when he began to write 'Childe Harold'
and finished it in 1818 when he was 25—when he wrote the 4th
Canto he was Courting one Martha Turner the Daughter of Mr
Will[m] Turner of Walk[d] Lodge—he began it one Sunday afternoon and finished it in three or four hours under an Ash Tree in
her Father's Home

Clare
Byron

Those clear blue eyes looked on me with a ray like May's skies
in Spring water soft and mild

   Mary Allen   Northborough
   Sarah Ann

'Wife Wife what Wife' a Comedy in Five acts
Is Jane Jewel a Wife
Yes by Marriage

1555

   Mary Castledine
   Mary Hives
   Sophy Hives
   Susan Hives
   Bekky Harrington
   Rachael Harrington
   Maria Harrington
   Mary Howell
   Mary Woolidge   Ufford
   Sally Derby
   Mary Moles
   Amelia Moles   Woodcroft
  Susan Lenton   Emma Betts—
  Susan Jayes   Payne's Tennant
   Miss Brooks's Tennant
   Eliza Dadford
   Mary Collingwood
   Mary Abbott

Ann Clare   Loop under Hill
I can't be myself
let me do as I will
I think till I'm
blind and feel willing
to die
but my true love has
left me and there remains
still
Mary Ann Appleby
Mary Ann Boyfield
Mary Boyd
Mary Ann True
Elenor Preston
Ann Pool   Glinton
He kissed me and left me
And nor do I know why

Then, some pages later, the names roll on as Clare drifts towards his identification with great men, such as the Iron Duke and the victor of Trafalgar:

Wellington
Albert
Nelson and Bronte
Prince of Wales
For her I live and love and sigh
My lovely Mary Neale ...
Lord Nelson (John Clare) on Board the 'L'Orient' Flagship receiving the Swords of the Enemy.

And on the final page and the inside back cover of the notebook:

Fell on the Deck of the Belerophon where his brains was knocked out with a Crowbar by the Crew
                    Horatio Nelson
          Hester Rolph
          Betsey Nottingham   Helpston
          Betsey Newbon   Ashton
          Betsey Nottingham   Bainton

> Jany 23 1850 Saw my Wife Patty in a Dream she looked well—
> with little Billy and an Infant carried by someone else all
> looked healthy and happy
>
> John Clare

On the flyleaf at the back of the first of his two precious volumes of transcriptions of the asylum poems, William Knight copied out a couplet, dated 27 August 1848, that he had found on a bit of blank paper in Clare's pocket: 'Some pretty face remembered in our youth / Seems ever with us wispering Love and Truth'. One of the last poems transcribed by Knight was a sonnet of farewell that ends with the words 'How can I forget?'—the same words that Clare had used when he returned home out of Essex and found no Mary. But the lists in the notebooks suggest that Clare spent many hours in the asylum remembering other pretty faces. About 150 women are named in the grubby pocket book that ends with the dream about Patty and little Billy. Mary Joyce is not among them.

The man who sits in an asylum writing of 'Lord Nelson (John Clare) on Board the "L'Orient" Flagship receiving the Swords of the Enemy' may deserve the name of 'lunatic'. But he is the same man who wrote this:

A VISION

> I lost the love of heaven above,
> I spurn'd the lust of earth below,
> I felt the sweets of fancied love—
> And hell itself my only foe.
>
> I lost earth's joys, but felt the glow
> Of heaven's flame abound in me
> 'Till loveliness and I did grow
> The bard of immortality.
>
> I loved, but woman fell away,
> I hid me from her faded fame,

I snatch'd the sun's eternal ray—
And wrote 'till earth was but a name.

In every language upon earth,
On every shore, o'er every sea,
I gave my name immortal birth
And kept my spirit with the free.

On the day that this poem was written, 2 August 1844, the Northampton General Lunatic Asylum witnessed a triumph, not a desolation. There is a thin partition between the delusion of madness and the highest reach of humankind's imaginative vision. This was Shakespeare's point that the lunatic and the poet are compacted by the tricks of strong imagination.

Through his poetry Clare was sometimes able to soar above the confines of earth, to break free from the shackles of the asylum: 'disdaining bounds of place and time', he 'could travel o'er the space / Of earth and heaven'. Byron at his most sublime had proposed a similar flight for the poet. At other times, though, poetry was for Clare the place of something more earthbound and ultimately more essential, more existential. It was where, as William Knight put it, he employed himself so that Clare could continue to be Clare. 'I feel I am;— I only know I am', he began his sonnet 'I Am'. And he ended it: 'But now I only know I am,—that's all.'

That 'all' of existential assertion was enough to lay the ground for the vision of reconnection to earth and sky, to childhood and eternity, ultimately to the divine, that he expressed in the very act of acknowledging his isolation, his shipwreck, in what is rightly his most famous lyric, the 'Lines: I Am' (written around the same time as the sonnet that is also called 'I Am'). Thomas Inskip arranged for publication in the *Bedford Times* on New Year's Day 1848:

I am—yet what I am, none cares or knows;
My friends forsake me like a memory lost:
I am the self-consumer of my woes—
They rise and vanish in oblivion's host

Like shadows in love-frenzied stifled throes——
And yet I am, and live——like vapours tossed

Into the nothingness of scorn and noise,
　　Into the living sea of waking dreams,
Where there is neither sense of life or joys,
　　　But the vast shipwreck of my life's esteems;
Even the dearest that I love the best
Are strange——nay, rather, stranger than the rest.

I long for scenes where man hath never trod,
　　A place where woman never smiled or wept,
There to abide with my Creator, God,
　　　And sleep as I in childhood sweetly slept,
Untroubling and untroubled where I lie,
The grass below——above, the vaulted sky.

When he was a child Clare set out to walk to the horizon, that magical line where sky meets earth. But the horizon is always beyond reach. As it receded, all he could imagine was an abyss at the edge of the world. Poetry took him to a better place. In imagination, even in the asylum, he could complete the circle of vision, undoing his troubles by laying himself to rest between grass and 'vaulted sky'. He longs at once for both childhood and the grave.

Plato tells in the *Symposium* of how when we are engendered we are split in two, with the result that we spend our lives wandering the earth in pursuit of our lost other half: such is the origin of desire. More than any other writer, Clare——the poet of circular motions—— lived out this Platonic quest. Perhaps that was because he was in a more literal sense split at birth, due to the early death of his twin sister. In 'Lines: I Am', he imagines himself back into an unbroken circle (a womb?) where he is himself without his cares. He finds a place anterior to the smiles and tears of erotic desire, the longed-for home where he was one with his other half who never grew to be a woman.

March 8th 1860

Dear Sir

I am in a Madhouse
& quite forget your
Name or who you are
You must excuse
me for I have nothing
to communicate or tell
of & why I am shut up
I don't know I have
nothing to say so I conclude
yours respectfully

John Clare

Mr J Hopkins

CHAPTER TWENTY-THREE

'WHY I AM SHUT UP I DONT KNOW'

The rest is near silence.

Inskip died late in 1849 and early the next year William Knight moved to a post in Birmingham, taking with him the two stout volumes into which he had transcribed the poems that Clare had composed during his first eight years in the Northampton asylum. There were more than eight hundred lyrics. Clare always veered between bursts of creativity and long periods of inertia, but his productivity averages out at a minimum of one hundred poems a year, or two per week. About 3,500 poems survive from the thirty-five years between the purchase in 1814 of the blank book that he entitled 'A Rustic's Pastime in Leisure Hours' and the final copies made by Knight into the manuscript book that he entitled 'Poetry by John Clare written by him while an Inmate of the Northampton General Lunatic Asylum'. By startling contrast, not a single poem survives from the years 1852 to 1859.

One hundred poems a year is a conservative estimate because we know that there were others that have not survived. By the same account, Clare may have gone on writing sporadically or even prolifically through the 1850s. It may simply be that the absence of a figure such as Knight meant that there was no one to preserve his work. We may even fantasise about the reappearance of a cache of lost manuscripts. But there is other evidence to suggest a withdrawal into silence. Clare's family kept his letters from the asylum: there is a yawning gap between one addressed to 'My dear daughter Sophy' in October 1852 and another to 'My dear Wife' in March 1860. And the asylum secretary, John Godfrey, said that for several years prior to 1860 Clare did not write a single line. 'I have forgotten how to write', he would say, and 'I'll write no more'.

In the first few months after Knight's departure, Clare kept in touch with him by letter. He sent a handful of new poems, written in pencil. Knight also ensured that his Northampton friend Joseph Stenson went on providing Clare with a supply of tobacco and books. For a time, Clare continued to enjoy news of the literary world. 'How do you get on at Birghmingham', he asked Knight, 'remember me to the Literary Lady you mention in your Letter—though I do not know her I know some of her friends Miss Landon Miss Cook Mrs Hemans and Mary Howitt and Remember them still perfectly'. Mary Howitt certainly visited Clare in the asylum and Eliza Cook may well have done, but he only 'knew' Miss Landon and the best-selling Mrs Hemans insofar as he knew their work.

Back in the 1820s, he had been 'uncommonly pleased' with the poetry of the famously fluent Laetitia Elizabeth Landon. He had been embarrassed when an editor assumed that one of his friendship poems addressed to Eliza Louisa Emmerson, 'E. L. E.', was meant for the much better known 'L. E. L.' He was not aware that at the height of her poetic popularity Landon had married, gone to West Africa and died of an overdose of prussic acid (accident?—more probably suicide) at the same age as Lord Byron, thirty-six.

Eliza Cook, self-educated daughter of a tinsmith, was an indefatigable poet and journalist who single-handedly published a weekly penny-halfpenny paper called *Eliza Cook's Journal*. Around this time, she devoted a lead article to the case of Clare and the proposition that 'The gifts of nature are of no rank or order . . . It is not necessary to graduate at a University to see Nature with a poetic eye.' She suggested, however, that it was rare for a 'peasant poet' to 'overleap the barriers of his class' and gain respect for his work purely on its

own merits. Eliza Cook found in Clare's poetry not only 'a perfect calendar of rural ongoings, of atmospheric beauties, of the life of the
flowers, woods, and fields', but also 'a loving eye for the common people among whom he lived—their customs, their griefs, and their
amusements'. His distinction lay in his unique combination of nature
and the people, linked together 'in one golden chain'. It was this that
made him the greatest of all the 'uneducated' poets.

Having mentioned the tragically premature deaths of such lower-
class poets as Burns, Kirke White and Robert Tannahill (a Scottish
silk-weaver and lyric writer—also admired by Clare—who drowned
himself at the age of twenty-six), Cook described the fate of Clare as
'the most unhappy of all'. He was 'a true child of genius—a born
poet, inspired by nature, but destroyed by the world'. She then told
her readers of how his 'nervous despondency' had eventually resulted
in 'complete unsettlement of the state of his mind'. She explained
that he still wrote poetry 'at lucid intervals' and that he was 'harmless and docile, though occasionally labouring under strange hallucinations'—as when he claimed to be a prize-fighter and spoke of his
great victories over long-dead rivals. 'He would also describe the
deaths, executions, and murders, of distinguished personages of former times, and fancy himself to have been an eye-witness of them.'
For Cook, all this was a sign that he was now living wholly in the place
where poetic genius had its origins: the imagination.

The exchange between Knight and Clare concerning 'literary
ladies', and the interest taken in his case by Eliza Cook, suggest a certain symmetry between the positions of the peasant poet and the
woman poet: each was struggling to make their voice heard in a literary world dominated by well-to-do, well-educated, well-connected
men. For some female readers today, the asylum notebooks make
Clare a repellent figure—one critic compares his lists of girls' names
to the documents of a 'sex-murderer'—yet his respect for the work of
Laetitia Landon and the spirit of shared poetic enterprise that ani-
mates his long correspondence with Eliza Emmerson tell a more
sympathetic story about his dealings with women.

In his letter to Knight of July 1850, Clare compared himself to the caged starling singing 'I cannot get out' in Laurence Sterne's novel *A Sentimental Journey*. He complained that he was lonely without the stimulation of Knight's company and that he was without books with which to kill time or inspire 'Prison Amusements' (i.e. poems) of his own. Nine months later he wrote again, enclosing an acrostic on the name of the artist George Maine. He continued to enjoy having his portrait taken.

The acrostic does not, however, seem to have been a new poem; it was probably written at the time of Maine's death over a year before. 'I heard U had broken your arm', Clare wrote in the accompanying letter, 'and now and then wish I was near U as usual to talk about Songs in which matters I have run myself out—I have scarcely read a good one since U left here so I don't know how to write one'. He keeps returning to his inability to write without the stimulation of nature or books or literary company. He is trapped and frustrated. For a second time he compares himself to Sterne's starling:

> I would try like the Birds a few Songs i' the Spring but they have shut me up and gave me no tools and like the caged Starnel of Stern 'I cant get out' to fetch any so I have made no progress at present—but I have written a good lot and as I should think nearly sufficient—so 'I rest from my labours and my works do follow me'—I love the 'rippling brook'—and 'the Singing of Birds'—But I cant get out to see them or hear them—while other people are looking at gay flower Gardens—I love to see the quaking bullrushes and the broad Lakes in the green meadows—and the sheep tracks over a fallowfield and a Land of thistles in flower—I wish I could make U a little book of Songs worth sending but after some trials I cant do it at present . . . I am in this d———d mad house and cant get out.

The phrase 'they have shut me up' following immediately upon an image of birdsong has extraordinary poignancy: Clare is not only a man enclosed but also a songster silenced. Yet it was not true that he was altogether deprived of his tools. The asylum had a library (though the Lunatic Commissioners complained about its poor stock) and pen and paper were obviously available to him. There may be a hint of paranoia in the projection of his silencing onto 'them', his keepers. Physical frailty and the depressive's lack of will-power, rather than cage-like confinement, are more likely reasons why he was no longer spending time outside the grounds of the asylum. There is no reason to think that he had become excessively violent or dangerously delusional by this time.

This moving letter to Knight is without a hint of 'lunacy'. Nor indeed does it manifest the decline of literary powers about which it complains: the bulrushes, sheep-tracks and thistles in flower could as well come from a poem. The presence of quotations are another reminder that Clare was as inspired by his reading as well as his walks in the fields. When thinking of how over the years he has composed 'a good lot', his mind turns to the image of a completed task, a finished life, in a verse from the Book of Revelation: 'Blessed are the dead which die in the Lord from henceforth: Yea, saith the Spirit, that they may rest from their labours; and their works do follow them.'

There were, nevertheless, vast stretches of silence during which the family must have wondered whether he was dead. His son Charles wrote in June 1850, asking how he was, anxious because they had not heard from him for 'a long time'. He mentioned that Joseph Henderson had left Milton Hall for the Fitzwilliam estate in Yorkshire, to which Clare replied just over a week later: 'I am sorry Mr Henderson has left the neighbourhood before I get back as I thought of going to see him when I got home—You may give him my best respects when you write to him and tell him I am still fond of Flowers and Birdnesting and all old amusements as usual.' To judge from this, he still imagined he would one day return home.

He asked after his family, including his father and his daughter Anna Maria, both of whom had died some years before. 'I would write you a long Letter only I have nothing to write about', he concluded, 'for I see Nothing and hear nothing'. And then in a postscript, 'I forgot to be kindly remembered to your Mother'.

Charles wrote again in May 1851:

My dear Father

It is now a very long time since we heard from you therefore Dear father I have written to you I hope to hear you are in Good health I have not got any thing to write about this time Dear Father when I have said that my Mother Brothers and Sisters are all well and send their kindest love to you also that my Brother John intends coming to see you again this Summer but I cannot say exactly when but I think Dear Father you need not expect him yet as it may be in the latter part of the summer or perhaps in autumn.

Clare replied that he was in his 'usual state of health' and that he had a particular message for his daughter Eliza: she should be sure to send her little ones to school. 'Do not forget that', he added. We do not know whether John made his intended visit later in the summer. He had certainly not gone to Northampton by July, when there was a further exchange of letters in which Clare said that he would be glad to see his son. Once again he asked after family members, friends and neighbours, some of whom had been dead for years. Among the names he recalled was that of his early sweetheart, Betsey Newbon.

It was soon after this that Charles Clare came down with tuberculosis. Sophy wrote in the autumn of 1852, but seems not to have told her father how serious her brother's condition was. Clare replied with the vain hope that Charles would soon be better. Within weeks he was dead. We do not know when—or indeed whether—Clare heard the news. Charles's death was a great blow to the family: as the most literate of the children, he had been the one with real prospects of advancement. The last surviving fragment in his hand is a letter to a correspondent who wanted to include a sample of Clare in a poetry anthology for schools. Charles replied that his father had been an inmate of an asylum for many years, '~~too much~~ Study having affected his Brain'. That striking-through of the phrase 'too much', as if to remove the smack of censure, offers a tiny revelation of Charles's sensitivity to his father's state.

The medical bill for Charles's treatment in his last days remained unpaid for two years. Patty treasured her lost boy's handwritten *Laws of Cricket*, while the task of corresponding with John Taylor fell to Sophy, the younger of Clare's two surviving daughters. Her handwriting, grammar and spelling were much rougher than Charles's. Several letters survive in which she sends the family's thanks for their half-yearly payments of five pounds from Earl Spencer, received via Mossop.

Throughout the asylum years, Clare's trust fund continued to be administered by Taylor and his associates. They did all they could for the family. In March 1850 Charles had requested money from Taylor to set up his older brother John (Jack) in business. Taylor replied that he did not have the power to use the trust fund for such a purpose. Jack was forced to leave the neighbourhood in pursuit of employment. He got a job as a carpenter undertaking railway construction work. In 1855 he was in Dorset, probably working on the construction of the Great Western Railway. He married Sarah Bartlett, a labourer's daughter, that February. In September she died in childbirth. The baby boy survived and was called Charles, after his recently deceased uncle. Jack took his son home to Northborough, to be cared for by Patty. We do not know how the infant was nourished on the journey across country with his father, but there is no doubt that he spent his childhood in the Northborough cottage. His was another mouth for Patty to feed.

In another exchange of correspondence concerning the family finances, Taylor had expressed regret that the other brother, William Parker, was idle. Charles had replied that 'he would not be idle if he could get any employ'. William Parker was a gardener and casual labourer who frequently couldn't get work for more than one day a fortnight, at the rate of one shilling and sixpence per day. One senses from Taylor's tone and Charles's defensiveness that he was a sullen presence: unlettered, usually out of work, stuck at home helping his mother keep house. We may recall that when Clare had dreamed of his three sons whilst in Dr Allen's asylum, William was the one with whom he was 'in a wrack'.

Clare's letter home in autumn 1852 was written out on his behalf by a fellow-patient. Clare explained that he could no longer write at any speed in his own hand. Rheumatism may well have been setting in: not a scrap of his handwriting survives from the next eight years. When the record resumes, his penmanship is shaky, without any of its old fluency. So it is that for the remainder of the 1850s we have only fragmentary glimpses. After about 1852, Clare was no longer well enough to walk into Northampton. He had become all but invisible to the outside world.

In 1854 Anne Elizabeth Baker, sister of the Northampton antiquary with whom Clare had corresponded years before, completed her *Glossary of Northamptonshire Words and Phrases*. It was published by subscription in two volumes. 'The dialectical peculiarities of our language are much less strongly marked than formerly, and are fast disappearing', explained Miss Baker in her preface, 'while various circumstances have conspired to render it most desirable to preserve in remembrance these remnants of our vernacular tongue.' She attributed the pace of change primarily to the advent of the railway.* Her desire to preserve a decaying tradition of local culture was of course an impulse strongly shared by Clare. The glossary has over five thousand entries, including about two thousand dialect words that had not been recorded in previous works of a similar kind. A high proportion of these were derived from the writing of Clare himself; he is credited with half of all the strictly Northamptonshire words.

Like *The Village Minstrel*, Baker's glossary included not only local words and 'examples of their colloquial use', but also an account of 'The Customs of the Country', such as Mumming plays and the Whitsun-ale festival. In the account of May Day festivities, there is a poem on the customs in and around Helpston that Clare wrote 'expressly for the present work'. This might indicate that he was still writing new material in the 1850s, but it is more likely that the poem was written on a visit to Anne Baker's house sometime in the 1840s

---

*Until the mid-nineteenth century, local time, determined by the position of the sun, varied from parish to parish, but the necessity for a nationwide railway timetable imposed uniformity upon time. By the same account, increased physical mobility diminished local linguistic diversity.

when Clare spent much of his time in the town of Northampton—the compilation of the glossary had been the work of many years, undertaken in collaboration with Miss Baker's brother, George, before his death in 1851.

Baker's preface gave particular thanks to the 'native' Northamptonshire poet Clare, 'who beautifully clothes his ideas in his own rustic idiom'. A considerable number of entries in the glossary were supported by quotation from manuscript poems that had 'all been written since his mental aberration, and during his confinement in the Northampton Asylum'. Fittingly, then, given Clare's passion for the language of his locality, many fragments of his asylum verses first reached print in the form of a dialect dictionary. So, for example, in illustration of *chimble*, 'To nibble or chew into small pieces, as vermin do anything within reach', we find

> The mice come out to *chimble* fruits,
> And take hips under ground;
> The husks of hips and haws lie round
> All *chimbled* seed and skin,
> There noses now peep from the ground,
> And there the tails bob in.

For *screed*, meaning 'shred', there is 'When *screeds* of sunshine gild the little yard, / A hive-bee humming by the wall is heard'. And for *whirlipuff*, 'a sudden gust of wind driving the dust into an eddy',

> Where the *whirlipuff* comes as if something was in't,
> And tazzles the grasses, and ruffles the corn,
> And runs o'er the corn-field in less than a minute.

In each case—and many others—the lines are ascribed to 'Clare's MS [manuscript] Poems'. By a happy twist of literary fortune, one of the most valuable offices that Anne Baker's glossary now performs is its elucidation of Clare's incomparably rich regional vocabulary and preservation of some of his last poems.

Thanks to writers such as Eliza Cook and Anne Baker, Clare's name was not forgotten in Northampton. He remained something of a local celebrity. G. C. Druce, who grew up to become an authority on the flora of the region, remembered how as a child he saw a small, dreamy-looking man gazing up at the sky. He was told it was Clare. Nationally, though, the Northamptonshire poet was steadily falling further into obscurity.

In 1851 a Congregational minister called Edwin Paxton Hood published a book called *Literature of Labour*. It included a substantial chapter on the life and poetry of Clare, arguing that he was the most remarkable of all labouring-class writers ('always excepting Burns'). Paxton Hood wrote incisively about Clare's art of particularity: 'Other poets select a river, or a mountain, and individualise it, but to Clare all are but parts of the same lovely Home, and as every part of the home is endeared—the chair, the shelf, the lattice, the wreathing flower, the fire-place, the table—so is every object in Nature a beloved object, because the whole is beloved.' Hood reported that Clare was now in the Northampton asylum, but that 'It is not to be supposed that the mind has really tottered from its throne: the fact appears to be that the body is too weak for the mind'. He made a pilgrimage to the poet's birthplace and was cordially received by the Reverend Mossop, who furnished him with 'the mournful details of the swan of Helpstone'. From there he went over to Northborough and spent a few minutes with Patty. He saw the old violin (the gift of Hessey) hanging on the wall, and Patty tearfully reminisced of the happiness of bygone days.

The combination of poignant biographical detail and high critical praise may have been calculated to revive Clare's reputation, but Paxton Hood's efforts met with little response. Clare's name is hardly to be found in print in the next few years. Among the handful of passing references were a brief mention in the 1856 edition of *Men of the Times: Biographical Sketches of Eminent Living Characters* to the effect that Clare had for many years been 'wholly lost to the world, without any hope of his restoration', and an anonymous magazine poem of 1857 in which he was described as an 'inoffensive lunatic'.

He was also mentioned in an article in the *Quarterly Review* by a Northamptonshire clergyman called Thomas James. This cultivated and philanthropic gentleman, whose unmarried sister shared his enthusiasm, had become interested in the work of the local asylum's most celebrated inmate. He regarded Clare as one of the county's two great poets, the other being the seventeenth-century laureate John Dryden. He delivered some public lectures to this effect. More than this, he approached John Taylor about putting together a selection of the poet's writings for the benefit of his family. He explained that he had access to some of Clare's unpublished poems—presumably through William Knight at the asylum—and inquired about rights to the published ones.

Taylor was delighted, but the scheme came to nothing.* The Reverend James had approached a Northampton publisher who, confusingly, was also called John Taylor. After expressing initial interest, this Taylor got cold feet, partly because he was conscious of a Mr Codgbrook of Northampton who, in order to get a pile of old copies of *The Village Minstrel* off his hands, had 'bound the two vols. in one, in a flashy red cloth binding, and lettered "Literary Souvenir." ' Codgbrook's ruse had not been a success and Taylor of Northampton thought this suggested there would not be enough of a market for anything else by Clare.

The article in the *Quarterly* had mentioned how Clare seemed a misfit when he was taken to London in the first year of his fame. A visitor to the asylum mentioned this to him and he replied, 'Yes, they wanted me to talk fine but I wouldn't'. The same visitor also recorded Clare's reply to the question of whether he had written anything recently: 'No, I haven't written a line for a hundred and fifty years; and I won't write any more. It has brought me into bondage, and I want my liberty'. He supposedly said that he wanted to be a farmer's boy again and to have the freedom to go back into Northampton. Then he 'wandered away into the wildest extravagances of his being a son of George III, and of his not being a man at all, but a spirit, that could stand fire and water; and of dragons that came and *flopped* down in

---

*Taylor mentioned in a letter around this time that he was thinking of going to Northampton the following day, with Hessey, presumably to see Clare. There is no record of the visit.

the yard with their great wings about them'. At this, 'the surgeon stopped him by a touch on the shoulder, and "Ah! Mr Clare, that will do" '.

The most authoritative recollection of Clare in the 1850s is that of Dr Nesbitt, medical superintendent of the asylum from 1845 to 1858. He noted the persistent 'visionary ideas and hallucinations': 'He may be said to have lost his own personal identity as with all the gravity of truth he would maintain that he had written the works of Byron, and Sir Walter Scott, that he was Nelson and Wellington, that he had fought and won the battle of Waterloo, that he had had his head shot off at this battle, whilst he was totally unable to explain the process by which it had again been affixed to his body'. At other times, though, the patient remained perfectly aware of his own identity, speaking of his love of wild flowers and the way that his poetry 'came to him whilst walking in the fields'. He said that he 'kicked it out of the clods'. Nesbitt remembered being presented with a scrap that read 'Where flowers are, God is, and I am free'.

The overriding impression was of passivity and defensiveness: 'He was generally docile and tranquil, but would brook no interference—anything approaching to this last would excite his ire in a torrent of ejaculation of no ordinary violence in which imprecations were conspicuous; but this was an exceptional state of things. Seated on a bench, and with his constant friend a quid of Tobacco, he would remain silent for hours.' Several visitors to the asylum mentioned seeing him thus.

The more dramatic delusions explain why some critics and biographers have speculated that Clare was schizophrenic or had a 'multiple personality' disorder. But, as I have suggested, his general behaviour does not conform to the usual patterns of schizophrenia. Typically, schizophrenics are easily distracted, unable to concentrate—yet Clare's characteristic mood was a state of intense absorption in his immediate environment. The 'negative' symptoms of schizophrenia do not accord with the Clare who was, in Dr Nesbitt's words, 'essentially a kind-hearted, good-feeling man'. Episodic hallucinations and delusions of the kind experienced by Clare in his later years are perfectly consistent with the view that his condition was what we now call manic depression of increasingly severe, and ultimately psychotic, magnitude.

Clare was always deeply influenced by his environment: this, after all, was what made him such a superb poet of the natural world. It is therefore hardly surprising that he took on some of the characteristics of true 'madness' (if that is the world we wish to use) in the course of more than twenty years in the lunatic asylum among inmates some of whom did undoubtedly suffer from such schizophrenic symptoms as extreme paranoia, the hearing of alien voices, and deluded beliefs about their own identity. One of Clare's fellow-patients believed he was God Almighty, another the Queen of the Fairies. If Nesbitt was right in saying that Clare sometimes believed 'with all the gravity of truth' that he was Byron or Nelson, then there were times when he was as 'mad' as these other sufferers. In modern psychiatric practice, a key question about psychosis is whether during 'normal' behaviour the patient is aware of his or her periodic 'abnormal' behaviour: unfortunately we do not have sufficient clinical evidence to establish whether there were phases when Clare knew that his personae such as Byron and Nelson were delusions or whether he eventually lost the ability to distinguish between reality and his fantasies.

Nesbitt's casebooks have been lost, but Frederick Martin saw them when researching his biography immediately after Clare's death, and he noted certain records to the effect that Clare 'was violent etc. on such a day and was treated in such and such a way.' What comes across especially strongly in the accounts that do survive is Clare's desire not to be disturbed. Long before the asylum years, he had complained of the 'friendly interferences' with which he always had to contend. Given his history, it is perfectly understandable that as an old man he 'would brook no interference'. His outbursts of swearing—very typical in people who have been institutionalized—were a form of defence. This may also have been the case with such stories as the one about having his head shot off at the battle of Waterloo: it was as good a way as any to make people leave him alone.

Whatever degree of conscious control Clare did or did not have over his fantasies, they clearly reveal his aspirations and his sufferings. To say that he had written the works of Byron and Scott was but an extreme way of saying he had written works that he hoped might one day be regarded as the equal of those of Byron and Scott. The Lord and the Baronet were the two most famous writers of the age: the Peasant wanted to be in their company, but was held back by his social status and economic impoverishment. These are facts, not delusions. Equally, the figure of the prize-fighter and the imagery of battle are in one sense dramatisations of the fact that Clare spent his life fighting battles—for his poetry, for recognition, for survival, against his inner demons.

In February 1860 Clare took up his pen again. He sketched a sheet of grotesque heads and then composed a handful of short lyrics, including a sonnet addressed 'To John Clare':

> Well, honest John, how fare you now at home?
> The spring is come and birds are building nests,
> The old cock robin to the sty is come
> With olive feathers and its ruddy breast,
> And the old cock with wattles and red comb
> Struts with the hens and seems to like some best,
> Then crows and looks about for little crumbs
> Swept out by little folks an hour ago.
> The pigs sleep in the sty; the bookman comes,
> The little boys lets home-close nesting go
> And pockets tops and taws where daisy blooms
> To look at the new number just laid down
> With lots of pictures and good stories too
> And Jack the Giant-killer's high renown.

Despite the decade's silence, Clare has lost none of his poetic lucidity and accomplishment. Like many of the 'Midsummer Cushion' and Northborough sonnets, these lines have an utterly original and carefully controlled rhyme scheme. And, as in so many of Clare's best poems, the different elements in the scene are held together through a pattern of repetition and variation—from cock robin to cock in the yard, sty to pig, birds building nests to bird's-nesting boys. In a typical Clare move, the cyclical motions of the natural world are then interrupted by a human intrusion: with the arrival of the pedlar selling penny books, the boys turn from nature to art, from outdoor games to reading of old adventures.

It has always been assumed that this poem is addressed by Clare to himself and is therefore further evidence of a split in his identity: the old man in the asylum is imagining his own younger self back home at Helpston. The arrival of the itinerant bookseller was indeed a treat in his childhood; reading stories in old chapbooks was just as much an originating force for his poetry as were bird's-nesting and walking out where daisies bloomed. There is, however, an alternative or additional reading of the poem. A few weeks after writing it, Clare wrote a letter to his family in which he referred to his elder surviving son as 'Champion John Junr': it is quite possible that 'honest John' refers to John Junior and that the sonnet is to be imagined as an address to his son. 'How fare you now at home?' would then be less a fantasy that his own spirit was still in its old home and more a tender inquiry after the well-being of his loved ones back in Northborough as winter comes to an end.

The letter home, dated 7 March 1860, was addressed to Patty and signed 'your loving husband till Death'—this from a man who had not seen his wife for twenty years. Its content suggests some confusion in both Clare's short-term memory and the extent of his knowledge of family affairs. He asked after his father, mother and son Frederick, all of whom had died many years before. Yet he did not mention Charles, so perhaps he did know about, and recall, the death of his beloved youngest son.

There were still occasional inquiries from well-wishers. A Westminster gentleman called James Hipkins wrote at this time. Dr Wing, who had succeeded Nesbitt as asylum superintendent in 1858, replied that the poet was 'still living and in good bodily health though very feeble in mind and still the subject of many mental delusions'. He tried to persuade Clare to write a poem for Hipkins, without success. All he could elicit was the following brief letter:

> Dear Sir
> I am in a Madhouse and quite forget your Name or who you are—you must excuse me for I have nothing to commu[n]icate or tell of and why I am shut up I dont know—I have nothing to say so I conclude
> Yours respectfully John Clare

This is a voice not of madness but of quiet despair.

Daughter Sophy replied to Clare's letter home. Was there anything they could send? There was no particular news. She had the tact not to mention that his sister, her namesake, had died back in 1855. The letter merely states that Aunt Sophia's family were all well and sent their love (she had left five children). 'We think of coming to see you in the course of a Month or two if the Lord spares us', added Sophy, but as far as we know, no family member did manage to make the journey to Northampton in the remaining four years of Clare's life.

His reply to Sophy is his last surviving letter. He again asked after his parents and his sister, who had not been mentioned in Sophy's letter because they were dead. A further name was added after 'Aunt Sophy': 'and Mary'. The delusion of the two wives had not entirely left him. 'I shall be glad to see You when you come—God bless you all', he wrote in response to the prospect of a visit. But his answer to the inquiry as to whether he needed anything seems to have a double meaning: 'I want nothing from Home to come here'. The memory of home had to be kept inviolate from the sights and sounds of the asylum.

Two further sonnets on the subject of spring followed some weeks later. The botanical detail is still there—crocus, 'patty kay' (colloquialism for *hepatica*), heart's-ease, polyanthus, pilewort—and the mind's eye for tiny things is sharp as ever: a brook spangling in the sunshine, 'hedges leafing with the green spring tide', a 'grass green' linnet, a beetle, a fly resting on a leaf. John Godfrey, asylum secretary, was surprised by 'the refreshing sweetness' of these poems, given the poet's 'desponding condition', but it was clear to the staff that in early 1860 his mind was in a more settled state than it had been for a long time. The improvement only lasted for a few months. Godfrey recalled that in the middle of the year 'the pen was resolutely laid aside, and the former misanthropic ideas were resumed'.

Agnes Strickland was co-author with her sister of an early Victorian multi-volume bestseller, *The Lives of the Queens of England*. She moved in the very best society. In 1860, after her usual summer season in London, she did an autumn round of country-house parties. First a visit to the mansion of Lady Emily Foley, sister of the Duke of Montrose, where she immersed herself in a copy of the *Anti-Tobacco Journal* and wrote to a friend complaining about the cigar and pipe smoke of the gentlemen. Then on to Stanford Hall near Rugby to stay with a robust dowager who had recently turned ninety-three. But then came an invitation to one of the grandest residences in England: Althorp House. Her host was the fifth Earl Spencer, at that time Groom Stole to Prince Albert. She revelled in the picture gallery and the library. She mingled comfortably at dinner with the Marquess of Exeter, the Earl of Euston, Lord Pomfret and her Ladyship's brother, General Seymour of the Rifle Brigade. 'The youthful lord and lady are so kind,' she wrote, 'that I feel quite at home with them—and Lady Sarah Spencer is quite a darling.'

The occasion of the party was a display by the riflemen of the Northamptonshire Volunteers—shades of Clare's enlistment nearly half a century before. But the rain poured down, the field became a mire and other amusements had to be found for the ladies. An outing to Burghley House with Lady Spencer provided the chance to see more old master paintings. After this, his Lordship proposed a visit to the local lunatic asylum, of which he was a benevolent patron. They went on 28 August, with General Seymour in attendance. Miss Strickland was amused to see how 'the poor madmen in the convalescent ward' crowded round Spencer, 'for they are all so very fond of him'. Then she was brought up short:

> I saw poor Clare, the celebrated Northamptonshire poet, among
> them. He is sullen and sad, but not violent. He told me he was
> much happier when he worked hard with his hands, for then he
> was strong and healthy. It was literature that had turned his
> brain and he put his hand on his head. His remark and action
> gave me the he artache.

The anti-tobacco activist does not say whether the poet was chewing
his customary quid.

Clare gave her a poem, 'The daisy is a happy flower', dated 25 July.
Reminiscent of the early work that had brought him fame, it was a
routine performance, tripping lightly with the motion of bee and
butterfly, then suddenly darkening to end on the fall of 'evening
shadows'. Miss Strickland expressed her pleasure, but Clare did not
raise his eyes, saying only, 'Ugh it is a tidy little thing'. We may sense,
as she did not, his frustration at being able to do no more than reproduce the simplicities of his early poetic manner.

She tried to carry on the conversation: 'I am glad you can amuse
yourself by writing.' 'I can't do it,' he replied, 'they pick my brains so.'
And then, one of the most haunting of his asylum sayings: 'Why, they
have cut off my head and picked out all the letters in the alphabet—
all the vowels and all the consonants and brought them out through
my ears—and then they want me to write poetry! I can't do it.'

Is this a symptom of persecution mania—the idea that 'they' had
it in for him? Or is it the agony of the artist who has been confined
away from the world while the words of poetry have gone on ringing
so intensely in his head that they have ceased to relate to things and
have instead been reduced to their raw components, *b*'s and *e*'s and *s*'s
and *t*'s which are like physical things that can be picked out of the
head one by one? Is it the regime of the asylum—the babel of his
fellow-inmates' voices and then the demand to perform for visitors—
that has cut off his head for poetry? Or should we number among the
'they' that whole succession of booksellers and publishers, patrons
and well-wishers, doctors and clergymen who tried to help Clare, to
sort him out in one way or another?

Or was it the poetry itself that drove him to the asylum? When

Agnes Strickland asked whether he preferred the life of the poet or that of the agricultural labourer, he had no hesitation in replying, 'I like hard work best, I was happy then. Literature has destroyed my head and brought me here.' In saying this, he was tacitly assenting to the diagnosis of Dr Skrimshire on the committal papers: it was not society or poverty or physical illness but the years of addiction to 'poetical prosing' that had turned his mind. He seems to be admitting that his head full of vowels and consonants could not make its way in the outside world.

For Miss Strickland, the moral was obvious: 'Alas! For the tragedy of authorship to men of low degree. How many lunatics, drunkards and suicides may date their calamities from the evil hour when literary ambition was roused and excited by a flattering and fickle world.' She returned from the county asylum to the great house, where she wrote a trifling poem of her own on the subject of 'The Meeting of the Rifle Volunteers in Althorp Park': 'Young Spencer calls his volunteers / To dine in festive glee, / Like Rupert and his cavaliers / Under the greenwood tree.'

Light versifying such as this comes easily enough to a genteel amateur, whereas Clare's despair in 1860 owed much to the sheer difficulty he was experiencing in completing to his own professional satisfaction even a poem so brief and simple as 'The Daisy'. In addition to the fair copy given to Miss Strickland, there are four other manuscripts of the lines in Clare's hand, each with variants and corrections. He had been working on it back in February and again in March. He tinkered with it once more in January 1863, after two and a half years during which he appears to have written nothing.

Agnes Strickland was not the last visitor. Others came in the final years. The artist Thomas Grimshaw returned to Northampton after a long absence. Clare immediately recognised him and they talked with some satisfaction about the portrait that had been painted nearly twenty years before. Grimshaw thought that Clare had 'quite his young look again', though this is hard to credit if one looks at the grizzled photograph of him that was taken in 1862 or the sketches done by a fellow-patient, George Duval Berry, which give him the unkempt and sorrowful look of a King Lear, his head bald on top but with side-whiskers and long white locks falling to his shoulders.

Another gentleman present on the occasion of Grimshaw's visit read out some verses by a former acquaintance who had moved to Australia. Clare's sullen look seemed to say, 'That is not poetry'. Godfrey, who shepherded the visitors, sought to ease the embarrassment of the moment by reciting some lines from Gray's 'Elegy Written in a Country Churchyard'. He asked Clare if he knew that. 'Know that?' he replied. 'To be sure I do; it's Gray, I knew Gray well'. According to Godfrey, if any of Clare's favourite poets were mentioned, 'he would immediately say that he knew him well or that he was a particular friend of his—evidently fully believing that his favourite authors were also his old earthly friends.' In his aged mind there was now no distinction between reality and the life of his imagination. But is it really 'madness' to say that one *knows* a favourite author, or a poem committed to memory, as well as one knows a neighbour or casual acquaintance?

In 1861 a Northampton poet called John Plummer visited the asylum and found Clare reading in the window recess of a comfortable room, 'the sitting chamber of the better class of patients'. There were mahogany chairs, table and couch, a soft carpet and warm fire. Clare was taciturn: he looked at his visitors with a vacant gaze for a moment, and then went on reading his book. Yet the attendant said that in general he was 'good humoured, obedient and cheerful'. 'Blithe and talkative' were the words that Plummer used in a later report on his visit. The variation of mood even this late in life suggests that he never escaped what modern clinicians would call his 'cyclothymic' condition.

He scratched his last poem onto a double sheet of foolscap. In a shaky hand, he scribbled down some half-remembered verses from Burns's 'Tam o'Shanter' that conjure up a stormy, windy night. As if in reply to his early poetic mentor, he then evoked a contrasting scene, a sunny spring day in the countryside he loved. John Godfrey recorded that the poem was composed about six months before Clare's death.

If that is correct, it was written very late in 1863, perhaps during a winter storm that reminded him of the lines in Burns. One final effort of imagination released him from the night and the storm, enabling him to recall his own springtime and to gather the fragments of memory with which to build the last of his poetic 'Birds Nests':

> 'Tis Spring warm glows the South
> Chaffinchs carry the moss in his mouth
> To the filbert hedges all day long
> And charms the poet with his beautifull song
> The wind blows blea o'er the sedgey fen
> But warm the sunshines by the little wood
> Where the old Cow at her leisure chews her cud

The manuscript is marked with more corrections than usual and the handwriting shows that the use of the pen had become, in Godfrey's words, 'a most laborious task'. As far as we know, these calm and poised lines were the last that Clare ever wrote.

Dr Wing's casebooks survive in the archive of the asylum. On 29 August 1861 he recorded an accident: 'Mr Clare in getting up immediately after dinner today fell, probably from a slight apopleptic seizure, of which he has had several, hit his head against the sharp edge of the table, causing an irregular jagged wound of about 3 inches in length and in depth through the integument to the periosteum which was uninjured—the wound was dressed with dry lint and plaster and he was put to bed.' *Apopleptic seizure* was the term used for a stroke. A series of mild strokes is the most likely cause of Clare's diminished mobility, impaired memory and difficulty with writing in his final years.

His next appearance in Wing's casebook was on 1 February 1863: 'Became very giddy and appeared to lose the use of his legs just before dinner time today, so he was put to bed. His delusions about his personal identity are as strong as ever, sometimes fancying himself Lord Byron, at others a Sea Captain, etc., His language is at times very bad.' There are several further entries over the following months: 'His habits are becoming very dirty and scarcely a day passes without his having to be changed on this account—otherwise he is much the same'; 'Is a trifle stronger than he was in the winter and he is occasionally taken out amongst the flowers to view the beauties of that nature of which he was wont to be so fond, but without apparently awakening any pleasurable emotions'; 'Was somewhat improved in general health lately, but mentally there is but little change, phantoms still haunt him and he will often swear most coarsely at the creatures of his own disordered fancy, his left side being usually where they locate themselves'.

Early in 1864 Wing reported that Clare's condition was more or less unchanged: better than he was nine months before, 'but yet very helpless and quite childish'. There came a time when he could no longer dress himself. Presiding over his ward was Sergeant George Bacon, a Crimean war veteran who also served as asylum bandmaster. He took particular care of the old man, not least because he had poetic aspirations of his own. Towards the end, Bacon moved Clare from a 'single dormitory' to his own room, so that he could check on him at night. This seemed to please him, though Bacon's recollection was that 'he never used to talk'.

On Good Friday (25 March), he was taken into his beloved outdoors for the last time, pushed in a Bath chair. In April, Wing noted a marked decline. The symptoms of stroke had become more severe:

> His general health has not been so good lately and the right side had more than once shown distinct signs of paralysis. His language is still often very bad indeed and he sometimes becomes so excited when swearing, that always having a quid in his mouth the piece finds its way into his larynx which brings on a dreadful fit of coughing and his face and head become perfectly scarlet and give strong fears of a sudden apoplexy.

In the day-room, he could still walk slowly to his favourite seat, looking out on the asylum's spacious gardens, but on 16 May he was confined to his bed due to the formation of a boil near his anus.

He lay quietly for three days. Godfrey believed that he had long since lost the will to live. As in the week of his birth, there was a heat wave. The perspiration rolled off him in streams as he lay in bed. On the morning of 20 May, 'he was found to be completely comatose'. At five to five that hot afternoon, 'he simply ceased to breathe'. The cause of death was formally recorded as apoplexy. In his last years he had often said 'I have lived too long' and 'I want to go home'.

PART FIVE

The Eternity of Song

In every language upon earth,
On every shore, o'er every sea,
I gave my name immortal birth
And kept my spirit with the free.

just about the middle of the ground where the Morning & Evening Sun can linger the longest on my Grave I wish to have a rough unhewn stone something in the form of a mile stone so that the playing boys may not break it in their heedless pastimes with nothing more on it then this Inscription.

I desire that no date be inserted thereon as I wish it to live or dye with my poems & other writing which if they have merit with prosperity it will & if they have not it is not worth preserving

HERE
Rest the
HOPES
and Ashes
of
JOHN CLARE

October
8th
1824.
"Vanity of vanity
all is Vanity"

Memorandums Continued

I once signed an agreement made out by Drury a long while back but I was reluctant at the first

CLARE'S INSTRUCTIONS FOR HIS TOMBSTONE

CHAPTER TWENTY-FOUR

REMAINS

J ohn Clare narrowly avoided a pauper's burial. The letter informing Patty of his death was sent to Helpston rather than Northborough. Good fortune intervened. The news quickly reached
William Bellars, son of the couple for whom the young Clare had
worked as a ploughboy at Woodcroft Castle. By coincidence, he was in
the process of buying the poet's old cottage. On discovering that the
asylum authorities intended to bury him at minimal expense in the
local cemetery in Northampton, Bellars and his wife Fanny immediately took it in hand to bring Clare's remains home to Helpston.

Bellars was a churchwarden, so well placed to make the arrangements. Together with Mr Spencer, the new tenant of Woodcroft Castle, he paid for the transportation of the body. Back at the asylum,
fellow-patient George Berry had sketched some simple and serene
line drawings of the corpse, and a death-mask had been taken, probably by Dr Wing, who duly noted Clare's death in his annual report
for 1864:

> Though ailing for some time, yet not in a degree to excite seri-
> ous apprehension of immediate danger, [Clare] was suddenly
> cut off by apoplexy on the 20th of May. It had been my purpose,
> had space and my physical strength permitted, to have written
> somewhat at length on the character of his insanity, and to have

pointed out the frequent connection between mental aberration and genius, and especially as illustrated by some of our noted poets. Latterly his intellect had become sadly clouded, yet there were periods when the shadow would be temporarily lifted.

Wing himself died the following year; it is regrettable that he did not write at greater length on the character of his patient's insanity.

The body of John Clare reached Helpston railway station on a sunny afternoon four days after his death, accompanied by asylum secretary John Godfrey. The coffin was laid out for the night in the Exeter Arms, the face visible through a thin glass plate. Clare would probably have been pleased that his mortal remains spent their last night above ground in a pub. Fanny Bellars, meanwhile, drove Godfrey to Northborough and the news was broken to Patty.

The funeral took place the next day. Forty years earlier, Clare had expressed the desire 'to lie on the North side the Church yard just about the middle of the ground where the Morning and Evening sun can linger the longest on my Grave'. In his early sonnet 'A Wish', published in *The Village Minstrel*, he had expressed the hope that he would eventually be laid to rest beneath a beloved sycamore tree. His favoured shady plot being occupied, he was buried on the south side, close to the church wall and beside his parents.

The vicar of Helpston was away in Scotland, so the burial service was read by the curate of Glinton. We may assume that he would have collected his vestments and prayer book from the Glinton Church vestry where Clare had attended school with Mary Joyce. Patty led the mourners, together with her son William Parker and his wife, who now shared the cottage in Northborough,* and her daughter Eliza Louisa (plus granddaughter). Little Charles, Jack's son by his first marriage, was there too. Also present were the Reverend Charles Mossop, who had buried Clare's parents but had by this time moved

---

*William Parker Clare married an Elizabeth Pateman in 1862; they had three children. The Northborough cottage remained in the hands of this family until 1920.

from Helpston to Etton; Jane Mossop, who was still close to her brother; Mr and Mrs Bellars; Mr and Mrs Spencer of Woodcroft; a Mr Edgson of Market Deeping, who had taken an interest in the family; and three friends from Clare's youth, Richard Royce (now ninety-three), Baxter Langley the village tailor, and Ann Price, widow of the late innkeeper of the Exeter Arms. Many of the villagers were there, and the local schoolchildren came out from class to watch. The coffin was made of the best oak, with a brass plate bearing the words 'John Clare, born July 13 1793, died May 20 1864.' It was reported that the funeral expenses had been defrayed by Earl Fitzwilliam.

There were some notable absentees from the ranks of the mourners. Clare's son Jack, the railway carpenter, was working far away to the west in the Welsh border county of Shropshire. He had remarried and fathered six more children. Like many of the Clares, he lived to a great age. On his death an obituary in the local newspaper reported, 'He was employed by the Cambrian Railway as foreman of the bridge carpenters and was greatly respected by the workmen under him. He was on the Oswestry and Ellesmere section at the commencement of the making of the line and was in the service of the Company nearly 50 years when he received his pension.' His father's only railway journey, by contrast, was the one taken by his body to Helpston for burial. The distance was such that Jack would not have heard of his father's death until after the funeral, but he visited his mother in Northborough about ten weeks later.

Clare's sister Sophy had died in 1855. Four years later, the other Sophy, his daughter, had become engaged to Lord Milton's gamekeeper, a Mr Harker. She reassured John Taylor that he was 'a steady man'. But the match fell through because her mother 'did not approve of the Man'. Patty seems to have had inappropriately great expectations for her youngest daughter. It was foolish to prevent the marriage of a girl who was nearly thirty. Deep bitterness comes across in Sophy's letters of this period. She was living with a cousin in Market Deeping, though still writing letters on her mother's behalf. The cousin was very kind to her but died suddenly in July 1863, leaving no will.

Bereft of companionship, money and work, Sophy wrote to Taylor for assistance. She was 'ashamed to ask' but had 'no other Friend'. He sent a post office order for three pounds. She moved in with a kindly aunt in Barnack, but then this woman was taken ill. Taylor asked her why she did not move back to her mother's. She replied, 'my youngest Brother is at Home with her she cannot do without him to manage her Cottage he has a Wife therefore I thought she did not require me'. Sophy's health was very poor by the late summer of 1863: 'I am always ill . . . it is more than two years since I was afflicted [and I] have required *medical* aid more or less ever since'. She died, aged thirty-three, soon after writing to this effect. There are signs that she shared her father's depressive tendency. Had she not preceded him to the grave by a few months, she might well have followed his path to the asylum.

John Taylor himself, Clare's first publisher and most loyal supporter, died just six and a half weeks after the poet. He had been ill for a long time, so he would have been unable to attend the funeral even if word of Clare's death had reached London before his burial, which it did not. But as Taylor lay dying, he was still working on Clare's behalf: he was in the middle of negotiations with Joseph Whitaker, whose family firm had published *The Rural Muse*, regarding a posthumous edition of the collected works.

A couple of months later, Whitaker went to Northborough and made an agreement with the family that in return for an annuity of ten pounds a year, he would acquire Clare's manuscripts and 'the right to publish anything printed or unprinted.' Whitaker called on Patty several times over the years, and even paid for her to visit London in 1867 with her niece Eliza (daughter of Clare's sister Sophy). There is no record of Patty's impressions of the great city.

A letter published in the local *Mercury* newspaper made public the information that the Earl Spencer had generously agreed to continue paying an annuity to Patty and that a forthcoming illustrated edition of Clare's works would also assist the poet's widow. Mrs Higgins, a pioneering Stamford photographer, would contribute pictures of Clare's two cottages, the Helpston village cross, the church, the grave and the sycamore tree under which it had not been possible to lay the body. Whitaker's plans were advancing.

An auspicious moment for publication would have been April 1865, when there was a festival of readings and music in the poet's honour in Stamford, in aid of a fund to erect a memorial in Helpston village. The festival announcement promised that a letter from the Poet Laureate commending the scheme would be read out. One assumes that Alfred Tennyson did not allude to the fact that many years before he had been a guest in Dr Allen's asylum at the same time as Clare. The evening was a success. The organisers ensured that events were brought to a conclusion before the last train left for Helpston. The monument was duly built, just over the road from the village cross. Adorned with quotations from the poems, all on the theme of mortality, it still stands today.

But there was no sign of the Whitaker edition. He had not found an editor willing or qualified to undertake the formidable task of untangling Clare's chaotic manuscripts. He had, however, found an employee at Macmillan who was interested in writing Clare's biography: Frederick Martin. A Berlin-born Jew who had previously been an amanuensis for Thomas Carlyle, Martin had taken British citizenship in the year of Clare's death. He proved his worth at Macmillan by producing an edition, with memoir, of Chatterton's poems.

The decision was taken to publish Clare's 'life' separately from the 'works'. Martin finished his work with remarkable speed, and the biography appeared just a year after the poet's death. *The Life of John Clare* is invaluable for its immediacy, though highly unreliable in its factual particulars. The preface painted a vivid outline of Clare's story: how he was brought forward as 'the Northamptonshire Peasant' and 'the English Burns', 'was duly petted, flattered, lionized, and caressed—and, of course, as duly forgotten when his nine days were passed', after which 'poverty, neglect, and suffering broke his heart'.

Frederick Martin was himself an exile, an outsider, a writer struggling to support a wife and family, a drinker: he had good reason to identify with Clare and he accordingly took the trouble to glean as much as he could from the original manuscripts that were in his hands. He embellished and romanticized his material, approaching it more in the manner of a novelist than a scholar.

Though Martin cannot be trusted in matters of detail, he conveys a strong sense of the shape of Clare's life. He made a symbolic start by calling Clare the English Burns and by studying his life alongside Chatterton's. In the poem 'Resolution and Independence' William Wordsworth had summoned up the memory of Chatterton ('the marvellous Boy') and Burns, the ploughman-turned-poet whose dissipation was supposed to have hastened his end. The premature demise of these two writers provoked in Wordsworth a conclusion which haunts every biographer of Clare: 'We Poets in our youth begin in gladness; / But thereof comes in the end despondency and madness'. Clare's tragedy was the longevity of the decline: he had the misfortune to live to twice the age of Burns and four times that of Chatterton.

This first biography laid the foundations for both the enduring myths and some of the key truths about Clare. Mary Joyce was a key figure in both his poetry and his delusions, but it is doubtful that she was really 'the deepest, noblest, and purest love of his whole life ... the Mary of all his future songs, ballads, and sonnets'. The Helpston of his childhood was not quite so illiterate as Martin makes out, but it was nevertheless a place of grinding rural poverty. Clare's London acquaintances treated him better than Martin implies, but he certainly felt disoriented in the city. Drink was an important factor in his decline, but probably not as uniquely important as Martin suggests. Perhaps the book's most notable achievement was the inclusion of a full, albeit poorly transcribed, text of the 'Journey from Essex', which made known to the public for the first time the extremity of what Clare endured. Martin's quotation of 'Lines: I Am', together with the incorrect assertion that it was the last poem that Clare ever wrote, made this his most famous work. It was the only one of his poems included in Sir Arthur Quiller-Couch's much-reprinted *Oxford Book of English Verse*.

Copious extracts from Martin's biography were reprinted in journals and provincial newspapers. As late as 1893 the entire book was serialised in a Peterborough local paper. The overall effect might be summed up as good for Clare's fame but bad for his reputation. Charles Dickens damned Martin for his 'preposterous exaggeration of small claims', whilst a searing review in the *Examiner* castigated the 'bastard picturesque' of his style and enumerated some of his many errors.

Patty was hurt by what she heard of Martin's account. Meanwhile, the Northampton publisher who shared the name of John Taylor decided to press ahead with a rival book: Clare's literary 'Remains', to be produced in a format matching the volumes published in the poet's lifetime. William Knight gave permission for the use of his transcriptions of the asylum poems.

Early in 1866, Taylor of Northampton concluded his purchase of Clare's library and those manuscripts not taken by Whitaker. Two donkey-carts were hired to carry the books, papers and even the bookcase to Helpston railway station. A subscription was arranged, allowing the printed books to be presented to the Northampton Museum. Taylor himself donated the bookcase. It can still be seen in the Northampton Central Library, with Clare's books on glass-fronted shelves beside it. Henry Burlowe's plaster bust of Clare, painted to look like bronze, is also there—Frederick Martin had bought it at auction in March 1865 and it was purchased from his daughter by the Northampton Public Libraries Committee in 1913. Grimshaw's portrait hangs on the wall, a donation from the family of the Mayor of Northampton, who had owned it during Clare's last years.

Clare's manuscripts were now dispersed. Whitaker had the majority of them, some obtained from Patty and others from Taylor of London, while Taylor of Northampton had many of the most valuable. Whitaker claimed the exclusive right to publish them, but, having bankrolled Martin's biography for little reward, was reluctant to proceed any further with an edition.

Nothing more was heard of publication plans until 1871, when an antiquarian named J. L. Cherry, who had once visited Clare in the Northampton asylum, agreed to edit the volume of 'Remains' for Taylor of Northampton. He hoped to dedicate the book to Tennyson, until he discovered in the course of his research that Clare's own desire was for his posthumously published poems to be dedicated to the Earl Spencer. The fifth Earl was contacted in Dublin, where he was serving as Lord-Lieutenant of Ireland. He replied with a graceful letter of agreement.

The project was dogged by various disputes—first over Cherry's editorial fee and then over the question of Whitaker's claim on the Clare copyright—but the book finally appeared early in 1873 under the title *Life and Remains of John Clare*. Cherry refused to return the manuscripts of Clare's correspondence until he received his ten-pound fee. When he eventually did so, Taylor sold Clare's incoming letters to the trustees of the British Museum. They remain in the British Library: twelve hundred letters in six bound volumes, a goldmine for the biographer.

Cherry's book followed the popular Victorian 'life and letters' format. A 130-page memoir, which unobtrusively corrected many of Martin's sentimental excesses and factual errors, was interspersed with samples of the poetry, extracts from Clare's journal of 1824–5 and a selection of letters to the poet, with an emphasis on such London acquaintances as Eliza Emmerson, Henry Cary and Charles Lamb. Over a hundred pages of 'Asylum Poems' then followed, including such favourites of later anthologists as 'Graves of Infants' and 'Little Trotty Wagtail'. 'Lines: I Am' was included at the climax of the narrative section, not with the other poems. The 'Remains' were rounded off with a miscellany of other poems, some of which had been previously published in the newspapers and annuals, a selection of the 'Old Songs and Ballads' that Clare had collected, and some prose fragments including the 'Confession of Faith' and 'Essay on Popularity'.

Cherry's volume was widely reviewed. Its principal importance was in making readers aware that Clare had carried on writing a considerable body of poetry whilst in the asylum. The *Remains* gave reviewers the opportunity to give general estimates of his poetic development. These ranged from the dismissive—'We doubt very much if the selection was worth making, much more whether it was worth publishing. At all events, if the poems of a lunatic are published, they should be given, if indeed with omissions, yet most certainly without corrections. But with one or two exceptions the poems seem to us poor'—to the sympathetic, if condescending:

> There is all the unaffected simplicity, the quiet love of nature, and the quaint use of local phrases, which gave such a peculiar colour to his earlier works. There is a clearness, a sanity, and now and then a perfection of expression, which could never suggest aberration of any kind. Clare was always sweet, with a sustained lingering intensity of tone. His poems only needed a quantum of strength to have claimed the title of great.

In 1893 Whitaker, in his seventies and close to death, sold all his Clare papers to the Peterborough Museum. They formed the centrepiece of a major exhibition there in celebration of the centenary of Clare's birth and subsequently of the largest collection of the poet's manuscripts, which is still held by the Peterborough Museum and Art Gallery Society.

Clare left very few possessions at his death: his books and papers, a few gifts from Mrs Emmerson and other well-wishers, Hessey's violin, a Wedgwood inkstand, ivory knife, pocket microscope, and a small collection of ornamental snuff-boxes that were put on show in the exhibition. Given how little he owned himself, it is ironic that Cherry's work on the *Life and Remains* should have provoked a contention regarding the ownership of his copyright so soon after his death. But neither Whitaker nor John Taylor of Northampton was solely in the business of making money for himself out of Clare's name. John Taylor of London's support for the family in his own last days was especially generous, but nearly all the parties involved with Clare and his family in the years immediately before and after his death treated him and his memory with the utmost respect and esteem. They were motivated above all by a desire to serve his memory, his work and his loved ones.

Patty and her family remained popular in the village of Northborough. She would sometimes take dinner to children who were sick, even if all she could afford to give them was a piece of bread. On 5 February 1871 she died of 'Disease of Heart', whilst staying with her daughter in Spalding. She was described on her death certificate as 'Widow of John Clare the Northamptonshire Peasant Poet'. She was buried not with her husband in Helpston, but in Northborough churchyard with her children. The graves are just behind the church, still in good condition.

William Parker Clare died in 1887, aged fifty-nine, and Eliza Louisa Sefton, the girl named after Mrs Emmerson, in 1906, aged eighty-four. The Sefton children contributed greatly to the 1893 exhibition. Last to die was John Clare the younger (Jack), the railway carpenter, away in Welshpool in 1911, aged eighty-five. Among Clare's grandchildren, one of Eliza Louisa's daughters, Martha Matilda (known as 'Patty'), lived from 1852 to 1952, while William Parker's firstborn of 1863, John Frederick Clare, lived until 1955. It is strange to think of Clare, born two years before Keats and only four after the storming of the Bastille, having grandchildren who survived into the 1950s.

J.A. Hessey, the other partner in the firm that brought Clare to fame, died in 1870, having long since retired from the book trade and become a schoolmaster. Joseph Henderson, the poet's gardener friend, died in Yorkshire in 1866, aged about seventy-five. The Reverend Charles Mossop, born the same year as Clare, lived until he was ninety. William Knight continued to work in Birmingham at the Borough Asylum (later called Winson Green) until 1892.

The Helpston cottage is now a single family home, rather than a row of tenements. It bears a plaque in the poet's memory. The shades of Parker and John Clare, both such keen gardeners, would smile to see their garden, for it is beautifully kept and displays a riot of colour in high summer. The soil remains exceptionally good. Every July, on the Saturday closest to Clare's birthday, Helpston hosts a festival in his honour, and the present owners of the cottage open the garden to all.

Clare would be less happy to know that the waste ground at the bottom of his garden, where he so often followed the path called Crossberry Way, has been given over to '43 detached, link-detached and mews-style three and four-bedroomed houses in Twigden Homes' brand new Cambridge range of house styles'. The estate is called Marymede, explained the housing developers, because 'this is where peasant poet John Clare met and fell in love with Mary Joyce, the muse of his creativity'. Real estate has its own poetic licence—never mind that Mary was a Glinton girl.

The Northborough cottage is also in private hands. New houses have been built around it, but one still gets a sense of how Patty at least must have appreciated the move from the Helpston tenement to a detached property in its own grounds. Where Clare's orchard once was, there is now a gift shop specialising in teddy bears.

Allen's private asylum no longer stands. On its site are a Scout camp and a field study centre for schoolchildren. The Northampton General Lunatic Asylum is still a mental health institution, now known as St Andrew's Hospital. Its beautifully manicured front lawn hosts the Northampton Croquet Club and there is a golf course in the grounds.

The asylum had its second brush with literary history some thirty years after Clare's death. J. K. Stephen could hardly have come from a more different background: born into a distinguished literary family, gilded youth (sporting star at Eton, 'Apostle' at Cambridge), noted wit and author of a best-selling book of light verse. But then one day his landlady found him 'standing at his bedroom window naked and quite mad throwing all his things out of the window and singing'. He was dispatched to the Northampton asylum, where he swung between violence and depression, refused to eat and starved himself to death within three months. Some time later, Dr (later Sir) George Savage, the man who had signed the committal papers, became doctor to Stephen's cousin, Virginia Woolf.

And what of Clare's physical remains? He was buried without a stone to mark his grave, but in 1867 a fund was established to remedy this. William Bellars and Mr Spencer of Woodcroft Castle were the principal subscribers. Sufficient money was raised to pay for a low-coped monument of Ketton stone to be placed over the grave. Enough was left over to renovate the adjacent headstone of Clare's mother's grave and to add to it an inscription recording his father's death. Parker had been buried beside Ann, but at that time there was no money to alter the stone.

The wording on Clare's long low stone was simple. On one side was written 'Sacred to the Memory of John Clare The Northamptonshire Peasant Poet Born July 13 1793 Died May 20 1864.' and on the other 'A poet is born not made', words translated from the famous Latin tag that had been applied to Clare by Frederick Martin in his biography: 'Of *Poeta nascitur non fit* there never was a truer instance than in the case of John Clare.' It was a fitting gesture that the architect who designed the coped stone was Michael Drury of Lincoln, son of Edward Bell Drury, the man who may justly be said to have discovered Clare. The stonework remains in good condition. Clare would have taken pleasure in stooping to observe that it is dappled with many species of lichen.

His own wishes for his remains had been slightly different:

> I wish to have a rough unhewn stone something in the form of a mile Stone so that the playing boys may not break it in their heedless pastimes with nothing more on it than this Inscription.

HERE

Rest the

HOPES

And Ashes

of

JOHN CLARE

> I desire that no date be inserted thereon as I wish it to live or dye with my poems and other writings, which if they have merit with posterity it will and if they have not it is not worth preserving.

CHAPTER TWENTY-FIVE

THE POET'S POET

John Clare called Robert Bloomfield 'the greatest Pastoral Poet England ever gave birth to'. He was wrong: if we take 'pastoral' to mean 'showing a deep knowledge of nature and rural life', then that title belongs to himself. Clare knew his environment with a lived intimacy that sets him apart from well-born pastoral poets. And he was without question the greatest labouring-class poet England ever gave birth to. Yet it has taken a long time for him to win his place, in Keats's phrase, 'among the English poets'.

Clare's admiration for Bloomfield reminds us that 'peasant poetry' was a popular vogue in the early nineteenth century. The search was on for an English Burns. Hundreds of impoverished men and women found their way into print. Many of them wrote on the same themes as Clare and some endured tougher lives than his. James Chambers was a Suffolk pedlar who wandered from village to village, accompanied by his faithful dogs, 'always sleeping in the fields, an outhouse, or under some hedge, wherever night happens to overtake him'. He managed to get his *Poetical Works* published by subscription in the same year as Clare's first book.

More typically, labouring poets were men and women of similar background to Clare's. Thus John Nicholson, 'The Airedale Poet', born in 1790: he had some rudimentary schooling and then educated himself through such books as he could find, while he supported his family by working long hours as a journeyman wool-comber. Inspired by the landscape of the Yorkshire moors, he became a poet and published his works by subscription. Among his subjects were the cares of life (as in Clare's early success, 'What is Life?'), a lyric called 'I will love thee, Mary!', an elegy on the death of Lord Byron, and a poem 'On the ascent of Mr Green's Balloon from Halifax, April 19, 1824' (as it happens, the same balloon floated over Clare's garden the following summer).

Clare was conscious of several other rural poets springing up in his own county. He was always keen to set himself apart from such rhymers. For all the self-doubt that plagued him, he knew that he was better than his rivals. After all, he was published in London by the leading literary house of Taylor and Hessey. In the 1820s he did not have to rely on subscription lists and provincial printers. He did not think well of his local competitors, noting in his journal in 1824: 'Looked over a new vol of provincial poems by a neighbouring poet—Bantum's "Excursions of Fancy"—and poor fancies I find them—there is not a new thought in them—four years ago a poet was not to be heard of within a century [hundred miles] of Helpstone and now there is a swarm.' A letter to his publisher the following year enumerates the swarm: 'I think I have about nine neighbour Poets who have printed their trifles by subscription.' He was especially scornful of the man he called 'Bantum', John Banton, a parish clerk from a village over in Rutland 'who had the impudence to style his poems "Visits from the Muses" and dedicated it to the "University of Cambridge" because two or three boys (the sons of Clergymen round his own village) had [subscribed to] it'.

His critical instincts were powerful: he knew how to distinguish false poetry from true. In his own mature work—thanks to both his own genius and the able assistance of his friends—John Clare achieved a technical accomplishment, a range of styles and subjects, a distinctiveness of voice and a visionary power unmatched by anyone of his class before or since.

Who else could claim the title of England's greatest lower-class poet? The majority of the English poets whose work has endured have belonged to the gentry and professional classes. Even those labelled by their contemporaries as having 'low' origins—Shakespeare, Blake, Keats, Hardy—have generally been from a 'trade' or small-business background. From the twentieth century, one might single out the coal-miner's son D. H. Lawrence, an under-rated poet if over-rated novelist. But Lawrence had far greater educational opportunities than Clare: he went to college and became a schoolteacher. We need to look to the Scottish and Irish traditions to find figures more comparable to Clare: Burns, Hogg, Kavanagh. Among the great *English* poets Clare is unique in having been born and remained a labourer—until he became a 'lunatic'.

And there's the rub. He came to fame as 'the Northamptonshire Peasant Poet'. When he died he was remembered as 'poor Clare', who had suffered from lunacy for over twenty years. Peasant poets and mad poets were considered to be freaks of nature. If they had genius, that was a matter of divine chance, not conscious art. In Scotland, Burns became a national institution. In England, Clare was consigned to the margins. No one has ever suggested that there should be a national Clare Night every 13 July. Perhaps someone would have done if the scale of Clare's achievement had been more visible—and England a less class-conscious country.

Late Victorian critical opinion was profoundly condescending towards him. Virginia Woolf's redoubtable father, Sir Leslie Stephen, summed up the 'official' view in the *Dictionary of National Biography*: 'Though Clare shews fine natural taste, and has many exquisite descriptive touches, his poetry does not rise to a really high level and though extraordinary under the circumstances, requires for its appreciation that the circumstances should be remembered.' In defence of Sir Leslie, we should remember that only about a fifth of Clare's prodigious poetic output was available to him. Much of his greatest poetry—most notably 'The Parish', 'The Moors', the uncut 'Midsummer Cushion' collection, and the Northborough sonnet sequence—remained invisible.

Equally, although Martin had published the 'Journey from Essex' and Cherry a few other fragments of prose, no nineteenth-century reader had any conception of Clare's genius as a pen-portraitist of people and places, fauna and flora. Just as many of his greatest poems remained unpublished, so did his two greatest (if unfinished) prose works, the lost 'Autobiography of John Clare' and the book that would have been called either 'A Natural History of Helpstone' or 'Biographies of Birds and Flowers'.

But even in the work that was published, there was enough for certain critics, usually men who were also poets themselves, to take a different view from the orthodox one epitomized in the *DNB*. Francis Turner Palgrave was both an Oxford professor of poetry and the author of several volumes of lyric verse. In 1861 he published the century's most influential anthology, *The Golden Treasury of Songs and Lyrics*. Palgrave excluded living writers from his collection, but in his preface he named the two contemporary English poets whom he believed would, in time, 'no doubt claim and obtain their place among the best'. One was his friend Alfred Tennyson, who in 1850 had succeeded Wordsworth as Poet Laureate. The other was John Clare, whose poetry had not been published in book form since 1835 and who had been in the Northampton asylum for twenty years.

At the turn of the century another minor poet, Norman Gale, edited a selection from the previously published poems with a gushing introduction in which Clare was described as a worshipper of Nature, whose best poems indisputably belonged 'to the excellent things of this earth'. Then a few years later, a much more considerable literary figure threw his weight behind Clare. Arthur Symons was a friend of W. B. Yeats and an accomplished lyric poet in the impressionist style. His *The Symbolist Movement in Literature* (1899) was a key influence on the development of Modernism, introducing British and American writers to such experimental French poets as Stéphane Mallarmé and Jules Laforgue. In 1908 Symons produced an edition of *Poems by John Clare*, which included judicious selections from the four volumes that had appeared in the poet's lifetime and from the asylum verses, as well as a substantial number of hitherto unpublished poems from the 'Manuscript Book' of *The Rural Muse*, including such crucial pieces as 'The Progress of Rhyme' and 'Remembrances'.

Symons's was the first selection to give some sense of Clare's poetic development and the range of his achievement. Furthermore, the introduction to the book raised the critical appreciation of Clare to a higher plane. Symons described the early poetry as 'more definitely the work of the peasant than perhaps any other peasant poetry'. 'No one before him,' he continued, 'had given such a sense of the village'. The later poetry was understood in terms of memory and loss. Symons was the first to perceive the full importance of Clare's alienation from his native place and the paradox that 'what killed him as a human mind exalted him as a poetic consciousness'. Symons perhaps understood this duality because he was himself torn between his Celtic origins—he was part Welsh, part Cornish—and the metropolitan sophistication of London and Paris. So it was that he regarded the asylum poetry as 'of a rarer and finer quality than any of the verse written while he was at liberty and at home'.

Equally impressive was Symons's recognition of Clare's considerable book-learning ('I am inclined to doubt the stories of the illiterate condition of even his early manuscripts'), his technical sophistication, and his advance from eighteenth-century to more contemporary styles (in *The Shepherd's Calendar* 'one even realises that he has read Keats much more recently than Thomson'). Symons was also the first to recognise the damaging effects of editorial intervention upon Clare's originals. He noted that Clare's manuscript sonnets were unpunctuated and saw this as an anticipation of the modernistic fluidity of Mallarmé rather than a symptom of poor education. He was disappointed not to find the original manuscripts of the asylum poems, 'which I would have liked to have printed exactly as they were written, having convinced myself that for the most part what Clare actually wrote was better than what his editors made him write'.

Symons's selection impressed the Anglo-Welsh man of letters Edward Thomas. In first his *Feminine Influence on the English Poets* and then his *Literary Pilgrim in England*, Thomas wrote with great sensitivity of the process whereby the figure of Mary Joyce became the symbolic muse of the asylum poems, whilst also noting Clare's preference for 'waste places' over cultivated land and praising his music of local place-names and country lore. 'No man', he memorably affirmed, 'ever came so near to putting the life of the farm, as it is lived, not as it is seen over a five-barred gate, into poetry.' The discovery of Clare was one part of the alchemy that transformed Thomas himself from prose writer to poet during the course of the First World War. His poetry, written on the Western Front, shares with Clare's a responsiveness to the seasons, a care for small things such as birds' nests and ponds, and an alertness to the power of memory to lodge itself in the seemingly inconsequential, as when he notices dust on 'Tall Nettles' in the corner of a farmyard. Thomas learned from Clare how emotional intensity could be buried below apparent simplicity of natural description.

Thomas was killed at Arras in 1917, whereas the poet and critic Edmund Blunden survived the Great War. He too had discovered Clare through the Arthur Symons collection, which he carried with him on the Western Front. Soon after returning to civilian life, Blunden became one of the first to work in detail on Clare's manuscripts in the Peterborough collection. 'To this day', announced his collaborator Alan Porter (literary editor of the *Spectator*) in 1920, Clare's 'best and most personal work is unpublished': 'two months ago the manuscripts lay for the greater part untouched in the ramshackle archive-cupboard of a provincial museum, black with dust, mouldered and worm-eaten, slowly fading beyond the power of man to decipher'. Clare's homemade ink had 'spread and eaten like saltpetre along the paper'.

The fruit of Blunden and Porter's labours in the archive was *John Clare: Poems chiefly from Manuscript*, published in 1920. They had examined over two thousand of Clare's poems, 'of which over two-thirds have not been published'. Their selection included ninety previously unpublished lyrics, together with a substantial biographical introduction by Blunden. A long and favourable review in the

Times Literary Supplement by the influential critic John Middleton Murry—husband of Katherine Mansfield, friend of D. H. Lawrence—contributed further to the revaluation of Clare and in particular the association of him with Keats. Blunden produced a further selection of unpublished lyrics in 1924, under the title *Madrigals and Chronicles*. In the preface to the latter, *The Rural Muse* was described as 'one of the richest and most melodious Collections ever published by an English Poet'. Blunden also obtained from Frederick Martin's daughter the original manuscript of 'Sketches in the Life of John Clare, written by Himself'. He published this in 1931, together with other autobiographical fragments such as Clare's accounts of the literary Londoners.

Blunden's work paved the way for the husband-and-wife team of John and Anne Tibble. They devoted two lifetimes' scholarship to the Peterborough and Northampton manuscripts, producing a biography of Clare (1932), a large two-volume collection of the poems (1935), a selection of the prose (1951) and an edition of the letters (1951). But their endeavours failed to enlist the most influential mid-twentieth-century critics—F. R. Leavis, William Empson, the American New Critics—in support of Clare.

In the mid-century, it was again the poet-critics who made Clare's poetry more available and his stature more apparent. Shortly after the Second World War, Geoffrey Grigson—poet, countryman, editor of the influential 1930s magazine *New Verse*, husband of the great cookery writer Jane Grigson—recovered more of the asylum poems. In 1949 he published a new selection of *Poems of John Clare's Madness*, with a remarkable fifty-page biographical introduction. A *Selected Poems* followed the next year, with a briefer but equally percipient introduction. Grigson understood that for Clare poetry was not an occupation but a compulsion: 'The making of poems was part of him, like laughing, feeling sad or feeling elated, like waking and sleeping. Indeed it was most of him. And this is worth saying, obvious as it may be, because so much poetry is always so diseased by being, not a willed product, but a willed product outside the nature of the poet.'

In the 1950s James Reeves, an especially fine children's poet, was editor of the Heinemann Poetry Library, a series of selections much used in schools. Three of his first four volumes were devoted to poets who had been made highly fashionable by T. S. Eliot, F. R. Leavis and their successors: John Donne, Gerard Manley Hopkins and D. H. Lawrence. But the fourth was a superbly chosen selection of Clare, with a brief introduction that pierces straight to the heart of the matter: 'No one was ever more continuously and unremittingly a poet', writes Reeves. 'He wrote because he could not help it'. In this sense, 'There never was a more helpless and more completely possessed victim of poetry'.

Clare has often been presented as the victim of his social circumstances, his patrons and his publishers. Reeves was closer to the truth when he portrayed him as victim of his own Muse. 'Poetry, nature, love: these formed the triple constellation by which the tempestuous course of Clare's life was directed.' Clare was not the first nature poet, Reeves notes, but no other poet has brought so fully to his relationship with nature that mark of the true lover, the capacity to 'lose his identity in the contemplation of the object of his love'.

From Symons to Blunden to Grigson to Reeves, then, it was the poets who both edited Clare and wrote most eloquently of his enduring power. During the years when the reading public's exposure to the works of Wordsworth, Coleridge, Blake, Shelley and Keats were increasingly being mediated by professional critics and university teachers, Clare stood apart. For the purposes of literary history and the teaching of English, he was classified as a 'minor' poet among the Romantics. But he went on speaking directly to the hearts of living poets. Robert Graves summed up the feelings of many fellow-writers when he admitted, in an almost confessional tone,

> I find myself repeating whole poems of Clare's without having made a conscious effort to memorize them. And though it was taken as a symptom of madness that he one day confided in a visitor: 'I know Gray—I know him well,' I shall risk saying here, with equal affection: 'I know Clare; I know him well. We have often wept together.'

A similar perception was articulated in verse by Sidney Keyes, a highly accomplished young poet who was killed in action in North Africa during the Second World War. His 'Garland for John Clare' suggests that Clare's self-identification with Byron and Shakespeare might be understood not as madness but as a profound perception of the kinship between all true poets:

> When London's talkers left you, still you'd say
> You were the poet, there had only ever been
> One poet—Shakespeare, Milton, Byron
> And mad John Clare, the single timeless poet.
> We have forgotten that. But sometimes I remember
> The time that I was Clare, and you unborn.

Clare, then, was not only a poet in himself. He has also been the cause of poetry in others. From Chauncey Hare Townsend and Eliza Emmerson onwards, his readers have turned their response to him into poetry of their own.

When Edmund Artis took a life-mask of the poet in 1822, Henderson the gardener composed some accompanying verses that praised Clare for his unaffected language:

> Or can you trace the genius here
> That pictures rural scenes so clear
> And gives to common, copse and green
> The charms of an Arcadian scene
> In language clear, devoid of art,
> Paints the best feelings of the heart
> And gathers sweets from every grove
> To weave the tender song of love?

A century later, one of Edmund Blunden's poems was inspired by another plaster-cast, the death-mask of Clare that was taken at the asylum. The mask was given to the Corporation of Northampton in 1918. Blunden saw in it a 'rich, sweet, serious gaze' and something like a smile.

That other poet-editor, James Reeves, wrote a meditation on John

Clare called 'The Savage Moon'. Like many poems that begin from admiration for an earlier poet, it made its subject into a ghost who haunts the later writer:

> The shadow of that small man haunts me still.
> I see him unappeased,
> His russet form stumping the road uphill,
> Weathered, yet pale of face, his forehead's height
> Unusual, his blue eyes dangerously bright.
>
> Continually he haunts me, unappeased
> Among the beanfields and the cottage rows.
> Rhyming and scribbling without cease he goes,
> Catching words from the wind,
> From the air fanning his high cheek
> Where the fever glows.
> A meadow brook flows in his mind like rhythm.
> He lifts his head to the autumn sky
> For a colour or a look . . .

Reeves ended his poem with a similar question to the one he asked in the introduction to his edition of Clare: 'Is poetry a punishment or a crime?'

Though Clare was so much a poet of locality, for later writers he has taken on a kind of universality as, in Keyes's phrase, 'the single timeless poet'. He has spoken with particular poignancy to poets who have themselves suffered from mental illness. The manic-depressive and suicidal American Theodore Roethke wrote a brief lyric called 'Heard in a violent ward' in which he placed Clare in a trinity of divinely driven 'lunatic' geniuses, the others being William Blake and Christopher Smart:

> In heaven, too,
> You'd be institutionalized.
> But that's all right,—
> If they let you eat and swear . . .

It is not only confessional poets such as Roethke who have turned to Clare. The urbane, abstract New Yorker John Ashbery has a prose

poem 'For John Clare' that improvises on his voice in a manner akin
to that of jazz:

> It is possible that finally, like coming to the end of a long, barely
> perceptible rise, there is mutual cohesion and interaction. The
> whole scene is fixed in your mind, the music all present, as
> though you could see each note as well as hear it. I say this be-
> cause there is an uneasiness in things just now. Waiting for
> something to be over before you are forced to notice it. The pol-
> larded trees scarcely bucking the wind—and yet it's keen, it
> makes you fall over. Clabbered sky. Seasons that pass with a
> rush.

Ashbery remarked in a lecture that it was Clare's prose fragment on
house-flies that got him thinking about the possibility of writing
prose poetry. 'For John Clare' is thus a tribute-poem in form as well as
substance. In the same lecture, Ashbery described Clare as someone
he has found himself turning to 'when I really needed to be reminded
yet again of what poetry is'. 'The effect of Clare's poetry, on me at
least,' he explained, 'is always the same—that of re-inserting me in
my present, of re-establishing "now." '

English affection for Clare—that of Blunden, say—is bound up
with nostalgia for the lost Arcadia of an imagined rural past of organic rootedness in the land. By contrast, when we see his poems
through the eyes of Ashbery, the haze of pastoral is burned away and
we are left with a bright precision of language. To the New Yorker,
Clare's 'nakedness of vision' is a sign of his remarkable modernity.

The sense that Clare was a marginal man, never quite at ease in the
London literary mainstream, has also made him attractive to other
poets who have been conscious of how their own language and location have been regarded as marginal. Patrick Kavanagh was born in
1904 in the townland of Mucker, in the parish of Inniskeen, County
Monaghan, in the west of Ireland. He grew up among smallholding
farmers who struggled to scrape a living from the land. His father
had a sideline as a cobbler. Like Clare, then, he came from genuine
'peasant' stock. Like Clare, he left school by the time he was thirteen,

with the expectation that he would plough the land rather than write about it. But, again like Clare, he educated himself from such books as he could find. He came to love poetry, though initially he had no conception that it was possible to make poetry out of the life of the farms and fields around him, or to write it in an earthy vernacular style. His discovery of Clare was crucial to the liberation of his own poetic voice. His first volume of verse, *Ploughman and other Poems* (1936), includes a tribute-poem to Clare, called 'Mary', in allusion to Mary Joyce:

> Her name was poet's grief before:
> Mary, the saddest name
> In all the litanies of love
> And all the books of fame.
>
> I think of poor John Clare's beloved
> And know the blessed pain
> When crusts of death are broken
> And tears are blossomed rain . . .

Two years later Kavanagh published an autobiography with a title that would have been equally apt for a life of Clare: *The Green Fool*. In his later poems, most notably *The Great Hunger*, he wrote of the Irish peasant in a manner that stripped rural life of the romantic veneer that wealthier-born poets had applied to it. He could not have done so but for the example of Clare.

Several subsequent Irish poets have also made Clare's cause their own. In 1993, the bicentenary of his birth (the year in which a plaque in his honour was finally placed in Westminster Abbey's Poets' Corner), Seamus Heaney gave a lecture in which he spoke of Clare's 'exacting and intuitive discipline', of 'the painterly thickness of the world' captured in the poems, of his combination of 'dreamwork' and 'photography', of how at their best Clare's pentameters 'take hold on the sprockets of our creatureliness', and of how in a poem such as 'The Lament of Swordy Well' the channels of expression are opened exhilaratingly by 'the removal of every screen between the identity of the person and the identity of the place'. Heaney could be speaking of his own best poetic work.

Again, the Ulster poet Michael Longley has reimagined the 'Journey out of Essex' in a lyric that begins with a stanza beautifully attuned to Clare's own voice:

> I am lying with my head
> Over the edge of the world,
> Unpicking my whereabouts
> Like the asylum's name
> That they stitch on the sheets.

And another Ulster writer, Tom Paulin, has been a powerful advocate of Clare's vernacular voice, notably in essays called 'John Clare in Babylon' and 'Strinking Dropples: John Clare' in his collections *Minotaur: Poetry and the Nation-State* (1992) and *Writing to the Moment* (1996). Paulin's poem 'The Wind Dog' weaves words from Clare together with a meditation on his life and place into a 'sound cento' that was composed for BBC radio, while 'The Writing Lark' is a poetic 'Letter to John Clare' that delights in his rough dialect:

> Dear Mr Clare
> Dear John Clare
> I'll start with *pudge*
> —pudge not budge
> pudge
> because pudge is a smashed puddle
> A muddy puddle on a track
> Or a whole clatter
> Scattered like broken plates
> —shiny plates
> on scoggy scroggy marshland
> —each pudge
> is like piss cupped in a cow-clap
> so I imagine a boot . . .

These lines are written with an intuitive understanding of the elemental quality of Clare's language and rhythms—and of the fact that he was at root a *walking* poet. Paulin is also fascinated by the near-misses and coincidental conjunctions that symbolise Clare's exclusion. We have seen how he just missed meeting Keats and Bloomfield, how he chanced upon Byron's funeral and shared Dr Allen's hospitality with Tennyson. Paulin reminds us that Chauncey Hare Townsend, who befriended Clare, later became the dedicatee of *Great Expectations*. So perhaps Townsend provided Dickens with the seed for the story of Pip's path from the marshes to London to despair: could that seed have been the life of Clare, who—like both Pip and Joe Gargery—lived 'the split between speech and print'. For poets, there is always a secret freemasonry of incidental connectedness. Paulin clinches the Irish connection with the discovery that Lucia, beloved 'mad' daughter of James Joyce, also died in the Northampton asylum.

Clare has inspired novelists, dramatists and painters as well as poets. John McKenna's *Clare: A Novel* (1993) offers haunting imaginary impersonations of the consciousnesses of Clare's wife Patty, his sister Sophy and a figure loosely based on Eliza Emmerson. Edward Bond's play *The Fool: Scenes of Bread and Love*, first performed at the Royal Court Theatre in 1975, is a dramatisation of the life that mingles fact and fiction in order to set Clare into the context of the contemporaneous Littleport food riots in a neighbouring district of East Anglia, so making him the victim of class oppression. Several painters have taken on the 'Journey from Essex'; the Oxford editions of Clare published in the 1960s were graced by David Gentleman woodcuts that finely caught the spirit of his rural world; and in the 1990s, the artist Carry Akroyd produced a series of paintings and prints that simultaneously evoked Clare's words and the fragility of the landscape of his fenland environment as it is now ravaged by intensive farming. Actors, too, seem to have a special affection for Clare. They have a tendency to recite 'Lines: I Am' from memory, their eyes filling with tears.

But he remains above all the poets' poet. R. S. Thomas, the Anglo-Welsh poet and priest who served in parishes among a North Wales peasantry whose working lives were not so very far from the world of

Clare's own community, began his tribute-poem by making the traditional link between lunacy and the moon. Written for the 1993 bicentenary of Clare's birth, which coincided with Thomas's own
eightieth year, the poem elides the full moon and the high forehead
of the balding dome of the older Clare's head in the 1844 Grimshaw
portrait. It then looks back to the youthful Clare whose feeling for nature was the purest kind of love. In the vision of R. S. Thomas, the lunatic, the lover and the poet are indeed of imagination all compact:

> Young, he was in his own
> sky, rising at mornings
> over unbrushed dew,
> with no-one to introduce
> him to earth's bustling creatures
> but his love. It was love
> brought him, as it brings
> all of us in the end, face
> against glass, to demand
> brokenly of the anonymous: Who am I?

But even during the long asylum years Clare knew—at least he knew
for most of the time—who he was:

> A silent man in life's affairs
> A thinker from a boy
> A Peasant in his daily cares
> The Poet in his joy.

'Genius', wrote Jean-Paul Sartre, 'is not a gift, but the way out a person invents in desperate circumstances.'

■■■

APPENDIX

ABBREVIATIONS

NOTES

SUGGESTIONS FOR FURTHER READING

ACKNOWLEDGEMENTS

INDEX

A P P E N D I X

C L A R E ' S   T E X T

The 'presentation' of Clare and his writings has been discussed at many points in this book, but something needs to be said about the twentieth-century editorial tradition—especially since readers will wish for some guidance as to the relative merits of the various modern editions of the poems.

J. W. and Anne Tibble performed a great service to Clare's memory through their pioneering mid-twentieth-century editions of his poems, prose and letters.* But their transcriptions of the manuscripts were riddled with errors. The text of the asylum verse in Geoffrey Grigson's *Poems of John Clare's Madness* (1949) was also inaccurate. Partly for this reason, a reaction set in during the 1960s: first Clare's text had been 'tidied up' by Taylor and Hessey, now it was being botched by modern editors, so the time was ripe to publish his works in a form absolutely true to what he wrote.

These were the guiding principles of the scholars Geoffrey Summerfield and Eric Robinson when they began transcribing the

---

The Poems of John Clare (2 vols., 1935), *The Prose of John Clare* (1951), *The Letters of John Clare* (1951).

Northampton and Peterborough manuscripts and publishing them word for word. If Clare did not punctuate, neither would Robinson and Summerfield; since his spelling was erratic, so would be that of their text. The initial result was editions of *The Later Poems of John Clare* (1964), *The Shepherd's Calendar* (1964) and *Selected Poems and Prose* (1966), which presented 'raw Clare' for the first time. The stripping away of editorial interference was especially effective in the case of the cycle of poems on the months of the rural year published in *The Shepherd's Calendar*. Since this had been the most heavily edited of Clare's works in his lifetime, the 'un-editing' of it was like the restoration of an over-varnished canvas to its original colours. Clare's language was revealed in all its freshness and immediacy.

During the next thirty-five years, this process of 'un-editing' or 'textual primitivism' (that is to say, a return to the 'pure' form of the early manuscripts) was applied to the entire body of Clare's poetry in the multi-volume complete Oxford Clare, edited by Eric Robinson, David Powell and Paul Dawson. The aim of this edition was to reproduce every one of Clare's three and a half thousand poems with absolute fidelity to the original manuscripts and full attention to textual variants in different drafts. First of all, two volumes were devoted to *The Later Poems* (published in 1984, covering the asylum years). Then two further volumes, published in 1989, restored *The Early Poems* from youthful work through to 1822. *The Poems of the Middle Period*, from 1822 to 1837, filled five more volumes (published between 1996 and 2003). In all, the Oxford edition runs to well over five thousand pages. It is an astonishing feat of scholarship. The letters and major prose writings, meanwhile, were given the same treatment in a succession of comparable editions.*

---

*John Clare's Autobiographical Writings, ed. Eric Robinson (1983), *The Natural History Prose Writings of John Clare*, ed. Margaret Grainger (1983), *The Letters of John Clare*, ed. Mark Storey (1985).

'Raw Clare' has been disseminated more widely thanks to a number of paperback volumes published by Carcanet Press in conjunction with the Mid Northumberland Arts Group. Four of these are exceptionally valuable: the full text of the carefully prepared manuscript of *The Midsummer Cushion* (edited by Kelsey Thornton and Anne Tibble, 1979); the *Northborough Sonnets* (edited by Eric Robinson, David Powell and P. M. S. Dawson, 1995); a collection of autobiographical prose writings, *John Clare by Himself* (edited by Robinson and Powell, 1996, superseding Robinson's *John Clare's Autobiographical Writings*); and a gathering of poems and prose selections on broadly political themes under the editorial title *A Champion for the Poor* (edited by Dawson, Robinson and Powell, 2000).

With the completion of the monumental scholarly work of Eric Robinson and his collaborators, the full range of Clare's poetic achievement became visible for the first time. But at a price: the Oxford texts and their Carcanet offspring are not easy to read and they make Clare look different from every other poet in the English language. No other writer has been accorded the honour of a 'standard edition' stripped of all punctuation and replete with misspellings, slips of the pen and so forth. Is this what Clare would have wanted? Setting aside the question of whether he would have wished his every line—including poems scored through in his manuscripts and marked 'Such as are crossed in this part are intended to be kept out of sight and not to be published'—to be enshrined in an academic monument at a published price of around seven hundred pounds, it is at the very least doubtful that he ever intended to make his deficiencies of formal written presentation apparent to his readers.

Advocates of 'raw Clare' frequently quote his remarks about the tyranny of grammar and the inconsistency of those who lay down the law on punctuation:

> Do I write intelligible—I am gennerally understood tho I do not use that awkard squad of pointings called commas colons semicolons etc and for the very reason that altho they are drilled

hourly daily and weekly by every boarding school Miss who pre-
tends to gossip in correspondence they do not know their proper
exercise for they even set gramarians at loggerheads and no one
can assign them their proper places for give each a sentence to
point and both shall point it differently.

If even the experts disagree about punctuation, demanded Clare,
then 'how should such a novice as I do it'? He explained to a correspondent that he 'omitted this awkard squad that you may drill my
sentences in your own way and understand me the better'. Readers of
the Oxford Clare are accordingly asked to drill his sentences in their
own way. The question is whether this policy really does allow them
to understand him better.

The passage quoted above was Clare's apology to the theatrical im-
presario William Robertson for the absence of punctuation in a private letter. Clare never stated that he wanted his poems to be
published without punctuation. Indeed, in his own note to his publisher with respect to his wishes for the transmission of his manuscripts into print, he explained that he had not attempted his own
'*Stops or Punctuation*' and that 'Bad spelling may be corrected by the
amanuensis, but no word is to be altered'. His clear implication is that
stops and spellings *should* be corrected by the professional scribe, but
that his lexical choices are to be respected.

His lack of confidence over 'stops' was partly due to his lack of formal education, but it should be noted that the manuscripts of those
Eton- and Harrow-educated poets Lord Byron and P. B. Shelley were
also slapdash in presentation and frequently minimalist in punctuation. It was common practice in the early nineteenth century to leave
'accidentals' such as punctuation to the discretion of the printer. As
for spelling, the instruction to his publisher makes clear that Clare
expected it to be corrected. He saw his work printed in books, anthologies, newspapers and magazines. Sometimes he protested vigorously over editorial rewording, but he never complained about such
regularizations as *I'm* for *Im* and *called* for *calld*.

There is also a mistaken modern assumption that the rejection of punctuation was somehow a political gesture. This view of Clare was born in the 1960s, in tandem with revolutionary ideas about the teaching of English in schools. Children and Clare, it was implied, should be treated in the same way: they should be left to express themselves, not drilled in deadening rules.* Clare was celebrated as a 'member of the awkward squad' in the sense of someone who refused to conform, a person of admirable independence. For Clare himself, though, the 'awkward squad' was a reference to his time in the militia: it referred to the incompetent recruits who were kept back for further training. His use of the phrase in the context of punctuation is a symptom of diffidence, not rebellion.

For Clare, the crucial matter was that he did not want his editors to alter whole words. In particular, he was keen for his local dialect to be retained. The note to his publisher gives an example: ' "egs on" in the "address to the Lark" wether provincial or what I cannot tell but it is common with the vulgar (I am of that class) and heartily desire no word of mine to be altered'. And he was equally committed to his attempts to reproduce what he called 'the language of Nature': 'The word 'twitatwit" (if a word it may be calld) you will undoubtedly smile at but I wish you to print it as it is for it is the language of Nature and that can never be disgusting'.

Editors of Clare from his own time until the 1950s added punctuation and corrected spelling, in accordance with the poet's expectations. But John Taylor and his successors also changed words, phrases and whole sequences. The process of *normalisation* thus became entangled with that of *alteration*. Furthermore, the poor quality of Clare's penmanship and the inadequacies of his writing instruments meant that errors and misreadings were frequently introduced into the text.

Consider two sequences chosen at random from 'October' in *The Shepherd's Calendar*. This is how Clare described birds in flight at dusk (a puddock is a kite):

*Geoffrey Summerfield was an inspirational originator not only of the return to Clare's original texts, but also of the creative use of poetry in education.

> The starnel crowds that dim the muddy light
> & puddock circling round its lazy flight
> Round the wild sweeing wood in motion slow
> Before it perches on the oaks below

But this is how these lines appeared in the published text of 1827:

> And whirr of starling crowds, that dim the light
> With mimic darkness, in their numerous flight;
> Or shrilly noise of puddocks' feeble wail,
> As in slow circles round the woods they sail.

The alteration of dialect *starnel* to standard English *starling*, the substitution of the poeticising 'mimic darkness' for the down-to-earth 'muddy light', the removal of the evocatively 'sweeing' (swaying) trees, the rewriting of whole phrases: changes of this nature angered and frustrated Clare. Given Taylor's treatment of such lines as these, one fully understands Summerfield and Robinson's desire to return to the original manuscripts.

But what about the following couplet, in which a cottager marshals his pigs through the woods? The Oxford text follows Clare's manuscript: 'The cotter journying wi his noisey swine / Along the wood ride were the brambles twine'. Here the reader is impeded by the spelling of *where* as *were*, while *journying* and *noisey* draw unnecessary attention to the irregularity of Clare's spelling. Clare would surely have wished Taylor and Hessey to normalise his English by printing the lines as 'The cotter journeying with [*or* wi'] his noisy swine, / Along the wood-ride where the brambles twine'. The trouble is, the 1827 printed text introduced an error—*side* for *ride* (in Clare's manuscripts it is often very hard to tell an *r* from an *s*). The frequency of errors such as this, in all editions prior to the 1960s, further encouraged the cry of 'back to Clare's manuscripts'.

Clare's own note to his publisher makes clear that there is a middle way: the best edition would be one which avoided errors and alterations, but provided light punctuation and regularised the spelling without diluting the dialect voice. As yet, however, no such edition exists for the great majority of the poems. The selection of poems I have edited to accompany this biography makes a start at the task of presenting Clare in this way.*

All but the most experienced readers are likely to assume that the multi-volume Oxford text, with its rigorous adherence to Clare's irregular spellings and lack of punctuation, together with its elaborate apparatus of textual variants, is somehow definitive. But no printed text could ever reproduce the real singularity of Clare's manuscripts: the cheap paper, the hand-stitched leaves, the miscellanies made up of scraps of old envelopes and letter-backs, the splotches of ink, the crossing out and adding in, the mix of pen and pencil, the sketches and doodles in the margins, the handwriting that ranges from rapid scrawl to painstaking fair copy, above all the manifestations of the need to cover every page—to turn a page sideways and write along the margins, to turn a notebook upside-down and start it again from the back, filling in all the gaps. That need grew equally from Clare's poverty (no scrap of paper could be wasted) and his compulsion to write.

Consider the very first few pages of the first volume of the Oxford Clare. *The Early Poems of John Clare* begins, as a manuscript-based text should, with the poet's first important manuscript: Northampton Manuscript 1, the 'book of blank Paper' that Clare bought from Henson in 1814, and into which he carefully inscribed his imitation title-page, 'A Rustic's Pastime, in Leisure Hours'. When Clare began work on this manuscript, he left blank the inside cover and the leaves before and after his handwritten title-page. The first poem that he copied into the book was 'Lines, written while viewing some Remains, of an Human, Body; in Lolham Lane' (in the attempt to pro-

---

*Interestingly, although Geoffrey Summerfield was one of the scholars who began the return to 'raw Clare', late in his life he argued for a limited degree of editorial intervention—see his *John Clare: Selected Poetry* (Penguin, 1990). A lightly interventionist editorial hand is also apparent in R. K. R. Thornton's brief selection of *John Clare* for the Everyman's Poetry series (1997) and Simon Kövesi's selections of Clare's *Love Poems* and *Flower Poems* (Bangkok: M & C Services, 1999 and 2001), mentioned below in connection with the copyright dispute.

duce a 'fair' copy, he has added an excess of punctuation instead of the usual lack of it).

Some time later, no doubt short of paper, Clare made use of the blank pages at the beginning of the book. On the inside cover, which is now soiled and water-stained, he scribbled some lines descriptive of a summer evening. Further passages for the same poem were added at the end of the manuscript and fitted into spaces at various points in the middle of it. All were scored through once Clare had copied out the complete poem and sent it to his publisher (the completed text survives elsewhere under the title 'Summer Evening', in the hand of an amanuensis).

The page opposite the title was also originally left blank. Here Clare at a later time turned the book upside-down and wrote some lines beginning 'How varying is the taste of man'. They form part of a poem that occurs in a fuller version in a different manuscript under the title 'Somthing New'. On the blank opening after the title-page, Clare later added in two further poems. One is a very rough pencil draft beginning 'No hailing curry favourings tothers / Muses gins my story / Blunt'. The other, in ink and more finished, is a robust expression of indignation at the cruelty of an unnamed local gentleman who has locked up the parish pump (the only water supply for the villagers). It ends with a bluntness that makes it very different from Clare's typical early poems: if the 'Marngrel curs' who do such things got the idea that a 'f—t' would be of any charitable use, he writes, 'They'd even burst before they'd set it loose!'

A scholar skilled in the conventions of textual bibliography would, with time and effort, be able to work out most of the above account from the Oxford edition, but the ordinary reader gains the impression that the first four poems in 'A Rustic's Pastime, in Leisure Hours' were 'Summer Evening', 'Somthing New', 'No hailing curry' and 'On Mr ——— Locking up the Public Pump'. Yet none of these was in the original collection. All are later poems that only appear in Manuscript 1 because there happened to be space to add them in (furthermore, none of them has a title in this manuscript). The Oxford edition does not offer the reader the assistance that would have been provided by a note explaining that these were rough drafts and that the fair-copy collection of 1814 only begins with the 'Lines' on seeing some human remains in Lolham Lane.

The textual status of the poems from these 'Lines' onward is manifestly superior to that of the fragments scrawled in later, but such is the Oxford editors' resistance to the idea of Clare's polishing his work for publication that they actually remove nearly all the punctuation from the poems that he wrote out in his best hand. These are described as 'over-punctuated' and Clare's attempts at pointing are banished to an appendix at the back of the volume. Granted that his over-punctuation was extremely clumsy, it was part of his attempt to present his work in a form suitable for potential publication. The Oxford edition accords more respect to the fragments that Clare chanced to scribble into the spaces in his manuscript-book than to the neatly copied poems that were the book's *raison d'être*!

I have needed nearly two pages to offer a summary account of how the impression given by the Oxford text distorts the first half-dozen pages of Clare's first substantial manuscript. What would it take to present a similar analysis for the entire body of nine thousand or more manuscript pages in the Peterborough and Northampton collections?

The difficulties of editing Clare's texts extend far beyond the question of regularisation. His intentions have frequently been misunderstood. The 'Midsummer Cushion' manuscript of 1832 has been painstakingly transcribed and published, giving the impression that this was the collection of his best work that he wanted in print. But his correspondence makes clear that he regarded that manuscript as a starting-point from which, with the assistance of Taylor and Emmerson, he would make a *selection* for publication. His own selection was the 'Manuscript Book' seen by Arthur Symons and now in the Pforzheimer Collection in the New York Public Library. This has never been published as a volume in its own right. Then there are the even more formidable problems presented by the writings begun in

Dr Allen's asylum at High Beech: the manuscripts of 'Child Harold' are so confused and fragmentary that no two modern editions of the poem print the stanzas in the same order!

The Oxford editors would not deny that their astonishing labours in the archive represent a new beginning for the editing of Clare, not an end to it. But an unusual impediment has remained in the way of the production of a normalised but not 'improved' text of the kind that I have suggested Clare would have wished for, and that would make his poems most accessible to ordinary readers.

It is not uncommon for there to be differences of opinion among scholars as to how literary works should be edited, especially when there has been authorial revision and press-correction. With the texts of Wordsworth and Coleridge, for instance, favour has fluctuated between the final version printed in the author's lifetime, the first version printed in book form, the first version printed in any form (e.g. newspaper and magazine publication), the final completed manuscript version, the earliest surviving manuscript version, and so forth. New editors come forward; they compare earlier editions with the manuscripts and produce texts of their own. The process of textual understanding proceeds by slow incremental steps.

Clare is like Wordsworth in that the great majority of his manuscripts are held close to his original home. As Wordsworth's are in Grasmere, so Clare's are in Peterborough and Northampton. But there is a crucial difference: whereas the Wordsworth Trust owns both the physical manuscripts of Wordsworth and the copyright in them, the Northampton Library and Peterborough Museum are under the impression that they own Clare's papers, but not the copyright in them. The copyright is claimed by none other than Professor Eric Robinson, chief editor of the Oxford Clare. Anyone wishing to edit Clare, or indeed to quote more than a few lines from him, supposedly needs the permission of the copyright holder.

So it is that the question of the presentation of Clare's text has become bound up with the ownership of his copyright. All the Oxford volumes of Clare's poetry bear the copyright of Eric Robinson.

Nearly all other modern editions of Clare carry the following acknowledgement: 'Copyright in the unpublished and much of the published work of John Clare is owned by Professor Eric Robinson who has together with Oxford University Press authorized this publication.' That is to say, copyright is asserted not only in the texts published by Oxford but also in the original manuscripts. I know of no comparable case among pre-twentieth-century English writers. How did Clare stumble into the bizarre distinction of still being 'owned' nearly a century and a half after his death?

He is a special case because only about four hundred of his poems were published in his lifetime. The 1842 Copyright Act, which was in force at the time of his death, only made provision in respect of published works. Unpublished poems came within the purview of the common law: the author of any writing, or his personal representative after his death, had complete and perpetual power over his work so long as it was unpublished. When the Oxford editors began their work in the early 1960s, over two thousand of Clare's poems still remained unpublished and therefore technically in copyright. Furthermore, the extent of editorial 'interference' with some of those that had appeared was so great that it was arguable that they had never been published in their true form.

As was shown in Chapter 24, the posthumous copyright in Clare's unpublished poetry was purchased by Joseph Whitaker in return for an annuity paid to Patty Clare. It is not entirely clear whether the purchase was properly completed (the Reverend Mossop, one of Clare's legal representatives, was distinctly uncertain about it) or indeed whether or not Whitaker dropped his copyright claim when he gave up on his plans to publish an edition of Clare. Nothing was said about copyright in the various editions that did appear in the first sixty years of the twentieth century.

Then in 1965 Eric Robinson purchased from the Whitaker family firm, which was still in the publishing trade, 'all rights whatsoever possessed by the company in the published and unpublished works of John Clare'. He paid the nominal sum of one pound. 'I foresaw several decades of work ahead of me and my co-editors,' he explained many years later, 'and I did not want people cribbing from our editions and claiming that they had worked from the manuscripts.' In 1873 Joseph Whitaker had insisted that J. L. Cherry's 1873 *Life and Remains of John Clare* should include an acknowledgement of his claim to the copyright. From the 1970s until the end of the twentieth century, Eric Robinson insisted that all printed selections from Clare should include an acknowledgement of *his* claim to the copyright.

The need to seek Robinson's permission, and in some cases to pay a copyright fee, together with the (not entirely accurate) perception that he would be hostile to any editorial approach other than his own method of rigorous fidelity to every particular of the manuscripts, weighed against the production of other substantial editions of Clare's poems. At the best of times there is hardly any money to be made in publishing scholarly editions of dead poets: it is easy to see why the proprietorial spectre of Professor Robinson proved itself a disincentive to other scholars and publishers from making a major investment in competing editions of Clare.

Of course Robinson had every right to protect the fruits of his years of scrupulous work deciphering and transcribing Clare's chaotic and often barely legible manuscripts. It was, however, a strange situation for the text of a long-dead poet to be under the legal protection of a single person who had no direct connection to his family or original publishers. And one might question the natural justice of Robinson's personal claim on the copyright of works by Clare that were first transcribed by other people, including his fellow-editors such as Geoffrey Summerfield.

Robinson believed that by reproducing the manuscripts exactly he was restoring the authentic voice of Clare, freeing him from the kind of control that had been exercised over his work by Taylor and the other early editors. But some Clare scholars argued to the contrary that Robinson's control of the copyright was perpetuating the situation whereby Clare was 'owned'. They suggested that this was acutely ironic in the light of Clare's passionate outbursts against the imposition of ownership brought about by the enclosure of Helpston. As Clare spoke for freedom and the right of all to share the common land, so his poems should be free for all to quote and reproduce without the payment of fees or the deferential acknowledgement of copyright ownership.

It was on the basis of an argument along these lines that around the turn of the millennium a young Clare scholar called Simon Kövesi deliberately challenged Professor Robinson's copyright claim by publishing unauthorised selections of Clare's love poems and flower poems. The controversy aroused considerable interest in the press and a bitter correspondence in the pages of the *Times Literary Supplement*. The resulting legal case is dormant but unresolved at the time of writing. The international dimension of copyright law is highly complex, especially in the light of recent European Union legislation. Kövesi provocatively muddied the waters further by publishing his edition in Bangkok, well beyond the reach of European copyright law!

The John Clare Society thrives. Schoolteachers have discovered that his 'nature' writing is an ideal way to introduce children to poetry. Enthusiasm for the work and fascination with the life may be found among a startling array of common readers, many of them far beyond the academic environment in which poetry is often confined. At long last, John Clare is in good health. But we still await a balanced presentation of the full range of his texts.

Autobiog   John Clare's draft autobiography, in *The Prose of John Clare*, ed. J. W.
and Anne Tibble (London: Routledge and Kegan Paul, 1951).

Baker   Anne Elizabeth Baker, *Glossary of Northamptonshire Words and
Phrases*, 2 vols. (London: John Russell Smith, 1854; facsimile repr.,
Thetford: Lark Publications, 1995).

CH   *Clare: The Critical Heritage*, ed. Mark Storey (London and Boston:
Routledge and Kegan Paul, 1973).

Cherry   J. L. Cherry, *Life and Remains of John Clare* (London: Warne, 1873;
Chandos Classics repr., London: Warne, and New York: Scribner,
n.d.).

CP   John Clare, *A Champion for the Poor: Political Verse and Prose*, ed.
P. M. S. Dawson, Eric Robinson and David Powell (Ashington: Mid
Northumberland Arts Group, and Manchester: Carcanet, 2000).

Deacon   George Deacon, *John Clare and the Folk Tradition* (London: Sinclair
Browne, 1983).

DRO   Uncatalogued papers of John Taylor at Derbyshire Record Office,
Matlock (9 boxes, ref. D1561).

Eg.   Correspondence of John Clare (letters to Clare): British Library
Egerton Manuscripts 2245–50, cited by manuscript and folio
number.

EP   *The Early Poems of John Clare*, ed. Eric Robinson and David Powell,
2 vols. (Oxford: Clarendon Press, 1989).

ERO   Documents pertaining to Matthew Allen's asylum at High Beach,
Essex Record Office.

J   John Clare's journal, 6 September 1824 to 11 September 1825 (with
brief supplementary entries, February 1828), NMS 15, published
in *JCBH* and *NHPW*, cited by date of entry.

JCBH   *John Clare by Himself*, ed. Eric Robinson and David Powell
(Ashington: Mid Northumberland Arts Group, and Manchester:
Carcanet, 1996). Supersedes *John Clare's Autobiographical*

	Writings, ed. Eric Robinson (Oxford: Oxford University Press, 1983).
JCSJ	*John Clare Society Journal*, annually since 1982, cited by vol. number and page reference for individual articles.
L	*The Letters of John Clare*, ed. Mark Storey (Oxford: Clarendon Press, 1985).
LP	*The Later Poems of John Clare*, ed. Eric Robinson and David Powell, 2 vols. (Oxford: Clarendon Press, 1984), through pagination.
LY	*John Clare: The Living Year 1841*, ed. Tim Chilcott (Nottingham: Trent Editions, 1999).
Martin	Frederick Martin, *The Life of John Clare* (London: Macmillan, 1865; repr. with introduction and notes by Eric Robinson and Geoffrey Summerfield, London: Cass, 1964).
MC	John Clare, *The Midsummer Cushion*, ed. Kelsey Thornton and Anne Tibble (Ashington: Mid Northumberland Arts Group and Manchester: Carcanet, 1979, repr. 1990). Transcription of PMS A54.
MP	John Clare, *Poems of the Middle Period*, ed. Eric Robinson, David Powell and P. M. S. Dawson, 5 vols. (Oxford: Clarendon Press, 1996–2003).
NGLA	Documents in the archive of the former Northampton General Lunatic Asylum (now St Andrew's Hospital, Northampton).
NHPW	*The Natural History Prose Writings of John Clare*, ed. Margaret Grainger (Oxford: Clarendon Press, 1983).
NMS	Northampton Manuscripts. Reference numbers as in David Powell, *Catalogue of the John Clare Collection in the Northampton Public Library* (Northampton: Northampton Public Library, 1964).
NRO	Documents in the Northamptonshire Record Office, Wootton Hall Park, Northampton (including Helpston parish records, materials relating to enclosure, Fitzwilliam miscellaneous papers).
NS	John Clare, *Northborough Sonnets*, ed. Eric Robinson, David Powell and P. M. S. Dawson (Ashington: Mid Northumberland Arts Group, and Manchester: Carcanet, 1995).
PDRLS	John Clare, *Poems, Descriptive of Rural Life and Scenery* (London: Taylor and Hessey, and Stamford: E. Drury, 1820).
Pforz	John Clare manuscripts in the Carl H. Pforzheimer Library Collection, New York Public Library, cited by Pforzheimer Miscellaneous Manuscript number.
PMS	Peterborough Manuscripts. Reference numbers (in each case a letter and a number) as in Margaret Grainger, *A Descriptive Catalogue of the John Clare Collection in Peterborough Museum and Art Gallery* (Peterborough: printed for Earl Fitzwilliam, 1973).

Prose   *The Prose of John Clare*, ed. J. W. and Anne Tibble (London: Routledge and Kegan Paul, 1951).

RM   John Clare, *The Rural Muse: Poems* (London: Whittaker, 1835).

SC   John Clare, *The Shepherd's Calendar; with Village Stories, and Other Poems* (London: for John Taylor by James Duncan, 1827; facsimile repr., Oxford and New York: Woodstock, 1991).

Sketches   *Sketches in the Life of John Clare by Himself*, ed. Edmund Blunden (London: Cobden-Sanderson, 1931). Edited text of NMS 14.

VM   John Clare, *The Village Minstrel, and Other Poems*, 2 vols. (London: Taylor and Hessey, and Stamford: E. Drury, 1821).

NOTES

The serious study of Clare begins with the huge manuscript collections in the Peterborough Museum and Art Gallery (PMS) and the Northampton Central Library (NMS). A near-complete set of microfilm reproductions of both collections has been published by Microform Academic Publishers of East Ardsley, Wakefield, West Yorkshire (NMS in 1974; PMS in 1980). Most of my references to Clare's writings are followed by both a Northampton or Peterborough manuscript number and a page reference to an appropriate modern edition. As explained in the Preface, the majority of quotations are lightly edited for clarity; this means that they frequently differ in accidentals from the transcriptions of Clare's manuscripts in the editions of Eric Robinson and his collaborators.

John Clare by Himself (*JCBH*) offers the fullest and most accurate printed texts of the autobiographical writings, but in order to make clear when I am quoting from Clare's 1821 memoir and when from the autobiography that he began drafting in 1824, references in my notes are to *Sketches in the Life* for the former (*Sketches*) and J. W. and Anne Tibble's edition of Clare's *Prose* for the latter (*Autobiog*). The autobiography survives only in the form of fragments, most of them scored through to indicate that they have been copied: the fair copy is lost. Although the Tibbles' text splices together passages from several different manuscripts and is highly inaccurate in its transcriptions, their arrangement of these fragments into a sequential narrative offers a readable approximation to the probable form of the lost fair copy.

DEDICATION

v 'As new things meet': 'To Anna three years old', PMS A41; *MP*, 2.143.

PREFACE

xviii 'In writing such Biographs': Pforz 198, p. 136.

3 'The man whose daughter': NMS 8; *LY*, p. 152n.

4 'Returned home': NMS 8, dated 23 July; copied into NMS 6, dated 24 July; *LY*, p. 147; also *JCBH*, p. 265, though printed there at end rather than beginning of 'Journey out of Essex'.

4 '1st Day': NMS 6; *LY*, p. 150n.

4 'So here I am': NMS 6; *LY*, p. 154.

4 'preceded by any severe': PMS F4. Skrimshire's spelling of *prosing* was *prossing*.

7 'I was a lover': PMS A25; *Autobiog*, p. 44.

9 'What are the supposed causes': PMS F4.

9 'Some thirty years previous': Martin, p. 3.

10 'My father was one of fate's': NMS14; *Sketches*, pp. 45–6.

11 'I cannot trace my name': PMS A32; *Autobiog*, pp. 11–12.

11 at least two Clare families: for the poet's ancestry, see *John Clare's Family Tree*, compiled by Mary Moyse (Helpston: John Clare Society, 1988); also her article in *JCSJ* 8 (1989):24–30. Alice, his grandmother, died at the age of eighty-two, not eighty-six, as Clare himself claimed.

12 'as soon as': Clare to Henry Behnes, 29 December 1828, *L*, p. 448.

12 swarthy in appearance ... ill-tempered: Edward Drury described her in 1819 as 'cross in her looks, and gipsey-like in her appearance' (NMS 43, letter 2).

12 'Both my parents was': NMS 14; *Sketches*, p. 46.

13 'the superstitious tales': ibid.

13 'tolerable good voice': ibid.

13 the earliest folk-song collector: Deacon, p. 18.

13 steep-roofed thatched tenement: for a much fuller account of the cottage, see my article 'New Light on the Life of Clare', *JCSJ* 20 (2001): 41–54.

13 'as roomy and': PMS B3; *Autobiog*, p. 12.

14 'hut': *L*, p. 379.

14 'when the rain': *L*, p. 576.

14 'the tree is an old': Clare to Hessey, 20 January 1823, NMS 32; *L*, p. 260.

14 'their peculiar flavour': NMS 32; *L*, p. 262.

15 'the unfortunate delusion': *Lincoln, Rutland, and Stamford Mercury*, 19 July 1793.

16 'What advantages': *Gentleman's Magazine* 63 (1793): 952.

16 'peculiarly serviceable': *Stamford Mercury*, 19 July 1793.

16 'sultry days and dewy nights': first version of 'July', intended for *SC*, line 2 (PMS A20; *MP*, 1:84).

16 'the gadfly's': 'July', line 94 (PMS A20; *MP*, 1:87).

16 'laid': 'July', line 590 (PMS A20; *MP*, 1:105, and note at 1:360).

17 'as much to the contrary': NMS 14; *Sketches*, p. 46.

17 'Bessey—I call thee': 'To an infant sister in heaven' (*L*, p. 195). Published in *London Magazine*, August 1821, as 'Sonnet. To a Twin-Sister who died in Infancy', with *untamed* for *untaind* (Clare's original word evokes both *unstained* and *untainted*).

CHAPTER TWO: CHILDHOOD

19 'ups and downs': PMS B5; *JCBH*, p. 34.

19 'surely the garden': PMS B8; *JCBH*, p. 36.

19 'real simple soul-moving': PMS A46; *JCBH*, p. 37.

21 'Our fancies': 'Childhood', PMS A40; *MC*, p. 99.

21 'Harken that': 'Evening Schoolboys', PMS A54; *RM*, p. 116; first published in *Stamford Champion*, 20 April 1830. Early printed texts follow Taylor's emendations of the opening ('Hark to') and 'schoolboy friendships' ('friendly schoolboys').

22 'and round the fire': 'Childhood', PMS A40; *MC*, p. 103.

22 'a good scholar': NMS 14; *Sketches*, p. 47.

22 'The youth, who leaves': 'May', *SC*, p. 44.

22 'Though one of the weakest': NMS 14; *Sketches*, p. 48.

23 'Giants, Hobgobblins': ibid.

23 'how Johnny Armstrong . . . And by imbibing': 'Lines on the Death of Mrs Bullimore', NMS 1; *EP*, 1:197–9.

23 'Robin Hood's Garland': PMS A31; *Autobiog*, p. 14.

24 'more known among . . . was that it was full': NMS 14; *Sketches*, pp. 64–5. For the uncle as the source of the book, see Edward Drury's 1819 memoir of Clare, transcribed by Mark Storey, *JCSJ* 11 (1992): 15.

24 'was always surprised': NMS 14; *Sketches*, p. 48.

25 'I got the prizes': NMS 22; *JCBH*, p. 33.

25 'For thou it was . . . Through Mathematics': NMS 1; *EP*, 1: 57.

25 'His place of rest': C. Carr to Clare, 29 June 1822, Eg. 2246, fo. 66.

25 One of Clare's school exercise books: NMS 11.

26 'I have a Superficial': NMS 22; *JCBH*, p. 33.

26 'felt an itching': NMS 14; *Sketches*, p. 53.

26 'persevered so far': NMS 14; *Sketches*, p. 54.

27 'luckily abandoned': ibid.

27 'a knotty question . . . that pleasure I have witnessed': NMS 14; *Sketches*, pp. 49–50.

27 'Study always left': NMS 22; *JCBH*, p. 32.

27 'Mathematics Particularly Navigation': ibid.

27 'Grammer I never': NMS 22; *JCBH*, p. 33.

28 'The romance of "Robinson Crusoe" ... new Crusoes': NMS 14; *Sketches*, pp. 64–5.

28 'some fancying it': NMS 14; *Sketches*, p. 50.

29 'sweeing ... to watch the rising': PMS A34; *JCBH*, pp. 37–8.

29 'marbles on the smooth-beaten ... The fields were ... into the quiet love': PMS A34; *Autobiog*, p. 12.

29 'the lighter hues': This and subsequent quotations and paraphrase from PMS A34; *Autobiog*, pp. 24–6; *JCBH*, pp. 38–9.

30 'When a boy': PMS A49; *JCBH*, p. 44.

30 'boughs from the trees': PMS B8; *JCBH*, p. 47.

31 'broken up by some': PMS A33; *JCBH*, p. 42.

31 'Playing at soldiers': PMS B3; *JCBH*, p. 166.

31 Like a bird building a nest: see further, 'Nests, Shells, Landmarks', chap. 6 of my *The Song of the Earth* (London: Picador, and Cambridge, Mass.: Harvard University Press, 2000).

31 'I felt the water choke me ... mine getting': PMS B7; *Autobiog*, pp. 14–15.

32 'I attempted it ... I lay for a long time': PMS B7; *Autobiog*, p. 15; *JCBH*, p. 43.

32 'yet when I was alone ... magnified it': PMS D2; *Autobiog*, pp. 40–1.

32 'if I deny': *L*, p. 61.

33 'Fakenham Ghost': Bloomfield, *Rural Tales*, quoted from 5th ed. (London, 1806), pp. 70–7.

33 'would brighten up ... for he would come down': PMS A46; *NHPW*, p. 86.

33 presumably to be drowned: see Anne Barton, 'Clare's Animals: The Wild and the Tame', *JCSJ* 18 (1999): 6.

33 'something or other': PMS A49; *NHPW*, p. 52. Compare *SC*, 'January: A Winters Day', lines 189–95.

34 'skilled in huswife': PMS A25; *JCBH*, p. 51.

34 'talk in rapture': 'As lingers winter', PMS A15; *EP*, 2:496. See also chap. 6 of Clare's projected autobiography (*Autobiog*, p.42; *JCBH*, p. 49).

34 'Elegy Humbly attempted': NMS 1; *EP*, 1:119. Several other poems, including 'Sorrows for a Friend' (*VM*, 2:151), were also written in memory of Turnill.

34 'the first whose loss': 3 September 1821, *L*, p. 212.

35 'made an instrument': PMS A25; *Autobiog*, p. 43.

35 one of Clare's early poems: 'To Mr J. Turnill', NMS 1; *EP*, 1:104.

35 a notice to quit: preserved in NRO (information from Oscar Turnill, descendant).

35 'he would not have been': introduction to *PDRLS*, repr. in *CH*, p. 46.

35 Turnill modestly regarded: letter to Clare, Eg. 2246, fo. 105.

36 'It was platonic affection ... the first creator': NMS 14; *Sketches*, p. 87.

37 'for the sake of meeting ... a tear would hang': PMS A25; *Autobiog*, p. 44.

37 'others might laugh it ... I cannot forget': PMS A53; *Autobiog*, p. 44.

37 'When she grew up': PMS A25; *Autobiog*, p. 44.

38 'Childish Recollections': *VM*, 2:14–18; *EP*, 2:298–301.

38 'Childhood': 'The past it is a magic word . . .', *Stamford Bee*, in three parts, February–March 1831; *MC*, pp. 96–106.

39 'Childhood': 'O dear to us ever', NMS 20 (I), dated 15 October 1848; *LP*, p. 651.

CHAPTER THREE: HORIZONS

41 'I had imagined . . . the hedge cricket': PMS A34; *Autobiog*, pp. 13–14; *JCBH*, pp. 40–1.

41 'To the worlds end': 'Birds Nesting', PMS B8; *MP*, 2:168.

43 'Send him to Norborrey': PMS A46; *JCBH*, p. 48.

44 'There is no direct': Drury to Taylor, NMS 43 (17).

44 John Scott: see Patrick O'Leary, *Regency Editor: Life of John Scott* (Aberdeen: Aberdeen University Press, 1983).

46 'For so long as the Miltons': Pforz 198; *JCBH*, p. 48.

46 'Inclosing Lands in the Parishes': 49 Geo III *Sess*. 1809, final 'Award of the Commissioners', dated 13 March 1820.

47 'open-field sense of space': John Barrell, *The Idea of Landscape and the Sense of Place 1730–1840: An Approach to the Poetry of John Clare* (Cambridge: Cambridge University Press, 1972), p. 103.

49 an angry poem of loss: 'In my native field two fountains run / All desolate and naked to the sun' (PMS A57).

49 'The vulgar tyrants': PMS A18; *MP*, 2:11.

50 'Clare may be described': E. P. Thompson, *Customs in Common* (London: Penguin, 1993), pp. 180–1. The whole of chap. 3, 'Custom, Law and Common Right', is highly relevant to Clare.

50 'By Langley Bush': 'Remembrances', *MC*, p. 370.

50 'A not unpicturesque country': De Wilde's *Rambles Roundabout* (1872), quoted in Cherry, p. 2.

51 'the old Roman road': Martin, p. 2.

52 ten thousand pounds: F. M. L. Thompson, *English Landed Society in the Nineteenth Century* (London: Routledge and Kegan Paul, 1963), p. 223.

52 'a Company of miserable Hibernians': prose sketch headed 'Vanity of Harbouring Foolish Wishes', NMS 1, pp. 145–6.

53 Irish immigrants feature: e.g. 'The Irish Emigrant', NMS 22; *EP*, 2:433.

53 'petticoats of banded plad': 'July' (first version, excluded from *SC*), lines 187–218, PMS A20; *MP*, 1:91–2.

54 'O Langley Bush': *VM*, 1:164–5; for manuscript text, see *EP*, 2:250.

54 'I hope [that] is not': Taylor to Clare, 11 February 1821, Eg. 2245, fo. 287, apropos of the poem published in *VM* as 'Cowper Green'.

54 skull and bones: 'On seeing a skull on Cowper Green', *RM*, pp. 41–4; see also *JCBH*, p. 244.

54 turned into a poem: 'The Lodge House', PMS B2; *EP*, 2:233–47.

54 'I remember with what': PMS A34; *JCBH*, p. 102.

55 'It is a curious old place': PMS B8; *JCBH*, p. 69.

56 'ah Helpstone I ween': 'Woodcroft Castle', stanza 5, in 'Village Minstrel' at stanza 101, NMS 3; *EP*, 2:165.

56 'slashed off': 'Woodcroft Castle', stanza 10.

56 'I believe the reading': NMS 14; *Sketches*, pp. 88–9.

57 'I was in earnest': PMS D2; *JCBH*, p. 164.

57 'with the old dish': NMS 14; *Sketches*, p. 88.

57 'England, with all thy': Cowper, *The Task*, 2:205–8, quoted by Clare, 'England' (*EP*, 2:69).

57 'I think I shall stand': *L*, p. 51.

58 'The conservative culture of the plebs': Thompson, *Customs in Common*, p. 9.

58 'I reverence the church': NMS 14; *Sketches*, p. 88.

59 'When I was a boy': PMS B5; *JCBH*, pp. 34–5.

59 'though young we was not': PMS B8; *Autobiog*, pp. 16–17.

59 'how we would make': PMS B8; *Autobiog*, p. 17.

60 'thronged round with stalls': ibid.

60 'and those that are': Clare's draft letter on village customs to Hone's *Every-day Book*, Pforz 198; Deacon, p. 283. Hone reproduced the account of the dumb-cake and porch-watching rituals, attributing it to 'a correspondent near Peterborough'—*Every-day Book*, 1 (1825), p. 523.

61 'The young men': Pforz 198; Deacon, p. 285.

61 The sheep-shearing ... frumenty: 'June' in *SC* has a vivid account of the 'feast of furmety' at 'clipping' time.

61 'Anon the fields': PMS B6, first four lines quoting revision in margin of p. 14; *MP*, 1:133.

61 'a common custom': Pforz 198; Deacon, p. 286.

62 'a dirty reality': Pforz 198; Deacon, p. 287.

62 'the shepherd cuts his journeys ... the beauties and horrors': 'The Woodman or the Beauties of a Winter Forest', NMS 1; *NHPW*, pp. 3–4.

62 'The Woodman': *VM*, 2:20–8.

63 'jagged leaves ... His eye also catches': NMS 1; *NHPW*, pp. 6–7.

CHAPTER FOUR: GARDENER, SOLDIER, LIME-BURNER

64 'There is William and John Close': NMS 30; *L*, p. 663.

65 William Bradford ... Tom Clare: information from 1841, 1851 and 1861 Census Books, Public Records Office, HO.107/815/13, HO.107/1747, R.G.9/969.

65 'My scholarship was': PMS B8; *Autobiog*, p. 18.

66 'little deformed fellow': PMS B8; *JCBH*, p. 64.

66 'did not much relish': PMS B8; *Autobiog*, p. 18.

66 'an odd young man': PMS B8; *JCBH*, p. 65.

66 the *Salsette*: but, as so often in the life of Clare, verification proves impossible—Farrow's name is not recorded in the muster of the *Salsette* or any of the other ships on which Byron hitched his rides around the Mediterranean.

67 'coddled up ... silly shanny': NMS 14; *Sketches*, p. 54. *Shanny* means 'shamefaced'.

67 'though I had clumb ... I felt timid': PMS B8; *Autobiog*, p. 18.

67 'meet manhood': PMS B8; *Autobiog*, p. 19.

67 'sent for to drive plough': PMS B8; *Autobiog*, p. 20.

67 'fancied that I should': PMS B8; *Autobiog*, p. 20.

68 'Wisbeach was a foreign ... the figure I should make': PMS B3; *Autobiog*, pp. 20–1.

68 'people stared at me': PMS B3; *Autobiog*, p. 21.

69 'look up boldly': PMS A43; *Autobiog*, p. 21. Subsequent dialogue from same source.

69 'taking portraits': PMS A43; *Autobiog*, p. 22.

69 'melancholy smile': ibid.

70 'as well as if': NMS 14; *Sketches*, p. 55.

70 'always the same': PMS D2; *Autobiog*, p. 23.

70 'a habit for thinking': PMS A43; *Autobiog*, p. 23.

70 'was warily on the watch': NMS 14; *Sketches*, p. 57. *Glegging* means 'peeping'.

70 'a fine lady': PMS A43; *Autobiog*, p. 23.

70 'I always turn': NMS 14; *Sketches*, p. 60.

70 Bill Manton: Clare only calls him 'Manton' in PMS B3; 'Bill' is supplied by Martin (p. 28). Unless the name is invented, this is one of the details suggesting that Martin had access to material that is now lost.

71 'a gentleman of great': NMS 14; *Sketches*, p. 60.

71 'I often thought': PMS A34; *Autobiog*, p. 26.

71 to the gardener 'as if': PMS A34; *Autobiog*, p. 26.

71 'a gentleman so bepowdered': Robert Heyes, '"Looking to Futurity": John Clare and Provincial Culture', unpublished Ph.D. thesis (Birkbeck College, University of London, 1999), p. 27, quoted from *Abercrombie's Practical Gardener* (1817); Clare owned the 1823 edition.

71 'out of which sum': Martin, pp. 29–30. The specificity with which Martin details the wage again suggests that he was working from a now-lost version of Clare's autobiography.

72 'I have him in my mind's eye': PMS A34; *Autobiog*, p. 27.

72 'at all hours': ibid.

72 'to give him his due': NMS 14; *Sketches*, p. 61.

73 'I even was foolish': PMS A34; *Autobiog*, p. 28.

73 'as white as a sheet': PMS A34; *Autobiog*, p. 30. PMS A34 gives two conflicting accounts of this first enlistment attempt.

73 'I could not stop': PMS A25; *Autobiog*, p. 32.

74 'which he had found': PMS A25; *JCBH*, p. 60.

75 'young chaps ... called colting': PMS B7; *Autobiog*, pp. 34–5.

75 'indisposition ... The ghastly paleness': NMS 14; *Sketches*, pp. 70–1.

77 'Two Jurneys': 'Disbostments of The Churchwardner Thos Drake for the Year 1810', in 'Helpston Churchwardens' Accounts 1780–1840', NRO 163p/29, fo. 65.

77 'was seized': *Stamford Mercury*, 9 August 1811.

77 'The country was': PMS B7; *Autobiog*, p. 46.

77 Scott ... Wordsworth: see Kenneth Johnston, *The Hidden Wordsworth* (New York and London: Norton, 1998), pp. 802–6.

77 'go for nothing': *Autobiog*, p. 47. See further, Bob Heyes, 'John Clare and the Militia', *JCSJ* 4 (1985): 48–54.

78 'For a week': Martin, p. 45.

78 'He was presently': PMS B7, *Autobiog*, p. 48.

79 'to be sent': PMS B7, *Autobiog*, p. 50.

79 'No person will hire': letter from a Northamptonshire correspondent to the Board of Agriculture, 1816, quoted, Heyes, 'Militia', p. 52.

80 'a corner of one room': PMS B3; *JCBH*, p. 117.

80 'his exertions and exposure': Taylor's introduction to *PDRLS*.

80 in receipt of Parish Poor Relief: surviving Poor Books in the Fitzwilliam Papers reveal that Parker Clare received relief in 1814 and was still on it in 1825 (NRO Fitzwilliam Misc. Vols. 573, 690). Clare's poem 'A simple effusion address'd to my lame father' (Pforz 197; *EP*, 1:544) refers to the receipt of 'Parish bounty'.

80 'greatest despair ... pottered about': NMS 14; *Sketches*, p. 70.

81 'Extra Labourers': Manuscript Account Book, 'Park and Plantations / Extra Labourers / Commencing 7th September 1816' (continuing to 7 April 1821), uncatalogued archive, Burghley House. For reasons why I believe the employee was the poet, not a different John Clare, see my article 'New Light on the Life of Clare', *JCSJ* 20 (2001): 41–54.

81 'What wonders strike': stanza from 'Wanderings in June' (published in the *London Magazine* of July 1822 and the 1827 *Shepherd's Calendar*, p. 195). In Clare's original manuscript, *Silvery* was *filmy* (*MP*, 1:314), an adjective more suggestive of something in the water that makes the pond need scouring.

82 'Closes of greensward': NMS 6, p. 20; *LY*, p. 162.

83 'He had an odd taste': PMS A34; *Autobiog*, p. 29. It is not clear whether Clare met Cousins when working as a boy in the kitchen-garden or as a man on the estate—or both.

83 'utterly cast down': PMS B3; *JCBH*, p. 117.

84 'It was a pleasant lively': PMS A32; *JCBH*, p. 81.

84 'I was in love': PMS B7; *Autobiog*, p. 55.

84 'succeeded so far': PMS B7, *Autobiog*, p. 55.

85 His poetry helped him: details from 'Song', *VM*, 2:46–7.

85 'still a fine': S. T. Hall, essay on 'Bloomfield and Clare' (1866), in his *Biographical Sketches of Remarkable People* (1873), repr. in *CH*, p. 281.

85 'pleasant shapings': PMS B7; *Autobiog*, p. 55.

85 'artless': 'Song', *VM*, 2:46–7.

86 'Confusion mingling fear': 'Ballad' (PMS B2) in *VM*, 1:143–6 (printed version omits a stanza about his 'freedoms', which concludes 'I gaind her love and provd it sweet / Beyond what words can tell').

86 'bare ground beaten': PMS B7, *Autobiog*, p. 56.

86 'heaths and woods': PMS B7; *Autobiog*, p. 57.

87 'approved of': PMS A32, *Autobiog*, p. 56.

87 'When John came': quoted in J. W. and Anne Tibble, *John Clare: A Life* (1932; rev. ed. London: Michael Joseph, 1972), p. 82.

87 'Such was the tide': PMS A32, *Autobiog*, p. 56.

CHAPTER FIVE: 'IN LEISURE HOURS'

89 '*That* is true fame!': Hazlitt's recollection of Coleridge, 'My first Acquaintance with Poets' (1823), in William Hazlitt, *The Fight and other Writings*, ed. Tom Paulin and David Chandler (London: Penguin, 2000), p. 262.

89 'twitter of joy': NMS 14; *Sketches*, p. 57. Clare was not sure that he remembered the year correctly.

89 'Come, gentle Spring': quoted in NMS 14; *Sketches*, p. 57.

90 ''twas reckoned nothing': NMS 14; *Sketches*, p. 58.

90 'and what with reading': NMS 14; *Sketches*, p. 59.

90 'The Morning Walk': neither this poem nor 'The Evening Walk' survives, though given Clare's tendency to revise and recycle his work there may be odd traces of them in such later poems as 'A Morning Walk' (PMS A29; *MP*, 3:350) and 'Recollections after an Evening Walk' (*VM*, 2:30; *EP*, 2:326).

91 'perhaps twenty times': NMS 14; *Sketches*, p. 59.

91 'humoured her mistake': NMS 14; *Sketches*, p. 62.

91 'Aye boy': NMS 14; *Sketches*, p. 63.

92 'a person who knew nothing': NMS 14; *Sketches*, p. 68.

92 'For I had hardly': ibid.

92 'finding a jumble': ibid.

92 'So in the teeth': NMS 14; *Sketches*, p. 69.

92 'enough of grammar ... correct placing': unpublished fragment, Pforz 198, p. 48.

92 'before I was 20': PMS B5, p. 89.

93 'The whole of music': PMS A9, quoted in Deacon, p. 10.

93 'Song taken': PMS B7; *EP*, 1:527.

93 'My odd habits': PMS A25; *Autobiog*, p. 32. *Sooty crew* was a conventional poetic phrase for gypsies, used by Clare in 'Langley Bush' (quoted in Chapter 3).

94 'in singular pomp': PMS A25; *Autobiog*, p. 35. Funeral noted in *Stamford Mercury*, 15 October 1824.

94 'by the ear': PMS A25; *Autobiog*, p. 35. For Gray, see Silvester Gordon Boswell, *The Book of Boswell: Autobiography of a Gypsy*, ed. John Seymour (London: Gollancz, 1970), p. 169.

94 'Finished planting': J, 3 June 1825.

94 oblong music books: NMS 12 and 13. Tunes transcribed in Deacon, pp. 307–80.

95 'Everything that is bad': PMS A25; *Autobiog*, p. 35.

95 newspaper report of a case: see *Northampton Mercury*, 30 January and 20 February 1819.

95 *Fireside Magazine*: I am very grateful to Sharon Floate for this reference, for the information (based on the recollection of Alfred Adams) on Boss and Young in Australia, and for genealogies of the Smiths.

96 'An ignorant iron-hearted': PMS A25; *Autobiog*, p. 35.

97 'Wasp weed': PMS A25; *Autobiog*, pp. 37–8.

97 'I had a great desire myself': PMS A25; *Autobiog*, p. 36.

97 'To me how wildly': 'The Gipsy's Evening Blaze', *PDRLS*, p. 191. 'Begun when I was 14 or 15' (PMS A32; *JCBH*, p. 110); 'before he was seventeen' (Taylor's introduction to *PDRLS*, p. xxii).

98 'The snow falls deep': 'The Gipsy Camp', published in *English Journal*, 29 May 1841; *LP*, p. 29.

99 'It was a sort of meeting house': PMS A25; *Autobiog*, p. 38.

99 'an unfinished sentence ... felt the accusations': PMS A53; *JCBH*, p. 88.

100 'first love reality ... I felt a sudden': PMS A25; *Autobiog*, p. 45.

100 'believed the explanations': PMS A25; *Autobiog*, p. 46.

100 'a strict observer': NMS 14; *Sketches*, p. 72.

101 'Bless me': PMS A25; *JCBH*, p. 53.

101 'he felt as happy': ibid. It is just possible that this passage refers to John Billings, but the manuscript context makes Porter much more likely.

101 'never caught': PMS A25; *Autobiog*, p. 51.

102 'anticipation is': PMS A34; *JCBH*, p. 57.

102 'a true story': PMS A25; *Autobiog*, p. 51.

102 'Bloomfield's Poems': ibid.

103 'dark system': ibid.

103 'systematic symbols': PMS B3; *Autobiog*, p. 53.

103 'a collection of dried': PMS B5; *JCBH*, p. 62.

103 'poetry, natural history': PMS A25; *Autobiog*, p. 51.

104 'ignorant appearance': PMS B3; *JCBH*, p. 103.

105 'a genius powerful': NMS 1; *EP*, 1:17.

105 'Parnas hill ... Sweet Songstress': 'To Mrs Anna Adcock', NMS 1; *EP*, 1:35.

105 'very middling': *L*, p. 333, in a letter to his publisher which says that 'Cottage Stories' would have been a good title for the volume that became *The Shepherd's Calendar; with Village Stories, and Other Poems*, but that it resembled Adcock's *Cottage Poems* too closely.

106 'The Lamentations of Round-Oak Waters': NMS 1; *EP*, 1:228–34.

106 'The Critics speaks': PMS B3; *JCBH*, p. 115.

106 'Hail England': NMS 1; *EP*, 1:38. Other poems mentioned: *EP*, 1:54, 208, 125.

107 'On the Death of a Quack': NMS 1; *EP*, 1:330.

107 'was very importunate ... decamped': PMS A25; *Autobiog*, p. 52. A longer early poem is called 'The Quack and the Cobler' (Pforz 197; *EP*, 1:164–70). Clare noted that it was a 'true tale' which offered 'exact portraits of his manners and Character' of a joking, yarn-spinning Helpston cobbler: this sounds very like Farrow, suggesting that the occasion with Parker Clare was not his only run-in with a quack doctor.

107 'was in great fame': PMS B6; *JCBH*, p. 101; 'Death of Dobbin', *EP*, 1:84–90; comprehensively revised in 1820, *EP*, 2:630–6.

107 'A moment's rapture': NMS 1; *EP*, 1:110.

108 'The Wish': NMS 1; *EP*, 1:43–50.

108 'I had got': *L*, p. 131.

109 'I always wrote': PMS A32; *JCBH*, p. 100. On the idea of Clare as a 'trespasser', see the excellent essay by John Goodridge and Kelsey Thornton in *John Clare in Context*, ed. Hugh Haughton, Adam Phillips and Geoffrey Summerfield (Cambridge: Cambridge University Press, 1994), pp. 87–129.

CHAPTER SIX: 'HOW GREAT ARE MY EXPECTATIONS!'

110 'a political pamphlet': PMS A31; *JCBH*, p. 103.

110 'congregational dissenters': PMS A31; *JCBH*, p. 104.

111 'dirty doings': ibid.

111 'detested the thoughts': NMS 14; *Sketches*, p. 73.

111 'whether *Religious, moral*': Henson to Clare, 7 November 1818, Eg. 2245, fo. 6.

112 'prosing thoughts ... hastily scratted': NMS 14; *Sketches*, p. 76.

112 'And what is life?': PMS A13, p. 69; *PDRLS*, p. 37.

112 'The man looked a little': NMS 14; *Sketches*, p. 77.

113 'The least touch': the address was reprinted in Taylor's introduction to *VM*, 1:xiii.

113 'I scarcely knew it': PMS A32; *Autobiog*, p. 59.

114 'Sir/ I send you some': *L*, p. 3 (the text actually survives only in the form of a copy made by Henson, Eg. 2245, fo. 75).

114 'carried so many': J. Simpson, *Obituary and Records for the Counties of Lincoln, Rutland, and Northampton* (Stamford: W. R. Newcomb, 1861), p. 335. One of many references I owe to Bob Heyes.

114 Other known subscribers: see Bodleian Library MS Don d. 36, fo. 4; *JCSJ* 11 (1992): 16.

115 'had not 15 pence': NMS 14; *Sketches*, p. 78.

115 'love matters ... strong tether': PMS A32; *Autobiog*, p. 60.

115 'the money was what': NMS 14; *Sketches*, p. 79.

116 ' "John Clare must come home" ': Martin, p. 71.

117 'The Two Soldiers': poetic versions in PMS A44, A59, prose in PMS A43, A46; *MP*, 1:291–301, 1:365–9.

117 'If you get the manuscripts': NMS 14; *Sketches*, p. 81.

118 'place full and undivided': Drury to Clare, 24 December 1818, Eg. 2245, fo. 10. My reconstruction of the sequence of events at this time is based on Drury's letters and Clare's *Sketches*. The account in Clare's later *Autobiog* differs in some particulars.

118 'bagatelles ... moral and rural': Drury to Clare, Eg. 2250, fos. 116, 135.

119 'sent them back': PMS A32; *Autobiog*, p. 62.

119 'became an errand boy': Drury to Clare, Eg. 2250, fo. 118.

119 'made one cold ... very pretty': PMS A32; *JCBH*, pp. 109–10.

120 'A Northamptonshire': *L*, p. 4.

120 'scribbling etc.': NMS 14; *Sketches*, p. 84.

120 'a literary gentleman': Eg. 2250, fo. 149.

120 'quiet inoffensive': PMS A25; *JCBH*, p. 56.

120 'to Enquire after': *L*, p. 5.

120 'as he thought': PMS A25; *JCBH*, p. 56.

121 'Putting the Correct': *L*, p. 12.

121 'Gent: of Learning ... I ask not': *L*, pp. 5–6.

121 'crampt the Imagination': *L*, p. 13.

121 'most contemptible ... *very bad*': Eg. 2250, fo. 119.

122 'Tasteful Illuminations': PMS A3; *EP*, 1:414; Macclesfield text identified by David Powell, *John Clare Society Newsletter*, September 1995.

122 'Poems in England': *L*, p. 8—but the gentleman was not Dr Bell, as asserted in the editorial note there (see PMS A32; *Autobiog*, p. 63).

122 'they were in the hands ... These things': PMS A32; *Autobiog*, p. 64.

123 'They are written ... In reading the work': NMS 43 (letter 1).

124 'a piece of dirty paper': NMS 43 (2).

124 'I procured a horse': ibid.

125 'I hope you have not': note in PMS A3; cf. letter to Holland (*L*, p. 19).

125 'Your hopes': NMS 43 (2).

125 'No where': NMS 43 (4).

126 'He is no drunkard': NMS 43 (4).

126 'rubbish ... gentleman-editor': NMS 43 (4). Clare's approval of Taylor's changes is commented on in NMS 43, letters 5, 6 and especially 29: 'he agrees with hearty satisfaction that he has such capital help'.

126 'Idea of his Deserts': NMS 47 (memorandum by Taylor).

127 cockney genius ... country one: Taylor mentioned Keats and Clare in the same breath in a letter of 21 July 1819 to the political philosopher James Mackintosh—see catalogue of Sotheby's English Literature and History sale (L00205), 13 July 2000, p. 52.

127 'I am not against': note in PMS 3.

127 'rural subjects': NMS 43 (8).

127 'D——d stuff': PMS B1.

127 'Those marked': ibid.

128 'My Rule': NMS 44 (2).

128 'My First Atempts': L, p. 15.

128 'Inform him': L, p. 19.

129 'I left it with regret': PMS A32; *Autobiog*, p. 65.

129 'the horizon sweeping': 'Written in April at Walk Lodge', NMS 3; *EP*, 2:121.

129 'very pleasant address': PMS B6; *Autobiog*, pp. 92–3.

131 'Nothing could exceed': *London Magazine*, January 1820; *CH*, p. 57.

131 'The lower orders': *Stamford Mercury*, 19 November 1819, quoted in Heyes, 'Looking to Futurity', p. 67n.

131 'The Invitation': *London Magazine*, January 1820; *CH*, pp. 41–2.

131 'without Emolument': letter of 30 November 1819, cited in NMS 47.

131 'too Refined': L, p. 18 (22 November 1819).

132 'friendless Case': Taylor to Drury, 28 December 1819, NMS 44 (1).

132 'I shall send you': Eg. 2245, fo. 15.

132 he appreciated the concert: It may have been the occasion that inspired Clare's poem 'After hearing a Lady sing "Banks o' Doon" ' (PMS B2; *EP*, 2:232).

132 'for I dare say': NMS 44 (1).

133 'A labouring clown': PMS B2; *EP*, 2:382.

133 'an unhanged rogue': Gilchrist to Taylor, 24 February 1820, NMS 44 (11).

133 'knavish Attorney': Taylor to his brother Jem, 13 March 1820, DRO. Mark Storey (L, p. 36n) asserts that this was the same Thompson from whom Drury took over the bookshop, but I have not found evidence to support this identification.

133 'Drury has persuaded': L, p. 486, copied by Clare from his 'journal at the time' (which is, alas, lost).

133 'secession from their society': NMS 43 (9).

133 'I found the lower orders': PMS D2; *JCBH*, p. 133.

134 'a heedless': PMS A32; *Autobiog*, p. 64.

134 'I don't wish': MS of 'Betty Sell' in Fitzwilliam Museum, Cambridge; see *EP*, 1:581.

134 'dealings with love ... temptations': NMS 14; *Sketches*, pp. 85–6.

135 'affection that made': PMS A32; *Autobiog*, p. 64.

135 'to leave them': PMS A32; *Autobiog*, p. 65.

136 'with a former love ... My long-smothered': PMS A32; *Autobiog*, p. 64.

136 'I felt awkwardly': ibid.

136 'let these poor': NMS 3; *EP*, 2:103.

136 'all despoiled': PMS B2; *EP*, 2:308. 'To the Lass of the Valley (under a cloud)' is a variant text of the same poem (PMS A8; *EP*, 2:399): this title makes it clear that the poem refers to 'Patty of the Vale'.

136 'Past is the scene': PMS B2; *EP*, 2:217.

137 'O say not love': PMS A11; *EP*, 2:452.

137 'S': PMS A16; *EP*, 2:499. The title 'S' is very faint, and might conceivably be a 'P', but, in contrast to the poems addressed to Patty, this one is about longing and unattainability ('As I love her could she love me / Enough of bliss were given, / An earthly immortality, / I'd want no more of heaven').

137 'Bessey's the top': PMS B2; *EP*, 2:204.

137 voice of a sailor: PMS A10; *EP*, 2:417.

137 'Jenny Young': PMS B2; *EP*, 2:376.

137 'How can I kiss': PMS B2; *EP*, 2:228.

137 'Mary leave': PMS A40; *EP*; 2:51.

138 Among the poems written around this time: *PDRLS*, p. 82; *VM*, 1:177, 2:140.

138 pointedly omitted: pointedly, insofar as the poems adjacent to them in Clare's manuscripts *were* published.

138 'Fate's bonds': PMS B2; *EP*, 2:81.

138 'But never o never': 'Ballad', PMS B2; *EP*, 2:89.

138 'When I prest': 'Ballad', PMS B2; *EP*, 2:90.

138 sheet of songs and ballads: see *L*, p. 23. The sheet is now at Oundle School.

138 'queen of my heart': *EP*, 2:366.

139 three other manuscripts: PMS A2, PMS A11, PMS B2.

PART TWO: FAME (1820–1827)

141 'At length 'twas known': 'The Fate of Genius'; Morgan Library MA1320; *EP*, 2:669.

CHAPTER SEVEN: PRESENTING THE PEASANT POET

143 ' "A happy new year" ': Gilchrist's article is repr. in *CH*, pp. 35–42.

145 'Mr G. has *picturesqued*': NMS 43 (30).

145 'taken by the hand': PMS F1; *Stamford Mercury*, 14 January 1820.

146 'The disgusting conceit': Taylor to his father, 19 January 1820, DRO.

146 'Ways of a Village': see *L*, pp. 60, 82, 90, 95, 107. Taylor had proposed 'Week in a Village' as the title (Eg. 2245, fo. 25).

146 'It is to be greatly feared': NMS (11).

147 'A slight word': NMS (10).

147 '[I cannot] think nor compose': PMS A3.

147 'Taylor is fearful': Eg. 2245, fo. 27.

148 'the least favoured': Taylor's introduction is repr. in *CH*, pp. 43–54.

148 'He loves the fields': *CH*, p. 50.

149 'the unmixed and unadulterated': *New Times*, 21 January 1820; *CH*, p. 55.

149 'much more agricultural': 'The Poems of John Clare', *Stamford Mercury*, 21 January 1820.

149 'Crazy Nell': *PDRLS*, p. 208 (in later editions this poem was moved to the opening section of miscellaneous poems). 'Crazy Nell was taken from a narrative in the Stamford Mercury nearly in the same manner it was related—I was very pleased with it and thought it one of the best I had written and I think so still' (PMS A32; *JCBH*, p. 110).

149 'terrific and pathetic Scenery': PMS D1.

150 'To Religion': *PDRLS*, p. 204. Cf. 'Christian Faith' (*PDRLS*, p. 189 and repr. in *Gentleman's Magazine*, March 1820).

150 'An Effusion to Poesy': *PDRLS*, p. 123.

151 'I love all wild flowers': *NHPW*, p. 23, identified as greater stitchwort.

151 'the growth of a poet's mind': Wordsworth's title for *The Prelude*.

151 'In those low paths': *PDRLS*, p. 148.

152 *Grandeur ... Oblivion*: examples from 'Elegy on the Ruins of Pickworth' (*PDRLS*, p. 65).

152 'The Fountain': *PDRLS*, p. 59.

152 Among the manuscripts he was filling: NMS 11; NMS 1; PMS A1, PMS A2, NMS 2; PMS A3; PMS A4, PMS A5, NMS 5.

152 'How beautiful e'en seems': NMS 7; *EP*, 1:501.

152 'To the Fox Fern': PMS D2; *EP*, 1:469.

154 'Sweet smiling village': Goldsmith, *The Deserted Village* (1770), lines 35–9, 51–6.

154 'Now all laid waste': 'Helpstone', *PDRLS*, p. 9.

155 'so he had a most': Drury to Taylor, NMS 43 (12).

155 'customers in high life': ibid.

155 'unstrung': NMS 43 (13).

155 'I must tell you candidly': Eg. 2245, fo. 27.

155 'impurities (and even impieties)': *Anti-Jacobin Review*, June 1820; *CH*, p. 106.

156 'the author's ardent attachment': *London Magazine*, March 1820; *CH*, p. 79.

156 lukewarm ... reacted against: e.g. *Monthly Review* and *Monthly Magazine* in March 1820; *Guardian* in May, *British Critic* and *Blackwood's Edinburgh Magazine* in June. See *CH*, pp. 54–106.

156 Drury's brother Michael: see letter from Taylor to Michael Drury, in *The Keats Circle*, ed. H. E. Rollins, 2 vols. (Cambridge, Mass.: Harvard University Press, 1965), 1:101.

156 'He looks abroad': *Quarterly Review*, May 1820; *CH*, p. 98.

156 'for it is not': NMS 43 (14).

156 'very drunk indeed': ibid.

157 'clear clean shirt': Eg. 2245, fo. 35.

158 'for fear of seeming': PMS A55; *Autobiog*, p. 68.

159 'a slow sententious manner': NMS 43 (15), letter from Drury to Taylor that is main source for this account.

159 'enquired minutely respecting': ibid.

159 'His Talents are very': Fitzwilliam to Taylor, 20 February 1820, DRO.

159 'would be in a dirty': PMS A55; *Autobiog*, p. 68.

160 'They expected you': ibid.

160 '[I] went upstairs': PMS A55; *Autobiog*, p. 69.

160 'eyeing the door': ibid.

160 'went off scarcely': PMS A32; *JCBH*, p. 119.

161 'The gates flew open': *Complete Works of William Hazlitt*, ed. P. P. Howe, 21 vols. (London: Dent, 1930–4), 10:68.

162 'until the attendants': Eg. 2245, fo. 179. Drury also sent Clare the report of the Earl's marriage from the *Monthly Magazine* (1797).

162 'How do I know': reported by Taylor in letter of 13 March 1820, DRO.

162 'Good men don't like': *L*, p. 34.

162 distinguished naval career: see D. W. Prowse, *A History of Newfoundland* (London, 1895), pp. 372–3, 418–19.

163 'take this little volume': 'Lines Written by a Lady, and presented with a volume of "Clare's Poems"—to a Noble Friend', Eg. 2245, fo. 33.

163 'Of your Poems': Eg. 2245, fo. 39.

164 'They flow from the heart': PMS F1 (6 July 1820).

164 'Sir W.S.': ibid.

164 'some two or three poems': *Morning Post*, 11 February 1820.

164 'when the baby's': PMS A4; *EP*, 1:80.

165 'dirty verse': NMS 43 (18).

165 'Lord Radstock still exerts': 15 February 1820, DRO.

166 'the novelty created': PMS A33; *Autobiog*, p. 79.

166 'the road was lined': PMS B3; *Autobiog*, p. 80.

166 Theatre Royal Drury Lane: Vestris was contracted here, and this is the location given on the broadside publication of the song (Deacon, p. 66), but Clare misremembered the location as Covent Garden.

166 'uncommonly astonished': PMS A33; *Autobiog*, p. 80.

166 'I felt often when walking': PMS A31; *Autobiog*, p. 81.

166 'Oh Christ': NMS 65 (Simpson family recollection).

167 'and when I opened them': PMS A31; *Autobiog*, p. 81.

167 'unwilling to play': Martin, p. 112.

167 'But Clare refused': ibid.

168 'the back shop': Eg. 2245, fo. 154.

168 'C in alt': Hood, *Works* (London, 1882), 2:376.

168 'Did you ever see': 'C. Van Vinkbooms [pseudonym of Wainewright], his Dogmas for Dilettanti', *London Magazine*, December 1821, p. 658.

169 'James Augustus Hessey': Taylor to his father, DRO; Chilcott, *A Publisher* *and his Circle: The Life and Work of John Taylor, Keats's Publisher* (London: Routledge and Kegan Paul, 1972), p. 8.

169 'He has the appearance': Cary to Rev. Thomas Price, 8 March 1820, quoted in R. W. King, *The Translator of Dante: The Life, Work and Friendships of Henry Francis Cary (1772–1844)* (London: Secker, 1925), p. 134.

169 'pleased us all': Taylor to his brother, 13 March 1820, DRO.

169 'A large man': PMS B6; *Autobiog*, p. 84.

170 'Clare at the first interview': Martin, p. 115.

170 'has been a very pretty woman': PMS A31; *Autobiog*, p. 85.

170 'On Leaving London': NMS 3; *EP*, 2:117.

171 'take it mighty hard': 'To the Muse', PMS B2; *EP*, 2:206.

171 'pride and presumption': from Mossop, 4 March 1820, Eg. 2245, fo. 51.

171 'at Half past Eight': Eg. 2245, fo. 59.

172 poem of fond farewell: 'On some Friends leaving a Favourite Spot', PMS A30; *MP*, 2:55–9.

172 'I shall *treasure* it': Eg. 2245, fo. 61.

CHAPTER EIGHT: THE PRICE OF FAME

173 'choose a bit of ground': *L*, p. 53.

173 'independant': *L*, p. 55.

173 'Do you find yourself': Eg. 2245, fo. 162.

174 'I held out': PMS A32; *Autobiog*, p. 65.

174 'prove a better bargain': Clare to Hessey, *L*, p. 82.

174 'domestic troubles': Eg. 2245, fo. 196.

174 'Patt and myself': to Taylor, *L*, p. 165.

175 'occasional Remittances': Eg. 2245, fo. 90. Radstock's proposal was reported to Clare by Emmerson: Eg. 2250, fo. 173.

176 'Sense of Superiority': Eg. 2245, fo. 202.

176 'John Clare has been': NMS 43 (28).

176 'I think too highly': survives in copy by Taylor, 30 March 1820, DRO.

176 'Beware, beware': Radstock's inscription in Francis Gastrell, *The Christian Institutes*, sent to Clare 17 February 1820, NMS 218.

176 'What a contrast': *L*, p. 153.

177 'A gentleman came in': *L*, p. 96.

177 'repeated it over': *L*, p. 103.

177 'used to cut': PMS A32; *Autobiog*, p. 63.

178 'his cottage at Helpstone': British Library Althorp Papers; see Paul Chirico, 'Writing for money: The correspondence of John Clare and Earl Spencer', *TLS*, 17 November 2000, p. 14.

178 'I am sought after': *L*, p. 215.

178 'I had the works': PMS B7; *Autobiog*, p. 71.

179 'He then asked me ... We have a Bible': PMS A33; *Autobiog*, p. 72.

180 'Dear Bardie': Eg. 2246, fo. 208.

180 'your brilliant ophthalmic': Eg. 2246, fo. 180–3.

181 'on such a morning ... the whistle was a song tune': PMS A25; *Autobiog*, pp. 75–7.

182 'A little river': PMS A32; *Autobiog*, p. 73.

182 'an old enemy': PMS A25, deleted.

183 'There is a vivid': *Morning Post*, 15 May 1820; *CH*, p. 59.

184 'I told him': PMS B6; *Autobiog*, p. 71.

184 'He mimicked': PMS B6; *Autobiog*, pp. 71–2.

184 'The plasters you sent': *L*, p. 92.

185 'the inmates of a whole': Martin, p. 118.

185 'sensible Gent': *L*, pp. 184–5. For the Artis connection, see Heyes, 'Looking to Futurity', pp. 171–2.

186 'I never expected': Hessey to Taylor, 15 November 1820, DRO.

186 'I was very unwilling': *London Magazine*, November 1821; *CH*, p. 158.

186 'On a projecting wall': *CH*, p. 162.

187 'Do you know personaly': Clare to Sherwill, 12 July 1820, *L*, pp. 86–7.

187 'writes about the peasantry': *L*, p. 302.

188 'Nursery rhyme': *L*, p. 221.

188 'sought to hallow': De Quincey, as reported by Richard Woodhouse, who was there. Robert Morrison, 'Richard Woodhouse's *Cause Book*: The Opium-Eater, the Magazine Wars, and the London Literary Scene in 1821', *Harvard Library Bulletin*, n.s. 9 (1998): 26.

188 parody of ... Westminster Bridge: PMS A18; *MP*, 2:7.

188 'even in this season': De Quincey, 'Sketches of Life and Manners', *Tait's Edinburgh Magazine*, December 1840; *CH*, p. 246.

188 'Give my sincere Respects': *L*, pp. 36–7.

188 'the beautiful in poetry': *L*, p. 541 (the 'beautiful' is here opposed to the 'sublime'—of which he couldn't think of a good example).

188 'striking': *L*, pp. 81–2.

189 'a constant allusion': PMS B5; *L*, p. 519, draft letter of 1830 to Herbert Marsh, elder son (who later died insane) of the Bishop of Peterborough. On poetic nightingales as against Clare's, see Hugh Haughton, 'Progress and Rhyme: "The Nightingale's Nest" and Romantic poetry', in *John Clare in Context*, pp. 51–86.

189 'the Description': Taylor to Clare, Eg. 2245, fo. 62.

189 'Keats is on the Water': Eg. 2245, fo. 225–6.

189 'thrown away ... stubborness': *L*, p. 99.

190 'I hope poor Keats': ibid.

190 'One of the very few': Eg. 2245, fo. 305.

190 'apathy of mellancholly': *L*, p. 175.

190 'there are many things': Eg. 2245, fo. 99. For a detailed account, see Eric Robinson, 'John Clare (1793–1864) and James Plumptre (1771–1832), "A

Methodistical Parson"', *Transactions of the Cambridge Bibliographical Society* 11 (1996): 59–88.

191 'Keep as you are': Eg. 2245, fo. 126.

191 'To Mr Clare': Eg. 2245, fo. 186.

191 'If we were still': 3 May 1822, Martin, p. 140, corrected from original MS in possession of Bob Heyes.

192 'Why did not you come': Eg. 2250, fo. 238.

192 'he is the most original poet': *L*, pp. 300–1.

CHAPTER NINE: 'EXPUNGE EXPUNGE!'

193 'not as amicable . . . Have you any Letters': Eg. 2245, fo. 66.

194 'I humbly conceive': 28 March 1820, NMS 43 (20).

194 'very unsatisfactory': 30 March 1820, DRO.

194 'So you are again': 27 April 1820, Eg. 2245, fo. 103.

194 'at least *half* ': NMS 47; *L*, p. 685.

195 'One great thing': Eg. 2245, fos. 115–17.

195 'If I am not mistaken': NMS 43 (23).

195 'Earl Spencer has lost': Eg. 2250, fo. 115.

195 'The surgeon can hardly': NMS 43 (26).

196 'Are you "St Caroline"': *L*, p. 109–10.

196 'I'm of no party': *L*, p. 208.

197 a poem on this theme: 'Rich and Poor; or Saint and Sinner', *EP*, 2:518.

197 'Drakard the Editor': *L*, p. 159.

197 'Lord R——': 25 April 1821, Eg. 2245, fo. 95.

197 'How truly dear Clare is': Eg. 2245, fo. 118 (copy).

198 'If you are determined': ibid.

198 'It has been my anxious': Eg. 2245, fos. 118–19 (copy).

198 'Let me now entreat': Eg. 2245, fos. 118–20.

199 'And he wishes you': Eg. 2245, fo. 121.

199 'Dear Taylor': 16 May 1820, *L*, pp. 68–70.

200 'I like *your idea*': Eg. 2245, fo. 131.

200 'I am inclined': Eg. 2245, fo. 140. Taylor was a little disingenuous in implying that two thousand copies of the third edition had been freshly printed: in fact the edition consisted of the remainder of the second edition with pages 153–64 omitted.

200 'I like your Independence': Eg. 2245, fo. 139.

200 'oppressed and harrassed': Eg. 2245, fo. 159.

200 '*own private drawer*': Eg. 2245, fo. 169.

200 'domestic troubles': Eg. 2245, fo. 196.

200 'Would to God': Eg. 2245, fo. 210.

201 'cursed mad': *L*, p. 83.

201 'He says he does not': Woodhouse to Taylor, in *The Letters of John Keats*, ed.

H. E. Rollins, 2 vols. (Cambridge, Mass.: Harvard University Press, 1958), 2:163.

201 'I know his taste': *L*, p. 84. '[none]' is my emendation, where Clare has repeated 'all', almost certainly a slip of the pen.

201 'false or true': Eg. 2245, fo. 172.

201 'Lord R. had expressed': Eg. 2245, fo. 225.

202 'I will write': Eg. 2245, fo. 254 (copy).

202 'Unless you commission': Eg. 2245, fo. 259.

202 'extreme agitation': Eg. 2245, fo. 263.

203 'I am a blunt fellow': *L*, pp. 42–3.

205 'Theres T[aylo]r': PMS B2; *EP*, 2:67.

205 'the myth of solitary genius': see Jack Stillinger, *Multiple Authorship and the Myth of Solitary Genius* (New York: Oxford University Press, 1991), and, for application to Clare, Bob Heyes, 'Writing Clare's Poems: "The Myth of Solitary Genius"', in *John Clare: New Approaches*, ed. John Goodridge and Simon Kövesi (Helpston: John Clare Society, 2000), pp. 33–45.

206 '*breaks* and *pauses*': Eg. 2245, fo. 113.

206 'I have been trying songs': *L*, pp. 64–5.

206 'These leaves of scribbling': NMS 1, p. 8.

207 'a sweet strain': 3 January 1822, Eg. 2245, fo. 269.

207 'Wether I lay': *L*, p. 45; Gilchrist reports the fit in NMS 44.

207 'in the fit': *L*, p. 70.

207 'Follow Dr Skrimshire's': Eg. 2245, fo. 128.

208 'some effect of mind': *L*, p. 59.

208 'depressions ... demons': Eg. 2245, fo. 249.

208 'nervous fears ... nervous depression': Eg. 2245, fos. 279, 397, 97.

208 'the fact is': *L*, p. 114.

209 'My two favourite Elm trees': to Taylor, 7 March 1821, *L*, p. 161.

209 'I am in that muddy': *L*, p. 162.

209 'a radical man ... I am glad': Drury to Clare, 16 March 1821, Eg. 2250, fo. 131.

209 'monstrous': Eg. 2245, fo. 317.

209 'Expectation is at its height': *L*, p. 195.

210 'Its gone home agen': *L*, p. 199.

210 'We all Sympathise': Eg. 2247, fo. 301.

210 'the deep and sincere Sympathy': Eg. 2245, fo. 329.

211 '*cold decorum*': Eg. 2245, fo. 398.

211 'for the last twin childern': *L*, p. 209.

211 'I can't repine': PMS A31, p. 197.

212 'with cherubs': PMS A50; *EP*, 2:524.

212 'I have had the horrors': 11 August 1821, *L*, p. 206.

212 'beauty floating': 'A Dedication to ✳✳✳✳', PMS A30; EP, 2:540–4.

213 'one here and there': Eg. 2245, fo. 124. Copies sent to Taylor: probably PMS C1 and C2.

213 'you are blind': *L*, p. 70.

213 passed to Octavius Gilchrist: a manuscript book that was at some time broken up and is now PMS B2 and NMS 3.

213 Others remained in manuscript: many drafts from this period are preserved in PMS A7–A25.

214 'Garland': Eg. 2245, fo. 115.

214 'interfere with other compositions': NMS 43 (26). Hessey's reply: NMS 44.

214 'What is the importance': Eg. 2245, fo. 176.

215 'I should have protested': Eg. 2245, fo. 360.

215 'You must not mind': 18 April 1820, Eg. 2245, fos. 90–1.

216 'painting of Nature's deformity': 16 July 1820, NMS 43 (25).

216 'My cousin John': 19 August 1820, NMS 43 (28).

216 'first pastoral': lost in its original form, but later revised into the opening section of 'Going to the Fair' (*MC*, pp. 32–46). My thanks to Paul Dawson for clarification on the complicated manuscript situation here.

217 'Village Scenes': Morgan Library, New York, manuscript MA 1320.

217 'I get on cursed bad': *L*, p. 114.

217 'to make a respectable': Eg. 2245, fo. 260.

217 'your plan cannot': *L*, p. 133.

217 'This Evening I have completed': DRO.

218 'let it pass . . . it would constitute': Eg. 2245, fo. 271.

218 'some of the best rural': *L*, p. 136.

219 'radical Slang': NMS 3, p. 186; Eg. 2245, fo. 272.

219 'There once were lanes': NMS 3; *VM*, 1:50.

219 'without spoiling': DRO.

220 'We have but few': Eg. 2245, fo. 277.

220 'bold challenge': Eg. 2245, fo. 281.

221 'too like "English Minstrelsy"': Eg. 2245, fo. 285.

221 'I think your ending': *L*, p. 146.

221 'do as you have done': *L*, p. 152.

221 'Here the change': Eg. 2245, fo. 288.

221 'Perhaps you like . . . I did not like': Eg. 2245, fos. 287–8.

221 'your assistance': *L*, p. 167.

222 'you rogue you': *L*, p. 204.

222 'I had thought you': Eg. 2245, fo. 359.

223 'portion consisted': *VM*, 1:xviii.

224 'country sports and customs': *VM*, 1:xxi.

224 'Wood seers': *VM*, 2:211.

225 molehill: see Bob Heyes's wholly persuasive 'Little Hills of Cushioned Thyme', *JCSJ* 12 (1993): 32–6.

225 'oft he dropt him': *VM*, 1:11.

226 'Crusoe's lonely isle': *VM*, 1:17.

226 'Bred in a village': ibid.

226 'not a cowslip': *VM*, 1:58.

226 'describe the feelings': PMS B6; *JCBH*, pp. 113–14.

227 'And, hour by hour': *VM*, 2:129.

228 'such a favourite': *L*, p. 109.

228 'this cold morning': *L*, p. 116.

228 'The small wind whispers': 'Winter', *VM*, 2:183.

229 'raise the reputation': October 1821; *CH*, pp. 141–5. Subsequent quotations from same source.

230 'justify all the praise': October 1821: *CH*, pp. 145–7.

230 'We are willing to give': November 1821; *CH*, pp. 150–6.

230 'he can teach us': November 1821; *CH*, pp. 167–8.

231 'These poems breathe': January 1822; *CH*, pp. 168–71.

231 'humbug': PMS B5.

231 'as a stimulant': *L*, p. 229.

231 'the real Admirers': Eg. 2246, fo. 44.

232 'At length 'twas known': Morgan Library, MA1320; *EP*, 2:669.

233 'And 'midst the dreads': *London Magazine*, February 1822, repr. as 'The Dream', *SC*, pp. 210–18.

233 ''Twas Mary's voice': PMS A29 (with footnote acknowledging the influence of *The Opium-Eater*); *MP*, 1:337.

234 'leaden interaction': Eg. 2246, fo. 17.

234 'exquisite sensibilities': Eg. 2246, fo. 18.

234 'well informed men … Hague': PMS A18; *Autobiog*, pp. 74–5.

234 'Artis up to the neck': PMS A18; *Autobiog*, p. 75.

235 'Friend Clare': Eg. 2246, fo. 7.

235 'He was a man': *Gardeners' Chronicle and Agricultural Gazette*, 1 December 1866, quoted in Heyes, 'Looking to Futurity', pp. 192–3.

236 'J Henderson will be happy': Eg. 2250, fo. 220.

236 'I should been': Eg. 2250, fo. 86.

236 'History of favorite': Eg. 2246, fo. 480.

236 a report of the discovery: 'Roman Antiquities', *Stamford Mercury*, 28 December 1827; pencil draft in PMS A39 (*L*, pp. 191–2, misdated); see Heyes, 'Looking to Futurity', pp. 185–6.

237 'Should leasure permit': Eg. 2246, fo. 59–60.

237 'Poets Hall': *L*, p. 227.

237 'I live here among': *L*, p. 230.

237 'confounded lethargy': *L*, p. 234.

238 'nearly extinguished': *L*, p. 230.

238 'I take a great deal': *L*, p. 234.

239 'My journey up': 22 May 1822, addressed to Parker; *L*, p. 241.

240 'at half-past six': Wainewright's invitation to Cary, quoted in King, *The Translator of Dante*, p. 138.

240 'a very comical': PMS B3; *Autobiog*, p. 91.

240 'previous experience of life': *Memorials of Thomas Hood* (London, 1869), p. xx; quoted in Andrew Motion's ingenious fictionalised biography, *Wainewright the Poisoner* (London: Faber and Faber, 2000), p. 117.

241 'his bright, grass-coloured': 'Literary Reminiscences No. 4', in Thomas Hood, *Works*, 2 vols. (London, 1882), 2:374.

241 'A tallish spare man ... one of those men': PMS B3; *Autobiog*, p. 90.

241 'He is very fond of snuff': PMS B3; *Autobiog*, p. 89. 'Packman' is an error for 'Packwood', who published poetic advertisements for his razor-strops.

242 'all Philology ... there go Tom': Hood, *Works*, 2:375. See also Wainewright, 'Janus Weatherbound, or the Weathercock Steadfast for Lack of Oil', *London Magazine*, January 1823.

242 'over his glass': PMS B3; *Autobiog*, p. 91.

242 'a little too much elated': Taylor to his father, 19 June 1822, DRO.

242 'as a careless listener': PMS B3; *Autobiog*, p. 87.

243 'I have had my Company': DRO.

243 'guileless yet suspicious': note by Reynolds in copy of RM given to his niece; quoted in Tibble, *Life*, p. 175.

243 'How anxious': Eg. 2246, fo. 62.

243 'pains both': Eg. 2246, fo. 64.

243 'alas! *too short*': Eg. 2246, fo. 68.

244 'little but *powerful*': Eg. 2246, fo. 76.

244 Rippingille: see Peter Cox, '"A liking to use the pen": Edward Villiers Rippingille (*c.* 1790–1859) and John Clare', *JCSJ* 17 (1998):17–33.

244 'a rattling sort': PMS B3; *Autobiog*, p. 85.

244 'in great disgrace': Eg. 2246, fo. 73.

245 'the fashionable Bookseller': Taylor to his father, 19 June 1822, DRO.

245 'unpleasant recollections': Eg. 2250, fo. 183.

246 'in a dangerous State': Eg. 2246, fo. 88.

246 'a faded flower': Eg. 2246, fo. 74.

246 'at the thought': *L*, p. 243.

246 'analyze the legions': Eg. 2246, fo. 22.

246 'He cross examines': Eg. 2246, fo. 119.

247 'purely rustic manners': Drury to Clare, 3 August 1822, Eg. 2246, fo. 96.

247 'Since I saw you': Lamb to Clare, 31 August 1822, Eg. 2246, fos. 99–100.

247 'mental sufferings': Eg. 2246, fo. 132.

247 'pay almost a daily': *L*, p. 253.

247 'Many miles stretch': *L*, p. 257.

248 'infernal tribe': 13 January 1823, Eg. 2246, fo. 144.

248 'lost a son': *L*, p. 273.

248 'had I know': *L*, p. 278.

248 'To Anna three years old': PMS A41; *MP*, 2:143–5.

249 'I think I never': PMS A46; *MP*, 2:158.

249 '*love-sick* of late': 6 May 1823, Eg. 2246, fo. 186.

249 'Besides, first impressions': ibid.

250 'in a way that enables': *CH*, pp. 180–1; Clare's annotated copy: NMS 97.

250 'None have better': Kent, *Flora Domestica* (1823), p. xxii. Clare's copy, presented by his publishers, is NMS 271.

251 'I have apathy': *L*, p. 277.

251 'troublesome nothing': Eg. 2246, fo. 251.

251 'fiery torments': Eg. 2246, fo. 264.

251 'the addition to your family': Eg. 2246, fo. 268.

252 'The medical gentleman': Martin, p. 173.

252 'soliciting his Lordship's': Eg. 2246, fo. 262.

252 'quackery': to Taylor, *L*, p. 297.

253 'One day he stayed': Martin, p. 175.

253 'delighted with the *Muse*': Eg. 2246, fo. 319, a reply to a lost letter from Clare that described various literary enthusiasms, including the poetry of Allan Cunningham.

253 'a little work': Eg. 2246, fo. 321.

253 'religion of nature': Eg. 2246, fo. 123.

254 'a question about Faith': Eg. 2246, fo. 294.

254 'real practical Religion': Eg. 2246, fos. 321–2.

254 'a set of simple sincere': *L*, p. 294.

255 Primitive Methodist: see Mark Minor, 'John Clare and the Methodists: A Reconsideration', *Studies in Romanticism* 19 (1980): 31–50.

255 'my feelings are so unstrung': *L*, p. 294.

255 'persuasive tenderness': *L*, p. 296.

255 'thin death-like shadows': PMS B3; *Autobiog*, p. 94.

257 'of the old school': James Clarke, *Autobiographical Recollections* (London, 1874), p. 123.

257 'we Received': *L*, p. 299.

257 'the wandering pains': Eg. 2246, fo. 332.

258 'I shall be': Eg. 2246, fo. 348.

258 'I am requested': Eg. 2246, fo. 352.

258 'I am glad at length': Eg. 2246, fo. 360 (21 July 1824).

259 'Are you a poet, Sir?': PMS B3; *Autobiog*, p. 97.

259 'was shivered': Eg. 2246, fo. 368.

260 'brother poet': PMS B3; *Autobiog*, p. 98.

260 *The Stage-Coach Breakfast*: see Francis Greenacre, *The Bristol School of Artists* (Bristol: City Art Gallery, 1973), pp. 133–5.

261 'smoke, smocks': Eg. 2246, fo. 366. The significance of the French Theatre was first noted by C. V. Fletcher, 'The Poetry of John Clare, with partic-

ular reference to poems written between 1837 and 1864', unpublished
M.Phil. dissertation, University of Nottingham, 1973, pp. 32–9.

261 'Why will you stay': Eg. 2246, fo. 366.

262 'it is now eleven': Eg. 2247, fo. 420.

262 'The first jaunt': PMS B3; *Autobiog*, p. 96.

262 'boximania': see Tom Bates, 'John Clare and "Boximania"', *JCSJ* 13 (1994):
5–17; also Roger Sales, *John Clare: A Literary Life* (London and Basingstoke: Macmillan, 2002), pp. 130–44.

263 'Randall, John': Reynolds, *The Fancy* (London, 1820); Clare's copy, NMS
342.

264 'a fit partner': J, 17 September 1824.

264 'his words hung': PMS B3; *Autobiog*, p. 91.

264 'He sits a silent': PMS B3; *Autobiog*, p. 88.

265 'A little artless': PMS B3; *Autobiog*, p. 91.

265 'Taylor has lately': *Letters of Thomas Lovell Beddoes*, ed. Edmund Gosse
(London, 1894), p. 371.

266 'like an earthquake': *London Magazine*, August 1824, p. 119.

266 'Byron is dead!': Jane Welsh to Thomas Carlyle, quoted in Leslie Marchard,
Byron: A Portrait (London: John Murray, 1971), pp. 467–8.

266 'straggling groups': PMS B3; *Autobiog*, p. 99.

266 'but they wore': PMS B3; *Autobiog*, p. 100.

267 'He has gained': PMS B3; *JCBH*, p. 157.

267 'Time is his monument': NMS 17, p. 52.

CHAPTER TWELVE: BIOGRAPHIES, BIRDS AND FLOWERS

268 'I propose': NMS 15, title-page. Subsequent references in this chapter given
as 'J', with date of entry.

268 'I have determined': J, 6 September 1824.

270 'Took a walk': J, 29 September 1824.

270 'Tyrany and Cruelty': J, 7 September 1824.

270 'one may almost': J, 8 September 1824.

271 '2 verses of the Shipwreck': J, 17 September 1824.

271 'great favourites': J, 13 September 1824.

271 'what a soul-thrilling': J, 10 November 1824.

271 'the uninterrupted flow': J, 26 October 1824.

271 'natural and beautiful': J, 29 October 1824.

271 'the essence and simplicity': J, 5 November 1824.

271 'Sir Nightingale': J, 2 October 1824.

271 'several beautys': J, 3 October 1824.

272 'one of the very best': J, 22 October 1824.

272 'Recieved a Letter': J, 19 June 1825.

272 'shot under the hedges': J, 9 September 1824.

272 'Took a walk in the field': J, 16 April 1825.

273 'Met with an extrodinary': J, 13 May 1825.

273 'Found the old Frog': J, 28 May 1825.

273 'heartily sorry': PMS A46; *NHPW*, p. 89.

273 'a little drawing': Eg. 2246, fo. 433.

274 'the lasses do not lift': J, 21 September 1824.

274 'Very ill': J, 22 September 1824.

274 'A wet day': J, 23 September 1824.

274 'Tryd to walk out': J, 24 September 1824.

274 'Very ill to day': J, 8 October 1824.

274 'this is a hungry': J, 28 November 1824.

275 'he had eaten nothing': Martin, p. 194.

275 'There went the left': J, 5 October 1824.

275 'the worlds friendships': J, 25 November 1824.

276 'the Inclosure has left': J, 26 November 1824.

276 'I little thought': J, 4 June 1825. See further, V. A. Hatley, 'The Poet and the Railway Surveyors', *Northamptonshire Past and Present* 5 (1974): 101–6.

276 'love[d] wild things': to Elton, *L*, p. 310.

276 'Took a Walk': J, 2 January 1825.

276 'the authoress': J, 5 January 1825.

276 ' "A Natural History" ': J, 11 September 1824.

276 'On the sexual system': PMS A46; *NHPW*, pp. 101–3.

277 'the vulgar are always': to Hessey, Berg Collection, New York Public Library; *NHPW*, p. 16.

277 'heart's-ease ... Sparkler': to Hessey, Berg Collection; *NHPW*, p. 19.

277 'The Author is mistaken': *London Magazine*, August 1823, p. 148.

277 'Intend to call': J, 11 March 1825.

277 'Resumed my letters': J, 18 April 1825.

278 'You need not have told me': Eg. 2247, fo. 145.

278 'Birds Nesting': PMS A47 (lost); see *MP*, 2:163–84, and Eric Robinson, ed., *John Clare Birds Nesting, The Lost Manuscript* (Tern Books: Market Drayton, 1987).

279 'and when we came up': PMS A49; *NHPW*, p. 37.

279 'March 25th': PMS A46; *NHPW*, p. 83.

280 'Martin—': PMS A46; *NHPW*, pp. 147–8.

280 'was very plentiful': PMS A5; *NHPW*, p. 301.

280 fragment in a different notebook: PMS A31; *NHPW*, pp. 277–8.

281 wording of his will: in subsequent correspondence with Eliza Emmerson, this proved a matter for further concern, especially with regard to the fate of his unpublished writings. See my article 'New Clare Documents', *JCSJ* 21 (2002): 5–18.

281 one of which survives: NMS 29; *JCBH*, p. 247.

282 'for the next Chapter': PMS A32.

282 'I will read': Eg. 2246, fo. 453.

282 'very trifling ... most of the naritive': PMS D2; *JCBH*, pp. 159–60.

282 'I am getting worse': *L*, p. 304.

283 'keep the bowels': Eg. 2246, fo. 450.

284 'weakling flower': J, 2 June 1825.

284 'Coud not sleep': J, 6 May 1825.

284 'My family has increased': Pforz 198, p. 47.

284 'the poor man's friend': *Morning Post*, 7 June 1826; *MP*, 3:315.

285 'Billings and Cooings': 24 October 1825, Eg. 2247, fo. 92.

285 'an harlots ... Dost think': PMS A32, pp. 8–11.

285 'Make your conscience': Eg. 2247, fo. 112.

286 'You have been *wandering*': Eg. 2247, fos. 126–7.

286 'present infatuated': Eg. 2247, fo. 156.

286 'some *loadstone*': Eg. 2247, fo. 164.

287 'I am sure Patty': *L*, pp. 379–80.

287 'for the gratification': Eg. 2247, fo. 224.

287 'vïz. supplying': Eg. 2247, fo. 182.

289 'a Stand-Cart': Eg. 2246, fo. 11.

290 'And fairest daughter': Pforz 198, p. 65; *MP*, 1:318.

290 'I cannot mend': Eg. 2246, fo. 43.

290 'Your verse is a develish': *L*, p. 231.

290 'The winds, that late': *London Magazine*, March 1822, p. 216; also *SC*, p. 200.

290 'The first Stanza': Eg. 2246, fo. 33.

291 Clare drafted January, February: in, respectively, PMS A29, PMS A30, PMS A20; there are also rough early drafts in PMS A18 and A19.

291 sketches towards September: entitled 'A Morning in the last of Summer' and 'The Last of Summer' (PMS A30; *MP*, 2:41–54).

291 'How goes on your': Eg. 2246, fo. 152.

291 '*not* for *present*': Eg. 2246, fo. 167.

292 'reather too severe': Eg. 2246, fo. 198 (21 May 1823).

292 'No injury can possibly': PMS A40; *EP*, 2:698, quoting Pope's advertisement to 'Epistle to Dr Arbuthnot'.

292 'My Dear Sir': Eg. 2246, fo. 226.

292 'clap the town brand': PMS B3; *JCBH*, p. 117.

292 'Having no credit': PMS A40; *EP*, 2:743–5 (though text there incorporates a substantial later addition).

293 'The past and present': PMS A40; *EP*, 2:761.

293 'master, son and serving man': PMS A40; *EP*, 2:702.

293 'True Patriot': *EP*, 2:736–49, ninety-line section published in *Drakard's Stamford News*, 17 August 1827.

293 'good old Vicar': PMS A40; *EP*, 2:756–61. 'The Vicar' was first written as an independent poem in 1821.

293 Clare was informed: by Van Dyk, acting for Taylor and Hessey; PMS F1, p. 109.

294 'political opinions': Eg. 2246, fo. 473.

294 'crabbed name': J, 4 November 1824. On this journal, see further, D. B. Green, 'John Clare, John Savage, and "The Scientific Receptacle"', *Review of English Literature* 7 (1966): 87–98.

294 *'half profit, half loss'*: Eg. 2249, fo. 304.

295 'a Name which Spenser': Eg. 2246, fo. 228.

295 'too general to excite': Eg. 2246, fo. 245.

296 'The distresses of some classes': Eg. 2246, fo. 268.

296 'one hundred sonnets': *L*, p. 288. This project was begun in NMS 17, which Clare entitled 'A Collection of Sonnets Descriptive of Appearances in the Seasons And other Pictures in Nature'. The collection peters out after twenty-five sonnets, some of which are highly evocative vignettes (e.g. 'The Foddering Boy' and 'School Boys in Winter', *EP*, 2:585–6).

296 'of a very timid': PMS B3; *Autobiog*, p. 96.

296 'Your opinion of my verses': Van Dyk to Clare, 21 August 1824, PMS F1, p. 93.

297 'already described … Let your Descriptions': Eg. 2246, fo. 406.

297 'the MSS they have': Clare to Elton, December 1824, *L*, p. 310.

297 'I have taken great liberties': Van Dyk to Clare, 15 March 1825, PMS F1, pp. 113–14.

298 'I thought I had one': J, 9 March 1825.

298 'It is better to terminate': Eg. 2246, fo. 470.

299 'close with Taylor': Eg. 2247, fo. 25.

299 'I know that my temper': *L*, pp. 329–30.

299 'When Midsummer comes': Eg. 2247, fo. 34.

300 'Shall we insert the Descriptions': Eg. 2250, fo. 329.

300 'there is nothing': *L*, p. 333.

300 'He hears the wild geese': PMS A20; *MP*, 1:42.

301 'While, far above': *SC*, p. 31.

301 'pressure and tightness': Eg. 2247, fo. 65.

301 'this last five or six': Clare to Taylor, 15 September 1825, *L*, p. 347.

302 'the most celebrated writers': Eg. 2247, fo. 62.

302 'Mary! I dare not': *MC*, p. 302. 'The Confession', written at the same time and published in the *Literary Magnet*, June 1826, was another 'ballad to Mary' (PMS A31; *MP*, 2:342–4).

302 'I hope you will approve': Alaric Watts to Clare, Eg. 2250, fo. 342.

302 'As to the Poetical Almanacks': *L*, p. 349.

303 'common every day': Clare to Taylor, *L*, p. 352.

303 'Popularity in Authorship': *European Magazine*, November 1825; *Prose*, pp. 255–60. Original draft as part of *Autobiog*: PMS B3.

303 'unfit for Insertion': Eg. 2247, fo. 131.

303 'Heretofore I have submitted': letter split between Eg. 2247, fos. 132–3, and
     Eg. 2250, fo. 326, published in *L*, pp. 356–8.
304 'paper war': *L*, p. 361.
304 'complete Record': Eg. 2247, fo. 152.
305 'if a first copy': *L*, p. 367.
305 'very clever Imitations': Eg. 2250, fo. 325.
305 'in these hard Times': Eg. 2250, fo. 324.
305 'a *set* of *modern antiques*': Eg. 2247, fo. 199.
306 'long illness ... kind assistance': Eg. 2247, fo. 212.
306 'Slashing': ibid.
306 'unaffected Narrative': Eg. 2247, fo. 236.
306 '*Crucible* ... higher subjects': Eg. 2247, fo. 238.
307 'a meagre piece': Eg. 2247, fo. 279.
307 'nothing would appear': *L*, p. 488.
307 'pastoral poesy of painting': *L*, p. 423.
307 'in grateful remembrance': *SC*, p. v.
308 'has had comparatively': Eg. 2247, fo. 322.
308 'Novels and such': *L*, p. 394.
308 'poetry has had': Eg. 2247, fo. 387.
308 'Nothing': *CH*, p. 204.
308 'in accurate pictures': *CH*, p. 210.
309 'Shakspearian splendour': *CH*, p. 209.
309 'I like thoughts': PMS F1, p. 82.
310 'My wild field catalogue': PMS A20; *MP*, 1:65.
311 'All this is past': PMS A29; *MP*, 1:83.
311 'Old customs!': *SC*, p. 99.
312 'dreaming joys ... A high blue': examples cited in Eric Robinson and
     Geoffrey Summerfield, 'John Taylor's Editing of Clare's *The Shepherd's
     Calendar*', *Review of English Studies*, n.s. 14 (1963): 359–69. This essay
     opened the prosecution case against Taylor. The best defence advocates
     are Tim Chilcott, in chap. 4 of his *A Publisher and his Circle*, and Zachary
     Leader, in chap. 5 of his *Revision and Romantic Authorship* (Oxford:
     Clarendon Press, 1996).
313 'intruders and stray cattle': *L*, p. 303.
313 'Wi smutty song': PMS A20; *MP*, 1:85.
314 'college poets ... true pastorals': PMS A46; *Cottage Tales*, ed. Eric Robinson,
     David Powell and P. M. S. Dawson (Ashington and Manchester: Mid
     Northumberland Arts Group and Carcanet Press, 1993), p. 146.
314 'Oh! The first time': PMS A29; *SC*, p. 175. *SC* has 'thrill' for 'chill'—a poet-
     icism in place of a more accurate registering of the sensation.
314 'Her face to me': *SC*, p. 178.
316 well into the twentieth: The first draft (PMS A18) was published in *The Po-
     ems of John Clare*, ed. J. W. Tibble, 2 vols. (London: Dent, 1935), 1:419–20,

the revised version (Pforz 198) in *Clare: Selected Poems and Prose*, ed. Eric Robinson and Geoffrey Summerfield (Oxford: Oxford University Press, 1966, repr. 1967), pp. 169–71.

316 'Far spread the moory': Pforz 198; *MP*, 2:347–50.

317 'Shades of the prison-house': Wordsworth, 'Ode; Intimations of Immortality' (published 1807).

319 'I've left mine': 'The Flitting', *MC*, p. 216.

CHAPTER FOURTEEN: FRIENDSHIP'S OFFERINGS

321 'I have for these nine years': Pforz 198; *JCBH*, p. 161.

323 'passionate fondness for Solitude': *L*, p. 392.

323 'If you have no other medicine': Eg. 2247, fo. 249.

323 'If the weather': June 1830, Eg. 2248, fo. 239.

324 'Perhaps the honor': Eg. 2247, fo. 371.

324 'among the many': *L*, p. 396.

324 'bachelor's fare': Eg. 2247, fo. 247.

325 'a stimulus': Clare to Taylor, October 1831, *L*, p. 550.

326 'This was the first time': Behnes letter, 19 July 1827, Fairfax Murray Collection, John Rylands University Library, Manchester.

326 '*Botanical* pursuits': Eg. 2247, fo. 315.

326 'I have twice paid': Eg. 2247, fo. 318.

327 'sterling good sense': Eg. 2247, fo. 340.

328 'of the *newest*': Eg. 2247, fo. 359.

328 'I am very unwell': *L*, p. 411.

328 'the excitable': Eg. 2247, fo. 381.

328 rough sketches: PMS A27, pp. 25–6.

329 'As there is reason': Eg. 2247, fo. 466.

329 'For him the whole': Eg. 2247, fo. 396. Indicative of mood, but not strictly autobiographical, since included in 'The Parish' (lines 1844–7; *EP*, 2:766).

329 'Stanzas written': PMS A40; *MP*, 4:470–2.

329 'eruption': Eg. 2247, fo. 391.

329 'foolish follys': J, 7 February 1828.

330 'Jealous goodness': PMS A39, p. 12.

330 'Martha Turner': PMS A39, p. 36.

330 'folly': 'Companion of my cheated checkered life', PMS B4; *MP*, 2:265–7.

330 'Thou art gone the dark journey': Eg. 2248, fo. 45; *MP*, 3:435. For Henderson's praise, see Eg. 2247, fo. 348.

331 'Bonny Rosalie': PMS A36; 'Mary Lee' was printed in the *British Magazine*, 1830; also *MC*, p. 175.

331 'Valentine to Mary': *MC*, p. 165.

331 'To ++++': *MC*, p. 214, possibly for Clare's daughter Anna.

331 'one of your Songs': Eg. 2248, fo. 13.

332 'I wish that': Eg. 2247, fo. 407.

332 'He was short': S. C. Hall, *The Book of Gems: The Poets and Artists of Great Britain* (London, 1838), p. 162.

333 'Too bad Eliza': Eg. 2247, fo. 452.

333 'little manuscript book': Eg. 2247, fo. 445.

333 'coxcomb': *L*, p. 426.

333 'I have no objection': Eg. 2247, fo. 413.

334 'intellectually lost': Eg. 2247, fo. 424.

334 'You cannot conceive': Eg. 2247, fo. 399.

334 'Magnificent Lunar Rainbow': Eg. 2248, fo. 51.

334 'a lady': *L*, p. 450.

335 'At the commencement': Martin, p. 266.

336 'had not been long seated': Mossop to Martin, 4 April 1865, NMS 58.

336 'I hope in God!': Eg. 2248, fo. 251.

336 'dreadfully ill': *L*, p. 512.

336 'she is never': *L*, p. 516.

337 'The last of ': NMS 29; *JCBH*, p. 244.

337 'Clare sent me': DRO (Clare's letter is lost). Cf. a contemporaneous letter to Emmerson (also lost) that was 'full of affection, philosophy, Religion, and sweet Poesy' (Eg. 2248, fo. 280).

337 'a charming picture': Eg. 2248, fo. 303.

337 'I awoke in dreadful': *L*, p. 537.

337 'stupid ... nerves ... evil spirits': Eg. 2248, fo. 385 (August 1831).

338 'My family increases': *L*, p. 512 (July 1830).

338 'though it be': Eg. 2248, fo. 22.

338 'I like a man': Eg. 2248, fo. 29.

339 '*bird-nesting descriptions*': Eg. 2249, fo. 34.

339 'Slavery is an abominable': Clare to Mary Anne Read, 16 May 1826, John Rylands Library; not in *L*.

339 'ten pounds per sheet': Eg. 2248, fo. 39.

339 'as hard to catch': Eg. 2248, fo. 223.

340 'Nothing you write': Eg. 2248, fo. 23.

340 'by promises': *L*, p. 512.

340 'as much land': *L*, p. 390.

340 'revelling afterwards': Eg. 2248, fo. 33.

340 'head over ears': *L*, p. 460.

340 'Clare cutting a hedge': unpublished note, Burghley House.

341 'I have my antipathys': *L*, p. 427.

341 'pomposity and fudge ... I can see': *L*, p. 429. The Rydes were satirised by Clare in a passage on 'Mr Puff' that modern editors have incorporated into 'The Parish' (lines 2128–82; *EP*, 2:776–8).

343 'In this cash account': PMS F3.

344 'of course, this Picture': Eg. 2248, fo. 175.

344 'I consider that': Eg. 2248, fos. 175–6.

344 '*you know* that I never': *L*, p. 472.

344 'pathetic pretensions': *L*, p. 485.

345 'You need never': Eg. 2248, fo. 207.

345 'I am no publisher': Eg. 2248, fo. 208.

345 'In this *half yearly*': *L*, p. 511.

346 'neglected and forgotten': *L*, p. 517 (September 1830, to Hessey, who was with Hazlitt when he died).

CHAPTER FIFTEEN: 'I NEVER MEDDLE WITH POLITICS'

348 'common fame': *European Magazine*, November 1825.

348 'as old as England': ibid.

348 'I commenced ... but when': NMS 18; Deacon, p. 43.

348 'the lower orders': PMS A49; Deacon, p. 43.

349 'National and Provincial Melodies': PMS A41.

350 'a prose tale': *L*, p. 421.

350 'the strides towards': PMS A43; the whole essay is transcribed by P. M. S. Dawson in *JCSJ* 20 (2001): 23–34.

350 'Politics may be defined': PMS A18, p. 241.

351 'forced down the throats': PMS A18, p. 253.

351 'Every discontented tradesman': 'Essay on Pretention', PMS A42, p. 146.

351 'to be wyse': PMS A43, p. 74.

351 'I was once invited': PMS A43, p. 21.

352 'every day matters': Eg. 2248, fo. 199.

353 'I should like to see the effect': Pforz 198; *CP*, p. 296.

353 'Christmas Boxes': PMS D14, p. 7.

354 'Vote for *those*': PMS B5, p. 25.

354 'bustle and bother ... country meeting mania': *L*, p. 497.

354 'Thus the Country': Eg. 2248, fo. 207.

355 his position was more complicated: see *CP*; also P. M. S. Dawson, 'John Clare—Radical?', *JCSJ* 11 (1992): 17–27, and 'Common Sense or Radicalism? Some Reflections on Clare's Politics', *Romanticism* 2 (1996): 81–97; also Alan Vardy, 'Clare and Political Equivocation', *JCSJ* 18 (1999): 37–48.

355 'I never meddle': PMS A46; *CP*, p. 298.

355 'nothing more or less': ibid.

355 'The Farmer as usual': *L*, p. 498. Subsequent quotations from same letter to Taylor (1 February 1830).

356 'a politically inspired': Eg. 2248, fo. 198.

357 'Some said it was Cobbett': *Stamford Champion*, 11 January 1831; *MP*, 4:524.

357 'most terrific and destructive': *Stamford Champion*, 21 December 1830.

358 'God forbid': *L*, p. 533.

358 'mob impulse ... threatening': *L*, p. 544.

358 '3 numbers of Cobbett's': Eg. 2248, fo. 413.

358 'I look upon Cobbett': *L*, p. 560.

358 'present grievances': PMS B5; *CP*, p. 299.

359 'Nothing can equal': PMS B5; *CP*, p. 86.

359 'Apology for the Poor': PMS A46; *CP*, pp. 267–9. Probably published in one of three numbers of the 1830 *Stamford Champion* that have disappeared from the archival record.

359 'Cant, humbug': PMS A46; *CP*, p. 287.

359 'Truth is always asserted': PMS A18; *CP*, p. 289.

360 'Its Principles': Eg. 2248, fo. 370.

360 'I wish success heartily': *L*, p. 527.

361 'an Acre of Orchard': Eg. 2248, fo. 399.

361 'The old plum tree': *L*, p. 551.

361 'emigration ... a more independent': Eg. 2249, fo. 1.

361 'is a rogue': *L*, p. 571.

362 'finished, and beautifully': Eg. 2249, fo. 24.

362 'I would begin': Eg. 2249, fo. 26.

363 a visitor ... 'still lived': James Clarke, a London doctor and nephew of Thomas Clarke, editor of the *Bee; CH*, p. 242.

363 'The very molehills': *L*, p. 561.

363 'there is neither wood': ibid.

363 'On flitting': Pforz 198; *JCBH*, p. 101. 'Gentle reader' suggests that this fragment may have been part of an abandoned draft preface for *The Rural Muse*.

364 'There are some things': Pforz 198; *L*, p. 577.

CHAPTER SIXTEEN:
FROM MIDSUMMER CUSHION TO RURAL MUSE

365 'Visits': Clare to Hessey, January 1827; Clare to Cary, November 1827; *L*, pp. 391, 402.

365 His notebooks ... from 1827 to 1837: the principal post-*SC* but pre-Northborough manuscripts are NMS 18 (the collection of 'Old Songs and Ballads'), PMS A35–A39 (mainly fragments and rough drafts), PMS A40 (the 'blank book' bought in 1825 for fair copies of his best poems), PMS A41 (mainly poems intended for 'National and Provincial Melodies' and 'Tales and Trifles in Verse for the amusement of Young Minds chiefly written for and related to The Authors own children when under Ten years old'), PMS A42–A46 (some poetic drafts but also many prose fragments), PMS A47 (draft bird poems, manuscript now lost), PMS A48–A53 and PMS A55–56 (poems, prose, scraps, sketches, jottings, memoranda), PMS A54 (the *MC* manuscript), PMS B8 (new poems in an old volume of Taylor transcripts), Pforz 196 (the *RM* manuscript), and Pforz 197–8 (drafts and fragments of many poems). The fragmentariness, the multiple versions, the revisions of older work: all make it very difficult to quantify the total output—a rough estimate would be that Clare wrote nearly five hundred new or revised poems between 1827 and 1832.

367 'The Pleasures of Spring ... action': *L*, p. 445.

367 'There have been': March 1829; *Eg.* 2248, fos. 129–30.

367 'to insert the best': *J*, 19 March 1825.

368 'Such as are': PMS A40, fo. 40.

368 Fanny apologised: *Eg.* 2250, fo. 316. Bob Heyes was the first to see that this letter refers to the *MC* manuscript.

368 'fugitives': *L*, p. 538.

368 'making some preparation': *L*, p. 543.

368 'the most exquisite': *Eg.* 2249, fo. 126.

368 'On reading': *Eg.* 2249, fo. 118.

369 'Up this green woodland': *MC*, p. 201.

369 'Just by the wooden': *MC*, p. 239.

369 'and you and I': *MC*, p. 240.

370 'I regret to say': *Eg.* 2249, fo. 14.

370 'Poetry is in a Consumption': *Eg.* 2248, fo. 395.

370 'Proposals for publishing': PMS B8; *Athenaeum*, August 1832; and elsewhere.

371 'kindness to my lame': *L*, p. 582.

371 'a beard ... The poet conversed': *New-York Mirror: A Reflex of News, Literature, Arts, and Elegancies of our Time*, 5 (10 October 1846), p. 12. Probably by C. F. Briggs, who was in England in late summer 1832. See D. B. Green, 'Three Early American Admirers of John Clare', *Bulletin of the John Rylands Library* 50 (1968): 365–86.

371 'a manufacturing district': *Eg.* 2249, fo. 155.

372 'staff of independence ... John I should': Clare to Taylor, September 1832; *L*, p. 592.

372 'the country subscribers': *Eg.* 2249, fo. 102.

372 'let your selection': *Eg.* 2249, fo. 103.

372 'The Midsummer Cushion': PMS A54; *MC*, p. xvii.

373 'It is a very old custom': *MC*, p. xxi.

373 'the *key* to all': *Eg.* 2249, fo. 175.

374 'the Rural Muse': *Eg.* 2249, fo. 175.

374 The manuscript still survives: Pforz 196.

375 'I shall be quite satisfied': *L*, p. 614.

375 'My chief Corrections': *Eg.* 2249, fo. 233.

376 'If this little volume': *Eg.* 2249, fo. 291.

376 ecstatic in his praise: reported by Taylor, *Eg.* 2249, fo. 295.

377 'rich and various ... We do not believe': *Blackwood's*, July 1835; *CH*, p. 226.

The American visitor who met Clare at Milton Hall in 1832 said that Wilson was present on this occasion, but the review does not mention any personal acquaintance.

377 'We do not believe': *CH*, p. 229.

377 'entirely distinguishable': *CH*, p. 240.

377 'light-blue ... animated': *CH*, p. 243.

378 'There is a cruelty': PMS A58; *NS*, p. 4.

378 'wide and common sky': *RM*, p. 50.

378 'All Nature owns': 'Nature's Hymn to the Deity', *RM*, p. 61. Compare Addison's hymn, 'The spacious firmament on high'. The uncut *MC* also has several poems in this vein of natural religion, such as a pair of sonnets on 'Nature's Melody'.

378 'My creed': NMS 30; Cherry, p. 307.

378 'The Eternity of Nature': *RM*, pp. 34–7.

379 'The Nightingale's Nest': *RM*, pp. 30–3. See Hugh Haughton's brilliant analysis of this poem in *John Clare in Context*, pp. 51–86.

379 'wrinkle ... wild and luxuriant': Baker, 1:157, 2:157. *RM* (like *SC*) has no glossary, but Baker's dictionary effectively constitutes one.

381 'Come Eliza and Anna': *MC*, p. 168, revised from 'A Walk in the Fields', an earlier poem (in which the children do not figure).

381 'With axe at root': *MC*, pp. 192–3.

382 'The white-nosed bee': 'Wild Bees', *MC*, p. 200.

382 'sweet spots': 'Bushy Close', *MC*, p. 207.

383 'I pick out pictures': *MC*, p. 208.

383 'four eggs': *MC*, p. 211.

383 'In poesy's spells': *MC*, p. 131.

384 'Progress of Rhyme': *MC*, pp. 224–32.

384 '—"Chew-chew"': *MC*, p. 229; cf. various attempts in 1832 to transcribe birdsong (PMS A58; *NHPW*, p. 312).

385 'Pastoral Poesy': *MC*, pp. 291–4.

385 'So would I my own': *MC*, p. 294.

CHAPTER SEVENTEEN: THE FLITTING

387 'a pleasant three miles': G. J. De Wilde, *Rambles Roundabout and Poems* (Northampton, 1872), p. 37.

388 some confusion and embarrassment: see Paul Chirico, 'Writing for money: The correspondence of John Clare and Earl Spencer', *TLS*, 17 November 2000, pp. 14–15.

389 'I've left my own': *RM*, p. 171.

389 'seems to feel itself': *MC*, p. 216 ('from home' revised to 'alone' in *RM*).

389 'Vague unpersonifying': *MC*, p. 218.

390 'words are poor': *MC*, p. 369.

390 'I ha'n't a friend': 'The Lament of Swordy Well', PMS A59; *CP*, p. 219.

390 'Lover of swamps ... I see the sky': Pforz 196; *MP*, 4:574–7.

391 'One unembodied thought': 'The Woods', *MC*, p. 260.

391 'Like a bird': *RM*, p. 108.

391 'Opening of the Pasture': copied at PMS B8, p. 61.

391 woman on a pedestal: PMS B8, p. 53.

391 'I love to see': NMS 419; *L*, p. 636.

392 'Pleasures ... Black melancholly': Pforz 196, p. 141; *MP*, 4:582–3.

393 'your opinion': *L*, p. 579.

393 sonnet about its gravel walks: PMS A59; *NS*, p. 13.

393 'a few useful tools': Eg. 2249, fo. 38.

393 'give the Blue devils': Eg. 2249, fo. 55.

394 'your vivid description': Eg. 2249, fos. 57–8.

394 'in the shape of a soul-stirring': 'A Remarkable Dream', PMS B5; *JCBH*, p. 253. Subsequent quotations from same fragment.

396 'I loved thee': NMS 30, p. 58.

396 'either elevated': *L*, p. 586.

396 'a handsome house': *Athenaeum*, 25 August 1832, p. 555.

397 'Officious interferences': *L*, p. 588.

397 'I wish to live': *L*, p. 590.

397 'labouring, with a wife': *Alfred*, 30 September 1832.

397 'the Whigs are not': *Stamford Bee*, 5 October 1832.

397 'a *political cats paw*': Eg. 2249, fo. 102.

398 'It will give me sincere': Eg. 2249, fo. 122.

398 'I now stop': *L*, p. 599.

398 'Last night my very brains': *L*, p. 604.

399 'In the first place': PMS B5, p. 90.

399 take the beating himself: according to Clare's grandchildren, as recorded by J. W. and Anne Tibble in their 1932 biography.

399 'sound affects me': *L*, p. 615.

400 'In a Memorandum': Eg. 2249, fo. 269.

400 letter of thanks: Emmerson's draft (Eg. 2250, fo. 175) is more fulsome than Clare's letter (L, pp. 625–6).

400 'My dear Sir, I am very': *L*, p. 629, probably to Captain Sherwill, who had written after long silence, or possibly to James Clarke, who had reviewed *RM* (Sherwill is more likely because Clarke *knew* that Clare had a 'great orchard and garden'—he had visited in 1832 and been shown the empty nightingale's nest).

401 'loved as nothing': Eg. 2249, fo. 339.

401 'I hear you are suffering': Eg. 2249, fo. 340.

401 never saw him again: unless he was the old friend who accompanied Cyrus Redding on his visit to Clare in Dr Allen's asylum at High Beech (I owe to Bob Heyes the information that Redding and Rippingille were acquainted).

CHAPTER EIGHTEEN:
'AND SO IN SPITE OF MYSELF I RYHME ON'

402 'I am sorry . . . that my writings': *L*, p. 626.

402 principal manuscripts of this period: PMS A57–A61, PMS B9, NMS 7.

403 'But I can do nothing': *L*, p. 633.

403 'little things': *L*, p. 596.

403 'common things': PMS A59, p. 60.

403 'Oh could I feel': PMS A59, p. 30.

403 'What a night': PMS A59; NS, p. 7.

403 'Oh take this world': PMS A59, p. 101.

403 'O love what is love': PMS A59, p. 39.

403 'Free from the world': PMS A61; *NS*, p. 55.

404 'idle fame': PMS A59, p. 36.

404 'after fame': PMS A57, p. 84.

404 'the eternity of song': ibid.

404 'treeless fens . . . not a hill': 'Wandering by the river's edge', PMS A57, p. 14.

405 'He falls as dead': PMS B9; *NS*, p. 28.

405 'rule and compass': *L*, p. 80.

405 'I dreaded walking': PMS A61; *NS*, p. 83.

405 poems that begin . . . begins with *dread*: see John Goodridge and Kelsey Thornton, 'John Clare: the trespasser', in *John Clare in Context*, p. 99.

406 'who is very ill': Taylor to Jem Taylor, 15 November 1836, DRO.

406 'I set off': Taylor to Elizabeth Taylor, 9 December 1836, DRO.

407 'Passion may a moment': PMS A60, p. 1.

407 'He throws the thorns': PMS A61, p. 104.

407 Family tradition: reported in J. W. and Anne Tibble's 1932 biography, p. 331.

407 'I was much pleased': Eg. 2249, fo. 359.

407 'by authority of his wife': 'Minutes of Visitors of Houses Licensed for the Reception of Insane Persons in the County of Essex', entry dated 15 July 1837, ERO, Q/Alp7.

408 'the Bearer . . . Medical Care': Eg. 2249, fo. 377.

408 '*mania*, or *madness*': Skrimshire, *The Village Pastor's Surgical and Medical Guide* (London, 1838), p. 196. Summary and subsequent quotations from pp. 196–203.

410 'had its origin': NMS 58.

411 'got his rock off': PMS A59, p. 88.

411 *On Nervous and Mental Conditions*: by William Willis Moseley (1838).

411 'intense application . . . too great activity': Arnold, *Observations on the Nature, Kinds, Causes, and Prevention of Insanity*, 2 vols. (2d ed., London, 1806).

412 posthumously diagnosed as schizophrenic: see especially Geoffrey Grigson's introduction to his *Poems of John Clare's Madness* (London: Routledge and Kegan Paul, 1949), pp. 23–5.

413 lunatic, lover and poet ... empirical support: see Daniel Nettle, *Strong Imagination: Madness, Creativity and Human Nature* (Oxford: Oxford University Press, 2001).

414 'little expenses occurred': PMS E4.

415 fellow-patient ... Jesus Christ: see Matthew Allen, *Essay on the Classification of the Insane* (London, n.d. [1835–7?]), p. 100.

415 'self-identity': NMS 6; *JCBH*, p. 271.

416 'he suffered': *London Magazine*, March 1820, p. 250.

416 'when I am ill': *London Magazine*, March 1820, p. 254.

416 'I became fond of scribbling': to Thomas Pringle, March 1832, Brotherton Library, University of Leeds, first published in my 'New Clare Documents', *JCSJ* 21 (2002):5–18.

417 'I shrank': *L*, p. 571.

417 'write on ... ambition ... If I have': *L*, p. 594.

417 'if you laugh': *L*, pp. 595–6.

PART FOUR: THE ASYLUM YEARS (1837–1864)

419 'My dear wife': *L*, p. 657.

CHAPTER NINETEEN: DR BOTTLE-IMP AND BOXER BYRON

421 'Moral Treatment': Samuel Tuke, *Description of the Retreat* (York, 1813), chap. 5. Subsequent quotations from same source.

422 Matthew Allen: for his early career, see Margaret C. Barnet, 'Matthew Allen, M.D. (Aberdeen), 1783–1845', *Medical History* 9 (1965): 16–28.

423 'I was the first': NMS 51.

423 'many Water Closets': 'Explanation to accompany the Plans' for the asylum at High Beech, ERO, Q/S Bb495/5/3. Subsequent quotations from same source.

424 'the retirement ... amusements': ERO, Bb495/5/4.

425 'to be used occasionally': Allen's plans, ERO, Q/Alp3/2.

425 Carlyle ... Jane: see R. B. Martin, *Tennyson: The Unquiet Heart* (London: Faber and Faber, 1983), p. 237.

425 'This asylum': 'Minutes of Visitors of Houses Licensed for the reception of Insane Persons in the County of Essex', ERO, Q/Alp7, entries for 1832–3.

425 *Allen versus Dutton*: London, 1833. I know of only two surviving copies; I have used the one in the Wellcome Library for the History of Medicine.

426 'mild system': Allen, *Classification of the Insane*, p. ix. See further, Valerie Pedlar, '"No Place like Home": Reconsidering Matthew Allen and his "Mild System" of Treatment', *JCSJ* 13 (1994): 41–57.

426 'unless their own conduct': Allen, *Classification of the Insane*, p. 30.

426 'the uncontrolled over-excitement': Allen, *Classification of the Insane*, p. 41.

428 'My dear Wife': *L*, p. 642.

429 'improved and improving': Eg. 2250, fo. 14.

429 entry in Clare's notebook: NMS 8; *LY*, p. 142.

429 'in his best State': Eg. 2250, fo. 12.

429 'Sir,—I observe': Allen to the Editor of *The Times*, 23 June 1840.

431 'a renewed appeal': *Athenaeum*, 27 June 1840, p. 516.

431 'it is confidently expected': *Athenaeum*, 8 May 1841.

431 Nothing was added: in 1854, the capital still stood at £393 15s., the sum recorded in 1841 (Taylor notebook, DRO).

432 'Why do you wear': R. B. Martin, *Tennyson*, p. 253.

433 'I can prove ... You can claim': *L*, p. 645 (probably April 1840—speculatively dated April 1841 in *L*, but lacking the capitalization characteristic of his writings that spring).

433 'a sweet Nurse': NMS 27; *LP*, pp. 3–5.

433 'and formed such': 'Relics of John Clare', *Overland Monthly*, February 1873, pp. 134–41, repr. in Green, 'Three Early American Admirers of John Clare', p. 382.

433 'I long to forget': *Overland Monthly*; *LP*, p. 14.

434 'Love One Another ... A Very Pleasant ... To Her Who': *L*, pp. 643–4.

435 'My Dearest Mary': *L*, p. 645.

437 'At The Easter Hunt': NMS 8; *LY*, pp. 141–2.

437 'Boxer Byron': NMS 8; *LY*, p. 142.

438 'Jack Randall': NMS 8; *LY*, p. 143.

438 'The architect': Pierce Egan, *Boxiana*, 4 vols. (London, 1818), 2:262.

438 'attenuated and pale': Redding, in *English Journal*, 15 May 1841; *CH*, p. 248.

438 'in a manner': *CH*, p. 248.

439 'The principal token': ibid.

439 'Clare's mind': Redding, 'John Clare', in *Past Celebrities whom I have Known* (London, 1866), p. 135.

439 'care for his subsistence': *CH*, p. 249.

440 'an old wide awake': NMS 8; *LY*, p. 148.

440 'all plain sailing': ibid.

440 'John Clare's Poems': NMS 8, p. 1.

440 'I awoke': Tom Moore, *Letters and Journals of Lord Byron*, 2 vols. (Paris, 1829), 1:258.

440 'I twine': *Childe Harold's Pilgrimage*, 4.9. For Clare and Byron, see further, Anne Barton, 'John Clare reads Lord Byron', *Romanticism* 2 (1996): 127–48; Frederick Burwick, *Poetic Madness and the Romantic Imagination* (University Park: Pennsylvania State University Press, 1996), pp. 254–75; and Philip Martin, 'Authorial Identity and the Critical Act: John Clare and Lord Byron', in *Questioning Romanticism*, ed. John Beer (Baltimore: Johns Hopkins University Press, 1995), pp. 71–91.

441 'Books Lent': NMS 7, p. 55.

441 'the licentiousness': *London Magazine*, October 1824, pp. 338–9.

442 'My Mind Is Dark': NMS 8; *LY*, p. 2.

442 'Plain Honesty': NMS 8; *LY*, p. 3.

442 'love and home': NMS 8, stanza 16; *LY*, p. 22.

442 'First love's dream ... prison': stanzas 25–6; *LY*, p. 30.

442 'Essence': stanza 20; *LY*, p. 24.

442 'Love is the main spring': NMS 8; *LY*, p. 42.

442 'My life hath been': ibid.

442 'Say What Is Love': NMS 8; *LY*, p. 4.

443 'I saw her': NMS 8; *LY*, p. 28.

443 'I have had many': NMS 8; *LY*, p. 46.

443 'my dear': stanza 20; *LY*, p. 24.

443 'Sweet Bessey': stanza 13; *LY*, p. 10.

443 'Where are my friends': stanza 18; *LY*, p. 32.

443 'Mary and Martha': stanza 22; *LY*, p. 26.

443 'My soul is apathy': NMS 8; *LY*, p. 50.

443 'I live in love ... Smile on': NMS 8; *LY*, p. 52.

444 'on the sacred ... *real old*': *Byron's Letters and Journals*, ed. Leslie A. Marchand, 12 vols. (London: John Murray, 1973–82), 4:220.

444 'while mental': *London Magazine*, March 1820, p. 321.

445 'all created things': *London Magazine*, March 1820, p. 322.

445 '"Poets are born"—and so are whores': NMS 8; *LY*, p. 37.

445 'there's such putting in': NMS 8; *LY*, p. 39.

445 'snuff box': NMS 8; *LY*, p. 41.

446 'Children are fond': NMS 8; *LY*, p. 39.

446 'the French actresses': De Quincey on Clare, *CH*, p. 246.

446 'I really can't tell': NMS 8; *LY*, p. 39.

446 'But I have seen': NMS 8; *LY*, p. 43.

447 'I have two wives': ibid.

447 'Though laurel': NMS 8; *LY*, p. 53.

447 'Lord Byron poh': NMS 8; *LY*, p. 51.

447 'Now this ... Next tuesday': ibid.

447 'sweet Eliza Phillips': NMS 8; *LY*, p. 45.

447 'My dear Eliza Phillips': NMS 8; *LY*, p. 147.

448 'Theres Docter Bottle': NMS 8; *LY*, p. 49.

449 'Nigh Leopards hill': NMS 8, p. 21 (previous editors have not included the blessing as part of the poem).

CHAPTER TWENTY: JOURNEY FROM ESSEX

451 Account of Clare's walk home paraphrased and quoted from his 'Reccolections etc of journey from Essex': partial draft in NMS 8 (notebook carried on the road); full fair copy in NMS 6 (foolscap blank book begun on return home); published inaccurately in Martin, pp. 282–9, and accurately in *JCBH*, pp. 257–65, and *LY*, pp. 147–54.

455 an objection noted: by John Noake of Worcester, who visited Clare in 1844 (*Worcester Journal*, 29 August 1844).

455 'you told me somthing': *L*, p. 651.

457 'She was up early': *Lincolnshire Chronicle*, 6 April 1838.

457 'I've wandered': NMS 8; *LY*, p. 56.

458 'July 23rd 41': NMS 8, p. 22.

458 'To Mary Clare—Glinton': NMS 6; *LY*, pp. 154–5.

459 'Marriage is nothing': NMS 6; *LY*, pp. 55–6.

459 'but his Wife': Allen to Walton, quoted in Edmund Blunden, *Keats's Publisher: A Memoir of John Taylor* (London: Cape, 1936), p. 209.

460 'A lonely man': final Northborough addition to 'Child Harold', NMS 6; *LY*, p. 124.

460 'My heart my dear Mary': fragment in PMS A62; *LY*, p. 107.

460 'thou partner of my life': Northborough addition to 'Child Harold', NMS 6; *LY*, p. 92.

460 'distant objects': Hazlitt, 'Why Distant Objects Please', in his *Table Talk* (1822).

460 'they Seldom': NMS 1; *EP*, 1:155. See discussion in Adam Phillips's superb essay, 'The exposure of John Clare', in *John Clare in Context*, pp. 178–88.

460 'To live with others': PMS A62, p. 13.

461 'My dear Sir': *L*, p. 650.

461 'I can be miserably': ibid.

461 'one of my fancys ... to be to myself': *L*, pp. 650–1.

462 'discharged': 'Minutes of Visitors', ERO, Q/Alp7, p. 161.

462 'I am glad': Eg. 2250, fos. 21–2.

463 ''Tis martinmass': Bodleian Library MS Don.c.64; *LP*, p. 102.

464 'immense flock': 4 November 1841, PMS A62.

464 'solitary persons': NMS 6; *LY*, pp. 159–62.

464 'so much / depends': Williams, 'The Red Wheelbarrow'.

464 'Anxiety ... My dear Mary': NMS 7.

464 'Found a Cowslip ... Thou'rt': PMS A62, p. 14.

464 'William found': PMS A62, p. 1.

465 incomplete fair copy: NMS 6.

465 'Though slave dealers': Bodleian Library MS Don.c.64; *LY*, p. 137.

465 'conversing ... the want of restraint': Mossop to Reid, NMS 420.

CHAPTER TWENTY-ONE: AMONG THE BABYLONIANS

466 'endeavour to elucidate': PMS F4.

467 'On the ground': Martin, pp. 291–2.

468 'Board, Washing ... List of Private Patients': *Annual Reports*, NGLA.

469 'limeburner': 1851 Census, Public Record Office, H.O. 107/1739.

469 'poet': 1861 Census, Public Record Office, R.G.9/937.

469 'not mad': G. J. De Wilde to J. W. Dalby, letter printed in *TLS*, 30 June 1921.

469 'occasional musical': *Annual Report for 1856*, NGLA. See further, Arthur Foss and Kerith Trick's history of *St Andrew's Hospital Northampton: The First 150 Years (1838–1988)* (Cambridge: Granta, 1989).

470 'Poor Clare': Eg. 2250, fo. 32.

470 'His gait': G. J. De Wilde to Frederick Martin, NMS 58.

470 'John Clare is': Eg. 2250, fo. 35.

471 'delighted in showing': Hall, 'Bloomfield and Clare', in his *Biographic Sketches of Remarkable People* (Burnley, 1873), repr. in *CH*, p. 279.

471 'rather burly': *CH*, p. 280.

472 'a long and favourite': *CH*, pp. 280–1.

473 'Yes ... I'm John Clare': PMS G5 (William Jerom's memoir of Clare).

473 'nautical phrases': Mary Russell Mitford, *Recollections of a Literary Life* (London, 1852), p. 195.

473 'That was ... he is quite': 'Rev. J. C. Westbrook' (real name John Hopeful), 'John Clare: A Reminiscence', *The Cheltenham Literary Annual* (Cheltenham, 1857), pp. 99–102. As in many reminiscences of Clare in the asylum, there is considerable journalistic licence in this account: the 'Song to Liberty' could not have been newly inspired around 1847, since Knight dated it 9 July 1844.

474 'We walked': De Wilde to Dalby.

474 'I saw Clare': De Wilde to Frederick Martin, 25 February 1865; NMS 58.

475 'It was an apartment': J. R. Dix, 'A Visit to John Clare', in his *Pen and Ink Sketches of Authors and Authoresses* (London, 1852), p. 80. Possibly apocryphal.

475 'agreeableness of disposition': Jerom, 'Reminiscences of Clare by a Fellow Patient', PMS G5; partially printed in *TLS*, 27 December 1941, p. 657.

476 'Also Kerseymere': ibid.

476 'Clare had a great knack': ibid.

477 'quite lost in reveries': *L*, p. 661.

477 tuberculosis: NMS 420; also Anna Maria's death certificate.

478 'a thrilling pleasure': NMS 14; *Sketches*, p. 50.

478 'Wordsworths Works': NMS 407.

478 'I am very happy': *L*, p. 654.

479 'unless it would give': *L*, p. 655.

479 'Angling is a Recreation': *L*, p. 656.

480 'My dear wife': *L*, p. 657.

481 'I am now': *L*, p. 661.

481 'I very much want': *L*, p. 664.

481 'I should hope': NMS 19; *L*, p. 661.

482 'A life of dreams': Dalby, 'John Clare', in his *Tales, Songs and Sonnets* (1866), repr. in *CH*, pp. 273–4.

483 'He is a short': Dudley, 'John Clare, the Peasant Poet', in his *Pictures of Life* *in England and America* (Boston, 1851), repr. in Green, 'Three Early American Admirers of John Clare', pp. 368–70.

484 'Where flowers are': *L*, p. 670, varying last line of 'Poets love nature' (NMS 20; *LP*, p. 313).

486 'glossy raven hair': NMS 19; *LP*, p. 197.

486 lists of girls' names: examples from NMS 19.

486 'Infants ... The present': NMS 19; *LP*, pp. 165, 173.

486 'Poetry by John Clare': NMS 20 (1); *LP*, p. 269.

487 'Thus John': Knight to Joseph Stenson, 3 March 1846, in 'John Clare: Some Unpublished Documents of the Asylum Period', *Northamptonshire Past and Present* 3 (1964), 192.

488 Inskip's replies: quotations from Inskip letters in NMS 52.

488 'I have often': Eg. 2250, fo. 239.

489 'every scrap': NMS 52, 31 January 1847.

489 'do you consider': NMS 52, 12 February 1847.

489 'in one or two': NMS 52, 29 April 1847.

490 'all the attempts': ibid.

490 'Even the Rural Muse': NMS 52, 23 July 1847.

490 'weird and mysterious': Mr Jesse Hall of Wimbledon, who described his 1848 visit to Clare in the *Literary World*, 22 September 1893.

490 'Wilt thou go': NMS 20; *Bedford Times*, 29 January 1848; *LP*, pp. 348–9.

492 'I find his poetry': NMS 52, 23 July 1847.

492 imitation of a Shelley lyric: 'Sweet Jessy', *Northampton Mercury*, 30 April 1842, imitating the 'Dirge' in Shelley's 'Ginevra'. For imitation more generally, see Greg Crossan, *A Relish for Eternity* (Salzburg: Universität Salzburg, 1976), appendix 2, and the same author's 'Clare's Debt to the Poets in his Library', *JCSJ* 10 (1991):27–41.

493 'three or four Volumes': *L*, p. 662.

493 'I will pay': ibid.

493 'I have many': Eg. 2250, fo. 40.

494 'My hopeless nerves': 'Stanzas', NMS 20; *LP*, p. 337.

494 'I always see': NMS 20; *LP*, p. 557.

495 'The crumping': NMS 20; *LP*, p. 570.

495 'The dew drops': NMS 20; *LP*, p. 909.

495 'A Raphsody': NMS 20; *LP*, pp. 992–8.

495 'always sang': PMS G5.

495 Patty ... Mary: e.g. *LP*, pp. 326, 649 (Patty); 344, 508, 509 (Mary); but 512 ('Mary a Ballad') repeats a poem previously addressed to 'Jessy'!

495 'sorrow is my joy': NMS 19; *LP*, p. 191.

496 'True love lives': 'Song', NMS 20; *LP*, p. 398.

496 'Black absence': NMS 20; *LP*, p. 293.

496 'I sleep with thee': NMS 20; *LP*, p. 294.

497 'On the seventeenth': NMS 20; *LP*, pp. 733–4.

498 'I long to see you': *L*, p. 666.

498 'How I long': *L*, p. 668.

498 'gently John gently John': NMS 10.

498 'M Drst Mr Cllngwd': NMS 9; *L*, p. 672.

499 'My Dearest': *L*, p. 673, first decoded in Eric Robinson and Geoffrey Summerfield, 'John Clare: An Interpretation of Certain Asylum Letters', *Review of English Studies*, n.s. 13 (1962): 135–46.

499 another of his lists: in PMS H23.

500 '1850 May 12th': NMS 9, p. 12.

501 'Lord Byron was 16': NMS 10, pp. 92–4.

502 'Wellington': NMS 10, pp. 116–18.

502 'Fell on the Deck': NMS 10, p. 186.

503 'Some pretty face': NMS (1), p. 403; *LP*, p. 664.

503 'How can I forget?': NMS 20 (2), p. 442; *LP*, p. 1090.

503 'A Vision': NMS 20; *LP*, p. 297.

504 'disdaining bounds': 'Sonnet: *I Am*', NMS 20; *LP*, p. 397.

504 'I am': NMS 20; *LP*, pp. 396–7. *Bedford Times* text has minor variants.

CHAPTER TWENTY-THREE:
'WHY I AM SHUT UP I DONT KNOW'

508 'I have forgotten': NMS 65, PMS G2 (Godfrey recollection).

508 'How do you get on': *L*, p. 678.

508 'uncommonly pleased': *L*, p. 313.

508 'The gifts of nature': *Eliza Cook's Journal*, no. 94, 15 February 1851, pp. 241–2. Subsequent quotations from same source.

509 'sex-murderer': Lynne Pearce, 'John Clare's *Child Harold*: The Road Not Taken', in *Feminist Criticism: Theory and Practice*, ed. Susan Sellers (New York and London: Harvester Wheatsheaf, 1991), p. 147.

510 'I cannot get out': *L*, p. 678.

510 'I heard U had broken': *L*, p. 679.

510 'I would try': ibid.

511 'Blessed are the dead': Revelation 14:13.

511 'a long time': NMS 411.

511 'I am sorry': *L*, p. 677.

512 'My dear Father': Eg. 2250, fo. 54.

512 'usual state of health': Eg. 2250, fo. 56.

512 'too much Study': to Alexander Spiers, Eg. 2250, fo. 63, replying to Eg. 2250, fo. 323.

513 'he would not be idle': NMS 54 (unpaginated).

514 'The dialectical peculiarities': Baker, 1:xi.

514 'expressly for the present': Baker, 2:423.

515 'who beautifully clothes … all been written': Baker, 1:xv.

515 'The mice come': Baker, 1:112.

515 'When *screeds* of sunshine': Baker, 2:205.

515 'Where the *whirlipuff*': Baker, 2:395.

516 'wholly lost': *CH*, p. 266.

516 'inoffensive lunatic': *London Journal*, November 1857, p. 192.

517 'bound the two vols.': John Taylor of Northampton, letter to *Northampton Herald*, 2 September 1893. Codgbrook's volumes were actually entitled *Poetic Souvenir*.

517 'Yes, they wanted … No, I haven't': George Kearley, *Links in the Chain; or Popular Chapters on the Curiosities of Animal Life* (n.d., c. 1862), chap. 11. See Bob Heyes, 'A Neglected Account of Clare in the Asylum', *JCSJ* 13 (1994), 59–60.

518 'He may be said': NMS 58 (Nesbitt to Martin).

518 'He was generally': ibid.

519 God Almighty … Fairies: noted in letter from Inskip to Knight, NMS 52.

519 'was violent etc.': NMS 58.

520 'Well, honest John': PMS D24; *LP*, p. 1102.

521 'Champion John Junr': *L*, p. 683.

521 'your loving husband': ibid.

521 'still living': NMS 40.

522 'Dear Sir': NMS 40; *L*, p. 683.

522 'We think of coming': PMS F11; *L*, p. 684.

522 'and Mary … I shall be glad': NMS 422; *JCBH*, p. 283. Dated 9 March 1860 by Clare, but clearly a reply to Sophy's letter of 15 March, so perhaps written 19 March?

522 'hedges leafing': PMS D26; *LP*, p. 1105.

523 'the refreshing sweetness … the pen': PMS G2.

523 'The youthful lord': Una Pope-Hennessy, *Agnes Strickland: Biographer of the Queens of England 1796–1874* (London: Chatto & Windus, 1940), p. 259.

524 'I saw poor Clare': Agnes Strickland's manuscript account of her visit to Clare, Berg Collection, New York Public Library. Subsequent quotations from same source, which was published with some variations in *Life of Agnes Strickland* by her sister, Jane Margaret Strickland (London, 1887). This book reports (it is unclear on what basis) that 'Some of Clare's near relatives had been insane' (p. 268).

524 'The daisy is a happy flower': Berg Collection, New York Public Library; *LP*, p. 1101.

525 'Alas! For the tragedy': Strickland's 'Autograph Book', quoted in Pope-Hennessy, *Agnes Strickland*, p. 261.

525 'quite his young look': PMS G2.

526 'That is not poetry': ibid.

526 'Know that?': ibid.

526 'he would immediately': ibid.

526 'the sitting chamber': Plummer, in *Once a Week*, May 1861; *CH*, p. 269.

526 'blithe and talkative': *Northampton Mercury*, 24 June 1861.

527 ''Tis spring': PMS D27; *LP*, p. 1106.

527 'a most laborious task': PMS G2.

527 'Mr Clare in getting up': Wing's casebooks in NGLA are partially quoted in Arthur Foss and Kerith Trick, *St Andrew's Hospital, Northampton: the First 150 Years (1838–1988)* (Cambridge: Granta, 1989), pp. 138–9.

527 'His habits are': Wing's entries for 8 April, 2 July, 1 October 1863, NGLA.

528 'but yet very helpless': Wing, 11 January 1864, NGLA.

528 'he never used to talk': NMS 66 (Bacon recollection).

528 'His general health': Wing, 5 April 1864, NGLA.

529 'he was found': Wing, 20 May 1864, NGLA.

529 'he simply ceased': NMS 65, PMS G2 (Godfrey recollection).

PART FIVE: THE ETERNITY OF SONG

531 'In every language': 'A Vision', NMS 20; *LP*, p. 297.

CHAPTER TWENTY-FOUR: REMAINS

533 'Though ailing': *Annual Report of the Northampton General Lunatic Asylum for 1864*, NGLA.

534 The funeral took place: for this account see *Northampton Mercury*, 3 June 1864.

534 'to lie on the North': NMS 15; *JCBH*, pp. 245–6.

535 'He was employed': Moyse, 'John Clare's Family Tree', p. 29. See further, Moyse, 'New light on John Clare's eldest surviving son', *JCSJ* 17 (1998): 59–63.

535 'a steady man ... did not approve': NMS 54.

536 'ashamed to ask ... my youngest': ibid.

536 'I am always ill': ibid.

536 Joseph Whitaker: The family firm was Whittaker and Company, but Joseph signed his name 'Whitaker'.

536 'the right to publish': PMS G11. The story of Whitaker, Taylor of Northampton, and the copyright is very complicated: see my article 'John Clare's Copyright 1854–1893', *JCSJ* 19 (2000): 19–32 (abbreviated version also in *TLS*, 'Commentary', 21 July 2000).

537 'Northamptonshire Peasant ... was duly petted': Martin, p. vii.

537 an exile, an outsider: for details of Martin's own life, see Robinson and Summerfield's introduction to the 1964 reprint of his *Life of John Clare*. Correspondence indicating the assiduity of Martin's research survives in the Clare archives (e.g. NMS 57, NMS 58, PMS G7).

538 'the marvellous Boy ... We Poets': Wordsworth, 'Resolution and Independence', first published in *Poems, in Two Volumes* (1807).

538 'the deepest, noblest, and purest': Martin, p. 21.

539 'preposterous exaggeration': Dickens, letter to John Forster, 15 August 1865, quoted in *CH*, p. 15.

539 'bastard picturesque': *Examiner*, 5 August 1865, *CH*, p. 15.

541 'We doubt very much': *Saturday Review*, 5 April 1873, *CH*, p. 290.

541 'There is all the unaffected': *Noncomformist*, 19 February 1873, *CH*, p. 289.

543 '43 detached, link-detached': *Peterborough Evening Telegraph*, 2 February 2000.

543 'standing at his bedroom window': letter from George Duckworth to Julia Stephen, quoted, Hermione Lee, *Virginia Woolf* (London: Vintage, 1997), p. 65.

544 'Of Poets': Martin, p. 5.

544 'I wish to have': NMS 14; *JCBH*, p. 246.

CHAPTER TWENTY-FIVE: THE POET'S POET

545 'the greatest Pastoral Poet': *L*, p. 300.

545 'among the English poets': Keats to George and Georgiana Keats, 14 October 1818—'I think I shall be among the English Poets after my death'.

545 'always sleeping': *Suffolk Garland*, quoted in C. R. Johnson's invaluable bibliography, *Provincial Poetry 1789–1839* (London: Jed Press, 1992), no. 177. For an introductory selection of writings by such figures, see *English Labouring-Class Poets 1700–1900*, ed. John Goodridge et al., 6 vols. (Hull: Pickering and Chatto, 2001–2).

546 'Looked over a new': J, 19 October 1824. *Excursions of Fancy* (Stamford, 1824) is still in Clare's library. It has the signature of Mossop the vicar— presumably Clare borrowed it and forgot to return it. On the publication of Clare's first book, another local poet, Samuel Messing, wrote to greet him 'as a Brother Poet' (Eg. 2245, fo. 48).

546 'who had the impudence': *L*, p. 334.

547 Stephen: 'Clare, John', in *Dictionary of National Biography* (1887), repr. in *CH*, p. 298. The *DNB* article is riddled with biographical errors.

548 'no doubt claim': Palgrave, *Golden Treasury* (1861, repr. London: Thomas Nelson, n.d.), p. viii.

548 'to the excellent things': Gale, introduction to *Poems by John Clare* (Rugby, 1901), repr. in *CH*, p. 299.

549 'Manuscript Book': i.e. Pforz 196.

549 'more definitely the work': Symons, introduction to *Poems by John Clare* (1908), repr. in *CH*, p. 301. Subsequent quotations from Symons: *CH*, pp. 302–7.

550 'No man': Thomas, *A Literary Pilgrim in England* (1917), repr. in *CH*, p. 319.

550 'To this day': Alan Porter, *Oxford Outlook* (May 1920), *CH*, p. 320.

551 'one of the richest': *Madrigals and Chronicles: being newly found poems written by John Clare* (1924), preface by Blunden, p. xi.

551 'The making of poems': Grigson, introduction to *Selected Poems of John Clare* (1950), repr. in *CH*, pp. 411–12.

552 'No one was ever … lose his identity': James Reeves, introduction to *Selected Poems of John Clare* (London: Heinemann, 1954), pp. xvi, xxi, xiii.

552 'I find myself repeating': Graves, in his *The Crowning Privilege* (1955), repr. in *CH*, p. 415.

553 'Garland for John Clare': Keyes, *Collected Poems*, ed. Michael Meyer (London and New York: Routledge, 1988), pp. 29–30.

553 'Or can you trace': Joseph Henderson, 'Inscription, for the pedestal of a bust of John Clare, executed by E. T. Artis'. See further, Charles Roach Smith, 'Unpublished Lines on Artis's Bust of John Clare the Poet', *Reliquary* 18 (1877–8): 240.

553 'rich, sweet': Edmund Blunden, 'The Death Mask of John Clare', quoted from *For John Clare: An Anthology of Verse*, ed. John Lucas (Helpston: John Clare Society, 1997), p. 6.

554 'The shadow of that small man': James Reeves, 'The Savage Moon: A Meditation on John Clare', quoted from *For John Clare*, p. 11.

554 'Heard in a violent ward': from *The Far Field* (1964), repr. in *Collected Poems of Theodore Roethke* (New York: Doubleday, 1966), p. 220.

555 'For John Clare': in Ashbery's *The Double Dream of Spring* (1969), repr. in his *Selected Poems* (London: Paladin, 1987), p. 107.

555 'when I really needed': 'John Clare: "Grey Openings Where the Light Looks Through"', the first of Ashbery's Charles Eliot Norton Lectures at Harvard, published as *Other Traditions* (Cambridge, Mass.: Harvard University Press, 2000), p. 5.

555 'The effect of Clare's poetry': *Other Traditions*, p. 19.

555 'nakedness of vision': *Other Traditions*, p. 15.

556 'Her name': repr. in *For John Clare*, ed. John Lucas (Helpston: John Clare Society, 1997), p. 7.

556 Heaney gave a lecture: published in *John Clare in Context*, pp. 130–47, and repr. as 'John Clare's Prog' in Heaney's lecture collection, *The Redress of Poetry* (London: Faber and Faber, 1995).

557 'I am lying': Longley, 'Journey out of Essex or, John Clare's Escape from the Madhouse', in his *No Continuing City* (1969), repr. in *Poems 1963–1983* (Harmondsworth: Penguin, 1986), p. 56.

557 'The Writing Lark': published in *JCSJ* 17 (1998): 5–15.

559 'Young, he was': R. S. Thomas, 'Lunar', JCSJ 12 (1993); 62, repr. in *No Truce with the Furies* (Newcastle-upon-Tyne: Bloodaxe, 1995).

559 'A silent man': 'The Peasant Poet', NMS 20; *LP*, p. 845.

559 'Genius': Sartre, *Saint Genet: Comédien et Martyr* (Paris: Gallimard, 1952), p. 645, my translation.

565 'Such as are crossed': PMS A40, p. 40a. For the case against the publication of Clare's poems in their 'raw' form, see Zachary Leader, 'John Taylor and the Poems of Clare', in his *Revision and Romantic Authorship* (Oxford: Clarendon Press, 1996), pp. 206–61; Hugh Haughton, 'Revision and Romantic Authorship: The Case of Clare', *JCSJ* 17 (1998): 65–73; and my review of *Poems of the Middle Period III–IV, JCSJ* 18 (1999): 79–83.

565 'Do I write': PMS A46, draft of letter to William Robertson (*L*, p. 497).

566 'how should such . . . omitted': *L*, p. 497.

566 '*Stops or Punctuation . . .* Bad spelling': PMS A3, p. 1.

567 ' "egs on" ': PMS A3, p. 32.

567 'The word "twitatwit" '. PMS A3, p. 32.

568 'The starnel crowds': PMS A29; *MP*, 1:142.

568 'And whirr of starling crowds': *SC*, p. 86.

568 'The cotter journying': PMS A29; *MP*, 1:138.

568 'The cotter journeying': *SC*, p. 84.

573 It is not entirely clear: Eric Robinson asserts that on Whitaker's death in 1895 the copyright passed to his son, whereas in 1894 the Peterborough Museum Society recorded in its annual report that Whitaker had given them 'a great number of MS.S. Books, etc., belonging to John Clare, together with the absolute right of publication' (see R. K. R. Thornton, 'The John Clare Exhibition of 1893', in *Peterborough's Past: The Journal of the Peterborough Museum Society* 3 (1988): 40–4). It is also curious that the acknowledgement of copyright that Whitaker insisted should be included in J. L. Cherry's *Life and Remains of John Clare* (1873) was withdrawn from the second edition of that work.

573 'I foresaw several decades': Robinson, letter to *Times Literary Supplement*, 1 September 2000.

574 The controversy aroused: see further, the selection of materials from the controversy at <http://human.ntu.ac.uk/clare/copyright.htm>.

SUGGESTIONS FOR FURTHER READING

Those who already have some familiarity with John Clare's work will gain a feel for the 'raw' manuscripts by way of Geoffrey Summerfield's excellent *John Clare: Selected Poetry* (London: Penguin, 1990, repr. 2000). The more advanced student will wish to move on to the Oxford Clare and its spin-offs, as described in my Appendix.

Further reading in the life should begin with the autobiographical materials gathered in *John Clare by Himself* (*JCBH* in my abbreviations and notes). Then Frederick Martin's 1865 biography should be read and enjoyed, but not trusted. J. W. and Anne Tibble's *John Clare: A Life* (1932; revised repr., London: Michael Joseph, 1972) was pioneering but suffers from many errors and omissions. June Wilson's *Green Shadows: The Life of John Clare* (London: Hodder and Stoughton, 1951) is more accurate, but very thin on the poetry. Roger Sales's *John Clare: A Literary Life* (London and Basingstoke: Macmillan, 2002) is polemical in tone but valuable for its contextual material regarding Regency literary culture, boxing, labouring-class poetry and nineteenth-century mental health regimes. For commentary on the biographical tradition, see Greg Crossan, 'The nine *Lives* of John Clare', *John Clare Society Journal* 5 (1986): 37–46, and my essay, 'John Clare: Prologue to a New Life', in *Romantic Biography*, ed. Arthur Bradley and Alan Rawes (Aldershot: Ashgate, 2003).

The most important relationship in Clare's publishing career is discussed at length in Edmund Blunden, *Keats's Publisher: A Memoir of John Taylor* (London: Cape, 1936), and Tim Chilcott's admirable *A Publisher and his Circle: The Life and Work of John Taylor, Keats's Publisher* (London: Routledge and Kegan Paul, 1972). The best account of Clare's manic depression is Evan Blackmore, 'John Clare's Psychiatric Disorder and its Influence on his Poetry', *Victorian Poetry* 24 (1986): 209–28, but for a warning against the dangers of retrospective analysis of 'madness', see Roy Porter's essay in *John Clare in Context* (cited below).

Readers seeking modern literary-critical analysis of Clare might begin with the essays by the poets Tom Paulin, Seamus Heaney and John Ashbery cited in Chapter 25, then proceed to the excellent collection *John Clare in Context*, ed. Hugh Haughton, Adam Phillips and Geoffrey Summerfield (Cambridge: Cambridge University Press, 1994), and thence to John Barrell, *The Idea of Landscape and the Sense of Place 1730–1840: An Approach to the Poetry of John Clare* (Cambridge: Cambridge University Press, 1972); Timothy Brownlow, *John Clare and Picturesque Landscape* (Oxford: Clarendon Press, 1983); Tim Chilcott, *'A Real World & Doubting Mind': A Critical Study of the Poetry of John Clare* (Pickering: Hull University Press, 1985); Johanne Clare, *John Clare and the Bounds of Circumstance* (Kingston and Montreal: McGill-Queens University Press, 1987); Mark Storey, *The Poetry of John Clare, A Critical Introduction* (London: Macmillan, 1974); and Janet Todd, *In Adam's Garden: A Study of John Clare's Pre-Asylum Poetry* (Gainesville: University of Florida Press, 1973).

For further references, see Barbara H. Estermann, *John Clare: An Annotated Primary and Secondary Bibliography* (New York: Garland, 1985), supplemented by John Goodridge, 'A Chronological Survey of Clare Criticism, 1970–2000', in *John Clare: New Approaches*, ed. John Goodridge and Simon Kövesi (Helpston: John Clare Society, 2000), pp. 202–250, also on the worldwide web at <http://human.ntu.ac.uk/clare/critbib.html>, with annual updates. This webpage also has an exceptionally valuable 'First-line Index to the Poetry of John Clare', compiled by John Goodridge, listing manuscript and print locations of nearly all of Clare's poems: <http://human.ntu.ac.uk/clare/flindex.htm>.

ACKNOWLEDGEMENTS

It would not have been possible to make sense of the Clare archives without the work of those who have catalogued them (notably David Powell in Northampton and the late Margaret Grainger in Peterborough) and the editors who have made the majority of his writings available in printed form: Eric Robinson, Geoffrey Summerfield, David Powell, P. M. S. Dawson, J. W. and Anne Tibble, Kelsey Thornton and Tim Chilcott for the poems and autobiographical prose, the Tibbles and Mark Storey for the letters. Eric Robinson in particular has devoted a lifetime's scholarship to Clare; his monumental editorial labours will ensure that his name will be linked to Clare's in perpetuity. I gratefully acknowledge his support for my undertaking. All modern Clare scholars also owe a debt to the pioneers who set about recovering his work and restoring his reputation in the early twentieth century, especially Arthur Symons, Edmund Blunden, and J. W. and Anne Tibble.

The members of the John Clare Society have been unfailingly supportive. For twenty years, the *John Clare Society Journal* has published new research of an exceptionally high calibre on both the life and the work. I have drawn on it extensively. The officers of the society have shared with me their deep knowledge and infectious enthusiasm: I am especially grateful to Peter Cox, John Goodridge, Peter and the late Mary Moyse (in addition to providing me with photographs of his own, Peter gave me access to Mary's transcriptions of archival material concerning Clare's family and his Helpston context). Bob Heyes probably knows more about Clare's life than anyone else. He has most generously shared his unpublished research with me as well as assisted in tracking down books; copies of his transcriptions of many of Clare's incoming letters greatly expedited my work at the British Library. I am also very grateful to David Powell for answering queries and more specifically for copies of his transcriptions of the Inskip letters.

Bob Heyes and Paul Dawson undertook the onerous task of reading drafts of my entire typescript. They saved me from many errors and offered exactly the right mix of caution and encouragement.

The following pointed me in the direction of valuable material or helped me with particular details: Terry Baker of the Stamford Fair Society, John Barnard, Peter Beal of Sotheby's, John Blagden, Russell Carter, Tim Chilcott, Tracey Crawley at the Stamford Museum, Greg Crossan, Sharon Floate (for matters Romany), Charles Forsdick, Dr Hugh Godfrey (for matters medical), John Hodgson, Ian Huish (for professional comments on my account of Clare's manic depression), Simon Kövesi, Tom Lockwood, John Mackintosh, Rob Morrison, Tom Paulin, Adam Phillips (critic and psychoanalyst *par excellence*), Nicholas Roe, Mark Storey, John Styles, Angela Taylor, Cathy Taylor, Geoff Ward, John Worthen—with thanks and apologies to others not listed here. Mrs Robin Goodfellow was immensely kind in showing me round Clare's cottage, which is now her home. Oscar Turnill was most generous in both providing me with information about Clare's friend Richard Turnill and tracing documents for me at the Public Record Office and the Family Records Centre.

My greatest personal debt is to the Leverhulme Trust for the award of a Leverhulme Personal Research Professorship, which released me from all teaching and administrative duties for the specific purpose of researching and writing this book. Special thanks to the former Director, Professor Barry Supple, for his particular interest in the project. A generous annual research expense allowance from the Trust allowed me to read manuscripts in Peterborough, Northampton, London and further afield, and to purchase twenty reels of manuscript material on microfilm.

The enthusiasm of my agent David Godwin and the faith of two great literary publishers, Peter Straus at Picador in London and Jonathan Galassi at Farrar, Straus and Giroux in New York, made it all happen. Jonathan read the book with both the attention of an ideal editor and the eye of a poet, so suggesting innumerable improvements. The production process was a pleasure, thanks to the talents of James Wilson, Annie Wedekind and Elaine Chubb at FSG, together with Ursula Doyle at Picador.

Dr Christopher Ridgway was the first to show me the true range and greatness of Clare. Dr Paula Byrne sustained my spirit and helped in more ways than can be counted—especially when, unable to see the wood for the trees, I was struggling with my final revisions of the typescript. Tom and Ellie, meanwhile, came banging on the door of my study and kept my feet on the ground in a way that would have been thoroughly understood by that devoted father John Clare.

INDEX

Abbott, Mary Ann, 486

Abercrombie, John, 71

Ackermann, Rudolph, 339

Adcock, Anna, 106

Addison, Joseph, 378

Akroyd, Carry, 558

Alfred (newspaper), 396, 397

Allen, Dr. Matthew: background, 407, 413, 422–28; Clare writes to, 461–62; desire to have Clare return to Essex, 459–60; as Dr Bottle-Imp, 448; observation of Clare, 429–30; private asylum today, 543; subscription scheme for Clare's poetry, 429–32

Allen, Revd W., 250

Amulet (annual), 302, 338

Analectic Magazine, 156

Anti-Jacobin Review, 155

Armour, Jean, 171

Arnold, Dr. Thomas, 76, 252–53, 411

Artis, Edmund Tyrell: as archaeologist and antiquarian, 103, 235; background, 235; as Clare friend and companion, 236, 238, 276, 278, 323, 325; as house steward at Milton Hall, 185, 234–35, 287; takes Clare's life mask, 553

Ashbery, John, 554–55

Ashby, Betsey, 498

Athenaeum, 377, 396, 398

Austen, Jane, 101

'Autobiography of John Clare' (unpublished), 276, 281–82, 548; *see*

also 'Sketches in the Life of John Clare'

Averey, Mary Ann, 498

Bachelors' Hall, 99, 116, 117, 124

Bacon, George, 528

Bain, James, 64

Baker, Anne Elizabeth, 514–15

Baker, Antony (Tant), 72, 128

Banton, John, 546

Barbauld, Anna, 283

Barr, Ben, 60

Barrell, John, 47

Bartlett, Sarah, 513

Beal, Mary, 496

Beattie, James, 220

Beddoes, Thomas Lovell, 265

Bedford Times, 489, 504

Bee, see *Stamford Bee*

Behnes, Henry, 325–26, 328, 332, 333, 336, 341, 367, 372; changes name, 393; *see also* Burlowe, Henry

Behnes, William, 325, 393

Belcher, Tom, 264

Bell, Dr J. G., 177–78

Bellamy, Councillor, 68–69

Bellars, Mr and Mrs, 67, 533, 535

Bellars, William, 533–34, 544

Bennion, Thomas, 239–40, 244, 246

Berry, George Duval, 525–26, 533

Bewick, Thomas, 404

Billings brothers, 59, 64, 99, 237, 285

Blackley, William, 255

PERMISSIONS ACKNOWLEDGEMENTS

I am deeply grateful to the Peterborough Museum and Art Gallery and the Northamptonshire Libraries and Information Service for permission to consult the manuscripts in their possession. Special thanks are due for the assistance of Terry Bracher, Local Studies Librarian in Northampton, and Glenys Wass, Collections Manager in Peterborough. I have quoted extensively from the comprehensive microfilm editions of these two collections, produced by Microform Academic Publishers (1974, 1980), with thanks to Paul Knights for generous permission to do so. Most of the manuscripts have now been transcribed and collated in the editions of Eric Robinson and his collaborators, and I am very grateful to Professor Robinson and his publishers, Oxford University Press and Carcanet Press/Mid Northumberland Arts Group, for these works of exemplary scholarship, against which I have checked my quotations from the microfilm edition. Thanks also to Mark Storey and Kelsey Thornton for allowing me to benefit from their respective editions of the letters and *The Midsummer Cushion*. I am also grateful to the British Library for permission to quote extensively from the letters *to* Clare in the Egerton manuscripts. Claire Blunden gave her generous permission for me to quote from works first published by Edmund Blunden, including the indispensable *Sketches in the Life of John Clare Written by Himself*.

Other unpublished manuscript material is cited by kind permission of the following: the Berg Collection at the New York Public Library; the Brotherton Collection at Leeds University Library; the Burghley Collection (thanks to Jon Culverhouse, Felix Pryor and especially the archivist, Michael Shepherd); Derbyshire Record Office (thanks to Judith Phillips, reference librarian at Matlock); Essex Record Office; Northamptonshire Record Office; the Carl H. Pforzheimer Collection of Shelley and His Circle, New York Public Library (Astor, Lenox and Tilden Foundations); John Rylands University Library, Manchester; and St Andrew's Hospital (formerly the Northampton General Lunatic Asylum). I have also made use of the Bodleian Library; Cambridge University Library; Gypsy Collection, Sydney Jones Library, Liverpool University; Houghton Library, Harvard University; Huntington Library, San Marino, California; Central Reference Library and Usher Gallery, Lincoln; and Wellcome Library for the History of Medicine.

Illustrations in copyright are reproduced by kind permission of the following: British Library (16, 17, 24, 25); Department of Prints and Drawings, British Museum (7, 10, 11, 12); Essex County Record Office (22, 23); National Trust Photo Library / A. C. Cooper (14); Northamptonshire Record Office (3, 5); Northamptonshire Libraries and Information Service (2, 4, 18, 19, 27–28, 31, 32; text illus. pages 20, 88, 268, 452, 506, 532); Peterborough Museum and Art Gallery (30; text illus. pages 322, 366); Sydney Jones Library, University of Liverpool (6, 20). Photographs by Peter Moyse ARPS (1, 3, 5, 8, 13, 19). Other items are from the author's personal collection; thanks also to Harvest Studios of Northampton and Ian Qualtrough of the University of Liverpool for photographic work.

The lines from John Ashbery's poem 'for John Clare' are reproduced by kind permission of the author.